T0301454

Microeconomic Foundations I

Microeconomic Foundations I

Choice and Competitive Markets

David M. Kreps

PRINCETON UNIVERSITY PRESS | PRINCETON AND OXFORD

Published by Princeton University Press, 41 William Street,
Princeton, New Jersey 08540

In the United Kingdom: Princeton University Press, 6 Oxford Street,
Woodstock, Oxfordshire OX20 1TW

pup.princeton.edu

Library of Congress Cataloging-in-Publication Data

Kreps, David M.
Microeconomic foundations / David M. Kreps
p. cm.
Includes bibliographical references and index.
ISBN 978-0-691-15583-8 (hbk.) 1. Microeconomics. I. Title.
HB172.K744 2013
338.5–dc23
2012011926
British Library Cataloging-in-Publication Data is available

This book has been composed in Helvetica, Palatino, and Computer Modern typefaces.

The publisher would like to acknowledge the author of this volume for providing the camera-ready copy from which this book was published.

1 3 5 7 9 10 8 6 4 2

To Kenneth J. Arrow

Contents

Preface

This book is for aspiring academic economists and those in related fields. It provides a rigorous treatment of some of the basic tools of economic modeling and reasoning, bundled together with enough commentary and reflection so that the reader can appreciate both the strengths and weaknesses of these tools. The target audience (to whom this preface is directly addressed) consists of first-year graduate students who are taking the standard "theory sequence" and would like to go more deeply into a selection of foundational issues, as well as students who, having taken a first-year graduate course out of one of the standard textbooks, would like a deeper dive. At the Stanford Graduate School of Business, this book (more or less) has been the basis of the first-quarter, first-year theory course for Ph.D. students, many of whom had taken a course out of the admirable textbook by Mas-Colell, Whinston, and Green,[1] and so for whom this is an opportunity to review and extend their command of that material.

The objective of the book is captured by the word "command." In my experience, most students emerge from the standard first-year graduate theory course with an understanding of the material that is good but not great. There is little doubt that almost any student would benefit from a structured review of this material using her original text. But, in my opinion, the standard textbooks are not written with command or mastery of the material as their primary objective. Because they are written to serve very broad audiences, breadth of coverage is stressed over depth, and the authors sometimes omit technical details, to avoid panicking less well-prepared readers. This book sacrifices breadth for depth, avoids compromises about details (with a few exceptions), and tries to explain to the reader both why economic foundations are done the way they are done and what are some of the limitations in how things are done.

Clearly, words like "command" and "mastery" must be taken with many grains of salt. If your career objectives are to do research in any topic covered by this book, the coverage here is inadequate to bring you to the level of understanding you will require. Every chapter in this book could be expanded to a book-length treatment on its own and, even then, important work on the topic would be left out. In some cases, the book comes closer to the research frontier than in others; perhaps not surprisingly, this is true on topics on which I myself have made contributions. But in no case will you finish a chapter and be prepared to tackle frontier research on the topic of that chapter.

Instead, when I use the terms "command" and "mastery," I have in mind something less ambitious. The foundations of economics are abstract and mathematical (more about this momentarily), and as with any abstract, mathematics-based dis-

[1] *Microeconomic Theory*, Oxford: Oxford University Press, 1995.

cipline, the more comfortable you are with the foundations, the more likely it is that you will use those foundations well. Errors in thought are much more likely the closer you are working to the frontiers of your understanding. If you ever find yourself leaning on formal mathematics that you don't fully understand—if you find yourself thinking, "I'm not sure why my model generates this result, but that's what emerges"—you are in grave danger. You should understand the tools you use deeply enough so that you aren't fooled by them.

So that's the objective here: to bring you (closer) to command level on a relatively limited set of results, rather than to a nodding-acquaintance level with a broader set. *If* you understand a few things deeply, you will understand what it means to acquire deep understanding, and then you can strive for a similar depth of understanding on whatever (other) subject is of interest to you. My objective is to turn that "if" into a "when," while covering a selection of important microeconomic foundations.

Given this objective, can this book be used as a primary text in the first-graduate-theory course? It is used that way for some of the students at the Stanford GSB, so of course I think the answer is yes. But bear in mind the book's trade-off of breadth for depth. You should complement this book with one that provides broader coverage. Indeed, since this material is part of the foundation of what (I expect) you hope to be your career, you should in any case invest in multiple perspectives. And, having given you that advice in general, let me be a bit more specific: One of the many virtues of Mas-Colell, Whinston, and Green (*ibid.*) is its enormous breadth. You ought to have a copy on your shelf, if not your desk.[2]

Volume I?

The title is *Microeconomic Foundations I* with subtitle *Choice and Competitive Markets*, suggesting that further volumes are in preparation. "In preparation" is an overstatement, as I write these words; "planned" is more accurate, and I plan not only *II: Strategic Interaction, Information, and Imperfect Competition*, but also *III: Institutions and Behavior*. The volume you are holding deals with economic foundations that existed in (nearly) finished form in the mid 1970s: various models of individual choice; consumer and producer theory (for price-taking or competitive consumers and firms); and (some) general equilibrium theory. The intended second volume will cover material that entered the mainstream of economic thought and practice from the mid 1970s to, say, 1990: information economics and noncooperative game theory, in particular. The third piece is the most speculative: I have in mind a volume that will wrap together developments in behavioral and institutional economics, with (perhaps) transaction cost economics playing a central (but not *the* central) role. I am trying to write this so that each volume would correspond to one ten-week course, fitting the academic calendar of Stanford University. But that's an ambitious agenda; only time will tell if the second and third parts ever appear.

[2] Of course, many other excellent treatments of these topics can be found; I make no attempt to list them all. But one resource that may be harder to find is a sequence of excellent notes on a variety of topics in microeconomics and related mathematics, prepared by Kim Border. Go to the URL http://www.hss.caltech.edu/~kcb/Notes.shtml for a list of these notes.

Mathematics in this book and in economics

The approach of this book is resolutely mathematical, because the foundations of economics are resolutely mathematical. The level of mathematics required is not *extremely* high; nearly everything takes place within finite-dimensional Euclidean space. This is a deliberate choice: I have tried to hold the mathematics employed to a level that most graduate students in economics will have. With exceptions limited to a few topics, to navigate this book you must know the sort of mathematics covered in an undergraduate course on real analysis, plus the first few weeks of an undergraduate course in abstract algebra (concerning binary relations).[3] You will need to know more about some specific mathematics, notably some convex analysis, some theory of correspondences, and basics of constrained optimization. But most of the prerequisite mathematics and all of these specific topics are reviewed in a series of appendices at the end of the book.[4]

However, while high-level mathematics is not required, what is commonly called "mathematical sophistication" is needed from start to finish. To make it through the book, you need to be comfortable with mathematical abstraction and with a definition–proposition–proof style of presentation. For students with a strong background in mathematics, this will not be problematic and may even be comforting; but for many students, this will be the real barrier to using this book. I make no apologies for imposing this hurdle, because this, in my opinion, is essential to command-level understanding of the mathematical tools economists employ. I take proofs seriously, providing in most cases details or at least an outline of the proof. (I will sometimes skip steps or "leave the proof to the reader." In every case where this happens, if you aren't sure you see how to fill in the gaps, then you really should take the time to figure out how to do so.)

Each chapter comes with some problems, often including requests that you provide proofs that I leave to the reader. You won't achieve mastery of this material if you don't do them. So do them. Answers to problems with asterisks—as in, *2.3, meaning Problem 3 in Chapter 2—are provided in a *Student's Guide*, which also gives summaries of each chapter. (This includes roughly half the problems and, in most cases, problems where I ask you to fill in gaps left in the text.) You can freely download chapter-by-chapter pieces of the *Student's Guide* at the URL http://www.microfoundations1.stanford.edu/student.[5]

Concerning mathematics and its role in economics: Some first-year graduate

[3] So my earlier claim that I have tried to avoid compromises is, at best, a relative statement. And sometimes the lure of going beyond finite-dimensional Euclidean spaces is irresistable: in a very few places, I employ some measure-theoretic probability theory; to do some of the problems, you must know some theory of stochastic processes; toward the end of the book, I informally discuss economies with a continuum of agents. But none of this material is essential for the main expositional flow of the text. I also expect all readers to be reasonably facile with spreadsheets; I employ MSExcel.

[4] I also provide a very detailed appendix on the methods of dynamic programming, which I expect few readers will have seen before. This material is not used in this book except in the problems connected to Chapter 7, but these are useful tools in modern macroeconomics and in topics to be discussed in the second volume, and it seemed appropriate to cover these methods in connection with Chapter 7, which concerns dynamic choice.

[5] Solutions to the other problems are provided in an *Instructor's Manual*, which also provides my

students are utterly turned off by their first-year theory courses. They have come to the study of economics to understand real-world phenomena and, perhaps, to make a difference in the real world, not to study mathematics. To those students, my response is that if you plan to use economic techniques to understand the real world and to see how to make a difference, your effectiveness will depend in part on how well you understand those techniques; doing all this math builds your understanding of the techniques. Aspiring novelists or essayists may not see the value in learning to diagram sentences in fifth grade, but if diagramming sentences in fifth grade improves the clarity of their sentences—and I think it does—it is an important drill along the way to becoming a novelist or essayist.

A different objection is that economics is a poorer discipline *because of* its reliance on mathematical models. To be tractable—a word you are likely to come to dislike—mathematical models must be relatively simple. So mathematics forces all sorts of simplifications on economic models that make the models less realistic. Because of this, some critics decry the study of mathematical models in economics; they say it is indoctrination of the young into a false and limiting faith.

Mathematical modeling is a mixed blessing for economics. Mathematical modeling provides real advantages in terms of precision of thought, in seeing how assumptions are linked to conclusions, in generating and communicating insights, in generalizing propositions, and in exporting knowledge from one context to another. In my opinion, these advantages are monumental, far outweighing the costs. But the costs are not zero. Mathematical modeling limits what can be tackled and what is considered legitimate inquiry. You may decide, with experience, that the sorts of models in this book do not help you understand the economic phenomena that you want to understand. Since, as I write these lines, I don't know what phenomena you want to understand, I can't say that you are surely wrong. And the position is defensible. But, based on my own experiences, you are probably wrong. In any case, you are more likely to succeed in convincing others and changing the way economists as a whole do business if you have mastered the sort of mathematical models presented here, which continue to be the foundation of modern economics.

Conventions

Within each chapter, propositions, definitions, lemmas, and so forth are numbered sequentially. That is, if the first such item in Chapter 6 is a definition, it is Definition 6.1; if the second such item in Chapter 6 is a proposition, it is Proposition 6.2. Figures in a chapter are also numbered sequentially, but in a different list. So the first figure in Chapter 6 is Figure 6.1. Problems are numbered sequentially in still another list, and equations in still another list.

The use of third-person singular pronouns in books such as this has become an exercise in political correctness. I use *she*, *her*, and *hers* when only one actor is

recommendations about teaching out of this volume. The *Instructor's Manual* is also available via the internet, but access is limited: instructors who wish access can get more information at the URL http://www.microfoundations1.stanford.edu/instructor.

involved; the second actor is *he, him,* and *his*. Keeping with PC requirements, when there are two actors and a logical status ordering, *she* has higher status, as in: *she is the employer, he is the employee*. With a tip of the hat to Robert Aumann, in some places she is Alice and he is Bob.

Having paid my dues to PC as outlined in the previous paragraph, the dollar is the standard currency in this book.

Acknowledgments

Many generations of Ph.D. students at the Stanford Graduate School of Business have suffered through typo-laden drafts of pieces of this volume, and they have done quite a lot to reduce (not to zero, I'm sorry to say) the number of typos. I thank them.

As I was wrapping up the final version of the manuscript, Alejandro Francetich took on the task of reading for internal consistency. He did much more, finding a host of both typos and think-os, including some that are best described as howlers. I don't know that he got them all, but he improved the final product immensely.

In a world of email, it is very easy to "reach out" to colleagues with a specific question. When writing a book of this sort, which encompasses a lot of material about which I am *not* an expert, the urge to ask colleagues who are experts has been too much for me to resist, and the equally good grace and advice of many colleagues have made this a far better book. I am bound to have forgotten some individuals in this category (to whom I apologize), but among those who have been generous with their time and expertise are Kenneth Arrow, Susan Athey, Robert Aumann, Kim Border, Eddie Dekel, Erwin Diewert, Yossi Feinberg, Faruk Gul, Matt Jackson, Jim Jordan, Vijay Krishna, Sunil Kumar, Mark Machina, Michael Ostrovsky, Phil Reny, John Roberts, Tom Sargent, José Scheinkman, Andy Skrzypacz, Hugo Sonnenschein, and Peter Wakker.

The production of this book required the efforts of a number of folks at Princeton University Press, who were very patient with a crazy, opinionated, and stubborn author. I'm particularly grateful to acquisition editor Seth Ditchik, production editors Ben Holmes and Kathleen Cioffi, copy editor Richard Isomaki, indexer Sheila Bodell, and senior book designer Lorraine Doneker.

I produced this book using TeXtures, an implementation of TeX by Blue Sky TeX Systems. The people at Blue Sky have always been there for me when I have had technical issues. Figures were produced using Adobe Illustrator.

This volume records the contributions of many economists, some of whom it has been my privilege to know as role models and friends. I am grateful to them all, and I take this opportunity to recognize one in particular:

Given the nature of this book and my unbounded admiration for both the individual and his work, it is a pleasure and honor to dedicate this volume to Kenneth Arrow.

Microeconomic Foundations I

Chapter One

Choice, Preference, and Utility

Most people, when they think about microeconomics, think first about the slogan *supply equals demand* and its picture, shown here in Figure 1.1, with a rising supply function intersecting a falling demand function, determining an equilibrium price and quantity.

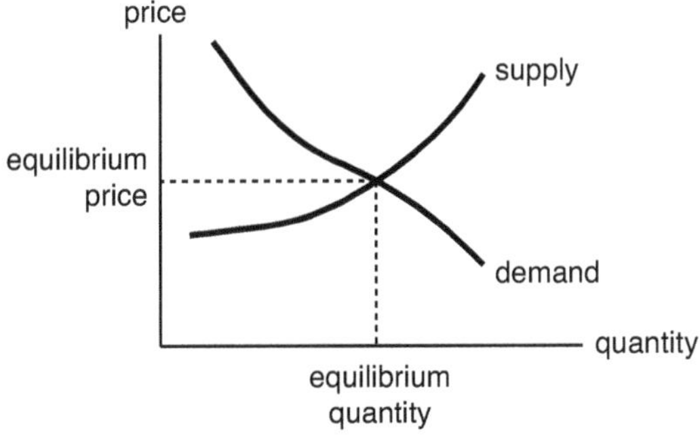

Figure 1.1. Supply equals demand

But before getting to this picture and the concept of an equilibrium, the picture's constituent pieces, the demand and supply functions, are needed. Those functions arise from *choices*, choices by firms and by individual consumers. Hence, microeconomic theory begins with choices. Indeed, the theory not only begins with choices; it remains focused on them for a very long time. Most of this volume concerns modeling the choices of consumers, with some attention paid to the choices of profit-maximizing firms; only toward the end do we seriously worry about equilibrium.

1.1. Consumer Choice: The Basics

The basic story of consumer choice is easily told: Begin with a set X of *possible objects that might be chosen* and an individual, the consumer, who does the choosing. The consumer faces limits on what she might choose, and so we imagine some collection $\mathcal{A}$ of nonempty subsets of X from which the consumer might choose. We let A denote a typical element of $\mathcal{A}$; that is, A is a subset of X. Then the choices of our consumer are denoted by $c(A)$.

The story is that the consumer chooses *one* element of A. Nonetheless, we think of $c(A)$ as a subset of A, not a member or element of A. This allows for the possibility that the consumer is happy with any one of several elements of A, in which case $c(A)$ lists all those elements. When she makes a definite choice of a single element, say x, out of A—when she says, in effect, "I want x and nothing else"—we write $c(A) = \{x\}$, or the singleton set consisting of the single element x. But if she says, "I would be happy with either x or y," then $c(A) = \{x, y\}$.

So far, no restrictions have been put on $c(A)$. But some restrictions are natural. For instance, $c(A) \subseteq A$ seems obvious; we do not want to give the consumer a choice out of A and have her choosing something that is not in A. You might think that we would insist on $c(A) \neq \emptyset$; that is, the consumer makes some choice. But we do not insist on this, at least, not yet. Therefore...

A ***model of consumer choice*** *consists of some set X of possible objects of choice, a collection $\mathcal{A}$ of nonempty subsets of X, and a choice function c whose domain is $\mathcal{A}$ and whose range is the set of subsets of X, with the sole restriction that $c(A) \subseteq A$.*

For instance, we can imagine a world of k commodities, where a *commodity bundle* is a vector $x = (x_1, \ldots, x_k) \in R^k_+$, the positive orthant in k-dimensional Euclidean space. (In this book, *the positive orthant* means all components nonnegative, or $R^k_+ = \{x \in R^k : x \geq 0\}$. *The strict positive orthant,* denoted by R^k_{++}, means elements of R^k all of whose components are strictly positive.) If, say, $k = 3$ and the commodities are (in order) bread, cheese, and salami, the bundle $(3, 0, 0.5)$ means 3 units of bread, no cheese, and 0.5 units of salami, in whatever units we are using. We can also imagine prices p_i for the commodities, so that $p = (p_1, \ldots, p_k)$ is the price vector; for convenience, we assume that all prices are strictly positive, or $p \in R^k_{++}$. And we can imagine that the consumer has some amount of income $y \geq 0$ to spend. Then the consumer's choice problem is to choose some affordable bundle given these prices and her income; that is, a typical set A is a budget set

$$\{x \in R^k_+ : p \cdot x \leq y\}.$$

A model of consumer choice in this context is then a choice function that says which bundles the consumer would be willing to accept, as a function of the prices of the goods p and her level of income y.

This is not much of a model, yet. Economic modeling begins with an assumption that the choices made by the consumer in different situations are somewhat coherent. Imagine, for instance, a customer at a café asking for a cup of coffee and a piece of pie. When told that they have apple and cherry pie, she opts for apple. Then the waiter tells her that they also have peach pie. "If you also have peach," she responds, "I would like cherry pie, please." We want to (and will) assume that choice in different situations is coherent enough to preclude this sort of behavior; we'll formalize this next page, in Definition 1.1b.

This is one sort of coherence. A second is that the consumer's choices are in accord with utility maximization, for some utility function defined on X. That is, there is a function $u : X \to R$, such that for every A,

$$c(A) = \{x \in A : u(x) \geq u(y) \text{ for all } y \in A\}. \tag{1.1}$$

A third sort of coherence involves a *preference relation* over X. A preference relation expresses the consumer's feelings between pairs of objects in X. We denote the preference relation by $\succeq$ and imagine that for every pair x and y from X, the consumer is willing to say that either $x \succeq y$, meaning x is at least as good as y, or not. For any pair x and y, then, one of four mutually exclusive possibilities holds: (1) the consumer says that $x \succeq y$ and that $y \succeq x$; (2) $x \succeq y$ but not $y \succeq x$; (3) $y \succeq x$ but not $x \succeq y$; or (4) neither $x \succeq y$ nor $y \succeq x$. Then, with these preferences in hand, a consumer chooses from a set A precisely those elements of A that are at least as good as everything in A, or

$$c(A) = \{x \in A : x \succeq y \text{ for all } y \in A\}. \tag{1.2}$$

When you look at (most) models in microeconomics that have consumers, consumers make choices, and the choice behavior of the consumer is modeled by either (1) a utility function and the (implicit) assumption that choice from any set A is governed by the rule (1.1) or (2) a preference relation and the (implicit) assumption that choice from any set A is governed by the rule (1.2). (Discrete choice models in econometrics have so-called random utility models, in which choices are stochastic. And in some parts of behavioral economics, you will find models of choice behavior that don't quite fit either of these frameworks. But most models have either utility-maximizing or preference-maximizing consumers.)

The questions before us in this chapter are: How do these different ways of modeling consumer choice compare? If we restrict attention to coherent choice, does one imply the other(s)? Can they be made consistent?

The basic answer is that *under certain coherence assumptions, the three ways of modeling consumer choice are equivalent.* We begin with the case of finite X. (We worry a lot about infinite X later.) To keep matters simple, we make the following assumption for the remainder of this chapter (but see Problems 1.15 and 1.16).

Assumption. *$\mathcal{A}$ is the set of* ***all*** *nonempty subsets of X.*

Two properties of choice functions and two properties of a preference relation must be defined:

Definition 1.1.

a. *A choice function c satisfies* ***finite nonemptiness*** *if $c(A)$ is nonempty for every finite $A \in \mathcal{A}$.*

b. *A choice function c satisfies* ***choice coherence*** *if, for every pair x and y from X and A and B from $\mathcal{A}$, if $x, y \in A \cap B$, $x \in c(A)$, and $y \notin c(A)$, then $y \notin c(B)$.*

c. *A preference relation on X is* ***complete*** *if for every pair x and y from X, either $x \succeq y$ or $y \succeq x$ (or both).*

d. *A preference relation on X is **transitive** if $x \succeq y$ and $y \succeq z$ implies that $x \succeq z$.*

Some comments about these definitions may be helpful: Concerning a, if X is finite, finite nonemptiness of c means that $c(A)$ is nonempty for all subsets of X. Later in the chapter, the restriction to finite A will have a role to play. Choice coherence is the formalization intended to preclude the apple, cherry, and peach pie vignette: If apple is the (sole) choice out of {apple, cherry}, then cherry cannot be chosen from {apple, cherry, peach}. An equivalent (contrapositive) form for b is: *For every pair x and y from X and A and B from $\mathcal{A}$, if $x, y \in A \cap B$, $x \in c(A)$, and $y \in c(B)$, then $y \in c(A)$ and $x \in c(B)$.*[1]

Proposition 1.2. *Suppose that X is finite.*

a. *If a choice function c satisfies finite nonemptiness and choice coherence, then there exist both a utility function $u : X \to R$ and a complete and transitive preference relation $\succeq$ that produce choices according to c via the formulas (1.1) and (1.2), respectively.*

b. *If a preference relation $\succeq$ on X is complete and transitive, then the choice function it produces via formula (1.2) satisfies finite nonemptiness and choice coherence, and there exists a utility function $u : X \to R$ such that*

$$x \succeq y \text{ if and only if } u(x) \geq u(y). \tag{1.3}$$

c. *Given any utility function $u : X \to R$, the choice function it produces via formula (1.1) satisfies finite nonemptiness and choice coherence, the preference relation it produces via (1.3) is complete and transitive, and the choice function produced by that preference relation via (1.2) is precisely the choice function produced directly from u via (1.1).*

In words, choice behavior (for a finite X) that satisfies finite nonemptiness and choice coherence is equivalent to preference maximization (that is, formula (1.2)) for complete and transitive preferences, both of which are equivalent to utility maximization (via formulas (1.1) and (1.3)). However expressed, whether in terms of choice, preference, or utility, this conglomerate (with the two pairs of assumptions) is the standard model of consumer choice in microeconomics.

A much-used piece of terminology concerns display (1.3), which connects a utility function u and a preference relation $\succeq$. When (1.3) holds, we say that the utility function u *represents* the preference relation $\succeq$.

In terms of economics, Proposition 1.2 is the story of this chapter. Several tasks remain:

1. We prove the proposition.

[1] If it isn't clear to you that this restatement is equivalent to b in the definition, you should verify it carefully. Stated in this alternative form, Mas-Colell, Whinston, and Green (1995) call property b *the weak axiom of revealed preference*, although their setting is a bit different; cf. Problem 1.15. In previous books, I have called property b *Houthakker's Axiom of Revealed Preference*, but I no longer believe this is a correct attribution; the first appearance of this property for choice out of general sets (that is, outside the context of price-and-income-generated budget sets) of which I am aware is Arrow (1959).

2. We consider how (and whether) this proposition extends to infinite X. After all, in the one example we've given, where $X = R_+^k$, we have an infinite X. Most economic applications will have an infinite X.

3. We have so far discussed the binary relation $\succeq$, known as *weak preference*, which is meant to be an expression of "at least as good as." In economic applications, two associated binary relations, *strict preference* ("strictly better than") and *indifference* ("precisely as good as") are used; we explore them and their connection to weak preference.

4. We comment briefly on aspects of the standard model: What if $\mathcal{A}$ does not contain all nonempty subsets of X? What is the empirical evidence for or against the standard model? What alternatives are there to the standard model?

1.2. Proving Most of Proposition 1.2, and More

Parts of Proposition 1.2 are true for all X, finite or not.

Proposition 1.3. *Regardless of the size of X, if $u : X \to R$, then*

a. the preference relation $\succeq_u$ defined by $x \succeq_u y$ if $u(x) \geq u(y)$ is complete and transitive, and

b. the choice function c_u defined by $c_u(A) = \{x \in A : u(x) \geq u(y) \text{ for all } y \in A\}$ satisfies finite nonemptiness and choice coherence.

Proof. (a) Given any two x and y from X, either $u(x) \geq u(y)$ or $u(y) \geq u(x)$ (since $u(x)$ and $u(y)$ are two real numbers); hence either $x \succeq_u y$ or $y \succeq_u x$. That is, $\succeq_u$ is complete.

If $x \succeq_u y$ and $y \succeq_u z$, then (by definition) $u(x) \geq u(y)$ and $u(y) \geq u(z)$; hence $u(x) \geq u(z)$ (because $\geq$ is transitive for real numbers), and therefore $x \succeq_u z$. That is, $\succeq_u$ is transitive.

(b) Suppose $x, y \in A \cap B$ and $x \in c_u(A)$. Then $u(x) \geq u(y)$. If, moreover, $y \notin c_u(A)$, then $u(z) > u(y)$ for some $z \in A$. But $u(x) \geq u(z)$ since $x \in c_u(A)$ implies $u(x) \geq u(z)$ for all $z \in A$; therefore $u(x) > u(y)$. Since $x \in B$, this immediately implies that $y \notin c_u(B)$, since there is something in B, namely x, for which $u(y) \not\geq u(x)$. This is choice coherence.

If A is a finite subset of X, then $\{r \in R : r = u(x) \text{ for some } x \in A\}$ is a finite set of real numbers. Every finite set of real numbers contains a largest element; that is, some $r^* = u(x^*)$ in the set satisfies $r^* \geq r$ for all the elements of the set. But this says that $u(x^*) \geq u(x)$ for all $x \in A$, which implies that $x^* \in c_u(A)$, and $c_u(A)$ is not empty. ∎

Proposition 1.4. *Regardless of the size of X, if $\succeq$ is a complete and transitive binary relation on X, the choice function $c_\succeq$ defined on the set of all nonempty subsets of X by*

$$c_\succeq(A) := \{x \in A : x \succeq y \text{ for all } y \in A\}$$

satisfies finite nonemptiness and choice coherence.

Proof. Suppose $x, y \in A \cap B, x \in c_{\succeq}(A)$, and $y \notin c_{\succeq}(A)$. Since $x \in c_{\succeq}(A)$, $x \succeq y$. Since $y \notin c_{\succeq}(A)$, $y \not\succeq z$ for some $z \in A$. By completeness, $z \succeq y$. Since $x \in c_{\succeq}(A)$, $x \succeq z$. I claim that $y \not\succeq x$: Assume to the contrary that $y \succeq x$, then $x \succeq z$ and transitivity of $\succeq$ would imply that $y \succeq z$, contrary to what was assumed. But if $y \not\succeq x$, then since $x \in B$, $y \notin c_{\succeq}(B)$. That is, $c_{\succeq}$ satisfies choice coherence.

I assert that if A is a finite (and nonempty) set, some $x \in A$ satisfies $x \succeq y$ for all $y \in A$ (hence $c_{\succeq}(A)$ is not empty). The proof is by induction[2] on the size of A: if A contains a single element, say, $A = \{x\}$, then $x \succeq x$ because $\succeq$ is complete. Therefore, the statement is true for all sets of size 1. Assume inductively that the statement is true for all sets of size $n-1$ and let A be a set of size n. Take any single element x_0 from A, and let $A' = A \setminus \{x_0\}$. A' is a set of size $n-1$, so there is some $x' \in A'$ such that $x' \succeq y$ for all $y \in A'$. By completeness of $\succeq$, either $x' \succeq x_0$ or $x_0 \succeq x'$. In the first case, $x' \succeq y$ for all $y \in A$, and we are done. In the second case, $x_0 \succeq x_0$ by completeness, and $x_0 \succeq y$ for all $y \in A'$, since $x' \succeq y$, and therefore transitivity of $\succeq$ tells us that $x_0 \succeq y$. Hence, for this arbitrary set of size n, we have produced an element at least as good as every other element. This completes the induction step, proving the result. ∎

Proposition 1.5. *Regardless of the size of X, suppose the choice function c satisfies finite nonemptiness and choice coherence. Define a binary relation $\succeq_c$ on X by*

$$x \succeq_c y \text{ if } x \in c(\{x, y\}).$$

Define a new choice function $c_{\succeq_c}$ by

$$c_{\succeq_c}(A) = \{x \in A : x \succeq_c y \text{ for all } y \in A\}.$$

Then $\succeq_c$ is complete and transitive, $c_{\succeq_c}$ satisfies choice coherence and finite nonemptiness, and for every subset A of X, either

$$c(A) = \emptyset \text{ or } c(A) = c_{\succeq_c}(A).$$

Before proving this, please note an instant corollary: If X is finite and c satisfies finite nonemptiness, then $c(A) \neq \emptyset$ for all $A \subseteq X$, and hence $c(A) = c_{\succeq_c}(A)$ for all A.

Proof of Proposition 1.5. Since c satisfies finite nonemptiness, either $x \in c(\{x, y\})$ or $y \in c(\{x, y\})$; hence either $x \succeq_c y$ or $y \succeq_c x$. That is, $\succeq_c$ is complete.

Suppose $x \succeq_c y$ and $y \succeq_c z$. I assert that choice coherence implies that $x \in c(\{x, y, z\})$. Suppose to the contrary that this is not so. It cannot be that $y \in$

[2] See Appendix 1.

$c(\{x,y,z\})$, for if it were, then x could not be in $c(\{x,y\})$ by choice coherence: Take $A = \{x,y,z\}$ and $B = \{x,y\}$; then $x,y \in A \cap B$, $y \in c(A)$, $x \notin c(A)$, and hence choice coherence implies that $x \notin c(B)$, contrary to our original hypothesis. And then, once we know that $y \notin c(\{x,y,z\})$, choice coherence can be used again to imply that $z \notin c(\{x,y,z\})$: Now $y,z \in \{x,y,z\} \cap \{y,z\}$, and if $z \in c(\{x,y,z\})$, since we know that $y \notin c(\{x,y,z\})$, this would imply $y \notin c(\{y,z\})$, contrary to our original hypothesis. But if x, y, and z are all not members of $c(\{x,y,z\})$, then it is empty, contradicting finite nonemptiness. Hence, we conclude that x must be a member of $c(\{x,y,z\})$. But then choice coherence and finite nonemptiness together imply that $x \in c(\{x,z\})$, for if it were not, z must be in $c(\{x,z\})$, and choice coherence would imply that x cannot be a member of $c(\{x,y,z\})$. Hence we now conclude that $x \in c(\{x,z\})$, which means that $x \succeq_c z$, and $\succeq_c$ is transitive.

Since $\succeq_c$ is complete and transitive, we know from Proposition 1.4 that $c_{\succeq_c}$ satisfies finite nonemptiness and choice coherence.

Now take any set A and any $x \in c(A)$. Let y be any other element of A. By finite nonemptiness and choice coherence, x must be in $c(\{x,y\})$, because, if not, then y is the sole element of $c(\{x,y\})$ and, by choice coherence, x cannot be an element of $c(A)$. Therefore, $x \succeq_c y$. This is true for every member y of A; therefore $x \in c_{\succeq_c}(A)$. That is, $c(A) \subseteq c_{\succeq_c}(A)$.

Finally, suppose $x \in c_{\succeq_c}(A)$ and that $c(A)$ is nonempty. Let x_0 be some member $c(A)$. By the definition of $c_{\succeq_c}$, $x \succeq_c x_0$, which is to say that $x \in c(\{x_0,x\})$. But then $x \notin c(A)$ is a violation of choice coherence. Therefore, $x \in c(A)$, and (assuming $c(A)$ is nonempty) $c_{\succeq_c}(A) \subseteq c(A)$. This completes the proof. ∎

1.3. The No-Better-Than Sets and Utility Representations

If you carefully put all the pieces from Section 1.2 together, you see that, to finish the proof of Proposition 1.2, we must show that for finite X, if c satisfies finite nonemptiness and choice coherence, some utility function u gives c via the formula (1.1), and if $\succeq$ is complete and transitive, some utility function u represents $\succeq$ in the sense of (1.3). We will get there by means of an excursion into the no-better-than sets.

Definition 1.6. *For a preference relation $\succeq$ defined on a set X (of any size) and for x a member of X, the* ***no-better-than*** *x* ***set****, denoted* NBT(x)*, is defined by*

$$\text{NBT}(x) = \{y \in X : x \succeq y\}.$$

In words, y is no better than x if x is at least as good as y. We define NBT(x) for any preference relation $\succeq$, but we are mostly interested in these sets for complete and transitive $\succeq$, in which case the following result pertains.

Proposition 1.7. *If $\succeq$ is complete and transitive, then* NBT(x) *is nonempty for all* x. *In particular,* $x \in$ NBT(x). *Moreover,* $x \succeq y$ *if and only if* NBT$(y) \subseteq$ NBT(x), *and if* $x \succeq y$ *but* $y \not\succeq x$, *then* NBT(y) *is a proper subset of* NBT(x). *Therefore, the collection of* NBT *sets nest; that is, if* x *and* y *are any two elements of* X, *then either* NBT(x) *is a proper subset of* NBT(y), *or* NBT(y) *is a proper subset of* NBT(x), *or the two are equal.*

This is not hard to prove, so I leave it to you in case you need practice with these sorts of exercises in mathematical theorem proving.

Proposition 1.8. *If* X *is a finite set and* $\succeq$ *is complete and transitive, then the function* $u : X \to R$ *defined by*

$$u(x) = \textit{the number of elements of } \mathrm{NBT}(x)$$

satisfies $u(x) \geq u(y)$ *if and only if* $x \succeq y$.

Proof. This is virtually a corollary of the previous proposition, but since I failed to give you the proof of that proposition, I spell this one out. Suppose $x \succeq y$. Then by Proposition 1.7, NBT$(y) \subseteq$ NBT(x), so $u(y) \leq u(x)$; that is, $u(x) \geq u(y)$.

Conversely, suppose $u(x) \geq u(y)$. Then there are at least as many elements of NBT(x) as there are of NBT(y). But, by Proposition 1.7, these sets nest; hence NBT$(y) \subseteq$ NBT(x). Of course, $y \in$ NBT(y), and hence $y \in$ NBT(x) so $x \succeq y$. ∎

To finish off the proof of Proposition 1.2, we need to produce a utility function u from a choice function c in the case of finite X. Here is one way to do it: Assume X is finite and c is a choice function on X that satisfies finite nonemptiness and choice coherence. Use c to generate a preference relation $\succeq_c$, which is immediately complete and transitive. Moreover, if $c_{\succeq_c}$ is choice generated from $\succeq_c$, we know (since X is finite; hence $c(A)$ is nonempty for every A) that $c_{\succeq_c}$ is precisely c. Use the construction just given to produce a utility function u that represents $\succeq_c$. Because, for any A,

$$c(A) = c_{\succeq_c}(A) = \{x \in A : x \succeq_c y \text{ for all } y \in A\},$$

we know immediately that

$$c(A) = c_{\succeq_c}(A) = \{x \in A : u(x) \geq u(y) \text{ for all } y \in A\}.$$

Done.

Although a lot of what is proved in this section and in Section 1.2 works for any set X, in two places we rely on the finiteness of X.

1. In the proof of Proposition 1.8, if NBT(x) can be an infinite set, defining $u(x)$ to be the number of elements of NBT(x) does not work.

2. In several places, when dealing with choice functions, we had to worry about $c(A) = \emptyset$ for infinite A. We could have added an assumption that $c(A)$ is never empty, but for reasons to be explained, that is a bad idea.

We deal with both these issues in Sections 1.5 and 1.6, respectively, but to help with the exposition, we first take up issues related to preference relations.

1.4. Strict Preference and Indifference

In terms of preferences, the standard theory of choice deals with a complete and transitive binary relation $\succeq$, often called *weak* preference. The statement $x \succeq y$ means that the consumer judges x to be at least as good as y; that is, either x and y are equally good or x is better than y.

For any pair x and y, completeness implies that of the four mutually exclusive possibilities ennumerated in the first paragraph of page 3, one of the first three must hold, namely

1. both $x \succeq y$ and $y \succeq x$, or
2. $x \succeq y$ but not $y \succeq x$, or
3. $y \succeq x$ but not $x \succeq y$.

In case 1, we say that the consumer is *indifferent* between x and y and write $x \sim y$. In case 2, we say that x is *strictly preferred* to y and write $x \succ y$. And in case 3, y is strictly preferred to x, written $y \succ x$.

Proposition 1.9. *Suppose weak preference $\succeq$ is complete and transitive. Then*

a. $x \succ y$ if and only if it is not the case the $y \succeq x$.

b. Strict preference is ***asymmetric****: If $x \succ y$, then it is not the case that $y \succ x$.*

c. Strict preference is ***negatively transitive****: If $x \succ y$, then for any third element z, either $z \succ y$ or $x \succ z$.*

d. Indifference is ***reflexive****: $x \sim x$ for all x.*

e. Indifference is ***symmetric****: If $x \sim y$, then $y \sim x$.*

f. Indifference is transitive: If $x \sim y$ and $y \sim z$, then $x \sim z$.

g. If $x \succ y$ and $y \succeq z$, then $x \succ z$. If $x \succeq y$ and $y \succ z$, then $x \succ z$.

h. Strict preference is transitive: If $x \succ y$ and $y \succ z$, then $x \succ z$.

Proof. Asymmetry of strict preference is definitional: $x \succ y$ if $x \succeq y$ and not $y \succeq x$, either of which implies not $y \succ x$. Indifference is reflexive because $\succeq$ is complete; hence $x \succeq x$ for all x. Indifference is symmetric because the definition of indifference is symmetric. Indifference is transitive because $\succeq$ is transitive: If $x \sim y$ and $y \sim z$, then $x \succeq y$, $y \succeq z$, $z \succeq y$, and $y \succeq x$, and hence $x \succeq z$ and $z \succeq x$, so $x \sim z$. This leaves a, c, g, and h to prove.

For g, if $x \succ y$ then $x \succeq y$. If in addition $y \succeq z$, then $x \succeq z$ by transitivity. Suppose $z \succeq x$. Then by transitivity of $\succeq$, $y \succeq z \succeq x$ implies $y \succeq x$, contradicting the hypothesis that $x \succ y$. Therefore, it is not true that $z \succeq x$, and hence $x \succ z$. The other half is similar.

For h, if $x \succ y$ and $y \succ z$, then $y \succeq z$. Apply part g.

For a, if $x \succ y$, then $x \succeq y$ and not $y \succeq x$ by definition, so in particular not $y \succeq x$. Conversely, not $y \succeq x$ implies $x \succeq y$ by completeness of $\succeq$, and these two together are $x \succ y$ by the definition of $\succ$.

For c, suppose $x \succ y$ but not $z \succ y$. By part a, the second is equivalent to $y \succeq z$, and then $x \succ z$ by part g. ∎

We began with weak preference $\succeq$ and used it to define strict preference $\succ$ and indifference $\sim$. Other textbooks begin with strict preference $\succ$ as the primitive and use it to define weak preference $\succeq$ and indifference $\sim$. While the standard theory is based on a complete and transitive weak preference relation, it could equally well be based on strict preference that is asymmetric and negatively transitive:

Proposition 1.10. *Suppose a binary relation $\succ$ is asymmetric and negatively transitive. Define $\succeq$ by $x \succeq y$ if not $y \succ x$, and define $\sim$ by $x \sim y$ if neither $x \succ y$ nor $y \succ x$. Then $\succeq$ is complete and transitive, and if we defined $\sim'$ and $\succ'$ from $\succeq$ according to the rules given previously, $\sim'$ would be the same as $\sim$, and $\succ'$ would be the same as $\succ$.*

Proving this makes a good exercise and so is left as Problem 1.9.

1.5. Infinite Sets and Utility Representations

This section investigates the following pseudo-proposition:

If $\succeq$ is a complete and transitive binary relation on an arbitrary set X, then some function $u : X \to R$ can be found that represents $\succeq$; that is, such that $x \succeq y$ if and only if $u(x) \geq u(y)$.

Proposition 1.3 tells us the converse: If $\succeq$ is represented by some utility function u, then $\succeq$ must be complete and transitive. But is the pseudo-proposition true? The answer is no, of course; we would not call this a pseudo-proposition if the answer were yes. I do not give the standard counterexample here; it is found in Problem 1.10.

Rather than give the standard counterexample, we look for fixes. The idea is to add some assumptions on preferences or on X or on both together that make the proposition true. The first fix is quite simple.

Proposition 1.11. If $\succeq$ is a complete and transitive binary relation on a ***countable*** set X, then for some function $u : X \to R$, $u(x) \geq u(y)$ if and only if $x \succeq y$.

(A set X is countable if its elements can be enumerated; that is, if there is a way to count them with the positive integers. All finite sets are countable. The set of integers is countable, as is the set of rational numbers. But the set of real numbers is not countable or, in math-speak, is uncountable. Proving this is not trivial.)

Proof. Let $\{x_1, x_2, \ldots\}$ be an enumeration of the set X. Define $d : X \to R$ by $d(x_n) = \left(\frac{1}{2}\right)^n$. Define, for each x,

$$u(x) = \sum_{z \in \mathrm{NBT}(x)} d(z).$$

(The series $\{\frac{1}{2}, \frac{1}{4}, \frac{1}{8}, \ldots\}$ is absolutely summable, so the potentially infinite sum being taken in the display is well defined. If you are unclear on this, you need to review [I hope it is just a review!] the mathematics of sequences and series.) Suppose $x \succeq y$. Then $\mathrm{NBT}(y) \subseteq \mathrm{NBT}(x)$, so the sum that defines $u(x)$ includes all the terms in the sum that defines $u(y)$ and perhaps more. All the summands are strictly positive, and therefore $u(x) \geq u(y)$.

Conversely, we know that the NBT sets nest, and so $u(x) \geq u(y)$ only if $\mathrm{NBT}(y) \subseteq \mathrm{NBT}(x)$. Therefore $u(x) \geq u(y)$ implies $y \in \mathrm{NBT}(y) \subseteq \mathrm{NBT}(x)$; $y \in \mathrm{NBT}(x)$, and hence $x \succeq y$. ∎

Compare the proofs of Propositions 1.8 and 1.11. In Proposition 1.8, the $u(x)$ is defined to be the size of the set $\mathrm{NBT}(x)$. In other words, we add 1 for every member of $\mathrm{NBT}(x)$. Here, because that might get us into trouble, we add instead terms that sum to a finite number, even if there are (countably) infinitely many of them, making sure that the terms are all strictly positive so that more summands means a bigger sum and so larger utility.

The hard part is to go from countable sets X to uncountable sets. A very general proposition does this for us.

Proposition 1.12. *Suppose $\succeq$ is a complete and transitive preference relation on a set X. The relation $\succeq$ can be represented by a utility function if and only if some countable subset X^* of X has the property that if $x \succ y$ for x and y from X, then $x \succeq x^* \succ y$ for some $x^* \in X^*$.*

Proof. Suppose X^* exists as described. Enumerate X^* as $\{x_1^*, x_2^*, \ldots\}$ and let $d(x_n^*) = \left(\frac{1}{2}\right)^n$. For each $x \in X$, define

$$U(x) = \sum_{\{x^* \in X^* \cap \mathrm{NBT}(x)\}} d(x^*).$$

If $x \succeq y$, then $\mathrm{NBT}(y) \subseteq \mathrm{NBT}(x)$; hence $\mathrm{NBT}(y) \cap X^* \subseteq \mathrm{NBT}(x) \cap X^*$. The sum defining $u(x)$ is over at least as large a set as the sum defining $u(y)$, and all the summands are positive, so $u(x) \geq u(y)$.

To show the converse, we use the contrapositive: If not $y \succeq x$, then not $u(y) \geq u(x)$. Not $y \succeq x$ is equivalent to $x \succ y$, and not $u(y) \geq u(x)$ is $u(x) > u(y)$. But if $x \succ y$, then there is some x^* in X^* such that $x \succeq x^* \succ y$. Hence x^* is in the sum that defines $u(x)$ but not in the sum that defines $u(y)$. Otherwise, every term in sum defining $u(y)$ is in the sum defining $u(x)$ (see the previous paragraph), and therefore $u(x) > u(y)$.

You may wish to avoid on a first reading the proof that if $\succeq$ is represented by the utility function u, then such a countable set X^* exists. This proof is somewhat technical and filled with special cases.

Let $\{I_n\}$ be an ennumeration of all closed intervals with rational endpoints; that is, each I_n is an interval of the form $[\underline{q}_n, \bar{q}_n]$ where $\bar{q}_n > \underline{q}_n$ are rational numbers. (The set of rational numbers is countable and the cross product of two countable sets is countable.) Let $u(X)$ denote the set of real numbers $\{r \in R : r = u(x)$ for some $x \in X\}$. Consider three possibilities:

1. If $u(X) \cap I_n$ is nonempty, pick some single $x \in X$ such that $u(x) \in I_n$ and call this x_n.

2. If $u(X) \cap I_n$ is empty, let $\bar{r}_n = \inf\{r \in u(X) : r > \bar{q}_n\}$. If $u(x) = \bar{r}_n$ for some $x \in X$, choose one such x and call this x_n.

3. If $u(X) \cap I_n$ is empty and $\bar{r}_n \neq u(x)$ for all $x \in X$, then do not bother defining x_n.

Let X^* be the set of all x_n created in cases 1 and 2. Since there are countably many intervals I_n and at most one x_n is produced for each I_n, X^* is a countable set.

Now suppose $x \succ y$ in X. Since u represents $\succeq$, $u(x) > u(y)$. Choose some rational number q in the open interval $(u(y), u(x))$. Let $\bar{r} = \inf\{r \in u(X) : r > q\}$. Clearly, $u(x) \geq \bar{r}$, since $u(x)$ is in the set over which we are taking the infimum. There are two cases:

1. If $u(x) > \bar{r}$, let q' be some rational number such that $u(x) > q' > \bar{r}$, and let n be the index of the interval $[q, q']$. By construction, $u(X) \cap [q, q'] \neq \emptyset$ (you may have to think about that one for a minute); hence there is $x^* \in X^*$, namely x_n, with $u(x^*) \in [q, q']$, which means $u(x) > u(x^*) > u(y)$. Done.

2. If $u(x) = \bar{r}$, then let q' be some rational number such that $q > q' > u(y)$, and let n be the index of the interval $[q', q]$. If $u(X) \cap [q', q] \neq \emptyset$, then there is $x^* \in X^*$ with $u(x) \geq q \geq u(x^*) \geq q' > u(y)$, and therefore $x \succeq x^* \succ y$. Alternatively, if $u(X) \cap [q', q] = \emptyset$, then the interval $[q', q]$ fits into category 2 above, and in particular, there is some $x^* \in X^*$, namely x_n, such that $u(x^*) = \bar{r} = u(x)$. But for this x^*, $u(x) = u(x^*) > u(y)$; hence $x \succeq x^* \succ y$. Once again, done. ■

Proposition 1.12 gives a necessary and sufficient condition that, in addition to $\succeq$ being complete and transitive, provides for a utility representation. This proposition is, therefore, the most general such proposition we can hope for. But general or not, it is not hugely useful, because the condition—the existence of the countable subset X^*—is not very practical. How can you tell, in a particular application, if such a countable subset exists?

For practical purposes, the usual method is to make *topological* assumptions about X and $\succeq$. To illustrate this method, and also to take care of the vast majority of applications you are likely to encounter in a career in economics, I'll specialize to the case where $X = R_+^k$, with the interpretation that there are k commodities and $x \in X$ is a bundle of goods. In this context, the following definition makes sense:

Definition 1.13. *Complete and transitive preferences $\succeq$ on $X = R_+^k$ are* **continuous** *if, for every pair x and y from X with $x \succ y$, we can find an $\epsilon > 0$ such that for every bundle $x' \in X$ that is less than ϵ distant from x and for every bundle $y' \in X$ that is less than ϵ distant from y, $x' \succ y'$.*

In this definition, the distance between two points is the length of the line segment that joins them; that is, we use Euclidean distance.[3]

The idea is captured by Figure 1.2. If $x \succ y$, then of course $x \neq y$. Denote the distance between them by d. If we take a small enough ϵ, say ϵ equal to 1% of d, then everything within ϵ of x will be very close to being as good as x, and everything within ϵ of y will be very close to being as good (or bad) as y. Since $x \succ y$, if we make the balls small enough, everything in the ball around x should be strictly better than everything in the ball around y.

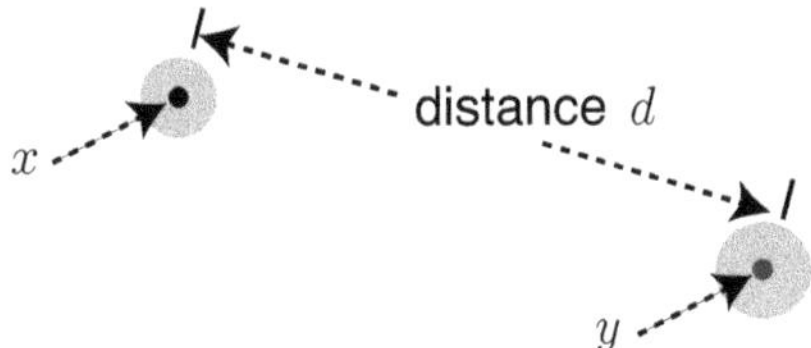

Figure 1.2. Continuity of preferences. Suppose $x \succ y$, and the distance between x and y is d. If preferences are continuous, we can put a ball around x and a ball around y, where you should think of the diameters of the balls being small relative to d, such that for all x' in the ball around x and for all y' in the ball around y, $x' \succ y'$.

This definition of continuity of $\succeq$ provides us with a very nice picture, Figure 1.2, but is neither mathematically elegant nor phrased in way that is useful in proofs of propositions that assume continuous preferences. The next proposition provides some equivalent definitions that are both more elegant and, in many cases, more useful.

---

[3] This is the first time that the distance between two bundles is mentioned, so to be very explicit: Suppose we are looking at the two bundles $(10, 20, 30)$ and $(11, 18, 30)$ in R^3. The most "natural" way to measure the distance between them is *Euclidean* distance, the square root of the sum of the squares of the distances for each component, or $\sqrt{(11-10)^2 + (20-18)^2 + (30-30)^2} = \sqrt{1+4+0} = \sqrt{5}$. But it is equivalent in terms of all important topological properties, to measure the distance as the sum of absolute values of the differences, component by component—in this case, $|11-10|+|20-18|+|30-30| = 1+2+0 = 3$—or to measure the distance as the maximum of the absolute values of the differences, component by component, or $\max\{|11-10|, |20-18|, |30-30|\} = 2$. For each of these distance measures, two bundles are "close" if and only if they are close in value, component by component; this is what makes these different ways of measuring distance topologically equivalent. It is sometimes useful to have these different ways of measuring distance—so-called norms or metrics—because a particular proposition may be easier to prove using one rather than the others. For more on this, and for many of the real analytic prerequisites of this book, see Appendix 2.

Proposition 1.14. *Continuity of preferences $\succeq$ on R_+^k imply the following, and any one of the following imply that preferences $\succeq$ on R_+^k are continuous. (Therefore, continuity of preferences could equivalently be defined by any one of the following, each of which implies all the others.)*

a. *If $\{x_n\}$ is a sequence from R_+^k with $x_n \succeq y$ for all n, and if $\lim_{n\to\infty} x_n = x$, then $x \succeq y$. If $\{x_n\}$ is a sequence from R_+^k with $y \succeq x_n$ for all n, and if $\lim_{n\to\infty} x_n = x$, then $y \succeq x$.*

b. *If $\{x_n\}$ is a sequence from R_+^k with $\lim_{n\to\infty} x_n = x$, and if $x \succ y$, then for all sufficiently large n, $x_n \succ y$. And if $\lim_{n\to\infty} x_n = x$, and $y \succ x$, then for all sufficiently large n, $y \succ x_n$.*

c. *For all $x \in R_+^k$, the sets* NBT(x) *and* NWT$(x) = \{y \in R_+^k : y \succeq x\}$ *are both closed sets. (NWT is a mnemonic for No Worse Than.)*

d. *For all $x \in R_+^k$, the sets* SBT$(x) = \{y \in R_+^k : y \succ x\}$ *and* SWT$(x) = \{y \in R_+^k : x \succ y\}$ *are both (relatively, in R_+^k) open sets.*[4] *(SBT is a mnemonic for Strictly Better Than, and SWT stands for Strictly Worse Than.)*

The proof of this proposition is left as an exercise, namely Problem 1.11. Providing the proof is a good diagnostic test for whether you understand concepts of open and closed sets and limits in Euclidean spaces. If you aren't sure that you can provide a proof, you should review these basic topological (or, if you prefer, analytical) concepts until you can prove this proposition; I provide a written-out proof in the *Student's Guide.*

The reason for the definition is probably clear:

Proposition 1.15. *If $X = R_+^k$ and preferences $\succeq$ are complete, transitive, and continuous on X, then $\succeq$ can be represented by a utility function u; that is, $u(x) \geq u(y)$ if and only if $x \succeq y$.*

Proof. The proof consists of showing that there is a countable subset X^* of X that does the trick, in the sense of Proposition 1.12. For instance, let X^* be all bundles $x \in X$ all of whose components are rational numbers. There are countably many of these bundles. Suppose $x \succ y$. Look at the line segment that joins x to y; that is, look at bundles that are convex combinations of x and y, or bundles of the form $ax + (1-a)y$ for $a \in [0,1]$. Let $a_1 = \inf\{a \in [0,1] : ax + (1-a)y \succeq x\}$. It is easy to see that $a_1 > 0$; we can put a ball of some size $\epsilon > 0$ around y such that every bundle in the ball is strictly worse than x, and for small enough a, convex combinations $ax + (1-a)y$ all lie within this ball. Let x_1 denote $a_1x + (1-a_1)y$; I

[4] The set Y is *relatively open* in another set X if Y is the intersection of X and an open set in the "host space" of X. Since $\succeq$ is assumed to be defined on R_+^k, which is a closed set in R^k, we need the notion of "relatively open" here. It is perhaps worth noting, in addition, that while Definition 1.13 and this proposition are constructed in terms of preferences $\succeq$ defined on R_+^k, they both generalize to binary relations defined on more general sets X. But if you are sophisticated enough to know what I have in mind here, you probably already realized that (and just how far we can push this form of the definition and the proposition).

claim that $x_1 \sim x$. To see this, consider the other two possibilities (both of which entail $a_1 \neq 1$, of course): If $x_1 \succ x$, then there is a ball of positive radius around x_1 such that everything in the ball is strictly preferred to x, but this would mean that for some convex combinations $ax + (1-a)y$ with $a < a_1$, $ax + (1-a)y \succeq x$, contradicting the definition of a_1. And if $x \succ x_1$, then a ball of positive radius around x_1 will be such that everything in the ball is strictly worse than x. This ball includes all convex combinations $ax + (1-a)y$ with a a bit bigger than a_1, again contradicting the definition of a_1.

Since $x_1 \sim x$, $x_1 \succ y$. There is a ball of positive radius around x_1 such that everything in the ball is strictly better than y. This includes convex combinations $ax + (1-a)y$ that have a slightly smaller than a_1. But by the definition of a_1, all such convex combinations must be strictly worse than x. Therefore, we know for some a_2 less than a_1, and for $x_2 = a_2x + (1-a_2)y$, $x \succ x_2 \succ y$. Now we are in business. We can put a ball of positive radius around x_2 such that everything in the ball is strictly worse than x, and we can put a ball of positive radius around x_2 such that everything in the ball is strictly better than y. Taking the smaller of these two radii, everything z in a ball of that radius satisfies $x \succ z \succ y$. But any ball of positive radius contains bundles all of whose components are rational; hence some $x^* \in X^*$ satisfies $x \succ x^* \succ y$. Done. ■

This proof uses the original definition of continuity. Can you construct a more elegant proof using one of the alternative characterizations of continuity of preferences given in Proposition 1.14?

Proposition 1.15 says that continuous preferences have a utility representation. We might hope for something more, namely that continuous preferences have a utility representation where the function u is itself continuous. We have not proved this and, in fact, the utility functions that we are producing in this chapter are wildly discontinuous. (See Problem 1.12.) In Chapter 2, we see how to get to the more desirable state of affairs, where continuous preferences have a continuous representation.

1.6. Choice from Infinite Sets

The second difficulty that infinite X poses for the standard theory concerns the possibility that $c(A) = \emptyset$ for infinite sets A. One of the two properties of choice functions that characterize the standard model is that $c(A)$ is nonempty for finite sets A; we could simply require this of all sets A; that is, assume away the problem. But this is unwise: Suppose, for instance, that $X = R^2_+$, and define a utility function u by $u(x) = u((x_1, x_2)) = x_1 + x_2$. Consider the subset of X given by $A = [0,1) \times [0,1)$; that is, A is the unit square, but with the north and east edges removed. The set $\{x \in A : u(x) \geq u(y) \text{ for all } y \in A\}$ *is* empty; from this semi-open set, open on the "good" sides, no matter what point you choose, there is something better according to u. If we insisted that c is nonempty valued for all A, we wouldn't be consistent with utility maximization for any strictly increasing utility function, at least for sets

A like the one here.

A different approach is to define choice only for some subsets of X and, in particular, to restrict the domain of c to subsets of X for which it is reasonable to assume that choice is nonempty; then strengthen finite nonemptiness by dropping its restriction to finite sets. See Problem 1.15 for more on this approach.

We can leave things as they are: Proposition 1.5 guarantees that if c satisfies finite nonemptiness and choice coherence, then for infinite A,

$$c(A) = \emptyset \quad \text{or} \quad c(A) = c_{\succeq_c}(A),$$

for $\succeq_c$ defined from c. As long as $c(A)$ is not empty, it gives the "right" answer. But still, it would be nice to know that $c(A)$ is not empty for the appropriate sorts of infinite sets A. For instance, if X is, say, R^k_+ and c generates continuous preferences, $c(A)$ should be nonempty for compact sets A, at least. (Why should this be true? See Proposition 1.19.) And in any setting, suppose we have a set A that contains x and that is a subset of NBT(x). Then $c(A)$ ought to be nonempty, since it should contain x.

These are nice things to have, but they can't be derived from finite nonemptiness and choice coherence; further assumptions will be needed to have them. To demonstrate this, imagine that c is a well-behaved choice function; it satisfies finite nonemptiness and choice coherence and is nonempty for all the "right" sorts of infinite sets A. Modify c, creating c', by letting $c'(A) = \emptyset$ for an arbitrary collection of infinite sets A. For instance, we could let $c'(A) = \emptyset$ for all compact sets that contain some given x^*, or for all sets A that are countably infinite, or for all sets that contain x^* or are countably infinite but not both. When I say "for an arbitrary collection of infinite sets," I mean "arbitrary." Then c' satisfies finite nonemptiness (of course, since it is identical to c for such arguments) and choice coherence. The latter is quite simple: Suppose $x, y \in A \cap B$, $x \in c'(A)$, and $y \notin c'(A)$. Since $c'(A) \neq \emptyset$, $c'(A) = c(A)$; since c satisfies choice coherence, $y \notin c(B)$. If $c'(B) \neq \emptyset$ then $c'(B) = c(B)$ and hence $y \notin c'(B)$. On the other hand, if $c'(B) = \emptyset$, then $y \notin c'(B)$.

There are lots of assumptions we can add to finite nonemptiness and choice coherence, to ensure that c is well-behaved on infinite sets. But perhaps the most general is the simplest. Begin with a choice function c that satisfies finite nonemptiness and choice coherence. Generate the corresponding preference relation $\succeq_c$. Use that preference relation to generate, for each $x \in X$, NBT$_{\succeq_c}(x)$, where I've included the subscript $\succeq_c$ to clarify that we are beginning with the choice function c. Then,

Assumption 1.16. *If $x \in A \subseteq$ NBT$_{\succeq_c}(x)$, $c(A) \neq \emptyset$.*

Let me translate this assumption into words: If faced with a choice from some set A that contains an element x, such that everything in A is revealed to be no better than x when pairwise comparisons are made (that is, $x \in c(\{x, y\})$ for all $y \in A$), then the consumer makes *some* choice out of A. (Presumably that choice includes x, but we do not need to assume this; it will be implied by choice coherence.)

Proposition 1.17. *A choice function c that satisfies finite nonemptiness and choice coherence is identical to choice generated by the preferences it generates—that is, $c \equiv c_{\succeq_c}$—if and only if it satisfies Assumption 1.16.*

Proof. Suppose $c \equiv c_{\succeq_c}$ and A is a set with $x \in A \subseteq \text{NBT}_{\succeq_c}(x)$. Then by the definition of $c_{\succeq_c}$, $x \in c_{\succeq_c}(A)$. Since $c \equiv c_{\succeq_c}$, this implies that $c(A)$ is nonempty. (Therefore, in fact, $c(A) = c_{\succeq_c}(A)$ by Proposition 1.5.) Conversely, suppose c satisfies Assumption 1.16. Take any A. Either $c_{\succeq_c}(A) = \emptyset$ or $\neq \emptyset$. In the first case, $c_{\succeq_c}(A) = c(A) = \emptyset$ by Proposition 1.5. In the second case, let x be any element of $c_{\succeq_c}(A)$. Then $x \in A$ and, by the definition of $c_{\succeq_c}$, $A \subseteq \text{NBT}_{\succeq_c}(x)$. By Assumption 1.16, $c(A)$ is nonempty, and Proposition 1.5 implies that $c(A) = c_{\succeq_c}(A)$. ■

An interesting complement to Assumption 1.16 is the following.

Proposition 1.18. *Suppose that c satisfies finite nonemptiness and choice coherence. If A is such that, for every $x \in A$, $A \not\subseteq \text{NBT}_{\succeq_c}(x)$, then $c(A) = \emptyset$.*

That is, the collection of sets in Assumption 1.16 for which it is assumed a choice is made is the largest possible collection of such sets, if choice is to satisfy finite nonemptiness and choice coherence. The proof is implicit in the proof of Proposition 1.17: If $c(A) \neq \emptyset$, then $c(A) = c_{\succeq_c}(A)$ by Proposition 1.5, and for any $x \in c(A) = c_{\succeq_c}(A)$, it is necessarily the case that $A \subseteq \text{NBT}_{\succeq_c}(x)$.

What about properties such as, c is nonempty valued for compact sets A? Let me state a proposition, although I reserve the proof until Chapter 2 (see, however, Problem 1.13):

Proposition 1.19. *Suppose $X = R^k_+$. Take a choice function c that satisfies finite nonemptiness, choice coherence, and Assumption 1.16. If the preferences $\succeq_c$ generated from c are continuous, then for any nonempty and compact set A, $c(A) \neq \emptyset$.*

1.7. Equivalent Utility Representations

Suppose that $\succeq$ has a utility representation u. What can we say about other possible numerical representations?

Proposition 1.20. *If u is a utility-function representation of $\succeq$ and f is a strictly increasing function with domain and range the real numbers, then v defined by $v(x) = f(u(x))$ is another utility-function representation of $\succeq$.*

Proof. This is obvious: If u and v are related in this fashion, then $v(x) \geq v(y)$ if and only if $u(x) \geq u(y)$. ■

The converse to this is untrue: That is, it is possible that v and u both represent $\succeq$, but there is no strictly increasing function $f : R \to R$ with $v(x) = f(u(x))$ for all x. Instead, we have the following result.

Proposition 1.21. *The functions u and v are two utility-function representations of weak preferences $\succeq$ if and only if there is a function $f : R \to R$ that is strictly increasing on the set $\{r \in R : r = u(x)$ for some $x \in X\}$ such that $v(x) = f(u(x))$ for all $x \in X$. Moreover, the function f can be taken to be nondecreasing if we extend its range to $R \cup \{-\infty, \infty\}$.*

Problem 1.14 asks you to prove this.

These results may seem technical only, but they make an important economic point. Utility, at least as far as representing weak preferences is concerned, is purely ordinal. To compare utility differences, as in $u(x) - u(y) > u(y) - u(z)$, and conclude that "$x$ is more of an improvement over y than y is over z," or to compare the utility of a point to some cardinal value, as in $u(x) < 0$, and conclude that "x is worse than nothing," makes no sense.

1.8. Commentary

This ends the mathematical development of the standard models of choice, preference, and utility. But a lot of commentary remains.

The standard model as positive theory

At about this point (if not earlier), many students object to utility maximization. "No one," this objection goes, "chooses objects after consulting some numerical index of goodness. A model that says that consumers choose in this fashion is a bad description of reality and therefore a bad foundation for any useful social science."

Just because consumers don't actively maximize utility doesn't mean that the model of utility-maximizing choice is a bad descriptive or positive model. To suppose that individuals act *as if* they maximize utility is not the same as supposing that they consciously do so. We have proven the following: If choice behavior satisfies finite nonemptiness and the choice coherence, then (as long as something is chosen) choice behavior is *as if* it were preference driven for some complete and transitive weak preference relation. And if the set of objects for which choice is considered is countable or if revealed preferences are continuous, then preference-driven choice is *as if* it were done to maximize a numerical index of goodness.

Utility maximization is advanced as a descriptive or positive model of consumer choice. Direct falsification of the model requires that we find violations of nonemptiness or choice coherence. If we don't, then utility maximization is a perfectly fine as-if model of the choices that are made.

Incomplete data about choice

Unhappily, when we look at the choices of real consumers, we do see some violations of choice coherence and nonemptiness (or, when we ask for preference judgments, of completeness and transitivity). So the standard model *is* empirically falsified. We will discuss this unhappy state of affairs momentarily.

But another problem should be discussed first. The assertion of two paragraphs ago fails to recognize the empirical limitations that we usually face. By this I mean, to justify utility maximization as a model of choice, we need to check the consumer's choice function for every subset A of X, and for each A we need to know all of $c(A)$. (But see Problem 1.15 for a slight weakening of this.) In any real-life situation, we will observe (at best) $c(A)$ for finitely many subsets of X, and we will probably see something less than this; we will probably see for each of a finite number of subsets of X *one* element out of $c(A)$; namely, the object chosen. We won't know if there are other, equally good members of A.

To take seriously the model of utility maximization as an empirically testable model of choice, we must answer the question: Suppose we see $c(A)$, or even one element from $c(A)$, for each of a finite number of subsets A of X. When are these data consistent with utility maximization?

The answer to this question at the level of generality of this chapter is left to you to develop; see Problem 1.16. In Chapter 4, we will provide an answer to a closely related problem, where we specialize to the case of consumer demand given a budget constraint.

Now for the bigger question: In the data we see, how does the model do? What criticisms can be made of it? What does it miss, by how much, and what repairs are possible? Complete answers to these questions would take an entire book, but I can highlight several important categories of empirical problems, criticisms, and alternatives.

Framing

In the models we have considered, the objects or consumption bundles x are presented abstractly, and it is implicitly assumed that the consumer knows x when she sees it. In real life, the way in which we present an object to the consumer can influence how she perceives it and (therefore) what choices she makes. If you find this hard to believe, answer the following question, which is taken from Kahneman and Tversky (1979):

> As a doctor in a position of authority in the national government, you've been informed that a new flu epidemic will hit your country next winter and that this epidemic will result in the deaths of 600 people. (Either death or complete recovery is the outcome in each case.) There are two possible vaccination programs that you can undertake, and doing one precludes doing the other. Program A will save 400 people with certainty. Program B will save no one with probability $1/3$ and 600 with probability $2/3$. Would you choose Program A or Program B?

Formulate an answer to this question, and then try:

> As a doctor in a position of authority in the national govenment, you've been informed that a new flu epidemic will hit your country next winter. To fight this epidemic, one of two possible vaccination programs is to be chosen, and undertaking one program precludes attempting the other. If Program X is

adopted, 200 people will die with certainty. Under Program Y, there is a 2/3 chance that no one will die, and a 1/3 chance that 600 will die. Would you choose Program X or Program Y?

These questions are complicated by the fact that they involve some uncertainty, the topic of Chapter 5. But they make the point very well. Asked of health-care professionals, the modal responses to this pair of questions were: Program A is strictly preferred to B, while Program X is worse than Y. To be clear, the modal health-care professional strictly preferred A to B and strictly preferred Y to X. The point is that Program A is precisely Program X in terms of outcomes, and Programs B and Y are the same. They sound different because Programs A and B are phrased in terms of saving people, while X and Y are phrased in terms of people dying. But within the context of the whole story, A is X and B is Y. Yet (by the modal response) A is better than B, and X is worse than Y. Preference judgments certainly depend on frame.

The way bundles are framed can affect how they are perceived and can influence the individual's cognitive processes in choosing an alternative. Choice coherence rules out the following sort of behavior: A consumer chooses apple pie over cherry if those are the only two choices, but chooses cherry when informed that peach is also available. Ruling this out seems sensible—the ruled-out behavior is silly—but change the objects and you get a phenomenon that is well known to (and used by) mail-order marketers. When, in a mail-order catalog, a consumer is presented with the description of an object, the consumer is asked to choose between the object and her money. To influence the consumer to choose the object, the catalog designer will sometimes include on the same page a slightly better version of the object at a much higher price, or a very much worse version of the object at a slightly lower price. The idea is to convince the consumer, who will compare the different versions of the object, that one is a good deal, and so worthy of purchase. Of course, this strikes directly at choice coherence.

The point is simple: When individuals choose, and when they make pairwise preference judgments, they do so using various processes of perception and cognition. When the choices are complex, individuals simplify, by focusing (for example) on particularly salient features. Salience can be influenced by the frame: how the objects are described; what objects are available; or (in the case of pairwise comparisons) how the two objects compare. This leads to violations of choice coherence in the domain of choice, and intransitivities when consumers make pairwise preference judgments.

Indecision

Indecision attacks a different postulate of the standard model: finite nonemptiness or, in the context of preference, completeness. If asked to choose between 3 cans of beer and 10 bottles of wine or 20 cans of beer and 6 bottles of wine, the consumer might be unable to make a choice; in terms of preferences, she may be unable to say that either bundle is as good or better than the other.

An alternative to the standard model allows the consumer the luxury of indecision. In terms of preferences, for each pair of objects x and y the consumer is assumed to choose one (and only one) of four alternatives:

x is better than y or y is better than x or

x and y are equally good or I can't rank them.

In such a case, expressed strict preference and expressed indifference are taken as primitives, and (it seems most natural) weak preference $\succeq$ is defined not as the absence of strict preference but instead as the union of expressed strict preference and expressed indifference. In the context of such a model, transitivity of strict preference and reflexivity of expressed indifference seem natural, transitivity of expressed indifference is a bit problematic, and negative transitivity of strict preference is entirely problematic: The whole point of this alternative theory is that the consumer is allowed to say that 4 cans of beer and 11 bottles of wine is strictly better than 3 and 10, but both are incomparable to 20 cans of beer and 6 bottles of wine. In terms of choice functions, we would allow $c(A) = \emptyset$—"a choice is too hard"—even for finite sets A, although we could enrich the theory by having another function b on the set of subsets of X, the *rejected set* function, where for any set A, $b(A)$ consists of all elements of A for which something else in A is strictly better.

Inconsistency and probabilistic choice

It is not unknown, empirically, for a consumer to be offered a (hypothetical) choice between x and y and indicate that she will take x, and later to be offered the same hypothetical choice and indicate that she prefers y. This can be an issue of framing or anchoring; something in the series of questions asked of the consumer changes the way she views the relative merits of x and y. Or it can be a matter of indecision; she is not really sure which she prefers and, if forced to make a choice, she does so inconsistently. Or it could be simple inconsistency. Whatever it is, it indicates that when we observe the choice behavior of real consumers, their choices may be stochastic. The standard model assumes that a consumer's preferences are innate and unchanging, which gives the strong coherence or consistency of choice (as we vary the set A) that is the foundation of the theory. Perhaps a more appropriate model is one where we suppose that a consumer is more likely or less likely to choose a particular object depending on how highly she values it "innately," but she might choose an object of lower "utility" if the stars are in the right alignment or for some other essentially random reason.

To deal empirically with the choices of real consumers, one needs a model in which there is uncertainty in how they choose—how can you fit a model that assumes rigid consistency and coherence to data that do not exhibit this?—the likelihood functions just do not work—and so, especially in the context of discrete choice models, microeconomists have developed so-called random utility or probabilistic-choice models. In these models, choice in different contexts exhibits coherence or consistency statistically, but choices in specific instances may, from the perspective of the standard model, appear inconsistent.

The determinants of preference

The standard model makes no attempt to answer the question, Where do preferences come from? Are they something innate to the individual, given (say) genetically? Or are they a product of experience? And if they are a product of experience, is that experience primarily social in character? Put very baldly, does social class determine preferences?

These questions become particularly sharp in two contexts that we reach in this book. The first concerns dynamic choice. If the consumer's experiences color her preferences for subsequent choices, having a model of how this happens is important for models of how the consumer chooses through time. This is true whether her earlier choices are made in ignorance of the process or, more provocatively, if her earlier choices take into account the process. We will visit this issue briefly in Chapter 7, when we discuss dynamic choice theory; it arises very importantly in the context of cooperation and trust in dynamic relationships (and is scheduled for discussion in that context in Volume 3).

These questions are also important to so-called welfare analysis, which we meet in Chapter 8. Roughly, a set of institutions will be "good" if they give consumers things they (the consumers) prefer. Those who see preferences as socially determined often balk at such judgments, especially if, as is sometimes supposed, members of an oppressed class have socially determined tastes or preferences that lead them to prefer outcomes that are "objectively" bad. In this book, we follow the principles of standard (western, or capitalist, or neoclassical) economics, in which the tastes and preferences of the individual consumer are sovereign and good outcomes are those that serve the interests of individual consumers, as those consumers subjectively perceive their own interests. But this is not the only way one can do economics.

The range of choices as a value

To mention a final criticism of the standard model, some economists (perhaps most notably, the Nobel Laureate Amartya Sen) hold that standard theory is too ends-oriented and insufficiently attentive to process, in the following sense: In the standard theory, suppose $x \in c(A)$. Then the individual is equally well off if given a choice from A as if she is simply given x without having the opportunity to choose. But is this correct? If individuals value being able to choose, and there is ample psychological evidence that they do (although there is also evidence that too much choice becomes bad), it might be sensible to use resources to widen the scope of choice available to the individual, even if this means that the final outcome chosen is made a bit worse evaluated purely as an outcome.

I call the standard model by that name because it is indeed the standard, employed by most models in microeconomics. The rise of behavioral economics and the development of random-choice models in empirical work make this less true than it was, say, a decade ago. But still, most models in microeconomics have utility-maximizing or preference-maximizing consumers. Certainly, except in a very few and brief instances, that is what is assumed in the remainder of this book.

My point, then, in raising all these caveats, criticisms, and possible alternatives to the standard model is not to indicate where we are headed. Instead, it is to remind you that the standard model starts with a number of assumptions about human choice behavior, assumptions that are not laws of nature. Too many economists learn the standard model and then invest in it a quasi-religious aura that it does not deserve. Too many economists get the idea that the standard model defines "rational" behavior and any alternative involves irrational behavior, with all the pejorative affect that the adjective "irrational" can connote. The standard model is an extremely useful model. It has and continues to generate all manner of interesting insights into economic (and political, and other social) phenomena. But it is just a model, and when it is time to abandon it, or modify it, or enrich it, one should not hesitate to do so.

Bibliographic Notes

The material in this chapter lies at the very heart of microeconomics and, as such, has a long, detailed, and in some ways controversial history. Any attempt to provide bibliographic references is bound to be insufficient. "Utility" and "marginal utility" were at first concepts advanced as having cardinal significance—the units mean something concrete—but then theory and thought evolved to the position that (more or less) is taken here: Choice is primitive; choice reveals preference; and utility maximization is solely a theoretician's convenient mathematical construct for modeling coherent choice and/or preference maximization. If you are interested in this evolution, Robbins (1998) is well worth reading. Samuelson (1947) provides a classic statement of where economic thought "wound up." Samuelson's development is largely in the context of consumer choice in perfect markets, subject to a budget constraint; that is, more germane to developments in Chapters 4 and 11. As I mentioned within the text of the chapter, to the best of my knowledge, Arrow originated what I have called "choice coherence" and its connection to preference orderings in the abstract setting of this chapter; this was done while writing Arrow (1951a), although the specific results were published in Arrow (1959).

Problems

Most problems associated with the material of this chapter involve proving propositions or constructing counterexamples. Therefore, these problems will give you a lot of drill on your theorem-proving skills. If you have never acquired such skills, most of these problems will be fairly tough. But don't be too quick to give up. (Reminder: Solutions to problems marked with an asterisk [such as *1.1] are provided in the *Student's Guide*, which you can access on the web at the URL http://www.microfoundations1.stanford.edu/student.)

■ *1.1. A friend of mine, when choosing a bottle of wine in a restaurant, claims that he always chooses as follows. First, he eliminates from consideration any bottle that costs more than $40.

Then he counts up the number of bottles of wine still under consideration (price $40 or less) on the wine list that come from California, from France, from Italy, from Spain, and from all other locations, and he chooses whichever of these five categories is largest. If two or more categories are tied for largest number, he chooses California if it is one of the leaders, then France, Italy, and Spain, in that order. He says he does this because the more bottles of wine there are on the list, the more likely it is that the restaurant has good information about wines from that country. Then, looking at the geographical category selected, he compares the number of bottles of white, rosé, and red wine in that category that cost $40 or less, and picks the type (white/rosé/red) that has the most entries. Ties are resolved: White first, then red. He rationalizes this the same way he rationalized geographical category. Finally, he chooses the most expensive bottle (less than or equal to $40) on the list of the type and geographical category he selected. If two or more are tied, he doesn't care which he gets.

Assume every bottle of wine on any wine list can be uniquely described by its price, place of origin, and color (one of white/rosé/red). The set of all wine bottles so described (with prices $40 or less) is denoted by X, which you may assume is finite. (For purposes of this problem, the same bottle of wine selling for two different prices is regarded as two distinct elements of X.) Every wine list my friend encounters is a nonempty subset A of X. (He never dines at a restaurant without a wine list.)

The description above specifies a choice function c for all the nonempty subsets of X, with $c(A) \neq \emptyset$ for all nonempty A. (You can take my word for this.) Give an example showing that this choice function doesn't satisfy choice coherence.

■ 1.2. Two good friends, Larry and Moe, wish to take a vacation together. All the places they might go on vacation can be described as elements x of some given finite set X.

Taken as individuals, Larry and Moe are both standard sorts of homo economicus. Specifically, each, choosing singly, would employ a choice function that satisfies finite nonemptiness and choice coherence. Larry's choice function is c_{Larry}, and Moe's is c_{Moe}.

To come to a joint decision, Larry and Moe decide to construct a "joint choice function" c^* by the rule

$$c^*(A) = c_{\text{Larry}}(A) \cup c_{\text{Moe}}(A), \text{ for all } A \subseteq X.$$

That is, they will be happy as a pair with any choice that either one of them would make individually.

Does c^* satisfy finite nonemptiness? Does c^* satisfy choice coherence? To answer each of these questions, you should either provide a proof or a counterexample.

■ *1.3. Disheartened by the result (in Problem 1.2) of their attempt to form a joint choice function, Larry and Moe decide instead to work with their preferences. Let $\succeq_{\text{Larry}}$ be Larry's (complete and transitive) preferences constructed from c_{Larry}, and let $\succeq_{\text{Moe}}$ be Moe's. For their "joint" preferences $\succeq^*$, they define

$$x \succeq^* y \quad \text{if} \quad x \succeq_{\text{Larry}} y \text{ or } x \succeq_{\text{Moe}} y.$$

In words, as a pair they weakly prefer x to y if either one of them does so. Prove that $\succeq^*$ is complete. Show by example that it need not be transitive.

■ 1.4. What is the connection (if any) between c^* from Problem 1.2 and $\succeq^*$ from Problem 1.3?

■ 1.5. Amartya Sen suggests the following two properties for a choice function c:

$$\text{If } x \in c(A) \text{ and } x \in B \subseteq A, \text{ then } x \in c(B). \qquad (\alpha)$$

$$\text{If } y \in B \text{ and, for } B \subseteq A, y \in c(A), \text{ then } c(B) \subseteq c(A). \qquad (\beta).$$

Paraphrasing Sen, (α) says "If the best soccer player in the world is Brazilian, he must be the best soccer player from Brazil." And (β) says: "If the best soccer player in the world is Brazilian, then every best soccer player from Brazil must be one of the best soccer players in the world."

Suppose (for simplicity) that X is finite. Show that choice coherence and finite nonemptiness imply (α) and (β) and, conversely, that (α) and (β) together imply choice coherence.

■ *1.6. Suppose $X = R_+^k$ for some $k \geq 2$, and we define $x = (x_1, \ldots, x_k) \succeq y = (y_1, \ldots, y_k)$ if $x \geq y$; that is, if for each $i = 1, \ldots, k$, $x_i \geq y_i$. (This is known as the Pareto ordering on R_+^k; it plays an important role in the context of social choice theory in Chapter 8.)

(a) Show that $\succeq$ is transitive but not complete.

(b) Characterize $\succ$ defined from $\succeq$ in the usual fashion; that is, $x \succ y$ if $x \succeq y$ and not $y \succeq x$. Is $\succ$ asymmetric? Is $\succ$ negatively transitive? Prove your assertions.

(c) Characterize $\sim$ defined from $\succeq$ in the usual fashion; that is, $x \sim y$ if $x \succeq y$ and $y \succeq x$. Is $\sim$ reflexive? Symmetric? Transitive? Prove your assertions.

■ *1.7. Suppose that $X = R_+^3$, and we define weak preference by $x \succeq y$ if for at least two out of the three components, x gives as much of the commodity as does y. That is, if $x = (x_1, x_2, x_3)$ and $y = (y_1, y_2, y_3)$, then $x \succeq y$ if $x_i \geq y_i$ for two (or three) out of $i = 1, 2, 3$.

(a) Prove that this expression of weak preference is complete but not transitive.

(b) Define strict preference from these weak preferences by the usual rule: $x \succ y$ if $x \succeq y$ but not $y \succeq x$. Show that this rule is equivalent to the following alternative: $x \succ y$ if x gives strictly more than y in at least two components. Is $\succ$ asymmetric? Is $\succ$ negatively transitive?

(Hint: Before you start on the problem, figure out what it means if y is *not* weakly preferred to x in terms of pairwise comparison of the components of x and y. Once you have this, the problem isn't too hard.)

■ 1.8. Prove Proposition 1.7.

■ 1.9. Prove Proposition 1.10.

■ *1.10. Consider the following preferences: $X = [0,1]\times[0,1]$, and $(x_1, x_2) \succeq (x_1', x_2')$ if either $x_1 > x_1'$ or if $x_1 = x_1'$ and $x_2 \geq x_2'$. These are called *lexicographic* preferences, because they work something like alphabetical order; to rank any two objects, the first component (letter) of each is compared, and only if those first components agree are the second components considered. Show that this preference relation is complete and transitive but does not have a numerical representation.

■ *1.11. Prove Proposition 1.14.

■ 1.12. Propositions 1.12 and 1.15 guarantee that continuous preferences on R_+^k have a utility representation. This problem aims to answer the question, Does the construction of the utility representation implicit in the proofs of these two propositions provide a continuous utility function? (The answer is no, and the question really is, What sort of utility function is produced?) Consider the following example: Let $X = [0,1]$ (not quite the full positive orthant, but the difference won't be a problem), and let preferences be given by $x \succeq y$ if $x \geq y$. The proof of Proposition 1.12 requires a countable subset X^*; so take for this set the set of rational numbers, enumerated in the following order:

$$\left\{0,\ 1,\ \frac{1}{2},\ \frac{1}{3},\ \frac{2}{3},\ \frac{1}{4},\ \frac{3}{4},\ \frac{1}{5},\ \frac{2}{5},\ \ldots\right\}.$$

First prove that this set X^* suits; that is, if $x \succ y$, then $x \succeq x^* \succ y$ for some x^* from X^*. Then to the best of your ability, draw and/or describe the function u produced by the proof of Proposition 1.15. This function u is quite discontinuous; can you find a continuous function v that represents $\succeq$?

■ *1.13. (This problem should only be attempted by students who were enchanted by their course on real analysis.) Proposition 1.19 states that if preferences $\succeq_c$ generated from choice function c are continuous on $X = R_+^k$ and if c satisfies finite nonemptiness, choice coherence, and Assumption 1.16, then $c(A) \neq \emptyset$ for all compact sets A. In Chapter 2, this is going to be an easy corollary of a wonderful result known as Debreu's Theorem, which shows that continuous preferences can always be represented by a continuous function; with Debreu's Theorem in hand, proving Proposition 1.19 amounts to remembering that continuous functions on nonempty and compact sets attain their supremum. (Well, not quite. I've included Assumption 1.16 here for a reason. What is that reason?) But suppose we try to prove Proposition 1.19 without Debreu's Theorem. One line of attack is to enlist Proposition 1.14: If preferences are continuous, then for every x, the set $\{y \in X : x \succ y\}$ is (relatively, in X) open. Use this to prove Proposition 1.19.

■ 1.14. Concerning Proposition 1.21, suppose throughout that u and v are two utility representations of (complete and transitive) preference relations $\succeq_u$ and $\succeq_v$ on a given set X.

(a) Show that if $f : R \to R$ is such that $v(x) = f(u(x))$ for all $x \in X$ and if f is strictly increasing on $u(X)$, then $\succeq_u$ and $\succeq_v$ are identical.

(b) Show that if $f : R \to R$ is such that $v(x) = f(u(x))$ for all x in X and if $\succeq_u$ and $\succeq_v$ are identical, then f is strictly increasing on $u(X)$.

(c) Suppose that $X = [0, \infty)$, $v(x) = x$, and

$$u(x) = \begin{cases} x, & \text{for } x \leq 1, \text{ and} \\ x + 1, & \text{for } x > 1. \end{cases}$$

Show that if $f : R \to R$ is such that $v(x) = f(u(x))$ for all x, then f cannot be a strictly increasing function on all of R.

(d) Suppose that $\succeq_u$ and $\succeq_v$ are the same. For each $r \in R$, define $X_r = \{x : u(x) \leq r\}$ and $f(r) = \sup\{v(x) : x \in X_r\}$. Prove that f composed with u is v (that is, $f(u(x)) = v(x)$ for all $x \in X$) and that f is strictly increasing on $u(X)$. Prove that f is nondecreasing on all of R. Why, in the statement of Proposition 1.21, does it talk about how f might have to be extended real-valued (that is, $f(r) = \pm\infty$)?

■ 1.15. As we observed on page 16, one approach to the "problem" that choice on some subsets of a set X might be infinite is to restrict the domain of the choice function c to a collection $\mathcal{A}$ of subsets of X where it is reasonable to assume that $c(A) \neq \emptyset$ for all $A \in \mathcal{A}$. So suppose, for a given set X, we have a collection of nonempty subsets of X, denoted $\mathcal{A}$, and a choice function $c : \mathcal{A} \to 2^X \setminus \emptyset$ with the usual restriction that $c(A) \subseteq A$. Note that we just assumed that $c(A) \neq \emptyset$ for all $A \in \mathcal{A}$! Suppose that c satisfies choice coherence, and suppose that $\mathcal{A}$ contains all one-, two-, and three-element subsets of X. Prove: *For every pair $x, y \in X$, define $x \succeq_c y$ if $x \in c(\{x, y\})$. Then for every $A \in \mathcal{A}$, $c(A) = \{x \in A : x \succeq_c y$ for all $y \in A\}$.* In words, as long as c satisfies choice coherence and $\mathcal{A}$ contains all the one-, two-, and three-element sets (and possibly others in addition), choice out of any $A \in \mathcal{A}$ is choice according to the preferences that are revealed by choice from the one- and two-element subsets of X.[5]

[5] With reference to footnote 1, this is how Mas-Collel et al. tackle the connection between choice and preference.

■ *1.16. Proposition 1.5 provides the testable restrictions of the standard model of preference-driven choice for finite X; it takes a violation of either finite nonemptiness or choice coherence to reject the theory. But this test requires tht we have all the data provided by $c(\cdot)$; that is, we know $c(A)$ in its entirety for every nonempty subset of X.

Two problems arise if we really mean to test the theory empirically. First, we will typically have data on $c(A)$ for only some subsets of X. Second, if $c(A)$ contains more than one element, we may only get to see one of those elements at a time; we see what the consumer chooses in a particular instance, not everything she would conceivably have been happy to choose.

(a) Show that the second of these problems can reduce the theory to a virtual tautology: Assume that when we see $x \in A$ chosen from A, this doesn't preclude the possibility that one or more $y \in A$ with $y \neq x$ is just as good as x. Prove that in this case, no data that we see (as long as the consumer makes a choice from every set of objects) ever contradict the preference-based choice model. (This is a trick question. If you do not see the trick quickly, and you will know if you do, do not waste a lot of time on it.)

(b) Concerning the first problem, suppose that, for some (but not all) subsets $A \subseteq X$, we observe all of $c(A)$. Show that these partial data about the function c may satisfy choice coherence and still be inconsistent with the standard preference-based choice model. (Hint: Suppose X has three elements and you only see $c(A)$ for all two-element subsets of X.)

(c) Continue to suppose that we know $c(A)$ for some but not all subsets of X. Specifically, suppose that we are given data on $c(A)$ for a *finite* collection of subsets of X, namely for $A_1, \ldots, A_n$ for some finite integer n. From these data, define

$$x \succeq^r y \text{ if } x \in c(A_k) \text{ and } y \in A_k, \text{ for some } k = 1, \ldots, n, \text{ and}$$

$$x \succ^r y \text{ if } x \in c(A_k) \text{ and } y \notin c(A_k) \text{ for some } k = 1, \ldots, n.$$

The superscript r is a mnemonic for "revealed." Note that $x \succ^r y$ implies $x \succeq^r y$.

Definition 1.22. *The data* $\{c(A_k); k = 1, 2, \ldots, n\}$ *violate the* ***Simple Generalized Axiom of Revealed Preference*** *(or* ***SGARP****), if there exists a finite set* $\{x_1, \ldots, x_m\} \subseteq X$ *such that* $x_i \succeq^r x_{i+1}$ *for* $i = 1, \ldots, m-1$ *and* $x^m \succ^r x^1$*. The data satisfy SGARP if no such set can be produced.*

Proposition 1.23. *If the data* $\{c(A_k); k = 1, 2, \ldots, n\}$ *violate SGARP, then no complete and transitive* $\succeq$ *gives rise (in the usual fashion) to these data. If the data satisfy SGARP, then a complete and transitive* $\succeq$ *can be produced to rationalize the data.*

Prove Proposition 1.23. (This is neither easy nor quick. But it is important for things we do in Chapter 4, so you should at least read through the solution to this problem that is provided in the *Student's Guide*.)

■ 1.17. In this problem, we consider an alternative theory to the standard model, in which the consumer is unable/unwilling to make certain preference judgments. We desire a theory along the following lines: There are two primitive relations that the consumer provides, strict preference $\succ$ and positive indifference $\sim$. The following properties are held to be desirable in this theory:

1. $\succ$ is asymmetric and transitive;

2. $\sim$ is reflexive, symmetric, and transitive;

3. if $x \succ y$ and $y \sim z$, then $x \succ z$; and

4. if $x \sim y$ and $y \succ z$, then $x \succ z$.

For all parts of this problem, assume that X, the set on which $\succ$ and $\sim$ are defined, is a finite set.

(a) Prove that 1 through 4 imply: If $x \succ y$, then neither $y \sim x$ nor $x \sim y$.

(b) Given $\succ$ and $\sim$ (defined for a finite set X) with the four properties listed, construct a weak preference relationship $\succeq$ by $x \succeq y$ if $x \succ y$ or $x \sim y$. Is this weak preference relationship complete? Is it transitive?

(c) Suppose we begin with a primitive weak preference relationship $\succeq$ and define $\succ$ and $\sim$ from it in the usual manner: $x \succ y$ if $x \succeq y$ and not $y \succeq x$, and $x \sim y$ if $x \succeq y$ and $y \succeq x$. What properties must $\succeq$ have so that $\succ$ and $\sim$ so defined have properties 1 through 4?

(d) Suppose we have a function $U : X \to R$ and we define $x \succ y$ if $U(x) > U(y) + 1$ and $x \sim y$ if $U(x) = U(y)$. That is, indifferent bundles have the same utility; to get strict preference, there must be a "large enough" utility difference between the two bundles. Do $\succ$ and $\sim$ so constructed from U have any/all of the properties 1 through 4?

(e) Suppose we have $\succ$ and $\sim$ satisfying 1 through 4 for a finite set X. Does there exist a function $U : X \to R$ such that $U(x) = U(y)$ if and only if $x \sim y$ and $U(x) > U(y) + 1$ if and only if $x \succ y$? To save you the effort of trying to prove this, I will tell you that the answer is no, in general. Provide a counterexample.

(f) (Good luck.) Can you devise an additional property or properties for $\succ$ and $\sim$ such that we get precisely the sort of numerical representation described in part d? (This is quite difficult; you may want to ask your instructor for a hint.)

Chapter Two

Structural Properties of Preferences and Utility Functions

If you have taken a course in microeconomics, you almost surely have encountered the picture of Figure 2.1, in which a consumer's preferences are depicted by indifference curves. Chapter 1's categories of choice, preference, and utility establish the basic justification for this sort of picture, but the picture as typically drawn exhibits a number of characteristics that are not the product of anything in Chapter 1. Specifically,

1. In the usual picture, indifference curves are just that, curves; they aren't "thick" in the sense of containing an open set of points.
2. Moving northeast (increasing either or both components) takes you to a higher indifference curve.
3. Indifference curves are convex to the origin—more precisely, the set of points as good as a given point is convex—which is important when it comes to finding the consumer's demand.
4. Indifference curves are continuous; they don't jump around or run out except on the axes. (You may suspect, correctly, that this is connected to continuity of preferences, which was discussed in Chapter 1.)

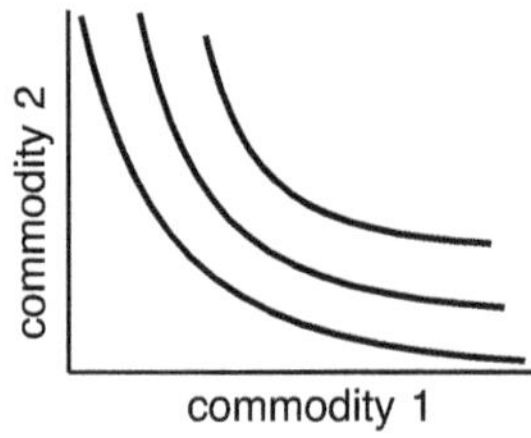

Figure 2.1. A consumer's indifference curves

This chapter ultimately concerns these properties and others like them. Throughout we consider the case $X = R^k_+$ for some integer k; preferences are defined over bundles of a list of k commodities, where the amount of each commodity in any bundle is required to be nonnegative. Consumer preferences are the fundamental primitive; complete and transitive weak preferences $\succeq$ on X are given, from which strict preferences $\succ$ and indifference $\sim$ are defined. Choice per se will not be an issue in this chapter, but think of choice as related to preferences in the fashion of Chapter 1.

This chapter makes extensive use of simple real analysis and the mathematics of convexity of sets and functions. Appendices 2 and 3 survey what you will need to know.

2.1. Monotonicity

In many cases, it is reasonable to assume that consumers prefer more to less—or at least they do not strictly prefer less to more. We have the following definitions and results:

Definition 2.1. *Preferences $\succeq$ are* ***monotone*** *(or* ***nondecreasing****) if for any two bundles x and y such that $x \geq y$, $x \succeq y$.*[1] *Preferences $\succ$ are* ***strictly monotone*** *(or* ***strictly increasing****) if for any two bundles x and y such that $x \geq y$ and $x \neq y$, $x \succ y$.*[2]

A function $u : X \to R$ is ***nondecreasing*** *if for any two bundles x and y such that $x \geq y$, $u(x) \geq u(y)$. And u is* ***strictly increasing*** *if for any two bundles x and y such that $x \geq y$ and $x \neq y$, $u(x) > u(y)$.*

Proposition 2.2. *If u represents preferences $\succeq$, these preferences are monotone if and only if u is nondecreasing, and these preferences are strictly monotone if and only if u is strictly increasing.*

The proof involves only a comparison of definitions and so is omitted.

Please take careful note of the implicit quantifiers in this result. The first part says that if *some* nondecreasing u represents $\succeq$, then $\succeq$ is monotone, while if $\succeq$ is monotone, then *every* u that represents $\succeq$ is nondecreasing. Therefore, if some u that represents a consumer's preferences is nondecreasing, every other u' that represents these preferences is nondecreasing. The second half implies the same sort of thing for strictly monotone preferences and strictly increasing utility representations. Problem 2.1 asks you to clarify all subsequent results along these lines.

Strictly monotone preferences for strict increases in the bundle

Also take careful note of how monotonicity and strict monotonicity of preferences are defined. In particular, note that in strict monotonicity, any increase in any one of the components of x (with no decreases in any components) leads to a strict

---

[1] For k-dimensional vectors x and y in R^k, $x \geq y$ means each component of x is at least as large as the corresponding component of y. When every component of x is strictly larger than the corresponding component of y, we will write $x > y$.

[2] In mathematics, "monotone" could mean increasing *or* decreasing. It would be more precise to say that preferences with the property of the definition are monotonically increasing (or nondecreasing). Indeed, while in this chapter I use "monotone" for preferences and "nondecreasing" for utility functions, later in the book I use "nondecreasing" more often than "monotone" and "strictly increasing" more often than "strictly monotone" when describing preferences.

preference improvement. An "intermediate" sort of monotonicity that is applied in some economic contexts is called "strict monotonicity for strict increases in the bundle," meaning that if $x > y$ (if x exceeds y in every component), then $x \succ y$. For instance, suppose preferences are represented by the utility function $u(x) = \min_{i=1,\ldots,k} u_i(x_i)$, where each $u_i : R_+ \to R$ is a strictly increasing function. The corresponding preferences are not strictly monotone (why?), but they are strictly monotone for strict increases in x (why?). Compare with, for instance, the classic Cobb-Douglas utility function $u(x) = \prod_{i=1}^{k} x_i^{\alpha_i}$, for $\alpha_i > 0$. The corresponding preferences are not strictly monotone (why?), but they are strictly monotone for strict increases in x (why?), and they are strictly monotone away from the axes in R^k (why?).

Global and local insatiability

Some commodities, such as week-old fish or contaminated water, are noxious; increased consumption makes the consumer worse off. Other goods are pleasant only up to some limit; very sweet foods are examples. Hence, it is preferable to avoid assuming strict monotonicity and even monotonicity if possible. But, for many important results to come, we will need to assume that the consumer is *insatiable*. Two versions of this assumption are used.

Definition 2.3.

a. *Preferences* $\succeq$ *are* ***globally insatiable*** *if, for every* $x \in X$, $y \succ x$ *for some other bundle* $y \in X$.

b. *Preferences* $\succeq$ *are* ***locally insatiable*** *if, for every* $x \in X$ *and for every number* $\epsilon > 0$, *there exists* $y \in X$ *that is no more than* ϵ *distant from* x, *such that* $y \succ x$.

Note that becoming satiated in one commodity or positively disliking another does not pose a problem for either global or local insatiability. All that is needed, for instance, for local insatiability is that, starting from any consumption bundle, the consumer would prefer a small increase (or decrease) in *some* of the commodities. These properties do not translate in any meaningful fashion into a statement about utility representations, except to restate the definition in those terms.

It is perhaps worth noting that if preferences are both locally insatiable and monotone, then they are (also) strictly monotone for strict increases in x, and if they are strictly monotone for strict increases in x, then they are locally insatiable. (You are asked to prove these two results and more besides in Problem 2.6, with the solution provided in the *Guide*.)

2.2. Convexity

The next set of properties that we consider revolves around the notion of *convexity* of preferences.

Definition 2.4.

a. *Preferences $\succeq$ are* ***convex*** *if for every pair x and y from X with $x \succeq y$ and for every number $a \in [0,1]$, the bundle $ax + (1-a)y \succeq y$.*

b. *Preferences $\succeq$ are* ***strictly convex*** *if for every x and y, $x \neq y$, such that $x \succeq y$, and for every $a \in (0,1)$, $ax + (1-a)y \succ y$.*

c. *Preferences $\succeq$ are* ***semi-strictly convex*** *if they are convex and if for every pair x and y with $x \succ y$ and for every $a \in (0,1)$, $ax + (1-a)y \succ y$.*

Why would one ever think that preferences are or should be convex? The story, such as it is, relates to the classic ideal of "moderation in all things." Under the assumption $x \succeq y$, we know that in moving along the line segment from y to x we will reach a point (x) at least as good as the point (y) from which we started. The various forms of convexity are variations on the general notion that at each step along this path, we are never worse off than where we began. That, precisely, is convexity. Semi-strict convexity maintains that if $x \succ y$, so we will be better off at the end of the journey, then we are strictly better off at each step than at the start. And strict convexity holds that even if $x \sim y$, if we are strictly between the two, we are better off than at the extremes.

Convexity of preferences is sometimes defined a bit differently. For each point $x \in X$, define the set $\text{NWT}(x) = \{y \in X : y \succeq x\}$. (NWT is a mnemonic for No Worse Than.)

Proposition 2.5. *Preferences $\succeq$ are convex if and only if, for every point x, the set NWT(x) is convex.*

The proof of this proposition is left as an exercise.

The benefits of convexity

Convexity is very convenient mathematically, because of what it says about a consumer who is choosing a consumption bundle from a convex set A.

Proposition 2.6. *If $\succeq$ is convex, the set of $\succeq$-best points in a convex set A—that is, $c_{\succeq}(A)$—is convex. (Of course, if A is infinite, $c_{\succeq}(A) = \emptyset$ is not precluded.)*[3] *If $\succeq$ is strictly convex, then $c_{\succeq}(A)$ contains at most one point; the consumer either chooses a single bundle or none at all.*

Proof. If both x and y are in $c_{\succeq}(A)$, then $x \sim y$. For any $a \in [0,1]$, convexity of A guarantees that $ax+(1-a)y \in A$, and convexity of $\succeq$ guarantees that $ax+(1-a)y \succeq x$ (and y). Since $x \in c_{\succeq}(A)$, $x \succeq z$ for all $z \in A$, and so by transitivity, $ax+(1-a)y \succeq z$ for all $z \in A$; hence $ax + (1-a)y \in c_{\succeq}(A)$. The set $c_{\succeq}(A)$ is convex.

Suppose $\succeq$ is strictly convex and x and y are distinct points in $c_{\succeq}(A)$. Then for any $a \in (0,1)$, $ax + (1-a)y \in A$ because A is convex and $ax + (1-a)y \succ x$, contradicting the $\succeq$-optimality of x and y in A. ∎

[3] Both by a strict interpretation of the definition and by convention, the empty set $\emptyset$ is a convex set.

Convexity and numerical representations

Now for the consequences of convexity of preferences in terms of utility representations. Begin with some definitions, which are repeated from Appendix 3:

Definition 2.7. *A function $f : A \to R$, where A is a convex set, is:*

a. ***concave*** *if for all $x, y \in A$ and $a \in [0,1]$, $f(ax + (1-a)y) \geq af(x) + (1-a)f(y)$;*

b. ***strictly concave*** *if for all $x, y \in A$, $x \neq y$, and $a \in (0,1)$, $f(ax + (1-a)y) > af(x) + (1-a)f(y)$;*

c. ***quasi-concave*** *if for all $x, y \in A$ and $a \in [0,1]$, $f(ax+(1-a)y) \geq \min\{f(x), f(y)\}$;*

d. ***semi-strictly quasi-concave*** *if it is quasi-concave and, for all $x, y \in A$, such that $f(x) > f(y)$ and $a \in (0,1)$, $f(ax + (1-a)y) > f(y)$; and*

e. ***strictly quasi-concave*** *if for all $x, y \in A$, $x \neq y$ such that $f(x) \geq f(y)$ and $a \in (0,1)$, $f(ax + (1-a)y) > f(y)$.*

Proposition 2.8.

a. *Preferences $\succeq$ represented by a concave function u are convex. Preferences represented by a strictly concave function u are strictly convex.*

b. *Suppose that u represents preferences $\succeq$. The utility function u is quasi-concave if and only if the preferences $\succeq$ are convex; u is strictly quasi-concave if and only if preferences $\succeq$ are strictly convex; and u is semi-strictly quasi-concave if and only if preferences $\succeq$ are semi-strictly convex.*

It is semantically unfortunate that con*vex* preferences go together with (quasi-) con*cave* utility functions. Things would be easier to remember if we talked about concave preferences. But, in Proposition 2.6, convexity of the NWT sets plays the crucial mathematical role. For this reason, preferences with convex NWT sets are said to be convex, even though they have (quasi-) concave representations.

Proof. I do not prove all of this, but here is enough to give you a taste of how the proofs run. Suppose u represents $\succeq$ and is concave. For any $x, y \in A$ such that $x \succeq y$ and $a \in [0,1]$, $u(ax+(1-a)y) \geq au(x)+(1-a)u(y) \geq \min\{u(x), u(y)\} = u(y)$; hence $ax + (1-a)y \succeq y$, and preferences are convex. If u is only quasi-concave, the inequality $u(ax+(1-a)y) \geq \min\{u(x), u(y)\}$ is directly implied; hence preferences are still convex.

Conversely, if preferences $\succeq$ are convex and u represents $\succeq$, then for any $x, y \in X$ such that $u(x) \geq u(y)$, $x \succeq y$ and thus for all $a \in [0,1]$, $ax + (1-a)y \succeq y$; hence $u(ax + (1-a)y) \geq u(y) = \min\{u(x), u(y)\}$, and so u is quasi-concave. And so on, for all the other parts. ∎

Note that part a of Proposition 2.8 runs in one direction only; if preferences have a concave representation, they are convex. But convex preferences can have numerical representations that are not concave. To see how, suppose that u is a concave function that represents $\succeq$. We know from Proposition 1.20 that if $f : R \to R$ is a strictly increasing function, then the function v defined by $v(x) = f(u(x))$ is another utility representation of $\succeq$. But it is quite easy to construct, for a given concave function u, a strictly increasing function f such that $f(u(\cdot))$ is not concave. Create such an example, if this isn't obvious to you.

In contrast, part b of the proposition says that *every* representation of convex preferences $\succeq$ is quasi-concave. Hence, we conclude that if u is a quasi-concave function and f is strictly increasing, $f(u(\cdot))$ is also quasi-concave.

One question is left open. We know (or, rather, you know if you constructed the example requested two paragraphs ago) that convex preferences can have numerical representations that are not concave functions. But perhaps we can show that *if preferences $\succeq$ are convex, they admit* ***at least one*** *concave numerical representation.* In fact, we cannot show this; examples of convex preferences that admit *no* concave representation can be constructed (see Problem 2.8).[4]

2.3. Continuity

In Chapter 1, continuity of preferences was defined and used as a sufficient condition for showing that preferences on infinite sets can have utility representations. But one might hope for more; namely, for a continuous utility representation u. Continuity is not preserved by strictly increasing rescalings of utility, so not every representation of continuous preferences will be continuous. Indeed, the representation produced in the proofs of Propositions 1.12 and 1.15 is typically discontinuous (cf. Problem 1.12). But some representations are continuous:

Proposition 2.9 (Debreu's Theorem). *If a continuous function u represents $\succeq$, then $\succeq$ is continuous. Conversely, if $\succeq$ is continuous, it has a continuous utility representation.*[5]

As with convexity, continuity of preferences has economic implications. Perhaps the most important is Proposition 1.19: If A is a compact set and preferences are continuous, then $c_{\succeq}(A)$ is nonempty. In other words, some $x \in A$ satisfies $x \succeq y$ for all $y \in A$. This can be proved directly; see the proof given in the solution to Problem 1.13 in the *Student's Guide*. But with Debreu's Theorem in hand, a simple proof is possible as long as you know the mathematical result that *a continuous function attains its supremum on a compact set:* If $\succeq$ is continuous, it has a continuous representation u. Since u is continuous, for some $x^* \in A$, $u(x^*) = \max\{u(y) : y \in A\}$, or $u(x^*) \geq u(y)$ for all $y \in A$; hence $x^* \succeq y$ for all $y \in A$ and so $x^* \in c_{\succeq}(A)$.

---

[4] In Chapter 6, we give an intuitive property about the consumer's preferences on *lotteries* of consumption bundles that ensures these preferences admit a concave numerical representation.

[5] I remind you that, throughout this chapter, we are assuming that the domain for preferences is R^k_+, the positive orthant of finite-dimensional Euclidean space. Many of the results in this chapter generalize beyond this setting, and many of the proofs apply to more general settings directly. But in proving Debreu's Theorem, we use some of the topological properties of Euclidean space in ways that may not be obvious to you if you don't understand all the details.

Proving Debreu's Theorem

It is relatively easy to prove the first sentence in Debreu's Theorem. Although it is somewhat clumsy, I use the original definition of continuity provided in Chapter 1. If $x \succ y$ and u is the continuous representation of $\succeq$, then $u(x) > u(y)$. Let $\delta = u(x) - u(y)$. By standard properties of continuous functions, we can put balls of positive diameter around x and around y so that for all x' in the ball around x, $|u(x) - u(x')| \leq \delta/3$, and for all y' in the ball around y, $|u(y) - u(y')| \leq \delta/3$. Therefore, for all x' and y' in the two respective balls, $u(x') - u(y') = u(x') - u(x) + u(x) - u(y) + u(y) - u(y') \geq u(x) - u(y) - |u(x') - u(x)| - |u(y) - u(y')| \geq \delta - \delta/3 - \delta/3 = \delta/3$; hence $x' \succ y'$. (The first inequality in this chain is justified as follows: Since $b \geq -|b|$ for all real numbers b, $a + b + c \geq a - |b| - |c|$ for all a, b, and c.)

Proving the second part of Debreu's Theorem is relatively simple and intuitive if we add a further assumption; namely, that preferences are monotone and strictly monotone for strict increases in the consumption bundle.[6] Without this additional assumption, the proof is quite difficult. So I will walk you through the steps of the proof with the additional assumption, emphasizing intuition and omitting details. Then I provide the details for the proof under the additional assumption. In the final problem of this chapter, I suggest how to prove the result without the additional assumption. A sketch of the details is then given in the *Student's Guide*. Only readers with considerable mathematical sophistication should attempt the problem or even try to follow the sketched proof in the *Guide*.

In $X = R_+^k$, the ray consisting of $x = (x_1, x_2, \ldots, x_k)$ where $x_1 = x_2 = \ldots = x_k$, is called the *diagonal* and is denoted by D. Let d denote the vector $(1, 1, \ldots, 1)$ so that, for $\alpha \in R_+$, αd is the diagonal vector $(\alpha, \alpha, \ldots, \alpha)$.

For any $x \in R_+^k$, we let $\mathrm{I}(x)$ denote the indifference class of x; that is, $\mathrm{I}(x) = \{y \in X : y \sim x\}$.

Now for the walk-through. There are five steps.

Step 1. Begin with a lemma:

Lemma 2.10. *Suppose $\succeq$ is continuous and $x \succeq x' \succeq x''$. Let $\phi : [0,1] \to X$ be a continuous function with $\phi(0) = x$ and $\phi(1) = x''$. Then for some $t \in [0,1]$, $\phi(t) \sim x'$.*

This has the following interpretation. Think of the function ϕ as tracing a path through X that starts at $x = \phi(0)$ and ends at $x'' = \phi(1)$. Because ϕ is continuous, this path is continuous. The lemma says that if preferences are continuous and $x \succeq x' \succeq x''$, this path must cross through $\mathrm{I}(x')$. Graphically, if you start in the region above the indifference curve of x' and go continuously along any path until you get to some point below this indifference curve (above and below defined in terms of preference), then continuity ensures that at some point along the way you must have crossed this indifference curve.

---

[6] If preferences are both continuous and strictly monotone for strict increases in x, then they are monotone—cf. Problem 2.6—so in fact in the context of Debreu's Theorem, where preferences are continuous, the assumption that preferences are monotone is redundant once we assume that they are strictly monotone for strict increases.

Step 2. Use the lemma and the assumption that preferences are monotone to show that every bundle $x \in X$ is indifferent to some diagonal bundle $y \in D$. Graphically, every indifference curve cuts through the diagonal.

Step 3. Because preferences are strictly monotone for strict increases in the bundle, if y and y' are any two bundles from D, then $y \succ y'$ if and only if y is further out along the diagonal. Therefore, if we define $u_D : D \to R$ by $u_D(\alpha d) = \alpha$, u_D represents $\succeq$ on D. Obviously, u_D is continuous on D.

Step 4. Define $u : X \to R$ by the following procedure. For each $x \in X$, let $(\alpha(x), \alpha(x), \ldots, \alpha(x))$ be the bundle along the diagonal indifferent to x. (Use Step 2 to see that at least one diagonal bundle exists having this property and Step 3 to show that there can be no more than one.) Then define $u(x) = \alpha(x)$. That is, measure the "utility" of any bundle by following its indifference curve into the diagonal, then set its utility equal to the place on the diagonal that is hit.

Step 5. Confirm that u so defined represents $\succeq$ (easy) and is continuous (a little harder).

That does it. To contruct a continuous representation of preferences, we measure how good x is by where its indifference curve hits the diagonal. Figure 2.2 shows this in a picture.

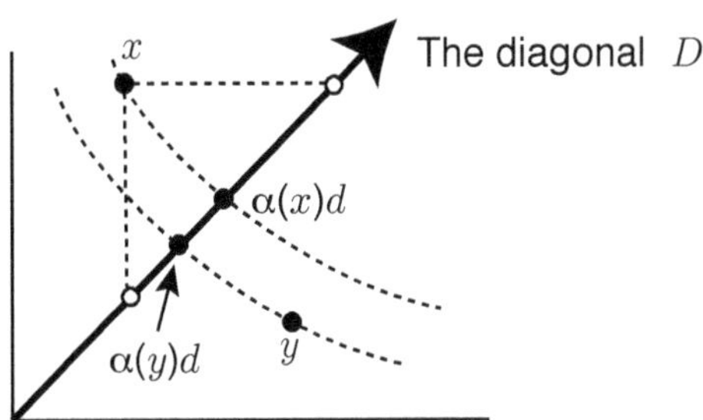

Figure 2.2. Debreu's Theorem with an extra assumption. With the extra assumption that preferences are monotone and strictly monotone along the diagonal, Debreu's Theorem is proved as follows. Any point such as x lies somewhere between the two points marked on the diagonal with open circles in terms of preference. Hence, by continuity, there is some point $\alpha(x)d$ along the diagonal that is indifferent to x; in other words, the indifference curve through x hits the diagonal at $\alpha(x)d$. The value of $\alpha(x)$ is unique because preference is strictly monotone along the diagonal. Similarly, for a point such as y, we can find the point $\alpha(y)d$ along the diagonal indifferent to y. Now $\alpha(x)d \succ \alpha(y)d$ if and only if $\alpha(x) > \alpha(y)$; strict monotonicity along the diagonal is used again. Hence by transitivity, $x \succ y$ if and only if $\alpha(x) > \alpha(y)$. Therefore, if we set $u(x) = \alpha(x)$ for each x, we have our utility function. We must prove that this $\alpha(\cdot)$ function is continuous, but that can be done, completing the proof.

Now for the details. First we prove the lemma. For the function ϕ as in the statement of the lemma, if $\phi(0) = x \sim x'$ or if $\phi(1) = x'' \sim x'$, there is nothing to prove, so we can assume that $x \succ x' \succ x''$. Let T^* be the set $\{t \in [0,1] : x' \succeq \phi(t)\}$, and let $t^* = \inf(T^*)$. Note that $0 \notin T^*$, because $\phi(0) = x \succ x'$. Moreover, since $\succeq$ is continuous, we can put an open ball around x such that every point in the ball is strictly preferred to x', and so we know that $t^* > 0$. On the other hand, $1 \in T^*$, since $x' \succeq \phi(1) = x''$.

I assert that $\phi(t^*) \sim x'$. To see this, note that for the sequence $\{t_n\}$ where $t_n = (n-1)t^*/n$, $t_n < t^*$; hence $\phi(t_n) \succ x'$, by construction. But then by continuity of the function ϕ, $\lim_{n\to\infty} \phi(t_n) = \phi(t^*)$, so by continuity of preferences, $\phi(t^*) \succeq x'$. On the other hand, there is some (nonincreasing) sequence of values $\{t'_n\}$ where $t'_n \in T^*$ (therefore, $x' \succeq \phi(t'_n)$) for each n and $\lim_n t'_n = t^*$; this follows from the definition of the infimum of a set of real numbers. By continuity of ϕ, $\lim_n \phi(t'_n) = \phi(t^*)$, and by continuity of preferences, $x' \succeq \phi(t^*)$. So $x' \succeq \phi(t^*) \succeq x'$, or $x' \sim \phi(t^*)$. This completes the proof of the lemma and step 1.

For Step 2, note that for any $x = (x_1, x_2, \ldots, x_k)$, if $\bar{x} = \max\{x_j; j = 1, \ldots, k\}$ and $\underline{x} = \min\{x_j; j = 1, \ldots, k\}$, then $\bar{x}d \succeq x \succeq \underline{x}d$ because preferences are monotone. By the lemma, some point on the line segment joining $\bar{x}d$ to $\underline{x}d$ is indifferent to x. This line segment is a piece of the diagonal D, and hence some point on the diagonal is indifferent to x.

Step 3 is a simple matter of marshalling definitions. For Step 4, we must show that for any $x \in X$, a unique $y \in D$ satisfies $y \sim x$. That $y \sim x$ for some $y \in D$ is Step 2. Suppose $x \sim y$ and $x \sim y'$ for distinct points y and y' from D. By transitivity, $y \sim y'$, contradicting Step 3.

Finally we have Step 5. Suppose x and x' are arbitrarily selected points from X. Then $x \sim u(x)d \in D$, and $x' \sim u(x')d \in D$. By transitivity of $\succeq$, $x \succeq x'$ if and only if $u(x)d \succeq u(x')d$ which, by Step 3, is true if and only if $u(x) \geq u(x')$. Thus u gives a representation of $\succeq$.

To show that u is continuous, suppose $\{x_n\}$ is a sequence in X with limit x. We need to show that $\lim_n u(x_n) = u(x)$. If not, then for some $\delta > 0$ and some subsequence $\{n'\}$, $\lim x_{n'} = x$, and either $u(x_{n'}) > u(x) + \delta$ for all $n' \geq N$ for some large N, or $u(x_{n'}) < u(x) - \delta$ for all $n' \geq N$ for some large N. Take the former case. For all $n' > N$, $x_{n'} \sim u(x_{n'})d \succ (u(x) + \delta)d$ and thus, by continuity of preferences, $x \succeq (u(x) + \delta)d$. But $x \sim u(x)d$, which would contradict Step 3. The second case, where $u(x_{n'}) < u(x) - \delta$ for all sufficiently large n', is similar. It follows that $\lim u(x_n) = u(x)$, completing the proof with the extra assumptions. ■

2.4. Indifference Curve Diagrams

Consider the standard indifference curve diagram from intermediate microeconomics, depicted in Figure 2.1. There are two commodities; that is, $X = R^2_+$. The figure depicts a consumer's indifference curves, the sets $\text{I}(x)$ for various x. At the start of this chapter, several characteristics of this diagram are listed, which can now be justified.

1. The indifference classes are "thin" curves; they have no depth; they contain no ball of positive radius. This is a consequence of local insatiability: Suppose there was a ball of radius ϵ wholely contained within some indifference curve. Let x denote the center of the ball. If preferences are locally insatiable, there is some y within $\epsilon/2$—that is, within the ball—that is strictly preferred to x, a contradiction.

2. The indifference curves are strictly decreasing as we move from left to right. In symbols, if $y = (y_1, y_2) \sim x = (x_1, x_2)$ and $y_1 > x_1$, then $y_2 < x_2$. This is true if preferences are strictly monotone: If $y_1 > x_1$ and $y_2 \geq x_2$ (and preferences are strictly monotone), then $(y_1, y_2) \succ (x_1, x_2)$.

3. The indifference curves are continuous and don't "run out" or end abruptly except on the boundaries of X. That is, if we start at any point $x \geq x'$ and follow a continuous path to a point $x'' \leq x'$, we cross the indifference curve of x'. This is true if preferences are monotone and continuous; if they are monotone, $x \geq x' \geq x''$ implies $x \succeq x' \succeq x''$; hence Lemma 2.10 applies. Continuity of preferences alone is insufficient; see Problem 2.7.

4. The indifference curves are strictly convex. That is, if distinct points x and y lie along the same indifference curve and $a \in (0, 1)$, then $ax + (1 - a)y$ lies on a higher indifference curve. This, of course, is strict convexity.

The indifference curves in Figure 2.1 have one further property: They are smooth, without kinks or sudden changes in derivatives. Nothing that we have said or done in this chapter gets us to this sort of property, although we see in later chapters that this property has some nice consequences.

2.5. Weak and Additive Separability

We now turn to properties of preferences and utility functions that are useful analytically. These properties turn up frequently in examples, but they are rarely justified. I hope that the discussion of these three properties convinces you that they involve strong assumptions indeed.

The first sort of property is associated with the term *separability*. To motivate this, suppose that consumption bundles $x \in R_+^k$ consist of bundles of foodstuffs and other items. Specifically, for $x = (x_1, \ldots, x_k)$, items 1 through j are levels of food, while $j + 1$ through k (for some $j < k$) are items of clothing, housing, recreation (other than eating), and so on. You might imagine that how a consumer feels about various combinations of food—so many steaks, so much corn, so many potatoes, so much lettuce—is all bound together in a complicated fashion, but how the consumer feels about different combinations of food doesn't depend on the amounts of other items (clothing, housing) that she consumes. If she prefers two steaks, two ears of corn, three potatoes, and no lettuce, to one steak, five ears of corn, no potatoes, and three kilograms of lettuce, she has those preferences whether she is wearing a skirt or a pair of jeans.

A ton of notation is required to formalize this idea in reasonable generality. Write K for the set $\{1,\ldots,k\}$; that is, K is the list of commodity names. For any subset $J \subseteq K$, write x_J for a commodity vector for the commodities named in the list J. So, for example, if $K = \{1,2,3\}$, thinking of the three commodities as cans of beer, bottles of wine, and loaves of bread, respectively, and if $J = \{1,3\}$, the bundle $x_J = (4,5)$ means four cans of beer and five loaves of bread. For any $x \in R^k_+$, write x_J for the components of x on the list J, and we write R^J_+ for the set of all such sub-consumption bundles (consisting only of commodities from the list J). That is, if $x = (4,3,5)$ and $J = \{1,3\}$, then $x_J = (4,5)$. Note that x_K is just the same as x, in this peculiar system of notation. If J and J' are disjoint subsets of K, write $(x_J, x_{J'})$ for the commodity bundle with commodity levels specified by x_J for commodities named in list J and by $x_{J'}$ for those named in list J'. For $J \subseteq K$, write J^C for the complement of J in K. Thus (x_J, x_{J^c}) is a completely specified commodity bundle (levels specified for every commodity named on the list $K = \{1,\ldots,k\}$).

Definition 2.11. *Let $J_1,\ldots,J_N$ be a list of N mutually exclusive subsets of K. That is, $J_n \cap J_m = \emptyset$ for $n \neq m$. Preferences $\succeq$ are **weakly separable** into $J_1,\ldots,J_N$ if for any $n = 1,\ldots,N$, x_{J_n} and x'_{J_n} from $R^{J_n}_+$, and $x_{J_n^C}$ and $x'_{J_n^C}$ from $R^{J_n^C}_+$*

$$(x_{J_n}, x_{J_n^c}) \succeq (x'_{J_n}, x_{J_n^c}) \quad \textit{if and only if} \quad (x_{J_n}, x'_{J_n^c}) \succeq (x'_{J_n}, x'_{J_n^c}).$$

To paraphrase, think of J_n as the list of food indices. Then, if $(x_{J_n}, x_{J_n^c}) \succeq (x'_{J_n}, x_{J_n^c})$, this means that the food sub-bundle x_{J_n} is preferred (weakly) to the food sub-bundle x'_{J_n} when the full bundle is filled out with $x_{J_n^c}$. When we compare $(x_{J_n}, x'_{J_n^c})$ and $(x'_{J_n}, x'_{J_n^c})$, we are changing how we fill out the full bundle, but we are comparing the same two food sub-bundles. The definition says that the comparison of food sub-bundles doesn't change with the filling-out. And it says more besides: The same property holds separately for each of the sub-bundle lists $J_1,\ldots,J_N$.

Proposition 2.12. *Suppose that u represents $\succeq$. Preferences $\succeq$ are weakly separable into J_1 through J_N, if and only if there exist functions $u_n : R^{J_n}_+ \to R$ (for $n = 1,\ldots,N$) and, for $u_n(R^{J_n}_+)$ the image set of u_n, $v : u_1(R^{J_1}_+) \times \ldots \times u_N(R^{J_N}_+) \times R^{(J_1\cup\ldots\cup J_N)^C}_+ \to R$ such that v is strictly increasing in its first N arguments, and*

$$u(x_K) = v\big(u_1(x_{J_1}), u_2(x_{J_2}), \ldots, u_N(x_{J_N}), x_{(J_1\cup\ldots\cup J_N)^C}\big).$$

It looks much worse than it is. Think of $N = 2$, J_1 being the list of food items, and J_2 being the list of, say, clothing items. Therefore, $(J_1 \cup J_2)^C$ is the list of all nonfood, nonclothing items. Suppose we have preferences that are weakly separable into food and clothing items. Then we can find sub-utility functions u_1 and u_2 defined for food and clothing sub-bundles, respectively, so that overall utility is given by a function of food sub-utility, clothing sub-utility, and the amounts of the other items, in a way that is strictly increasing in both food and clothing sub-utility levels. (All that stuff about the image set is just saying that we are only defining v for values that are needed for the representation.)

Proof. If we have a utility representation u taking this form, weak separability is shown as follows: For any n, x_{J_n}, x'_{J_n}, and $x_{J_n^C}$, $(x_{J_n}, x_{J_n^C}) \succ (x'_{J_n}, x_{J_n^C})$ implies that $u_n(x_{J_n}) > u_n(x'_{J_n})$, which implies that $(x_{J_n}, x'_{J_n^C}) \succ (x'_{J_n}, x'_{J_n^C})$ for all $x'_{J_n^C}$.

For the converse, suppose u represents $\succeq$, and $\succeq$ is weakly separable into J_1 through J_N. Fix some bundle x^*. For each n, define a function $u^n : R_+^{J_n} \to R$ by $u^n(x_{J_n}) = u(x_{J_n}, x^*_{J_n^C})$. For $(r_1, \ldots, r_N)$ such that $r_n = u_n(x_{J_n})$ for some x_{J_n} (for each n), and for any $x_{K'}$ where K' is used as temporary shorthand for $(J_1 \cup \ldots \cup J_N)^C$, define $v(r_1, \ldots, r_N, x_{K'}) = u(x_{J_1}, \ldots, x_{J_N}, x_{K'})$. The key step in the proof is to show that this definition doesn't depend on the particular x_{J_n} chosen (as long as $u_n(x_{J_n}) = r_n$). That is, if $\{x'_{J_n}\}$ is another collection of sub-bundles with $u_n(x'_{J_n}) = r_n$ for each n, then $u(x_{J_1}, \ldots, x_{J_N}, x_{K'}) = u(x'_{J_1}, \ldots, x'_{J_N}, x_{K'})$. This is where weak separability comes in:

$$u((x_{J_n}, x^*_{J_n^C})) = u_n(x_{J_n}) = u_n(x'_{J_n}) = u((x'_{J_n}, x^*_{J_n^C}))$$

implies $(x_{J_n}, x^*_{J_n^C}) \sim (x'_{J_n}, x^*_{J_n^C})$. Apply weak separability, replacing $x^*_{J_n^C}$ with $(x_{J_1}, \ldots, x_{J_{n-1}}, x'_{J_{n+1}}, \ldots, x'_{J_N}, x_{K'})$, and we get

$$\begin{aligned}(x_{J_1}, x_{J_2}, \ldots, x_{J_{n-1}}, x_{J_n}, x'_{J_{n+1}}, \ldots, x'_{J_N}, x_{K'}) \sim \\ (x_{J_1}, x_{J_2}, \ldots, x_{J_{n-1}}, x'_{J_n}, x'_{J_{n+1}}, \ldots, x'_{J_N}, x_{K'}).\end{aligned} \tag{2.1n}$$

Note that there are n indifference relations here, for $n = 1, \ldots, N$, and that the right-hand term in the nth of them is the left-hand term in the $n+1$. Thus the left-hand term in the first is indifferent to the right-hand term in the Nth, by transitivity of indifference. This is

$$(x_{J_1}, \ldots, x_{J_N}, x_{K'}) \sim (x'_{J_1}, \ldots, x'_{J_N}, x_{K'}),$$

which is just what we want.

It remains to show that v so defined is strictly increasing in its first N arguments. I leave this to you. Begin with the hypothesis that $u_n(x_{J_n}) = r_n \geq r'_n = u_n(x'_{J_n})$ for each n, with a strict inequality for some n. You have to show under this hypothesis that $(x_{J_1}, \ldots, x_{J_N}, x_{K'}) \succ (x'_{J_1}, \ldots, x'_{J_N}, x_{K'})$, and (therefore) $u((x_{J_1}, \ldots, x_{J_N}, x_{K'})) > u((x'_{J_1}, \ldots, x'_{J_N}, x_{K'}))$. To do this, repeat the argument in the previous paragraph, but with a chain of $\succeq$s and one $\succ$ in place of all the $\sim$s. ∎

Next comes additive and strong separability. The property on preferences is called strong separability; additive separability refers to the structure of the representation.

Definition 2.13. *Let $J_1, \ldots, J_N$ partition K. That is, $J_n \cap J_m = \emptyset$ for $n \neq m$, and $J_1 \cup \ldots \cup J_N = K$. Preferences $\succeq$ are* **strongly separable** *in $J_1, \ldots, J_N$ if for every $L = J_{n_1} \cup J_{n_2} \cup \ldots J_{n_\ell}$, for some set of indices $\{n_1, \ldots, n_\ell\}$ drawn from $\{1, \ldots, N\}$, $(x_L, x_{L^C}) \succeq (x'_L, x_{L^C})$ for some x_{L^C} implies that $(x_L, x'_{L^C}) \succeq (x'_L, x'_{L^C})$ for all x'_{L^C}.*

In words, we have strong separability when we have weak separability not only for the individual groups of commodities (food, clothing, shelter, etc.), but also for all unions formed out of those groups (food and clothing together are weakly separable from everything else). Not only is the consumer's preference over food items independent of what he wears and what quality housing he has, but the trade-offs he makes between food and clothing are independent of his housing, the trade-offs he makes between food and housing are independent of his clothing, and the trade-offs he makes between housing and clothing are independent of his food. All this independence adds up to a very nice result.

Before giving the result, we need a minor definition. Suppose we have strong (or even weak) separability with commodity index sets J_1 through J_N. For each of the J_n, we say that $\succeq$ is *nontrivial on* J_n if there exists a pair of J_n sub-bundles x_{J_n} and x'_{J_n} and some full bundle x^* such that $(x_{J_n}, x^*_{J^C_n}) \succ (x'_{J_n}, x^*_{J^C_n})$. (Weak separability tells us that the bundle x^* used to "fill out" the sub-bundles is actually irrelevant to this definition.)

Proposition 2.14. *Suppose preferences $\succeq$ are continuous and strongly separable in J_1 through J_N. Suppose further that $\succeq$ is nontrivial on at least three of the commodity index sets J_1 through J_N. (Therefore, $N \geq 3$ is certainly required.) Then we can find continuous functions $u_n : R^{J_n}_+ \to R$ such that*

$$u(x) = \sum_{n=1}^{N} u_n(x_{J_n})$$

is a utility representation of $\succeq$. Conversely, if preferences are represented by a utility function u taking the form $\sum_{n=1}^{N} u_n(x_{J_n})$, for $u_n : R^{J_n} \to R$, then preferences are strongly separable.

In words, with strong separability into three or more sets of indices, we can find an additively separable utility function, where to find the utility of an entire bundle, we sum the sub-utilities of the sub-bundles (for special sub-utility functions).

One direction—that an additively separable representation implies strong separability of preferences—is easy to prove, but the converse is difficult. I won't try even to sketch its proof; see Debreu (1960).

2.6. Quasi-linearity

Quasi-linearity is a functional form for utility that is extensively used in applications. It involves a commodity space, R_+^K that is divided into two pieces, a single distinguished commodity, and all the others. We will assume that the distinguished commodity is the Kth, and we will write commodity bundles as (x, m), where $x \in R_+^{K-1}$ gives the levels of all but the last commodity, and $m \in R_+$ gives the last. The symbol m is a mnemonic for money: In the usual application of quasi-linearity, the consumer's preferences are specified for a (usually small) subset of the commodities and money left over to buy the others; that is, x gives the levels of consumption of the small subset, and m the amount of money left over to buy everything else. Since this is overwhelmingly the standard application of quasi-linearity, the terminology "money left over" is used here.

Definition 2.15. *Preferences $\succeq$ on R_+^K are* ***quasi-linear in the Kth commodity*** *if they can be represented by a utility function of the form*

$$U(x, m) = u(x) + m,$$

for some sub-utility function $u : R_+^{K-1} \to R$. In such cases, we also say that the utility function U has a quasi-linear form.

In words, the utility of a bundle (x, m) is the sub-utility of the sub-bundle x plus the amount m of money left over.

Proposition 2.16. *Preferences $\succeq$ on R_+^K have a quasi-linear representation in the Kth commodity if and only if the following properties hold:*

a. *For every $x \in R_+^{K-1}$ and m and $m' \in R_+$, $(x, m) \succeq (x, m')$ if and only if $m \geq m'$.*

b. *For every x and $x' \in R_+^{K-1}$ and m and $m' \in R_+$, $(x, m) \succeq (x', m')$ if and only if $(x, m + m'') \succeq (x', m' + m'')$ for all $m'' \in R_+$.*

c. *For every x and $x' \in R_+^{K-1}$, $(x, m) \sim (x', m')$ for some m and $m' \in R_+$.*

The proof is left as an exercise. See Problem 2.11 for hints (which make the proof fairly simple), and the *Student's Guide* for the detailed proof.

Property b is the key in terms of economics. It says that trade-offs between the other goods and money don't change with equal increases in the amount of money; in other words, there are no "wealth effects." If the consumer is willing to trade x and \$10 to get x', he is willing to make this same net trade whether it leaves him with \$0 (hence $(x', 0) \succeq (x, 10)$) or it leaves him with \$100,000 (hence $(x'$, 100,000$) \succeq (x$, 100,010$)$). This powerful property simplifies analysis tremendously in applications. Of course, it is also quite a dubious property on first principles; if you use it in applications, you must justify doing so.

While we have emphasized b, the roles of a and c should be discussed briefly. Property a says that more money is better than less, which is easy to accept. Property c combines two ideas: First, no matter how much better than x' is the sub-bundle x, some amount of money compensates for getting x' instead of x. That is, notwithstanding the old cliché, money *can* buy happiness. Moreover, money can be used to calibrate the difference in worth of any two sub-bundles of the other goods; by adjusting the amount of money used in compensation, we can always get precise indifference.

Back in Chapter 1, we said that it didn't make sense to ascribe meaning to differences in utility; that is, if $u(x, m) - u(x', m') > u(x', m') - u(x'', m'')$, we shouldn't conclude that the difference from (x, m) to (x', m') is "bigger" than the difference from (x', m') to (x'', m''). But if our utility function is quasi-linear, differences in utility *on that particular scale* have a very concrete interpretation: $u(x, m) - u(x', m')$ is the amount of money left over needed to compensate the consumer for going from (x, m) to (x', m'). That is, letting $m^* = u(x, m) - u(x', m')$, $(x, m) \sim (x, m' + m^*)$.

2.7. Homotheticity

The final special property for preferences and utility functions that we explore is homotheticity.

Definition 2.17. *Preferences $\succeq$ are **homothetic** if $x \succeq y$ implies $\lambda x \succeq \lambda y$ for all $x, y \in X$ and $\lambda \geq 0$.*

Homotheticity is not a very natural property intuitively, at least in a world where there are some goods that promote the consumer's well-being (taken in moderation) and others that are and remain "fun." To take an example, imagine that $k = 2$ and the two goods are cod liver oil (measured in teaspoons) and manna (measured in kilograms). Imagine that this particular form of manna lacks a single mineral that promotes health, a mineral that can be obtained from a single teaspoon of cod liver oil. But except for that mineral, manna is much more desirable than cod liver oil, being tastier. Then it is reasonable to suppose that $(1, 2) \succ (0.2, 2.8)$ (where the first component is the amount of cod liver oil, measured in teaspoons)—the consumer prefers to get her teaspoon of cod liver oil—and yet $(5, 10) \prec (1, 14)$—this consumer doesn't want more than one teaspoon of the oil.

Despite its lack of intuitive appeal, homotheticity has its value for some types of analysis, so we investigate its consequences for utility representations. We begin with mathematical definitions.

Definitions 2.18. *A subset A of R^k is a **cone** if $x \in A$ implies $\lambda x \in A$ for all scalars $\lambda \geq 0$.*

*If A is a cone in R^k, a function $f : A \to R$ is **homogenous of degree** $\alpha \geq 0$ if $f(\lambda x) = \lambda^\alpha f(x)$ for all $\lambda \geq 0$ and $x \in A$. In the case $\alpha = 1$, we often say (simply) that the function is **homogeneous**.*

Proposition 2.19. *Preferences $\succeq$ are continuous and homothetic if and only if they can be represented by a continuous and homogeneous utility function.*

The proof is left for you to do as Problem 2.12.

Bibliographic Notes

Most of the results in this chapter are relatively straightforward; there is no particular place to send you for further reading. But the exceptions are Debreu's Theorem on continuous representations of continuous preferences, and Proposition 2.14, on strong and additive separability, which is also due to Debreu. The classic references are Debreu (1954) and (1960), respectively.

Problems

■ *2.1. (a) The form-of-representation results that are at the heart of this chapter take different forms because corresponding to each $\succeq$ are many different representing utility functions U. In one direction, we have results such as *Preferences $\succeq$ are monotone implies **all** utility function representations are nondecreasing;* but we also have results for different properties of $\succeq$ and U where the ***all*** is replaced by ***some***. In the converse direction, a typical result is that *Preferences are monotone is implied if **some** utility function representation is nondecreasing.* So that you have all such results compiled in one place, fill in the table in Table 2.1 following the example in the first line.

Preferences are	implies	is implied if	utility function representation(s) is/are
monotone	all	some	nondecreasing
strictly monotone			strictly increasing
convex			concave
strictly convex	????		strictly concave
convex			quasi-concave
semi-strictly convex			semi-strictly quasi-concave
strictly convex			strictly quasi-concave
continuous			continuous
weakly separable			weakly separable form (see note 2)
strongly separable			additively separable (see note 3)
such that they satisfy the 3 properties in Prop. 2.16			quasi-linear form (see note 4)
continuous and homothetic (see note 5)			continuous and homogeneous

Table 2.1. Problem 2.1: Fill in the table (but see the notes below first)

Notes: 1. Do not attempt to fill in the box marked ????. You were not given this information in the chapter. (In fact, I don't know what is correct to put in this box.)
2. u takes the form $v(u_1(x_{J_1}), u_2(x_{J_2}), \ldots, u_N(x_{J_N}), x_{K\setminus(J_1\cup\ldots\cup J_N)})$ for v strictly increasing in its first N arguments.
3. u takes the form $\sum_{n=1}^{N} u_n(x_{J_n})$.
4. U takes the form $u(x) + m$.
5. In this row, a maintained hypothesis is that preferences are continuous.

(b) A subtle distinction between *if $\succeq$ has property ..., then all utility functions that represent $\succeq$ have property ...,* and *if $\succeq$ has property ..., then some utility function that represents $\succeq$ has property ...,* is that the first is consistent with the case that $\succeq$ admits *no* representation, while in the second, a representation *must* exist. (For this reason, results of the first type are *not* stronger than results of the second type.) To see this distinction at work, which of the properties in the left-hand column of Table 1 are satisfied by the lexicographic preference relation defined in Problem 1.10 (which, of course, has no numerical representation)? Is your answer to this question consistent with what you supplied in the second-from-left-hand column?

■ 2.2. Proposition 2.6 leaves open the unhappy possibility that, for convex preferences and a convex set A, $c_{\succeq}(A) = \emptyset$; there are no $\succeq$-best elements of A. This is a real possibility: Consider $A = (1,5)$ or $A = (3,\infty)$ as subsets of R_+, with strictly monotone preferences. But suppose A is convex and compact?

Show by example that even if preferences are strictly convex, it is possible that $c_{\succeq}(A) = \emptyset$ for a compact set A. (Hint: Examples are possible with $X = R_+$. Obviously, these preferences cannot be continuous, and the real point of this problem is to have you think about how convexity of preferences connects with continuity of preferences.)

■ *2.3. Prove that if preferences $\succeq$ are globally insatiable and semi-strictly convex, then they are locally insatiable. Show by example that this isn't true for globally insatiable preferences that are only convex.

■ 2.4. Prove Proposition 2.5.

■ *2.5. (a) Give an example of a concave function $u : R^k_+ \to R$ (for some integer k) and a strictly increasing function $f : R \to R$ such that $f(u(\cdot))$ is not concave. (Examples with $k = 1$ are certainly possible.)

(b) Give an example of a continuous function $u : R^k_+ \to R$ (for some integer k) and a strictly increasing function $f : R \to R$ such that $f(u(\cdot))$ is not continuous.

■ *2.6. Prove that continuous preferences are strictly monotone for strict increases in all components—that is, if x and y are such that $x_i > y_i$ for all i, then $x \succ y$—if and only if preferences are monotone and locally insatiable. What can you say along these lines if we remove the assumption that preferences are continuous?

■ 2.7. Most pictures of indifference curves have the property that if $x \geq x' \geq x''$, then any continuous path from x to x'' cuts through the indifference curve of x'. That is, if $\phi : [0,1] \to R^k_+$ is a continuous function with $\phi(0) = x$ and $\phi(1) = x''$, and if $x \geq x' \geq x''$, then there is some $t \in [0,1]$ such that $\phi(t) \sim x'$. We remarked in the text that this is true if preferences are monotone and continuous; if preferences are monotone, $x \geq x' \geq x''$ implies $x \succeq x' \succeq x''$, then continuity of preferences combined with Lemma 2.10 gives the result. Show by example that continuity of preferences is insufficient for this result; if you can, show that even if preferences are continuous and locally insatiable, this result fails.

■ 2.8. *Part a is not too hard if you know the required mathematics. Part b is extremely difficult.*

(a) Consider the following two utility functions defined on R^2_+:

$$U_1(x_1, x_2) = \begin{cases} x_1x_2 & \text{if } x_1x_2 < 4, \\ 4 & \text{if } 4 \le x_1x_2 \le 8, \text{ and} \\ x_1x_2 - 4 & \text{if } 8 \le x_1x_2. \end{cases}$$

$$U_2(x_1, x_2) = \begin{cases} x_1x_2 & \text{if } x_1x_2 < 4, \\ 4 & \text{if } x_1x_2 = 4 \text{ and } x_1 \ge x_2, \\ 5 & \text{if } x_1x_2 = 4 \text{ and } x_1 < x_2, \text{ and} \\ x_1x_2 + 1 & \text{if } x_1x_2 > 4. \end{cases}$$

Show that the corresponding two preferences are both convex. Show that neither could be represented by a concave utility function. Are either or both of the corresponding preferences semi-strictly convex? Are either or both of the corresponding preferences continuous?

(b) There are preferences that are both semi-strictly convex and continuous but that don't admit any concave numerical representations. One such utility function is

$$U_3(x_1, x_2) = \begin{cases} \frac{2(1+x_2)}{2-x_1} - 1 & \text{if } x_1 + x_2 \le 1, \text{ and} \\ x_1 + x_2 & \text{if } x_1 + x_2 \ge 1. \end{cases}$$

Prove that preferences given by this utility function cannot be represented by any concave function.

■ *2.9. (a) Consider the utility function on $X = R^2_+$ given by $u(x) = u((x_1, x_2)) = \alpha x_1 + \beta x_2$, for α and β strictly positive constants. What do the indifference curves corresponding to this utility function look like? Are these preferences monotone? Strictly monotone? Locally insatiable? Convex? Strictly convex? Semi-strictly convex? Continuous?

(b) Consider the utility function on $X = R^2_+$ given by $u(x) = u((x_1, x_2)) = \min\{x_1/\alpha, x_2/\beta\}$, for α and β strictly positive constants. What do the indifference curves corresponding to this utility function look like? Are these preferences monotone? Strictly monotone? Locally insatiable? Convex? Strictly convex? Semi-strictly convex? Continuous?

■ 2.10. (This one is for math jocks.) In Chapter 1, we proved that continuous preferences had a representation in two steps. We showed (in the proof of Proposition 1.15) that if preferences $\succeq$ defined on R^k_+ are continuous, then the set of points with rational coefficients (which we can write as Q^k_+, where Q stands for the rationals) is order-dense, in the sense of Proposition 1.12. And then we relied on the proof of

Proposition 1.12. This means that, if we let $\{q^1, q^2, \ldots\}$ be an ennumeration of Q^k_+ (we know that Q is countable, so Q^k_+ is also countable), and we define

$$u(x) := \sum_{\{q^i \in Q^k_+ : x \succeq q^i\}} \frac{1}{2^i}$$

for $x \in R^k_+$, then $u : R^k_+ \to R$ represents $\succeq$. Prove that, if $\succeq$ is continuous (and complete and transitive), then u defined in this manner is upper semi-continuous.

■ *2.11. Prove Proposition 2.16. If you would like a challenge, try to prove it without reading the following hint, which gives the game away. (Hint: Fix some x^0. For each x, use property c from the proposition to find m and m' such that $(x, m) \sim (x^0, m')$. Define $u(x) = m' - m$.)

■ 2.12. Prove Proposition 2.19. It simplifies matters to assume that the preferences involved are strictly monotone, as well as continuous, and you may make this assumption if you wish, although it isn't necessary to the proof. (Hint: Given this assumption, mimic the proof of Debreu's Theorem given in this chapter.)

■ 2.13. Suppose $k = 2$, and we have a consumer whose preferences are continuous and strictly monotone. If you are given a single indifference curve for this consumer, how much of her preferences can you construct if her preferences are also homothetic? What if, in addition to being strictly monotone and continuous, her preferences are quasi-linear in the second commodity?

■ *2.14. The objective in this problem is to prove Debreu's Theorem without the extra assumption that preferences are monotone and strictly monotone along the diagonal. (The extra assumption was stated a bit differently in the text, but this is what it comes down to.) The proof for the general case takes a fair amount of work, but if you are able to do real analysis, there is nothing particularly fancy about it. I outline the proof here; in the *Student's Guide*, I provide a few more of the details.

To set the stage, let us briefly review the two places we used the extra assumption in the proof given in the text. First, it was used to ensure that for every $x \in X$, there exist y and y' from D such that $y \succeq x \succeq y'$. This, together with Lemma 2.10, ensured that we could find for each $x \in X$ some $\alpha(x)d \in D$ such that $x \sim \alpha(x)d$. Thus once we produced a numerical representation of $\succeq$ on D, we could extend it to all of X. Second, the assumption made it very easy to produce a continuous utility function on the diagonal: We could simply define $U_D(\alpha d) = \alpha$.

The general proof will follow this basic line of attack. First, we produce a one-dimensional continuous "curve," which we denote by Z, such that for all $x \in X$ there exists z and z' from Z such that $z \succeq x \succeq z'$.

(a) You should begin by producing such a Z. Use the fact that $\succeq$ has a numerical representation (albeit not necessarily continuous) and think in terms of a "curve" Z that looks something like a connect-the-dots diagram. (Further hint: Consider the following two-by-two collection of cases: For V a numerical representation, either $\sup V(Z)$ is attained or is not, and either $\inf V(Z)$ is attained or is not. If both the sup and inf are attained, your connect-the-dots picture will consist of one line segment. If either is not attained, you will have countably many dots to connect.)

(b) Now apply the lemma to conclude that for every $x \in X$ there is some $z(x) \in Z$ such that $x \sim z(x)$.

(c) Using part (b), prove that if U_Z is a continuous representation of $\succeq$ restricted to Z, you can extend U_Z to all of X to get a continuous representation of $\succeq$ on X.

So what remains is to produce a continuous representation on Z.

Let Z' be a countable dense subset of Z. If Z contains a best and / or a worst element, be sure that these are in Z'. Ennumerate Z' as $\{z'_1, z'_2, \ldots\}$. Take each z'_n in turn and define $U_{Z'}(z'_n)$ as follows: If $z'_n \sim z'_m$ for $m < n$, then $U_{Z'}(z'_n) = U_{Z'}(z'_m)$ (which was defined in an earlier step). If $z'_n \succ z'_m$ for all $m < n$, let $U_{Z'}(z'_n) = \max_{m<n} U_{Z'}(z'_m)+1$. If $z'_m \succ z'_n$ for all $m < n$, let $U_{Z'}(z'_n) = \min_{m<n} U_{Z'}(z'_m)-1$. And if z'_n satisfies $z'_m \succ z'_n \succ z'_p$ for $m, p < n$ but z'_n is indifferent to nothing that has lower index, define

$$U_{Z'}(z'_n) = \frac{\min\{U_{Z'}(z'_m); m < n, z'_m \succ z'_n\} + \max\{U_{Z'}(z'_m); m < n, z'_n \succ z'_m\}}{2}.$$

That is, give z'_n a value halfway between the values of next lowest and next highest points whose values have already been assigned.

(d) Show that this produces a numerical representation of $\succeq$ on Z'.

(e) Let I be the smallest interval containing $U_{Z'}(z')$ for all $z' \in Z'$. Show that the set of values $\{r = U_{Z'}(z'); z' \in Z'\}$ is dense in I.

(f) Take any $z \in Z$ and let $\{z'_n\}$ be a sequence out of Z' with limit z. Show that $\limsup_n U_{Z'}(z'_n) = \liminf_n U_{Z'}(z'_n)$. Then show that $\lim U_{Z'}(z'_n)$ (which we now know exists) is finite. (Hint: Use continuity of $\succeq$ and steps (d) and (e).)

(g) Define $U_Z : Z \to R$ by $U_Z(z) = \lim U_{Z'}(z'_n)$ for any sequence $\{z'_n\}$ out of Z' with limit z. Why is this well defined? (Invoke (f).) Prove that U_Z so defined gives a continuous representation of $\succeq$ on Z.

■ 2.15. (This problem requires that you know some measure theory.) In Chapter 1, we proved the existence of numerical representations of complete and transitive preferences on finite sets by counting the size of $\text{NBT}(x)$ and, on countable sets, by computing $\sum_{y \in \text{NBT}(x)} a(y)$, where $\{a(y) : y \in X\}$ was a summable sequence of numbers. In roughly that spirit, suppose that $X = R^k_+$, $\succeq$ is complete, transitive, and continuous, and μ is a finite and positive measure on X such that $\mu(A) > 0$ for every (measurable) set A that has positive Lebesgue measure. In this setting, define $u : X \to R$ by $u(x) = \mu(\text{NBT}(x))$. Prove that u is a utility representation of $\succeq$ and is upper semi-continuous, but not necessarily continuous. Can you find further conditions on $\succeq$ that will imply that u is continuous?

Chapter Three

Basics of Consumer Demand

The prototypical application in economics of the material from Chapters 1 and 2 is to *consumer demand in a competitive marketplace.* The individual consumer chooses a consumption bundle $x \in R_+^k$, subject to a budget constraint. This chapter gives the basics of the model; many following chapters contribute further pieces to this story.

3.1. The Consumer's Problem

The consumer's problem—the focus of this chapter and many to follow—is formulated as follows:

- The *space of consumption bundles* X is R_+^k, the positive orthant of k-dimensional Euclidean space, where k, a positive integer, is the number of commodities.
- The consumer has a fixed amount of money to spend on her consumption bundle. This amount of money is commonly referred to as the consumer's *income* and is denoted here by y.[1] We assume y is nonnegative throughout.
- The price of a unit of the jth commodity is denoted by p_j, for $j = 1, 2, \ldots, k$. We write p for a typical price vector $(p_1, \ldots, p_k)$. Throughout this chapter, all prices are assumed to be strictly positive; therefore p is an element of R_{++}^k, the strictly positive orthant in R^k.
- The consumer takes prices as given. She assumes she can buy any amount of a commodity at its market price, without changing that market price. Therefore, if prices are given by the price vector $p = (p_1, p_2, \ldots, p_k)$, the total cost of the commodity bundle $x = (x_1, x_2, \ldots, x_k)$ is $p_1x_1 + p_2x_2 + \ldots + p_kx_k = p \cdot x$, where $p \cdot x$ is the dot or scalar or inner product of the two k-vectors p and x.
- The consumer operates under the constraint that the bundle she purchases costs no more than the income she has to spend, or $p \cdot x \leq y$. Also, the consumer is constrained to consume nonnegative amounts of each commodity, or $x \geq 0$. For given prices p and income y, we denote by $\mathbf{B}(p, y)$ the set $\{x \in R_+^k : p \cdot x \leq y\}$, calling this the *budget set* or the *set of budget-feasible consumption bundles.*
- Subject to these constraints, the consumer endeavors to select the best bundle she can, according to her preferences. Following developments in Chapter 1, we

[1] The use of the term "income" is traditional, although "wealth" or "resources" may give more appropriate connotations.

assume that the consumer has complete and transitive preferences $\succeq$, which are always continuous in this chapter. This guarantees the existence of a continuous function u on the domain R^k_+ that represents $\succeq$ (cf. Proposition 2.9).

Therefore, the consumer's problem (abbreviated CP) given prices p, income y, and her utility function u, is to choose x to

$$\textit{Maximize } u(x), \quad \textit{subject to } p \cdot x \leq y \textit{ and } x \geq 0. \tag{CP}$$

Note that three things "define" a particular CP: the consumer's utility function u, the price vector p, and the consumer's income y.

You are probably familiar with the picture that goes with the CP; for purposes of comparison with other pictures later, I reproduce it here. For a two-commodity world, preferences are depicted by indifference curves, and the budget set is a triangle with vertices at $(0,0)$, $(y/p_1, 0)$, and $(0, y/p_2)$. The consumer tries to find the highest indifference curve that still intersects the budget set. Figure 3.1 captures all this.

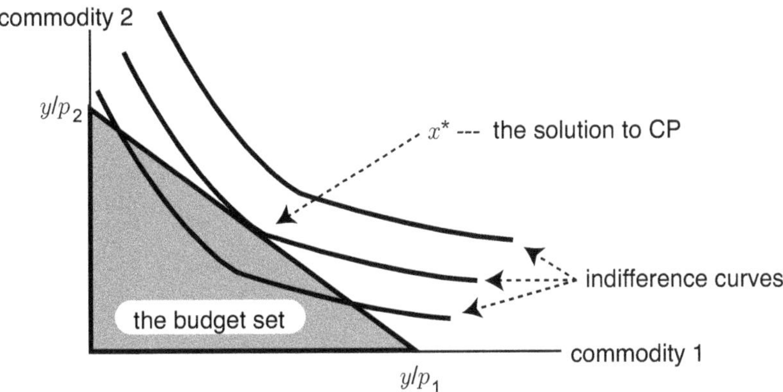

Figure 3.1. The consumer's problem (or the CP) in a picture

The assumption of constant prices

The assumption that the consumer faces constant prices—she pays $p_j y_j$ for y_j units of good j, no matter what is the size of y_j and no matter what are her other consumption decisions—has two components.

1. The consumer believes (and it is in fact true in the model) that her consumption decisions are on such a small scale that they do not affect the prices p_j that are charged for various commodities.

2. The consumer receives no quantity discounts, nor does she pay a premium for large-scale purchases. In the jargon of economics, she faces linear prices. Being "small" in the sense of the previous paragraph doesn't guarantee this; my

personal household consumption of water and telephone services is small on the scale of my local water utility and phone company, yet I pay an increasing amount on the margin the more water I use, and the average cost to me of phone services decreases with the number of phone calls I make. Very small consumers sometimes face nonlinear prices.

Despite these examples, linear prices are the starting point for most economic theory, rationalized by the possibility of resale. If a single consumer could lower her average price by purchasing more and more, some consumer (the rationale goes) would purchase in bulk and resell the goods to other consumers at a profit. If a single consumer faces higher prices as her scale of purchases increases, she would get friends to purchase in small lots and resell to her. To maintain nonlinear prices, the vendor must be able to control resale (which both my water utility and phone company can do, to a large extent). For now we assume the vendor cannot control resale and, for that reason if for no other, prices are linear.

Savings

The CP makes no provision for savings. The consumer has an amount of income y to spend, every penny of which is spent on consumption if this maximizes utility. This is neither reasonable nor descriptive. A consumer taking a trip to her local grocery rarely spends every penny in her pocket or in her checking account on groceries. Considerations of savings and trips to one store among many take us into the realm of dynamic choice, which we study only in Chapter 7. For now, think of CP as describing the shopping expedition of a mythical consumer who makes one trip to one store in her lifetime, then spends the rest of her life consuming her one-time purchases.

3.2. Basic Facts about the CP

Figure 3.1 is the typical picture drawn for the CP but is special in three ways:

1. The CP has a solution.
2. The solution is unique.
3. The solution involves spending all the consumer's income.

Drawing a picture where the CP has no solution is a challenge—you need very strange (essentially, discontinuous) indifference curves—but it is easy to draw pictures where the CP has multiple solutions or where the solutions involve spending less than y; see Figures 3.2a, b, and c.

On the other hand, it is easy to give conditions that guarantee 1 through 3.

Proposition 3.1. *Fix a continuous utility function u, and consider the CP for various strictly positive prices p and nonnegative income levels y.*

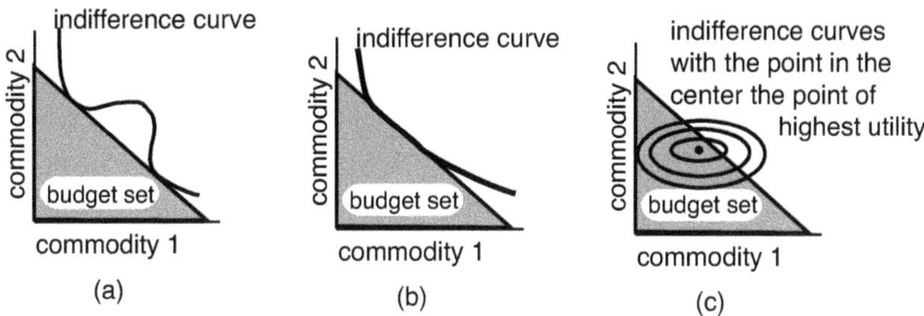

Figure 3.2. Variations on Figure 3.1. In panel a, the CP has two solutions because preferences are not convex. In panel b, preferences are convex but not strictly convex, and the CP has a convex set of solutions. In panel c, preferences are not locally insatiable, and the solution to the CP is interior to the budget set (that is, at the solution, the consumer spends less than y).

a. *If x is a solution of the CP for a given p and y, then x is also a solution for $(\lambda p, \lambda y)$, for any strictly positive scalar λ.*

b. *The CP for each p and y has at least one solution; some $x \in \mathbf{B}(p, y)$ maximizes $u(x)$ over $\mathbf{B}(p, y)$.*

c. *If u is quasi-concave (preferences are convex), the set of solutions to the CP for any p and y is convex. If u is strictly quasi-concave (if preferences are strictly convex), then the CP for each p and y has a unique solution.*

d. *If preferences are locally insatiable and if x is a solution to the CP at (p, y), then $p \cdot x = y$.*

Proof.

a. For any strictly positive λ, $p \cdot x \le y$ if and only if $\lambda p \cdot x \le \lambda y$; hence $\mathbf{B}(p, y) = \mathbf{B}(\lambda p, \lambda y)$. The objective function doesn't change with λ; hence the set of solutions for (p, y) is the same as the set of solutions for $(\lambda p, \lambda y)$.

b. If we show that $\mathbf{B}(p, y)$ is nonempty and compact (closed and bounded), then b follows from the continuity of u. Nonemptiness of $\mathbf{B}(p, y)$ is trivial; $0 \in \mathbf{B}(p, y)$ for all p and y. To show that $\mathbf{B}(p, y)$ is compact, note first that $x \to p \cdot x$ is a continuous function. Hence for any convergent sequence $\{x^n\}$ of points from $B(p, y)$ with limit x, $p \cdot x^n \le y$ and $x^n \ge 0$ for each n imply that $p \cdot x \le y$ and $x \ge 0$. Therefore, $x \in \mathbf{B}(p, y)$, and $\mathbf{B}(p, y)$ is closed. Let $\delta = \min\{p_i; i = 1, \ldots, k\}$; since prices are strictly positive, $\delta > 0$. If $x \in \mathbf{B}(p, y)$, then $p \cdot x \le y$; hence for each i, $p_i x_i \le y$ (because the cost of all other goods cannot be negative), so each $x_i \le y/p_i \le y/\delta$. Therefore if $x \in \mathbf{B}(p, y)$, $x_i \le y/\delta$ for all i, and $\mathbf{B}(p, y)$ is bounded.

c. The constraint set $\mathbf{B}(p, y)$ is convex because convex combinations of nonnegative vectors are nonnegative and the function $p \cdot x$ is linear in x. Therefore, if $p \cdot x \le y$ and $p \cdot x' \le y$, for any $a \in [0, 1]$, $p \cdot (ax + (1 - a)x') = a(p \cdot x) + (1 - a)(p \cdot x') \le ay + (1 - a)y = y$. Now apply either Proposition 2.6 or Proposition A3.21.

d. Suppose preferences are locally insatiable and x solves the CP, but $p \cdot x < y$. Let $\beta = y - p \cdot x$, $\gamma = \max\{p_i; i = 1, \ldots, k\}$, and $\epsilon = \beta/(k\gamma)$. By local insatiability, some x' within ϵ of x is strictly preferred to x; that is, $u(x') > u(x)$. But $p \cdot x' = \sum_{i=1}^{k} p_i x'_i \leq \sum_{i=1}^{k} p_i(x_i + \epsilon) \leq p \cdot x + k\gamma\epsilon = p \cdot x + \beta = y$. That is, x' is affordable at prices p with wealth y, and it is strictly preferred to x, contradicting the supposed optimality of x for prices p and income y. ∎

A simple picture goes with the proof of part d. See Figure 3.3 and the accompanying caption.

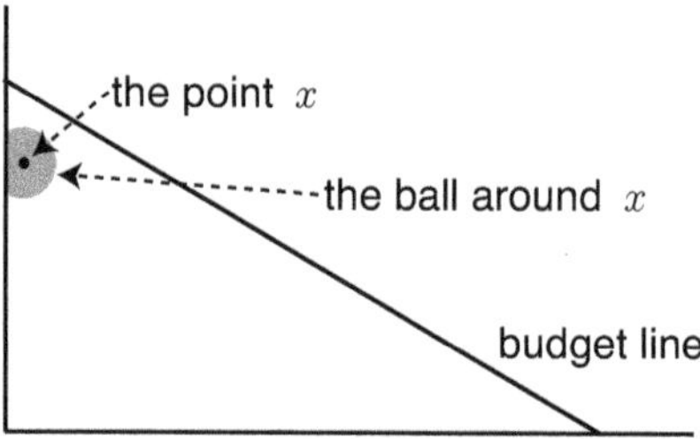

Figure 3.3. The picture for the proof of Proposition 3.1d. If $p \cdot x < y$, then x lies "below" the budget line, and we can put a ball of strictly positive radius around x such that $p \cdot x' \leq y$ for every x' inside the ball. Local insatiability ensures that no matter how small the radius of this ball, as long as it is strictly positive, some (nonnegative) point inside the ball must be strictly better than x, which contradicts the optimality of x at the given prices and income.

3.3. The Marshallian Demand Correspondence and Indirect Utility Function

Fix the utility function u for a particular consumer. Assume u is continuous, reflecting this consumer's continuous preferences. For each set of strictly positive prices p and nonnegative income level y, we have a version of the CP for this consumer. By virtue of Proposition 3.1b, we know that the CP has a solution. Let $\mathbf{D}(p, y)$ denote the set of solutions for the fixed u, as a function of p and y, and let $\nu(p, y)$ denote the value of the optimal solution; that is, $\nu(p, y) = u(x^*)$ for any $x^* \in \mathbf{D}(p, y)$. ($\mathbf{D}$ is a mnemonic for *demand*.)

Definition 3.2. *Fixing u, the set $\mathbf{D}(p, y)$ is called **Marshallian demand** at prices p and income y, and the correspondence $(p, y) \Rightarrow \mathbf{D}(p, y)$ is called the **Marshallian demand correspondence**. The number $\nu(p, y)$ is called the **indirect utility** at p and y, and the function $(p, y) \to \nu(p, y)$ is called the **indirect utility function**.*

Proposition 3.3 (Berge's Theorem applied to the consumer's problem).

a. *For all $p \in R^k_{++}$, $y \geq 0$, and $\lambda > 0$, $\mathbf{D}(p, y) = \mathbf{D}(\lambda p, \lambda y)$ and $\nu(p, y) = \nu(\lambda p, \lambda y)$.*

b. *The Marshallian demand correspondence is upper semi-continuous. If, for some open set of prices and income, Marshallian demand is singleton valued (that is, the CP has a* *unique solution for all price-income pairs inside that open set), then the function that describes the solution as a function of (p, y) is a continuous function.*

c. *The indirect utility function is continuous.*

If the notion of a correspondence or an upper semi-continuous correspondence is new to you, or if you have never heard of Berge's Theorem, also known as the Theorem of the Maximum, please consult Appendix 4 before attempting to understand either the statement of this proposition or its proof.

Proof. Part a of the proposition is a simple corollary of Proposition 3.1a. As for parts b and c, these come from a straightforward application of Berge's Theorem, given in Appendix 4 as Proposition A4.7. Since this is our first application of this important general result, I spell out the details: The consumer's problem is a parametric constrained maximization problem

$$\text{maximize } u(x), \quad \text{subject to } x \in \mathbf{B}(p, y).$$

The variable in the problem is x, and the parameter is the vector (p, y). Berge's Theorem tells us that the solution correspondence is nonempty valued if, for each set of parameters, the constraint set is nonempty and compact and the objective function is continuous in the variables; moreover, the solution-set correspondence is upper semi-continuous and the value-of-the-solution function is continuous, both in the parameters, as long as the objective function is jointly continuous in the variables and the parameters and the constraint-set correspondence is locally bounded and continuous in the parameters. (The version of Berge's Theorem given in Appendix 4 is somewhat more robust than this simple rendition, but the simple rendition is adequate for now.)

In this particular application, the objective function is independent of the parameters and assumed continuous in the variables. Therefore, the objective function presents no problem. We already showed that each $\mathbf{B}(p, y)$ is nonempty and compact. So once we show that $(p, y) \Rightarrow \mathbf{B}(p, y)$ is a continuous and locally bounded correspondence, the conditions of Berge's Theorem are met, and its conclusions are established. To begin with local boundedness, fix a pair (p, y), and let

$$\epsilon = \frac{1}{3} \min_{i=1,\ldots,k} p_i.$$

For all (p', y') within ϵ of (p, y), $x \in \mathbf{B}(p', y')$ must solve $p' \cdot x \leq y'$. Since in the sum $p' \cdot x$ each term is nonnegative and $y' \leq y + \epsilon$, this inequality implies that $p'_i x_i \leq (y + \epsilon)$; hence $x_i \leq (y + \epsilon)/p'_i$. But $p'_i \geq p_i - \epsilon \geq \frac{2}{3} p_i \geq 2\epsilon$; therefore $x_i \leq (y + \epsilon)/(2\epsilon)$, which provides a uniform bound for $x \in \mathbf{B}(p', y')$.

Continuity of the constraint correspondence is shown by proving separately that the correspondence is upper and lower semi-continuous. To show upper semi-continuity (having shown local boundedness), we take a sequence $\{(x^n, p^n, y^n)\}$

with $x^n \in \mathbf{B}(p^n, y^n)$ for each n and with limit $\{(x, p, y)\}$.[2] (We are using superscripts here because subscripts denote components of the vectors x and p.) Of course, $x^n \geq 0$ for each n, and since the positive orthant is closed, this implies that $x \geq 0$. Moreover, $p^n \cdot x^n \leq y^n$ for each n; using continuity of the dot product, this implies that the limit of the left-hand side, $p \cdot x$, is less than or equal to the limit of the right-hand side, y. Therefore, $p \cdot x \leq y$ and $x \in \mathbf{B}(p, y)$. This establishes upper semi-continuity.

To show lower semi-continuity, for each sequence $\{(p^n, y^n)\}$ with limit (p, y) and a point $x \in \mathbf{B}(p, y)$, we must produce a sequence $\{x^n\}$ with limit x and such that $x^n \in \mathbf{B}(p^n, y^n)$ for each n. If $y = 0$, then $x = 0$ (prices are strictly positive); therefore $x^n = 0$ for all n works. If $x = 0$, the same choice of x^n will do. Therefore, we can assume that $y > 0$, $x \neq 0$ and, by going far enough out in the sequence, that the $p^n \cdot x$ are uniformly bounded away from zero. Let

$$x^n = \frac{y^n}{y} \frac{p \cdot x}{p^n \cdot x} x.$$

Since $y^n \to y$ and $p^n \to p$, continuity of the dot product implies that $x^n \to x$. It remains to show that $x^n \in \mathbf{B}(p^n, y^n)$. Nonnegativity of x^n is no problem, since x^n is just a scale copy of x. Moreover,

$$p^n \cdot x^n = \frac{y^n}{y} \frac{p \cdot x}{p^n \cdot x} p^n \cdot x = \frac{y^n}{y} p \cdot x \leq y^n.$$

■

3.4. Solving the CP with Calculus

When economists build models populated by consumers, it is common practice to specify the individual consumer's utility function and to solve the CP analytically, using calculus. (It is also common to begin directly with the consumer's demand function, or even with a demand function that aggregates the demands of a population of consumers. We discuss these alternative practices in later chapters.) To build and work with such models, you must be able to carry out this sort of analytical exercise. In this section, we discuss how this is done, and (more important to future developments) how to interpret pieces of the exercise.

The CP is a problem of constrained optimization: A numerical objective function (utility) is to be maximized, subject to some inequality constraints (the budget constraint, and all variables nonnegative). Assuming the objective function and constraint functions are differentiable and otherwise well behaved, the standard theory of constrained optimization establishes necessary and sufficient conditions

[2] In proving upper and lower semi-continuity, we look at sequences of parameters—in this case, sequences $\{p^n, y^n\}$—that converge to points in the domain of the correspondence. Therefore, the limit price vector p here must be strictly positive.

for a solution. The rudiments of the general theory (or, rather, those rudiments that are germane to applications in this book) are given in Appendix 5. Adapting them to this context yields the following.

Definition 3.4. *Consider the CP for a differentiable utility function u, strictly positive prices p, and strictly positive income y.*[3] *A consumption bundle x^* is said to satisfy the* ***(first-order/complementary-slackness) optimality conditions*** *for the problem if:*

a. $p \cdot x^* \leq y$;

b. for some $\lambda \geq 0$,

$$\left.\frac{\partial u}{\partial x_j}\right|_{x^*} \leq \lambda p_j \text{ for each } j,$$

with equality if $x_j > 0$; *and*

c. if $p \cdot x^* < y$, *then* $\lambda = 0$.

Proposition 3.5. *Consider the CP for a differentiable utility function u, strictly positive prices p, and strictly positive income y.*

a. If x^* is a solution of this problem, then the optimality conditions must hold at x^*.

b. If u is concave and if x^* satisfies the optimality conditions, then x^* solves the CP.

To paraphrase, the optimality conditions are necessary for a solution, and they are sufficient for concave utility functions.[4]

Compared to the general form of first-order/complementary-slackness conditions given in Appendix 5, the optimality conditions are given here in somewhat compact form. In case you are new to constrained optimization, it may help to derive these specific conditions following the step-by-step recipe from the appendix.

Step 1. Form the Lagrangian. Let λ be the multiplier on the budget constraint $p \cdot x \leq y$ and let μ_j (for $j = 1, \ldots, k$) be the multiplier on the constraint $x_j \geq 0$. The Lagrangian is

$$u(x) + \lambda\left(y - \sum_{j=1}^{k} p_j x_j\right) + \sum_{j=1}^{k} \mu_j x_j.$$

Step 2. Obtain the first-order conditions for the x_j variables. These are

$$\frac{\partial u}{\partial x_j} - \lambda p_j + \mu_j = 0, \quad \text{or} \quad \frac{\partial u}{\partial x_j} + \mu_j = \lambda p_j.$$

[3] If $y = 0$, the problem is trivial. The only budget-feasible bundle is $x = 0$.

[4] See Problem 3.11 for a partial extension of part b to quasi-concave utility functions.

Step 3. List all constraints, including constraints on the multipliers. The multipliers are all constrained to be nonnegative and, of course, the solution must obey the original constraints $p \cdot x \le y$ and $x \ge 0$.

Step 4. Give the complementary-slackness conditions:

$$\lambda(y - p \cdot x) = 0 \quad \text{and} \quad \mu_j x_j = 0 \text{ for } j = 1, \ldots, k.$$

Now to simplify these conditions. Since $\mu_j \ge 0$, the first-order condition for x_j can be rewritten

$$\frac{\partial u}{\partial x_j} \le \lambda p_j,$$

where the difference $\lambda p_j - \partial u / \partial x_j$ is just μ_j. The complementary-slackness condition $\mu_j x_j = 0$ is, therefore, $\lambda p_j = \partial u / \partial x_j$ if $x_j > 0$. Finally, the complementary-slackness condition $\lambda(y - p \cdot x) = 0$ can be rephrased, If $y > p \cdot x$, then $\lambda = 0$. This gives the specific optimality conditions defined above.

Parts a and b of the proposition, therefore, correspond to Propositions A5.3 and A5.4, respectively. To apply Proposition A5.3, we must ensure that the constraint qualification holds. The details are left to you; strict positivity of p and y is the key. To apply Proposition A5.4, we must check that the constraint functions are all quasi-convex. Here they are linear, so we have no problems with quasi-convexity. A few remarks on the formulation are in order:

1. Differentiability of the utility function means continuous differentiability. Similar results can be given for utility functions that have left- and right-hand (partial) derivatives everywhere; after you absorb the discussion of the intuition of these conditions that follows, you may wish to formulate this sort of result.

2. Differentiability also entails finite partial derivatives everywhere.

3. On the boundaries of the consumption region—where $x_j = 0$ for some or several j—continuous differentiability is defined as follows: Right-hand partial derivatives along the boundary exist, are continuous, and are approached continuously by partial derivatives along paths from the interior. It is common in parametric specifications of utility functions for u to have infinite partial derivatives along the boundary. For example, the simplest standard parameterization of a consumer's utility function is the Cobb-Douglas utility function, $u(x) = \prod_{j=1}^{k} x_j^{\alpha_j}$, for $0 \le \alpha_j$. Supposing, as is common, that $\alpha_j < 1$, the partial derivative of u in x_j at $x_j = 0$ (and all other components strictly positive) is infinity.

   Infinite derivatives at the boundary (only) pose no problem in the following sense. If $\partial u / \partial x_j = \infty$ at x^*, the optimality condition requires that $\lambda = \infty$. Therefore, $p \cdot x^* = y$. Assuming $y > 0$, this means that $x_j^* > 0$ for some j. Assuming u doesn't have infinite partial derivatives in x_j for $x_j^* > 0$, the optimality conditions could not hold for j with $\lambda = \infty$, a contradiction. In other words, when in specific parameterizations (such as Cobb-Douglas utility) the finite-derivative condition is violated along the boundary of the positive orthant, solutions to the optimality conditions are never found along those boundaries.

A simple example: Cobb-Douglas utility

To see Proposition 3.5 in action, imagine a consumer whose utility function takes the Cobb-Douglas form

$$u(x) = \prod_{j=1}^{k} x_j^{\alpha_j},$$

for strictly positive constants α_1 through α_k. Note that if $x_j = 0$ for any component j of x, $u(x) = 0$, whereas (for any strictly positive y) positive expenditure on each good gives strictly positive utility; we know a priori that the solution x^* to the CP for any p and $y > 0$ will be strictly positive in all components. Therefore, if λ is the multiplier on the budget constraint, the combined first-order, complementary-slackness optimality condition for x_j is

$$\left.\frac{\partial u}{\partial x_j}\right|_{x^*} = p_j\lambda.$$

Evaluating the partial derivative for this utility function u, we get

$$\alpha_j (x_j^*)^{\alpha_j - 1} \prod_{j' \neq j} (x_{j'}^*)^{\alpha_{j'}} = p_j\lambda,$$

and multiplying the right and left sides of this equation by x_j^*, we find that (as a necessary condition for optimality),

$$\alpha_j u(x^*) = p_j x_j^* \lambda.$$

It is clear that $\lambda > 0$. (Hence we know that the consumer must spend all of y, although we know this on first principles anyway, since u is locally insatiable.) We can divide both sides by λ and get, as a necessary condition for optimality,

$$\frac{u(x^*)}{\lambda} = \frac{p_j x_j^*}{\alpha_j}.$$

The left-hand side of this last equation is independent of j (is the same for every j), so a necessary condition for optimality is

$$\frac{p_1 x_1^*}{\alpha_1} = \frac{p_2 x_2^*}{\alpha_2} = \ldots = \frac{p_k x_k^*}{\alpha_k},$$

or

$$p_{j'}x^*_{j'} = \frac{\alpha_{j'}}{\alpha_j} p_j x^*_j, \text{ for all } j \text{ and } j'.$$

The consumer must spend all of her income, or

$$y = p_1 x^*_1 + p_2 x^*_2 + \ldots p_k x^*_k.$$

In this last equation, substitute $(\alpha_{j'}/\alpha_j)p_j x^*_j$ for $p_{j'}x^*_{j'}$ (for $j' = 1, \ldots, k$), to get $y = \sum_{j'}(\alpha_{j'}/\alpha_j)p_j x^*_j$, which can be solved for x^*_j:

$$x^*_j = \left[\frac{\alpha_j}{\sum_{j'} \alpha_{j'}}\right]\left[\frac{y}{p_j}\right].$$

In other words, the monetary expenditure $p_j x^*_j$ on good j at the solution is proportional to y, the level of income, where the constant of proportionality is obtained by "normalizing" the coefficient α_j (dividing α_j by $\sum_{j'} \alpha_{j'}$, so that the sum of the constants of proportionality is one).

Do we know this is the solution? We do indeed, and two arguments show this. First, if $\sum_j \alpha_j \leq 1$, the function u is concave, and the optimality conditions are sufficient for a solution. "What," you may be asking, "if the sum exceeds 1?" Then replace α_j by $\alpha_j / \sum_{j'} \alpha_{j'}$.[5] This is a strictly monotone transformation of the utility function (why?), so it gives the same preferences and choices (hence the same solutions to the CP), and the transformed utility function is concave. (Of course, the solution x^* we derived is unchanged by this transformation.)

Or, if that argument doesn't appeal to you, try this one: Because u is continuous, we know that the CP has a solution. We know that the optimality conditions are necessary; they must hold at the solution. But the optimality conditions uniquely yield the solution x^* derived above. So this uniquely derived x^* must be the solution.

Note in passing that a Cobb-Douglas consumer has remarkably simple demand. For each good, a fixed percentage of her income goes to purchase that good, regardless of the price of the good or the prices of other goods. Of course, the price of the good enters into the amount of the good purchased: If (say) $\alpha_1 / \sum_j \alpha_j = 0.1$, then 10% of the consumer's income goes to good 1, and the amount of good 1 purchased is $0.1y/p_1$. But the amount of good 1 purchased is utterly independent of the prices of other goods.

Because of the simplicity of demand by a Cobb-Douglas consumer, this particular utility function is much favored by economists who wish to illustrate simple points about consumer demand and who need little flexibility in the actual properties of demand. On the other hand, it is remarkably inflexible for some purposes;

[5] Or see Problem 3.3.

notably, as a parametric family of utility functions (parameterized by the coefficients α_j), it will rarely fit actual consumer demand very well. For econometric purposes, it is too simple. In the problems, you are asked to solve the CP for other utility functions that give slightly more flexible demand. The cost of this flexibility, of course, is that you must to work a bit harder to solve the CP.

Interpreting the optimality conditions

If we know that $\lambda > 0$, the optimality conditions can be rewritten as follows: If goods i and j are consumed in positive amounts at the optimum,

$$\frac{\partial u}{\partial x_i} \Big/ \frac{\partial u}{\partial x_j} = p_i/p_j.$$

In words, the ratio of marginal utilities equals the ratio of prices. This may be familiar to you from intermediate microeconomics, or you may recall *The marginal rate of substitution of good i for good j (along an indifference curve) equals the ratio of their prices*, which is the same thing. Even if $\lambda = 0$ we have this relationship, as long as we recognize that when $\lambda = 0$, the first-order conditions read that $\partial u/\partial x_i = 0$ for goods that are consumed in positive amounts, and we interpret $0/0$ as being any number we wish.

Whether or not $\lambda > 0$, yet another way to rewrite and interpret the optimality conditions involves the ratio of $\partial u/\partial x_j$ to p_j. Let MU_j denote $\partial u/\partial x_j$ and let $\mathrm{MU}_j(x)$ denote this partial derivative evaluated at the point x. MU_j here is a mnemonic for the *marginal utility of good j*, or the rate at which utility accrues per unit increase in the amount of good j consumed.

Call the ratio $\mathrm{MU}_j(x)/p_j$ the *bang for the buck* of good j (at the point x). The reason for this name is: Suppose the consumer spends \$1 more on good j, where I use the dollar as the numeraire. \$1 more spent on good j means an increase of $1/p_j$ in the amount of good j consumed. To a first-order approximation, this means $(\mathrm{MU}_j(x))(1/p_j)$ more units of utility. Hence $\mathrm{MU}_j(x)/p_j$ is the bang in utility for the (extra) buck spent on good j.

The optimality conditions can be paraphrased: If x_j and $x_{j'}$ are both strictly positive, then $\mathrm{MU}_j(x)/p_j = \mathrm{MU}_{j'}(x)/p_{j'} = \lambda$, and if $x_j > 0$ and $x_{j'} = 0$, then $\mathrm{MU}_j(x)/p_j = \lambda \geq \mathrm{MU}_{j'}(x)/p_{j'}$. Or, in words, at the solution to the CP, the bangs for the buck of goods consumed in strictly positive amounts should be equal, and these bangs for the buck must be at least as large as the bangs for the buck of goods whose level of consumption is zero. Or, to rephrase in words one final time, if good j is consumed at a strictly positive level, its bang for the buck must be at least as large as the bang for the buck of any other good (whether consumed or not).

Why? Suppose this failed. That is, suppose that at some feasible (nonnegative and budget-feasible) consumption bundle x^*, $x_j^* > 0$, but the bang for the buck of good j was strictly less than that of some other good, say good i. Consider spending $\delta > 0$ dollars less on good j and δ dollars more on good i, where δ is small. This means δ/p_j less of good j, and δ/p_i more of good i. Because $x_j^* > 0$, for some small enough δ, this reduction in the consumption of good j is feasible; the constraint $x_j \geq 0$ won't be violated. (None of the other nonnegativity constraints can be violated, since we are adding to the amount of good i consumed, and we are leaving the rest alone.) Also, this small change does not affect budget feasibility; we are spending just as much as we were before. By Taylor's Theorem, we know that the impact of this variation on the level of utility is to move us from $u(x^*)$ to

$$u(x^*) + \text{MU}_j(x^*)\Big(-\frac{\delta}{p_j}\Big) + \text{MU}_i(x^*)\Big(\frac{\delta}{p_i}\Big) + o(\delta).$$

(If you don't know Taylor's Theorem or the mathematical language of little-o's, all that this says is, The utility level changes, to a first-order approximation, by the change in the amount of good j times its marginal utility, plus the change in the amount in good i times its marginal utility.) Therefore, the change in utility is

$$\delta\Big(\frac{\text{MU}_i(x^*)}{p_i} - \frac{\text{MU}_j(x^*)}{p_j}\Big) + o(\delta).$$

By assumption, $\text{MU}_i(x^*)/p_i > \text{MU}_j(x^*)/p_j$, and so this is strictly positive for sufficiently small δ. Therefore, x^* cannot be the solution to the consumer's problem.

Note well, if you can cross i's and dot t's when it comes to using Taylor's Theorem, we just proved Proposition 3.5a: The argument just given says that if the optimality conditions fail at x^*, then x^* cannot be a solution to the CP. This is the contrapositive to, The optimality conditions are necessary at a solution. (If $p \cdot x^* < y$, then the bangs for the buck must all be 0, which is λ. Can you see how to adapt the argument above to show this?) And whether you can cross i's and dot t's, the intuition should be apparent: If good j has a lower bang for the buck than good i at x^*, the consumer will do better to decrease the consumption of good j and spend the money saved on good i. The only thing that can prevent this is if the consumption of good j cannot be decreased, which is to say, if $x_j^* = 0$.

Let me ring one further change on this. Suppose the consumer has y to spend and, at the given prices, finds that the optimal consumption bundle for her is x^*. Suppose that we then give her \$1 more to spend (where you should think of \$1 as small on the scale of y). What should she do with the extra \$1? To a first-order approximation, she can divide the extra \$1 among all the goods j with $x_j^* > 0$ in any fashion she pleases, and she is close to the optimum. More precisely, if she allocates any of the extra \$1 to a good whose bang for the buck is less than the bang for the buck of some other good, she will be doing less well than she might. Now recall that λ, the multiplier on the budget constraint, is (by the optimality conditions) just this maximal bang for the buck. *The marginal utility accruing from an extra bit of income is just the multiplier on the budget constraint.* If you increase the consumer's income by \$3 and if she spends the extra optimally, her utility will rise by 3λ, to a first-order approximation. (If you have had prior exposure to constrained optimization, you may recall that the multiplier on a constraint is the "shadow value" on that constraint; that is, the rate at which the objective function improves per unit relaxation of the constraint. If you have never seen or heard this, you have now seen it in a specific context.)

Assuming you understand intuitively the previous paragraph, let me now warn you, it isn't quite correct. Assuming u is differentiable, the loose and informal argument given there can be tightened down to a formal proof (with a formal statement) *if* we know that the optimal solution to the CP at income $y + 1$ is "close" to the solution at income level y. The reason we need to know this is that the argument, when fleshed out, works (only) for small changes in consumption levels from x^*. But what if the solution jumps discontinuously? (Can the solution jump discontinuously?) This takes us deeply into the mathematics of constrained optimization problems, which I want to leave alone until Chapter 10. So for now, I hope the intuition behind the previous paragraph is clear, and (as well) that you recognize that, as an argument that is relying on calculus, it is only about how the objective function responds to local variations in the consumption bundle.

Differentiability of utility

Throughout this section, we have assumed that u is (continuously) differentiable. Nothing like this appeared in Chapter 1 or 2, so a few remarks on this assumption are in order.

Differentiability of u is not easy to justify. If u is differentiable, for strictly increasing $f : R \to R$, $v(x) = f(u(x))$ may not be, so no property of preferences[6] will guarantee differentiability of *every* numerical representation. Of course, the same is true about continuity; we are content in that case with the result that if preferences are continuous, they have at least one continuous representation. Similarly, we would be content with *If preferences have property (fill in the blank), they have a continuously differentiable representation.* Unhappily, I know of no reasonably intuitive property that fills the blank and makes this statement correct.[7]

Differentiability of u, then, should be regarded solely as an analytical convenience; one that holds in all manner of parametric specifications of utility that economists use, but not one with a firm axiomatic basis.

Bibliographic Notes

The theory of the consumer is one of the cornerstones of microeconomic theory, and a full bibliographic note would run for many pages. I'm unable to do full justice to the subject here, and so will refrain from trying altogether.

Almost every textbook on microeconomic theory will have a chapter or more devoted to the subject. My recommendations here (and throughout the rest of our discussion of these ideas) are: Kreps (2004) for readers who desire an "intermediate

---

[6] Except $x \succeq y$ for all x and y.

[7] (1) The blank can be filled in by asking the consumer for her preferences over gambles with prizes in X; see Chapters 5 and 6. (2) *If* preferences can be represented by a concave function u, then we are almost there: A concave function u is "almost everywhere" continuously differentiable. But convexity of $\succeq$ is insufficient to guarantee that a concave u can be found to represent $\succeq$, and in any case this doesn't give us differentiability everywhere.

micro" level treatment of the subject; Mas-Colell, Whinston, and Green (1995) and Varian (1992) for alternative treatments at roughly the level of this book; and Katzner (1970) for a full-blown, all-the-math development.

Problems

■ *3.1. Imagine a consumer whose preferences are strictly decreasing. That is, if $x_i \leq x'_i$ for all commodities i, with a strict inequality for at least one commodity, then $x \succ x'$. The solution to the CP for this consumer, for any prices p and income level y, is clearly to consume the bundle $0 = (0, 0, \ldots, 0)$. Hence from part d of Proposition 3.1, we know these preferences are not locally insatiable. Give a direct argument for this implication.

■ 3.2. Suppose that in a world with k goods, a locally insatiable consumer's preferences $\succeq$ have the following property. Her preferences are strictly convex in the first j goods. That is, if x^1 and x^2 are two distinct bundles of goods with $x^1 \succeq x^2$ and $x^1_i = x^2_i$ for all $i = j+1, j+2, \ldots, K$, and if $a \in (0,1)$, then $ax^1 + (1-a)x^2 \succ x^2$. And she has no use whatsoever for the goods with index above j. If x^1 and x^2 are two bundles of goods with $x^1_i = x^2_i$ for $i = 1, 2, \ldots, j$, then $x^1 \sim x^2$. Show that if prices are strictly positive, this consumer's solution to the CP is unique.

■ 3.3. (a) Suppose that $u(x) = \sum_{j=1}^{k} \beta_i \ln(x_i)$, where $\beta_i > 0$. Fixing prices p and income y, what is the consumer's demand?

(b) How does your answer to part a compare with demand by a consumer with Cobb-Douglas utility?

(c) In footnote 5, I suggested that you look at this problem. What was I thinking of? How could you rewrite the paragraph in the text that contains this footnote, in view of your answer to part b?

■ *3.4. Suppose that $k = 3$, $u(x) = \ln(x_1 + 2) + 2\ln(x_2 + 3) + 4\ln(x_3 + 2)$. If prices are $p_1 = 2$, $p_2 = 3$, and $p_3 = 1$, what does the consumer demand at $y = 5$? At $y = 16.4$? At $y = 100$?

■ 3.5. Suppose that $u(x) = \prod_{j=1}^{k} (x_j + \gamma_j)^{\beta_j}$, for strictly positive constants β_j and nonnegative constants γ_j $(j = 1, \ldots, k)$. Describe a procedure (graphical or algebraic) to find the consumer's demand at prices p and income y. (Hint: Warming up to this problem with Problem 3.4 might help.)

■ *3.6. (a) Suppose that $u(x) = \sum_{j=1}^{k} \alpha_j x_j$, for strictly positive constants α_j. What is consumer demand at prices p and income y?

(b) Suppose that $u(x) = \min\{\alpha_1 x_1, \ldots, \alpha_k x_k\}$, for strictly positive constants α_j. What is consumer demand at prices p and income y? (Note that this utility function isn't differentiable, so you can't use Proposition 3.5.)

■ 3.7. Suppose that $u(x) = \left[\sum_{j=1}^{k} \alpha_j x_j^{\mu}\right]^{1/\mu}$, for strictly positive constants α_j, $j = 1, \ldots, k$, and $\mu < 1$, $\mu \neq 0$. What is consumer demand at prices p and income y?

What happens when $\mu = 1$? What happens as μ approaches zero? (This utility function is called the *constant elasticity of substitution*, or CES, utility function.)

■ *3.8. Suppose $u(x_1, \ldots, x_k) = \sum_{i=1}^{k} u_i(x_i)$, where each u_i is strictly concave, continuously differentiable, and strictly increasing, with $u_i'(0) < \infty$. Devise a graphical procedure for finding $x(p, y)$, given p and y.

■ *3.9. Suppose $u(x_1, \ldots, x_k) = \sum_{i=1}^{k-1} u_i(x_i) + x_k$, where each u_i is strictly concave, continuously differentiable, and strictly increasing, and with $u_i'(0) < \infty$. Describe to the fullest extent you can what this consumer will demand at prices p and income level y.

■ 3.10. (a) Which of the utility functions in the problems 3.3 through 3.9 represent homothetic preferences?

(b) Complete and prove the following proposition: *Suppose a consumer has homothetic preferences. If she demands x at prices p and income y (i.e., if x solves the CP at these prices and income level), then her demand at prices p and income y' is...*

■ 3.11. Proposition 3.5b says that for concave utility functions u, the optimality conditions are sufficient for solutions of the CP; i.e., if for a given x there exists a multiplier λ such that x and λ satisfy the optimality conditions, then x solves the CP. But as we saw in Chapter 2, concavity of u is not "natural"; convexity of preferences goes more naturally with quasi-concavity of the utility function.

(a) Suppose u is quasi-concave and $\partial u/\partial x_1 > 0$, at all levels of consumption. Prove that the combined first-order/complementary-slackness conditions are sufficient to guarantee optimality.

(b) Show by example that if u is locally insatiable and quasi-concave, being a solution of the combined first-order/complementary-slackness conditions is not sufficient to guarantee optimality. (Hint: The simplest example you can give is for the case $k = 1$!)

■ *3.12. It is a useful thing to know, a priori, that the multiplier λ found in solving the CP will be strictly positive. Give an example to show that this is something to worry about; specifically, give a utility function u that is strictly increasing and represents strictly convex preferences, strictly positive prices p, and a strictly positive income level y^0, such that at the unique solution to the CP at prices p and income y, the multiplier λ must be zero. (Hint: This can be done with a very small number of commodities.)

■ 3.13. Suppose that u is not continuously differentiable, but it is "piecewise differentiable." That is, at every $x \in R_+^k$ and for every $j = 1, \ldots, k$, u has right- and left-hand partial derivatives in x_j. (You should assume that u is continuous.) In the spirit of Proposition 3.5a, give necessary conditions for an optimal solution to the CP.

■ 3.14. Robinson Crusoe is marooned on a desert island with only a supply e of seedcorn. He will be rescued two years from now (he knows this), and so his problem is to allocate the e units of seedcorn between current consumption and planting for second-period consumption. If he plants x units of corn, he will get back a crop of size $f(x)$, for a function f that is nondecreasing and satisfies $f(0) = 0$. So if he chooses to plant x units, his consumption stream will be $e - x$ in the first period and $f(x)$ in the second, for total utility $U(e-x, f(x))$, and his maximization problem is

$$\text{Maximize } U(e - x, f(x)) \text{ in the variable } x, \text{ subject to } 0 \leq x \leq e.$$

a. What can you tell me about the existence and character of a solution to this problem, for fixed e? That is, make whatever assumptions you need to prove that a solution exists.

b. Find assumptions that guarantee that the set of solutions to this problem is convex.

c. Find assumptions that guarantee that this problem has a unique solution. (There is more than one answer to this part, so see if you can find multiple answers.)

d. Let $v(e)$ be the value of the solution as a function of e and let $X^*(e)$ be the set of solutions. What can you tell me (about continuity, upper- and/or lower-semicontinuity) about v and X^*? That is, find assumptions that guarantee that v is a continuous function and X^* is an upper semi-continuous correspondence. How about assumptions that make X^* lower semi-continuous?

Chapter Four

Revealed Preference and Afriat's Theorem

This chapter concerns a consumer who, we hypothesize, is solving the CP for a number of different prices and incomes. We observe the consumer's choices and ask, What can we say about this consumer? In particular, are her choices consistent with the standard model of preference-driven, utility-maximizing choice? What patterns can we expect to see in the choices she makes, as we (say) vary one price only or her level of income? The emphasis here is on what can be discerned from a finite number of actual choices; Chapter 11 concerns the entire array of choices the consumer might make, for every possible level of income and every possible set of prices.

4.1. An Example and Basic Ideas

The main point of this chapter is illustrated by the following example. Imagine a consumer who lives in a three-commodity world and makes the following three choices.

- When prices are $(10, 10, 10)$ and income is 300, the consumer chooses the consumption bundle $(10, 10, 10)$.
- When prices are $(10, 1, 2)$ and income is 130, she chooses the consumption bundle $(9, 25, 7.5)$.
- When prices are $(1, 1, 10)$ and income is 110, she chooses the consumption bundle $(15, 5, 9)$.

Are these choices consistent with the standard model of the CP, in which the consumer has complete and transitive preferences and solves the CP for each set of prices and income?

This question is somewhat artificial. The story of the CP is that the consumer makes a single consumption choice, at one time, for all time. How then could we observe three different choices that she makes? The best we can do is to suppose that we have posed a set of hypothetical questions to the consumer of the form, If prices were p and your income was y, what would you purchase?[1]

[1] A different way to try to make the story realistic is to suppose (1) that the consumer shops, say, each week, (2) has a fixed budget for each week, and (3) has preferences that are weakly separable from one week to the next and that are unchanging from week to week. Then our three pieces of data could be the results of three weeks of shopping. But suppositions 2 and 3 are rather incredible.

Setting this artificiality to one side, a trivial affirmative answer to the question is possible. Imagine a consumer who is indifferent among, say, all bundles that give her less than 1000 units of each of the three goods. Since at these three sets of prices, the incomes she has are insufficient to purchase any bundle with 1000 units of each good, any choices—in particular, the choices she has made—are consistent with utility maximization, as long as they respect her budget constraint, which these do. This trivial answer may seem fanciful, but the point is not. To falsify the standard model, we must be able to use the data to conclude that some bundle is strictly preferred to some other(s). Otherwise, complete indifference is consistent with any pattern of choice that satisfies feasibility.

One way we might proceed is to ask whether the choices observed are consistent with preference maximization for strictly convex preferences. If a consumer with strictly convex preferences chooses the bundle x^* when prices are p and income is y, then the consumer strictly prefers x^* to any other bundle x such that $p \cdot x \leq y$, since we know that with strictly convex preferences and a convex choice set, the chosen bundle is strictly preferred to all feasible alternatives.

We take a slightly different path in this chapter, asking whether the observed choices are consistent with preference maximization for *locally insatiable* preferences. Local insatiability gives us cutting power according to the following lemma.

Lemma 4.1. *Suppose a consumer with complete, transitive, and locally insatiable preferences $\succeq$ chooses the consumption bundle x^* facing prices p with income y. Then we know that $x^* \succeq x$ for all bundles x such that $p \cdot x = y$. And we know that $x^* \succ x$ for all bundles x such that $p \cdot x < y$.*

Proof. The first part is obvious: If $p \cdot x = y$, x is feasible. Since x^* is chosen, it must be at least as good as x. The second part uses local insatiability: If $p \cdot x < y$, local insatiability ensures that there is some bundle x' near enough to x so that $p \cdot x' \leq y$, with $x' \succ x$. This means x' is feasible; hence $x^* \succeq x'$. But then $x^* \succeq x' \succ x$ gives the desired conclusion. ∎

Now back to the example. From the data given above, we calculate the cost of each of the three selected bundles at each of the three sets of prices. This is done for you in Table 4.1.

		Prices		
		(10,10,10)	(10,1,2)	(1,1,10)
	(10,10,10)	300	130	120
Bundle	(9,25,7.5)	415	130	109
	(15,5,9)	290	173	110

Table 4.1. Cost of three bundles at three sets of prices.

In each case, the bundle selected exhausts the income of the consumer. This is required for these choices to be consistent with local insatiability: A locally insatiable consumer always spends all of her income; if a consumer ever chooses a bundle that costs strictly less than the income she has available, she cannot be maximizing locally insatiable preferences.

Beyond this, the important things to note are:

- When $(10, 10, 10)$ was chosen (at prices $(10, 10, 10)$ and income 300), the bundle $(15, 5, 9)$ could have been purchased with some money left over. Apparently, this consumer strictly prefers $(10, 10, 10)$ to $(15, 5, 9)$.
- At the second set of prices $(10, 1, 2)$, since $(10, 10, 10)$ and $(9, 25, 7.5)$ both cost 130 and $(9, 25, 7.5)$ was selected, the latter must be at least as good as $(10, 10, 10)$.
- At the third set of prices $(1, 1, 10)$, the bundle $(9, 25, 7.5)$ costs 109, while $(15, 5, 9)$ costs 110. And we are told that with income 110, the consumer chose $(15, 5, 9)$. Hence, $(15, 5, 9) \succ (9, 25, 7.5)$.

The data tell us that $(10, 10, 10) \succ (15, 5, 9)$, that $(9, 25, 7.5) \succeq (10, 10, 10)$, and that $(15, 5, 9) \succ (9, 25, 7.5)$. We can string these three deductions from the data together in the order $(10, 10, 10) \succ (15, 5, 9) \succ (9.25, 7.5) \succeq (10, 10, 10)$, which by transitivity (if the consumer has complete and transitive preferences) tells us that $(10, 10, 10) \succ (10, 10, 10)$. These data are therefore inconsistent with consumer behavior based on the standard preference-maximization model with locally insatiable preferences. On the other hand, suppose the third piece of data was instead:

- At prices $(1, 2, 10)$ and income 115, the bundle selected is $(15, 5, 9)$.

Then we would have come to no negative conclusions. At the first set of prices and income, the bundles $(10, 10, 10)$ and $(15, 5, 9)$ are affordable, and as the first bundle is selected and the $(15, 5, 9)$ does not exhaust the budget constraint, $(10, 10, 10)$ is revealed to be strictly preferred to $(15, 5, 9)$. At the second set of prices and income level, $(10, 10, 10)$ and $(9, 25, 7.5)$ are precisely affordable and $(9, 25, 7.5)$ is selected, so it is revealed to be weakly preferred to $(10, 10, 10)$. This is just as before. But now, at the third set of prices and income level, of the three bundles only $(15, 5, 9)$ is affordable. Knowing that it is selected tells us nothing about how it ranks compared to the other two; it could well come at the bottom of the heap. In fact, the other two choices tell us that $(15, 5, 9)$ *must* come bottom among these three; the data are consistent with preferences among the three bundles that have $(9, 25, 7.5) \succ (10, 10, 10) \succ (15, 5, 9)$, as well as preferences where $(9, 25, 7.5) \sim (10, 10, 10) \succ (15, 5, 9)$.

Of course, this argument doesn't tell us for sure that these three pieces of data are consistent with locally insatiable preference maximization; we need locally insatiable preferences for *all* of R^3_+ that support these three choices. But it is not hard to imagine that we can fill in preferences consistent with these data. The main result of this chapter, Afriat's Theorem, shows that we can construct preferences supporting these choices that are complete, transitive, and locally insatiable, and, in addition, strictly increasing, convex, and continuous.

4.2. GARP and Afriat's Theorem

To generalize the example, three definitions are needed. The setting throughout is one with k commodities, so that consumption bundles lie in R^k_+, prices are from R^k_{++}, and income levels come from R_+.

Definition 4.2.

a. *Take any finite set of (feasible) demand data:* $x^1 \geq 0$ *chosen at* (p^1, y^1), $x^2 \geq 0$ *chosen at* (p^2, y^2), …, *and* $x^J \geq 0$ *chosen at* (p^J, y^J), *where, in addition,* $p^j \cdot x^j \leq y^j$ *for each* j. *If* $p^i \cdot x^j \leq y^i$, *the data* ***reveal directly that*** x^i ***is weakly preferred to*** x^j, *written* $x^i \succeq^d x^j$. *And the data* ***reveal directly that*** x^i ***is strictly preferred to*** x^j, *written* $x^i \succ^d x^j$, *if* $p^i \cdot x^j < y^i$. *(The superscript* d *is for* directly.*) Note that* $x^i \succ^d x^j$ *implies* $x^i \succeq^d x^j$.

b. *Suppose that for some* x^i *and* x^j, *there is a chain of direct revelations of weak preferences that start with* x^i *and end with* x^j. *That is, for some* $x^{i_1}, \ldots, x^{i_m}$, $x^i \succeq^d x^{i_1} \succeq^d x^{i_2} \succeq^d \ldots \succeq^d x^{i_{m-1}} \succeq^d x^{i_m} \succeq^d x^j$. *Then the data* ***indirectly reveal that*** x^i ***is weakly preferred to*** x^j, *written* $x^i \succeq^r x^j$. *If some one or more of the steps in the chain is a direct relevation of strict preference, the data* ***indirectly reveal that*** x^i ***is strictly preferred to*** x^j, *written* $x^i \succ^r x^j$. *(The superscript* r *is for* revealed.*) In this definition, we allow for the case in which no intervening steps are required;* $x^i \succeq^d x^j$ *implies* $x^i \succeq^r x^j$, *and* $x^i \succ^d x^j$ *implies* $x^i \succ^r x^j$.

c. *The data satisfy the* ***Generalized Axiom of Revealed Preference****, abbreviated* ***GARP****, if no strict revealed preference* ***cycles*** *exist. That is, for no* x^i *is it the case that* $x^i \succ^r x^i$.

Part c sometimes confuses students, so let me be explicit on two grounds. First, suppose that for some x^i, p^i, and y^i, $p^i \cdot x^i < y^i$. Then according to part a of the definition, $x^i \succ^d x^i$; hence by part b, $x^i \succ^r x^i$, and hence GARP is violated. In words, GARP is violated if any bundle chosen at given prices and income costs less at those prices than the level of income. Second, suppose $x^i \succeq^r x^j$ and, simultaneously, $x^j \succ^r x^i$, for some pair x^i and x^j. That is, there is a chain of revealed weak preferences from x^i to x^j and a chain of revealed weak preferences, at least one of which is also strict, from x^j back to x^i. Then according to part b of the definition, $x^i \succ^r x^i$ and $x^j \succ^r x^j$, and this is also true for any element in either of the two chains of revealed preference. The two chains join together in a cycle, so there is a chain going from any link in the chain back to that link, with one of the links direct strict preference. Satisfaction of GARP is equivalently stated as: No such cycle can be found in the data.

Proposition 4.3 (Afriat's Theorem). *If a finite set of demand data violates GARP, these data are inconsistent with choice according to locally insatiable, complete, and transitive preferences. Conversely, if a finite set of demand data satisfies GARP, these data are consistent with choice according to complete, transitive, strictly increasing (hence, locally insatiable), continuous, and convex preferences.*

Before giving the proof, two comments are in order.

1. GARP concerns weak and strict revealed preferences among the finite collection of bundles that are chosen. We need not compare chosen bundles with those that never are chosen. *No violations of GARP among the set of chosen bundles* is necessary and sufficient for standard (locally insatiable) preferences for *all* of R^k_+.

2. If the data contain a violation of GARP, then no locally insatiable, complete, and transitive preferences can rationalize or explain the data. But if the data satisfy GARP, then not only can we produce locally insatiable, complete, and transitive preferences, but preferences which *in addition* are strictly increasing, continuous, and convex. In other words, given a finite collection of demand data, we cannot falsify the hypothesis that the consumer's preferences are strictly increasing or continuous or convex without throwing away the entire model of choice by locally insatiable, complete, and transitive preferences. The three extra properties add no testable restrictions.

   Please be careful in interpreting this. This does not say that it is impossible to falsify strictly increasing or convex preferences empirically. (I'm unwilling to make a claim one way or the other about continuity; whether continuity can be tested empirically depends on your definition of a valid empirical test.) Suppose, for instance, I ask a consumer to rank order the three distinct bundles x, x', and $0.5x + 0.5x'$, and she says the convex combination is definitely the worst of the three. Then we know she doesn't have convex preferences. Suppose I ask her to rank order three distinct bundles x, x', and x'' where x' and x'' are both $\geq x$ and neither $x' \geq x''$ nor $x'' \geq x'$, and she says x' is worst of the three. Then we can reject the hypothesis that she has strictly increasing preferences (and even nondecreasing preferences), without (yet) rejecting local insatiability. The point is, these are not questions about market demand data. What is asserted here is that, with a finite collection of *market demand* alone, I can't reject the three properties without simultaneously rejecting that her preferences are complete, transitive, and locally insatiable.

The proof of Afriat's Theorem

The first "half" of the proposition is easy. If the data are generated from locally insatiable, complete, and transitive preferences $\succeq$, then $x^i \succ^d x^j$ implies $x^i \succ x^j$, and $x^i \succeq^d x^j$ implies $x^i \succeq x^j$. The argument is the one given in Lemma 4.1. Therefore, by standard transitivity properties of strict and weak preferences, $x^i \succ^r x^i$ implies $x^i \succ x^i$, which violates the asymmetry of strict preference.

The proof of the second half of the proposition is long and very technical. The proof I am about to give is due to Varian (1982). I am unaware of any other use for these proof techniques in economics; to my knowledge, they give you no technique that can be usefully transferred to any other situation you will enounter. Therefore, I think you can almost surely skip this proof without risk of missing something later on. On the other hand, if you are an aficionado of very elegant proofs, this is one to see. Assume throughout that we have J demand choices—$x^j \geq 0$ chosen at prices p^j with income y^j, such that $p^j \cdot x^j \leq y^j$, for $j = 1, \ldots, J$—that collectively satisfy GARP.

As we remarked informally a page ago, for each j, $p^j \cdot x^j = y^j$; if $p^j \cdot x^j < y^j$, then $x^j \succ^d x^j$ according to the definition, which is a violation of GARP.

Lemma 4.4. *For each i, let $n(i)$ be the number of indices j such that $x^i \succ^r x^j$.*

a. If $n(i) < n(j)$, then $p^i \cdot x^i < p^i \cdot x^j$.

b. If $n(i) = n(j)$, then $p^i \cdot x^i \leq p^i \cdot x^j$.

c. At least one i satisfies $n(i) = 0$.

Proof. For both a and b, we prove the contrapositives. (a) If $p^i \cdot x^i \geq p^i \cdot x^j = y^j$, then $x^i \succeq^d x^j$ by definition. But then if $x^j \succ^r x^k$ for any k, it follows that $x^i \succ^r x^k$, and hence the set of indices k such that $x^j \succ^r x^k$ is a subset of the indices such that $x^i \succ^r x^k$; $n(j) \leq n(i)$ follows immediately.

(b) And if $p^i \cdot x^i > p^i \cdot x^j$, then $x^i \succ^d x^j$. We know that every k such that $x^j \succ^r x^k$ also satisfies $x^i \succ^r x^k$, and there is at least one k, namely j itself, such that $x^i \succ^r x^j$ but not $x^j \succ^r x^j$. (If $x^j \succ^r x^j$, GARP is violated.) Hence $n(i) > n(j)$. The contrapositive to this that $n(i) \leq n(j)$ implies $p^i \cdot x^i \leq p^i \cdot x^j$, and b then follows as a special case.

(c) If $n(i) \geq 1$ for every i, then for each i we can produce another index j such that $x^i \succ^r x^j$. Starting from any i, this gives us a chain $x^i = x^{i_1} \succ^r x^{i_2} \succ^r x^{i_3} \succ^r \ldots$. Since there are only J possible values for the bundles, this chain must eventually cycle, which would violate GARP. ■

Lemma 4.5. *Real numbers v^i and $\alpha^i > 0$ for $i = 1, \ldots, J$ can be found such that, for all i and j,*

$$v^i \leq v^j + \alpha^j [p^j \cdot x^i - p^j \cdot x^j]. \tag{4.1}$$

Proof. We use induction on J. The result is trivially true for $J = 1$. Suppose it is true for all sets of data of size $J - 1$ or less. Take a set of data of size J (with no violations of GARP), and (renumbering if necessary) let 1 through I be the indices with $n(i) = 0$. By Lemma 4.4c we know that $I \geq 1$. Therefore, the set of indices $I + 1, \ldots, J$ gives us $J - 1$ or fewer pieces of data (with no violations of GARP). (The case where $I = J$ is handled by an easy special argument.) Hence we can produce v^i and α^i as needed for i from $I + 1$ to J, and inequality (4.1) holds for i and j both from $I + 1$ to J.

We extend to a full set of v^i and α^i as follows. Set

$$v^1 = v^2 = \ldots v^I = \min_{i=1,\ldots,I;j=I+1,\ldots,J} v^j + \alpha^j [p^j \cdot x^i - p^j \cdot x^j].$$

By this definition, (4.1) will hold for i from 1 to I and j from $I+1$ to J.

To get (4.1) for i from $I+1$ to J and j from 1 to I, we use α^j. Note that by Lemma 4.4a, for such i and j, since $n(i) > 0$ and $n(j) = 0$, we know that $p^j \cdot x^i > p^j \cdot x^j$. Therefore, we can select (for each $j = 1, \ldots, I$) α^j large enough so that these strictly positive terms give us the desired inequalities.

Finally, Lemma 4.4b tells us that for i and j both from 1 to I, $p^j \cdot x^i \geq p^j \cdot x^j$. Therefore, since $v^i = v^j$, no matter what (positive) values we chose for α^j, we have (4.1). This completes the induction step and the proof of Lemma 4.5. ∎

The rest is easy. Define

$$u(x) = \min_{i=1,\ldots,J} v^i + \alpha^i[p^i \cdot x - p^i \cdot x^i].$$

Note that u is the minimum of a finite set of strictly increasing, affine functions; hence u is strictly increasing, concave, and continuous. (Math facts: The (pointwise) minimum of a finite set of strictly increasing functions is strictly increasing. The minimum of a finite set of concave functions is concave. The minimum of a finite set of continuous functions is continuous. If you did not know these facts, prove them.)

From (4.1), $u(x^i) = v^i$. This is a simple matter of comparing (4.1) with the definition of u.

We are done once we show that u rationalizes the data. To do this, take any observation (x^j, p^j, y^j). Because GARP is satisfied, $p^j \cdot x^j = y^j$. We know that x^j gives utility v^j. And it is evident from the definition of u that for any x such that $p^j \cdot x \leq y^j = p^j \cdot x^j$,

$$u(x) = \min_{i=1,\ldots,J} v^i + \alpha^i[p^i \cdot x - p^i \cdot x^i] \leq v^j + \alpha^j[p^j \cdot x - p^j \cdot x^j] \leq v^j.$$

That does it. ∎

WARP: The Weak Axiom of Revealed Preference

In many economic textbooks, the so-called Weak Axiom of Revealed Preference, or WARP, is discussed. It may be helpful to make (brief) connections with what we have done here.

The *Weak Axiom of Revealed Preference* says that if x^* is chosen at (p, y), then x^* is strictly preferred to any other bundle x such that $p \cdot x \leq y$. This is almost a special case of GARP. It is a *special* case because it refers only to direct revelation of preference. GARP, on the other hand, looks at chains of revealed preference. But it is only *almost* a special case because it is a bit stronger than local insatiability allows; following Lemma 4.1, we can conclude only that when x^* is chosen at (p, y), then x^* is strictly preferred to any other bundle x such that $p \cdot x < y$, and is weakly preferred to x if $p \cdot x = y$.

The difference comes about because we are augmenting the standard model of preference maximization with local insatiability; WARP "works" if we augment the standard model with the maintained hypothesis that solutions to the CP are always unique, for example, if preferences are strictly convex.

4.3. Comparative Statics and the Own-Price Effect

Comparative statics is a term used by economists for questions (and answers to those questions) of the form, How does some economic quantity change as we change underlying parameters of the situation that generates it? Much of the empirical content of economics lies in the comparative statics predictions it generates. If within a model we can show that quantity x must rise if parameter z falls, and if the data show a falling z accompanied by a falling x, then we reject the original model.

In terms of consumer demand, the natural comparative statics questions are: How does demand for a particular good change with changes in income, holding prices fixed? How does demand for a good change with changes in the price of some other good, holding all other prices and income fixed? And—the so-called *own-price effect*—how does the demand for one good change with changes in the price of that good, holding other things fixed?

Everyday experience indicates that the theory on its own will not have much to say about income effects. There are goods the consumption of which declines as the consumer's wealth increases, at least over some ranges—public transportation is a commonly cited example. And there are goods the consumption of which rises with the consumer's wealth—taxicab rides, or skiing trips to the Alps. Goods whose consumption falls with wealth are called *inferior goods*, while those whose consumption rises with wealth are called *superior*. Moreover, when the percentage of income expended on a good rises as wealth rises, the good is called a *luxury* good; nonluxury goods are called *necessities*.

Of course, most goods do not fall neatly into a single one of these categories. Demand for public transportation by a given consumer rises as the consumer moves away from improverishment, and then falls as the consumer moves toward being rich. Indeed, since demand for all goods must be zero when $y = 0$, only a good that is never consumed in positive levels could qualify for *always* being inferior. Hence while a *superior good* is one the consumption of which never falls with rising income, an *inferior good* is one where the level of consumption *sometimes* falls with rising income.

As for the effect on the consumption of commodity i of a change in the price of commodity j, there is (again) little the bare theory of preference maximization can tell us. Demand for nails falls as the price of lumber rises, and the demand for corn rises with increases in the price of wheat. Roughly speaking, nails and lumber are complementary goods, while corn and wheat are substitutes. (This is rough for reasons that are discussed in later chapters, when precise definitions will be given.)

The best hope for a strong comparative statics prediction from the standard theory concerns own-price effects; everyday experience suggests that a consumer will demand less of a good as its own price rises. This is so strongly suggested by most people's experiences that goods for which this is true are called *normal*, while goods that are not normal—the demand for which sometimes rises as the price of the good rises—are called *Giffen* goods (named for Scottish economist Sir Robert Giffen, to whom the notion is attributed by Alfred Marshall).

The question is, if we look at demand by a preference-maximizing consumer, will demand for a good inevitably fall as the price of that good rises, holding everything else fixed? The answer, which you probably know from intermediate microeconomics, is no. One can draw pictures of indifference curves that support an increase in the consumption of a good as its own price rises.

With Afriat's Theorem, we can rigorize these pictorial demonstrations. Fix prices p, income y, and demand x at these prices and income. Choose some commodity (index i), and let p' be a price vector where all the prices except for good i are the same as in p, and $p'_i > p_i$. Let x' be demand at p' and y. Since (assuming local insatiability) $p \cdot x = y$ and p' is greater than p, as long as $x_i > 0$, $p' \cdot x > y$. *As long as $p' \cdot x' = y$, it doesn't matter what x' is—in particular, it doesn't matter whether $x'_i \leq x_i$ or $x'_i > x_i$—GARP will not be violated by these two data points.* Afriat's Theorem tells us that convex, strictly increasing, and continuous preferences can be found to support the existence of a Giffen good. Indeed, if we have any finite sequence of demand data for a fixed income level y and a succession of prices that involve (successive) rises in the price of good i only, as long as the demanded bundles satisfy the budget constraint with equality, GARP will not be violated.

A positive result

Consider the following alternative comparative statics exercise. Ask the consumer for her choice at prices p and income y. Suppose x is her choice. Now replace p with p', where p' is the same as p, except that the price of good i has been strictly increased, and *simultaneously* replace y by $y' = p' \cdot x$. Let x' be the chosen bundle at p' and y'. Suppose $x'_i > x_i$.

Since x is feasible at (p', y') by construction, we know that x' must be weakly preferred to x. But at the same time,

$$p' \cdot x' = \sum_{j \neq i} p'_j x'_j + p'_i x'_i = \sum_{j \neq i} p'_j x_j + p'_i x_i = p' \cdot x.$$

Rewrite the inner two terms as

$$\sum_{j \neq i} p_j x'_j + p'_i x'_i = \sum_{j \neq i} p_j x_j + p'_i x_i,$$

invoking the fact that $p'_j = p_j$ for $j \neq i$. Since $p'_i > p_i$ and $x'_i > x_i$, we know that $(p'_i - p_i)x'_i > (p'_i - p_i)x_i$; subtract the larger left-hand term from the left-hand side of the previous display, and the smaller right-hand term from the right-hand side of the display, and we see that $p \cdot x' < p \cdot x$. Therefore, for locally insatiable preferences, x is strictly preferred to x'. Oops. This demonstrates the following formal result.

Proposition 4.6. *Suppose x is chosen by the consumer facing prices p and income y, and x' is chosen at prices p' and income $p' \cdot x$, where p' is p except for an increase in the price of good i. If these choices are made according to the standard model with locally insatiable preferences, then $x'_i \leq x_i$.*

In other words, if we ask this pair of questions of a consumer and find the consumption of good i rising, we have refuted (for this consumer) the standard model, augmented with local insatiability.

Giffen goods must be inferior

Before commenting on the result just derived, let me gather up one more "fact."

Proposition 4.7. *Suppose i is a Giffen good for some preference-maxiziming consumer with locally insatiable preferences. That is, for some income level y, price vectors p and p' such that p is identical to p' except that $p_i < p'_i$, and consumption bundles x and x' such that x is chosen at (p, y), x' is chosen at (p', y), $x'_i > x_i$. Then good i must be (sometimes) inferior for this consumer. More specifically, $y' = p \cdot x' < y$, and if x'' is a choice by the consumer facing (p, y'), then $x''_i > x_i$.*

Proof. Since $p' \cdot x' = y$ and $x'_i > x_i \geq 0$, we know that $y' = p \cdot x' < y$. Now suppose x'' is a bundle chosen at (p, y'). (To be completely rigorous about this, we ought to have insisted on augmenting the standard model of complete and transitive preferences with local insatiability *and continuity*, the latter to ensure that some bundle is chosen at every price and income combination.) Comparing x' and x'', we have that x' is chosen at (p', y), and x'' is chosen at $(p, p \cdot x')$, where p is p' except for a reduction in the price of good i. By an argument similar to that in the proof of Proposition 4.6, we conclude that $x''_i \geq x'_i$. But $x'_i > x_i$ by assumption; therefore $x''_i > x_i$. ∎

Discussion

Why are Giffen goods possible? How could the consumption of good i rise with increases in its price? Roughly, the reason is that when the price of good i rises, two things happen. The relative price of good i, relative to the prices of other goods, is increased. Our expectations that the consumption of good i will fall (or, at least, not rise) stems from this; as the relative price of good i rises, the consumer ought to substitute other goods for it. But also the "level of real wealth" of the consumer falls; her income y is no longer sufficient to purchase the bundle x that she chose before the rise in p_i. A poorer consumer may choose more of good i because good i is inferior, and this implicit income effect may overcome the effect of the increased relative price of good i.

Indeed, the first alleged instance of a Giffen good concerned potatoes in Ireland during the great potato famine: The shortage of potatoes caused the price of potatoes, the staple crop of the working class, to rise precipitously. This so impoverished the working class that their diet came to consist almost entirely of ... potatoes; they could no longer afford to supplement potatoes with other goods. The effect was so strong, it was claimed, that they purchased more potatoes. (Careful empirical evidence has been offered to refute that this did in fact happen.)

Proposition 4.7 supports this intuitive explanation, by showing that if a good is Giffen, it must be inferior. Or, to put it the other way around, if the good is superior—if there is no chance that reduced income leads to an increase in its consumption—then it cannot be Giffen; a rise in its price cannot lead to a rise in its level of consumption.

And Proposition 4.6 pretty much clinches the argument. Recall how the comparative statics exercise worked. We began with prices p, income level y, and a choice x by the consumer. The price of good i was increased, giving new prices p'. This makes the consumer worse off in real terms—she can no longer afford x (if $x_i > 0$)—so to compensate her, we increase her wealth to $y' = p' \cdot x$, just enough so that she could purchase x if she wanted to. Now the income effect of lower real wealth is controlled for, leaving only the relative price effect, and the consumer must choose a bundle x' with no more of good i than before.

Compensating the consumer in this fashion—giving her enough income so that at the new prices she can purchase the bundle at the original prices—is called Slutsky compensation. We pick up the story of compensated demand in Chapter 10, but for now we conclude with a final proposition, which is left for you to prove.

Proposition 4.8. *For a consumer with locally insatiable, complete, and transitive preferences, suppose that x is chosen at prices (p, y), and x' is chosen at prices p' and income $p' \cdot x$, for any other price vector p'. Then $(p' - p) \cdot (x' - x) \leq 0$.*

Coming attractions

We are far from finished with the classic theory of consumer demand, but we are going to take a break from it for a while. My personal prejudices are to undertake further foundations of models of choice—under uncertainty, dynamic, and social—before finishing the story. You (or your instructor) may feel differently about this, in which case you may wish to move to Chapters 10 and 11, concerning the dual consumer's problem, Roy's identity, the Slutsky equations, and integrability. But if you do this, a warning: The mathematical developments in Chapters 10 and 11 build on methods first employed in the theory of the profit-maximizing firm, in Chapter 9. So you should probably tackle Chapter 9 before Chapters 10 and 11.

Bibliographic Notes

Afriat's Theorem is given in Afriat (1967). The proof given here is taken directly from Varian (1982). The axioms of revealed preference discussed here are applied as well in the literature to demand *functions*, full specifications of consumer demand for all strictly positive prices and income levels; this part of the literature will be discussed in Chapter 11.

Problems

■ *4.1. In a three-good world, a consumer has the Marshallian demands given in Table 4.2. Are these choices consistent with the usual model of a locally insatiable, utility-maximizing consumer?

Prices			Income	Demand		
p_1	p_2	p_3	y	x_1	x_2	x_3
1	1	1	20	10	5	5
3	1	1	20	3	5	6
1	2	2	25	13	3	3
1	1	2	20	15	3	1

Table 4.2. Four values of Marshallian demand.

■ 4.2. There are a few details to clean up in the proof of Afriat's theorem. First, show that the minimum over a finite set of concave functions is concave, the minimum over a finite set of strictly increasing functions is strictly increasing, and the minimum over a finite set of continuous functions is continuous. Second, show how to proceed if, in the proof of Lemma 4.5, you find that $n(i) = 0$ for all i, and (hence) $I = J$.

■ 4.3. For a two-good world, create an indifference curve diagram that shows the (theoretical) possibility of a Giffen good.

■ *4.4. Prove Proposition 4.8.

Chapter Five

Choice under Uncertainty

Economic decisions often have uncertain consequences. When you purchase a car, you don't know its quality. When you choose an education, you are unsure about your abilities, later opportunities, and the skills of your instructors. In financial and insurance markets, uncertainty is almost the essence of the transaction.

The theory of consumer choice developed so far can be applied directly to such commodities. A can of Olympia beer is a definite thing—a share of General Motors is another—and we can work with consumer's preferences for bundles that contain so many cans of beer, so many shares of GM, and so on. But *because* "a share of GM" has a special structure (or, rather, because we can model it as having a special structure), we are able to enlist specialized models of choice that take advantage of that structure.

In this chapter and the next, we develop and then apply the standard specialized models. This chapter concerns the basic theories of choice in uncertain situations; Chapter 6 provides applications.

5.1. Two Models and Three Representations

This is a very long chapter and it is easy to get lost in the details. To help you keep track, I begin with a discussion of where we are headed and how, conceptually, we get there.

The state-space model

The first thing to settle is how to model things with uncertain consequences. In economics, two standard models of uncertainty are used. The first is variously called the *state-space, states-of-nature,* or *contingencies* model. (It is also called the model with subjective uncertainty, but the explanation for this name comes only when we get to the representation theorem.)

In this approach, the consumer chooses from a set of available *actions* or *acts*. Each act has uncertain consequences, depending on the realization of uncertain factors. The formal model consists of a set X of *consequences* (or prizes) and another set S of *states of nature* or *contingencies*. Each state of nature gives a complete description of how all pertinent uncertainty resolves—what is the weather, the results of whatever coin flips might be taken, and so on. The *state space* S is a list of states s that are both mutually exclusive—*at most* one $s \in S$ will occur—and exhaustive—*at least* one $s \in S$ will occur. Because each $s \in S$ is a complete description of all relevant uncertainty, the state and the act taken completely determine the consequences. Therefore, each act a is described by a function from S to X, where $a(s) = x$ means that the act a gives outcome $a(s) = x$ if the state of nature is s. The set of functions from S to X, denoted X^S, is called the (universal) space of acts, denoted by A.

A given consumer has preferences $\succeq$ over the space of acts A. In choosing from a subset of A, the consumer selects some $\succeq$-best element of the set of available acts, as in Chapter 1. As in Chapter 1, we seek a utility function representation of $\succeq$, a function $u : A \to R$ such that $u(a) \geq u(a')$ if and only if $a \succeq a'$ (where, remember, both a and a' are functions). As in Chapter 2, we assume more of $\succeq$ than that it is complete and transitive, and we hope in consequence to get out a nicer utility representation.

As a concrete example, suppose the acts under consideration are various bets on a two-horse horse race, where the two horses are Secretariat and Kelso. The amount won or lost in a given bet or act is determined by the winner of the race, where a dead heat (tie) is a real possibility. We have

$$S = \{\text{Secretariat wins, Kelso wins, dead heat}\}.$$

I'll abbreviate these three states as s_1, s_2, and s_3, respectively.

Suppose each act results in a dollar prize from the set $X = \{\$-2, \$0, \$1.20, \$3\}$, where $\$-2$ means a net loss of \$2. A typical bet or act would be a', given by

$$a'(s) = \begin{cases} \$1.20, & \text{if } s = s_1, \\ \$-2, & \text{if } s = s_2, \text{ and} \\ \$0, & \text{if } s = s_3. \end{cases}$$

In words, a' is a bet of \$2 that pays back \$3.20, so you net \$1.20, if Secretariat wins, nothing if Kelso wins, and returns your stake if the race ends in a dead heat.

Acts can be depicted as in Figure 5.1: We draw a chance node (or circle with three arms coming out of it), where each arm represents and is labeled by one of the three states; at the end of each arm we give the prize. Hence the act in Figure 5.1a is the bet a' from the previous paragraph, while the act in Figure 5.1b is the constant act that gives prize \$3 no matter how the race ends.

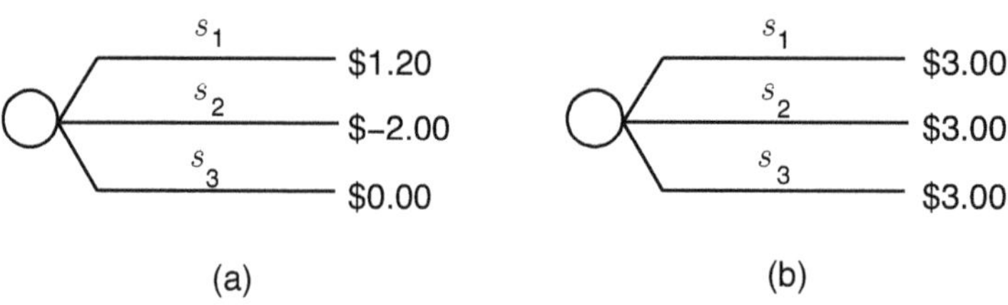

Figure 5.1. Two acts or gambles

The consumer, of course, can access only a few of all possible acts. For instance, it is the rare race track that will offer the \$3-net-prize-no-matter-how-the-race-ends bet. But we *imagine* that the consumer has preferences over all conceivable acts—she will probably like the \$3-for-sure act rather a lot—and we seek a utility function representation for those preferences.

Two representations for the state-space model

In Chapter 1, we settled for any numerical representation of $\succeq$. In this chapter, following the general idea of Chapter 2, we look for additional properties of $\succeq$ that guarantee a "nice" numerical representation. In particular, we look for one of two sorts of representations. (Assume for now that S is finite.) The first is *additively separable across states*:

For each $s \in S$, there is a function $u_s : X \to R$ such that

$$u(a) = \sum_{s \in S} u_s(a(s)) \tag{5.1}$$

represents $\succeq$.

The second, which is a special case of the first, is called a *subjective expected-utility* representation:

For some probability distribution p on S and function $U : X \to R$,

$$u(a) = \sum_{s \in S} p(s) U(a(s)) \tag{5.2}$$

represents $\succeq$.

This is a special case of an additively separable representation, because, in (5.2), each state-specific sub-utility function u_s of (5.1) is a scaled copy $p(s)U$ of some single utility function U.

Savage's Sure-Thing Principle

What does it take to get either of these representations? We already know that $\succeq$ must be complete and transitive, so the question really is, *What more?* The classic answer is given in Savage (1954). This is a relatively complex result, and we settle (in Section 5.3) for the simpler development in Anscombe and Aumann (1963). But a brief discussion of the most important of Savage's axioms—which he calls the Sure-Thing Principle[1]—is in order.

---

[1] Savage (1954, p. 22) explains why he calls this the Sure-Thing Principle; I cannot say that I find his explanation convincing. My preference would be to call it *independence*, which is sometimes used or, even better, *state-separability*, which does not seem to be used at all. Savage's original name is most commonly used, however, so I will stick with it.

From our discussion in Section 2.5 of additive separability, you should be able to anticipate this axiom: Think of each act a as a vector of consequences, where each component corresponds to a state $s \in S$. For additive separability state-by-state, it must be that preference is separable into T and T^C, for every subset T of S. (Recall that T^C is the complement of T.) To write this more formally:

Axiom 5.1 (Savage's Sure-Thing Principle). *Suppose a, a', b, and b' are four acts, and $T \subseteq S$ is a subset of the state space, such that $a(s) = a'(s)$ and $b(s) = b'(s)$ for all $s \in T$, and $a(s) = b(s)$ and $a'(s) = b'(s)$ for all $s \in T^C$. Then $a \succeq b$ if and only if $a' \succeq b'$.*

This is really quite simple. The supposition is that a and b agree on T^C. Hence if we compare a and b, it is "natural" to look at how they differ where they differ, namely on T. But a' and b' also agree on T^C, and since $a \equiv a'$ and $b \equiv b'$ on T, how a and b differ where they differ is identical to how a' and b' differ where *they* differ. Hence the ranking of a and b should be the same as that of a' and b'.

Or to put it more in the language of weak separability, a and b are identical on T^C. The axiom says that *how* they are the same doesn't matter. If we change both of them on T^C so that they continue to agree there, without changing how they (potentially) disagree on T, and hence getting to a' and b', we haven't affected how they compare.

When we introduced weak and strong separability in Chapter 2, we proposed them as very special properties. Now we are proposing a form of strong separability as being entirely natural and intuitive. The difference can best be seen by comparing two situations: acts based on the two-horse race; and meals composed of an entrée, a main course, and dessert. To take the latter first, we think of meals that are three-dimensional vectors, such as *(shrimp, steak, cake)*, meaning shrimp for an entrée or appetizer, steak for a main course, and cake for dessert. In this setting, separability of the first two components from the third is not natural: How the consumer feels about *shrimp* vs. *melon* for a starter depends on whether there is fruit for dessert. That is, it is entirely natural to suppose that

$$\textit{(shrimp, steak, fruit)} \succ \textit{(melon, veal, fruit)}, \qquad \text{but}$$

$$\textit{(shrimp, steak, cake)} \prec \textit{(melon, veal, cake)}.$$

In this setting, the consumer gets all three components to eat, and interactions between them may (very naturally and intuitively) matter. But if we write acts based on the two-horse race as three-dimensional vectors, such as $(10, -5, -1)$, meaning win 10 in state is s_1, lose 5 in state s_2, and lose 1 in state s_3, then in this setting the consumer gets only one of the three components. Suppose the consumer proclaims

$$(5, -2, -1) \succeq (2, 2, -1),$$

and then we tell her, You can still have your choice between those two acts/gambles, except that if the race is a dead heat (state s_3), we will give you 2 instead of taking

1 from you. Since the race is either a dead heat or not, and since her choice doesn't affect her prize if it is a dead heat in either case, she naturally won't change her ranking:

$$(5, -2, 2) \succeq (2, 2, 2).$$

Or so Savage's Sure-Thing Principle—and the two representations—would have us assume.

Two examples where the representations fail

To sharpen your understanding of the two representations and what they entail, consider the following two examples.

1. Imagine you are marketing a particular product and trying to decide how much advertising to do. To keep things simple, imagine that the product will either sell 1000 units or 10,000. If it sells 1000, you will lose \$1000, not including the cost of advertising. If it sells 10,000, you will make \$3000 less the cost of any advertising. You can either advertise a lot or not at all. Not advertising costs you nothing, while advertising a lot costs you \$1000.

   Create the following model. The prize is your net profit. Possible values are \$–2000, \$–1000, \$2000, and \$3000, so these four dollar amounts constitute X. The states are your level of sales: You sell 1000 units (state s_1) or 10,000 (state s_2). Hence there are two states in S. The two acts you can consider are: "advertise," which we denote by a, where $a(s_1) = \$-2000$ and $a(s_2) = 2000$; and "don't advertise," which we denote by a', where $a'(s_1) = \$-1000$ and $a'(s_2) = \$3000$.

   As long as your state-dependent utility functions u_s are increasing in profits, if an additively separable representation holds you never choose to advertise. Whether the state is s_1 or s_2, a' always gives a better outcome (by the \$1000 cost of advertising). The problem is easiest to see if we look at the representation (5.2). In this story, your choice of an act presumably influences how many units you sell. But in (5.2), the probabilities of the states do not depend on the act chosen. That is, we don't write $p(s; a)$ or anything like that. In an additively separable representation this is a bit more subtle, but (essentially) the same problem arises: The functions u_s are not affected by the overall act you take. So in cases where acts themselves influence the state that arises, we couldn't expect representations of either form to hold.

   (In this example, a simple cure is available. We need three states: s_1, the state that the product sells 1000 units whether you advertise or not; s_2, the state that the product sells 1000 units if you don't advertise and 10,000 units if you do; and s_3, the state that the product sells 10,000 whether you advertise or not. [If there is a chance that advertising will anger potential customers, we would add a fourth state.] The question of whether to advertise becomes one of how likely is the state s_2, in which you increase your profits by \$3000 if you do advertise, compared to the "lost" \$1000 in advertising fees in states s_1 and s_3.)

2. A second example shows the difference between (5.1) and (5.2). Imagine that you are thinking of undertaking one of two acts. In the first, you will be given an umbrella if it is raining and suntan lotion if the sun is shining. In the second, you are given the umbrella if the sun is shining and suntan lotion if it is raining. We create a model of this with states of nature that describe the possible states of the weather and with prizes that include *umbrella* and *suntan lotion*.

   Do we expect the representation (5.2) to hold in this case? Suppose in our model there are two states, s_1 for *rain* and s_2 for *sunny*. And suppose that you assess that these two states are equally likely. Then representation (5.2) would require that you are indifferent between the two acts; each gives you probability 0.5 of having an umbrella and probability 0.5 of having suntan lotion, and whatever are the (state-independent!) utilities of those two prizes, the expected utilities of the two acts are identical. But, of course, the first act is preferable (unless you have perverse preferences), because the umbrella is better than suntan lotion when it rains, while suntan lotion is better than the umbrella when the sun is shining. The first act is better state by state, so it is better overall.

   This would not be a problem in the representation (5.1). It is natural to think that $u_{s_1}(\text{umbrella}) > u_{s_1}(\text{suntan lotion})$, since s_1 is *rain*, and $u_{s_2}(\text{umbrella}) < u_{s_2}(\text{suntan lotion})$, since s_2 is *sunny*. As long as this is so, the first act is better than the second, per any representation of the form (5.2).

   In (5.1), but not in (5.2), the value of a prize can depend on the state in which it is received. Representation (5.2) is appropriate *only* when prizes are modeled in a way that makes their relative values independent of the state in which they are received. If, instead of *umbrella* and *suntan lotion*, the prizes were things like *dry but sunburned, wet and without sunburn* and *dry without a sunburn*, (5.2) might be reasonable. It is getting a bit ahead of ourselves, to material that belongs to Chapter 6, but it is worth saying at this point: In a lot of economics, model (5.2) is used, where the prizes are money: you gamble (or invest), and your reward is, depending on the state of nature, so many dollars, which presumably are used to purchase consumption goods. You should be wary of such applications, insofar (for instance) as the money prizes have different consumption-good-purchasing-power in different states of nature in the model. An investment that pays a big nominal return when overall economic times are good and a smaller return when times are bad may be less risky than models of the (5.2) variety indicate, if good economic times are accompanied by a higher cost of living. (But the same investment may be worth less than (5.2) indicates, if good economic times mean that other sources of income that you have are higher; see the discussion at the end of this chapter on portfolio or correlation effects.)

Objective probabilities and von Neumann–Morgenstern expected utility

The second standard model of choice under uncertainty is usually referred to as the model with *objective uncertainty*, and the representation as *(objective) expected utility* or *von Neumann–Morgenstern expected utility.*

In this approach, the choices available to the consumer are represented by probability distributions over a given prize space; these objects are called *lotteries* and *gambles*, as well as probability distributions. Formally, we have a space X of prizes or consequences (just as in the first approach), out of which a space P of probability distributions / lotteries / gambles over X is formed. The consumer's preferences are given by a preference relation $\succeq$ on the space P, and we seek well-structured numerical representations of those preferences.

To keep the discussion simple, we will work (until the end of Section 5.2) with probability distributions that have only finitely many possible prizes:

Definition 5.2. *A* ***simple probability distibution*** π *on* X *is specified by*

a. a finite subset of X*, called the* **support** *of* π *and denoted by* $\text{supp}(\pi)$*, and*

b. for each $x \in \text{supp}(\pi)$ *a number* $\pi(x) > 0$*, with* $\sum_{x \in \text{supp}(\pi)} \pi(x) = 1$.

The set of simple probability distributions on X *will be denoted by* Π*. For* $\pi \in \Pi$*, we "extend" the domain of* π *to all of* X*, writing* $\pi(x) = 0$ *for any* $x \notin \text{supp}(\pi)$.

For $x \in X$*, we let* δ_x *be that element of* Π *with* $\text{supp}(\delta_x) = \{x\}$ *and (of course)* $\delta_x(x) = 1$.

Please note: The set X can be infinite in this definition. But we only look at probability distributions on X with finite support.

We will depict simple probability distributions by chance nodes in the style of Figure 5.2 (where the prize space $X = R^2_+$); there is a chance node (circle) with as many arms emerging as there are elements of the support of the distribution, the prizes are listed at the ends of the arms, and the probabilities of the prizes are given in parentheses along the arms. So, for example, the chance node in Figure 5.2 represents the simple lottery π with $\text{supp}(\pi) = \{(10, 2), (4, 4)\}$, $\pi((10, 2)) = 1/3$, and $\pi((4, 4)) = 2/3$.

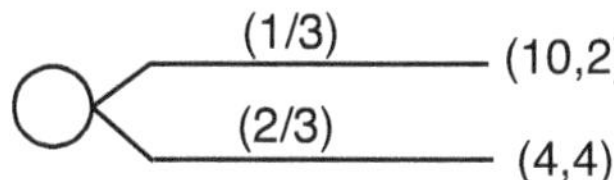

Figure 5.2. A simple probability distribution

Compare this model with the state-space model described previously. In particular, imagine that the consumer must decide between three bets on the horse race: (a) bet \$2 on Secretariat to win, where a win pays \$3.20; (b) bet \$2 on Kelso to win, where a win pays \$5.00; and (c) make no bet. In the state-space model, we formalize this by forming the three-element state space described earlier and supposing that the consumer must choose between the three acts or gambles depicted in Figure 5.3. The consumer has preferences over all of A, and she chooses whichever of the three she most prefers.

In this second model (or model technique), we *assume* that each of the three gambles can be described adequately by a probability distribution over monetary

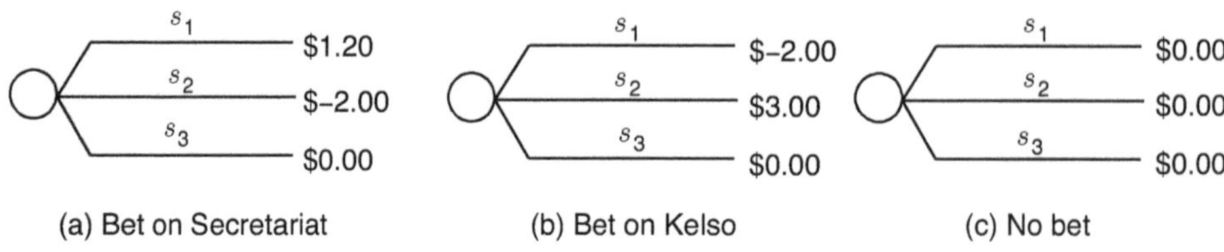

Figure 5.3. Three state-contingent acts/bets

prizes, for instance as in Figure 5.4. The consumer has preferences over Π. And she chooses whichever probability distribution she most prefers.

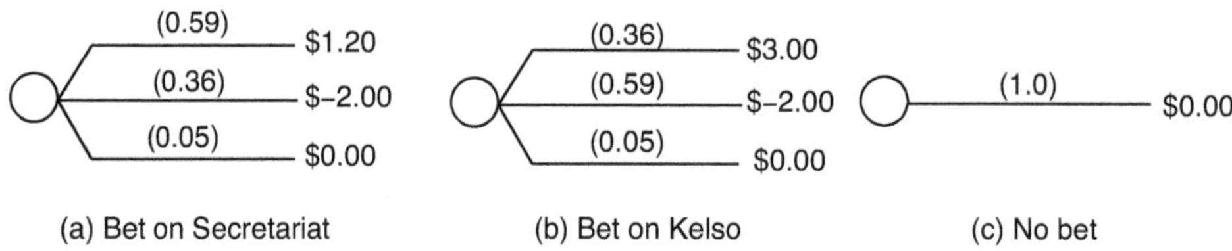

Figure 5.4. Three probability distributions/gambles

The obvious question concerning the second model technique is, Where did the probabilities come from? Moreover, I've written out probability distributions where the probabilities of a \$0 prize in the first and second gamble are equal, and where the probability of getting \$1.20 in the first equals the probability of the outcome \$−2.00 in the second. Is this necessarily entailed? The answers are: (1) We don't say (within this sort of model) where the probabilities come from. (2) No, these cross-lottery restrictions on the probabilities are not entailed by the model per se. In this second sort of model, the probabilities are exogenous; they are part of the description of the lottery. It might be sensible or good modeling technique to add restrictions on these out-of-thin-air probabilities such as, The probability of \$1.20 in the first gamble equals the probability of \$−2.00 in the second. But that is a question of model building and not of the application of this specific model, which begins with probability distributions.

There is a subtle point here. In the state-space approach, we can distinguish between preferences representable as in Equation (5.1) and those representable as in Equation (5.2). The issue, essentially, is whether the value of a prize is independent of the state in which it is received. That issue cannot and does not arise in the second modeling approach, because all we have formally are prizes and their probabilities. The idea of "the state in which a prize is received" may be in the back of our minds as we put together a formal model of this second type, but it stays in back.

Compound lotteries

When we have two simple probability distributions, say π and ρ, and a number a between zero and one, we can take the a-convex combination of π and ρ, written $a\pi + (1-a)\rho$, in two steps:

1. The support of this new probability distribution is the union of the supports of π and ρ.[2]
2. If x is a member of this union, then the probability given by $a\pi + (1-a)\rho$ to x is $a\pi(x) + (1-a)\rho(x)$, where $\pi(x)$ is understood to be zero if x is not in the support of π, and similarly for ρ.

An example may help. Suppose π gives probabilities .3,.1, and .6 to prizes x, y, and z, respectively, and ρ gives probabilities .6 and .4 to prizes x and w, respectively. We form, say, $(1/3)\pi + (2/3)\rho$ as follows: The support of $(1/3)\pi + (2/3)\rho$ is $\{x, y, z, w\}$, and the probabilities it gives to its four possible prizes are, respectively,

$$\begin{aligned}
&\text{for } x,\ (1/3)(.3) + (2/3)(.6) = .5 \\
&\text{for } y,\ (1/3)(.1) + (2/3)(0) = .0333\ldots \\
&\text{for } z,\ (1/3)(.6) + (2/3)(0) = .2 \\
&\text{for } w,\ (1/3)(0) + (2/3)(.4) = .26666\ldots
\end{aligned}$$

When we depict probability distributions such as $(1/3)\pi + (2/3)\rho$ in the example just given, we sometimes will draw a *compound lottery*. For example, in Figure 5.5a, we show $(1/3)\pi + (2/3)\rho$ as a compound lottery: a lottery whose outcomes are the lotteries π and ρ. In Figure 5.5b, we depict the one-stage lottery to which this compound lottery reduces. *In our formal setup, the objects depicted in Figures 5.5a and b are precisely the same thing, which is "more correctly" the lottery in 5.5b. When we say that the consumer has preferences over Π, it is implicit that the consumer regards the lotteries in 5.5a and b as precisely the same object.* We can imagine a theory in which these two lotteries are distinguished in the mind of the consumer, and she prefers one to the other. But this isn't that theory. It doesn't matter how probabilities arise here—what are the states, or whether there are compound lotteries or not—because the formal model isn't rich enough to incorporate such considerations. All this theory has is prizes and their probabilities.

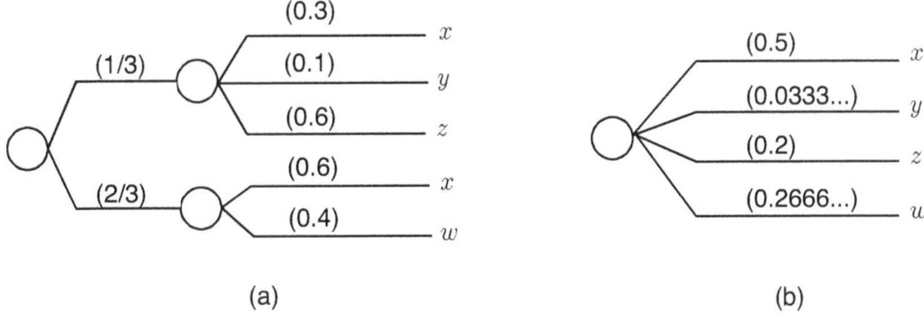

Figure 5.5. Compound and reduced lotteries. The compound lottery in panel a reduces to the single-stage lottery in panel b by the laws of probability theory. In our theory, the consumer either *identifies* these two as being the same object or, at least, is indifferent between them.

[2] To be fanatically precise, $\text{supp}(a\pi + (1-a)\rho) = \text{supp}(\pi)$ if $a = 1$, $\text{supp}(\pi) \cup \text{supp}(\rho)$ if $0 < a < 1$, and $\text{supp}(\rho)$ if $a = 0$.

The representation and axioms

Within this setting, we seek a *von Neumann–Morgenstern expected-utility representation*:

Proposition 5.3. *A preference relation $\succeq$ on the set Π of simple probability distributions on a set X satisfies*

a. $\succeq$ is complete and transitive,

b. for all π, ρ, φ, and φ' from Π and $a \in [0,1]$, $a\pi + (1-a)\varphi \succ a\rho + (1-a)\varphi$ if and only if $a\pi + (1-a)\varphi' \succ a\rho + (1-a)\varphi'$, and

c. if $\pi \succ \rho$, then for any third lottery φ there exists $a^* \in (0,1)$ such that $a\pi+(1-a)\varphi \succ \rho$ and $\pi \succ a\rho + (1-a)\varphi$ for all a such that $a^* < a \leq 1$,

if and only if

$$\pi \succeq \rho \quad \textit{if and only if} \quad \sum_{x \in \mathrm{supp}(\pi)} U(x)\pi(x) \geq \sum_{x \in \mathrm{supp}(\rho)} U(x)\rho(x)$$

for some function $U : X \to R$. Moreover, if U provides a representation of $\succ$ in this sense, then V does as well if and only if $V(\cdot) = AU(\cdot) + B$ for constants $A > 0$ and B.

This is quite a mouthful, so let's take it in pieces. First, a, b, and c provide three axioms or properties for preferences $\succeq$ that give the representation. Axiom a should come as no surprise after Chapter 1. Axiom b is often called the *independence* or *substitution axiom* in this setting. Axiom c essentially says that preferences are continuous in probabilities.

Second, these three axioms are necessary and sufficient to give an expected-utility representation; that is, $\succeq$ is represented by a function $u : \Pi \to R$ which has the form

$$u(\pi) = \sum_{x \in \mathrm{supp}(\pi)} \pi(x)U(x), \tag{5.3}$$

for some function $U : X \to R$.

Third, functions $U : X \to R$ that work in this fashion for given preferences $\succeq$ are all positive affine transformations of one another.

Compare with the subjective expected-utility representation (5.2). In both, prizes from X have associated utility levels $U(x)$, and the value of an act/probability distribution is the mathematical expectation of the utilities of the prizes. In Equation (5.2), utilities are weighted by subjective probabilities of states. In Equation (5.3), the exogenously given probabilities (that describe each π) are used. (Since the probabilities are not a subjective product of the person whose preferences we are representing, but instead are presumably the product of an objective modeler, they are called *objective* probabilities, to be distinguished from the *subjective* probabilities of (5.2).)

Comparisons between Savage's Sure-Thing Principle and property b are immediate. Think of $T \subseteq S$ (in the state-space approach) as an event of probability a, and $a\pi + (1-a)\varphi$ is, roughly, "π on T and φ on T^C." If we make this rough and informal translation, when we compare $a\pi + (1-a)\varphi$ with $a\rho + (1-a)\varphi$, we are comparing two gambles that differ on the a-probability event T and are the same on the complement of this event. Savage's Sure-Thing Principle says that in terms of how the two compare, it doesn't matter how they are the same. So, in this setting, it doesn't matter that they are both φ on this complementary event, or that they are both φ'.

The continuity property c can be stated in many ways; the one here was chosen to look the most like continuity as defined in Chapter 1. It says that as we move from π to φ by taking convex combinations $a\pi + (1-a)\varphi$ of the two, for a close enough to 1 (so the convex combination is close to π), the combination is "close" in preference to π.

The rest of the chapter

This completes our survey of the basic models—how they differ, what sorts of representations are used, and what properties of preference drive the representations. We now have to justify what we've said. In Section 5.2, we prove Proposition 5.3 by first proving a very general (and useful) result known as the *Mixture-Space Theorem*; then we discuss how to extend Proposition 5.3 to probability distributions that are not simple. In Section 5.3, we discuss how to get representations (5.1) and (5.2); note that we have not yet stated a formal proposition leading to those representations. Section 5.4 discusses subjective vs. objective probabilities. And we wrap up in Section 5.5 with a brief discussion of empirical and theoretical problems with these models.

5.2. The Mixture-Space Theorem

The proof of Proposition 5.3 enlists a general result known as the Mixture-Space Theorem. The setting for this result is an abstract space Z, in which it is possible to take *mixtures* or convex combinations of items: For all pairs z and z' in Z and for all $a \in [0,1]$, there is an element $az + (1-a)z'$ in Z. It is assumed that the "usual" rules of convex combinations hold, such as $1z + 0z' = z$, $az + (1-a)z = z$, $a(a'z + (1-a')z') + (1-a)(a''z + (1-a'')z') = (aa' + (1-a)a'')z + (1 - aa' - (1-a)a'')z'$, and $az + (1-a)z' = (1-a)z' + az$.[3]

The space of simple probability distributions Π over an arbitrary space X is a mixture space. We use two other classes of examples in this chapter.

[3] Formal and abstract definitions of a mixture space concern a space Z and, for each $a \in [0,1]$, a map $h_a : Z^2 \to Z$ such that $h_1(z, z') = z$, $h_a(z, z) = z$ for all a, and so forth. I am being less formal than this and, in particular, writing $az + (1-a)z'$ for the abstract $h_a(z, z')$, since in all the examples of mixture spaces we consider, the informal notation is more intuitive and suggestive of what is going on and is easier to work with. But beware: In formal treatments, it is not assumed that $h_a(z, z') = h_{1-a}(z', z)$ or, in informal notation, that $az + (1-a)z' = (1-a)z' + az$. This property isn't needed to prove the Mixture-Space Theorem, although it holds in all practical examples of which I am aware and makes life a bit simpler when it comes to proofs. So I assume it.

1. Any space of probability distributions over some space X of prizes that is closed under the taking of convex combinations is a mixture space. Suppose, for instance, that $X = R$. If Z is the space of probability distributions on X with continuous density functions, or the space of probability distributions on X with countable support, or (if you know what this means) the space of Borel probability measures on X; if Z is any of those spaces, then Z is closed under the taking of convex combinations (the convex combination of two probability distributions with continuous density functions is a probability distribution with a continuous density function, etc.), and Z is therefore a mixture space.
2. Let S be a finite set, let X be an arbitrary set of prizes, let Π be the space of simple probability distributions on X, and let $H = \Pi^S$. That is, elements of H are S-dimensional vectors of simple probability distributions on X. We use the notation h to denote a member of H, $h(s)$ (for $s \in S$) to denote the s-component of h (therefore, $h(s) \in \Pi$), and $h(s)(x)$ (for $s \in S$ and $x \in X$) to denote the probability of the prize x according to the simple probability distribution $h(s)$. For h and h' members of H and for $a \in [0,1]$, let $ah+(1-a)h'$ be the member of H whose s component is $ah(s) + (1-a)h'(s)$; that is, take convex combinations component by component. This makes H a mixture space. (If you do not quite understand this example, we draw some helpful pictures later in this chapter.)

Although the elements of some mixture spaces are not probability distributions or lotteries in any sense, I use the term "lottery" informally to refer to a member of an arbitrary mixture space for the remainder of this section.

Proposition 5.4 (The Mixture-Space Theorem, Herstein and Milnor 1953). *A preference relation $\succeq$ on a mixture space Z satisfies*

a. *$\succeq$ is complete and transitive,*

b. *for all $z, z', \hat{z}$, and $\hat{z}'$ from Z and $a \in [0,1]$, $az + (1-a)\hat{z} \succ az' + (1-a)\hat{z}$ if and only if $az + (1-a)\hat{z}' \succ az' + (1-a)\hat{z}'$, and*

c. *if $z \succ z'$, then for any third lottery z'' there exists $a^* \in (0,1)$ such that $az+(1-a)z'' \succ z'$ and $z \succ az' + (1-a)z''$ for all a such that $a^* < a \leq 1$,*

if and only if a function $u : Z \to R$ exists such that

d. *$z \succeq z'$ if and only if $u(z) \geq u(z')$ (that is, u represents $\succeq$), and*

e. *$u(az + (1-a)z') = au(z) + (1-a)u(z')$ for all $z, z' \in Z$ and $a \in [0,1]$ (that is, u is linear in convex combinations in Z).*

Moreover, if u represents $\succeq$ in this sense, $v : Z \to R$ is another representation (that is linear in convex combinations) if and only if $v(\cdot) = Au(\cdot) + B$ for constants $A > 0$ and B.

The proof of this proposition comes in three pieces: (1) properties a, b, and c imply the existence of a function u that satisfies d and e; (2) a function u satisfying d and e implies that the corresponding preference relation satisfies a, b, and c; and (3) in either case, the representing u is unique up to positive affine transformations. The second of these three pieces is relatively straightforward, so I leave it to you to do.

Five lemmas

The first piece of the proof is the longest and hardest. It begins with five lemmas. The first of these is a simple matter of definitions, applied to property b. Since property b is stated as an if and only if, the negation of either side implies the negation of the other. Hence:

Lemma 5.5. *Property b is equivalent to*

b′. for all z and z' from Z and $a \in [0,1]$, if $az + (1-a)\hat{z} \succ az' + (1-a)\hat{z}$ for some $\hat{z} \in Z$, then $az + (1-a)\hat{z}' \succ az' + (1-a)\hat{z}'$ for all $\hat{z}' \in Z$,

both of which are equivalent to

b″. for all $z, z', \hat{z}$, and $\hat{z}'$ from Z and $a \in [0,1]$, $az + (1-a)\hat{z} \succeq az' + (1-a)\hat{z}$ if and only if $az + (1-a)\hat{z}' \succeq az' + (1-a)\hat{z}'$.

Moreover, any of b, b′, or b″ imply that for all $z, z', \hat{z}$, and $\hat{z}'$ from Z and $a \in [0,1]$, $az + (1-a)\hat{z} \sim az' + (1-a)\hat{z}$ if and only if $az + (1-a)\hat{z}' \sim az' + (1-a)\hat{z}'$.

Please note: because we assume $az + (1-a)z' = (1-a)z' + az$, each of b, b′, and b″, as well as their implication in the lemma just stated, could be stated where the substitution occurs in the first term of the convex combination. That is, b is equivalent to $a\hat{z}+(1-a)z \succ a\hat{z}+(1-a)z'$ if and only if $a\hat{z}'+(1-a)z \succ a\hat{z}'+(1-a)z'$, and so forth.

For the rest of the lemmas, it is assumed that $\succeq$ satisfies a, b, and c of the proposition.

Lemma 5.6. *If $z \succ z'$, then $z \succ 0.5z+0.5z' \succ z'$. If $z \sim z'$, then $z \sim 0.5z+0.5z' \sim z'$.*

Proof. Suppose $z \succ z'$ but, contrary to the statement in the lemma, $0.5z+0.5z' \succeq z$. Write $z = 0.5z+0.5z$, and apply property b″ to $0.5z+0.5z' \succeq 0.5z+0.5z$ by changing the "common" z to a z', to get $z' = 0.5z' + 0.5z' \succeq 0.5z' + 0.5z = 0.5z + 0.5z' \succeq z$. Hence, by transitivity of $\succeq$, $0.5z + 0.5z' \succeq z$ implies $z' \succeq z$, a contradiction. Similarly, if $z' \succeq 0.5z+0.5z'$, property b″ can be used to show that $0.5z+0.5z' \succeq z$ (do it if you don't see the steps), and then by transitivity, $z' \succeq z$, again a contradiction.

Suppose $z \sim z'$ but $0.5z + 0.5z' \succ z$. Rewrite the second part as $0.5z + 0.5z' \succ 0.5z+0.5z$, which (by b) implies that $z' = 0.5z'+0.5z' \succ 0.5z'+0.5z = 0.5z+0.5z' \succ z$; apply transitivity to derive a contradiction. The case $z \succ 0.5z + 0.5z'$ is handled similarly. ∎

Lemma 5.7. *If $z \succ z'$ and $a, b \in [0,1]$ are such that $a > b$, then $az + (1-a)z' \succ bz + (1-b)z'$. If $z \sim z'$, then $z \sim az + (1-a)z' \sim z'$ for all $a \in [0,1]$.*

Or, in words, when taking convex combinations of lotteries, one of which is strictly preferred to the other, preference is "strictly monotone" in the weight of the better lottery in the convex combination.

Proof. Suppose $z \succ z'$. By Lemma 5.6, $z \succ 0.5z + 0.5z' \succ z'$. I assert that if $0 \le k < j \le 2^n$ for k, j, and n integers, then $\frac{j}{2^n}z + (1 - \frac{j}{2^n})z' \succ \frac{k}{2^n}z + (1 - \frac{k}{2^n})z'$. The proof is by induction in n. Suppose the result is true for n, and take any integer ℓ such that $0 \le \ell < 2^n$. By the induction hypothesis applied to n, ℓ in the role of k, and $\ell + 1$ in the role of j,

$$\frac{\ell+1}{2^n}z + \left(1 - \frac{\ell+1}{2^n}\right)z' \succ \frac{\ell}{2^n}z + \left(1 - \frac{\ell}{2^n}\right)z';$$

hence by Lemma 5.6,

$$\frac{2\ell+2}{2^{n+1}}z + \left(1 - \frac{2\ell+2}{2^{n+1}}\right)z' \succ \frac{2\ell+1}{2^{n+1}}z + \left(1 - \frac{2\ell+1}{2^{n+1}}\right)z' \succ \frac{2\ell}{2^{n+1}}z + \left(1 - \frac{2\ell}{2^{n+1}}\right)z'.$$

A simple application of transitivity gives the induction step and the result.

Continue to suppose $z \succ z'$, and take any $a \in (0, 1)$. We know by property c that $a'z + (1 - a')z' \succ a'z' + (1 - a')z' = z'$ for all a' sufficiently close to one. Moreover, we can find such an a' such that $a = \frac{j}{2^n}a'$ for some integer j and n. Therefore, by the previous paragraph,

$$\frac{j}{2^n}(a'z + (1 - a')z') + \left(1 - \frac{j}{2^n}\right)z' \succ z',$$

which is $az + (1 - a)z' \succ z'$. By a similar argument, we can show that $z \succ az + (1 - a)z'$.

And now take arbitrary $a, b \in (0, 1)$ with $a > b$. By the previous paragraph, $az + (1 - a)z' \succ z'$. Applying the paragraph again, regarding $bz + (1 - b)z'$ as a convex combination of $az + (1 - a)z'$ and z', yields $az + (1 - a)z' \succ bz + (1 - b)z'$.

Next, in exactly the manner of the first paragraph of this proof, use induction and Lemma 5.6 to show that if $z \sim z'$, then $az + (1 - a)z' \sim z$ if a is of the form $k/2^n$ for integers k and n. Extend this to all $a \in [0, 1]$ as follows: suppose $z \sim z'$ but, for some $a \in (0, 1)$, $az + (1 - a)z' \succ z$. Property c implies that for all a' greater than but sufficiently close to a, $a'z + (1 - a')z' \succ z$. One such a' is of the form $k/2^n$, a contradiction. The case where $z \succ az + (1 - a)z'$ is handled similarly. ■

Lemma 5.8. *Suppose* $z \sim z'$. *For any third* z'' *and any* $a \in [0, 1]$, $az + (1 - a)z'' \sim az' + (1 - a)z''$.

Proof. Suppose that $z \sim z'$ but, for some a and z'', $az + (1 - a)z'' \succ az' + (1 - a)z''$. Apply property b to change the common z'' to z', getting $az + (1 - a)z' \succ az' + (1 - a)z' = z'$, which contradicts Lemma 5.7. A symmetric argument rules out $a'z + (1 - a)z'' \succ az + (1 - a)z''$. ■

Lemma 5.9. *Suppose* $z \succeq z' \succeq z''$. *Then for some* $a^* \in [0, 1]$, $a^*z + (1 - a^*)z'' \sim z'$. *And if, in addition,* $z \succ z''$, *then this* a^* *is unique.*

Proof. Taking the last statement first, the uniqueness of a^*, if it exists, is immediate from the first part of Lemma 5.7. As for the existence of a^*: If $z \sim z''$, then $z \sim z' \sim z''$ and any a^* will do. So we can assume that $z \succ z''$. If $z' \sim z$, $a^* = 1$ works; if $z' \sim z''$, $a^* = 0$ works; so we can assume that $z \succ z' \succ z''$.

Let $a^* = \inf\{a \in [0,1] : az + (1-a)z'' \succ z'\}$. Since $z \succ z' \succ z''$, property c ensures that $a^* \in (0,1)$.

Suppose that $a^*z + (1-a^*)z'' \succ z'$. By c, some strict convex combination of $a^*z + (1-a^*)z''$ and z'' is strictly preferred to z'. This would be $az + (1-a)z'' \succ z'$ for $a < a^*$. But the definition of a^* precludes this: For all $a < a^*$, $z' \succeq az + (1-a)z''$.

Or suppose that $z' \succ a^*z + (1-a^*)z''$. Then c implies that z' is strictly preferred to a strict convex combination of $a^*z + (1-a^*)z''$ and z, which is $az + (1-a)z''$ for $a > a^*$. But if $a > a^*$, then there is some $b \in [a^*, a)$ such that $bz + (1-b)z'' \succ z'$, and Lemma 5.7 implies that $az + (1-a)z'' \succ z'$, a contradiction.

The only possibility left is $a^*z + (1-a^*)z'' \sim z'$. ∎

Finishing the first piece of the proof

With these five lemmas, we can finish the first piece of the proof of the Mixture-Space Theorem; that a, b, and c imply the existence of a linear-in-convex-combinations representation u. In fact, here I am going to do something less. I will prove this with one extra assumption:

For some $\overline{z}$ *and* $\underline{z}$ *in* Z, $\overline{z} \succeq z \succeq \underline{z}$ *for all* $z \in Z$.

Or, in words, Z contains a best and worst element. This assumption is *not* necessary to prove the result, but it does simplify things. For the proof of the proposition without this assumption, see Problem 5.3.

If $\overline{z} \sim \underline{z}$, then every element of Z is as good as every other. Therefore, any constant function u works. Having disposed of this case, we move to the more interesting case where $\overline{z} \succ \underline{z}$.

Take any z in Z. By Lemma 5.9, there exists a unique $a \in [0,1]$ such that $z \sim a\overline{z} + (1-a)\underline{z}$. For each z, let $u(z)$ be this a; that is, for each $z \in Z$, $z \sim u(z)\overline{z} + (1-u(z))\underline{z}$.

By Lemma 5.7, u gives a numerical representation of $\succeq$ on Z: Compare z and z'. Because $z \sim u(z)\overline{z} + (1-u(z))\underline{z}$ and $z' \sim u(z')\overline{z} + (1-u(z'))\underline{z}$,

$$z \succeq z' \text{ if and only if } u(z)\overline{z} + (1-u(z))\underline{z} \succeq u(z')\overline{z} + (1-u(z'))\underline{z},$$

which, according to Lemma 5.7, is true if and only if $u(z) \geq u(z')$.

And u is linear in convex combinations of lotteries. Fix z, z', and $a \in [0,1]$. Because $z \sim u(z)\overline{z} + (1-u(z))\underline{z}$, by an application of Lemma 5.8,

$$az + (1-a)z' \sim a\big[u(z)\overline{z} + (1-u(z))\underline{z}\big] + (1-a)z',$$

and, by a second application of Lemma 5.8 based on $z' \sim u(z')\overline{z} + (1-u(z'))\underline{z}$, this is indifferent to

$$a\big[u(z)\overline{z} + (1 - u(z))\underline{z}\big] + (1 - a)\big[u(z')\overline{z} + (1 - u(z'))\underline{z}\big] =$$
$$\big[au(z) + (1 - a)u(z')\big]\overline{z} + \big[1 - (au(z) + (1 - a)u(z'))\big]\underline{z}.$$

Therefore, by the definition of u,

$$u(az + (1 - a)z') = au(z) + (1 - a)u(z'). \qquad \blacksquare$$

This proof is central to much of this chapter, so it pays to take a minute and reflect on how it works. Using the extra assumption, we use Lemma 5.9 to measure or calibrate every $z \in Z$ by finding the (unique!) convex combination of $\overline{z}$ and $\underline{z}$ that is indifferent to z. This gives a numerical representation of preferences, because we know (Lemma 5.7) that preferences are strictly monotone in probabilities when we take convex combinations of two lotteries, one better than the other. And this gives a representation that is linear in convex combinations because convex combinations are themselves linear, and Lemma 5.8 tells us that we can substitute any lottery in a convex combination with any other lottery indifferent to it; in particular, with the appropriate convex combination of $\overline{z}$ and $\underline{z}$.

The third piece of the proof of the Mixture-Space Theorem

Suppose u gives a mixture-space representation of $\succeq$. Define $v : Z \to R$ by $v(z) = Au(z) + B$ for constants $A > 0$ and B. Since v is a strictly increasing transformation of u, v represents $\succeq$ since u does. And it is straightforward to see that v is linear in convex combinations:

$$v(az + (1 - a)z') = Au(az + (1 - a)z') + B = A[au(z) + (1 - a)u(z')] + B$$
$$= a[Au(z) + B] + (1 - a)[Au(z') + B] = av(z) + (1 - a)v(z').$$

Suppose both u and v give mixture-space representations of $\succeq$. If $z \sim z'$ for all $z \in Z$, then u and v are both constant; hence $v(\cdot) = u(\cdot) + B$ for some constant B. So we can assume that $z \succ z'$ for some pair z and z'. Pick such a pair, denoting them by $\overline{z}$ and $\underline{z}$, respectively. (We are no longer assuming that these are best and worst in Z, but only that $\overline{z} \succ \underline{z}$.) Define $u^* : Z \to R$ and $v^* : Z \to R$ by

$$u^*(z) = \frac{u(z) - u(\underline{z})}{u(\overline{z}) - u(\underline{z})} \quad \text{and} \quad v^*(z) = \frac{v(z) - v(\underline{z})}{v(\overline{z}) - v(\underline{z})}.$$

The function u^* is a positive affine transformation of u; hence u^* represents $\succeq$ and is linear in convex combinations. Similarly, v^* is a positive affine transformation of v; therefore v^* represents $\succeq$ and is linear in convex combinations. Moreover, $u^*(\overline{z}) = v^*(\overline{z}) = 1$ and $u^*(\underline{z}) = v^*(\underline{z}) = 0$, by construction.

I assert that $u^*(z) = v^*(z)$ for *every* $z \in Z$. Once this assertion is proved, we are done with the third step: v is a positive affine transformation of v^* (find the constants if you are unsure about this), which is u^*, which is a positive affine transformation of u. Therefore, v is a positive affine transformation of u, which is what we want to show.

To prove the assertion that $u^*(z) = v^*(z)$ for every $z \in Z$, we take three cases:

1. If $\overline{z} \succeq z \succeq \underline{z}$, since $\overline{z} \succ \underline{z}$, Lemma 5.9 tells us that there exists a unique $a \in [0, 1]$ such that $a\overline{z} + (1 - a)\underline{z} \sim z$. Therefore,

$$u^*(z) = u^*(a\overline{z} + (1 - a)\underline{z}) = au^*(\overline{z}) + (1 - a)u^*(\underline{z}) = a,$$

where the first equality follows because u^* represents $\succeq$, the second because u^* is linear in convex combinations, and the third because $u^*(\overline{z}) = 1$ and $u^*(\underline{z}) = 0$. But exactly the same chain of logic shows that $v^*(z) = a$. Therefore, $u^*(z) = v^*(z)$ for every z such that $\overline{z} \succeq z \succeq \underline{z}$.

2. If $z \succ \overline{z}$, then $z \succ \underline{z}$, and Lemma 5.9 tells us that there is a unique $a \in (0, 1)$ such that $az + (1 - a)\underline{z} \sim \overline{z}$ and, therefore,

$$1 = u^*(\overline{z}) = u^*(az + (1 - a)\underline{z}) = au^*(z) + (1 - a)u^*(\underline{z}) = au^*(z).$$

Therefore, $u^*(z) = 1/a$. But the same argument applied to v^* will show that $v^*(z) = 1/a$.

3. If $\underline{z} \succ z$, then Lemma 5.9 tells us there is a unique $a \in (0, 1)$ such that $a\overline{z} + (1 - a)z \sim \underline{z}$, which means that $a + (1 - a)u^*(z) = 0$, or $u^*(z) = a/(a - 1)$ for this a. The same logic tells us that $v^*(z) = a/(a - 1)$.

Therefore, $v^* \equiv u^*$, and the third piece of the proof is done. ∎

Using the Mixture-Space Theorem to prove Proposition 5.3

Having proved the Mixture-Space Theorem, we can finish off the proof of Proposition 5.3. Again there are three pieces: that the three properties imply the existence of a function $U : X \to R$ such that expected utility computed with respect to U represents preferences; if preferences are represented by expected utility for some function $U : X \to R$, then preferences satisfy the three properties; and two utility functions U and V on prizes, both of which give expected utility representations of given preferences, are positive affine transformations of one another.

Again, I leave the second piece to you. As for the first piece, Π (the space of simple probability measures on X) is a mixture space and, if the three properties hold, the Mixture-Space Theorem guarantees that there is a function $u : \Pi \to R$ that represents $\succeq$ and that is linear in convex combinations. For $x \in X$, define $U(x) = u(\delta_x)$ (where δ_x, recall, is the probability distribution that gives x with probability 1). I assert that

$$u(\pi) = \sum_{x \in \text{supp}(\pi)} U(x)\pi(x),$$

for each $\pi \in \Pi$, which, once proved, gives the first step. To see that this is so, we induct on the size of the support of π. If the support of π contains a single element, so that $\pi = \delta_x$ for some $x \in X$, the result is true by the definition of U. Suppose the statement is true for any π with n or fewer elements in its support. Take some π with $n+1$ elements in its support. Let x_0 be any one of the elements in the support of π, so that $0 < \pi(x_0) < 1$. We can write

$$\pi = \pi(x_0)\delta_{x_0} + (1 - \pi(x_0))\rho$$

where ρ is a lottery with $\text{supp}(\rho) = \text{supp}(\pi) \setminus \{x_0\}$ and, for $x \in \text{supp}(\rho)$, $\rho(x) = \pi(x)/(1 - \pi(x_0))$.

Because u is linear in convex combinations,

$$u(\pi) = \pi(x_0)u(\delta_{x_0}) + (1 - \pi(x_0))u(\rho) = \pi(x_0)U(x_0) + (1 - \pi(x_0))u(\rho).$$

Because ρ has a support with n elements, the induction hypothesis applies to it, so

$$u(\rho) = \sum_{x \in \text{supp}(\rho)} \rho(x)U(x) = \sum_{x \in \text{supp}(\rho)} \frac{\pi(x)}{1 - \pi(x_0)} U(x); \text{ therefore}$$

$$u(\pi) = \pi(x_0)U(x_0) + (1 - \pi(x_0)) \left[\sum_{x \in \text{supp}(\rho)} \frac{\pi(x)}{1 - \pi(x_0)} U(x) \right] = \sum_{x \in \text{supp}(\pi)} \pi(x)U(x).$$

Only the third piece remains. Suppose U gives an expected utility representation of $\succeq$ on Π and $V(\cdot) = AU(\cdot) + B$ for constants $A > 0$ and B. Define u and v both from Π to R by

$$u(\pi) = \sum_{x \in \text{supp}(\pi)} U(x)\pi(x) \quad \text{and} \quad v(\pi) = \sum_{x \in \text{supp}(\pi)} V(x)\pi(x).$$

It is easy to see that both u and v are linear in convex combinations, and $v(\cdot) = Au(\cdot) + B$. Therefore, v gives the same preferences on Π as does u, which means that V gives the same expected utility representation on Π as does U. Conversely, if U and V give the same expected utility representations on Π, defining u and v as above and applying the Mixture-Space Theorem tells us that v is a positive affine transformation of u. Since $U(x) = u(\delta_x)$ and $V(x) = v(\delta_x)$ for all $x \in X$, V is a positive affine transformation of U. ∎

Expected utility for nonsimple lotteries

(This subsection requires substantially more mathematical sophistication than what precedes and what follows it. Apologies are tendered to readers who find this tough sledding.)

The proof of Proposition 5.3 establishes an *expected-utility* representation for simple probability distributions on an arbitrary prize space X. It would be nice to extend this result to more complex spaces of probability distributions; for instance, to the space of probability distributions with countable support on some arbitrary space X, or to the space of probability distributions on R with continuous density functions, or to the space of Borel probability measures on R^k, and so forth. Needless to say, to make this work, we must know what is meant by integration with respect to the probabilities in question (expected utility is, in general, a matter of integration). And we must worry about what do to if the expected utility of some probability distribution is either $+\infty$ or $-\infty$ or, worse, if the positive and negative parts of the integral both diverge.

But setting aside for the moment these "technical" concerns, is it clear that such extensions will be possible? That is, suppose $\succeq$ is defined on some rich space of probability distributions or measures on some prize set X. Assume that this space is closed under the taking of convex combinations, so that the space, denoted P, is a mixture space. Suppose $\succeq$ satisfies the three mixture-space properties, properties a, b, and c from Proposition 5.4. Does this imply that there is some function $U : X \to R$ such that expected utility calculated using U represents $\succeq$?

The Mixture-Space Theorem takes us a good deal of the way to a positive answer. Specifically, the three properties imply that some function $u : P \to R$ that is linear in convex combinations represents $\succeq$. But going from u defined on P to U defined on X in the manner of the proof of Proposition 5.3 is not going to work; the proof consisted (essentially) of using the linear-in-convex-combinations property finitely many times, which suffices only if the probability distributions in question have finite support. Of course, just because the proof we used does not work does not imply that the result is false. But the result *is* false, as the following example shows.

Let P be all probability distributions on $X = R$ that are convex combinations of simple probabilities and probabilities that have a continuous density that has compact support. That is, each $p \in P$ can be written as $a\pi + (1-a)f$, where $\pi \in \Pi$ and f is a continuous density that is zero outside of some compact set (that changes with f). To be very precise, the probability assigned by $p = a\pi + (1-a)f$ to any (measurable) subset $Y \subseteq R$ is

$$p(Y) = a \sum_{x \in Y \cap \mathrm{supp}(\pi)} \pi(x) \quad + \quad (1-a) \int_Y f(x)dx.$$

I assert that any such probability has a unique decomposition into its simple (or discrete) part and its continuous-density part. I further assert that this space is indeed closed under the taking of convex combinations; that is, it is a mixture space. (You are left the job of verifying these assertions.)

Define a function $u : P \to R$ by

$$u(a\pi + (1-a)f) \quad = \quad a \sum_{x \in \mathrm{supp}(\pi)} x\pi(x) \quad + \quad (1-a).$$

I assert that this function u is linear in convex combinations (more work for you), so we know that if preferences are defined by this utility function—that is, $p \succeq p'$ if $u(p) \geq u(p')$—then $\succeq$ must satisfy a, b, and c of the Mixture-Space Theorem. But I assert that these preferences cannot have an expected-utility representation. For if $U : X \to R$ gave an expected-utility representation, then by looking at probability distributions in P that are entirely simple (such that the a in $a\pi + (1-a)f$ equals 1), it is not hard to show that $U(x)$ must take the form $Ax + B$ for constants $A > 0$ and B. (Essentially, use the definition of u and the uniqueness part of Proposition 5.3.) But then consider $\hat{p} = \delta_2$—the simple probability distribution that gives 2 with certainty—and $\check{p}$ = any probability distribution that is purely a continuous-density probability with support $[3, 4]$. If $U(x) = Ax + B$ for $A > 0$, then the expectation of U taken with respect to $\hat{p}$ is $U(2) = 2A + B$, while the expectation of U taken with respect to $\check{p}$ can be no less than $3A + B$, because the integrand $U(x) \geq 3A + B$ for all x in the support of $\check{p}$. Expected utility will tell us that $\check{p} \succ \hat{p}$. But it is easy to compute that $u(\hat{p}) = 2$ and $u(\check{p}) = 1$, so $\hat{p} \succ \check{p}$. Oops.

The example suggests a possible cure for the problem it presents: In the example, the lottery $\hat{p}$ gives a prize of 2 with certainty. The lottery $\check{p}$ gives prizes between 3 and 4. That is, with probability 1, $\check{p}$ gives a prize that, taken as a sure thing, is strictly preferred to the (sole) prize possible under $\hat{p}$. And yet $\hat{p} \succ \check{p}$. How about adding to properties a, b, and c a property that rules this sort of thing out? (I hope you agree that this sort of thing constitutes unreasonable behavior in terms of someone's preferences.) In fact, this line of attack, suitably generalized, does work; you can see how in Fishburn (1970).

I prefer and will formalize a somewhat different cure. (At this point, the math level goes up another notch or two.) Assume that X, the set of prizes, is a nice subset of R^k for some k[4] and that P is the space of Borel probability measures on X. Add to a, b, and c of the Mixture-Space Theorem the assumption

Preferences $\succeq$ are continuous in the topology of weak convergence on P.

We have only discussed continuity of preferences for preferences defined on subsets of Euclidean space R^k, so to make sense of this assumption, we must identify this topology and define continuity of preferences. The second is not hard: *Preferences are continuous in a given topology if, for all p, the sets $\{p' : p' \succ p\}$ and $\{p' : p \succ p'\}$ are open.* As for the definition of this topology, *the sequence $\{p^n\}$ in P has limit p in this topology if and only if $\lim_n \int_X f(x)p^n(dx) = \int_X f(x)p(x)$ for all bounded and continuous functions f on R.* (The solution to Problem 5.7 in the *Student's Guide* provides more details.) It can be shown that, for any probability measure p on X, we can construct a sequence of simple probability measures $\{p_n\}$ such that $\lim_n p_n = p$ in this topology.[5] If we have a, b, and c from the Mixture-Space Theorem, we know

[4] I am being vague about what "nice" means here, but I have in mind that $X = R^k$, or $X = R^k_+$, or X is at least a "rectangle" in R^k.

[5] For instance, partition increasingly larger but bounded subsets of X into finitely many small "rectangles." If $X = R$, say, take rectangles of the form $(i/n, (i+1)/n]$ for $i = -n^2, \ldots, -1, 0, 1, 2, 3, \ldots, n^2$. Then, for any one of the rectangles, call it Z, let p_n place the measure $p(Z)$ on any single point from within Z, arbitrarily assigning the leftover probability to, say, the origin. This "discretization" of p

that there is a function $u : P \to R$, linear in convex combinations, that represents $\succeq$. We can define $U : X \to R$ by $U(x) = u(\delta_x)$; the continuity of $\succeq$ in this topology can be used to show that U is a continuous function. Finally, define $u' : P \to R$ by $u'(p) = \int_X U(x)p(dx)$. Use the argument from the proof of Proposition 5.3 that shows that $u(\pi)$ has the expected-utility form, to show that u and u' agree on all simple probability measures; then use continuity and the sort of approximation of any p by a sequence of simple p_n mentioned to show that u' does in fact give a representation of $\succeq$. If you have learned about this topology, the steps are not that hard. So I'll give this as a formal proposition, which I ask you to prove in Problem 5.7. (The proof is then given in the *Student's Guide*):

Proposition 5.10. *Suppose $X = R^k$ (or R^k_+) and P is the space of Borel probability measures on X. If preferences $\succeq$ defined on P satisfy a, b, and c of the Mixture-Space Theorem and are also continuous in the topology of weak convergence, then there exists a* ***bounded*** *and* ***continuous*** *function $U : X \to R$ such that*

$$u(p) = \int_X U(x)p(dx)$$

represents $\succeq$. (Conversely, for any bounded and continuous function $U : X \to R$, u defined in this fashion gives preferences that satisfy a, b, and c and that are continuous in the topology of weak convergence.)

Note that, in this proposition, the utility function U must be both bounded and continuous. If you know about the topology of weak convergence, continuity should not come as a surprise; if $\{x_n\}$ is a sequence of prizes with the limit x, then $\delta_{x_n} \to \delta_x$ in this topology. (This doesn't prove that U must be continuous, but it is the first step in a proof.) But the boundedness of U has to be rated as something of a ... disappointment, if we were planning to use this proposition for the sort of applications one finds littering the literature of economics, especially financial economics, in which the utility function of choice is the unbounded function $U(x) = -e^{-\lambda x}$ for some $\lambda > 0$, and probability distributions that are Normal are among the objects of choice.

The reason that Proposition 5.10 produces a bounded U is not too hard to see. The Mixture-Space Theorem produces a function $u : P \to R$. That is, the "utility" of each lottery or probability distribution must be finite. That, in turn, is something of a consequence of mixture-space property c, which says that no matter how good or bad is some p'', if $p \succ p'$, then mixtures of p' and p'' with most (but not all) of the weight on p' are worse than p (so p'' cannot be supergood) and mixtures of p and p'' with most (but not all) of the weight on p are better than p' (so p'' cannot be superbad).

Suppose, then, that U was unbounded. In the context of Proposition 5.10, P contains probability distributions that are discrete but with countable support.

gives a sequence of measures that converges to p in the topology of weak convergence, as the diameter of the rectangles goes to zero.

Suppose, specifically, that U is unbounded below. This means that for each $k = 1, 2, \ldots$, we can find some x_k such that $U(x_k) < -2^k$. Then construct the (countable support) probability distribution p^* whose support is $\{x_1, x_2, \ldots\}$ and that assigns probability $1/2^k$ to x_k. Expected utility for this probability distribution is $-\infty$. That is, $u(p^*)$ would have to be $-\infty$, which the Mixture-Space Theorem does not allow.

Nowhere in Proposition 5.3 does it say that U is bounded. No such restriction is needed (more precisely, is implied by the three mixture-space properties a, b, and c), because in Proposition 5.3, only simple (finite support) lotteries are allowed. Even if U is unbounded, you cannot produce within Π a supergood or superbad lottery (one with expected utility either $+\infty$ or $-\infty$). Put another way, when applied to a relatively "poor" mixture space like Π—poor in the sense that it does not contain a lot of probability distributions on X—property c is a lot less strong than when it is assumed for a "rich" space of probability distributions (those with unbounded support).

Still, there is that disappointment to deal with: To do lots of interesting financial economics, we want to have models in which utility functions take the form $U(x) = -e^{-\lambda x}$ and lotteries on prizes are Normally distributed. If you consult the literature of finance, you will quickly appreciate the analytical conveniences of this pair of parameterizations. Can we find some way to "legitimize" models that use this pair of parameterizations?

Without going into details, it can be done. The key is to find a mixture space P that is restricted enough that property c doesn't limit you to bounded U. In the context of $X = R$, if you assume that the P contains only distributions whose tails vanish on the order of, say, e^{-kx^2} (a space that includes all Normals and all finite mixtures of Normals), then you may have utility functions that are unbounded, as long as their rates of growth and decline are suitably limited. In particular, with tails that vanish on the order of e^{-kx^2}, growth/decline that is exponential or less is fine. Having said this, a comment on the literature is worth making. Results of the sort indicated in this paragraph are possible, and they would save the parameterizations that are much used and loved by financial economists and others. But if anyone has ever published such results, I am unaware of them.

Another version of the Mixture-Space Theorem

The independence and continuity properties b and c in Propositions 5.3 and 5.4 are not entirely standard. I chose a formulation of property b that makes comparisons with Savage's Sure-Thing Principle as straightforward as possible and eases (a bit) difficulties in the proof. But in place of b and c you will often find equivalent pairs of properties, such as b′ and c′ in the following proposition.

Proposition 5.11. *Suppose $\succeq$ defined on a mixture space Z is complete and transitive. Then $\succeq$ satisfies b and c of Proposition 5.4 if and only if $\succeq$ satisfies*

b′. If $z \succ z'$, then for all $a \in (0,1)$ and $z'' \in \Pi$, $az + (1-a)z'' \succ az' + (1-a)z''$, and c′. *If* $z \succ z' \succ z''$, *then there exist* $a, b \in (0,1)$ *such that* $az + (1-a)z'' \succ z' \succ bz + (1-b)z''$.

Therefore, b′ and c′ (with a) are necessary and sufficient for the mixture-space representation, which is unique up to positive affine transformations. In fact, an easy way to show that b and c imply b′ and c′ (if a holds as well) is to note that b and c give a mixture-space representation, which almost immediately can be shown to imply b′ and c′. Conversely, if you can show that b′ and c′ (with a) yield a mixture-space representation, then the converse half of Proposition 5.4 shows that b′ and c′ imply b and c. I won't give the proof of the Mixture-Space Theorem using b′ and c′ instead of b and c; see Kreps (1988) or Fishburn (1970) for the details.

5.3. States of Nature and Subjective Expected Utility

Now we return to the states-of-nature approach, looking for justifications for additively separable and subjective expected-utility representations (that is, representations of the forms (5.1) and (5.2)). As already noted, the classic way to get (5.2) is due to Savage. But Savage's development is fairly complex, so we use the alternative and somewhat easier development due to Anscombe and Aumann (1963).

Horse races and roulette wheels

We begin with set of prizes X and a set of states of nature S, out of which the set of acts $A = X^S$ is formed. Throughout this section, we assume that S is finite.[6] Consumer preferences are given over the set A.

Anscombe and Aumann enrich this setup. Let Π be the space of simple probability distributions on X, with a typical element written as π, and call $\pi \in \Pi$ *roulette lotteries*, thinking of π as a gamble that is based on objects such as well-balanced roulette wheels, very symmetric dice, and so on. That is, for lotteries π, the odds (probabilities) are objective because of the symmetry of the randomizing devices employed.

Preferences $\succeq$ are extended from the set of acts A to the space $H = \Pi^S$. Each $h \in H$ is a function with domain S and range Π; for each state s, h specifies a roulette lottery $h(s)$. The interpretation is that the states s represent the results of things like horse races (the weather, the resolution of technological uncertainty, and so on), and a *horse-race lottery* h is a gamble that, depending on the state of nature s, pays off in a roulette lottery.

For example, imagine a betting ticket that pays the following: In state s_1 (Secretariat wins), the consumer get $\$-2$ for sure. (That is, she loses \$2 for sure.) In state s_2 (Kelso wins), she gets \$3 with probability $1/2$ and \$1 with probability $1/2$. In state s_3 (a dead heat), she gets \$6 with probability $1/3$ and loses \$4 with

[6] The assumption of finite S would seem to limit the applicability of this approach. This limitation is more apparent than real: The extension of these results to general S is straightforward, albeit notationally cumbersome. However, this extension *only* takes you as far as finitely additive subjective probability, without a considerable upgrade in mathematical armament. Problem 5.6 gives details.

probability 2/3. This sort of creature is depicted by a compound chance node, as in Figure 5.6b, where the compounding is now an important part of the mathematical formalism. (Panels a and c of this picture will be explained momentarily.) In these pictures we use a solid node for the state-of-nature uncertainty and an open node for the roulette-based uncertainty.

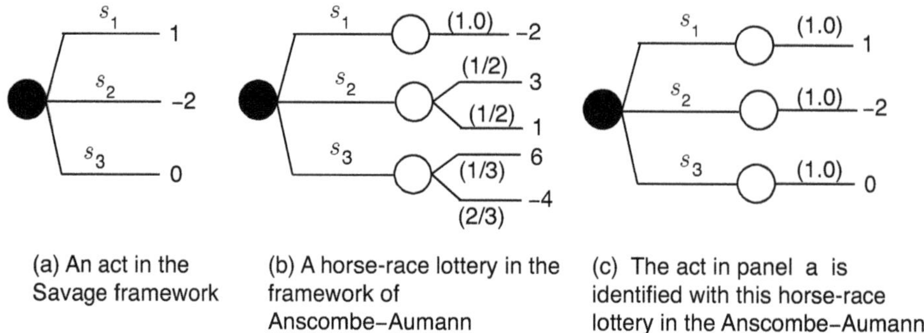

Figure 5.6. Acts and horse-race lotteries

Compare this with the setup with which we began. Previously, after the horse race was run and the state s was realized, the outcome was a prize $x = a(s)$. Now the "outcome" of the horse race is a lottery $h(s) \in \Pi$. Of course, A is something of a subset of H; included in H are horse-race lotteries that pay off, in each state, in degenerate (single prize) roulette lotteries. (See Figure 5.6 for all this said with pictures.) So you can think of this enriching of the space on which consumer preferences are given as a thought experiment: Our interest, ultimately, is in representing the consumer's preferences on acts from A. But we ask the consumer to rank more objects than these, because properties of preference on a larger space (insofar as those properties have the form *For all*...) will be stronger properties, giving us more to work with when seeking a representation.

Suppose h and g are two horse-race lotteries, and a is a number between zero and one. Define a new horse-race lottery, denoted $ah + (1-a)g$, as follows: For each state s, the new horse-race lottery gives as prize the roulette lottery $ah(s) + (1-a)g(s)$, where this last object is defined as the usual convex combination of the two probability distributions $h(s)$ and $g(s)$. Figure 5.7 gives an example of this sort of operation.

An additively separable representation

Proposition 5.12. *Suppose S is finite. Then preferences $\succeq$ on H satisfy*

a. $\succeq$ is complete and transitive,

b. for all $h, h', g,$, and g' from H and $a \in [0,1]$, $ah + (1-a)g \succ ah' + (1-a)g$ if and only if $ah + (1-a)g' \succ ah' + (1-a)g'$, and

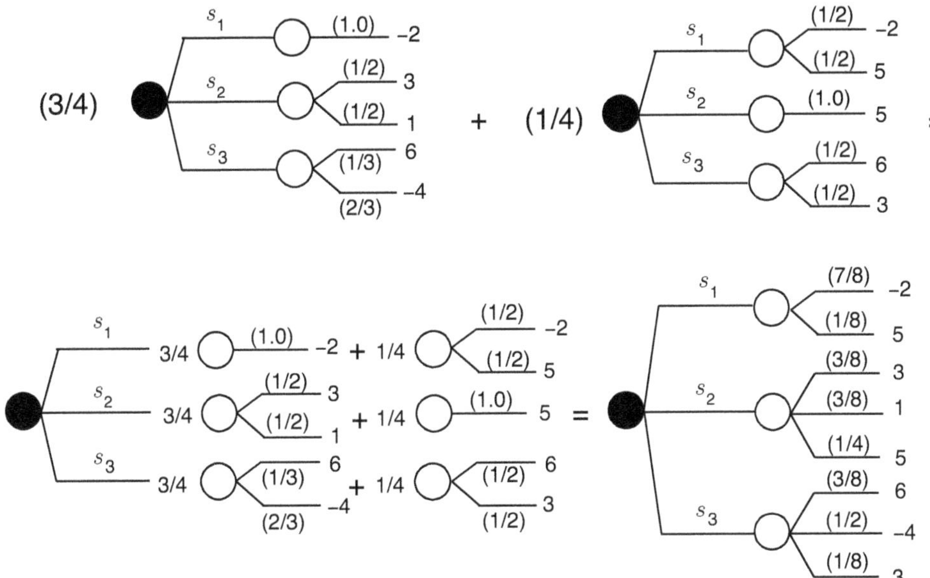

Figure 5.7. Taking mixtures of horse-race lotteries. When mixing horse-race lotteries, you mix the lotteries for each outcome of the horse race.

c. *if* $h \succ h'$, *then for any third horse-race lottery* g *there exists* $a^* \in (0,1)$ *such that* $ah + (1-a)g \succ h'$ *and* $h \succ ah' + (1-a)g$ *for all* a *such that* $a^* < a \leq 1$

if and only if there is a function $u : H \to R$ *such that*

d. u *represents* $\succeq$: $h \succeq g$ *if and only if* $u(h) \geq u(g)$, *and*

e. u *has the form*

$$u(h) = \sum_{s \in S} \sum_{x \in \text{supp}(h(s))} U_s(x)h(s)(x), \tag{5.6}$$

for functions $U_s : X \to R$, *for each* $s \in S$. *Moreover, if* v *is another such representation of* $\succeq$, *with accompanying state-utility functions* V_s, *then there exist constants* $A > 0$, B, *and* B_s *for* $s \in S$ *such that* $v(\cdot) = Au(\cdot) + B$ *and each* $V_s(\cdot) = AU_s(\cdot) + B_s$.

Some commentary is in order before getting to the proof.

1. It is probably obvious to you from a, b, and c that we are about to enlist the Mixture-Space Theorem again. But before doing so, you might want to consider whether, in the current context, a, b, and c are sensible assumptions to make about consumer preferences.

2. In the representation, we get additive separability across horse-race states $s \in S$, and within each state s, we get an expected-utility representation, although the utility function for state s can be quite different than that for s'. To evaluate a

horse-race lottery h, you must (1) use the state s utility function U_s to compute the expected utility of the roulette lottery $h(s)$, for each s separately, and then (2) add up the state-specific expected utilities. When restricted to horse-race lotteries whose roulette lotteries are all degenerate (sure-things), this specializes to the state-additive representation (5.1).

Proof. As we remarked when we first introduced the concept of a mixture space, the space H is a mixture space, where $ah + (1 - a)h'$ involves taking convex combinations for each state $s \in S$. Hence, the Mixture-Space Theorem, applied to this setting, would pretty much conform to the statement of the proposition, except that e would be replaced by

e′. u is linear in convex combinations

and we would not have the bit at the end concerning a comparison of the U_s and V_s. I leave it to you to prove that if $u : H \to R$ has the form (5.6), then u is linear in convex combinations; once that is shown, the Mixture-Space Theorem tells us that d and e imply a, b, and c. Instead, I'll assume a, b, and c, and pick up the story at the point where the Mixture-Space Theorem has been applied and we have produced a function $u : H \to R$ that represents $\succeq$ and is linear in convex combinations.

Fix (completely arbitrarily) some roulette lottery $\pi^0 \in \Pi$. For each $s \in S$, and $h \in H$, let $h^0(h, s)$ be the horse-race lottery that gives roulette lottery $h(s)$ in state s and the roulette lottery π^0 in all other states. Let h^0 be the horse-race lottery that gives π^0 in every state, and normalize u so that $u(h^0) = 0$. By straightforward algebra,

$$\sum_{s \in S} \frac{1}{N} h^0(h, s) = \frac{1}{N} h + \frac{N-1}{N} h^0, \tag{5.7}$$

where N is the number of states. Because u is linear in convex combinations, we therefore know that

$$\sum_{s \in S} \frac{1}{N} u(h^0(h, s)) = \frac{1}{N} u(h) + \frac{N-1}{N} u(h^0).$$

Since $u(h^0)$ has been normalized to be 0, the last term drops out. Multiply both sides of what remains by N, to get

$$\sum_{s \in S} \left[u(h^0(h, s)) \right] = u(h).$$

For each $s \in S$, define $u_s : \Pi \to R$ by

$$u_s(\pi) = u(h') \text{ where } h' \text{ is the horse-race lottery with } h'(s') = \begin{cases} \pi, & \text{if } s' = s, \text{ and} \\ \pi^0, & \text{if } s' \neq s. \end{cases}$$

With this definition, $u(h^0(h,s)) = u_s(h(s))$, since $h^0(h,s)$ is the horse-race lottery with π in s and π^0 in all other states. Hence

$$\sum_{s \in S} u_s(h(s)) = u(h).$$

Moreover, because u is linear in convex combinations on H, it is relatively easy to show that each u_s is linear in convex combinations on Π; hence (because Π consists of simple probabilities only) we know (from the argument back on pages 95 and 96) that each u_s has the form

$$u_s(\pi) = \sum_{x \in \mathrm{supp}(\pi)} U_s(x)\pi(x)$$

where $U_s : X \to R$ is defined by $U_s(x) = u_s(\delta_x)$. Putting everything together gives (5.6).

Suppose that u and v are two different linear-in-convex-combinations representations of $\succeq$. We know that $v(\cdot) = Au(\cdot) + B$ by the Mixture-Space Theorem. Construct U_s and V_s from u and v as above. Fix any x^0, and define $B_s = V_s(x^0) - AU_s(x^0)$. It is immediate that $\sum_s B_s = B$. Now take any $x \in X$ and $s' \in S$, and consider the horse-race lottery that gives x^0 with certainty for all $s \neq s'$ and x with certainty in state s'. Under v, this has value $V_{s'}(x) + \sum_{s \neq s'} V_s(x^0)$, while under u it has value $U_{s'}(x) + \sum_{s \neq s'} U_s(x^0)$. Since $v = Au + B$, this means

$$V_{s'}(x) + \sum_{s \neq s'} V_s(x^0) = A\left[U_{s'}(x) + \sum_{s \neq s'} U_s(x^0)\right] + B = AU_{s'}(x) + B_{s'} + \sum_{s \neq s'} [AU_s(x^0) + B_s].$$

Cancel the two summations, since they are identical term by term, to obtain $V_{s'}(x) = AU_{s'}(x) + B_{s'}$; since x is free here, this tells us that $V_{s'} \equiv AU_{s'} + B_{s'}$. ∎

The trick

This late in the chapter, you may be feeling a bit glassy-eyed and inclined to accept the short proof just given without worrying too much how it works. But diligent readers may feel a bit cheated by the proof. It isn't clear (to most first-time readers) how additive separability across states just popped out of a hat, like the proverbial rabbit.

Let me sharpen the point this way. Suppose instead of looking at horse races that pay off in roulette lotteries, we had gone to the casino first and then the racetrack; that is, we worked with the space of simple probability distributions over the space $A = X^S$. Since this is a space of simple probability distributions, it is a mixture space, and the Mixture-Space Theorem applies. But the conclusions of the Mixture-Space Theorem viewing things this way are much weaker than the conclusions of Proposition 5.12. In particular, we do not get anything close to additive separability across states. It is *vitally* important in this theory that the horses run first. (Can you figure out why on your own? If not, read on.)

The trick, if I may call it that, comes in the definition of convex combinations in H. Let me illustrate with a very specific example. Suppose the state space $S = \{s_1, s_2\}$, and the set of prizes X is $\{steak, chicken\}$, representing dinners you might have. Consider the following four horse-race lotteries: h_{ss} gives the consumer steak for sure in both states; h_{sc} gives her steak in s_1 and chicken in s_2; h_{cs} gives her chicken in state s_1 and steak in s_2, and h_{cc} gives her chicken for sure, regardless of the state.

Imagine that the two states are equally likely in the mind of this consumer, and she generally prefers steak to chicken. Imagine as well that this consumer's tastes in meals are not separable across states; that is, the value to the consumer of a steak dinner instead of chicken in one state is affected by what she gets to eat in the other state. To be very concrete, imagine that the value of steak instead of chicken is enhanced if it is paired with steak in the other state, while the value of a chicken dinner in one state is enhanced a bit if it is paired with chicken. Under all these assumptions, if we offered the consumer a 50-50 convex combination of h_{ss} and h_{cc} or a 50-50 convex combination of h_{sc} and h_{cs} (where 50-50 convex combinations mean, determined by the flip of a fair coin), we would expect her to prefer the former; that way she "benefits" by the enhancement of the value of steak when it is paired with steak and chicken when it is paired with chicken.

Since these preferences are not separable across states, they cannot be represented by a representation of the form (5.6). Accordingly, we might wonder, Which of a, b, and c is being violated in this example? The answer is, It isn't a, or b, or c, that rules this out. *It is the formulation itself that makes this impossible.* To see why, note that, in terms of H, a 50-50 convex combination of h_{ss} and h_{cc} *is identical to* a 50-50 convex combination of h_{sc} and h_{cs}; namely, each gives a coin-flip choice of steak or chicken in both states of nature. Our formal setup *identifies* these two convex combinations; since they are the same thing, our consumer must be indifferent between them. This is the key point, so let me say it again: When convex combinations are taken state by state, without regard to what each constituent horse-race lottery gives in the other states, state separability is implicitly invoked in the setup, before we get to the mixture-space properties a, b, and c.

Indeed, you see this rather blatantly in the proof at Equation (5.7). We take an arbitrary horse-race lottery h and "repackage" it in a convex combination with a reference lottery as the convex combination of lotteries each of which picks up a single state-component of h. The two convex combinations give the same overall lottery, so the consumer is forced to be indifferent between them. But the repackaging immediately gives us additive separability, because it takes "h plus a constant" and breaks this into a sum of terms, each of which depends on a single component of h.

If you are still fuzzy on this, I urge you to try Problems 5.4 and 5.5 (and, if possible, discuss your answers with your colleagues).

Subjective expected utility

Proposition 5.12 gets us additive separability over outcomes of the horse race and, for each outcome of the horse race, expected utility as in Proposition 5.3. But the state-dependent utility functions U_s needn't bear any particular relationship to one another. We are seemingly a long way from a representation of the form of (5.2).

Recall the discussion of umbrellas and suntan lotion from the first section, and you will see what is missing. The mixture-space properties a, b, and c do not speak to the question, Is the value of a prize independent of the state in which it is received? To finish the Anscombe-Aumann development, we need to assume that the answer to this question is yes.

This requires a bit more notation. For $\pi \in \Pi$ (a roulette lottery), write π as an element of H (a horse-race lottery) meaning the horse-race lottery that gives, regardless of the outcome of the horse race, the prize π.

Proposition 5.13. *For finite S, $\succeq$ satisfies a, b, and c of Proposition 5.12 and, in addition,*

f. for each $s \in S$ and π and $\rho \in \Pi$, $\pi \succeq \rho$ if and only if $h \succeq g$, where $h(s) = \pi$, $g(s) = \rho$, and $h(s') = g(s')$ for all $s' \neq s$,

if and only if $\succeq$ is represented by a function $u : H \to R$ taking the following form:

$$u(h) = \sum_{s \in S} \left[\sum_{x \in \text{supp}(h(\cdot|s))} U(x)h(s)(x) \right] \mathbf{p}(s), \tag{5.8}$$

where $U : X \to R$ and $\mathbf{p}$ is a probability distribution on S with $\mathbf{p}(s) > 0$ for all $s \in S$. Moreover, U is unique up to positive affine transformations, and if there exist x and x' such that $U(x) \neq U(x')$, then $\mathbf{p}$ is unique.

This is full subjective expected utility, with a state-independent utility function U and subjective probabilities for the states, given by $\mathbf{p}$.

The fourth assumption f is fairly blatant. Suppose π, ρ, s, h, and g are as in the statement of the assumption. Then h and g are identical on all states except s (hence, under a, b, and c, it doesn't matter how they are the same), and the consumer's preferences between h and g depends solely on how she feels about π vs. ρ contingent on state s. However she feels, the assumption is that she feels the same way between π-regardless-of-the-state and ρ-regardless-of-the-state. Comparisons of roulette lotteries are independent of state.

Proof. The previous paragraph almost gives the proof away. Suppose $\succeq$ satisfies properties a, b, and c. Then we know we get a representation of the form given in Proposition 5.12, specified by state-dependent utility functions U_s. Define for each state s the preferences $\succeq_s$ on Π that are created by U_s; i.e., $\pi \succeq_s \rho$ if $\sum \pi(x)U_s(x) \geq \sum \rho(x)U_s(x)$. These are expected-utility preferences in the sense of Proposition 5.3, and so satisfy a, b, and c there. Moreover, for h and g as in the statement of this proposition, $h \succeq g$ if and only if $\pi \succeq_s \rho$. But then f asserts that $\pi \succeq_s \rho$ if and only if $\pi \succeq_{s'} \rho$, for all π, ρ, s, and s'. Therefore, the uniqueness part of Proposition 5.3 tells us that if we fix some s^0, for each $s \neq s^0$ there exists $A(s) > 0$ and $B(s)$ such that $U_s(x) = A(s)U_{s_0}(x) + B(s)$. Define $U(x) = U_{s_0}(x)$ and $\mathbf{p}(s) = A(s)/\left(\sum_{s' \in S} A(s')\right)$ (where we interpret $A(s_0) = 1$). It is a matter of straightforward algebra to see that (5.6) becomes (5.8).

This leaves the converse part of the proposition—the representation implies the four properties—and the uniqueness claim. Both are left for you to do. ∎

It may be worth pointing out that in many treatments of Anscombe-Aumann, the possibility that $\mathbf{p}(s) = 0$ for some states is allowed. This takes a modification of f, to allow for states for which nothing (in terms of the lottery won in that state) matters.

5.4. Subjective and Objective Probability and the Harsanyi Doctrine

At the start of this chapter, I said that representations of the form (5.2) are sometimes called *subjective expected utility*. On the other hand, representations of the form (and in the setting) of Proposition 5.3 are often called *objective expected utility*. We can now explain what lies behind this terminology.

The probability distribution p in (5.2) or $\mathbf{p}$ in (5.8) is as much an expression of the personal preferences of the consumer as is the utility function u. To be very pedantic about this, consider betting on the next World Cup. We will look at gambles whose outcomes depend only on whether the winner of the next Cup comes from Europe (including Russia), from America (North or South), or from the rest of the world, so we take a three-element state space $S = \{s_1, s_2, s_3\}$ where s_1 is the state that a European team wins the next World Cup, s_2 is the state that an American team wins, and s_3 is the state that some other team wins.[7] We will take the prize space X to be $[0, 100]$, with numerical amounts representing dollars won. Imagine that we give a consumer her choice of the three gambles (from the Anscombe-Aumann version of H) depicted in Figure 5.8. Suppose she ranks the three as $h \succ h' \succ h''$. If her preferences conform to the Anscombe-Aumann axioms (and she prefers more money to less), we interpret this as: Our consumer assesses probability greater than .48 that an American team will win and probability less than .48 that a European team will win. By varying the probability in h' until we find the value that makes her indifferent between h and h' (as modified), we find her subjective probability that an American team will win. N.B., the subjective probability she assesses for s_2 is (only) a construct of the representation guaranteed by the Anscombe-Aumann axioms; it arises solely from her preferences for these lotteries. If a different consumer expresses the preferences $h'' \succ h' \succ h$, we conclude that the two consumers' preferences are represented by different assessments over the state space S; probability assessments (as an expression of preferences) are subjective.

[7] If I was being very careful, there would be a state of nature for ties, or for the case where no winner is named, and so on.

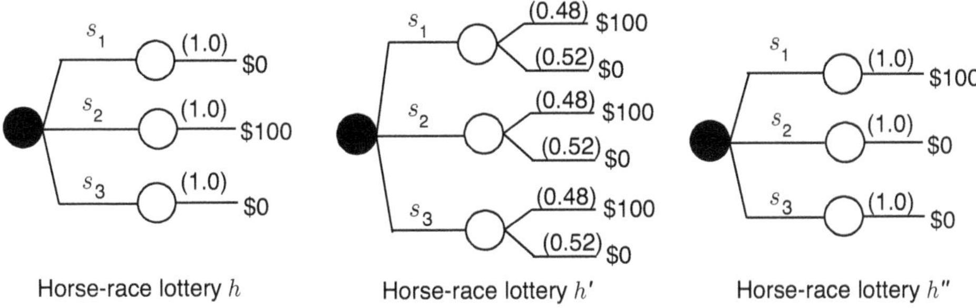

Figure 5.8. Three Anscombe-Aumann gambles. Within the Anscombe-Aumann framework, if a consumer prefers horse-race lottery h to h' and h' to h'', she is implicitly saying that she assesses probability greater than 0.48 for state s_2 and less than 0.48 for state s_1. Of course, this is implicit: She is only expressing preferences among horse-race lotteries; nowhere (in the theory) is she asked to assess a probability.

The probabilities in the roulette lottery parts of the gambles are meant, in this story, to be objective; i.e., reflecting the physical reality of well-balanced roulette wheels, symmetric dice, and so on (at least, to a reasonable degree of approximation). All consumers are meant to agree to these probabilities. Hence they can be used to calibrate subjective probabilities, just as we've done here.

The start-with-probability-distributions approach of Proposition 5.3 and Section 5.2 seemingly makes the most sense in a world of objective probabilities, because if probabilities are objective—reflecting physical reality and agreed upon by all consumers—it is clear where they come from. Hence that approach is labeled objective expected utility. Notwithstanding the label, this general approach can be (and often is) used with subjective probabilities, albeit bearing in mind that if there is no objective basis for the probabilities, they enter the model out of thin air.

Returning to the full subjective model, there is a final point to make. Economists (of a neoclassical stripe) rarely if ever insist that consumers have the same ordinal preferences over bundles of goods. Individual consumers are allowed to have individual preferences. In the same spirit, subjective probabilities—another part of the expression of personal preferences—should be allowed and even expected to vary across individuals. If this seems philsophically correct to you, and it certainly does to me, you are forewarned many eminent economists maintain as dogma (philosophy?) that two individuals *having access to the same information* will inevitably express the same subjective probability assessments. Any difference in subjective probability assessments must be the result of differences in information. Two consumers betting on the World Cup might order the gambles in Figure 5.8 differently, but only if they have been exposed to different pieces of information about the qualities of the various teams, etc. I leave it to others to defend this assumption—see, for example, Aumann (1987, section 5)—as I cannot do so. But you should be alerted to this modeling assumption, which has played an important role in parts of pieces of modern microeconomic theory; it is called both the *common prior assumption* and the *Harsanyi doctrine*.

5.5. Empirical and Theoretical Critiques

The models of expected utility maximization, with either subjective or objective probabilities, are the standard models of choice under uncertainty employed by economists. With the rise of behavioral economics and behavioral finance, it may no longer be appropriate to say that they are the overwhelming choice of economists who wish to model uncertain choices. But they are still chosen a very high percentage of the time, and certainly they still constitute the overwhelming percentage of models in the literature.

These models are used both normatively—as tools recommended for use by decision makers who themselves face a choice problem with uncertainty—and descriptively, meant to model how decision makers make real-life choices. I won't discuss the normative application of these models here; if you are curious to see a normative treatment, find a textbook on strategic decision making or decision analysis.[8] Instead, here we discuss the use of these models in descriptive economics.

In that context, the test is surely empirical: When we watch people making choices under uncertainty, in the field or in the lab, does their behavior conform to the models we have developed? Any number of studies have shown that the answer is, Not precisely. And, moreover, choice behavior has been observed that exhibits enough regularity so that one can contemplate better descriptive models than these.

A vast literature documents the empirical failings of these models, and I certainly will not try to catalog all the effects that have been observed. But I will point out three major themes or threads that appear.

In each of these threads, the evidence comes from the laboratory. Individuals are asked within the lab to make choices or statements of preference—"If you could choose between gamble A or B, which would you choose?"—or—"Do you prefer gamble A or gamble B?" They are asked to compare A with B and (later) A′ with B′, and we look at the data to see if these pairs of choices/preferences are internally consistent, according to the standard model. In some experiments, the choices are real; there is some chance the individual will actually get what she chooses/prefers. More often, though, the exercise is hypothetical.

Framing effects

Back in Chapter 1 (pages 22–3), we discussed the first of the three threads; the problem of framing. Individuals choose differently between the "same" pair of objects, depending on how those objects are framed (presented to them). We discussed in Chapter 1 the Kahnemann and Tversky (1979) example of vaccination programs, where the framing issue concerned whether outcomes were presented in terms of

[8] For an attempt to convince students of management that they should use expected utility, see Chapter 16 of Kreps (2004).

lives saved or people condemned to death. And we mentioned there tricks used by mail-order catalogs to convince you to buy their products.

Kahnemann and Tversky (1979) go on to develop further the example of the vaccination programs, in ways that are very significant for choices with uncertain outcomes. In the example of the vaccination programs, one way to think about what is happening is to think in terms of changes in the status quo: Is the status quo the position today, where no one has died, and so one vaccination program condemns some number of people to death; or is the status quo the no-vaccination program outcome of 600 deaths, in which case that program has the virtue of being sure to return some people to life?

Kahnemann and Tversky show evidence that, with monetary gambles, the status quo position, especially with regard to losses and gains, matters. They give their subjects choices such as

> Gamble A gives you \$400 for sure, while Gamble B provides \$600 with probability 2/3 and \$0 with probability 1/3

and they find a tendency to prefer the \$400 for sure. But then they reframe the choices:

> To begin, you will be given \$600 with which to gamble, which is yours to keep if you so choose. Then you can choose between Gamble A′, in which you lose \$200 for certain, and Gamble B′, in which you will lose nothing with probability 2/3 and \$600 with probability 1/3.

Framed this way, they find subjects who previously preferred Gamble A now preferring Gamble B′. In general, they present evidence that people are more inclined to gamble to avoid a loss than they are to record a large gain, calling this the "zero illusion."

The Allais Paradox and variations

The second theme traces from the work of Allais (1953) and concerns the model with objective probability. The classic so-called *Allais Paradox* asks an individual to choose between the two lotteries in Figure 5.9a and then between the two in Figure 5.9b.

A large fraction of the subjects express a preference for Gamble B in 5.9a and A′ in 5.9b, which is inconsistent with expected utility maximization for any utility function; letting U be the individual's utility function, a preference for Gamble B over A means that

$$
\begin{aligned}
0.33\,U(27500) + 0.66\,U(24000) + 0.01\,U(0) &< U(2400), \quad \text{and hence} \\
0.33\,U(27500) + 0.01\,U(0) &< 0.34\,U(24000), \quad \text{and hence} \\
0.33\,U(27500) + 0.67\,U(0) &< 0.34\,U(24000) + 0.66\,U(0),
\end{aligned}
$$

which implies a preference for B′ over A′. Kahnemann and Tversky (1979) go on to divide the Allais-type inconsistency (with the expected utility model) into two

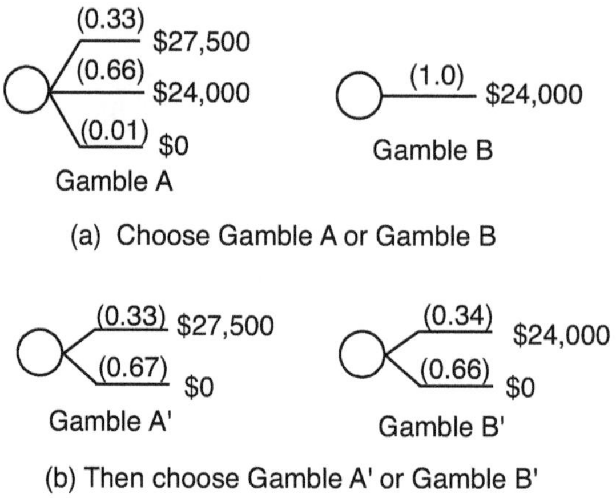

(0.33) $27,500
(0.66) $24,000
(0.01) $0
Gamble A

(1.0) $24,000
Gamble B

(a) Choose Gamble A or Gamble B

(0.33) $27,500
(0.67) $0
Gamble A'

(0.34) $24,000
(0.66) $0
Gamble B'

(b) Then choose Gamble A' or Gamble B'

Figure 5.9. The Allais Paradox. Many individuals prefer B to A and simultaneously say that they prefer A′ to B′. This is inconsistent with the expected utility model. (See text for further explanation.)

regular effects: individuals overvalue certainty; and they also overweight small-probability outcomes.

The Ellsberg Paradox

The third theme begins with the work of Ellsberg (1961) and draws a distinction between *uncertainty* and *risk*. These terms, used in this fashion, refer to a distinction that goes back in the literature to work by Keynes and Ramsey; *risk* is used when the gamble in question has "known odds," while *uncertainty* refers to situations where the odds are "unknown." I will not attempt to be precise about the meanings of known and unknown odds, but the spirit of the thing is that odds are known if they are determined by a fair coin or a balanced roulette wheel, or if they come from some random event that has been repeated enough so that the decision maker is confident she knows the chances of the various outcomes. The odds are unknown, basically, if they are not known; that is, if neither of these conditions hold. So, for instance, suppose I tell you I have a bent coin, and I ask you (without letting you examine the coin or experiment with it) to bet on whether the coin will land heads or tails. Since you don't know the odds of heads, you face uncertainty. If the coin is known a priori to be fair, or if you have been allowed to flip it, say, one million times, and it has come up heads 621,231 of those million, so the odds of heads are likely to be very close to 0.621231, then the odds are (approximately) known.[9]

In most interesting economic contexts of choice under uncertainty, where physical symmetry of the outcomes of random events is meaningless and where past

[9] Because the odds are "approximately" known in the second case, you can see that my "definitions" are woefully inadequate; it ought to be that from known to unknown—from risk to uncertainty—is a continuum, not a discrete distinction. By employing DeFinneti's Theorem, one can construct such a continuum; for an introduction to the DeFinneti's Theorem in roughly this context, see Kreps (1988, Chapter 11), although this introduces DeFinetti's Theorem; it does not construct the continuum or discuss the distinction between risk and uncertainty.

data are at best only a partial guide to the future, the decision maker faces at least some level of uncertainty. So, choice under uncertainty should be of greater concern to economists than is choice under conditions of risk.

The models of Savage and of Anscombe and Aumann (developed here) have the decision maker choosing according to expected utility, employing subjectively determined probabilities where there is uncertainty. Once probabilities are (subjectively) assigned to uncertain outcomes and events, no distinction is made between uncertainty and risk.

Ellsberg tested this as a descriptive model by posing the following hypothetical decision problem. He described to his subjects an urn containing 300 colored balls: 100 red, and 200 some (unknown) combination of blue and green. One ball is to be drawn at random from the urn. Then he asked:

> Would you prefer: (A) a bet in which you win \$100 if the ball drawn is red (and \$0 otherwise); or (B) a bet in which you win \$100 if the ball drawn is blue (and \$0 otherwise)?

And he asked:

> Would you prefer: (A′) a bet in which you win \$100 if the ball drawn is red or green (and \$0 if it is blue); or (B′) a bet in which you win \$100 if the ball drawn is blue or green (and \$0 if it is red)?

He asked this of fairly sophisticated decision makers, his colleagues at the RAND Institute. And he found that a sizeable fraction preferred A to B and B′ to A′.

The explanation of this pair of preferences is easy, given the distinction between risk and uncertainty. The probability of winning \$100 in A is 1/3; you know 100 balls out of 300 are red, so it stands to reason that the probability of a red ball being drawn is 1/3. But you don't know the number of balls that are blue—you only know that it is between 0 and 200—so the odds of winning \$100 in B are unknown. And in B′, you know that 200 balls are either blue or green, so the odds of \$100 are 2/3; this is a situation of risk. While in A′, you don't know how many balls are red or green—it could be as few as 100 or as many as all 300—so this is a gamble with uncertainty. If you are averse to uncertainty per se—that is, every thing else being equal (whatever that means), you prefer risk to uncertainty, you will prefer A to B and B′ to A′.

But, of course, this is inconsistent with the Savage and Anscombe-Aumann models of choice. It is perhaps easiest to see this by noting that the pair of preferences A better than B and B′ better than A′ is a direct violation of Savage's Sure-Thing Principle, Axiom 5.1 (page 82): Gambles A and B give the same outcome \$0 if the ball is green, and if we change that same outcome if green to \$100, we get A′ and B′, respectively.

So what?

Individuals deviate from the models of expected utility maximization that are developed in this chapter in systematic fashion, making those models less than ideal for descriptive purposes. Some apologists for the models argue that the deviations that are observed are not of economic significance (but try telling that to, for instance, the designers of mail-order catalogs, who employ framing effects in the their designs); others will argue that preferences expressed in a lab setting are not taken seriously by the subjects, and when it comes to serious economic decisions, conformity to the standard models is better.

But the evidence is strong and the effects are confirmed experimentally time after time, so it seems witless to pretend that the evidence isn't there. Two tasks are obvious:

1. Better models—better in the sense that the behavior modeled is closer to what we see empirically—should be developed. There are, in fact, large (perhaps not quite vast) literatures that address in various ways Allais-type and Ellsberg-type choice behavior. But, at least to my knowledge, none of the variations offered by these literatures has been accepted broadly as *the* right alternative.[10]

2. In specific applied settings, the economic implications of systematic deviations from the standard models should be explored. This has been the subject of recent work in the realms of behavioral economics and behavioral finance.

While awaiting further progress in these two directions, the models of (subjective and objective) expected utility maximization remain the standard (descriptive) models of choice under uncertainty. So we turn next chapter to a few of the standard applications.

Theoretical issues with the models

But before doing so, we must observe that objections on theoretical grounds can be made to the models of expected utility maximization, at least as applied by economists in some contexts. The two objections we raise here both arise from the same root cause, the application of the model to a "small world of choice" that is properly part of a broader choice context.

Imagine a consumer choosing whether to invest in, say, debt issued by a major corporation that is not doing well. Debt (in the form of corporate bonds) is meant, ideally, to be riskless, at least in terms of nominal (non-inflation-adjusted) payoffs. But in today's financial markets, that ideal is rarely met, and anyone contemplating an investment in debt instruments would take into account the odds of default, and so forth. Do we, therefore, model the decision process (whether to invest in this debt and, if so, how much debt to take on) by describing the probability distribution (subjectively determined, say) for the payoffs and then by comparing expected utility of the consumer with and without the debt? Students of finance will see immediately that the world of investments is more complex than this; one needs to think of the investor's full portfolio of financial investments. This debt

[10] A reviewer of the book suggests that reference-dependent, loss-averse preferences, as developed by Koszegi and Rabin (2006), has achieved the status of being at least *a* right alternative. I'm unsure I would go quite that far, but this model of preferences does have considerable power to explain a host of empirical "anomalies."

is worth less to the investor, in most cases, if it has positive correlation with other investments held by the investor, and it is worth more if the correlation is negative.

The moral is simple: When evaluating an investment, we know (at least, you know, once you've had an introductory course in finance) that one has to look at the investor's full portfolio; looking at a single investment in isolation is nonsensical, if one is thinking of employing the models of this chapter.

But this obvious principle is not so well honored in the literature if one expands the setting slightly. A cornerstone of financial theory, the Capital Asset Pricing Model (CAPM), divorces the investor's decision how to invest from the investor's human and real capital. As an employee of Stanford University, with a fair amount of my wealth tied up in a house that sits not too many miles from the San Andreas Fault, my investments in financial assets issued by California corporations and, especially, by firms in Silicon Valley should probably be somewhat tempered, at least relative to the investments of a colleague of mine from, say, Princeton University. A high-level executive in the Ford Motor Company should, perhaps, hold less financial wealth in assets that have positive correlation with the fortunes of the automobile industry than should a similarly placed executive in the financial sector. Yet when you go to the textbooks and papers that develop the CAPM, you won't always find due care taken of such considerations.

A second theoretical issue concerns so-called temporal resolution of uncertainty. Imagine that I will flip a fair coin and, if it is heads, give you a check for $100,000. If it is tails, you get nothing. As a graduate student (I'll assume), this is a nice thing, but to complicate it a bit, let me suppose that you will get the check, if the coin comes up heads, exactly twelve months from today. And, to add one further level of complication, consider the following three variations on this theme:

A. I will flip the coin today, and tell you the result of the flip today.

B. I will flip the coin in twelve months, so you only learn the outcome then.

C. I will flip the coin today, in the presence of some reliable witnesses. But I will only tell you the outcome in twelve months' time.

To give this a decision focus, suppose I offer you your choice of the gamble as described, or a sure-thing $20,000, also to be given to you in twelve months.

How you feel about the gamble versus the sure thing depends on a lot of subjective circumstances. But, if you are like most folks, you strictly prefer variation A to variations B and C, and you probably are indifferent between B and C. Indeed, for some folks, the gamble under variation A is preferred to $20,000 for sure, but $20,000 for sure is preferred to either variation where you don't learn the outcome for twelve months. This is so because the information will guide decisions you make over the next twelve months, such as how much to consume, whether to get your car repaired, whether to take a vacation in Hawaii in the interim, and so forth.

If we used the expected utility model applied to your utility for consumption streams (therefore employing some of the ideas we'll discuss in Chapter 7, when we get to dynamic choice), the differences between B and C on the one hand and A on the other would be obvious within the model. But if, in trying to decide whether you want to take the $20,000 for sure or the lottery without incorporating into our analysis all those intervening consumption decisions, we'd be unable to distinguish (within the model) between A on the one hand and B and C on the other. All three are 50-50 gambles with prizes $100,000 or $0, so in the (narrow scope) application of the models of this chapter, the three are the "same."

Moreover (and this is a good deal harder to see), even if we fix the resolution of uncertainty at some fixed date—we compare various lotteries among which you might choose, with the understanding that the uncertainty involved will resolve only in, say, twelve months' time, when payment is made—you might not satisfy the "substitution axioms" that are key to this chapter.[11]

In both these circumstances, no theoretical problem arises in the application of the models of this chapter *if* your model of the consumer's decision process is broad enough to encompass all the relevant factors. But in many applications of the models of this chapter, the economist doing the model chooses to economize on the scope of his or her model and, in so doing, raises good theoretical objections to the use of the model altogether.

Bibliographic Notes

The subject of choice under uncertainty is well covered in detail in a number of textbooks. I recommend Fishburn (1970) and Kreps (1988). For getting all the details of the standard model, Fishburn is highly recommended. Kreps omits some of the details of proofs, but is perhaps more immediately accessible than Fishburn. If you like to consult original sources, see von Neumann and Morgenstern (1944), Herstein and Milnor (1953), Savage (1954), and Anscombe and Aumann (1963).

On the topic of empirical objections to the models, the three classic references are (chronologically) Allais (1953), Ellsberg (1961), and Kahnemann and Tversky (1979). A good survey of alternatives that deal with the so-called Allais Paradox is Machina (1987); Wakker (2008) provides a survey of alternatives that deal with the Ellsberg Paradox.

Problems

■ *5.1. (a) Suppose a consumer who satisfies assumptions a, b, and c of Proposition 5.3 is choosing among the following gambles: (1) $10,000 with probability 1. (2) $3600 with probability 1/3 and $14,400 with probability 2/3. (3) $0 with probability 1/5, and $10,000 with probability 1/5, and $22,500 with probability 3/5. The consumer has utility function $U(x) = \sqrt{x}$. How does this consumer rank-order these three gambles?

---

[11] Why? Roughly, imagine that you are indifferent between lottery A and lottery B under these circumstances, but facing lottery A, you take a different immediate consumption decision than you do facing lottery B. Then you prefer A and B to a convex combination of them, since in the convex combination, you have to hedge your bets in terms of immediate consumption.

(b) Suppose a consumer whose preferences are represented as in equation (5.1) is choosing among the three acts or gambles shown in Figure 5.10. Her three state-dependent utility functions are $u_{s_1}((x_1, x_2)) = \sqrt{x_1 x_2}$, $u_{s_2}((x_1, x_2)) = 0.6 \min\{x_1, x_2\}$, and $u_{s_3}((x_1, x_2)) = 0.4\,(x_1 + x_2)$. How does this consumer rank order these three acts?

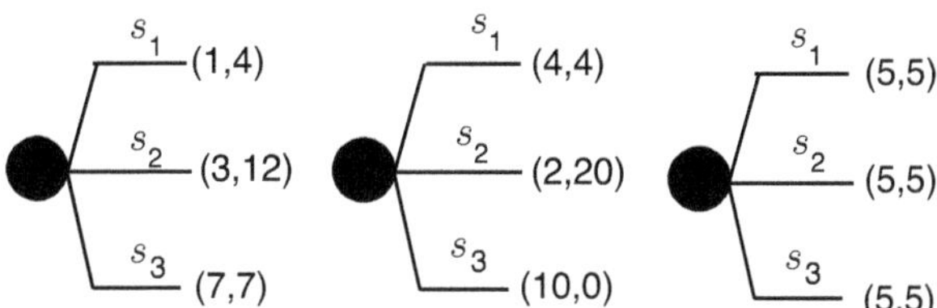

Figure 5.10. Problem 1b and c: Three acts

(c) Suppose a consumer whose preferences are represented as in Equation (5.2) is choosing among the three acts shown in Figure 5.10. Her subjective probability assessment is $p(s_1) = 0.5$, $p(s_2) = 0.3$, and $p(s_3) = 0.2$, and her utility function is $U((x_1, x_2)) = (x_1 x_2)^{0.25}$. How does this consumer rank order these three acts?

(d) Suppose a consumer who satisfies the assumptions of Proposition 5.12 must choose between the two acts (or, in this context, horse-race lotteries) in Figure 5.11. Her three state-dependent utility functions are $u_{s_1}((x_1, x_2)) = \sqrt{x_1 x_2}$, $u_{s_2}((x_1, x_2)) = 0.6 \min\{x_1, x_2\}$, and $u_{s_2}((x_1, x_2)) = 0.4\,(x_1 + x_2)$. Which horse-race lottery would this consumer choose?

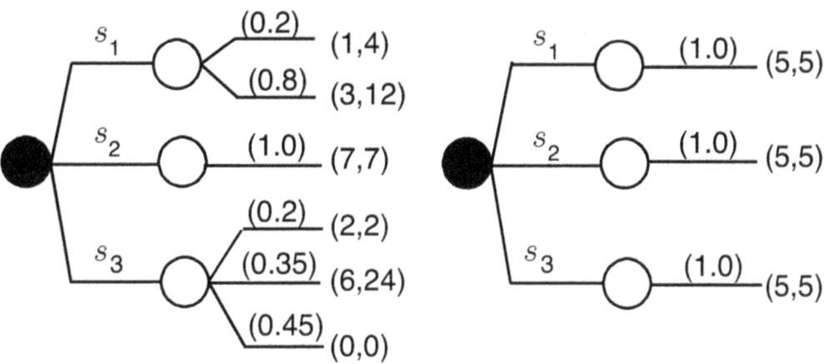

Figure 5.11. Problem 1d and e: Two horse-race lotteries

(e) Suppose a consumer who satisfies the assumptions of Proposition 5.13 must choose between the two horse-race lotteries in Figure 5.11. This consumer assesses $\mathbf{p}(s_1) = .5$, $\mathbf{p}(s_2) = .3$, and $\mathbf{p}(s_3) = .2$, and her utility function is $u((x_1, x_2)) = (x_1 x_2)^{0.25}$. Which horse-race lottery would this consumer choose?

■ 5.2. One will sometimes find mention of "state dependent subjective expected utility," meaning (in the context of preferences $\succeq$ on $A = X^S$) a representation of the form

$$u(a) = \sum_{s \in S} p(s) u_s(a(s)),$$

where p is a probability distribution on S and, for each s, $u_s : X \to R$. Is this representation stronger, weaker, or equivalent to the additive-across-states representation given in Equation (5.1)?

■ *5.3. The purpose of this problem is to explore the proof of Proposition 5.4 where we don't add the extra assumption about the existence of best and worst elements $\overline{z}$ and $\underline{z}$. Prove the Mixture-Space Theorem without this assumption. Of course, you are free to enlist Lemmas 5.5 through 5.9, none of which use this extra assumption.

This is a hard problem, so let me give you some assistance: If every element of Z is indifferent to every other element of Z, then u equal to any constant will do. So we can assume that there exist a pair $\overline{z}$ and $\underline{z}$ in Z such that $\overline{z} \succ \underline{z}$, although it is no longer true that $\overline{z} \succeq z \succeq \underline{z}$ for all $z \in Z$. Now *calibrate* each $z \in Z$ on a scale where $u(\overline{z}) = 1$ and $u(\underline{z}) = 0$; to see what this means, go back to page 95: If $\overline{z} \succeq z \succeq \underline{z}$, find the unique a such that $a\overline{z} + (1-a)\underline{z} \sim z$, and set $u(z) = a$. If $z \succ \overline{z}$, find the unique a such that $az + (1-a)\underline{z} \sim \overline{z}$, and set $u(z) = 1/a$. And if $\underline{z} \succ z$ ... well, case 3 on page 95 tells you what to do.

Now that we have u, we have to show that u represents $\succeq$ and is linear in convex combinations. You can try a brute force approach to this (and it will work), but be warned that there are a lot of cases to consider. Or you can be more clever: Take any pair z and z' from Z. Let z_1 be the $\succeq$-best out of z, z', and $\overline{z}$. Let z_2 be the worst out of z, z', and $\underline{z}$. Prove that $z_1 \succ z_2$ and that $z_1 \succeq \hat{z} \succeq z_2$ for $\hat{z}$ any one of z, z', $\overline{z}$, $\underline{z}$, and any convex combination of any of those four. Let $Z' = \{\hat{z} \in Z : z_1 \succeq \hat{z} \succeq z_2\}$. Is Z' a mixture space? (Yes, but you have to prove this.) If the three mixture-space axioms (a, b, and c from Proposition 5.3) apply to Z, do they apply to Z'? (Yes, but you have to say why.) Apply the argument in the proof in the text to Z' (it satisfies the extra assumption, of course), to produce a representing and linear-in-convex-combinations $v : Z' \to R$. Now rescale v so that the rescaled function, call it v', satisfies $v'(\overline{z}) = 1$ and $v'(\underline{z}) = 0$. How does v' compare with u on Z'?

■ 5.4. With regard to the "run the horses second" discussion beginning on the bottom of page 105, suppose that we let $A = X^S$ for some finite set S, we let Π be the set of simple probability distributions on A, and we assume that $\succeq$ on Π satisfies the (mixture-space) assumptions a, b, and c of Proposition 5.3. That is, we run the horses after conducting the roulette lottery. What result (in the spirit of the results in this chapter) do we get?

■ 5.5. To help you to understand what I call the trick in Anscombe-Aumann, investigate the following alternative setting. Let X be an arbitrary finite set of objects, and let Z be the set of all subsets of X. Assume a decision maker has complete and transitive preferences $\succeq$ over elements of Z. Since Z is finite, we've already made enough assumptions to ensure that $\succeq$ has a numerical representation $u : Z \to R$, but I'd like more.

To get more, and in the general spirit of Anscombe and Aumann, we can expand the domain for $\succeq$. One possibility is to look at the space of probability distributions on Z. Call this space P, and assume that $\succeq$ is defined on all of P and satisfies the three mixture-space axioms. (In this context, Z is a "subset" of P in the sense that, within P, there are probability distributions that have a one-element support.) What results? Does this help us to pin down the structure of u?

A second possibility is to define the space $Q := [0,1]^X$, where the interpretation of a $q \in Q$ is that, if the decision maker chooses q, then $q(x)$ is the probability that the decision maker gets x in the subset of objects out of X that she receives. (In this context, each element $z \in Z$ can be identified with that element $q \in Q$ that gives probability 1 to elements $x \in z$ and probability 0 to $x \notin z$.) The space Q is a mixture space, where $aq + (1-a)q'$ is defined by $(aq + (1-a)q')(x) = aq(x) + (1-a)q'(x)$. Suppose $\succeq$ is extented to all of Q and satisfies the three mixture-space axioms. What results? Does this help us to pin down the structure of u? (Hint: Yes, it does. You should be able to show that there exists a function $U : X \to R$ such that $u(z) = \sum_{x \in z} U(x)$.)

Why does the application of the Mixture-Space Theorem in the second possible approach give such a stronger result than its application in the first possible approach? How does this relate to the discussion of the trick in Anscombe-Aumann that is given in the book?

■ *5.6. The Anscombe and Aumann derivation of subjective expected utility relies on the set of states of nature S being finite. How would we extend it to infinite state spaces? This problem takes you (step by step) through one extension that, essentially, adapts the original proof. There is a lot of setup and notation involved, so if you tackle this, please be patient.

First, we provide a setup. Begin with an arbitrary state space S and an arbitrary prize space X. As in the text, let Π be the space of simple probability distributions on X. The setup also involves an *algebra* of subsets of S, denoted $\mathcal{A}$; an algebra of subsets is a set of subsets such that (1) $S \in \mathcal{A}$, (2) if $A \in \mathcal{A}$, then the complement of A, denoted A^C, is also $\in \mathcal{A}$, and (3) if $A, B \in \mathcal{A}$, then $A \cap B \in \mathcal{A}$. (If you've never worked with this concept before, you might want to prove: If $\mathcal{A}$ has properties (1) through (3), then $\mathcal{A}$ is also closed under unions.)

For finite S, we defined $H = \Pi^S$, the space of all functions from S into Π. Now, with an arbitrary set S, we "reduce" H somewhat: If $h \in H$, then there exists a finite partition $A_1, \ldots, A_n$ of S, with each $A_i \in \mathcal{A}$, such that h is constant over each A_i. That is, there is an equal-length list of objective-probability lotteries $\pi_1, \ldots, \pi_n$, such that $h(s) = \pi_i$ if $s \in A_i$.

Because of this, we can describe any $h \in H$ as

$$h = [\pi_1 \text{ on } A_1, \ldots, \pi_i \text{ on } A_i, \ldots, \pi_n \text{ on } A_n],$$

as long as $\{A_1, \ldots, A_n\}$ is a partition of S with each $A_i \in \mathcal{A}$.

H, so defined, is a mixture space: Suppose h is as described in the display just above, and

$$h' = [\pi'_1 \text{ on } A'_1, \ldots, \pi'_j \text{ on } A'_j, \ldots, \pi'_m \text{ on } A'_m].$$

For $a \in [0,1]$, we define

$$ah + (1-a)h' := [\ldots, a\pi_i + (1-a)\pi'_i \text{ on } A_i \cap A'_j, \ldots]_{i=1,\ldots,n;\, j=1,\ldots,m}.$$

That is, $a\pi + (1-a)\pi'$ is defined on the partition that is the meet or coarsest common refinement of the two partitions, which is formed by intersecting cells of the two partitions, and that, on the cell $A_i \cap A'_j$, is the obvious mixture of π_i and π'_j.

a. *Since H is a mixture space, what does the Mixture-Space Theorem say about a preference relation $\succeq$ defined on H, which satisfies the three mixture-space axioms?*

For $\pi \in \Pi$, when I write, for instance, $\pi \succeq h$ for some preference relation $\succeq$ on H, I am identifying π with that element of H that is π for all S or, in other symbols, $[\pi \text{ on } S]$. And for $x \in X$, if I write x where the context wants an element of Π, I will mean the objective-probability lottery that gives x with certainty; if I write x where the context wants an element of H, I mean $[x \text{ with probability 1 on } S]$.

Fix some element of X, which we'll denote by $\underline{x}$. In part a, you (presumably) said that if the three mixture-space axioms hold for $\succeq$, then $\succeq$ is represented by some function $F : H \to R$ that has certain useful properties. (I don't want to give away the whole answer to part a!) You also (presumably) said that such functions F can be rescaled by adding or subtracting any constant and by multiplying by a positive constant. (Right?) For the remainder of this problem, I want you to assume that $\succeq$ on H satisfies the three mixture-space axioms, and then fix such an F that is normalized so that $F(\underline{x}) = 0$.

Let A be any subset of S (from $\mathcal{A}$), and let H_A be functions from A into Π that take on at most finitely many values, on sets from $\mathcal{A}$. That is, $h_A \in H_A$ has the form: there is a partition $A_1, \ldots, A_m$ of A (all from $\mathcal{A}$) and $\pi_1, \ldots, \pi_m$, all from Π, such that $h_A(s) = \pi_j$ for $s \in A_j$. In this setting, define $F_A : H_A \to R$ by

$$F_A(h_A) := F([\pi_1 \text{ on } A_1, \ldots, \pi_m \text{ on } A_m, \underline{x} \text{ on } A^C])$$

Next, suppose that $A_1, \ldots, A_n$ is a finite partition of S, and suppose that $A_{i1}, A_{i2}, \ldots, A_{im}$ is a further finite partition of each A_i (all of this involving sets from the algebra $\mathcal{A}$).

(I really ought to write m_i, so that the further partition of A_i can have a different number of cells than the further partition of $A_{i'}$. But, at least formally, by putting in copies of the empty set into these further partitions, my notation is without loss of generality.) Let $\{\pi_{ij}; i = 1, \ldots, n,\ j = 1, \ldots, m\}$ be a list of elements of Π.

b. Prove that

$$F([\ldots, \pi_{ij} \text{ on } A_{ij}, \ldots]) = \sum_{i=1}^{n} F_{A_i}([\ldots, \pi_{ij} \text{ on } A_{ij}, \ldots]),$$

where in the sum on the right-hand side, for each i, you are looking at the element of H_{A_i} that assigns π_{ij} to sub-cell A_{ij}.

(Part b is the key step, and it comes right out of the proof of the basic Anscombe-Aumann result, where the normalization $F(\underline{x}) = 0$ makes everything a snap.)

c. Refer to Savage's Sure-Thing Principle, Axiom 5.1 in the text. Prove that (if $\succeq$ satisfies the three mixture-space axioms), then it satisfies Axiom 5.1 adapted to this context. (Part of this question is figuring out what I mean by "adapted to this context.")

d. For $A \in \mathcal{A}$ and $x \in X$, define $U_A(x) := F([x \text{ on } A, \underline{x} \text{ on } A^C])$. Prove that the function

$$U([\pi_1 \text{ on } A_1, \ldots, \pi_n \text{ on } A_n]) := \sum_{i=1}^{n} \sum_{x \in \text{supp}(\pi_i)} U_{A_i}(x)\, \pi_i(x)$$

provides a representation of $\succeq$ on H.

For the remainder of this problem, we assume that there exists some $\overline{x} \in X$ such that $\overline{x} \succ \underline{x}$. Given this $\overline{x}$, we fix the representing function F with which we've been working so that, in addition to $F(\underline{x}) = 0$, we have $F(\overline{x}) = 1$.

By virtue of part c above, it makes sense, for any set $A \in \mathcal{A}$, to speak of a preference relation $\succeq_A$, defined on Π, defined by

$$\pi \succeq_A \pi' \quad \text{if} \quad [\pi \text{ on } A, \text{anything at all on } A^c] \succeq$$
$$[\pi' \text{ on } A, \text{the same anything on } A^c].$$

That is, in part c, you showed that what was assigned on A^C was irrelevant, as long as it was the same anything. It should also be clear (if not, make it so) that $\succeq_A$ on Π satisfies the three mixture-space axioms.

Assume henceforth that, not only is $\overline{x} \succ \underline{x}$, but also $\overline{x} \succeq_A \underline{x}$ for all $A \in \mathcal{A}$. We do not preclude the possibility that $\overline{x} \sim_A \underline{x}$, in which case we say that A is *null*.

A finitely additive probability on $(S, \mathcal{A})$ is a function $\mathbf{p} : \mathcal{A} \to [0, 1]$ such that $\mathbf{p}(S) = 1$ and, if A and B are disjoint subsets from $\mathcal{A}$, then $\mathbf{p}(A \cup B) = \mathbf{p}(A) + \mathbf{p}(B)$.

e. Define

$$\mathbf{p}(A) := F([\overline{x} \text{ on } A, \underline{x} \text{ on } A^C]).$$

Prove that $\mathbf{p} : \mathcal{A} \to R$ *is a finitely additive probability on* $(S, \mathcal{A})$ *and that* $\mathbf{p}(A) = 0$ *if and only if* A *is null. (What happens to this result if we do not assume that* $\overline{x} \succeq_A \underline{x}$ *for all* A*?)*

f. We add one final assumption: If A *is null, then* $x \sim_A \underline{x}$ *for all* x*, and if* A *is not null, then* $\succeq_A$ *(viewed as a preference relation on* Π*) is the same as* $\succeq$ *(also viewed as a preference relation on* Π*). Prove that if this is true (and all our earlier assumptions are true), then there exists a single utility function* $U : X \to R$ *such that*

$$U([\pi_1 \text{ on } A_1, \ldots, \pi_n \text{ on } A_n]) := \sum_{i=1}^{n} \mathbf{p}(A_i) \sum_{x \in \mathrm{supp}(\pi_i)} U(x)\, \pi_i(x)$$

represents $\succeq$ *on* H*.*

This finishes the "more-or-less-staight-out-of-Anscombe-Aumann" extension to general state spaces S. We get subjective expected utility, where subjective probability is finitely additive, and the utility representation is for h that are "doubly simple": h is piecewise constant on a finite partition of S and, on each cell of the partition, π is simple (has finitely many prizes). We discussed in the text (near the top of page 109) how one might move to expected utility for nonsimple π (albeit without a state space) and the difficulties that are encountered because St. Petersburg paradoxes can arise if U is unbounded. In the same spirit, one can use continuity of preferences to extend $\mathbf{p}$ to a countably-additive probability on $(S, \mathcal{A})$ (assuming $\mathcal{A}$ is a sigma-algebra) and expected utility to more complex $h : S \to \Pi$. If you have sufficient mathematical sophistication to know about countable additivity, sigma-algebras, and the definition of integrals through limits, you should be able to do this. I invite you to do so, although the answer I give in the *Student's Guide* stops with part f.

*5.7. Prove Proposition 5.10. (You will need to know about the topology of weak convergence to do this, of course. The solution given in the *Student's Guide* provides some further information about this topology, if this is somewhat new to you.)

Chapter Six

Utility for Money

In many applications of the models of Chapter 5, the lottery prizes $x \in X$ are assumed to be amounts of money. In this chapter, we explore a number of developments specific to this context.

Throughout, the space of prizes X is an interval of the real line, and Π is the set of simple probability distributions on X. A consumer's preferences over Π are given by $\succeq$, which, we assume, satisfy the three mixture-space axioms (a, b, and c of Proposition 5.3), so that they are represented by expected utility for a utility function $U : X \to R$. Prizes are referred to as money, as income, or as wealth, depending on the context.

6.1. Properties of Utility Functions for Money

We first ask, If the prizes are monetary, what are reasonable (further) properties for $\succeq$ and what are the consequences of those properties for U?

More money is better

It seems entirely reasonable to assume that our consumer prefers more money to less. This has a straightforward consequence for the representation, which you should have no difficulty proving.

Proposition 6.1. *The utility function U is strictly increasing if and only if, for all x and y in X such that $x > y$, $\delta_x \succ \delta_y$.*[1]

Continuity

Continuity of the utility function U is useful for many purposes and is ensured by a fairly intuitive property.

Proposition 6.2. *The utility function U is continuous if and only if: For every prize x and gamble π such that $\pi \not\sim \delta_x$, there exists $\epsilon > 0$ such that either $\pi \succ \delta_{x'}$ for all x' within ϵ of x, or $\delta_{x'} \succ \pi$ for all such x'.*

In words, unless $\delta_x \sim \pi$, we can make small changes in the "for-certain" prize and not affect how the two compare. Very roughly, continuity of U is ensured if preferences are continuous when we make small changes in the prizes.

Proof. Suppose U is continuous and $\pi \succ \delta_x$. Then $u(\pi) = \sum_y U(y)\pi(y) > U(x)$. Let $\gamma = u(\pi) - U(x)$. By continuity of U, there is some ϵ such that for all x' within ϵ of

[1] Recall that for $x \in X$, δ_x denotes the lottery that gives prize x with probability 1.

x, $U(x') - U(x) < \gamma$, which implies $u(\pi) > U(x')$, or $\pi \succ \delta'_x$. A similar argument works for the case $\delta_x \succ \pi$.

Conversely, suppose that U is not continuous at a point x. Then there is some sequence $\{x_n\}$ with limit x such that $\lim_n U(x_n)$ exists (allowing limits ∞ or $-\infty$) and either $\lim_n U(x_n) > U(x)$ or $\lim_n U(x_n) < U(x)$. Write L for $\lim_n U(x_n)$, and suppose $L > U(x)$. If $L = \infty$, then $\delta_{x_n} \succ \delta_{x_N} \succ \delta_x$ for all large n and some fixed N, and we get a violation of the property in the proposition. If $L \neq \infty$, let $L - U(x) = \gamma$, and let x_N be such that $|L - U(x_N)| < \gamma/2$. Then the gamble π with prizes x_N and x, each with probability one-half, has expected utility no smaller than $L/2+U(x)/2-\gamma/4 = U(x)+\gamma/4$ and no larger than $L/2+U(x)/2+\gamma/4 = L-\gamma/4$. Thus $\pi \succ \delta_x$, but for all sufficiently large n, $\delta_{x_n} \succ \pi$, contradicting the property in the proposition. A similar argument works for the case $L < U(x)$. Therefore, if U is not continuous, the property fails. The contrapositive is, If the property holds, U must be continuous. ■

A few remarks about continuity of U are in order for the mathematically more sophisticated. We can talk about continuity in this setting in at least two ways; namely, continuity in probabilities and continuity in prizes. Continuity in probabilities means: If $\{\pi_n\}$ is sequence of simple lotteries, each having support contained in some finite set X', and if $\lim_n \pi_n(x)$ exists and equals $\pi(x)$ for each $x \in X'$, then $\pi \succ \rho$ implies $\pi_n \succ \rho$ for all large-enough n, and similarly for $\rho \succ \pi$. Note that in this form of continuity the probabilities of the prizes are changing with n, but the supports of the probability distributions (essentially) do not change.[2] Continuity of preferences in probabilities is guaranteed by the three assumptions of Proposition 5.3; note that the expected utility function $u(\pi) = \sum_{x \in \text{supp}(\pi)} U(x)\pi(x)$ is continuous in probabilities no matter how well- or ill-behaved is U.

Continuity of preferences in the prizes asks for a lot more. Now a "small change" in a lottery π can involve small shifts in the probabilities of the prizes, as before, but also small shifts in the prizes themselves. Of course, this means that we have to know what it means for there to be a small change in prizes; the prize space X must come with a notion of nearness, which is manifestly the case when X is an interval of the real line. A lottery with prizes 4 and 6 having probabilities 0.3 and 0.7 is "close" to a lottery with prizes 3.9 and 6.05 having probabilities 0.29 and 0.71. I won't try to give a formal definition of this sort of continuity, but you should (at least) see that continuity is a much stronger assumption if small changes in both probabilities and prizes are to be allowed.[3]

---

[2] We say *essentially* because this does allow for some change in the supports. Specifically, if $x \in \text{supp}(\pi)$, then x must be in the support of π_n for all large n. But there can be $x \in \text{supp}(\pi_n)$ and even in the supports of the π_n for infinitely many n that are not in the support of π, as long as (1) there are only finitely many such x and (2) $\lim_n \pi_n(x) = 0$ for every such n. Indeed, we can allow there to be infinitely many such x, *if* we know that there is a uniform bound on their utilities. See footnote 3 for more on this.

[3] I have in mind, roughly, continuity in the topology of weak convergence. But this is only roughly correct, because I am not assuming that U is bounded. For readers who know about the weak topology: Suppose U is unbounded, say, above. Let x_n be such that $U(x_n) > n$, and let π^n be the (two-outcome)

Risk aversion

The next property is *risk aversion*. First we need a piece of notation. For $\pi \in \Pi$, let $E\pi$ represent the expected value of π, or $E\pi = \sum_x x\pi(x)$.[4]

Proposition 6.3. *The utility function U is concave if and only if, for all lotteries π, $\delta_{E\pi} \succeq \pi$.*

A consumer who prefers, for every π, the expected value of π for sure (that is, $\delta_{E\pi}$) instead of π, and whose utility function is therefore concave, is said to be *risk averse*. We could also define a *risk-seeking* consumer as one for whom $\pi \succeq \delta_{E\pi}$ for all π; this sort of behavior goes with a convex utility function u. And a consumer is *risk neutral* if $\pi \sim \delta_{E\pi}$, which goes with an affine utility function. In economic theory, risk aversion, which includes risk neutrality as a special case, is typically assumed.

Proof of Proposition 6.3. Suppose U is not a concave function. Then for some $x, x' \in R$ and $a \in [0, 1]$, $U(ax + (1 - a)x') < aU(x) + (1 - a)U(x')$. Let π be the lottery that has prizes x and x' with probabilities a and $1 - a$; then $E\pi = ax + (1 - a)x'$. The expected utility of $\delta_{E\pi}$ is $U(ax + (1 - a)x') < aU(x) + (1 - a)U(x')$, which is the expected utility of π. Hence $\pi \succ \delta_{E\pi}$.

Conversely, suppose that U is a concave function. It is a relatively simple matter of induction to prove that if $x_1, \ldots, x_n$ is a list of real numbers, and $a_1, \ldots, a_n$ is a list of numbers between 0 and 1 such that $\sum_{i=1}^n a_n = 1$, then $U(\sum_{i=1}^n a_i x_i) \geq \sum_{i=1}^n a_i U(x_i)$. (This result is the discrete form of Jensen's inequality.) Applying this to any simple lottery π tells us that, if U is concave,

$$U\Big(\sum_{x \in \text{supp}(\pi)} \pi(x)x\Big) \geq \sum_{x \in \text{supp}(\pi)} \pi(x)U(x).$$

The left-hand side is the utility of the lottery $\delta_{E\pi}$, while the right-hand side is the expected utility of π; hence $\delta_{E\pi} \succeq \pi$. ∎

Figure 6.1 indicates what is going on. (Ignore the mention of certainty equivalents for now.) A concave utility function U is depicted, together with a line segment joining the two points $(x, U(x))$ and $(x', U(x'))$. Take any $a \in (0, 1)$, say $a = .6$, and consider the lottery $0.6\,\delta_x + 0.4\,\delta_{x'}$; that is, an 0.6 chance at x and a 0.4

lottery that gives (arbitrary) prize x_0 with probability $(n - 1)/n$ and prize x_n with probability $1/n$. The expected utility of π^n is at least $(n - 1)U(x_0)/n + 1$. Find some N such that $U(x_N) > U(x_0) + 1$, and construct a two-outcome lottery with prizes x_0 and x_N whose expected utility is $U(x_0) + 1/2$; since you can continuously vary the probabilities, this is easily done. Then for all sufficiently large n, $\pi^n \succ \pi' \succ \delta_{x_0}$, and yet $\pi^n \to \delta_{x_0}$ in the weak topology. Oops.

If U is bounded and continuous, then preferences are continuous in the weak topology. If U is continuous but not bounded, I only get continuity of preferences for sequences of (always simple) lotteries that (1) have uniformly bounded supports and (2) converge in the weak topology.

[4] We later will write $E\theta$ for the expected value of a random variable θ. No confusion should result.

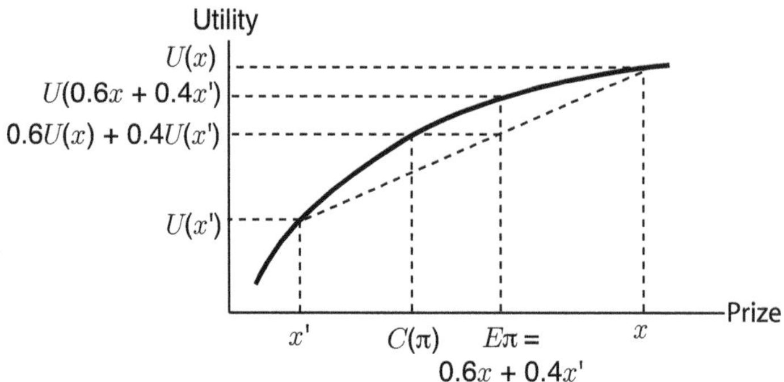

Figure 6.1. Concavity, risk aversion, and certainty equivalents. For a lottery π that gives prize x with probability .6 and x' with probability .4, we mark the expected value of the lottery as $E\pi$ and the certainty equivalent of the lottery as $C(\pi)$.

chance at x'. The expected value of π is $0.6x + 0.4x'$.[5] Does our consumer prefer $\delta_{0.6x+0.4x'}$ or the lottery $0.6\,\delta_x + 0.4\,\delta_{x'}$? Answer this by comparing the two expected utilities. For $\delta_{0.6x+0.4x'}$, we have expected utility $U(0.6x+0.4x')$, while the expected utility of $0.6\,\delta_x + 0.4\,\delta_{x'}$ is $0.6\,U(x) + 0.4\,U(x')$. By concavity, the former is at least as large as the latter, which is what we want. Of course, the property of risk aversion is meant to hold for all lotteries and not just those with supports of size two. But concavity of U is just what is needed, in general.

If U is a concave function on an interval of real numbers, it is automatically continuous on the interior of the interval (see Proposition A3.17g), although there can be a discontinuous drop in the value of the function at any endpoint the interval might possess. Therefore, risk aversion virtually implies continuity of U; we only need to worry about continuity at the endpoints of the interval, if any.

Certainty equivalents and risk premia

Because the utility function U in Figure 6.1 is continuous, we know (from the Intermediate-Value Theorem of calculus) that for every $a \in [0,1]$ there is some value x^* with $U(x^*) = aU(x) + (1-a)U(x')$. For any such x^*, we know from the expected utility representation that $\delta_{x^*} \sim \pi$. Such an x^* is called a *certainty equivalent* of π. In general,

Definition 6.4. *A* ***certainty equivalent*** *for a lottery π is any prize x such that $\delta_x \sim \pi$.*

Proposition 6.5. *If U is continuous, then every lottery π has at least one certainty equivalent. If U is strictly increasing, every π has at most one certainty equivalent.*

(The proof is left as an exercise. Remember that we assume throughout that X is an

---

[5] Careful! The lottery $0.6\,\delta_x + 0.4\,\delta_{x'}$ denotes a probability distribution with two possible outcomes, x and x', whereas $0.6x + 0.4x'$ is a number. And, appearing momentarily, $\delta_{0.6x+0.4x'}$ is a probability distribution with one possible outcome, namely $0.6x + 0.4x'$.

interval in R.) We henceforth assume that the utility function under consideration is strictly increasing, continuous, and concave, reflecting increasing, continuous, and risk-averse preferences. Hence every π has a unique certainty equivalent, which we denote $C(\pi)$. Note that risk aversion, in this setting, can be characterized by $C(\pi) \leq E\pi$. We write $R(\pi)$ for the difference $E\pi - C(\pi)$, calling $R(\pi)$ the *risk premium* of π; therefore another characterization of risk aversion is $R(\pi) \geq 0$ for all π.

Absolute (and relative) risk aversion

In a rough sense, $R(\pi)$ is a measure of the level of risk aversion of the consumer; the larger is $R(\pi)$, the greater is the extent to which the consumer "fears" the riskiness of π. (If $R(\pi) = 0$ for all π, then the consumer is risk neutral.) In this section, we use this concept to compare the levels of risk aversion of two different expected-utility maximizers, and then we look into the question, What happens to a single consumer's level of risk aversion as she grows wealthier?

Begin with two consumers, both of whom are expected-utility maximizers (for monetary prizes). The first consumer has utility function W and the second V, where for simplicity assume these functions are defined on the same interval of the real line. Assume as well that both W and V are strictly increasing, continuous, and concave. To economize on language, we will loosely use expressions such as "W is more risk averse than V" when we really mean, "The individual with utility function W is more risk averse than the individual with utility function V." But what could we mean by that idea, however expressed?

Definition 6.6. *W is at least as risk averse as V if, for any lottery π and sure-thing dollar amount x, if W (weakly) prefers π to x, then so does V.*

This may seem a natural definition, but at least one author, Ross (1981), criticizes it as inadequate.

Proposition 6.7. *W is at least as risk averse as V if and only if the function $W \circ V^{-1}$ is concave.*

Commentary and proof. First, to say a few words about this proposition: The symbol $\circ$ means functional composition. V is a strictly increasing function and continuous from some interval of the real line to some other interval of real numbers (use continuity). Since it is strictly increasing and onto, it possesses a continuous and strictly increasing inverse, which is denoted by V^{-1}, whose domain is the range of V and whose range is the domain of V, which by assumption is also the domain of W. Therefore, $W \circ V^{-1}$ transforms (in a strictly increasing manner) V into W; that is, $W(x) = (W \circ V^{-1}) \circ V(x)$.

Suppose $W \circ V^{-1}$ is concave. Fix any lottery π and sure thing x^0 such that W prefers the lottery, which is to say

$$W(x^0) \leq \sum_x \pi(x)\, W(x),$$

where the sum is over the support of π. Rewrite this as

$$(W \circ V^{-1}) \circ V(x^0) \leq \sum_x \pi(x)\,(W \circ V^{-1}) \circ V(x),$$

and use the concavity of $W \circ V^{-1}$ to conclude that

$$(W \circ V^{-1}) \circ V(x^0) \leq \sum_x \pi(x)\,(W \circ V^{-1}) \circ V(x) \leq (W \circ V^{-1})\Big(\sum_x \pi(x)V(x)\Big).$$

Since $W \circ V^{-1}$ is strictly monotone, this implies that

$$V(x^0) \leq \sum_x \pi(x)V(x),$$

which is to say that V prefers π to x^0.

Conversely, suppose $W \circ V^{-1}$ is not concave. Then there exist r_1 and r_2 in the domain of $W \circ V^{-1}$ (which is the range of V) and a scalar a between 0 and 1 such that

$$W \circ V^{-1}(ar_1 + (1-a)r_2) < a\,W \circ V^{-1}(r_1) + (1-a)\,W \circ V^{-1}(r_2).$$

Let x_1 and x_2 be the two elements of the domain of V that map into r_1 and r_2, respectively. Therefore, we can rewrite the previous inequality as

$$\begin{aligned} W \circ V^{-1}(ar_1 + (1-a)r_2) &< a\,W \circ V^{-1}(V(x_1)) + (1-a)\,W \circ V^{-1}(V(x_2)) \\ &= a\,W(x_1) + (1-a)W(x_2). \end{aligned}$$

Now let x_3 be the certainty equivalent of the lottery with prizes x_1 and x_2 and probabilities a and $1-a$, respectively. That is,

$$W(x_3) = a\,W(x_1) + (1-a)\,W(x_2).$$

Combine this with the previous inequality, and you get

$$W \circ V^{-1}(ar_1 + (1-a)r_2) < W(x_3).$$

Rewrite this as

$$W \circ V^{-1}(aV(x_1) + (1-a)V(x_2)) < W \circ V^{-1}(V(x_3)).$$

Since $W \circ V^{-1}$ is strictly monotone, this is

$$aV(x_1) + (1-a)V(x_2) < V(x_3).$$

Therefore, for this lottery and for the sure-thing x_3, W is indifferent between them, while V strictly favors the sure thing. If $W \circ V^{-1}$ is not concave, W is *not* at least as risk averse as V. ■

Now suppose that both W and V are twice continuously differentiable. We have no justification for this, other than that it leads to some nice results. We'll use notation V' and V'' to denote the first and second derivatives of V, respectively, and similarly for W. It is perhaps worth noting the mathematical fact that, if V is strictly increasing, continuously differentiable, and its derivative is never zero, then V^{-1} is also continuously differentiable, with derivative

$$\frac{dV^{-1}}{dy} = \frac{1}{V'(V^{-1}(y))}.$$

Proposition 6.8. *Suppose W and V are both strictly increasing, concave, and twice continuously differentiable, and their derivatives are never zero. Then W is at least as risk averse as V if and only if*

$$-\frac{W''(x)}{W'(x)} \geq -\frac{V''(x)}{V'(x)},$$

for all x in their (common) domain.

Proof. This is a matter of calculus. We want to show that the condition given (on the ratios of second derivatives to first derivatives) is equivalent to concavity of $W \circ V^{-1}$. This involves showing that this function is twice continuously differentiable and evaluating its second derivative; given the formula for the derivative of V^{-1} (and the fact that it is continuously differentiable), you should be able to do this, discovering that

$$\frac{d^2\,(W \circ V^{-1})}{dr^2} = \frac{W'(x)}{(V'(x))^2}\left[\frac{W''(x)}{W'(x)} - \frac{V''(x)}{V'(x)}\right],$$

where x is shorthand for $V^{-1}(r)$, for r in the domain of $W \circ V^{-1}$, which is the range of V. On the right-hand side, the terms outside the square brackets are all strictly positive, and so the second derivative of $W \circ V^{-1}$ is nonpositive everywhere (hence, $W \circ V^{-1}$ is concave) if and only if the terms inside the brackets are nonpositive, which is true if and only if the ratios of the second to first derivatives are ordered as in the statement of the proposition. ■

Despite the seemingly formidable math (more seeming than actual), what is going on here is straightforward conceptually. One utility function is at least as risk averse as another if it is "more concave" or more curved. Proposition 6.7 says that this holds as long as (and only as long as) the first utility function is gotten from the second by a strictly increasing and concave transformation. And Proposition 6.8 takes this to a "local" condition; the ratio of the second derivative to the first is, for real-valued functions of one variable, a measure of their curvature: it tells you how fast the second derivative is changing, normalized by the first derivative. Since the second derivative of a concave function is nonpositive, "more curved" at every point means putting a minus sign in front of these ratios and comparing as in Proposition 6.8.

A second way to view this ratio as a local measure of risk aversion is as follows:

Proposition 6.9. *Fix a strictly increasing and concave utility function U that is twice continuously differentiable at x^0, with $U'(x^0) > 0$. Consider the local lottery that has prizes $x^0 + \epsilon$ and $x^0 - \epsilon$, each with probability one-half. (Assume that $x^0 - \epsilon$ and $x^0 + \epsilon$ are both in the domain of U.) The risk premium for this gamble is $-[\frac{1}{2}U''(x^0)/U'(x^0)]\epsilon^2$, up to a term of order $o(\epsilon^2)$.*[6]

This is proven using Taylor's series expansions of the quantities involved; you are asked to supply the proof in Problem 6.3. This result and our discussion of the curvature of U justify the following definition.

Definition 6.10. *For a twice-continuously differentiable utility function U with strictly positive first derivative, the function*

$$\lambda(x) = -\frac{U''(x)}{U'(x)}$$

is known as the (local) ***coefficient of risk aversion.***[7]

Note that if $U' > 0$ and U is concave, $\lambda(x) \geq 0$.

Consider a lottery π and a (dollar) amount z. Write $\pi \oplus z$ for the lottery that gives prize $x + z$ with probability $\pi(x)$. That is, $\pi \oplus z$ is just the lottery constructed from π by increasing each prize of π by the amount z. Thinking of these prizes as the after-the-gamble wealth level of our consumer, as we increase z in $\pi \oplus z$, we increase the consumer's general wealth level. It seems somewhat natural to suppose that as someone becomes richer, she cares less and less about risks that she takes in given gambles. In symbols, this would say that as z increases, $R(\pi \oplus z)$ should not increase; the consumer's risk premium for a fixed gamble should not increase as the consumer becomes wealthier.[8] We formalize this notion and two related to it as follows:

---

6 This means that if you write $d(\epsilon)$ for the difference between the actual risk premium of this gamble and $-[\frac{1}{2}U''(x^0)/U'(x^0)]\epsilon^2$, then $\lim_{\epsilon \to 0} d(\epsilon)/\epsilon^2 = 0$.

7 It is sometimes known as the *Arrow-Pratt* coefficient or measure of risk aversion, after the two individuals who independently developed the concept. And, for reasons to be discussed, it is often referred to as the coefficient of *absolute* risk aversion.

8 Fixing a lottery π, as we shift the consumer's wealth level z and construct $\pi \oplus z$, we have to be careful that the prizes remain in the domain of the consumer's utility function U.

Definition 6.11. *For a fixed consumer with utility function U, if $R(\pi \oplus z)$ is nonincreasing in z, the consumer is said to be* ***nonincreasingly risk averse.***[9] *If $R(\pi \oplus z)$ is constant in z, we say that the consumer is* ***constantly risk averse*** *or has* ***constant risk aversion.*** *If $R(\pi \oplus z)$ is nondecreasing in z, then we say the consumer is* ***nondecreasingly risk averse.***

Economists generally assert that it is natural to assume consumers are nonincreasingly risk averse and that, over intervals of prizes that are not large relative to the individual's lifetime incomes, the individual is approximately constantly risk averse.

What does all this portend for the utility function U?

Proposition 6.12. *For a consumer with twice-continuously differentiable utility function U such that $U' > 0$ and corresponding risk aversion coefficient function $\lambda(\cdot)$, the consumer is nonincreasingly risk averse if and only if $\lambda(\cdot)$ is a nonincreasing function. The consumer is nondecreasingly risk averse if and only if $\lambda(\cdot)$ is a nondecreasing function. And the consumer has constant risk aversion if and only if $\lambda(\cdot)$ is a constant function λ, in which case the utility function U is a positive affine translate of the utility function $-e^{-\lambda x}$. (If λ is the constant zero, then U is a positive affine translate of the function x; the consumer is risk neutral.)*

This result follows as a corollary to Proposition 6.8. Take the single utility function U and two wealth levels z and z'. Construct from these two different utility functions: $W(x) := U(x + z)$ and $V(x) := U(x + z')$. How the U-utility function evaluates $\pi \oplus z$ is the same as how W evaluates π, and how U evaluates $\pi \oplus z'$ is the same as how V evaluates π. Being careful with definitions, you can show that U is nonincreasingly risk averse according to the first definition if and only if W is at least as risk averse as V whenever we have $z' \geq z$. But $-U''(z)/U'(z) = -W''(0)/W'(0)$, and $-U''(z')/U'(z') = -V''(0)/V'(0)$, so $\lambda(x) = -U''(x)/U'(x)$ being nonincreasing comes down to a comparison of the risk-aversion coefficients of W and V for $z' \geq z$. Proposition 6.8 then gives all of 6.12 except for the part about constant risk aversion being equivalent to the utility function $U(x) = A - Be^{-\lambda x}$ for constants A and $B > 0$, and that is a matter of simple integration of $-U''/U' =$ a constant λ.

A variation played on this theme concerns how a single consumer responds to proportional gambles with her wealth. Suppose that $X = (0, \infty)$, and the consumer's von Neumann–Morgenstern utility function U is concave, strictly increasing, and twice continuously differentiable. We imagine that the consumer has at her disposal an amount of wealth x, all of which she stakes in a gamble that pays a random *gross return*. Such a random gross return is specified by a simple probability distribution π with domain X, where our consumer's wealth after the gamble is θx (for $\theta \in \text{supp}(\pi)$) with probability $\pi(\theta)$. We can define a *certainty equivalent rate of return*, $CRR(\pi; x)$, which is that number $\hat{\theta}$ such that our consumer is indifferent between staking her wealth according to the gross return distribution

[9] Sloppy terminology is sometimes used: this property is called decreasing risk aversion, and we say that the function U has or exhibits nonincreasing/decreasing risk aversion.

π or taking $\hat{\theta}x$ for sure. And we can ask how $CRR(\pi;x)$ changes with changes in the consumer's initial level of wealth x. It is generally considered somewhat natural to suppose that $CRR(\pi;x)$ is nonincreasing in x; the richer our consumer is, the more conservative she becomes in staking all of her wealth. If we define $\mu(x) = -xU''(x)/U'(x)$, we can get results such as $CRR(\pi;x)$ is nonincreasing in x if and only if $\mu(x)$ is nonincreasing in x. The function μ is called the *coefficient of* ***relative*** *risk aversion*, as distinguished from $\lambda \equiv -U''/U'$, the coefficient of *absolute* risk aversion. For more on this, consult one of the references at the end of the chapter.

First- and second-order stochastic dominance

Because expected-utility maximizers in economic theory are nearly always assumed to have increasing and concave utility functions, these properties are used to create desirability-based partial orders on probability distributions according to the following definitions. (We continue to assume that all probability distributions are simple, although the theory about to be described generalizes to nonsimple probabilities.)

Definition 6.13. *Probability distribution π is* ***first-order stochastically dominant*** *over ρ, denoted $\pi \geq^1 \rho$, if, for every nondecreasing utility function $U : R \to R$, the expected utility of π computed with U is at least as large as the expected utility of ρ. That is, $\pi \geq^1 \rho$ if every expected-utility maximizer who has a nondecreasing utility function (weakly) prefers π to ρ. And probability distribution π is* ***second-order stochastically dominant*** *over ρ, denoted $\pi \geq^2 \rho$, if, for every nondecreasing and concave utility function U, the expected utility of π computed with U is at least as large as the expected utility of ρ. Or, put differently, $\pi \geq^2 \rho$ if every expected utility maximizer who has nondecreasing and (weakly) risk averse preferences over lotteries (weakly) prefers π to ρ.*

These two partial orders can be characterized directly in two ways: in terms of their cumulative distribution functions and in terms of jointly distributed random variables with π and ρ as their marginal distributions. First, for any simple probability distribution π, let $F_\pi : R \to [0,1]$ be the cumulative distribution function of π; that is, $F_\pi(r) = \sum_{x \in \text{supp}(\pi);\, x \leq r} \pi(x)$, which is (loosely) the probability under π of an outcome less or equal to r.

Proposition 6.14.

a. $\pi \geq^1 \rho$ if and only if, for all $r \in R$, $F_\pi(r) \leq F_\rho(r)$.

b. $\pi \geq^2 \rho$ if and only if, for r^0 a real number such that $F_\pi(r^0) = F_\rho(r^0) = 0$ and for all $r^1 \geq r^0$,

$$\int_{r^0}^{r^1} F_\pi(r)dr \leq \int_{r^0}^{r^1} F_\rho(r)dr.$$

(We'll discuss the proof of this proposition after we state the other characterization of first- and second-order stochastic dominance.)

The second characterization is most easily expressed in the terminology of random variables. Given two distributions π and ρ, we want to find a pair of random variables X_π and X_ρ defined on a single probability space, where the marginal distribution of X_π is π, the marginal distribution of X_ρ is ρ, and whose joint distribution has easy-to-interpret properties.

Proposition 6.15.

a. *$\pi \geq^1 \rho$ if and only if a pair of random variables X_π and X_ρ can be constructed (on a single probability space) such that X_π has marginal distribution π, X_ρ has marginal distribution ρ, and $X_\pi = X_\rho + Y$ for a random variable Y that is nonnegative with probability one. In words, X_π is X_ρ plus a nonnegative supplement.*

b. *$\pi \geq^2 \rho$ if and only if a pair of random variables X_π and X_ρ can be constructed (on a single probability space) such that X_π has marginal distribution π, X_ρ has marginal distribution ρ, and $X_\rho = X_\pi + Y$, where Y is a random variable that has conditional mean less than or equal to zero, conditional on X_π. In words, X_ρ is X_π plus a supplement which can be negative or positive but that, conditional on X_π, must have nonpositive mean.*

For readers unfamiliar with the concepts of random variables defined on a single probability space, the following restatement of Proposition 6.15 may help. Think of a probability-tree depiction of π; for instance, if π has a three-element support, $\{0, 5, 10\}$, with probabilities 0.4, 0.2, and 0.4, respectively, we'd depict π as in Figure 6.2a. Now, conditional on the outcome (one of 0, 5, or 10), we have a second round of uncertainty. As shown in Figure 6.2b, if the outcome of π is 0, this second-round supplement is either -3 or $+3$, each with probability 0.5; if π gives 5, the second round supplement is -2 or $+3$ with probabilities 0.75 and 0.25, respectively. And if π gives 10, the second round supplement is -2 or $+2$, with probabilities 0.5 and 0.5. In Figure 6.2c, we show the net of these two rounds, where we add the outcomes of the two rounds: the resulting probability distribution has support $\{-3, 3, 8, 12\}$, with probabilities 0.2, 0.35, 0.25, and 0.2, respectively. This distribution, which we'll call ρ, is the distribution of a random variable $X_\rho = X_\pi + Y$, where X_π has distribution π (the first round), plus the supplementary Y, whose mean conditional on each value of X_π is less than or equal to zero. Hence, according to Proposition 6.15, π second-order stochastically dominates ρ. Proposition 6.15 also tells us a distribution π second-order stochastically dominates ρ *only if* this sort of construction relating an X_π and an X_ρ is possible, and π first-order stochastically dominates ρ *if and only if* a construction of this nature is possible with the supplementary Y being nonpositive with probability one.[10]

[10] In Figure 6.2, the marginal distribution of the supplement Y is that it gives prize -3 with probability 0.2, -2 with probability 0.35, 2 with probability 0.2, and 3 with probability 0.25. But, for second-order stochastic dominance, it is the various conditional distributions of Y and not its marginal distribution that are important; specifically, the conditional distributions must all have nonpositive

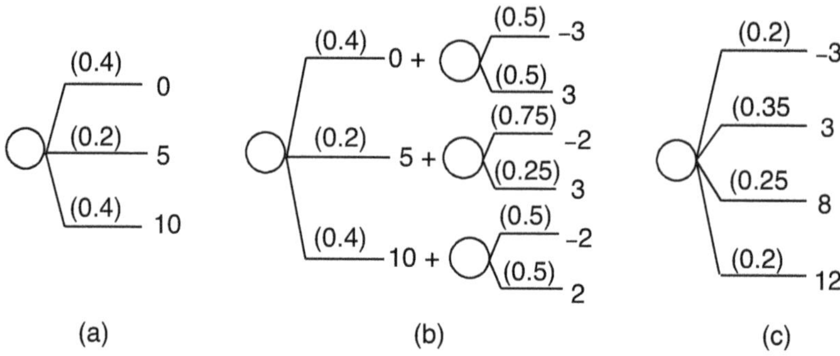

Figure 6.2. Second-order stochastic dominance. Does the three-outcome distribution depicted in panel a second-order stochastically dominate the four-outcome distribution depicted in panel c? It does. As shown in panel b, one can create a two-stage probability tree where the first stage is panel a and, for every outcome of the first stage, the second stage has (conditional) mean less than or equal to zero (conditional on the results of the first stage), where the sum of the two stages gives the distribution in panel c. Proposition 6.15 says that one distribution second-order stochastically dominates a second distribution if and only if we can construct the second distribution from the first plus a conditional-nonpositive-mean addition, in this fashion.

The proofs of Propositions 6.14 and 6.15 are left as exercises, as Problems 6.5 and 6.6. For the most part, these are not hard to prove, if you have the right tools handy (and the problems will supply the tools), with one exception: it is not easy to show that if π second-order stochastically dominates ρ, then ρ is π plus a conditional-nonpositive-mean noise term. (For this part, the problems will direct you to an ingenious constructive proof in the literature.)

6.2. Induced Preferences for Income

In the analysis conducted in the previous section, we interpreted prizes as amounts of money, using our intuition about likely properties for lotteries with dollar-valued prizes. But consumers don't eat money. Money is useful for the commodities one can buy with it. So a fairly obvious question is, If a consumer has von Neumann–Morgenstern preferences for consumption bundles and if her preferences for money arise entirely from the purchasing power of that money, what conditions on her preferences for consumption bundles will translate into the properties discussed in Section 6.1?

Suppose there are k commodities; the consumption space X for the consumer is R^k_+. Assume that the consumer, considering simple lotteries over the consumption bundles x that she might consume, conforms to the assumptions of Proposition 5.3. Let $U : X \to R$ be her (resulting) von Neumann–Morgenstern utility function

means. For first-order stochastic dominance, the marginal distribution of Y is sufficient; Y is nonpositive with (marginal) probability one if and only if it is conditionally nonpositive with probability one (conditional on every x in the support of π).

for simple lotteries on X. Note that U is a perfectly good ordinal representation for our consumer's preferences on sure-thing consumption bundles. That is, U could be used in all of the developments of Chapters 3 and 4; in particular, corresponding to U is an indirect utility function $\nu(p, y)$ that gives the amount of utility (on the scale of U) our consumer derives from income y at prices p. But U is more than just any ordinal numerical representation for preferences on X. We can use U (and positive affine transformations of U) to compute expected utilities for simple lotteries on X, to determine our consumer's preferences over those simple lotteries.

We also assume for the time being that prices are fixed and given by some price vector $p \in R^k_{++}$. (We will explore uncertain prices later.)

The question is, How does the consumer rank two lotteries concerning her level of income? We let y denote a level of income, drawn from the set of nonnegative numbers $[0, \infty)$, so that a (simple) lottery π on income is a (finite support) probability distribution over $[0, \infty)$.

Assume that the consumer learns how much income she has to spend before she purchases any part of her consumption bundle. Then if she has income y to spend, she purchases some $x \in \mathbf{D}(p, y)$ (her Marshallian demand), which gives her utility $U(x) = \nu(p, y)$. Accordingly, the expected utility she achieves from π is

$$\sum_{y \in \text{supp}(\pi)} \nu(p, y)\pi(y),$$

so that for two lotteries over her income, π and ρ, $\pi \succ \rho$ if and only if

$$\sum_{y \in \text{supp}(\pi)} \nu(p, y)\pi(y) > \sum_{y \in \text{supp}(\rho)} \nu(p, y)\rho(y).$$

That is to say, $\nu(p, y)$, viewed as a function of y for the fixed prices p, is a von Neumann–Morgenstern utility function for our consumer when she examines her preferences for lotteries over levels of income.

The assertions of the previous paragraph are more subtle than may be apparent, so don't go past them too quickly. For one thing, preferences over lotteries of income are *induced* from the consumer's primitive preferences over consumption lotteries. A lottery over income, together with the assumption that the consumer shops intelligently (maximizes her preference over consumption once she knows her income and the prices), determines a corresponding lottery over (well chosen) consumption bundles. And the consumer's ranking between two income lotteries is then inherited from or induced by her ranking between the two corresponding consumption lotteries. This probably seems to you the obvious way to analyze the problem, but it contains an assumption about how the consumer thinks about income lotteries: She goes through the calculations indicated. Or, at least and in the general spirit of positive economic modeling of choice, when choosing among income lotteries, she acts *as if* she did all these calculations.[11]

And there is an important timing issue here. Recall from Chapter 5 (page 115) the discussion about the timing of resolution of uncertainty. We have made the "right" assumption here, namely that all uncertainty about y resolves before the consumer must make any decisions about how she will spend y. This ensures that her induced preferences over income lotteries have an expected utility representation and so are themselves expected-utility preferences. Without this assumption, her induced preferences may not take an expected-utility form. (See Problem 6.7 for more on this point.)

Once we accept these modeling assumptions and assertions, questions about properties of the consumer's preferences over income lotteries and her corresponding utility function for income become questions about her indirect utility function. The following proposition, which summarizes the state of affairs, gives the basic results.

Proposition 6.16. *Suppose the consumer has preferences over lotteries of consumption bundles that satisfy the assumptions of Proposition 5.3. Let U be her utility function on consumption bundles and let $\nu(p, y)$ be the corresponding indirect utility function. Assume that U is continuous. Then the consumer's preferences over immediately-resolving lotteries pertaining to income satisfy the three mixture-space axioms, and $y \to \nu(p, y)$ is her utility function for income. Moreover:*

a. $\nu(p, y)$ is continuous in y.

b. If the consumer is locally insatiable, then $\nu(p, y)$ is strictly increasing in y.

c. If U is a concave function, then $\nu(p, y)$ is a concave function in y; that is, our consumer is risk averse concerning lotteries over income.

Proof. To begin, note that the preamble asserts that the consumer's preferences on income lotteries satisfy the three mixture-space axioms. We know this *because* her preferences over income lotteries have an expected utility representation; Proposition 5.3 states that the three assumptions are necessary and sufficient for expected utility.

Part a is (essentially) Proposition 3.3c.

For part b, suppose $y > y'$, and let $x' \in \mathbf{D}(p, y')$. (We are assuming that U is continuous, so the existence of x' is guaranteed.) Then $\nu(p, y') = U(x')$. Of course, $p \cdot x' \leq y'$ (in fact, $p \cdot x' = y'$, but we don't need that), and hence $p \cdot x' < y$. Therefore, if income is y, the consumer (at prices p) can afford some bundle strictly better than x'. The optimal bundle at prices p and income y can only be better than this, so $\nu(p, y) > U(x') = \nu(p, y')$.

For part c, take two income levels y and y' and $a \in (0, 1)$. Suppose $x \in \mathbf{D}(p, y)$ and $x' \in \mathbf{D}(p, y')$. Then $p \cdot (ax + (1 - a)x') = ap \cdot x + (1 - a)p \cdot x' \leq ay + (1 - a)y'$,

[11] This is the first manifestation of dynamic choice in this book, to which next chapter will be devoted: Before deciding that this way of modeling her preferences over income lotteries is obvious, please see what next chapter has to say.

which means that $ax + (1 - a)x'$ is feasible at prices p with income $ay + (1 - a)y'$. Hence $\nu(p, ay + (1 - a)y') \geq U(ax + (1 - a)x')$, and

$$\begin{aligned} a\nu(p, y) + (1 - a)\nu(p, y') &= aU(x) + (1 - a)U(x') \\ &\leq U(ax + (1 - a)x') \leq \nu(p, ay + (1 - a)y'), \end{aligned}$$

where the first inequality follows from the concavity of U. ■

Part c of the proposition requires that U, the consumer's utility function over consumption bundles, is concave. In Chapter 2, we said there is no particular reason to suppose that this is so, but in the current context it can be justified. Now we can ask our consumer: For any two bundles x and x', would you rather have the bundle $0.5x + 0.5x'$ (where we are taking the convex combination of the bundles) or a lottery where you get x with probability 1/2 and x' with probability 1/2? If our consumer always (weakly) prefers the sure thing, and if she conforms to the assumptions of expected-utility theory, then her von Neumann–Morgenstern utility function, which is a perfectly good representation of her (ordinal) preferences on X, will be concave.[12]

In the derivation above, we assume that prices are certain, given by a fixed p. What if there is uncertainty about prices? Specifically, imagine that our consumer enters into a lottery that determines her income y, and at the same time prices are determined by a lottery ρ. All uncertainty resolves, and then our consumer chooses what to consume.

If we want to speak of the consumer's preferences over lotteries (only) in her income in this setting, we must make some assumption about the statistical relationship between lotteries on y and on p. A simple example will illustrate the point. Consider a consumer who is evaluating an income lottery that gives her $10,000 with probability 1/2 and $20,000 with probability 1/2. Suppose that prices will be either p or $2p$, each with probability 1/2. If our consumer's income level is perfectly positively correlated with the price level, she faces no real uncertainty; her real purchasing power is unchanged. If, on the other hand, her income level is perfectly negatively correlated with the price level, she faces rather a lot of uncertainty in her purchasing power. It will be a rare consumer indeed who is indifferent between these two situations, even though in terms of the lotteries on (nominal) income, the two situations are identical. Either we must consider how the consumer feels about lotteries jointly on prices and income, or we have to make some assumption that prevents this sort of problem.

The simplest assumption we can make is that these lotteries are statistically independent. Then if we let ρ be the probability distribution on prices, the induced expected utility our consumer obtains from the probability distribution π on y is

---

[12] To deduce concavity, it isn't quite sufficient to check risk aversion only for gambles with two equally likely prizes; but if U is continuous, this is enough.

given by

$$\sum_{y \in \text{supp}(\pi)} \sum_{p \in \text{supp}(\rho)} \nu(p, y)\rho(p)\pi(y).$$

Therefore, the consumer's von Neumann–Morgenstern utility function for income, which we will now write $V(y)$, is

$$V(y) = \sum_{p \in \text{supp}(\rho)} \nu(p, y)\rho(p).$$

You can quickly check that, in this setting, Proposition 6.16 holds without any change except for this redefinition of the utility function on income.

A different question is, How does the consumer respond to uncertainty in the price level? Suppose we fix the consumer's income at y, and ask about her preferences over probability distributions over the prices p that she faces. By the same logic as before, $\nu(p, y)$, now viewed as a function of p for the fixed y, is her von Neumann–Morgenstern utility function for price vectors. We know that $\nu(p, y)$ will be continuous in p (if the underlying utility function is), and it can be shown that $\nu(p, y)$ is nonincreasing in p (but not strictly decreasing). But convexity / concavity properties are generally ambiguous. Specifically, suppose we ask whether a consumer (with concave von Neumann–Morgenstern utility function U for lotteries on consumption bundles) would prefer to face a lottery where prices are either p or p', each with probability 1/2, or to face the prices $(p + p')/2$. The answer will depend (in general) on the specific p and p'; sometimes the former is preferred (the consumer prefers to gamble over the prices she will face), and sometimes the latter is preferred. For more on this, see Problem 6.8.

6.3. Demand for Insurance and Risky Assets

The most prevalent and extensive applications of the models of the last chapter and this are to insurance and financial markets. Entire books and courses are devoted to these markets, and to deal with them in reasonably sophisticated fashion, one needs to take into account information and strategic action, ideas that are developed only in Volume II. But the simplest and most preliminary results are accessible at this point; in this section, these results are provided in the context of insurance; corresponding results concerning financial markets and risky assets are developed in problems at the end of the chapter.

Imagine a consumer whose income level is subject to some uncertainty. Specifically, her income will be y with probability π and y' with probability $1 - \pi$, where $y > y'$. Think of the difference $\Delta = y - y'$ as some loss the consumer might sustain, because of an accident, ill health, theft, or some other misfortune. An insurance company will insure against this loss; if the consumer pays a premium of δ, the insurance company will pay Δ back to the consumer if she sustains this loss. The consumer may buy partial coverage; if she pays $a\delta$, she gets back $a\varDelta$ if she sustains the loss. We do not restrict a to $[0,1]$. (There are good reasons why such a restriction or one even more severe might be in place, but they concern concepts and ideas for which we are not yet ready.)

Assume this consumer satisfies the three mixture-space axioms concerning her final level of income, net of any payments to/from the insurance company, and her utility function V is strictly increasing, concave, and differentiable. If the consumer buys a-fractional insurance, her expected utility is

$$v(a) = \pi V(y - a\delta) + (1-\pi) V(y' + a\varDelta - a\delta), \tag{6.1}$$

and her problem is to maximize $v(a)$ over a.

Proposition 6.17. *Consider the problem of maximizing $v(a)$ defined by (6.1) for $y > y'$, $\varDelta = y - y'$, and V a concave, strictly increasing, and differentiable function.*

a. If $\delta = (1-\pi)\varDelta$, then $a = 1$ is a solution of the problem.

b. If $\delta > (1-\pi)\varDelta$, then $a < 1$ for any solution of the problem.

Proof. If V is concave, then an application of the second half of Proposition A3.17b tells us that v is a concave function of a. If is easy to show that v is a differentiable function of a as well, so we know that the first-order condition for a maximum, $v'(a) = 0$, which is

$$\pi\delta V'(y - a\delta) = (1-\pi)(\varDelta - \delta)V'(y' + a\varDelta - a\delta), \tag{6.2}$$

is both necessary and sufficient for a to be a solution to the maximization problem.

(a) If $\delta = (1-\pi)\varDelta$, then $(1-\pi)(\varDelta - \delta) = (1-\pi)\varDelta - (1-\pi)\delta = \delta - (1-\pi)\delta = \pi\delta$, and (6.2) can be rewritten

$$V'(y - a\delta) = V'(y - (1-a)\varDelta - a\delta),$$

which obviously holds at $a = 1$.

(b) Let $b = \pi\delta/((1-\pi)(\varDelta - \delta))$. Then $\delta > (1-\pi)\varDelta$ implies $b > 1$. Rewrite (6.2) as

$$bV'(y - a\delta) = V'(y - (1-a)\varDelta - a\delta).$$

Because $b > 1$, this implies that

$$V'(y - a\delta) < V'(y - (1-a)\varDelta - a\delta)$$

if a is a solution. Since V is concave, its derivative is nonincreasing, and so this inequality implies

$$y - a\delta > y - (1-a)\Delta - a\delta,$$

which can only hold at $a < 1$. ∎

Note that $(1-\pi)\Delta$ is the expected payout of the insurance company. Accordingly, if $\delta = (1-\pi)\Delta$, the insurance company pays out on average just what it takes in as premium, and the contract it offers is said to be *actuarially fair*. Therefore, part a can be paraphrased: If the contract is actuarially fair, the consumer wishes to purchase full insurance.[13]

If $\delta > (1-\pi)\Delta$, the company takes in more than it expects to pay out on average; the contract is *actuarially unfair*. Part b is paraphrased: The consumer only partially insures if offered actuarially unfair insurance.[14]

Problem 6.9 continues this analysis, and Problems 6.10 through 6.12 develop similar results for the case of demand for risky (financial) assets.

Bibliographic Notes

The material on utility functions for money (and especially absolute and relative risk aversion) is further developed (in varying degrees) in Fishburn (1970) and Kreps (1988). The classic references are Arrow (1974) and Pratt (1964). The classic references on stochastic dominance are Hadar and Russell (1969) and Rothschild and Stiglitz (1970); in the problems to follow, I adopt the ingenious construction of Machina and Pratt (1997) for the one difficult step.

The economics of uncertainty (demand for insurance and risky assets) is developed in many different places. Borch (1968) provides a readable introduction; it is out of print, but libraries may have copies. Arrow (1974) contains a number of classic developments.

Problems

■ *6.1. (a) Prove Proposition 6.1.

(b) Provide the induction argument called for in the proof of Proposition 6.3.

(c) Prove Proposition 6.5.

■ 6.2. An expected-utility-maximizing decision maker professes to have constant absolute risk aversion over the range of (dollar) prizes from \$–1000 to \$5000. Faced

[13] Note that part a only says that $a = 1$ is *a* solution. There may be others. In particular, what happens if the consumer is risk neutral?

[14] Note that part b says only that $a < 1$ at a solution. It doesn't say that a solution exists. In particular, what happens if $\delta \geq \Delta$?

with a gamble with prizes \$5000 and \$0, each with probability 1/2, the decision maker says her certainty equivalent is \$2400. Which of the following three is most preferred by this decision maker: (a) \$2000 for sure; (b) \$5000 with probability 0.6 and $\$-1000$ with probability 0.4; or (c) \$5000 with probability 0.4, \$0 with probability 0.3, and \$1000 with probability 0.3.

■ *6.3. Provide the proof of Proposition 6.9. (You need to know Taylor's Theorem, concerning Taylor's series expansions, to do this.)

■ 6.4. A commonly employed family of von Neumann–Morgenstern utility functions (for strictly positive dollar prizes) is $U(x) = x^{\alpha}/\alpha$ for $\alpha < 1$ and $\alpha \neq 0$. What are the corresponding coefficients of absolute and relative risk aversion for these utility functions?

Problems 6.5 and 6.6 concern first- and second-order stochastic dominance and, in particular, the proofs of Propositions 6.14 and 6.15 (in the context of simple probability distributions). Problem 6.5, concerning first-order stochastic dominance, is not too difficult if you understand the trick that is described in part b of the problem. Problem 6.6 is a good deal more difficult, especially part c. If you get stuck on part c, go to the *Student's Guide*, where I provide further hints before giving the full solution.

■ *6.5. (a) Suppose that $\pi \geq^1 \rho$, as defined in Definition 6.13. Show that $F_\pi(r) \leq F_\rho(r)$ (where $F_\pi(r)$ is the cumulative distribution function for π, as defined on page 132) for all r.

(b) Suppose that U is a uniformly distributed random variable on the interval $[0,1]$. That is, U is a random variable where the probability that $U \leq r$ for $r \in [0,1]$ is r. Suppose that π is a simple probability distribution on R, and let the support of π be $\{x_1, x_2, \ldots, x_n\}$ where $x_1 < x_2 < \ldots < x_n$. Define a new random variable X from U by the rule $X = x_i$ if $U \in (F_\pi(x_{i-1}), F_\pi(x_i)]$, where for the case $U \leq F_\pi(x_1)$ we let $X = x_1$. Essentially, we are defining $X = F_\pi^{-1}(U)$. Show that X has the marginal distribution function π; that is, the probability that $X = x_i$ is $\pi(x_i)$.[15]

(c) Use part b to show that if F and G are two (simple) cumulative distribution functions such that $F(r) \leq G(r)$ for all r, then we can construct joint random variables X_F and X_G where X_F has cumulative distribution F, X_G has cumulative distribution G, and $X_F - X_G \geq 0$ with probability 1.

(d) Suppose that π and ρ are two (simple) probability distributions such that there exist joint random variables X_π and X_ρ where X_π has distribution π, X_ρ has distribution ρ, and $X_\pi - X_\rho \geq 0$ with probability 1. Then $\pi \geq^1 \rho$.

■ *6.6. (a) Suppose that $\pi \geq^2 \rho$, as defined in Definition 6.13. Let r^0 be any real

[15] This trick for creating a real-valued random variable X whose cumulative distribution function is a given F from a uniformly distributed random variable U by the rule $X = F^{-1}(U)$ works for general cumulative distribution functions and not only those that arise from simple probabilities.

number such that all values in the supports of π and ρ strictly exceed r^0. Show that for all $r^1 > r^0$,

$$\int_{r^0}^{r^1} F_\pi(r)dr \leq \int_{r^0}^{r^1} F_\rho(r)dr.$$

(Hint: Consider the utility function $U_{r^0,r^1}(x) = \min\{x - r^0, r^1 - r^0\}$.)

(b) Suppose that π and ρ are two (simple) probability distributions such that there exist joint random variables X_π and X_ρ where X_π has distribution π, X_ρ has distribution ρ, and the conditional expectation of $X_\rho - X_\pi$, conditional on each value of X_π, is nonpositive. Show that $\pi \succeq^2 \rho$.

(c) Suppose that ρ and π are two simple probability distributions on R such that, for some r^0 strictly less than every value in the supports of ρ and π and for every $r^1 \geq r^0$,

$$\int_{r^0}^{r^1} F_\pi(r)dr \leq \int_{r^0}^{r^1} F_\rho(r)dr.$$

Show that there exist joint random variables X_π and X_ρ where X_π has distribution π, X_ρ has distribution ρ, and the conditional expectation of $X_\rho - X_\pi$, conditional on each value of X_π, is nonpositive.

■ 6.7. Consider a consumer who divides her consumption between two goods and whose utility function is $U((x_1, x_2)) = \ln(x_1 + 1) + \ln(x_2 + 1)$. Moreover, she is an expected utility maximizer when it comes to (simple) lotteries over her consumption bundle, and U is her von Neumann–Morgenstern utility function. The prices of the two goods are both 1. Her income, used to finance purchases of the goods, is given by the variable y, and it may be random.

What sets this problem apart from what we did in the chapter is that our consumer must choose x_1 before any uncertainty about y, if there is uncertainty, resolves. (The values of x_1 and x_2 must be nonnegative; her choice of x_1 must be such that $x_2 \geq 0$ with probability one.) Suppose, therefore, that she faces a lottery in which $y = 98$ or $y = 178$, each with probability 1/2. What is her optimal choice for x_1? What is her expected utility? (You should be able to find the optimal level of x_1 analytically, but as you'll need numerical methods later in this problem, you might want to set this up numerically from the start. Compute her expected utility to at least four places past the decimal point.)

Next, suppose that y is certain; specifically, $y = 126.948391819$ with probability 1. What is her optimal choice of x_1, and what is her (expected) utility?

Finally, suppose that y takes on one of three values, 98, 178, or 126.948391819, each with probability 1/3. What is her optimal choice of x_1, and what is her expected utility? (Unless you can solve cubics analytically, you will need to do this numerically. You have to do it accurately enough so that you find expected utility to four places past the decimal point.)

In the first paragraph, it says "she is an expected utility maximizer..." But the answers you got should convince you otherwise. (Why do they convince you otherwise?) What is going on here?

*6.8. Fix a consumer with von Neumann–Morgenstern preferences over lotteries for consumption bundles, and fix this consumer's income at some level y. Given two strictly positive price vectors p and p', would the consumer rather be in an economy where prices are either p or p', each probability 1/2, or in an economy where the prices are sure to be $0.5p + 0.5p'$? We asserted that there is no clear answer to that question. In this problem, you are asked to develop two examples that indicate what can happen along these lines.

(a) Imagine that there are two goods, and the consumer's *ordinal* preferences are given by $u(x_1, x_2) = x_1 + x_2$. That is, the consumer's von Neumann–Morgenstern utility function is $U(x_1, x_2) = f(x_1 + x_2)$ for some strictly increasing function f on the real line. Suppose that $p = (1, 3)$ and $p' = (3, 1)$. Show that *regardless of what the function f is*, this consumer prefers to take her chances with the risky prices.

(b) Imagine that there are two goods and the consumer's von Neumann–Morgenstern utility function is $U(x_1, x_2) = f(\min\{x_1, x_2\})$ for some concave, strictly increasing function f on the real line. Assume that $f(0)$ is finite. Now suppose that the risk in prices is entirely risk in the overall price level: $p = (\gamma, \gamma)$ and $p' = (1/\gamma, 1/\gamma)$ for some scalar $\gamma > 1$. Prove that for fixed γ you can always find a function f such that the consumer prefers the certain prices $0.5p + 0.5p'$ to the risky prices. And prove that for every concave, strictly increasing function f with $f(0)$ finite there is a γ sufficiently large so the consumer prefers the risky prices to the certain prices.

■ 6.9. Suppose that an insurance policy compensates a victim for loss, but does so somewhat imperfectly. That is, imagine that in the story given about the insurance-buying consumer our consumer's income prior to any insurance is $y - \Delta$, where Δ is a simple random variable (a random variable with finite support) whose support includes 0 and some strictly positive amounts. The available insurance policy pays a flat amount B in the event of any loss, that is, in the event that Δ exceeds zero. The premium is still δ. Let $1 - \pi$ be the probability that the consumer sustains a loss. The contract is actuarially fair if $\delta = (1 - \pi)B$. Suppose this is so and that B is the expected amount of the loss, if there is a loss. If the consumer has a strictly concave and differentiable utility function, will she buy full insurance? Possible answers are yes, no, and it depends. (Use a simple parameterized example if you can't do this in general.)

Problem 6.10 through 6.12 concern the demand for risky assets. The setting for all these problems is provided in Problem 6.10, which goes on to ask you to provide results that parallel the results we gave in the chapter for insurance. The remaining problems take you further into this topic.

■ *6.10. Imagine a consumer who will do all her consuming one year hence. This consumer has w dollars to invest and no sources of income except for the proceeds from her investments with which to finance her (eventual) consumption. Let y denote the proceeds from her investments and assume that her preferences over lotteries with prizes y satisfy the von Neumann–Morgenstern assumptions, with $y \to V(y)$ her von Neumann–Morgenstern utility function, which is strictly increasing, concave, and differentiable.

This consumer can invest her money in one of two assets. The first of these is a riskless asset; for every dollar invested, the consumer gets back $r > 1$ dollars next year. The second asset is risky. Its gross return, denoted by θ, has a simple probability distribution π, so that $\pi(\theta)$ represents the probability that the risky asset has a gross return of θ. By gross return we mean a dollar invested in the risky asset returns θ dollars next year.

The consumer's problem, then, is to decide how much money to invest in each of the two assets. Since every dollar invested in the second asset is precisely one dollar less invested in the first, we can write her decision problem as a problem in one variable a, the amount of money she invests in the second, risky asset. If θ is the gross return on the risky asset, investing a in this asset means she will have

$$y = \theta a + r(w - a) = a(\theta - r) + rw$$

dollars to spend on consumption next period. So her problem is to

$$\max_a v(a) \quad \text{for} \quad v(a) = \sum_{\theta \in \text{supp}(\pi)} V(a(\theta - r) + rw)\pi(\theta), \tag{6.3}$$

subject to constraints we may choose to put on a. In particular, we will constrain a to be nonnegative, or $a \geq 0$. In the venacular of finance, this constraint says that the consumer cannot *short-sell* the risky asset, but she can *leverage* her investments in the risky asset by *borrowing* at the riskless rate. (If we let a be negative, we would be permitting short sales. If we constrained $a \leq 1$, we would be prohibiting leverage through borrowing.)

The following proposition parallels Proposition 6.17 in this context:

Proposition 6.18. *Consider the problem* (6.3) *with the constraint* $a \geq 0$. *Assume* V *is concave, differentiable, and strictly increasing.*

a. If $E\theta < r$, *then the solution, and the only solution, is* $a = 0$.

b. If $E\theta = r$, *then* $a = 0$ *is a solution, although there may be others.*

c. If $E\theta > r$, *then every solution* a, *if there is a solution, must be strictly positive.*

d. If the consumer is risk neutral—that is, $V(x) = Ax + B$ *for constants* $A > 0$ *and* B*—then there is no solution if* $E\theta > r$*, every* $a \geq 0$ *is a solution if* $E\theta = r$*, and* $a = 0$ *is the only solution if* $E\theta < r$*.*

e. Suppose $\theta \geq r$ *for all* $\theta \in \text{supp}(\pi)$*, with* $\theta > r$ *for at least one* θ *(such that* $\pi(\theta) > 0$*). Then there is no solution to the problem.*

f. If the consumer is strictly risk averse—that is, $V'(x)$ *is strictly decreasing in* x*—and if* $\text{supp}(\pi)$ *contains at least two elements, then the solution, if there is one, is unique. Hence under these conditions, if* $E\theta = r$*, then* $a = 0$ *is the unique solution.*

Prove the proposition.

■ 6.11. Now specialize Problem 6.10 as follows. Assume that the expected return on the risky asset is strictly greater than r, the riskless rate, and the support of π contains at least one value that is strictly less than r. And assume that the consumer has constant (absolute) risk aversion; that is, her utility function V is $V(x) = -e^{-\lambda x}$ for some strictly positive constant λ.

(a) Prove that the solution to the consumer's investment problem is finite and unique; denote this solution by $a(w, \lambda)$.

(b) Prove that $a(w, \lambda)$ is independent of w; no matter what her initial wealth, the consumer invests the same amount in the risky asset.

(c) Prove that $a(w, \lambda)$ is nonincreasing in λ; the more risk averse the individual, the less she invests in the risky asset.

■ *6.12. When more than one asset is risky and there is a riskless asset returning r, it is possible that a risky asset could have an expected return less than r and still be demanded and that an asset could have an expected return greater than r and not be demanded at all. (Recall that we are not allowing short sales of risky assets. To make matters a bit more easy, assume that short-selling the riskless asset is also forbidden.) Produce examples to support these claims. (Hints: For the first example, you want negative correlation between the returns on the two risky assets. For the second example, think of a case where each asset returns either $\bar{\theta} > r$ or $\underline{\theta} < r$, but with differing probabilities; you have to careful about the correlation between them, as well.)

When it comes to applications of the models of this chapter and last, a lot of attention is directed toward the effects of risk sharing, risk spreading, and diversification. The final two problems provide you with some basic themes from this literature on which to chew.

■ 6.13. (a) Consider an expected-utility maximizer whose utility function U is strictly increasing and concave. Imagine that this consumer has initial wealth w and is considering whether to buy a small share in a gamble whose payoffs are given by a simple probability distribution π. To be very precise, the consumer is choosing between staying with her wealth w, or supplementing this with an α share of the gamble, for $\alpha > 0$ but very small. Letting E be the expected value or mean of π—that is, $E = \sum_{x \in \text{supp}(\pi)} x\pi(x)$—shares in this gamble are priced at βE for a 100% share, for some $\beta < 1$. So if the consumer purchases an α share, her wealth (whose expected utility she seeks to maximize) will be $w + \alpha(x - \beta E)$ with probability $\pi(x)$, for each x in the support of π.

Assume that $E > 0$ and that the consumer's utility function U is continuously differentiable. (Since it is concave and strictly increasing as well, the derivative is everywhere strictly positive.) Show that for any fixed $\beta < 1$, the consumer prefers to buy an α share of the lottery on these terms, rather than stick with w, for α sufficiently close to zero.

(In words, if the lottery sells for less than its expected value, there is a small-enough share of the lottery that this consumer wishes to buy, even though she is risk averse. For small shares in a gamble, this consumer is "approximately risk neutral.")

(b) What happens to this result if the consumer's utility function is not differentiable at w? What happens if the consumer's initial position (to which a share α of the lottery might be added) is random, given by some lottery ρ on her wealth level w?

■ *6.14. The following bit of nonsense is often heard:

> Suppose I offered you, absolutely for free, a gamble where with probability .4 you win \$1000 and with probability .6 you lose \$500. You might well choose not to take this gamble (if the alternative is zero) if you are risk averse; although this gamble has a positive expected value (0.4)(\$1000) + (0.6)(\$ – 500) = \$100, it also has substantial risk. But if I offered you, say, 100 independent trials of this gamble, then you would certainly wish to take them; the law of large numbers says that you will wind up ahead. That is, risk aversion is perhaps sensible when a single gamble is being contemplated. But it is senseless when we are looking at many independent copies of the same gamble; then the only sensible thing is to go with the long-run averages.

Is this nonsense? Can you produce a particular "consumer" who is rational according to the von Neumann–Morgenstern axioms, and who would turn down all independent copies of this gamble, no matter how many were offered? Or would any von Neumann–Morgenstern expected-utility maximizer take these gambles if offered enough independent copies? (Hints: Either answer can be correct, depending on how you interpret the phrase "enough copies of the gamble." The problem is easiest if we read this phrase as: We offer the consumer a number of copies, fixed in advance, but very large. Then you should be able to produce a consumer who will not take any of the gambles. If you are worried about bankruptcy of this consumer, you may take your pick: [1] This consumer is never bankrupt — her utility function is defined for all monetary levels, however positive or negative; [2] this consumer is bankrupt if her wealth, which begins at a level of \$2,000, ever reaches \$0; and we will stop gambling with this consumer the moment she becomes bankrupt. Interpretation [1] is the easier to work with, but either is okay.)

And, if you like challenges, try to prove the following: Suppose that we play according to rule (2): The consumer is offered "up to N gambles" with the proviso that we stop gambling if ever the consumer's wealth falls to \$0. Assume that the consumer has a utility function for final wealth that is strictly increasing and that is finite at zero. (a) If the consumer's utility function is unbounded above, then there is an N sufficiently large so that, offered N gambles or more, the consumer will take them. (b) While if the consumer's utility function is bounded above, the result can go either way: The consumer might turn down the gambles, for all sufficiently large N; or the consumer might accept the gambles, for all sufficiently large N. If you can further characterize the two cases in (b), that would be better still. (To be able to answer this question in full, you will need to know a lot of the theory of stochastic processes: some basic theory of random walks; then the theory of martingales and, in particular, the Martingale Convergence Theorem.)

Chapter Seven

Dynamic Choice

This short chapter concerns two elaborations on the general theory of choice: dynamic choice, and static choice within a dynamic context.

To explain what this means, consider the following simple example. A decision maker is choosing her dinner in two stages: In the first stage, at time $t = 0$, she chooses a *menu* of meals. In the second stage, at time $t = 1$, she chooses a *meal* from the menu she selected at the first stage. To make this formal, start with a finite set X of meals, and form from it the set Z consisting of all nonempty subsets of X; Z is the set of menus. At time $t = 0$, she chooses a menu z from some available subset $A \subseteq Z$; at time $t = 1$, she chooses some x from the menu z she selected at the outset. Her *dynamic choice* is the sequence of two choices she makes, first z from A and then x from z. If we wanted to formalize dynamic choice with choice functions, we'd have, say, a pair of choice functions, c_0 a choice function defined on the subsets of Z, and c_1, a choice function defined on subsets of X (parameterized, if necessary, by things that happen between the two moments of choice). Or we might formalize things with preference relations $\succeq_0$ and $\succeq_1$, or with utility functions u_0 and u_1 to be maximized (with $\succeq_1$ or u_1 bearing any necessary parameters). If, on the other hand, we are interested solely in the first-stage choice of a menu, that is *static choice within a dynamic context*; the standard theoretical constructs of a choice function, a preference relation, or a utility function would be employed, all defined on Z, but (presumably) exploiting the special structure that Z possesses and taking into account the dynamic context of this first-stage choice.

This example illustrates what the terms mean, but it fails to do justice to the importance of the topic. Among the most important economic decisions made by individuals are savings and investment decisions, which fit fully into these categories. The term *investment* should be read broadly here, to include education decisions as well as any other decision to acquire information for later use. Job choice also fits, insofar as the choice of what work to do today both enables and constrains later opportunities for work. Indeed, it is hard to think of any significant economic decision that neither is part of a linked series of decisions (hence dynamic) nor has implications for later decisions (hence is taken within a dynamic context).

Given the importance of these sorts of choices, three questions are obvious:

1. *How should dynamic choice, or static choice within a larger dynamic context, be modeled?*

2. *Does the dynamic context provide structure that can be exploited, to refine the basic models of choice from Chapter 1?* For instance, in our example, first-period choice entails the choice of *sets* of objects. Letting $\succeq_0$ denote the decision maker's

preferences over elements of the set of menus Z, can we say anything about $\succeq_0$ for sets z and z' where z is a subset of z'? If $z \succeq_0 z'$, are there any implications for how $\succeq_0$ behaves on the union of these sets?

3. *Does the dynamic nature of the problem raise issues that push us to rethink and, perhaps, modify the basic models of choice from Chapter 1?* Do dynamics, per se, cast doubt upon the basic axioms and properties of our models of choice?

These may seem obvious questions, but they are rarely asked or explicitly answered. The answer to the first of these questions is deemed to be obvious, so obvious that the answer is only given implicitly (that is, the answer is assumed without any comment), and so the second two questions never arise. Recent developments in so-called behavioral economics have begun to direct attention to these questions, however. In this chapter, the "obvious answer" is presented, and then I will argue that it is anything but obvious and that, in consequence, all three questions deserve the attention they are beginning to receive.

7.1. The Standard Strategic Approach

The standard approach to dynamic decision making (and to decision making within a larger dynamic context) is to regard the decision problem as one of choosing, at the outset, an optimal overall *strategy* and then implementing it flawlessly. Optimality is determined according to the *outcome* engendered by the strategy; outcomes are (within the model) what matters to the decision maker, over which the decision maker has Chapter-1-style preferences (or utility). Let me illustrate with two examples:

Example 1: Menus and meals

Begin with the simple menus-meals example. An outcome in this case is (assumed to be) a meal, and the decision maker is assumed to have complete and transitive preferences over meals. Since X is finite, a utility function $u : X \to R$ can be constructed to represent those preferences. To make things very concrete, suppose that $X = \{c, s, f\}$, where c is a meal of chicken, s is steak, and f is fish, and suppose that the decision maker's preferences over X are represented by the utility function $u(f) = 2, u(c) = 1$, and $u(s) = 0$.

The space of menus, Z, is the space of all nonempty subsets of X so, in this case, Z has seven elements. A *strategy* is a complete plan of action for all choices that need to be made; a strategy in this case takes the form of "choose some z and then some x from the chosen z." So, for instance, if the decision maker has an initial choice of the four menus

$$\{c, s\}, \{c, f\}, \{f\}, \{f, s, c\},$$

then she has available eight strategies, among which are "choose $\{c, s\}$ and then

c," "choose $\{c, s\}$ and then s," and "choose $\{f\}$ and then f."[1] Let me temporarily number these as strategies 1, 2, and 3, respectively.

Each strategy gives an outcome. For instance, strategy 1 gives the outcome c, while strategy 3 gives the outcome f. And strategies are ranked according to the outcomes they engender. So from the utility function u on outcomes, we conclude that strategy 1 provides utility 1 (since it provides outcome c and $u(c) = 1$), while strategy 3 provides utility 2.

The optimal strategies are those that give the best outcome, measured in terms of preference or utility. In this case, there are three optimal strategies, namely, "choose $\{c, f\}$ and then f," "choose $\{f\}$ and then f," and "choose $\{f, s, c\}$ and then f." There is nothing mysterious here: A meal of fish is the best outcome, so the optimal strategies are precisely those that give this outcome (assuming that some strategy in the feasible set provides this outcome).

The standard model of dynamic choice, in this context, has the decision maker evaluating each available menu to find one that provides her the best meal according to her preferences; then she implements the (or, an) optimal strategy as time unfolds. If our interest was only in her static choice of a menu, the model begins the same way: Evaluate the menus to find one that gives the best meal, then (at the initial decision point) pick any menu that qualifies.

Example 2: Consumption-savings

A somewhat less trivial example concerns a decision maker who possesses \$1000 in wealth at time $t = 0$ and who must decide, at dates $t = 0, 1, 2, \ldots$, how much of her wealth to consume and how much to set aside in savings for future consumption. To keep the story relatively simple, we assume money not saved is directly consumed (that is, the decision maker "eats" money). Let w_t denote her wealth at time t (before she decides on time t consumption) and c_t, the amount she chooses to consume, so her savings exiting this time period are $w_t - c_t$. Given this savings decision, her savings w_{t+1} at time $t + 1$ are determined by a random process in which $w_{t+1} = 1.05w_t$ or $w_{t+1} = 1.12w_t$, each with probability $1/2$ and independent of past rates of return on her savings. (That is, she earns either 5% or 12% on her savings, determined by a coin flip.) At time t, when she is choosing c_t, she knows w_t but she doesn't know anything about future returns except the

[1] Readers with some training in game theory and/or in the methods of dynamic programming may wonder about the way the term "strategy" is interpreted here. A complete strategy for an extensive-form game or in a dynamic-programming analysis specifies how the decision maker will act in every situation in which she might conceivably be called upon to act, including situations that she herself might preclude by earlier actions she takes. In the current context, then, one complete strategy would be "choose $\{c, s\}$; if $\{c, s\}$ was chosen in the first stage, choose c; if $\{c, f\}$ was chosen in the first stage, choose f; if $\{f\}$ was chosen in the first stage, choose f; if $\{f, s, c\}$ was chosen in the first stage, choose s." That is, a complete strategy would specify the second-stage choice for all available menus, and not simply for the menu that is chosen in the first stage. Indeed, if you read Appendix 6, concerning the methods of dynamic programming, you will learn that those methods *require* this interpretation of a strategy to work. And, if we take this interpretation, then a decision maker with a first-stage choice from the four strategies given would have 48 strategies available instead of 8. For current purposes of somewhat informal discussion, either interpretation of the term "strategy" is fine, and I'll work with the one given in the body of the text, since it economizes on exposition.

probabilistic law just given; she does know her past consumption decisions, of course, and past rates of return.

An outcome for this decision maker is the sequence of her consumption levels, $(c_0, c_1, \ldots)$. Or, more precisely, since there is uncertainty in this problem, an outcome for her is a probability distribution over the sequence $(c_0, c_1, \ldots)$. It is assumed that her preferences over random consumption sequences are represented by expected utility, where the (von Neumann–Morgenstern) utility function $U(c_0, c_1, \ldots)$ for this decision maker is

$$\sum_{t=0}^{\infty} 0.9^t c_t^{1/2}.$$

That is, the decision maker makes consumption-savings decisions in whatever manner maximizes the expectation of this utility function.

A strategy in this example is a plan that says how much to consume and how much to save out of w_0 at time 0, how much to consume and how much to save at time 1, contingent on her time 0 decision and the return she got on her savings between times 0 and 1, and so on, for all t. Constraints are imposed: Consumption cannot be less than zero in any period, and (we assume) c_t must be no larger than w_t; the decision maker cannot borrow; she can only save. So, for instance, one strategy is to consume \$300 each period unless and until w_t falls below \$300; if and when it does (and, in fact, it is sure to do so, since savings grow by at most \$120 per period), consume 10% of current wealth until it falls to \$1 or less, if it ever does so; at which point consume all that is left immediately.[2]

Every strategy engenders a probability distribution on $(c_0, c_1, \ldots)$, which (in the standard approach) determines the quality of the strategy: strategies are evaluated according to the expected utility of the consumption sequence they engender. An optimal strategy is one that makes this expected utility as large as possible; our decision maker, per the standard approach to dynamic choice, follows the dictates of an optimal strategy (or *the* optimal strategy, if there is only one). Given the vast multitude of strategies, you might wonder if we could ever solve this problem. But we can: It turns out that, in this case, the optimal strategy is to set $c_0 = \$121.38$ (approximately) and, in later time periods, to set $c_t = 0.12138 w_t$ (again, approximately), whatever is w_t. That is, it is optimal to consume around 12.138% of one's wealth and save 87.862%, regardless of the value of w_t and regardless of how w_t got to be that level. (I'll explain the source of this particular rabbit-from-the-hat answer in a bit.)

These are but two examples; if you want to see some others, Appendix 6 provides a selection. They illustrate the standard approach to modeling dynamic

[2] This is a fairly complex strategy. Note, in particular, that c_t in this strategy is not simply a function of current wealth w_t: If w_t ever falls to, say, \$299, then the strategy calls for consuming \$29.90, and then there is probability 1/2 that, next period, w_{t+1} will exceed \$300. But the strategy, in this case, says to set $c_{t+1} = 0.1 w_{t+1}$, even though $w_{t+1} > 300$. I point this out to emphasize that there are a lot of strategies in this problem, and the decision maker is optimizing over *all* of them.

choice, which is to reformulate the problem as being a static or atemporal choice of an optimal strategy:

- The model specifies a space of outcomes of interest to the decision maker, as well as her preferences (typically represented by a utility function) over outcomes. As the consumption-savings example indicates, the term *outcome* here should be read broadly: outcomes are very typically probability distributions over some set of "prizes," with preferences that are (then) often of the expected-utility variety.
- The model also specifies the details of the decision maker's dynamic decision problem: when decisions/choices are called for; what options are available; and what information is available on which basis the decisions can be made. From these items, the full range of dynamic strategies available to the decision maker is constructed.
- The model describes the connection between strategies and outcomes: what outcome will be engendered by each strategy.
- The decision maker evaluates each strategy according to her preferences over the outcomes, and she identifies strategies that provide the best outcomes, where "best" reflects her preferences over outcomes. She then proceeds to implement (one of) the optimal strategy(ies).

Three implicit assumptions in this approach deserve to be made explicit.

1. The decision maker has (and acts on) fixed, atemporal preferences over outcomes. She will not change her mind about what she wants.
2. From the outset, the decision maker has full "strategic awareness" of what options she has and will have and how her decisions will translate into outcomes. All this is allowed to be dependent on the resolution of uncertain events. But unforeseen contingencies, previously unappreciated options, and the general law of unintended consequences are not (relevant) parts of her vocabulary and, in particular, she makes no allowance today for any such possibilities affecting her in the future.
3. She has the cognitive and computational abilities required to evaluate all the strategies she has available or, at least, to find one that is optimal.

7.2. Dynamic Programming

The third of these assumptions speaks to the proverbial rabbit I pulled out of a hat in the second example, when I announced that the optimal strategy in the consumption-savings problem is to consume 12.138% of one's wealth in each period. A lot of strategies are possible in the second example, and connecting them to the probability distributions over consumption sequences, evaluating the expected utility of each, and then finding the strategy that maximizes expected utility, would seem quite a chore. Happily, mathematical techniques can be employed that identify the optimal strategies for problems such as this one, techniques that fall under the general rubric of *dynamic programming*. Appendix 6 provides a primer on those techniques and, in particular, provides the solution of the consumption-savings problem as an example.

It is perhaps worth noting that these techniques identify optimal strategies, they don't find the value of all alternatives. I have no idea what expected utility is generated by the complex strategy (Start with c_0 = \$300 and then ...), but dynamic programming tells me that (a) the "spend 12.138...% of your wealth" strategy generates an expected utility of around 70.448 (if you start with \$1000) and (b) no alternative strategy does better than this.

You are invited to learn the techniques from the appendix if you don't already know them, but with two strong warnings: First, the appendix is around 50 pages long. And, second, even at 50 pages, it only provides techniques useful for solving a limited number of problems. It is true that the overlap between the problems that can be addressed with the techniques in the appendix and those tackled in the literature is substantial. But this is mostly because problems in the literature are there at least in part because they are simple enough to be solved. (I'll return to this point later.)

7.3. Testable Restrictions of the Standard Model

Since I keep referring to the standard model and the standard approach, I must have in mind alternatives. Since I went out of my way to highlight the three implicit assumptions listed above, my alternatives presumably involve violations of those assumptions.

To be precise about alternatives, begin with the question: What sort of observed behavior can we say is *inconsistent* with the standard model? Tackle this question in the context of the first sort of problem: A decision maker chooses an object from a finite set X in two stages. First, she chooses a subset of X; then she chooses an x from the subset chosen in the first stage. As before, Z is the set of all nonempty subsets of X.

By the standard model in this context, we mean: There are complete and transitive preferences $\succeq$ on X, such that at the first stage, the decision maker (weakly) prefers one menu z to another z' if and only if the $\succeq$-best meal in z is preferred to the $\succeq$-best meal in z'. Equivalently, for some function $u : X \to R$, the menu z is (weakly) preferred to z' if and only if $\max_{x \in z} u(x) \geq \max_{x \in z'} u(x)$. And, in the second stage, the decision maker chooses from z some meal that maximizes u over z.

The precise question we will answer is, Given the decision maker's choice behavior concerning menus, when is that choice behavior consistent with the standard model? As the previous paragraph makes clear, if stage-one choice is consistent with the standard model, it (to begin with) satisfies all the usual general rules of "rational" choice; that is, choice of a menu satisfies (finite) nonemptiness and choice coherence and (equivalently) can be rationalized by a complete and transitive binary relation on Z. We know this because first-stage choice corresponds to maximization of a real-valued function, namely $U : Z \to R$ defined by $U(z) = \max_{x \in z} u(x)$. In view of this, the proposition that answers this question will assume from the outset that first-stage choice behavior conforms to a complete and transitive relation $\dot{\succeq}$ on Z. We let $\dot{\succ}$ denote the corresponding strict preference relation and $\dot{\sim}$ the corresponding indifference relation.

Proposition 7.1. *Suppose first-stage choice conforms to a complete and transitive relation $\dot{\succeq}$ on Z. Then it conforms to the standard model of dynamic choice (as defined above, in this specific context) if and only if it satisfies the further condition that, for all z and z', if $z \dot{\succeq} z'$, then $z \dot{\sim} z \cup z'$.*

Proof. If first-stage choice of a menu conforms to the standard model, then it conforms to maximization of a function $U : Z \to R$ that, in turn, is given by $U(z) = \max_{x \in z} u(x)$ for some $u : X \to R$. But for any such U, $z \dot{\succeq} z'$ implies $U(z) \geq U(z')$ implies $\max_{x \in z} u(x) \geq \max_{x \in z'} u(x)$ implies $\max_{x \in z} u(x) = \max_{x \in z \cup z'} u(x)$, which is $U(z) = U(z \cup z')$, which is $z \dot{\sim} z \cup z'$.

Conversely, suppose first-stage choice of a menu conforms to preference maximization for a complete and transitive preference relation $\dot{\succeq}$ that has the further property: $z \dot{\succeq} z'$ implies $z \dot{\sim} z \cup z'$. Since Z is finite, $\dot{\succeq}$ has a numerical representation $U : Z \to R$; fix one such. For $x \in X$, define $u : X \to R$ by $u(x) = U(\{x\})$. I assert that $U(z) = \max_{x \in z} u(x)$ for this u; this is proved by induction on the size of z: It is true by definition for singleton sets z, so suppose inductively that it is true for sets of size $n - 1$ or less. Let z be any set of size $n > 1$. Let x^0 be any element of z, and let $z' = z \setminus \{x^0\}$. By the induction hypothesis, $U(z') = \max_{x \in z'} u(x)$. Consider two cases: $u(x^0) < U(z')$, and $u(x^0) \geq U(z')$.

In the first case $z' \dot{\succ} \{x^0\}$, so by the extra property, $z' \cup \{x^0\} = z \dot{\sim} z'$; hence $U(z) = U(z')$. But also in this case, $\max_{x \in z} u(x) = \max\{u(x^0), \max_{x \in z'} u(x)\} = \max_{x \in z'} u(x) = U(z')$, and hence $\max_{x \in z} u(x) = U(z)$.

And in the second case, $U(\{x^0\}) = u(x^0) \geq U(z')$, which implies $\{x^0\} \dot{\succeq} z'$; hence (by the extra property) $\{x^0\} \dot{\sim} \{x^0\} \cup z' = z$, and hence $u(x^0) = U(z)$. But also in this case $u(x^0) \geq U(z') = \max_{x \in z'} u(x)$, and therefore $u(x^0) = \max_{x \in z} u(x)$. Hence $U(z) = \max_{x \in z} u(x)$.

In either case, $U(z) = \max_{x \in z} u(x)$, establishing the induction step and the truth of this equality for all $z \in Z$. Which means that first-stage choice conforms to the standard model. ∎

The symbols may make a very simple idea seem complex. In the standard model of dynamic choice (in this context), a menu is as good as the best meal it contains, where "best" is in terms of the decision maker's atemporal preferences over outcomes. But then one menu is at least as good as a second if and only if the best meal in the first is at least as good as the best meal in the second, in which case one of the best meals in the union of the two menus is the best meal in the first, and the first menu is just as good as the union. This is the argument for why the extra property $z \dot{\succeq} z'$ *implies* $z \dot{\sim} z \cup z'$ is necessary for the standard model to hold; the argument that this extra property is also sufficient just turns this argument on its head.

Two comments are in order about the title given this section, "Testable Restrictions of the Standard Model."

First, we have both "the standard model of dynamic choice" and "the standard model of static choice (of a menu) in a dynamic context." The proposition is clearly about the latter object. It characterizes (only) the decision maker's first-stage choice of a menu, albeit bearing in mind that her choice of a menu is only the first stage in a two-stage choice process. We could instead speak of her first- and second-stage choice behavior, wondering whether they together conform to the standard model. But, in this simple context, if you know her first-stage preferences $\dot{\succeq}$ over menus, then you know what, according to the standard model, she must do in the second stage: In the standard model, her first-stage preferences among singleton-set menus $\{x\}$ tell you what preferences govern her second-stage choices.

Second, the "testable restrictions" part of the section title sounds like: We have empirical data about choices the decision maker has made. But the proposition imposes its test on something decidely more ephemeral, namely all of $\dot{\succeq}$. We've run into this issue previously, specifically, in Problem 1.16 and then in Chapter 4: Observing some choices actually made is not much grist for any empirical test of theories of choice that permit everything to be indifferent to everything else (in which case, any pattern of choice is consistent with the theory). One needs some data about strict preferences. Back in Problem 1.16 and Chapter 4, the emphasis was in seeing some (but not all) expressions of strict preference; here, in constrast, we have all the data about preferences, but in a context where the objects chosen are sets, and it is the set structure that gives us the needed grist.

As an alternative where we work with fewer but richer data, imagine embedding this two-stage choice problem into one slightly larger. Imagine that the individual is choosing pairs of the form: a menu z from which a later meal will be selected and an immediate, one-dimensional reward r for which more is unambiguously better. If we see an individual choose the menu z and immediate reward r when z' and r are available, but we also see her choose $z \cup z'$ together with $r - \epsilon$ for any positive ϵ when (z, r) is available, then we know that the standard model has a problem.[3] Under the standard model, the first choice tells us that a choice out of z, together with r, is at least as good as a choice out of z'. Why, then, is she willing to give up the valuable ϵ to maintain the flexibility provided to her by $z \cup z'$?

Or, with the same embedding, suppose that we look at two menus, z and z', where $z' \subseteq z$ but $z \neq z'$; that is, z' is a strict subset of z. Under the standard model,

[3] How can we also see this other choice? As in Problem 1.16 and in Chapter 4, the story, such as it is, is that we face the decision maker with a selection of hypothetical choices—"What would you choose if your feasible alternatives were ...? What if they were ...?"—and we look for consistency in these hypothetical choices.

there is no conceivable reason for her to choose z' and $r - \epsilon$ over z and r, for any positive ϵ. There is no reason, in other words, for her to devote valuable resources in order to restrict her own (subsequent) choice set.[4] This is a fairly general characteristic of the standard model of dynamic choice, one that transcends this simple context: The standard model presumes (pretty explicitly) that the decision maker has unchanging, atemporal preferences over outcomes, and she chooses strategies according to those preferences. Why, then, would she have (or exhibit) a strict preference for constraining her own choices?

7.4. Three Alternatives to the Standard Model

The possibilities raised in the previous two paragraphs lead to alternatives to the standard model that have been explored in the literature.

Changing tastes and self-control

Return to the very specific example where f is a meal of fish, c is chicken, and s is steak. Consider the first-stage preferences

$$\{f\} \dot{\sim} \{f, c\} \dot{\succ} \{c\} \dot{\succ} \{f, c, s\} \dot{\sim} \{f, s\} \dot{\sim} \{c, s\} \dot{\sim} \{s\}.$$

(Throughout this section, first-stage choice of menus will always be consistent with complete and transitive preferences, so you can use the standard transitivity rules to fill out the preference relation.) The decision maker with these first-stage preferences explains:

> I have a problem with my cholesterol levels and so should avoid steak. I know this, but I also know that if and when I get to the restaurant, if steak is on the menu, the temptation will be too much for me. Fish is best for me, and I can resist the temptation to have chicken instead of fish, if both are on the menu. But I'll give in to steak if it is there, so...

This individual's self-control issues can be thought of as a matter of an anticipated change in her tastes. At the moment she is choosing a menu, her preferences over meals (given, essentially, by her preferences over singleton menus) is $f \succ_0 c \succ_0 s$. But when she gets to the restaurant, her choices (if her initial choice of menu has left herself with any choice) reveal a different set of tastes: $s \succ_1 f \succ_1 c$. *Anticipating this*, at the first stage, she chooses menus in a way that serves her $t = 0$ tastes by constraining her later options: $\{f\}$ and $\{f, c\}$ are the best menus, because they will result in fish, followed by $\{c\}$ which will lead to chicken, followed by the four menus that have steak, since she anticipates that her later self will choose steak, and steak is the worst choice for her (in terms of her $t = 0$ tastes).

[4] With reference to the previous footnote, note that this is an inconsistency that we could see with a single choice. A dynamic decision maker who conforms to the standard model never expends valuable resources to constrain her later options. But see the next footnote for an important caveat to this statement.

This rationalization has three parts: (1) The decision maker's tastes will change between the times when she chooses a menu and when she chooses a meal. (2) She anticipates the change. (3) When she chooses a menu, she acts in a way that favors her current tastes among meals. First-stage preferences would be different if she didn't anticipate the change in her tastes, or if she anticipated those changes, but decided that her second-stage preferences should govern; if either of those were true, she wouldn't be in the business of constraining her own later choices.

In the economics literature, the idea that tastes may change in an anticipated manner and so, to favor current tastes, an individual may constrain her own later choices, goes back to original work by Strotz (1955-6). But the idea goes back much further than that; it is classic in the full sense of the word: In the *Odyssey*, Odysseus, wanting to hear the song of the Sirens but wanting not to throw himself onto the rocks, has his crew bind him to the mast, while they plug their own ears.

Note that there is more here than a realization that having chicken for lunch affects the desirability of chicken for dinner, or that drinking single-malt whisky today positively affects one's taste for single-malt whisky in the future. Those effects can be accommodated in models where tastes for consumption tomorrow are not separable (in the sense of Chapter 2) from what is consumed today but where one's preferences over consumption bundles through time are unchanging. If preferences for lifetime consumption bundles are unchanging, the decision maker never has an active preference for constraining her later self.[5]

Along the same lines, imagine the following first-stage preferences:

$$\{f\} \dot{\sim} \{f,c\} \dot{\succ} \{c\} \dot{\succ} \{f,c,s\} \dot{\sim} \{f,s\} \dot{\succ} \{c,s\} \dot{\succ} \{s\}.$$

The story behind these preferences begins the same way: This decision maker has problems with her cholesterol and should avoid steak for dinner. This decision maker also has self-control issues, but she is stronger willed than the previous individual; she will be able to order fish from $\{f, c, s\}$ and from $\{f, s\}$ and to order chicken from $\{c, s\}$. But the effort of resisting the lure of a steak dinner is costly to her, and she'd rather not have the temptation, so (for instance) $\{f, c\} \dot{\succ} \{f, c, s\}$.

In the first story, a characteristic of $\dot{\succ}$ is that, for all z and z' such that (without loss of generality), $z \dot{\succeq} z'$, either $z \cup z' \dot{\sim} z$ or $z \cup z' \dot{\sim} z'$. To explain, some x will be chosen from z in the second stage, and some x' from z'; $z \dot{\succeq} z'$ follows if $\{x\} \dot{\succeq} \{x'\}$; that is, if the first-stage preferences prefer the second-stage choice out of z. Assume

[5] This is true absent concerns of a wholely different sort: An individual with unchanging, atemporal tastes may choose to limit the actions she can take at a later date because of the impact this will have on the actions of others. Army generals from the ancient world are often described as taking actions—burning bridges behind themselves, placing their army with its rear to a river—that make retreat impossible. They do this both to imbue their own troops with a desire to fight, even if they are losing, since no retreat cuts off other options. And they do this to encourage their opponents not to press on: An army that cannot retreat is more likely to fight to the death. The conclusion that a decision maker will never strictly prefer to leave herself fewer options if her tastes are unchanging is correct in a single-person decision context; but not in general. When you see a decision maker taking actions that limit her later choices, you have to ask: Is she doing this because of the impact it will have on the actions of others, or because she fears what her own later self might do, given the opportunities she is eliminating?

this is so. When looking at $z \cup z'$, and assuming away for simplicity the issue of ties in second-stage preferences, the question is, Will the second-stage preferences result in x being chosen—in which case $z \cup z' \dot{\sim} z$—or will x' be chosen, resulting in $z \cup z' \dot{\sim} z'$? One of the two must hold, and therefore we have the stated property. (See Problem 7.3.) In the second story, where self-control may be possible but is psychologically wearing, we might have $z \dot{\succ} z'$ and $z \dot{\succ} z \cup z' \dot{\succ} z'$; a menu that is the union of z and z' might result in the preferred (in terms of stage-one preferences) meal, but at a pyschological cost from the effort at self-control.

And, in fact, these sorts of properties for $\dot{\succeq}$ can be shown to characterize, in the first case, a simple model of changing tastes (where the psychological costs of exercising self-control do not enter, because second-stage urges cannot be controlled), and in the second case, a more complex model with self-control costs. The theory is developed in Gul and Pesendorfer (2001).

Unforeseen contingencies and preference for flexibility

Now imagine a decision maker who, at the first stage, expresses the following preferences over menus:

$$\{c, s, f\} \dot{\sim} \{s, f\} \dot{\succ} \{f, c\} \dot{\sim} \{f\} \dot{\succ} \{s, c\} \dot{\sim} \{s\} \dot{\succ} \{c\}.$$

Since $\{f, c\} \dot{\succ} \{s\}$ and yet $\{s, f, c\} \dot{\succ} \{f, c\}$, this doesn't follow the standard model. Asked to explain, this decision maker tells the following tale:

> I am pretty sure that I would like to have fish for dinner, in preference to steak or chicken. In fact, I can't foresee any specific circumstance in which this wouldn't be so. But, in my life, I've sometimes met up with contingencies that I didn't foresee, and I suppose there is a chance that I might wind up preferring steak. Hence I hedge, with a slight preference for $\{c, s, f\}$ over $\{f, c\}$ (and, for that matter, over $\{f\}$). I reiterate, I don't foresee any specific reason that this might happen and, in consequence, these strict preferences are very slight. But however slight, they are there. And, since you are wondering why this same consideration doesn't have me rank $\{c, s, f\}$ over $\{s, f\}$ or $\{f, c\}$ over $\{f\}$, the answer is that I absolutely hate chicken, and I simply refuse to acknowledge even the slightest possibility of an unforeseen contingency in which chicken beats out fish.

The last part of this rationalization seems to me questionable: This decision maker appreciates the possibility, however slight, of one sort of unforeseen contingency but not another. But they are her preferences, and I want to focus on the first part. In the standard model, one implicit assumption was that the decision maker had full strategic awareness of the situation, which is a dubious assumption to make of anyone.[6] Recognizing that this may not be so, the decision maker just described is prepared to sacrifice (at least) a bit of resources to maintain her flexibility of choice.

---

[6] It is obvious, I hope, that the discussion of the last section is directed at the first implict assumption of fixed atemporal preferences.

This suggests that, as a general rule, preferences in the first stage ought to satisfy $z \dot{\succeq} z'$ if $z' \subseteq z$, which is implied by but a good deal weaker than the property developed in Proposition 7.1 that is observationally equivalent to the standard model. Consider, in this regard, the following:

$$z' \subseteq z \text{ and } z' \dot{\sim} z \quad \text{implies} \quad z' \cup z'' \dot{\sim} z \cup z'' \text{ for all } z'' \in Z.$$

In words, suppose z' is a subset of z but $z' \dot{\sim} z$. Then the extra flexibility afforded the decision maker in z instead of z' is deemed to be of no value whatseover. If this is so, then (presumably) the extra flexibility of $z \cup z''$ over $z' \cup z''$ is of no value—either something in z'' will be selected (and is available in either case), or we are back to the z versus z' comparison.

If a decision maker, in her first-stage preferences, exhibits general preference for flexibility but tempered by the property just displayed, her first-stage preferences over menus can be given a very simple representation that *suggests* a decision maker who admits the possibility of contingencies that are unforeseen and makes some allowance for them; that is, there are in the representation both exogenously given states of nature, representing contingencies that are foreseen, and also states of nature that arise endogneously (that are constructed from the individual's preferences) to explain the preference for flexibility. See Kreps (1979a, 1992).

Complexity and heuristics

Although the menus-and-meals problem is quite simple to solve according to the standard method of dynamic choice, most dynamic choice problems are complex. To solve the second example that is given, the consumption-savings problem, requires techniques that most first-year graduate students in economics will be seeing for the first time. And this problem is solvable because of some specific features in the formulation: The problem is stationary (Appendix 6 explains what this means); the distribution of returns in each period is known to the decision maker and independent of past returns; the utility function over consumption streams is additively separable, with a per-period utility function that takes a particularly convenient functional form. If any one of these assumptions is relaxed, the problem will probably become intractable.

In Chapter 1 it says, "Just because consumers don't actively maximize utility doesn't mean that the model of utility-maximizing choice is a bad descriptive or positive model. To suppose that individuals act *as if* they maximize utility is not the same as supposing that they consciously do so." In the current context, the argument would be: *Even if* dynamic decision problems are so complex that economists specially trained to solve them can do so only if a lot of simplifying assumptions are made, real-life dynamic decisions, made through guesswork and heuristics, come close to the decisions that would be made by ideal dynamic decision makers who followed the standard dynamic approach. Modeling with the standard approach may be an unattainable idealization, but it provides a good positive model of the somewhat messier reality.

That is an interesting assertion, but if it is to be taken seriously, either theoretical or empirical justification for it ought to be pursued. It isn't hard to model the sorts of heuristics that are employed in the face of complexity—at one end of the scale are simple psychological models of satisficing and goal setting; at the other end in terms of sophistication are the modeling and econometric/fitting techniques that economists themselves employ when trying to find optimal economic policies—and it should be possible to categorize environments in which a particular heuristic works well or not. In fact, work along these lines has been done: In the 1980s, a number of studies were made of how (well) decision makers would learn through time the relationship between equilibrium and prices, if that relationship co-evolved with what the decision makers were learning; in the 1990s, a modest literature was created about learning in the context of repeated play of games. Rust (1987) provides a marvelous empirical study (albeit very specific) of whether a real decision maker, through intuition or heuristics or whatever, approaches the optimal solution of a complex dynamic decision problem. But much more work of this sort should be done before we accept the assertion or, what is more likely to be the outcome, before we understand when the assertion is reasonable and when it is not.

And the complexities of dynamic decision problems raise another possibility. So far, in proposing alternatives to the standard model, we've looked at alternatives where, at least, choice at any single point in time (that is, static choice within a dynamic context) follows the rules of Chapter 1: Some large set of conceivable objects (menus, consumption levels) is given, and choice from a feasible subset of the larger set is according to complete and transitive preferences on the larger set. At the start of this discussion, we asked *Does the dynamic nature of the problem raise issues that push us to rethink and, perhaps, modify the basic models of choice from Chapter 1?* Do dynamics, per se, cast doubt upon the basic axioms and properties of our models of choice? At the level of choices made at a single point in time, the answer has been no.

But dynamic problems tend to be complex, and complexity could be a reason to doubt the basic choice constructs of Chapter 1. Faced with a complex decision problem, one in which there are many options and/or options whose eventual consequences are difficult to evaluate, the decision maker might resort to heurisitics or rules of thumb. When evaluating options from a large set of options, the decision maker might choose to focus on a limited set of characterisitics, where the characteristics chosen are influenced by the full set of immediately available options. This isn't a consequence of the dynamic context per se. But dynamic considerations breed complexity, and complexity breeds rules of thumb that could lead to violations of Chapter 1 principles.

A temporary bottom line

The economic importance of dynamic decisions and of static decisions made within a dynamic context cannot be questioned. If the models of choice that were developed in earlier chapters cannot be adapted to dynamic contexts, then they aren't of much use in exploring important economic issues. Economists have, for the most part, taken the models of Chapters 1, 2, 5, and 6, all of which are developed as static models of (once-and-for-all) choice, and adapted them to dynamic contexts through the standard method of regarding dynamic choice as being the static choice of an optimal dynamic strategy.

If you accept this, then what remains to do concerning dynamic choice is to learn how to solve the relatively complex optimization problems that arise in dynamic choice contexts. Or, what is in fact more accurate, one must jointly learn how to formulate problems that are sufficiently simple to be solved and then solve them. This is the purpose of Appendix 6.

But, especially in light of the importance of decisions made in dynamic contexts, it is important to understand the behavioral assumptions and limitations of this standard method and to study both the robustness of the standard method and alternatives to it. With the rise of behavioral economics, this has been an increasingly important part of economic theory. But a lot of work along these lines remains to be done.

Bibliographic Notes

Finding a precise statement of the standard strategic approach to dynamic choice in the literature is, I believe, impossible. It seems to have the status of folk wisdom; it has always been the way to do things. Methods for solving reasonably complex problems with this approach, methods of dynamic programming, were developed by a variety of authors in the 1950s and 1960s; important names in this development are Richard Bellman for the fundamental ideas and David Blackwell and Ralph Strauch for more formal developments. Textbook references are provided in Appendix 6.

The changing-tastes alternative entered the economics literature in R. Strotz (1955–6). Schelling (2006, Chapter 1) provides a fascinating discussion. Gul and Pesendorfer (2001) is the essential reference in the formal aspects of this line of research, which has been fairly active recently. (See also Gul and Pesendorfer, 2005.) "Preference for flexibility" and an interpretation of this as a manifestation of unforeseen contingencies is provided in Kreps (1979a, 1992). This is also a somewhat active topic. Models of heuristics employed in complex dynamic choice situations have tended to concern very specific contexts, such as rational expectations equilibria or learning in games: Sargent (1999) provides a wonderful application of these ideas to macroeconomic policy; Fudenberg and Levine (1998) summarizes and extends much of the literature related to game theory.

Problems

Appendix 6 gives a number of problems to be solved with the methods of dynamic programming (and works through many of them); you should certainly read through the solution of those for which solutions are provided (such as the consumption-savings example given in this chapter) and provide solutions for the rest. The problems provided here concern some of the alternatives to the standard approach to dynamic choice discussed in the chapter. As such, they constitute a further digression from the basic trajectory in this book and can be skipped without compromising your understanding of the rest of the text. For this reason, the first three of these problems are solved in the *Student's Guide,* and I provide a reference where you can find the solution to the last problem.

■ *7.1. Imagine a decision maker who must decide how much asparagus and how much broccoli to eat in each of two time periods, $t = 1$ and $t = 2$. Let a_t be the amount of asparagus consumed in period t, and b_t the amount of broccoli consumed in period t. Suppose the price of broccoli and asparagus are both a constant $1 (in both periods), and the decision maker has a total of $100 to spend on these four commodities.

(a) At time $t = 1$, the decision maker's preferences are given by the utility function

$$u(a_1, a_2, b_1, b_2) = \ln(a_1) + \ln(a_2) + \ln(b_1) + \ln(b_2).$$

If the decision maker is able to choose at time $t = 1$ (according to these preferences) how much of each vegetable to consume, what will she choose?

(b) Suppose instead that the decision maker chooses, at $t = 1$, the amounts of a_1 and b_1 to consume, and also the amount s_1 of savings to set aside for period 2 vegetable purchases. Then at time $t = 2$, she decides how to spend the s_1 she saved on a_2 and how much to spend on b_2. To be very clear, at time $t = 1$ she is choosing a_1, b_1, and s_1 subject to the budget constraint $a_1 + b_1 + s_1 \leq 100$, and at time $t = 2$ she is choosing a_2 and b_2 subject to the budget constraint $a_2 + b_2 \leq s_1$. (Her savings earn no interest. To keep matters simple, assume that all variables including s_1 are constrained to be nonnegative.) Assuming that her preferences are unchanging and the standard methods for dealing with dynamic choice problems are employed, what does she choose to do?

(c) Now suppose that asparagus is something of an acquired taste. What this means is that the utility she derives from consuming asparagus at time $t = 2$ increases with the amount of asparagus she consumes at time $t = 1$; her utility function is

$$u(a_1, a_2, b_1, b_2) = \ln(a_1) + (1 + a_1/25)\ln(a_2) + \ln(b_1) + \ln(b_2).$$

If she made all her vegetable purchases (to maximize this utility function) at the outset, what would she choose to do? If she made her vegetable purchases in two steps, as in part b, but with the objective of maximizing this utility function, what would she do? (You probably will need to solve this problem numerically rather than analytically.)

In parts d and e, we enter into the world of changing tastes. Specifically, at time $t = 1$, the decision maker's preferences over the outcome (a_1, a_2, b_1, b_2) are given by the utility function u from part a of the problem. But, if she has choices to make at time $t = 2$, she will act in a fashion to maximize

$$u_2(a_2, b_2; a_1) = (1 + a_1/25)\ln(a_2) + \ln(b_2).$$

Note that in posing her time $t = 2$ preferences in this fashion, we are implicitly assuming that a_1 and b_1 are already fixed and determined; any remaining choices concern a_2 and b_2 only. But the level of a_1 enters her preferences parametrically, affecting how much utility she gets from time 2 consumption of asparagus. In this case, rather than saying that asparagus is an acquired taste, we might describe what is going on by saying that asparagus is *addictive*, in that her tastes for a_2 (relative to the other goods) changes based on her experiences with a_1.

(d) Suppose that our decision maker chooses in the fashion of part b—at time 1, she chooses a_1, b_1, and s_1—but she does not anticipate at $t = 1$ that her tastes will change at time 2 in the fashion described. Instead, her choices at $t = 1$ are made under the mistaken belief that her tastes at time 2 will stay what they are at time $t = 1$. (In the literature of changing tastes, this is what is known as *naive* choice.) What happens?

(e) And suppose that our decision maker chooses in the fashion of part b, but she is aware of how addictive is asparagus: She anticipates at time $t = 1$ that, at time $t = 2$, she will seek to maximize u_2, and she chooses at time $t = 1$ to maximize her time $t = 1$ overall preferences with that anticipation. (In the literature of changing tastes, this is known as *sophisticated* choice.) What happens?

■ *7.2. Much of the recent literature connected to "changing tastes" concerns so-called hyperbolic discounting. This concerns problems in the intertemporal allocation of resources or, in simple form, consumption-savings problems. The idea is that if you ask someone, "Would you rather have $1 today or $1.20 tomorrow?" she wants the $1 today, but if the question is, "Would you rather have $1 tomorrow or $1.20 the day after?" the $1.20 is chosen. And, the point of this, this is true tomorrow as well, meaning: Tomorrow, $1 today is preferred to $1.20 tomorrow. In other words, people tend to discount the future, with the greatest discount applied between today and next period, and this remains true when next period comes around.

If this isn't clear, here's a problem: A decision maker has $100 to split between consumption today ($t = 0$), tomorrow ($t = 1$), and the day after ($t = 2$). Today, if c_t is the level of (dollar) consumption on date t, the decision maker's utility function is

$$u(c_0, c_1, c_2) = v(c_0) + 0.5v(c_1) + 0.4v(c_2),$$

for some strictly concave function v.

(a) Being very concrete, suppose $v(c) = c^{1/2}$ and suppose that the budget constraint facing the individual is $c_0 + c_1 + c_2 \leq 100$. (This budget constraint reflects no interest paid on savings. That is, \$1 saved today returns the same \$1 tomorrow, etc.) Assuming the decision maker can fix c_0, c_1, and c_2 today, subject to this budget constraint, what consumption plan maximizes her utility?

The decision maker cannot fix c_1 and c_2 today; at $t = 0$, she divides her \$100 between immediate consumption c_0 and savings s_0. If she saves s_0, when tomorrow rolls around, she has s_0 to divide between c_1 and s_1, and then she consumes $c_2 = s_1$ the day after tomorrow (at $t = 2$). If her relative tastes for consumption trade-offs between periods 1 and 2 don't change—if at $t = 1$ she chooses c_1 and s_1 to maximize $c_1^{1/2} + 0.8c_2^{1/2}$, her solution in the dynamic choice problem will give her the outcome you computed in part a of the problem. (You can take my word for this.) But, in the story of hyperbolic discounting, at date $t = 1$, she will choose c_1 and s_1 to maximize $c_1^{1/2} + 0.5c_2^{1/2}$.

(b) Given that this is so, if she acts naively about her changing intertemporal tastes (see part d of the first problem), what is the outcome?

(c) And if she acts in sophisticated fashion about her changing tastes (see part e of the first problem), what happens?

■ *7.3. Suppose X is a finite set and Z is the set of all nonempty subsets of X. Suppose that $\dot{\succeq}$ is a complete and transitive binary relation on Z that, in addition, satisfies the property that

$$\text{for all } z \text{ and } z',\ z \cup z' \dot{\sim} z \text{ or } z \cup z' \dot{\sim} z'.$$

We claimed in the text that this property characterized preferences over menus (members of Z) that can be explained by a changing-tastes model. This can be difficult to show in general, so to make it easy, assume as well that $\dot{\succeq}$, restricted to singleton sets, is anti-symmetric:

$$\text{for all } x, x' \in X,\ \text{if } \{x\} \dot{\succeq} \{x'\} \dot{\succeq} \{x\},\ \text{then } x = x'.$$

(In words, this means that the decision maker, if able to commit to a meal, is not indifferent between any pair of distinct meals.) Suppose that $\dot{\succeq}$ has these properties. Define $\succeq_1$ and $\succeq_2$ on X by

$$x \succeq_1 x' \text{ if } \{x\} \dot{\succeq} \{x'\},\ \text{and } x \succeq_2 x' \text{ if } \{x\} \dot{\sim} \{x, x'\}.$$

Show that both $\succeq_1$ and $\succeq_2$ are complete, transitive, and antisymmetric. Show that, by virtue of anti-symmetry, for each z there is a unique $x \in z$, such that $x \succeq_2 x'$ for all $x' \in z$; let $x_2(z)$ be this x. And then show that $z \dot{\succeq} z'$ if and only if

$x_2^*(z) \succeq_1 x_2^*(z')$. (This verifies the claim in the text, if we add the extra assumption. Gul and Pesendorfer (2005) proves the result without the extra assumption of anti-symmetry.)

■ 7.4. Suppose X is a finite set and Z is the set of all nonempty subsets of X. Suppose that $\dot{\succeq}$ is a complete and transitive binary relation on Z that, in addition, satisfies the two properties

$$z \subseteq z' \text{ implies } z' \dot{\succeq} z \quad \text{and} \quad z \subseteq z' \text{ and } z' \dot{\sim} z \text{ implies } z \cup z'' \dot{\sim} z' \cup z'' \text{ for all } z''.$$

Show that this is true if and only if there exists a finite set S and a function $U : X \times S \to R$ such that if we define $v : Z \to R^S$ by

$$(v(z))_s := \max_{x \in z} U(x, s),$$

then

$$z \dot{\succeq} z' \quad \text{if and only if} \quad u(v(z)) \geq u(v(z')) \text{ for a function } u : R^S \to R \text{ that is strictly increasing on the range of } v.$$

In words, the set S is a subjective state space, and $U(x, s)$ gives the utility of meal x is state s, so that $v(z)$ is the vector of utilities provided by picking, in each state, the meal that gives the highest utility in that state. The representation, then, is that $z \dot{\succeq} z'$ if and only if $u \circ v(z) \geq u \circ v(z')$, for a function u that is strictly increasing in the vector of state-dependent utilities. (In fact, one can show that the function u can be taken to be component-by-component addition—that is, $u(v(z)) = \sum_{s \in S} (v(z))_s = \sum_{s \in S} \max_{x \in z} U(x, s)$, but getting this additive form is something of a cheat, as explained in Kreps (1979a). You can find the proof of the proposition, both as formulated here and then in the additive form, in Kreps (1979a).)

Chapter Eight

Social Choice and Efficiency

Our concern so far has been in modeling choice by an individual. *Social choice* concerns choice made on behalf of a set of individuals.

The basic question is framed as follows: A *social state* or *outcome* x is to be chosen; X represents the set of all conceivable social states, while A often represents the subset of X of feasible states. The choice will affect a nonempty set of *individuals* or households, denoted by H. Each individual $h \in H$ has her own opinion about the various possible social states, given (for the time being) by a complete and transitive preference relation $\succeq_h$ on X. Since the choice of a social state x affects all the individuals, the choice "should" be made in a way that takes into account the preferences of the individuals. The question is, How? More specifically, suppose we want to construct a social ordering $\succeq$ on X that aggregates the preferences of the individuals. How "should" we do this?

Having put scare quotes around the word "should" twice, let me explain: This question raises the prospect of engaging in moral philosophy. As individuals typically have conflicting preferences among the social states, we presumably must look for principles that allow us to make good compromises or value judgments. Some economists are also excellent moral philosophers. But, as you'll learn in this chapter, economics, or at least mainstream economics, has by and large avoided the sort of value judgments that seem to be needed. Mainstream economics is unwilling to go beyond value judgments that seem, at least at first blush, to be utterly noncontroversial, leaving a theory of social choice that mixes negative results about strong social choice criteria with simple characterizations of the weak criteria that are left. That's the plot for this chapter.

8.1. Arrow's Theorem

Modern social choice theory begins, and in some senses ends, with a remarkable result variously known as Arrow's Possibility Theorem and Arrow's *Im*possibility Theorem. Arrow (1951a) is looking for what he calls a *social preference function.* This is a function that maps arrays of individual preferences, $(\succeq_h)_{h \in H}$, into a social preference relation $\succeq$.[1] The idea, in essence, is that, once we learn the preferences over the social states of each member h in a society H, the social preference function will tell us what preferences society should have as a function of those individual

[1] In fact, Arrow calls these objects *social welfare functions;* I use the alternative *social preference function* to prevent confusion with what later will be called a *social utility functional* and also to signal clearly that this is an object that maps arrays of preferences into social preferences.

preferences.[2]

To keep matters simple, I will assume (as does Arrow) that the set of possible social states X is finite, and the set of individuals H is finite. The symbol Φ will be used for a social preference function. The domain of a social preference function Φ consists of arrays of preferences, one for each individual $h \in H$, and the range provides preferences on X. Until further notice, we make the following assumptions about the domain and range of Φ:

Assumption 8.1. *The domain of Φ is the set of* **all** *H-tuples of preference relations $(\succeq_h)_{h \in H}$, where each $\succeq_h$ is a complete and transitive binary relation on X. The range consists of complete and transitive binary relations on X.*

Both parts of this assumption should be carefully considered. The assumption on the domain of Φ has two significant parts: First, we assume that each individual $h \in H$ has preferences over X that are standard in the sense of Chapter 1. We could, conceivably, be interested in social preferences when individuals have incomplete or intransitive preferences but, at least in this chapter, we don't consider this. Second, having assumed each individual has complete and transitive preferences, we impose no further restrictions on the *array* or *profile* or *constellation* of preferences. The social preference function must deliver a social verdict, for *every* H-tuple of complete and transitive preferences. And, the second part of the assumption, the verdict must take the form of coherent (that is, complete and transitive) preferences over all the social states so that, presumably, no matter what subset A of social states X is feasible, Φ will tell us, given the preferences of the individuals, what society prefers.[3]

In the usual fashion, if h's preferences are given by $\succeq_h$, then $\succ_h$ will denote her strict preferences and $\sim_h$ her indifference relation. When we want to compare one array of preferences with a second one, we'll use $\succeq'_h$, $\succ'_h$, and $\sim'_h$. For a given social preference function Φ, standard notational conventions would have us write $\Phi[(\succeq_h)_{h \in H}]$ for the value of the function Φ at the argument $(\succeq_h)_{h \in H}$. That is pretty clumsy, and we'll also want to be able to write down the strict preference and indifference relations generated from $\Phi[(\succeq_h)_{h \in H}]$. So, on expositional grounds, we'll denote $\Phi[(\succeq_h)_{h \in H}]$ simply by $\succeq$, with $\succ$ and $\sim$ the corresponding strict preference and indifference relations; we'll use $\succeq'$ for $\Phi[(\succeq'_h)_{h \in H}]$, and so forth. (Where confusion might result, I'll try to clarify.)

Now consider the following three properties for a social preference function Φ:

[2] You might wonder how we will get members of the society to tell us their preferences. If they know the rule by which their preferences will be mapped into a social preference relation and, thence, into some social state, mightn't they have the incentive to misrepresent how they feel? A remarkable variation of Arrow's Theorem, known as the Gibbard-Satterthwaite Theorem, takes up this question. This result properly belongs to Volume 2, and it is left for there.

[3] The first half of Assumption 8.1 is often called the *universal domain* assumption; the second half is sometimes called the *coherence* assumption (vaguely related to the terminology *choice coherence* from Chapter 1).

Definition 8.2.

a. *The social preference function Φ satisfies* ***unanimity*** *if, for any profile of individual preferences $(\succeq_h)_{h \in H}$ and any pair of social states x and y, if $x \succ_h y$ for each $h \in H$, then $x \succ y$ (where $\succ$ is the strict preference relation that goes with $\succeq = \Phi[(\succeq_h)_{h \in H}]$).*

b. *The social preference function Φ satisfies* ***independence of irrelevant alternatives (IIA)*** *if, for any two profiles of individual preferences $(\succeq_h)_{h \in H}$ and $(\succeq'_h)_{h \in H}$ and any two social states x and y such that $x \succeq_h y$ if and only if $x \succeq'_h y$ for all $h \in H$, $x \succeq y$ if and only if $x \succeq' y$.*

c. *The social preference function Φ is* ***dictatorial*** *if there is some $h^* \in H$ such that, for every profile of individual preferences $(\succeq_h)_{h \in H}$ and every pair of social states x and y, $x \succ_{h^*} y$ implies $x \succ y$.*

In words: (a) Φ satisfies unanimity if, whenever every individual strictly prefers x to y, then the social preference function has x strictly preferred to y. (b) Φ satisfies IIA if the social preference function's decision about x versus y depends *only* on how each individual feels about x versus y. (c) Φ is dictatorial if some individual's strict preferences about any two states x and y are decisive: if she strictly prefers x to y, then the social preference function says that society does as well, even if everyone else strictly prefers y to x.

It is hard to argue against unanimity as a desirable property for a social preference function, at least if the objective is to find a rule that respects the desires of the individuals involved. Surely, if everyone strictly prefers x to y, then society should do so as well.

Independence of irrelevant alternatives is also meant to be a desirable property. One way to think about it is to imagine that X is the set of all conceivable social states, but some subset $A \subseteq X$ is feasible. The social preference function generates a preference ordering over X so that society will choose in coherent fashion no matter what is A. Then: Suppose $A = \{x, y\}$. How society chooses between x and y—which depends on whether $x \succeq y$ or $y \succeq x$ or both—"ought to" depend only on how individuals feel about x versus y and not on any infeasible and therefore irrelevant alternative social state z. (A different way to think about this assumption has to do with intensity of preference, but I want to leave a discussion of that interpretation until after Arrow's Theorem is stated and proved.)

Finally, having a dictatorial social preference function is, a priori, meant to be bad. Think in particular of cases where H consists of many, many individuals. If Φ is dictatorial, with h^* as the dictator, then even in the profile $(\succeq_h)_{h \in H}$ for which $y \succ_h x$ for everyone except h^*, if $x \succ_{h^*} y$, then the social ordering produced by Φ has $x \succ y$. That hardly seems fair or reasonable.

To be clear, if Φ is dictatorial, with h^* the dictator, it isn't necessarily the case that social preferences $\succeq$ are identical to $\succeq_{h^*}$. If, for some pair x and y, the dictator is indifferent (that is, if $x \sim_{h^*} y$), then society's preferences (as determined by Φ and the full array of individual preferences) can have $x \succ y$ or $y \succ x$ or $x \sim y$. Being a dictator means: When the dictator has a strict preference for one social state over a second, society has that same strict preference. The converse need not be true.

Arrow's Theorem says: If there are three or more social states and you have a social preference function Φ that satisfies Assumption 8.1, unanimity, and IIA, then, as unhappy as it may be, it is also dictatorial. It is sometimes called Arrow's Possibility Theorem, because it limits what is possible in a "good" social preference function to dictatorship. And it is sometimes called the *Im*possibility Theorem because, since dictatorship is bad, it says that it is impossible to produce a "good" social preference function; where good means Assumption 8.1, unanimity, IIA, and no dictators. With either name, it is the same formal theorem.

Proposition 8.3 (Arrow's Theorem). *Suppose that X contains three or more elements. If Φ satisfies Assumption 8.1, unanimity, and IIA, then Φ is dictatorial.*

Proof. To keep the statement of the theorem as neat as possible, the proof of the theorem becomes a bit involved. You may wish to skip the proof on a first reading. But nothing in this proof is hard; it just involves being very clever in how you maneuver profiles of individual preferences. This isn't quite the proof originally given by Arrow, but the basic ideas all derive from his original argument.

Fix a social preference function Φ that satisfies Assumption 8.1, unanimity, and IIA.

For any pair x and y, a subset $H' \subseteq H$ is said to be *decisive* for x over y if, whenever $x \succ_h y$ for all $h \in H'$ and $y \succ_h x$ for $h \notin H'$, then $x \succ y$. By unanimity, H is decisive for x over y, for all x and y.

Now take in turn each (ordered) pair x and y, $x \neq y$ and, for this pair, a smallest set (measured by the number of elements in the set) $H_{x,y} \subseteq H$ that is decisive for x over y. I've written *a smallest set* instead of ***the** smallest set* because there may be ties; that is, there may be (for a particular x and y), three different five-member sets of individuals that are decisive for x over y, and no sets of individuals with four or fewer members that is decisive. Take one ordered pair x and y, $x \neq y$, and a smallest set $J \subseteq H$ decisive for x over y, such that J is smallest (measured by number of elements) among all the $H_{x',y'}$, as we vary x' and y'. Again, there may be many choices for x, y, and J; the point is to find an x, y, and J such that for any other pair x' and y', no set with fewer members than has J is decisive for x' over y'.

I assert that J must contain a single element. (By unanimity, J must have at least one element.) Suppose, by way of contradiction, that J has more than one element, and let J' and J'' be a partition of J such that both J' and J'' each contain at least one element. Let z be any element of X that is not x and not y. (We are assuming that X has at least three elements.) Consider any array of individual preferences where:

For $h \in J'$, $z \succ_h x \succ_h y$.
For $h \in J''$, $x \succ_h y \succ_h z$.
For $h \notin J$, $y \succ_h z \succ_h x$.

Since J is decisive for x over y, Φ produces social preferences for this array with

$x \succ y$. Now by negative transitivity, either $z \succ y$ or $x \succ z$. Take the two cases in turn.

Suppose $z \succ y$. Take any array of preferences $\succeq'_h$ such that $z \succ'_h y$ for $h' \in J'$ and $y \succ'_h z$ for $h' \notin J'$. The preferences for z versus y in $\succ'_h$ match those of $\succ_h$. So by IIA, Φ must produce the same result for z versus y at the argument $(\succeq'_h)_{h \in H}$ as it did at $(\succeq_h)_{h \in H}$. Since $z \succ y$, it must be that $z \succ' y$. But this means that J' is decisive for z over y, contradicting the minimality (in size) of J. Similarly, if $x \succ z$, IIA implies that J'' will be decisive for x over z, a contradiction. The only way out of this contradiction is if J is a singleton set.

So now we have a distinguished x and y, $x \neq y$, and $h^* \in H$ such that $\{h^*\}$ is decisive for x over y. The rest of the proof consists of showing that h^* is, in fact, a dictator.

First, we show that if $(\succeq_h)_{h \in H}$ is any profile in which $x \succ_{h^*} z$ for arbitrary $z \in X$, then $x \succ z$. Assume for the moment that $z \neq y$, and construct a profile of individual preferences $(\succeq'_h)_{h \in H}$ in which $x \succ'_{h^*} y \succ'_{h^*} z$ and, for all other h, $y \succ'_h x$ and $y \succ'_h z$, and x and z are ranked under $\succeq'_h$ for $h \neq h^*$ precisely as they are ranked under $\succ_h$. Since $\{h^*\}$ is decisive for x over y, $x \succ' y$. By unanimity, $y \succ' z$. Hence by transitivity, $x \succ' z$. But by IIA, since each $\succ'_h$ ranks x and z precisely as does $\succ_h$, this implies $x \succ z$.

And if $z = y$: Then take any element w of X that is not x and not y. The argument just given shows that for any array of individual preferences such that $x \succ_{h^*} w$ and $w \succ_h x$ for $h \neq h^*$, $x \succ w$. This means that $\{h^*\}$ is decisive for x over w. Now replace y with w in the preceding paragraph (remembering that z is y) to conclude that $x \succ z = y$.

Second, we show that if $(\succeq_h)_{h \in H}$ is any profile in which $z \succ_{h^*} y$, then $z \succ y$. Assume for the moment that $z \neq x$, and construct a profile of individual preferences $(\succeq'_h)_{h \in H}$ in which $z \succ'_{h^*} x \succ'_{h^*} y$ and, for $h \neq h^*$, $z, y \succ'_h x$ and z and y are ranked precisely as they are under $\succeq_h$. Since $\{h^*\}$ is decisive for x over y, $x \succ' y$. By unanimity, $z \succ' x$. By transitivity, $z \succ' y$. And then by IIA, $z \succ y$. Then, following the argument of the previous paragraph, you can take care of the case where $z = x$.

Third, we show that for any element w that is neither x nor y, $\{h^*\}$ is decisive for w over x. To do this, let $(\succeq_h)_{h \in H}$ be any array in which $w \succ_{h^*} x$ and $x \succ_h w$ for all $h \neq h^*$. Construct $(\succeq'_h)_{h \in H}$, which agrees with $(\succeq_h)_{h \in H}$ concerning x versus w and which places y as follows: $w \succ'_{h^*} y \succ'_{h^*} x$ and, for $h \neq h^*$, $y \succ'_h x \succ'_h w$. By unanimity, $y \succ' x$. By the previous paragraph, $w \succ' y$. Hence $w \succ' x$ by transitivity, and $w \succ x$ by IIA.

But then, since $\{h^*\}$ is decisive for w over x, if $z \succ_{h^*} x$ for arbitrary $z \in X$ in any array of individual preferences, the paragraph that begins "Second" (two paragraphs previous to this) shows that $z \succ x$.

Finally, suppose we have any two outcomes w and z such that $w \succ_{h^*} z$ in some array of individual preferences. If $w = x$, the paragraph that begins "First" shows that $w \succ z$. If $z = x$, the previous paragraph applies and we conclude that $w \succ z$. And if x is neither w nor z, then construct $(\succeq'_h)_{h \in H}$ so that each $\succ'_h$ agrees with $\succ_h$ on w versus z and so that $w \succ'_{h^*} x \succ'_{h^*} z$. (It doesn't matter what $\succeq'_h$

does concerning x versus w and z.) By the previous paragraph, $w \succ' x$. By the paragraph that begins "First," $x \succ' z$. By transitivity, $w \succ' z$. By IIA, $w \succ z$. Individual h^* is a dictator. ∎

This result must be viewed as a disappointment, if one had hoped to find a nice method for mapping individual preferences to social preferences. Each of the four properties that we've asked of Φ—that it work for every possible profile of individual preferences on social outcomes; that it deliver a complete and transitive social ranking of outcomes; that it satisfy unanimity and IIA—seems a reasonable request. But any Φ that satisfies all four is dictatorial, as long as there are more than two social outcomes.[4] And a dictatorial social preference function is surely not where one wishes to wind up.

There is nothing wrong with the proof, so there must be something wrong—at least in terms of the four properties—with social preference functions that seem naturally to suggest themselves. For instance, consider *majority rule*. To be precise, consider the social preference function Φ_{MR} that is defined as follows: For any pair x and y from X and for a profile of individual preferences $(\succeq_h)_{h \in H}$, say that $x \succeq y$ if $x \succeq_h y$ for half or more of the h. It is not difficult to show that Φ_{MR} so defined satisfies unanimity and IIA.[5] It certainly isn't dictatorial, at least for the case where H has two or more members. So, applied to the collection of all arrays of individual preferences, this must not be producing complete and transitive social preferences. In fact, as defined here, $\succeq$ is complete: For any pair x and y and for each h, either $x \succeq_h y$ or $y \succeq_h x$ (or both). Therefore, half or more of the h must have $x \succeq_h y$, or half or more must have $y \succeq_h x$. In the first case, $x \succeq y$ by majority rule; in the second case, $y \succeq x$ by majority rule.

So it must be that transitivity goes wrong. And it does: Suppose $X = \{x, y, z\}$ and $H = \{1, 2, 3\}$, and consider the array of individual preferences in which $x \succ_1 y \succ_1 z$, $y \succ_2 z \succ_2 x$, and $z \succ_3 x \succ_3 y$. (This famous counterexample has a name: It is the Condorcet cycle.) Two out of three people have $x \succeq_h y$, so $x \succeq y$. Two out of three have $y \succeq_h z$, so $y \succeq z$. Hence, for transitivity, $x \succeq z$ must hold. But only one out of the three individuals has $x \succeq_h z$; this doesn't hold.

This is only one way to implement the general principle of majority rule; other variants require supermajorities or use weighted voting. In most of these variations, the relationship between x and y socially depends (only) on how individuals rank x and y; IIA holds by design. And most sensible definitions will give you unanimity; it is hard to think of an implementation of majority rule that doesn't have that, if

[4] What if there are only two social outcomes? See Problem 8.2.

[5] Unanimity is defined in terms of strict preferences and since, as we are about to learn, the social preferences produced by majority rule are not complete and transitive, it isn't altogether obvious how one defines social strict preference. I'm using the following definition: For any binary relation $\succeq$ that is meant to represent weak preferences, the corresponding strict preference relation is defined by $x \succ y$ if it is not the case that $y \succeq x$. Hence, if $x \succ_h y$ for all h, where $\succ_h$ are strict preferences defined from the complete and transitive individual preferences $\succeq_h$ in the usual fashion, then $y \succeq_h x$ for no h, and so it is not true that $y \succeq x$ by majority rule (in fact, no one votes for this). Therefore $x \succ y$ in the social strict preferences; unanimity holds.

$x \succ_h y$ for every $h \in H$, then society strictly prefers x to y. Finally, most sensible definitions will not be dictatorial—however you implement majority rule, if one person has $x \succ_h y$ and everyone else has $y \succ_h x$, it is hard to produce a social strict preference for x over y.[6] So, per Arrow's Theorem, implementations of majority rule and its variants, when applied to a domain of all profiles of individual preferences, fail to produce complete or transitive social preferences. In most cases, the Condorcet example from the previous paragraph tells the unhappy tale.

A second possible social preference function, often used in athletic contexts to find consensus rankings of teams, is the Borda rule. Suppose there are N social states. For each individual $h \in H$, convert her preferences $\succeq_h$ in a given profile of individual preferences to a cardinal utility function as follows: Her highest ranked social state gets utility $u_h(x) = N$. Second highest gets $u_h(x') = N - 1$. And so forth, where ties get the average of their ranks.[7] And then, for each x, compute $U(x) = \sum_{h \in H} u_h(x)$, and let $\succ$ be the preference ordering given by U. This clearly produces complete and transitive social preferences, since it produces a numerical ranking. And it clearly satisfies unanimity: If everyone ranks Stanford's football team as strictly better than USC's, then Stanford will have a higher ranking in the poll. It clearly fails to be dictatorial, if H has more than one element. So, per Arrow's Theorem, it must violate IIA. And so it does: Suppose $H = \{1, 2\}$ and $X = \{a, b, c, d\}$. According to this social preference function:

$$\text{if } a \succ_1 b \succ_1 c \succ_1 d \text{ and } b \succ_2 c \succ_2 a \succ_2 d, \text{ then } b \succ a;$$

$$\text{and if } a \succ_1' c \succ_1' d \succ_1' b \text{ and } b \succ_2' c \succ_2' a \succ_2' d, \text{ then } a \succ' b.$$

The rankings of a versus b are the same in the two profiles of individual preferences, but changing the positions in 1's rankings of c and d relative to a and b changes the social ranking of a and b.

8.2. What Do We Give Up?

Arrow's Theorem is, without question, a disappointing result, but it does point the way forward for further analysis. Assume we are still interested in finding a "nice" social preference function. Assume that a dictatorial social preference function, for more than three social states, is not nice. Then Arrow's Theorem tells us that our definition of "nice" will have to do without one of the following: The domain of Φ consists of *every* H-tuple of preferences. The range is the space of complete and transitive preference orders on X. Unanimity is satisfied. IIA is satisfied. One of these, and perhaps more than one, has to go.

[6] You can do it with weighted majority rule, if one person has more than 50% of the weight. But that is just another way to define dictatorship.

[7] That is, if $N = 6$ and h has $x_1 \succ_h x_2 \sim_h x_3 \sim_h x_4 \succ_h x_5 \sim_h x_6$, then set $u_h(x_1) = 6$, $u_h(x_5) = u_h(x_4) = u_h(x_3) = (5 + 4 + 3)/3 = 4$, and $u_h(x_2) = u_h(x_1) = (2 + 1)/2 = 1.5$.

No one seems very interested in giving up unanimity. If every member of society thinks x is strictly better than y, it is hard to imagine that society should conclude otherwise, for any social preference function that is "nice."

One way forward, then, is to give up on the notion that the domain of Φ consists of every H-tuple of preferences on X. One idea here is that X has some geometric structure that precludes certain preferences. The paramount example here concerns so-called *single-peaked preferences*. One assumes that X is one-dimensional; to be concrete, assume that $X \subseteq R$, the real line.

Definition 8.4. *For $X \subseteq R$, a complete and transitive preference relation $\succeq$ on X is said to be single-peaked if, for all x, y, and z such that $x > y > z$, either $y \succ x$ or $y \succ z$ (or both).*

Single-peaked preferences are particularly interesting to political scientists. Think of social states being arrayed on a single left-wing-to-right-wing dimension. Each individual has her ideal point on this one-dimensional political spectrum, with preference falling off as the social state moves further and further (in one direction or the other) from the individual's ideal social state.

Proposition 8.5. *Suppose $X \subseteq R$, and suppose H has an odd number of elements. The majority-rule social preference function given last section, Φ_{MR}, produces complete and transitive social preferences for any profile of individual preferences for which each $\succeq_h$ is single-peaked and anti-symmetric (that is, if $x \succeq_h y \succeq_h x$, then $x = y$).*

The proof is left as an exercise. (It is Problem 8.3, and the solution is provided for you in the *Student's Guide.*) To interpret this: If we define a social preference function Φ as majority rule, in that for any profile of individual preferences $(\succeq_h)_{h \in H}$, Φ produces the majority-rule comparison rule as defined previously, then, in general, Φ satisfies unanimity and IIA, but it doesn't produce complete and transitive social preferences. (See the discussion last section.) But *if* X is one-dimensional and we restrict individual preferences in our profiles to be single-peaked and anti-symmetric, then Φ does produce complete and transitive preferences. (Adding in the assumption that each individual preference relation is anti-symmetric is an analytical convenience. Note that this was true in the example given last section; the real bite here is the assumption that preferences are single-peaked.) If we are allowed to restrict the domain of Φ (in this case to profiles of single-peaked and anti-symmetric preferences, where X has the geometric structure needed for this to make sense), we can get everything else desired while avoiding dictatorship.

The term "majority rule" here needs to be carefully interpreted. We use majority rule to make pairwise comparisons, and then use those pairwise comparisons to choose from a feasible subset of X. It is relatively easy to construct an example in which there are three options, x, y, and z, for which (a) pairwise comparisons lead to $x \succ y \succ z$ and yet (b) if we asked each h to vote for its favorite option of the three, option y would command a plurality of the vote. Most textbooks on the theory of voting systems will discuss the case of single-peaked preferences in detail.

This is only one example of what might be done by restricting the domain of the social preference function. For further results, see Caplin and Nalebuff (1988).

Alternatively, one might give up on the independence of irrelevant alternatives. We already provided one rationale for IIA, but here is a second: IIA is desirable because, knowing only each individual's ordinal ranking of social states, we have no way to make interpersonal comparisons of utility or utility differences. If we know, say, that half the population prefers x to y and the other half prefers y to x, we have no particular basis for preferring one or the other. But if we know that, for the people who prefer x to y, the difference is really important to them, while for those who prefer y to x, they are near to indifferent, then we might choose x. Since we have formulated our knowledge about individual preferences as ordinal preference relations, we have no direct knowledge about intensity of preferences. But, within the context of ordinally expressed preferences, if half the population puts y in, say, third place overall and x in fourth place, while the other half puts x in third place and y in fifteenth place—something that depends on how x and y compare to other social states—it might be thought legitimate to infer that the difference between x and y for the second group is greater and, on that basis, come to the social conclusion that x is preferable to y.

That, in essence, is what the Borda rule is doing. It is converting the ordinal ranking of an individual into cardinal measures of "worth" and then adding up those cardinal measures to get a social ranking. This means a violation of IIA, of course, but the violation is done to facilitate interpersonal comparisons.

The Borda rule, however, quite ad hoc. Why assign cardinal values $N, N-1, N-2, \ldots, 1$? Why not assign values $N^2, (N-1)^2, \ldots, 4, 1$? Why not use the $p_N, p_{N-1}, \ldots, 2$, where p_n is the nth prime? Or use Fibonacci numbers? Once you are in the business of assigning ad hoc cardinal values to "positions" in an order, a lot of assignments are possible, all of them equally meaningful (or meaningless, as you prefer). And, of course, it makes a difference to the final social outcome which you use.

If we want to be in the business of making interpersonal comparisons of utilities and utility differences, we should probably look for data that provide meaningful cardinal utilities directly. Introducing lotteries over social states might be a means for doing this; for a treatment along these lines, see Kaneko and Nakamura (1979). Or imagine that we are lucky enough to have utility functions that are quasi-linear in a transferable store of value (money). Then we can make interpersonal comparisons of utility differences by measuring everying in money and adding up dollar values. Indeed, in this case, we could imagine ameliorating disputes over which social state to implement by engaging in compensation; that is, in transfers from those who benefit from the selected social state to those who suffer. Arrow (1951a) provides a discussion of compensation. The bottom line here is: The formulation of the problem of social choice with which we began, and in particular the formulation of individual preferences ordinally, makes interpersonal comparisons of preferences and preference differences suspect. Giving up on IIA would seem to mean allowing for interpersonal comparisons, and that in turn seems best accomplished if you assume (as analyst) that you have access to data that permit meaningful interpersonal comparisons. With such data, Arrow's Theorem is *not* the end of the story of social choice.

8.3. Efficiency

But without more data (and if we are unwilling to make interpersonal comparisons based on individual ordinal rankings), if we won't give up unanimity or restrict the possible profiles of individual preferences, we are left with setting our sights lower: Instead of producing a complete and transitive social ordering of X, we look for something less.

This is the traditional stance of economics and economists: *x is comparable to y if and only if x is a Pareto improvement on y, in which case x is judged better than y. Within any subset A of X, we look for the Pareto-efficient (often just "the efficient") elements of A. And (as economists) we don't seriously try to judge the relative merits of two different efficient outcomes.* Let me define the new terms:

The setting is more or less as before, although X need not be a finite set. We continue to suppose that the set of individuals, H, is finite, and that each individual has complete and transitive preferences $\succeq_h$ on X, from which strict preferences $\succ_h$ and indifference $\sim_h$ are derived.

Definition 8.6. *The social state (or outcome) x is **Pareto superior to** y (or Pareto dominates y), if $x \succeq_h y$ for every h in H and $x \succ_h y$ for at least one $h \in H$. (In this case, we also say that y is Pareto **dominated** by or is Pareto **inferior** to x.) The social state x is **strictly Pareto superior to** y (or strictly Pareto dominates y) if $x \succ_h y$ for all h. For a subset A of X and a point $x \in A$, x is **Pareto efficient** (or just efficient) within A if there is no $y \in A$ that Pareto dominates x. The set of Pareto efficient points within A is called the **Pareto frontier** of A.*

Fixing the profile of individual preferences, Pareto superiority and strict Pareto superiority create binary relations among the social states: Write $x \dot{>} y$ if x is Pareto superior to y, and write $x \dot{\gg} y$ if x is strictly Pareto superior to y. With our maintained assumption that each $\succeq_h$ is complete and transitive, it is simple to establish the following result:

Proposition 8.7. *Both $\dot{>}$ and $\dot{\gg}$ are transitive and asymmetric. If $x \dot{\gg} y$, then $x \dot{>} y$.*

But, in general, $\dot{>}$ (and, therefore, $\dot{\gg}$) is not complete. As for the existence of Pareto-efficient points within a set $A \subseteq X$, we have:

Proposition 8.8. *A given set $A \subseteq X$ has a nonempty Pareto frontier (that is, there exist Pareto efficient points within A) if either (a) A is finite or (b) (if X is a subset of R^n or otherwise has a suitable topological structure) A is compact and each $\succeq_h$ is continuous.*

Proof. For notational convenience, I'll assume that the individuals (members of H) are denoted by $1, 2, \ldots, N$, for some finite N. In either case (a) or (b), let A_1 be the set of elements of A that are $\succeq_1$-best. (That is, A_1 consists of all the points that

$h = 1$ likes best among the points in A.) Results from Chapter 1 show that A_1 is nonempty. In case (a), it is obvious that A_1 is finite. In case (b), I assert that A_1 is compact: Boundedness of A_1 is immediate because A_1 is a subset of the bounded A. And A_1 is closed: Let x_n be a sequence of points in A_1 converging to x. Let y be any other point in A; then since x_n is in A_1, $x_n \succeq_1 y$. But then, by continuity, $x \succeq_1 y$. Since y is arbitrary in A, x is $\succeq_1$-best in A, and hence $x \in A_1$, showing that A_1 is closed.

Now let A_2 be the subset of A_1 consisting of all the $\succeq_2$-best points out of A_1. By the arguments just given, A_2 is nonempty and, in case (b), A_2 is compact. Proceed in this fashion for all $h \in H$; ending with A_N. The argument shows that A_N is nonempty; I assert that any $x \in A_N$ is Pareto efficient in A. Suppose, to the contrary, that $y \in A$ is Pareto superior to x. Then $y \succeq_1 x$, and since $x \in A_n \subseteq A_1$, y must also be in A_1. Proceeding along these lines, we find that $y \in A_2$, then A_3, and so forth. But for some lowest index h, $y \succ_h x$ (since y Pareto dominates x, we have to hit a strict preference somewhere down the line). Since $y \in A_{h-1}$, $x \in A_{h-1}$, and x is among the $\succeq_h$-best elements of A_{h-1}, we know that $x \succeq_h y$, a contradiction to $y \succ_h x$. No such y can exist, every $x \in A_N$ is Pareto efficient, and (therefore) the Pareto frontier of A is nonempty. ∎

(This is a good place to engage your intuition. We just showed that A_N is a subset of the Pareto frontier of A. A_N was constructed by taking the individuals in H in a particular order; presumably, if we permute the order, we'll wind up with a different subset of the Pareto frontier. So suppose we take all the possible permutations of the individuals and, for each permutation, construct a set analogous to A_N. Does the union of all these A_N-like sets give the entire Pareto frontier of A? No, it does not. In a few paragraphs, we'll see a picture that shows this clearly. But before we get to that picture, can you see what is going on here?)

8.4. Identifying the Pareto Frontier: Utility Imputations and Bergsonian Social Utility Functionals

In specific applications, although we (as economists) may be unwilling to select among Pareto-efficient outcomes, we often do want to find (or otherwise characterize) all the efficient outcomes. A methodology for doing this, in some applications, employs so-called utility imputations and *Bergsonian social utility functionals*.

Suppose that the profile of individual preferences is given by a collection of utility functions $u_h : X \to R$ for $h \in H$ that represent the individual's preference relations $\succeq_h$. In this case, we can map each social state x into the vector of utilities it provides for each individual in turn; formally, let $u : X \to R^H$ be defined by $(u(x))_h := u_h(x)$. The vector $u(x)$ is called the *utility imputation* for the social state x; the range of u is the set of *utility imputations*; if we have a subset $A \subseteq X$ of feasible social states, the set $u(A) = \{u(x); x \in A\}$ is called the set of feasible utility imputations, and so forth. In these terms, the state x is Pareto superior to y if and only if $u(x) \geq u(y)$ and $u(x) \neq u(y)$; the state x is Pareto efficient in $A \subseteq X$ if and only if there is no $v \in R^H$ such that $v = u(y)$ for some $y \in A$ and $v \geq u(x), v \neq u(x)$. Graphically, when H has two members (so that utility imputations are points in the plane), the Pareto frontier of A is the set of points $x \in A$ such that there is no other point in $u(A)$ to the northeast of $u(x)$; see Figure 8.1.

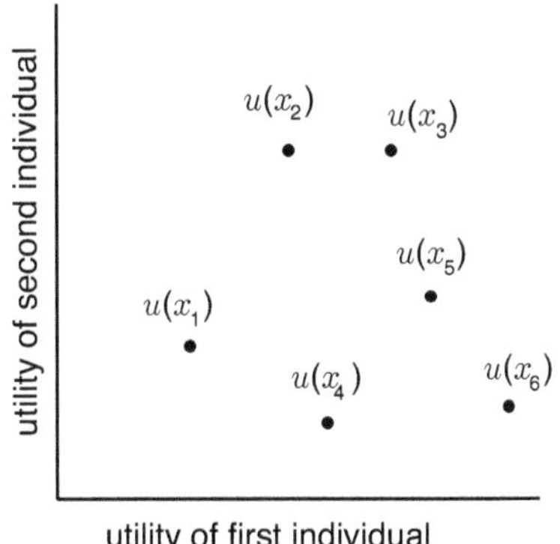

Figure 8.1. Pareto efficiency. Imagine that there are two individuals (H has two elements) and six social states, $x_1, \ldots, x_6$. For each social state x_i, we plot the utility imputation of the state, the point $u(x_i) = (u_1(x_i), u_2(x_i))$. From the picture, we see that x_1 is Pareto dominated by x_2, by x_3, and x_5; x_4 is Pareto dominated by x_3, x_5, and x_6; and—since $u_1(x_3) > u_1(x_2)$ and $u_2(x_3) = u_2(x_2)$—x_2 is Pareto dominated by x_3. The states x_3, x_5, and x_6 are Pareto efficient, and as a set they constitute the Pareto frontier.

Needless to say, the set of utility imputations in any specific context depends on the specific utility functions u_h chosen to represent the preferences of the individuals.

(Now go back to the proof of Proposition 8.8. Suppose that H has two elements, so there are two orders in which we can take the individuals. Which points in the Pareto frontier of X are selected by the procedure in the proof, if we take first one order and then the other? Can you identify the results for the example of Figure 8.1, if we assume that $A = X$?)

In this context, where individual preferences over social states X are given by some specification of individual utility functions u_h and where the vector function u is defined as above, we have the following obvious result:

Proposition 8.9. *Suppose that $W : R^H \to R$ is strictly increasing. If x is a solution to the problem*

$$\textit{Maximize } W \circ u(x), \quad \textit{subject to } x \in X,$$

then x is Pareto efficient.

Proof. We prove the contrapositive statement: If x is not Pareto efficient, some $y \in X$ is Pareto superior to it. But then $u(y) \geq u(x)$ and $u(y) \neq u(x)$. If W is strictly increasing, then $W(u(y)) > W(u(x))$, so x would not be a solution to the problem of maximizing $W \circ u$ over X. ∎

What about the converse? That is, if x is Pareto efficient, is there some strictly increasing W such that x solves the problem of maximizing $W \circ u$? Suppose the answer is yes. Then, at least in theory, we have a machine for finding the Pareto frontier of any X (or, more generally, of any $A \subseteq X$), namely: Solve the problem of maximizing $W \circ u$ for *every* strictly increasing function $W : R^H \to R$. And, in fact, the answer is yes. (See Problem 8.5, which is solved for you in the *Student's Guide*.)

But there are a lot of strictly increasing functions $W : R^H \to R$—some of them extremely ill-behaved—and in finding every Pareto-efficient point in a given X, you may need some of the ill-behaved ones: For instance, while you can limit yourself to continuous and strictly increasing W if X is a finite set, if X is infinite, it may take a discontinuous function W to get at a particular Pareto-efficient x. And even if we could limit attention to continuous and strictly increasing W—indeed, even if we could limit ourselves to W that are differentiable—there are a lot of such functions, and solving the problem of maximizing $W \circ u$ for all of them is not a very (excuse the adjective) efficient machine.

The following proposition comes to our rescue.

Proposition 8.10. *Suppose that the set $\{v \in R^H : v \le u(x)$ for some $x \in X\}$ is convex. Then every Pareto-efficient point $x^0 \in X$ is the solution to the problem*

$$\text{Maximize} \sum_{h \in H} \alpha_h u_h(x), \quad \text{subject to } x \in X,$$

for some set of nonnegative weights $(\alpha_h)_{h \in H}$, not all zero. Moreover, the set $\{v \in R^H : v \le u(x)$ for some $x \in X\}$ is convex if X is convex and if each u_h is a concave function (from X to R).

This proposition amalgamates two different results, and it may help to unpack them.

Taking the second half first, it provides conditions under which, in a specific application, the set of utility "imputations" is convex. The term utility imputations is put in scare quotes because, in fact, we are really concerned with vectors of utility levels that lie at or below the set of utility imputations; that is, we look at all vectors of utility levels $v \in R^H$ such that v is less or equal to $u(x)$, for some $x \in X$, the set of social states. Those conditions are: (1) The set of social states is a convex set. And (2) the individual utility functions are concave functions. This requires that the set of social states X have a geometric structure that allows us to talk about convexity: You can think of X being the subset of some finite-dimensional Euclidean space R^K, so that the definition of concavity of each u_h is just the definition given in Appendix 3. But for readers conversant with more general notions of convexity of a set (within a general linear space) and concavity of a real-valued function defined on such a set, it will be obvious from the proof that this part of the result is quite general.

As for the first part, *if* the set $\{v \in R^H : v \leq u(x) \text{ for some } x \in X\}$ is convex—in particular, *if* the conditions of the second half of the proposition hold—then the proposition tells us that we can identify the Pareto frontier by maximizing simple weighted averages of the utility functions of the individuals. Or, to be precise, it almost tells us that: It says that every Pareto-efficient point is the solution to a maximization problem for this sort of weighted average of utilities. And Proposition 8.9 tells us that if the weights are strictly positive (so this objective function is a strictly increasing function of the individual utilities) then every solution is Pareto efficient. But we have a bit of a middle ground left to discuss: To find all the Pareto-efficient points, we need to consider cases where some of the weights α_h are zero. But then solutions of the maximization problem are not guaranteed to be Pareto efficient. We'll discuss this middle ground after proving the proposition.

In the previous paragraph, the phrase *weighted averages of the utility functions* sounds as if we are imposing the condition that the weights sum to 1. In fact, we *could* impose that condition on the weights without changing the proposition: maximizing $\sum_h \alpha_h u_h(x)$ gives the same solutions as does maximizing $\sum_h \lambda \alpha_h u_h(x)$ for any strictly positive λ. So, for general weights $(\alpha_h)_{h \in H}$, if we let $\lambda = 1/\sum_h \alpha_h$, then we have weights that sum to 1. (Since not all the weights are zero, the sum is strictly positive.) As a practical matter, when we go to apply the proposition, what is important is that all relative weightings of the various individuals are considered; having the weights sum to 1 works or, in a problem where H is doubleton, setting one α_h to 1 and letting the other weight vary between 0 and ∞ will work (except for the weighting where the first individual gets 0 weight).

You may wonder why we stated the proposition in this two-stage manner. It would be cleaner, perhaps, to say "Suppose X is convex and all the u_h are concave. Then..." and give the conclusion of the first half. But for the conclusion of the first part to follow, convexity of the set $\{v \in R^H : v \leq u(x)\}$ is what is needed. Convexity of X and concavity of the u_h are sufficient for convexity of this set, and in almost every application of which I am aware, those are the sufficient conditions employed. But I don't want to preclude an application where, on other grounds, you know that the critical set is convex.

Finally (before we get to the proof), the proposition is stated in terms of the Pareto frontier of the set of all social states X. In many applications, we are concerned with the Pareto frontier of a subset $A \subseteq X$. The proposition works just as well for such applications; the first part follows if the set $\{v \in R^H : v \leq u(x) \text{ for } x \in A\}$ is convex, and convexity of this set is guaranteed if A is convex and the u_h are concave.

Proof of the second part of Proposition 8.10. We prove the second and easier part of the proposition first. Suppose that $v \leq u(x)$ for $x \in X$ and $v' \leq u(x')$ for $x' \in X$. We must show, for $\beta \in [0, 1]$, that $\beta v + (1 - \beta)v' \leq u(x'')$ for some $x'' \in X$. The obvious candidate (and one that works) is $x'' = \beta x + (1 - \beta)x'$. This is in X because X is assumed to be a convex set. And since each u_h is concave, $u_h(x'') = u_h(\beta x + (1-\beta)x') \geq \beta u_h(x) + (1-\beta)u_h(x') \geq \beta v_h + (1-\beta)v'_h$. This is true for each $h \in H$, so the vector $u(x'')$ is greater than or equal to the vector $\beta v + (1-\beta)v'$, which is what we needed to show. ∎

Proof of the first part of Proposition 8.10. The first part isn't hard to prove either, once you have the right mathematical hammer in your toolkit. That hammer is the *Separating-Hyperplane Theorem,* which is Proposition A3.10. This is, I believe, the first application in the text of the Separating-Hyperplane Theorem; it is far from the last, as I believe it is safe to say that no mathematical hammer gets more widespread use in the remainder of this book.[8]

Suppose x^0 is Pareto efficient. This implies that the sets $\{v \in R^H : v \leq u(x) \text{ for some } x \in X\}$ and $\{v \in R^H : v > u(x^0)\}$ are disjoint: If v were in the intersection of these sets, then $u(x^0) < v \leq u(y)$ for some $y \in X$, and y is Pareto superior to x^0, contradicting the assumption that x^0 is Pareto efficient. But the set $\{v \in R^H : v \leq u(x) \text{ for some } x \in X\}$ is convex by assumption, and $\{v \in R^H : v > u(x^0)\}$ is easily shown to be convex. Hence there exists a nonzero vector β and scalar γ that separates the two sets: That is, $\beta \cdot v \leq \gamma$ for all $v \in \{v \in R^H : v \leq u(x) \text{ for some } x \in X\}$, and $\beta \cdot v \geq \gamma$ for all $v > u(x^0)$. I assert that $\beta \geq 0$; if some coefficient of β, say β_h, is strictly less than zero, then taking v to be $u_{h'}(x^0) + 1$ for $h' \neq h$ and $v_h = u_h(x^0) + M$ for large M gives a vector $v > u(x^0)$ that, for M approaching infinity, has $\beta \cdot v$ approaching $-\infty$; hence eventually less than γ. That cannot be. And, I assert, $\beta \cdot v(x^0) = \gamma$: Take $v^n = u(x^0) + (1/n, 1/n, \ldots, 1/n)$, which is $> u(x^0)$. Therefore, $\beta \cdot v^n \geq \gamma$. But as n approaches infinity, $\beta \cdot v^n$ approaches $\beta \cdot u(x^0)$. Hence $\beta \cdot u(x^0) \geq \gamma$. On the other hand, $u(x^0)$ is in the set $\{v \in R^H : v \leq u(x) \text{ for some } x \in X\}$; hence $\beta \cdot u(x^0) \leq \gamma$.

But this means that $\beta \cdot u(x^0) = \gamma \geq \beta \cdot u(y)$ for all $y \in X$, since $u(y) \in \{v \in R^H : v \leq u(x) \text{ for some } x \in X\}$. Let the weights α_h be the components of the vector β, and you have the result. ∎

A picture of this proposition will help readers who are new to separating hyperplanes understand what is going on *and* help to shed light on the discussion we began about the middle ground caused by zero weights. The figure depicts a case where H has two members, so utility imputations lie in the plane. In Figure 8.2a, a set of utility imputations $u(X) = \{v \in R^2 : v = u(x) \text{ for some } x \in X\}$ is given. This set is *not* drawn as being convex, but it is "convex to the northeast"; this is not atypical of the situation where X is convex and the utility functions are concave (see Problem 8.6). But when we expand the set by including everything less or equal to a utility imputation—that is, when we look at $\{v \in R^2 : v \leq u(x) \text{ for some } x \in X\}$—then we get a convex set (when X is convex and the u_h are concave), as depicted

[8] I will use the Separating-Hyperplane Theorem, but readers who prefer can concoct an argument that enlists the Supporting-Hyperplane Theorem, Proposition A3.13. In fact, if you are new to arguments using separating hyperplanes, it might be good practice to construct the supporting-hyperplane version of the proof.

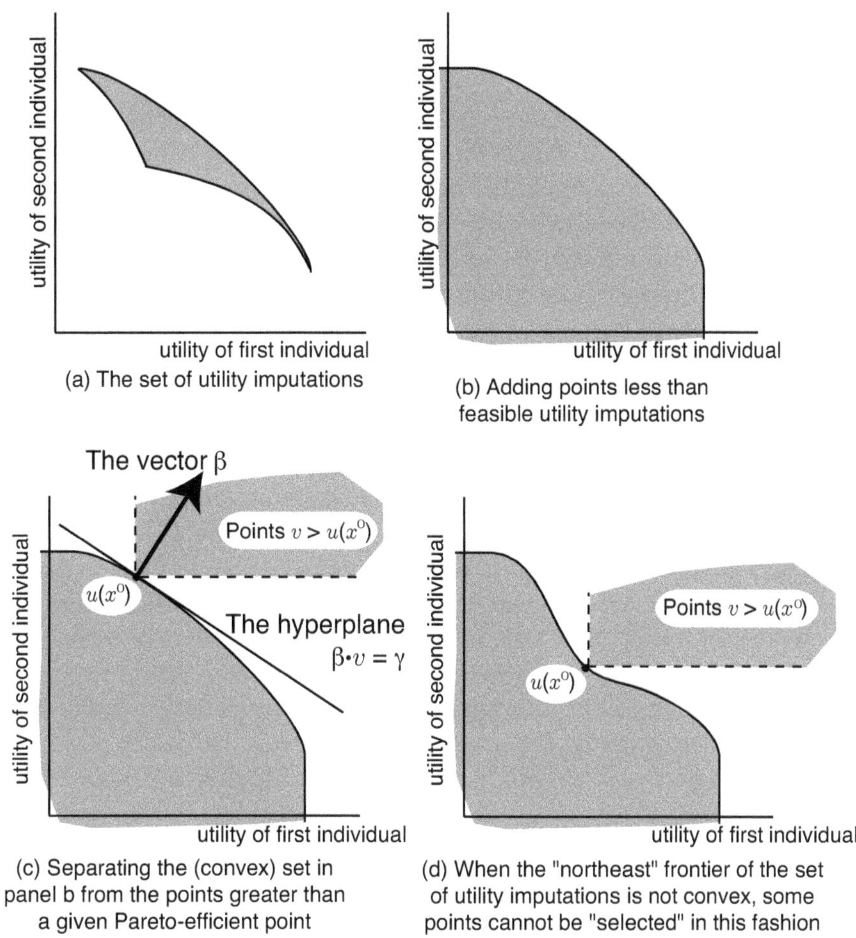

Figure 8.2. Proposition 8.10 in pictures. See the text for explanation.

in panel b. Now take any Pareto-efficient point x^0 and the corresponding utility imputation $u(x^0)$, and look at all points in the space of utility imputations that are strictly greater than $u(x^0)$. See panel c of Figure 8.2, where the dashed lines indicate that the second set is open along its boundaries. Precisely because x^0 is Pareto efficient—so that $u(x^0)$ lies along the northeast border of the set of utility imputations, the two sets depicted are disjoint. The two sets are convex, the set $\{v \in R^2 : v \leq u(x) \text{ for some } x \in X\}$ by assumption and the set $\{v \in R^2 : v > u(x^0)\}$ by a simple argument, so according to the Separating-Hyperplane Theorem, a hyperplane separates them. This is depicted by the line that separates the two sets in panel c, $\{v : \beta \cdot v = \gamma\}$, where the vector β is the normal to the line (see panel c) and the scalar γ gives the "height" of the line (in general, the hyperplane) perpendicular to this normal. You can imagine tracing out all of the Pareto frontier of X (or, more precisely, their utility imputations) by changing the slope of the hyperplane; as you make the hyperplane "flatter"—by making β more nearly vertical, which means more relative weight on the second component—you get points more to the north;

as the hyperplane becomes more nearly vertical—by making β more nearly horizontal, which means more relative weight on the utility of the first individual—you get points more to the east.

Panel d of Figure 8.2 shows why we need the second part of Proposition 8.10. If the set $\{v \in R^H : v \leq u(x) \text{ for some } x \in X\}$ is not convex, then there are Pareto-efficient points, with utility imputations such as $u(x^0)$ as shown, that can't be found as the solutions to a maximization problem where the objective function simply weights the individuals' utilities and adds. This point can be picked out by a fancier strictly increasing function of the utilities, but the proposition (and method it presents) is useful precisely because we can identify the entire Pareto frontier with a relatively simple collection of such functions.

These objective functions have a name: They are known as the Bergsonian social utility functionals. Definitions vary from source to source, so you should be careful when consulting a different book, but we'll define things as follows: A *social utility functional* is a function W from R^H to R that maps each utility imputation vector $u(x)$ into an overall level of "social utility" $W(u(x))$.[9] You can imagine, if you'd like, that a given social utility functional describes how a social planner or dictator decides on a social state: She learns what utility each individual ascribes to each possible social state x, then uses W to find the "social utility" of each x, and then (presumably) chooses whichever social state is feasible and maximizes social utility.

In most contexts, and following in the general spirit of the unanimity assumption, attention is restricted to social utility functionals that are increasing, at least weakly; the adjective *benevolent* is sometimes used to describe this. And Bergsonian social utility functionals (after the public choice economist Abram Bergson) are those that are simple weighted sums of the individuals' utilities.

Note that in Proposition 8.10, some (but not all) of the weights α_h are allowed to be zero. If this happens, if some of the weights are zero, the functional is not strictly increasing, and maximizing the social utility functional may lead to social states that are not Pareto efficient. Figure 8.3 illustrates why allowing zero weights may be necessary. As before, this is for the case where H has two members, and we are drawing sets of utility imputations. Panel a depicts a set of utility imputations for some set X, and panel b all points that are less than or equal to the set of these utility imputations. So that the first part of Proposition 8.10 can be enlisted, the set of utility imputations is convex to the northeast, so the set in panel b is convex. (In fact, I've drawn it so that the set of utility imputations is convex, but the essential feature is that it is convex to the northeast.) Focus attention on the utility imputations $u(x^0)$ and $u(x^1)$. I've drawn the picture so that x^0 is Pareto efficient and so that x^1 is not:

[9] As with the term *social preference function*, the term *social utility functional* is not standard, but I use it to help prevent confusion. Please note that the difference is not simply that one operates on preferences and the other on utilities: The domain of a social preference function is the space of arrays of preference relations and the range is a preference relation; the parallel concept would be a function operating on an array (an H-tuple) of utility functions, and mapping to a utility function. A social utility functional has a much less complex domain and range; it maps a subset of R^H into R. (Of course, a social utility functional implicitly creates a mapping from H-tuples of utility functions into a utility function; if $(u_h)_{h \in H}$ is an H-tuple of utility functions defined on some set X and $W : R^H \rightarrow R$, then $W \circ (u_h)_{h \in H}$ is a utility function on X.)

x^0 is strictly preferred by the first individual to x^1, while the second individual is indifferent between them (gives her the same utility). But I've also drawn the picture so that the Pareto frontier (in the space of utility imputations) approaches $u(x^0)$ in an "assymptotically flat" manner. (Think, for instance, of a Pareto frontier in the space of utility imputations that describes a quarter circle.)

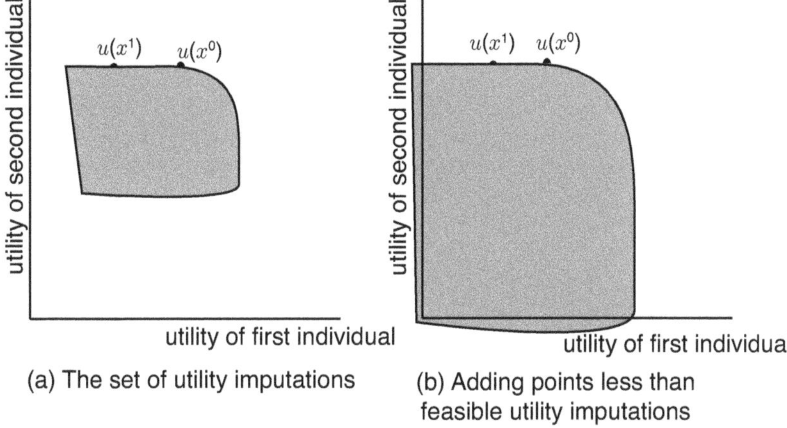

Figure 8.3. The need for and consequences of zero weights in Proposition 8.10. To pick out the Pareto-efficient point x^0 with a Bergsonian social utility functional, it is necessary to put zero weight on the utility of the first individual. But by putting zero weight on the utility of the first individual, we introduce Pareto-inefficient points such as x^1 as solutions to the problem, Maximize the Bergsonian social utility functional.

To separate the set in panel b from the set of utility imputations strictly greater than $u(x^0)$, we need a hyperplane that is horizontal, which means that the normal to the hyperplane is vertical, putting all its weight on the second individual. If we maximize this weighting of the individual utilities over X, x^0 emerges as an answer, but so does x^1. We can't produce x^0 with any other weights (in a simple linear weighting of utilities); if any strictly positive weight is put on the utility of the first individual, maximizing will push u down and to the right along the Pareto frontier. But giving the first individual zero weight gives answers that are not Pareto efficient.

There is, unhappily, nothing to be done about this. When you go to apply Proposition 8.10, either you can use only strictly positive weighting vectors, and potentially miss some of the Pareto-efficient social states; or you can use zero weights and be sure to find all the Pareto-efficient social states, but run the risk of finding some other, inefficient states besides.

After what we said about mainstream economics being unwilling to make interpersonal comparisons of utility, the direction we've taken in this section may be puzzling. When we maximize a Bergsonian social utility functional, we seem to be doing precisely what we said we would not do, and with a great deal of exactness: if we are maximizing with weights where $\alpha_h = 2\alpha_{h'}$, we are apparently saying h's utility is worth twice the utility of h'. We said we would eschew the use of cardinal representations of utility; now we have a section that is devoted entirely to specific numerical representations. What is going on?

The answer is, We are developing an analytically convenient way to find Pareto-efficient social states, at least for some applications, and we are moreover giving conditions under which this "machine" is guaranteed to find *all* the Pareto-efficient social states. *If* we went on to choose among the Pareto-efficient states that we identify—say, by giving special credit to the equal-weighting social utility functional, or by any other means—then we'd be breaking with what we said earlier. But unless and until we say that one efficient point is, on some grounds, better than another—as long as we are using this machine only to characterize the Pareto frontier—we are keeping to the notion that, as economists, efficiency is as far as we are willing to go.

8.5. Syndicate Theory and Efficient Risk Sharing: Applying Proposition 8.10

Proposition 8.10 is typically employed in the analysis of specific contexts, to find and/or characterize efficient arrangements in those contexts. To provide a model for how to attack such problems, in this section we characterize efficient risk sharing, following the treatment given by Wilson (1968) under the title syndicate theory.

A finite collection H of individuals has formed a syndicate that will share the proceeds from various risky ventures. To keep matters relatively simple, we imagine that there is a finite set S of states of nature, with generic element s, and the syndicate collectively holds a finite collection J of risky ventures or gambles, where z_{js} is the amount that venture j returns in state s. A *sharing rule* for the syndicate is an element $(y_{hs}) \in R^{H \times S}$ such that, for each state s, $\sum_{h \in H} y_{hs} \leq \sum_{j \in J} z_{js}$, with the interpretation that under the sharing rule (y_{hs}), y_{hs} is individual h's share of the total in state s.[10] You might imagine, for instance, that each individual h starts with a risky venture and that members of the syndicate pool these ventures and then share in the outcomes—this would mean that $j \in J$ corresponds in one-to-one fashion to $h \in H$. You might imagine further that each individual's venture involves only losses (that is, each $z_{js} \leq 0$), in which case the story suggests that the individuals are engaged in a mutual insurance scheme. Alternatively, the index set of ventures might bear no particular relationship to the list of individuals. Regardless of how these different ventures arise, what is important to the analysis to follow is that the returns from the different ventures are pooled and then shared out among the members of the syndicate. A *social state* x is then one of these sharing rules (y_{hs}), and we seek to answer the question: Which are the Pareto-efficient sharing rules?

Of course, to answer this, we need to know the preferences of the individuals

[10] Rather than the weak inequality $\leq$, you might want to insist on an equality constraint. But we'll shortly make assumptions on preferences that guarantee that, for any Pareto-efficient sharing rule, the inequality constraint will bind. Because we'll enlist the optimization techniques of Appendix 5, an inequality constraint is preferred.

concerning the sharing rules. Assume that each individual h is an expected-utility maximizer, with (cardinal, or von Neumann–Morgenstern) utility function $U_h : R \to R$, and with (subjective) probability assessment $\pi_h(s)$ that state s occurs. Assume that each individual h owns a private endowment amounting to e_{hs} in state s, which is not part of the pooled risky ventures but which represents resources that h can call upon to facilitate the risk sharing. Then the preferences of individual h are given by her subjective expected utility; that is, individual h evaluates sharing rule (y_{hs}) as having the utility

$$\sum_{s \in S} \pi_h(s) U_h(y_{hs} + e_{hs}).$$

We assume that the utility functions U_h are continuous, strictly increasing, and concave. To avoid pathologies, we assume that $\pi_h(s) > 0$ for all h and s; that is, each individual subjectively assesses positive probability for each state.

We also need to know whether there are any constraints that apply to feasible sharing rules. One constraint, the *adding-up* constraint, has already been mentioned: $\sum_h y_{hs} \leq \sum_j z_{js}$ for each s.[11] But beyond this, three other constraints seem worthy of discussion:

- $y_{hs} \geq 0$ for all h and s. Of course, for this to work, we'll need to have $\sum_j z_{js} \geq 0$ for each s, so if the story is one of mutual insurance, this constraint won't work. This constraint says that the sharing rule never asks an individual to contribute out of her private resouces, to make up the shares of others, beyond what is provided in the shared ventures.
- $y_{hs} + e_{hs} \geq 0$ for all h and s. If we assume that each e_{hs} is nonnegative, this relaxes the previous constraint: It allows for negative values in the sharing rule, but not so negative that the individual ends up, net of her own endowment, with a negative outcome. Depending on the domain of the utility function U_h, something like this may be necessary.
- $\sum_s \pi_h(s) U_h(y_{hs} + e_{hs}) \geq \sum_s \pi_h(s) U_h(e_{hs})$ for each h. This constraint, which would be implied by the first constraint (since each U_h is increasing) but which is neither implied by nor implies the second, says that the ex ante position of each individual after sharing rules are assigned leaves the individual at least as well off as if the individual gets nothing from the sharing rule. In the insurance interpretation, this would not be natural to assume: The individual h starts with some lottery with bad outcomes, so to say that her expected utility post-sharing should be at least as large as her expected utility if she faced no risk of this sort at all is ... optimistic. Indeed, if the individuals' outside endowments, given by the e_{hs}, are all constant, and if the shared gambles z_{js} are all nonpositive (and not identically zero), this constraint would make the problem infeasible.

[11] To follow up on footnote 10, since the U_h are strictly increasing, this constraint will bind for any Pareto-efficient sharing rule.

We'll have more to say about these constraints momentarily. But first we have the following result:

Proposition 8.11. *(Recall that we assume that each U_h is concave and strictly increasing.) No matter which subset of the three constraints above are imposed, the set of feasible sharing rules X is convex, and the individual utility functions are all concave.*[12] *Therefore, the first part of Proposition 8.10 applies to this problem.*[13]

Details of the proof are left to you to write out. (It is assigned as Problem 8.7, and the solution is provided in the *Student's Guide.*) To show the concavity of the function $\sum_s \pi_h(s)U_h(y_{hs} + e_{hs})$ in the sharing rule (y_{hs}), you may wish to enlist Proposition A3.17b.

Therefore, according to the proposition, if we want to find the family of Pareto-efficient sharing rules under some set of constraints, we should solve the problems

$$\text{Maximize} \sum_h \alpha_h \left[\sum_s \pi_h(s) U_h(y_{hs} + e_{hs}) \right],$$

where the maximization is over the variables (y_{hs}), subject to the adding-up constraints $\sum_h y_{hs} \leq \sum_j z_{js}$ for each s, plus any other of the constraints we wish to include. As we solve this problem, parametrically varying the weights $(\alpha_h)_{h \in H}$ (where the weights must be nonnegative), we are sure to pick off every Pareto-efficient sharing rule, although we may find solutions that are not Pareto efficient, if any of the weights have value 0. (In fact, for this specific problem, this won't happen. The explanation follows in a bit, but you may wish to see if you can figure out the reason on your own.)

The analysis is a bit clearer if we make a change of variables. Rather than work in terms of the sharing rules (y_{hs}), it is more convenient to work in terms of the net-of-endowment positions of the individuals, the vector $(x_{hs}) \in R^{H \times S}$, where $x_{hs} = y_{hs} + e_{hs}$. Making this substitution, and letting $W_s = \sum_h e_{hs} + \sum_j z_{js}$, the problem can be restated as

$$\text{Maximize} \sum_h \alpha_h \left[\sum_s \pi_h(s) U_h(x_{hs}) \right] \quad \text{subject to} \sum_h x_{hs} \leq W_s \text{ for each } s,$$

plus any additional constraints we care to impose. Please note that we have used the simple symbol x to denote a social state, which is a sharing rule. So, with this

[12] To be clear about what this means: To say that the individual utility functions are concave is *not* to say that the individual's von Neumann–Morgenstern utility functions U_h are concave, which we are *assuming*. Instead, thinking of a social state x as a sharing rule (y_{hs}), the proposition is saying that the function $u_h(x) = \sum_s \pi_h(s)U_h(y_{hs} + e_{hs})$ is a concave function of x. This uses the concavity of the U_h, of course, but still requires some proof.

[13] If we impose some of the constraints mentioned, depending on the parameters of the problem, there may be no feasible sharing rules. To cover this unhappy possibility, we follow the usual convention that the empty set is convex.

change of variables, we are thinking of $x = (x_{hs})$ as a social state or, equivalently, a net-of-endowments sharing rule. Also, for a given net-of-endowment sharing rule $x = (x_{hs})$, we write $u_h(x)$ for $\sum_s \pi_h(s)U_h(x_{hs})$, and $u(x)$ for the vector of utility imputations $(u_h(s))_{h\in H}$.

What about the constraints? In terms of the x_{hs} variables, they are

$$x_{hs} \geq e_{hs} \text{ for all } h \text{ and } s,$$

$$x_{hs} \geq 0 \text{ for all } h \text{ and } s, \text{ and}$$

$$\textstyle\sum_s \pi_h(s)U_h(x_{hs}) \geq \sum_s \pi_h(s)U_h(e_{hs}) \text{ for each } h.$$

I want to argue that the third type of constraint can be imposed post-analysis, so needn't be considered in the analysis, while the first is "uneconomical" in spirit; only the second sort of constraint should concern us.

To take up the third sort of constraint first: Each Pareto-efficient sharing rule $x = (y_{hs})$ and its equivalent net-of-endowment vector (x_{hs}) gives a utility imputation $u(x)$; this third type of constraint simply requires that the vector $u(x)$ satisfy $u(x) \geq v^0$, where $v^0 \in R^H$ is the vector whose h component is $v_h^0 = \sum_s \pi_h(s)U_h(e_{hs})$. The constraint takes the larger Pareto frontier (without it) and restricts attention to a subset, without changing the shape, structure, or character of social states in that subset. We can worry about whether a particular Pareto-efficient allocation gives each individual enough utility after we find the allocation; if h is not getting enough expected utility when we maximize for some weighting vector $(\alpha_h)_{h\in H}$, we can improve her situation by increasing her relative weight.

As for the first sort of constraint, suppose some sharing rule x is Pareto efficient with this constraint but not when the constraint is relaxed. That is, there is some sharing rule x' that Pareto dominates x, but that is ruled out because it violates this constraint. This means that x' is ruled out because it calls for some individual h to take resources provided by her endowment and, in some state, transfer them to another member of the syndicate. But since x' Pareto dominates x, this individual is just as well off, in terms of overall utility, as at x; presumably, the individual is compensated (and perhaps more) by a larger transfer (relative to what she gets under x) from the syndicate members in some other state(s). And someone is better off at x' than at x. In the context of this problem, we can find the individual who is strictly better off and, in at least one state, take a bit away from him and distribute that to every other individual in a way that makes *everyone* strictly better off than at x; that is, if x' Pareto dominates x, then there is some x'' that *strictly* Pareto dominates x. Now h is strictly better off than at x. Will h really object to drawing upon her private endowment in some states, if by doing so she winds up in a strictly better position overall? In fact, there may be good economic reasons for this, but they lie beyond the story we are telling here;[14] our objective for now

[14] Suppose that h's endowment is unknown to other members of the syndicate; in the terminology of Volume II, the endowments are private information to their owners. And suppose that which Pareto-efficient sharing rule the syndicate chooses is influenced by how well off are syndicate members overall; richer syndicate members are given less weight. Then h might want to hide her endowment if she

is to find efficient sharing rules, where we suppose we (and everyone) has all the information that makes up this problem, in which case it is difficult to justify the first sort of constraint.

To be clear, this argument completely blurs any distinction between the set of jointly owned ventures, given by (z_{js}), and the private endowments (e_{hs}). The syndicate may have formed to share in the risk of those jointly owned ventures. But once we start looking for efficient sharing rules, where Pareto efficiency inevitably involves the private endowments, since those endowments affect preferences, risk sharing of the private endowments enters the picture. Put it this way: Suppose that the jointly owned ventures didn't really exist, in the sense that $z_{js} \equiv 0$. If members of the syndicate H can engage in mutually beneficial risk sharing of their private endowments, then getting rid of constraints of the first type will have them do so (in Pareto-efficient sharing rules). The argument given in the previous paragraph essentially says (in this context): "If it makes everyone better off, why not?"

In comparison, constraints of the second type could be quite reasonable. What does it mean, that $x_{hs} < 0$ in some state s? Where does h obtain the resources to make good on this net debt? What if U_h is undefined for negative arguments?

This leaves us with two possible formulations of the problem; one with no constraint other than the adding-up constraint $\sum_h x_{hs} \leq W_s$ for each s; and one where we add the constraints $x_{hs} \geq 0$ for every h and s.

The decision whether to add the constraints $x_{hs} \geq 0$ or not should be made on grounds of what is right in terms of economics. But those constraints provide a measure of analytical convenience as well: With them, the space over which the maximum is taken—the space $\{(x_{hs}) \in R^{H \times S} : \sum_h x_{hs} \leq W_s$ for each s, $x_{hs} \geq 0$ for all h and $s\}$—is compact, and we are assured that the maximization problem has a solution for every weighting vector (α_h). Without the nonnegativity constraints, the set over which the maximum is taken is not compact, and for particular weights or even in general, the maximization problem may have no solution. Among the ways in which a solution may fail to exist are the following two:

- First, suppose individual h^0 is given no weight, or $\alpha_{h^0} = 0$. Then providing h^0 with an immensely negative share has no impact on the objective function and allows an individual with positive weight to have an immensely positive share. Depending on the behavior of the utility functions of individuals with positive weight (whether their utility functions are bounded above), this may or may not mean that unbounded objective-function values are possible. But as long as each U_h is strictly increasing (which we've assumed), it does mean that there cannot be a solution to the maximization problem.

  We may as well take this opportunity to deal with the issue of zero weights in the weighting function. As just discussed, if we do not have the constraints

is relatively rich, which might mean imposing this sort of constraint; the syndicate can only share in the resources its members hold jointly. But please note that this story imposes major difficulties on the project of finding efficient sharing rules: If h's endowment is not known to her fellow syndicate members, how would they know her level of risk aversion, unless we supposed that they assume she has constant risk aversion?

$x_{hs} \geq 0$ and if the weighting vector has some of weights equal to zero, then the maximization problem has no solution. On the other hand, if we do have the constraints $x_{hs} \geq 0$ and some $\alpha_{h_0} = 0$, then maximizing the weighted sum of utilities leads to $x_{h_0 s} = 0$ for all s: If $x_{h_0 s} > 0$ for any s, then transferring that share in state s to some h_1 with $\alpha_{h_1} > 0$, increases the utility of h_1, and hence the sum of utilities, with no impact through the decrease in expected utility for h_0. (If $U_{h_0}(0) = -\infty$, we have to worry about how to interpret $0 \cdot U_{h_0}(0)$, but the interpretation we'll adopt is that this is zero.) Therefore, if we do have these nonnegativity constraints, when maximizing the weighted sum with some zero weights, the thing to do is to give individuals with zero weights zero shares and maximize over everyone else. And the resulting solutions will necessarily be fully Pareto efficient. It isn't always true, but in this specific application of Proposition 8.10, we do *not* need to worry about producing Pareto-inefficient solutions when the weighting vector includes some zeros.

- Second, suppose individuals h^0 and h^1 differ in their assessment of some state. Suppose, in particular, that $\pi_{h^0}(s^0) > \pi_{h^1}(s^0)$. Since each individual's probabilities must sum to one, this means that

$$\pi_{h^1}(s^1) > \pi_{h^0}(s^1)$$

for some other state s^1. But then, if U_{h^1} and U_{h^0} are "insufficiently concave," we get existence problems for *nearly every* vector of weights. To be very specific, suppose both U_{h^1} and U_{h^0} are linear, so both individuals are risk neutral. Disagreeing as they do over the relative probabilities of states s^0 and s^1, you can construct a bet between them where h^1 wins if s^1 occurs and loses if s^0 occurs, and with h^0 taking the other side of this bet, which both of them view as having subjective positive expectation. If they are both risk neutral, increasing the scale of this bet between them, whatever else happens in the sharing rule, drives the expected utilities of both of them to $+\infty$, and regardless of the weighting vector, as long as it gives one or the other positive weight, this drives the objective function to $+\infty$; the problem has no solution. (If one or the other has zero weight, we already know from two paragraphs ago that there can be no solution.)

Please note carefully that while the maximization problem may not have a solution for some weighting vectors, this doesn't affect our earlier results: We still know that any Pareto-efficient social state will be a solution of this problem for some weights $(\alpha_h)_{h \in H}$, and every solution that we do manage to find will be Pareto efficient. So the plot remains the same: We want to characterize solutions to those maximization problems, as we parametrically vary the weighting vectors, since solutions are Pareto efficient and Pareto-efficient sharing rules correspond to solutions. And when it comes to looking for solutions to the maximization problems, the following result simplifies the task.

Proposition 8.12. $(x_{hs})_{h \in H; s \in S}$ *maximizes*

$$\sum_h \alpha_h \left[\sum_s \pi_h(s) U_h(x_{hs}) \right]$$

subject to the constraints $\sum_h x_{hs} \leq W_s$ *for all* s *(and, depending on the formulation,* $x_{hs} \geq 0$ *for all* h *and* s*) if and only if the net-of-endowments sharing rule for each state* s*, or* $(x_{hs})_{h \in H}$*, maximizes*

$$\sum_h \alpha_h \pi_h(s) U_h(x_{hs})$$

subject to the constraint $\sum_h x_{hs} \leq W_s$ *(and, depending on the formulation,* $x_{hs} \geq 0$ *for all* h*), for each state* s *independently.*

In other words, we can solve the maximization problem state by state and then paste the results together. Seeing that this is so is a matter of noting that

$$\sum_h \alpha_h \left[\sum_s \pi_h(s) U_h(x_{hs}) \right] = \sum_s \left[\sum_h \alpha_h \pi_h(s) U_h(x_{hs}) \right].$$

This just involves changing the order of the two summations. Maximizing the objective function (on the left-hand side of the last displayed equation) amounts to maximizing the right-hand side, and since none of the constraints cut across the states, this amounts to maximizing separately each term in the sum on the right-hand side.

At the risk of (once again) being overly pedantic, let me be clear what this is saying. Once we fix the weights $(\alpha_h)_{h \in H}$ and set out to maximize, to find Pareto-efficient sharing rules, we maximize on each state independently of what happens in the other states. But this is for fixed weights. When it comes to picking from among the Pareto-efficient sharing rules, if it ever does come to that, then a selection of which Pareto-efficient sharing rule is equitable will involve the computation of overall expected utilities, which cuts across states.

Now assume that each U_h is differentiable, with derivative denoted by U_h'. We are looking for solutions to

$$\text{Maximize } \sum_h \alpha_h \pi_h(s) U_h(x_{hs}), \quad \text{subject to } \sum_h x_{hs} \leq W_s,$$

plus possibly nonnegativity constraints. Letting λ_s be the multiplier on the adding-up constraint and noting that the adding-up contraint will bind at any optimum, the first-order, complementary slackness (FOCS) conditions for an optimum if we do not have the nonnegativity constraints are

$$\alpha_h \pi_h(s) U_h'(x_{hs}) = \lambda_s \quad \text{and} \quad \sum_h x_{hs} = W_s.$$

If we do have the nonnegativity constraints, the FOCS conditions change to

$$\alpha_h \pi_h(s) U'_h(x_{hs}) \leq \lambda_s, \text{ with equality if } x_{hs} > 0, \quad \text{and} \quad \sum_h x_{hs} = W_s.$$

Since the constraints are all linear and the objective function is concave, the FOCS conditions are sufficient for an optimum; since the constraint qualification holds, they are necessary. That is, these FOCS conditions characterize the Pareto-efficient net-of-endowment outcomes for each individual or, equivalently, the Pareto-efficient sharing rules. They can be used, for instance, to derive the following:

- Suppose every individual except possibly one is strictly risk averse. Then for each weighting vector, there is a unique solution to the maximization problem.
- With or without the nonnegativity constraints, the Pareto-efficient net-of-endowment outcome rules depend on the total endowment vector W_s and not on how the total endowment is divided between the income from the ventures held by the syndicate and the private endowments of each individual. Roughly put, while the syndicate may have been formed to share in income produced from risky ventures that are jointly held by the syndicate, Pareto-efficient sharing rules propel members of the syndicate into sharing the risks of their private endowments. (This is not true if constraints of the form $x_{hs} \geq e_{hs}$ are added.)
- Suppose individuals have common subjective probability assessments; that is, $\pi_h(s) = \pi_{h'}(s)$ for all states s and pairs of individuals h and h'. Then the (common) probability assessment is irrelevant to Pareto-efficient sharing rules; if the (common) probability assessment changed to some different but still common assessment, the set of Pareto-efficient sharing rules would not change at all.
- Suppose individuals have common subjective probability assessments and every individual except exactly one is strictly risk averse, and the one exception is risk neutral. Suppose as well that (at least) the risk-neutral party is not subject to the nonnegativity constraint. Then every Pareto-efficient rule has all the (strictly) risk averse individuals receiving a net-of-endowment outcome that is constant across the states, with the one risk-neutral individual absorbing all the risk. (The size of the various constant net-of-endowment outcomes determines where on the Pareto frontier the sharing rule is found.)
- Suppose individuals have common subjective probability assessments, nonnegativity constraints are not imposed, and every individual has a constant-absolute-risk-aversion utility function, or $U_h(x) = -e^{-\mu_h x}$. Let $\tau_h = 1/\mu_h$; τ_h is sometimes called the *coefficient of risk tolerence* of individual h. Let $T = \sum_h \tau_h$. Then Pareto-efficient rules have the form

  $$x_{hs} = \frac{\tau_h}{T} W_s + k_h,$$

  for constants k_h that sum to zero (and move the sharing rule from one point on the Pareto frontier to another).

Problem 8.10 provides you with the opportunity to prove each of these claims.

8.6. Efficiency?

By restricting attention to efficiency, economics avoids controversy. Surely, the argument goes, we can all agree that an inefficient social outcome is bad and should be replaced by an outcome that Pareto dominates it. Who would argue against moving from one social state to another, if the second social state is weakly preferred to the first by everyone and strictly preferred by some? Controversy arises when we debate among the Pareto-efficient states. But can there be any reason not to look for an efficient outcome?

Taken for what it says and not misused for what it doesn't say, this argument is largely unexceptional, which is why controversy-averse economists are fond of it. But (1) it can be and, in some instances, has been misused. And (2) some situations present complications or, at least, reasons to wonder about the appeal of efficiency defined in the fashion of this chapter.

The misuses arise when the focus is on the comparison of processes or policies or mechanisms, rather than on social outcomes. One process/policy/ mechanism may guarantee an efficient outcome. Another may offer no such guarantee; indeed, another process/policy/mechanism may guarantee a social outcome that is *inefficient*. Does this make the first better than the second? Suppose the first guarantees a social outcome that, while efficient, is vastly inequitable; the competing mechanism may provide an inefficient outcome that is substantially more equitable. To reject the second mechanism on grounds that it is "inefficient" is, in essence, to say that any efficient outcome is better than any inefficient outcome. The argument for efficiency in this chapter certainly doesn't imply that. To give a concrete example (for readers with background in the relevant parts of economics), free-trade policies may lead to efficient outcomes, while protectionism may lead to inefficient results. But this doesn't mean that everyone in the economy benefits when a society moves from protectionism to free trade. Don't misunderstand, I'm not saying that protectionism is better. (I'm also not trying to defend the proposition that free trade leads to efficient outcomes; that is a complex question that is well beyond the scope of this volume or even the material planned for subsequent volumes.) But, granting the assertion that free trade leads to an efficient outcome and protectionism does not, this is not, by itself, a compelling argument in favor of free trade. (This takes one into the issue of compensation, and I again recommend Arrow's chapter on the topic.)

The complications all have to do with the basic premise of Pareto efficiency, sometimes called *consumer sovereignty*, that the preferences of the individuals involved are all that matters.

1. Suppose the context is dynamic and, contrary to the standard models of dynamic choice/behavior, the preferences of the individuals involved change through time. Do we regard the individual's initial preferences as controlling the definition of efficiency, or her final preferences? Instead, perhaps we should define

efficiency as: One social outcome is Pareto superior to a second if each individual, at each point in time, regards the first as at least as good. And if this is the criterion employed, what if the choice of social state endogenously informs the way in which the individual's preferences change? That is, she has one set of "later" preferences in social state x, and a different set of "later" preferences in social state y. How do we compare x and y in such circumstances?

2. Changing preferences are *not* standard in economics, so item 1 might be regarded as something of a diversion from the mainstream of economic thought and practice. But, still in a dynamic context, suppose the choice of social state affects which *individuals* come into (later) existence. How do we treat the preferences of the not yet born if, under state x, they will be born, while in state y, they never will be?

3. A third dynamic effect concerns the distinction between ex ante and ex post utility or preferences. It is easiest to raise the issue with a story: Throughout the 1970s, the Institute for Mathematical Studies in the Social Sciences (or IMSSS) sponsored a biweekly series of seminars in economic theory at Stanford University. Speakers would talk for an hour, and then everyone would adjourn for coffee or tea and cookies in the lounge, after which the seminar would continue for another hour or so. In the lounge was a sofa with small pillows and, one day, two famous economic theorists, Joe and Bob, were arguing over the contents of the pillows. Joe maintained that the pillow had a natural down filling, while Bob thought a synthetic filling was more likely. Being famous economic theorists, they quantified their uncertainty, with Bob assessing probability 0.2 that the filling was natural and Joe assessing probability 0.9. They decided, therefore, to construct a bet about this: If the pillow had natural down, Bob would pay Joe $100, but if it had artificial down, Joe would pay Bob $200. The problem was that they could only discover the truth by cutting the pillow open, which would destroy it. A new pillow would cost $50, and after consulting their utility functions, they discovered:

   - Relative to not betting at all, Bob would prefer a bet in which he wins $150 if the pillow has artificial down filling and loses $100 if it did not (a 0.8 chance at $150 and a 0.2 chance at −$100).
   - Relative to not betting at all, Joe would prefer a bet in which he wins $50 if the pillow has natural filling and loses $200 if not (a 0.9 chance of $50 and a 0.1 chance of −$200 if it does not).

   They could conduct this bet, which would destroy the pillow but leave $50 in hand with which to buy a new pillow. Hence, from the ex ante perspective, betting is Pareto superior to not betting. But ex post, all that happens is that money has changed hands and a perfectly good pillow has been destroyed. Is this really what we mean by Pareto superiority?

4. The final complication, which is not specifically dynamic, goes right at the heart of consumer sovereignty and might be called *paternalism*. Few economists

would think of extending the idea that the individual's preferences are all that matters to, say, the preferences of children. This could be labeled as a manifestation of changing tastes (with a clear preference for what, one hopes, will be where tastes end up), or perhaps as preferences that are not adequately informed by all available information. But in the latter case, do we then define Pareto superiority in terms of what individuals would prefer *if* they had full information? What if the choice of social state affects what information individuals have? What if, for instance, the verdict is that social state x would be judged efficient if everyone had full information, but x precludes that everyone has full information, so that a number of individuals *regard* x as inferior to y? And what if it is not a question of information, but simply a case of pure paternalism: An individual prefers an outcome that, society strongly believes, is bad for that individual? (Suppose the individual is genetically predisposed to alcoholism, for instance. Or, to take an example that is a bit less extreme and certainly more controversial, suppose some members of society save too little for their own good, at least according to "experts.")

In mainstream economics, these sorts of issues rarely arise. So the general lure of efficiency in mainstream economics is and remains very strong. But, *rarely* is not *never*, and categories 2 and 4 given above are the starting point for some controversies. Especially as economics expands its grasp in the directions of behavioral phenomena, it is worthwhile to maintain a somewhat skeptical view of efficiency as defined by an economist.

Bibliographic Notes

The classic reference in the theory of social choice is Arrow (1951a). Another excellent monograph is Sen (1970). Syndicate theory is studied in Wilson (1968).

Problems

■ 8.1. In the text, we observed that if h^* is a dictator in the social preference function Φ, this doesn't imply that Φ produced social preferences $\succeq$ that are identical to $\succeq_{h^*}$. In particular, if h^* is indifferent between x and y, then Φ can produce strict preference in either direction, while still having h^* be a dictator according to Φ.

(a) We never settled the question of whether there is any social preference function that satisfies unanimity and IIA (and Assumption 8.1); Arrow's Theorem only shows that *if* there is such a social preference function, it must be dictatorial. So, please clear up the existence question by producing a social preference function that satisfies Assumption 8.1, unanimity, and IIA.

(b) Suppose that Φ works as follows: The individuals in H are sequenced arbitrarily as $h_1, h_2, \ldots, h_n$ (where n is the cardinality of H). For the array $(\succeq_h)_{h \in H}$, Φ gives social preferences $\succeq$ that work as follows: For every x and y, $x \succ y$ if: $x \succ_{h_1} y$; or

$x \sim_{h_1} y$ and $x \succ_{h_2} y$; or $x \sim_{h_1} y$ and $x \sim_{h_2} y$ and $x \succ_{h_3} y$; and so forth. If $x \sim_h y$ for all h, then $x \sim y$. In words, we have a *sequential dictatorship*: If h_1 has a strict preference, society adopts that; if h_1 is indifferent between x and y, we go on to consult h_2, and so forth. Does this social preference function satisfy Assumption 8.1, unanimity, and/or IIA?

(c) Suppose that X contains more than three elements. Does (b) exhaust the set of social preference functions that satisfy Assumption 8.1, unanimity, and IIA? (If so, you must prove it. If not, you can simply supply a social preference function that satisfies these properties and is not a sequential dictatorship.)

■ 8.2. Arrow's Theorem makes the assumption that X has at least three elements. What happens if X has two elements?

■ *8.3. (a) Prove Proposition 8.5.

(b) Give the sort of example described two paragraphs after the statement of Proposition 8.5. (You can do this even if you can't do part (a).)

■ 8.4. Prove Proposition 8.7.

■ *8.5. Prove that if x^0 is Pareto efficient in A and if, for each $h \in H$ (for a finite H), u_h is a utility function representing h's preferences, then there is a strictly increasing function $W : R^H \to R$ such that x^0 maximizes $W \circ u$ over the set A. (Warning: If A is infinite, the function W may have to be discontinuous.)

■ *8.6. I assert in the course of discussing Figure 8.2 (and the proof of Proposition 8.10) that even if X is convex and each u_h is a concave function, the set $\{v \in R^H : v = u(x)$ for some $x \in X\}$ may not be convex "to the southwest." (See Figure 8.2a, in particular.) Give an example to demonstrate this.

■ *8.7. Prove Proposition 8.11.

■ 8.8. Give proofs of the following three results claimed in the discussion of syndicate theory: (a) If constraints of the form $x_{hs} \geq 0$ are not imposed and if $\alpha_h = 0$ for some h, then the maximization problem has no solution. (b) If constraints of the form $x_{hs} \geq 0$ are imposed, then even if $\alpha_h = 0$ for some of the h, any solution of the maximization problem provides a Pareto-efficient sharing rule. (c) If some sharing rule x' Pareto dominates another sharing rule x, then some sharing rule x'' *strictly* Pareto dominates x. (Why are parts (b) and (c) connected?)

■ 8.9. In the formulation where the shares are not constrained, suppose that individuals h^1 and h^2 differ in their assessment of state s^0; specifically, suppose that $\pi_{h^1}(s^0) > \pi_{h_2}(s^1)$. And suppose that both h^1 and h^2 are risk neutral. In the text, a loose argument is given that this will mean that the maximization problem will have no solution, as long as either α_{h^1} or α_{h^2} is nonzero. Give a tight argument that this is so. (Since a different argument covers the case where any individual has zero weight, you may if you wish assume that both of them have strictly positive weight.) Then: in the discussion, it first says that this sort of thing will cause existence problems if U_{h^1} and U_{h^2} are "insufficiently concave." Show by example that existence problems can occur if both U_{h^1} and U_{h^2} are strictly concave, but still "insufficiently concave" (where part of the problem is to figure out what that vague phrase might mean).

■ *8.10. Prove each of the bullet-point claims on pages 191–2.

■ 8.11. Consider a two-person society in which there are two consumption goods, x_1 and x_2. Individual 1's utility function is $u_1(x_1^1, x_2^1) = 6 + 0.4\ln(x_1^1) + 0.6\ln(x_2^1)$, while individual 2's utility function is $u_2(x_1^2, x_2^2) = 8 + \ln(x_1^2) + \ln(x_2^2)$. The social endowent consists of 15 units of the first good and 20 units of the second good, to be split between the two.

What division of the social endowment between the two individuals maximizes the social utility functional $2\min\{u_1, u_2\} + \max\{u_1, u_2\}$?

Hint: What does Figure 8.4 depict, and how did I construct it?

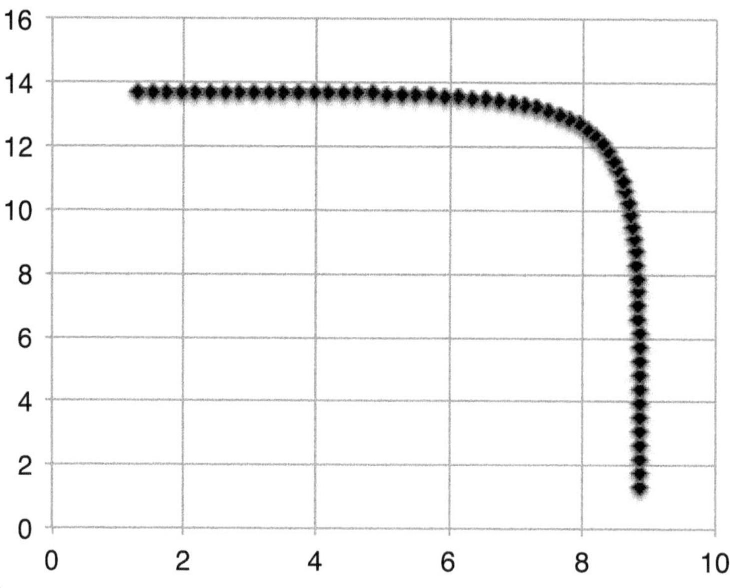

Figure 8.4. Hint for Problem 8.11.

Chapter Nine

Competitive and Profit-Maximizing Firms

Two categories of entities inhabit neoclassical microeconomic theory, consumers and firms. We've met consumers at length already, with more to come in Chapters 10 and 11. The story about firms is shorter and simpler; it can be contained within a single albeit lengthy chapter.

In neoclassical economics, firms are optimizing *entities*, similar to consumers. In more recent developments, firms are analyzed as *institutions*, within which individual optimizing agents (investors, managers, employees, and so forth) interact. In this volume and, in particular, in this chapter, we explore the neoclassical theory only, treating firms as entities.

Also, we will restrict our attention to the special case of a competitive (or price-taking), profit-maximizing firm. A large portion of the neoclassical theory of the firm concerns firms with the power to affect prices, in the so-called theories of monopoly, oligopoly, and monopolistic competition. Consumers, with the exception of people such as Bill Gates, are naturally thought of as being so small relative to the markets in which they participate, that their actions do not materially affect the prices they face; for firms, this assumption is certainly much less natural. Yet we will study only competitive firms and, moreover, firms that face linear prices for their inputs and outputs. For reasons to be discussed, we will study firms with a single objective function: maximization of profit. And we will restrict attention to the "static" theory of the firm: Firms, we will see momentarily, are entities that transform bundles of commodities into different bundles of commodities via *production*; we will deal only with instantaneous production, in which inputs are purchased, transformed, and sold in an instant of time.[1] We will have more to say on this point when we discuss the assumption that firms maximize their profits.

Finally, even within the context of competitive, static, and profit-maximizing firms, one finds a number of ways to model the capabilities of firms and the problem they face. Our attention in this chapter is almost entirely fixed on the firm's capabilities modeled as a *production-possibility set* from which it chooses a profit-maximizing production plan given the prices for inputs and outputs it faces. Alternatives include the problem of minimizing the cost of producing a fixed amount of output, using input-requirement sets and facing prices on inputs, or the profit-maximization

[1] By labeling commodities with the time at which they exist, the theory we develop here can be reinterpreted as a theory of dynamic production; see the discussion of general equilibrium, time, and uncertainty in Chapter 16. But for reasons that we will only be able to explain later, these extensions are not altogether satisfactory.

problem but with the firm's capabilities given by a production function. We briefly outline the theory of cost minimization and input-requirement sets near the end of the chapter.

9.1. The Production-Possibility Set

The commodity space is R^k. The (one) firm has the power to transform vectors of commodities into other vectors of commodities; we say that the firm engages in *production*. A *netput* vector is a vector from R^k, where a negative component connotes a net *input* into the firm's production process and a positive component connotes a net *output*. So, for instance, if $k = 5$, the netput vector $(-2, 0, 3, -1, 2)$ is interpreted as the firm transforming two units of the first commodity and one unit of the fourth into three units of the third and two units of the fifth. These are net input and net output amounts—the -2 in the first component could represent an initial input of three units, but with one unit "returned" at the end of the production process. In this idealization, production takes no time and, in fact, when we get to markets for inputs and outputs, the story will be that the firm buys its net inputs and simultaneously sells its net outputs, which doesn't leave a lot of time for the transformation to take place.

The firm is capable of some but not all netput vectors, and the full set of production possibilities for the firm is given by a set $Z \subseteq R^k$, the so-called *production-possibility set* or *set of feasible netput vectors* for this firm. It is typical to make assumptions on the shape of Z. Some common assumptions are:

- *No free production.* $Z \cap R^k_+ \subseteq \{0\}$. In words, the only nonnegative netput vector that could possibly be feasible is the zero vector. The firm can't turn nothing into something.
- *Free disposal.* If $z \in Z$ and $z' \leq z$, then $z' \in Z$. In words, if the firm can do z, it can get by with more net input and less net output (or even turning some net outputs into net inputs). Another paraphrase, very much in line with the term free disposal, is: Dumpsters are freely available and free to use.
- *The ability to shut down.* $0 \in Z$. Or, in words, the firm can choose to do nothing.
- *Convexity.* The set Z is convex.
- *Closedness.* The set Z is closed.
- *Increasing returns to scale.* If $z \in Z$ and $\alpha > 1$, then $\alpha z \in Z$.
- *Decreasing returns to scale.* If $z \in Z$ and $0 \leq \alpha < 1$, then $\alpha z \in Z$.
- *Constant returns to scale.* If $z \in Z$, then $\alpha z \in Z$ for all $\alpha \geq 0$.

These are fairly straightforward properties, although decreasing returns to scale may give you a moment's pause. The phrase "returns to scale" implicitly means "scaling up," and so increasing returns to scale says: The firm has the ability to scale up any feasible production plan. On the other hand, decreasing returns to scale says: If the firm can do some production plan, it can do the same plan on any (proportionally) smaller scale. It is when scale increases that feasible production plans may become infeasible. Also, "increasing" and "decreasing" here really mean "nondecreasing" and "nonincreasing," respectively, so that an alternative definition of constant returns to scale is that Z has *both* increasing and decreasing returns.

In a moment, we will introduce the firm's optimization problem, which is to maximize profit, a linear function of production. We will want, when the time comes, to make assumptions that guarantee the existence of a solution, at least for strictly positive prices, for which purpose the following property of Z comes into play.

- *The recession-cone property*. If $\{z^n\}$ is a sequence from Z such that $\|z^n\| \to \infty$, then every accumulation point of the set $\{z^n/\|z^n\|; n = 1, 2, \ldots\}$ lies in the negative orthant of R^k.[2]

This property deserves considerable pondering. In words, if we have a sequence of feasible production plans whose norms diverge, and if we normalize them by dividing each one by its norm, so the result lies on the unit circle, then the normalized vectors will only accumulate in the negative orthant. Rephrasing roughly, if we take any ray in R^k from the origin that has some strictly positive components (that doesn't run off into the negative orthant), this ray eventually "leaves" Z. Put this way, you can see that, except for cases where Z lies within the negative orthant (the firm can only destroy commodities), the recession-cone property is inconsistent with increasing (hence constant) returns to scale.

9.2. Profit Maximization

The production-possibility set Z describes the capabilities of the firm. The other piece of this chapter's model of the firm is the firm's objective function, which determines what the firm chooses to do. The firm, the model assumes, chooses z to maximize its profit: A vector of prices $p \in R^k_{++}$ is fixed, so that $p \cdot z$ is the firm's profit if it undertakes z; the firm chooses $z \in Z$ to maximize $p \cdot z$. Note well, $p \cdot z$ is the value in the market (at the given prices) of all net outputs (positive components of z) less the cost to the firm in the market of all its net inputs (negative components of z).

We've already said it, but to reiterate, this assumes:

- The firm's level of activities doesn't affect the price of any good, whether an input or an output.
- The firm faces linear prices.

And, as we've already said, especially when it comes to its outputs, it is less than completely sensible to assume that firms have no impact on the prices they face. General Motors has a pretty direct impact on the price of Cadillacs; it is perhaps

[2] The negative orthant in R^k is the set of $z \leq 0$; coordinate values of 0 are permitted.

less obvious, but still plausible, that agribusiness giant ADM affects the price of high-fructose corn syrup, one of its products, and perhaps (but less likely) the price of corn, an input. Those are real and interesting possibilities that are *not* considered in this chapter.

Even assuming that the firm has no effect on the prices it faces and that those prices are linear, it is by no means obvious that the firm chooses to maximize the profit it earns. Begin by thinking of a firm that is a sole proprietorship, where the person making decisions is the owner of the firm and, therefore, the residual claimant to the firm's profit. Why would this individual choose z to maximize profit? If, for instance, the sole proprietor has a particular interest in some activity—it is fun, say—might not the person engage in that activity, even at the cost of some profit? Or what if the firm has separation between owners and managers? The person(s) choosing the production plan is not the residual claimant(s) to the profit of the firm but instead her agent(s). What motivates the manager *cum* agent to choose a profit-maximizing plan? Finally, in real life (but not this model) firms exist for multiple periods. Profit is not a clearly defined concept in this case: Does it mean accounting earnings or income? And how should trade-offs be made between income in one period and in the next? (We will confront these issues in Chapter 16, when time is introduced into our models in a serious way.)

These are all good questions, and a large literature in economics exists to deal with them. It is impossible to do justice to this literature here, without expanding this chapter unreasonably and, in any case, some of the answers require pieces of economics that we haven't yet studied. So I'll plead simply that profit maximization is a modeling assumption, one with which economists are comfortable not as a law of nature but as an approximation to reality. Having said that, three specific points are worth making, albeit briefly.

- Profit maximization as an objective function for firms is a lot more specific than utility maximization for consumers. When we assume that a consumer maximizes her utility, we leave it up to the consumer how she feels about apples versus oranges. But, once prices are given, the trade-offs facing a firm are fixed if the firm maximizes profit. (On the other hand, the choice set of a consumer is fixed once prices are fixed and the consumer's income is given. For firms, the production-possibility set Z gives a lot of latitude to the modeler.)
- Accounting earnings or income is not economic profit. Accounting income does not include any return on capital equipment.
- The arguments in the literature for profit maximization when there is a division between managers and owners of the firm turn to some extent on a contention that managers act on behalf of the firm's owners, who prefer profit maximization. *Why* managers do this is usually the issue being studied in the literature. But it is worth noting that the assertion that owners prefer profit maximization is very bound up in the assumption that the firm has no impact on prices. When firms affect prices, and when owners of the firm consume (or are endowed with) the goods whose prices the firm affects, it is no longer clear that

the owners either should or do prefer profit-maximizing choices by firms.

9.3. Basics of the Firm's Profit-Maximization Problem

For most of the remainder of this chapter, then, we study the *firm's profit-maximization problem*: For a given $Z \subseteq R^k$ and $p \in R^k_{++}$,

$$\text{maximize } p \cdot z, \text{ subject to } z \in Z.$$

Fixing Z, we define

$$Z^*(p) = \text{arg max } \{p \cdot z : z \in Z\} \quad \text{and} \quad \pi(p) = \sup \{p \cdot z : z \in Z\}.$$

Elements of $Z^*(p)$ are called both *optimal netput vectors* and *optimal production plans* for the firm at prices p; the correspondence $p \Rightarrow Z^*(p)$ is the firm's *optimal netput correspondence*. The function π is called the *profit function*. For the remainder of this chapter, we assume that $Z \neq \emptyset$, so that $\pi(p) > -\infty$ for all p.

Because Z is not necessarily compact, we don't know, for a given price vector p, that a solution to this problem exists. A solution could fail to exist on either of two (general) grounds: $\pi(p)$ may be finite, but Z isn't closed. And $\pi(p)$ could be infinite: For each $n = 1, 2, \ldots$, there could be some $z^n \in Z$ such that $p \cdot z^n \geq n$. In either case, we would say that $Z^*(p) = \emptyset$. And, in the second case, we say that $\pi(p) = \infty$.

These are real possibilities, depending on what is assumed about Z. In particular, assumptions of increasing returns to scale are problematic.

Proposition 9.1. *Suppose that Z exhibits increasing returns to scale. Then for every $p \in R^k_{++}$, if $\pi(p) > 0$, then $\pi(p) = \infty$.*

Proof. Suppose $\pi(p) > 0$. Then for some $z^0 \in Z$, $p \cdot z^0 > 0$. But by increasing returns to scale, for each positive integer n, $nz^0 \in Z$, so $\pi(p) \geq p \cdot (nz^0) = n(p \cdot z^0)$, which goes to ∞ as n goes to ∞. ∎

Corollary 9.2. *Suppose that Z exhibits increasing returns to scale and $0 \in Z$. (In particular, if Z exhibits constant returns to scale, this is true.) Then for every $p \in R^k_{++}$, either $\pi(p) = 0$ or $\pi(p) = \infty$.*

Proof. If $0 \in Z$, then $\pi(p) \geq 0$ for all p. Apply the previous proposition. ∎

Results that work even if $Z^*(p) = \emptyset$ for some p

We know that $\pi(p)$ is either finite or $+\infty$ for all p.[3] Because $\pi(p) = -\infty$ has been ruled out, we can talk about π being convex and homogeneous of degree 1, even if it is sometimes infinite valued:

---

[3] A mathematician would say that π is an *extended real-valued* function, where the extended reals are the real numbers plus $\pm\infty$.

- The convex combination $\alpha\pi(p) + (1-\alpha)\pi(p')$ for $\alpha \in [0,1]$ equals $\pi(p)$ if $\alpha = 1$, $\pi(p')$ if $\alpha = 0$, the usual thing if $\alpha \in (0,1)$ and both $\pi(p)$ and $\pi(p')$ are finite, and ∞ if $\alpha \in (0,1)$ and either $\pi(p)$ or $\pi(p')$ or both are infinite.
- The term $\alpha\pi(p)$ for $\alpha \geq 0$ is defined to be 0 if $\alpha = 0$ (even if $\pi(p) = \infty$), the usual thing if $\alpha > 0$ and $\pi(p) < \infty$, and ∞ if $\alpha > 0$ and $\pi(p) = \infty$.

With these conventions, convexity and homogeneity are defined precisely as in the case of real-valued functions.

Proposition 9.3. *The function π is homogeneous of degree 1 and convex. For all p and $z^* \in Z$, $z^* \in Z^*(p)$ if and only if z^* is a subgradient of π at p.*

Proof. For homogeneity, take any p and $\alpha > 0$. If $\pi(p) < \infty$, then for each $\epsilon > 0$, there is some $z^\epsilon \in Z$ such that $p \cdot z^\epsilon \geq \pi(p) - \epsilon$. But then

$$\pi(\alpha p) \geq (\alpha p) \cdot z^\epsilon = \alpha(p \cdot z^\epsilon) \geq \alpha(\pi(p) - \epsilon) = \alpha\pi(p) - \alpha\epsilon.$$

Since ϵ is arbitrary here, this implies that $\pi(\alpha p) \geq \alpha\,\pi(p)$. If $\pi(p) = \infty$, then for any positive integer n, for some $z^n \in Z$, $p \cdot z^n \geq n$. But then $\pi(\alpha p) \geq (\alpha p) \cdot z^n = \alpha(p \cdot z^n) \geq \alpha n$, and since n is an arbitrary positive integer here, we again conclude that $\pi(\alpha p) \geq \alpha\pi(p)$. These are the only two cases, so $\pi(\alpha p) \geq \alpha\pi(p)$ unconditionally. Apply this to $p' = \alpha p$ and $\alpha' = 1/\alpha$, and you conclude that $\pi(p) \geq (1/\alpha)\,\pi(\alpha p)$, and combining the two inequalities shows that $\pi(\alpha p) = \alpha\,\pi(p)$.

This leaves the special case $\alpha = 0$. The function π has only been defined for $p \in R^k_{++}$, so in one sense, we don't have to worry about $\alpha = 0$; $0 \cdot p = 0$, so $\pi(\alpha p)$ for $\alpha = 0$ is not defined. But there is no problem in extending the domain of definition of π ($:= \sup_{z \in Z} p \cdot z$) to all nonnegative p (or even p with negative components); if we do this for $p = 0$, we get (of course) $\pi(0) = 0$. And our convention is that $0 \cdot \pi(p) = 0$, whether $\pi(p)$ is finite or infinite, so $\pi(\alpha p) = \alpha\pi(p)$ works for $\alpha = 0$.

Hence, the function π is homogeneous of degree 1.

To show that π is convex, we need to show that $\pi(\alpha p + (1-\alpha)p') \leq \alpha\,\pi(p) + (1-\alpha)\,\pi(p')$ for all $p, p' \in R^k_{++}$ and $\alpha \in [0,1]$. Let p'' denote $\alpha p + (1-\alpha)p'$ for the duration of this proof. The cases $\alpha = 0$ and $\alpha = 1$ are trivial. So suppose $\alpha \in (0,1)$. Suppose $\pi(p'') < \infty$. For every $\epsilon > 0$, there is (then) some $z^\epsilon \in Z$ such that $p'' \cdot z^\epsilon > \pi(p'') - \epsilon$. But then

$$\begin{aligned}\alpha\,\pi(p) + (1-\alpha)\,\pi(p') &\geq \alpha(p \cdot z^\epsilon) + (1-\alpha)(p' \cdot z^\epsilon) \\ &= (\alpha p + (1-\alpha)p') \cdot z^\epsilon = p'' \cdot z^\epsilon \geq \pi(p'') - \epsilon.\end{aligned}$$

Since $\epsilon > 0$ is arbitrary, this implies that

$$\alpha\,\pi(p) + (1-\alpha)\,\pi(p') \geq \pi(p'').$$

This leaves the case $\alpha \in (0,1)$ and $\pi(p'') = \infty$. If either $\pi(p) = \infty$ or $\pi(p') = \infty$, then $\alpha\pi(p) + (1-\alpha)\pi(p') = \infty$, and we are done. So we only need to worry about the case there both $\pi(p)$ and $\pi(p')$ are finite. But if both are finite, since $\pi(p'') = \infty$, we can find a $z^* \in Z$ such that $p'' \cdot z^* > \max\{\pi(p), \pi(p')\}$. That is,

$$\begin{aligned}\max\{\pi(p), \pi(p')\} &< p'' \cdot z^* = (\alpha p + (1-\alpha)p') \cdot z^* \\ &= \alpha(p \cdot z^*) + (1-\alpha)(p' \cdot z^*) \leq \alpha\pi(p) + (1-\alpha)\pi(p'),\end{aligned}$$

an obvious contradiction. This covers all cases; π is convex.

In general, subgradients of π at p are affine functions, but since we know that π is homogeneous of degree 1, Proposition A3.26 tells us that subgradients are linear; that is, they have the form $p \cdot z^*$ for some $z^* \in R^k$. And z^* is a subgradient at p if $p \cdot z^* = \pi(p)$ and $p' \cdot z^* \leq \pi(p')$ for all p' in the domain of π. Now as long as $z^* \in Z$ (which is part of the premise), $p' \cdot z^* \leq \pi(p')$ for all $p' \in R^k_{++}$ (the domain of π). So this part of the proposition comes down to: for p and $z^* \in Z$, $z^* \in Z^*(p)$ if and only if $p \cdot z^* = \pi(p)$. This is, pretty much, a definition of $Z^*(p)$.[4] ∎

It would be nice to be able conclude that if z^* is a subgradient of π at p, then $z^* \in Z^*(p)$, without assuming that $z^* \in Z$. But this isn't true. It isn't hard to construct examples where $z \in R^k$ is a subgradient of π at some p, but $z \notin Z$. (Let $k = 2$ and let $Z = \{(-1,1), (-3,2), (0,0)\}$. What is π?) However, while this isn't true, it is sort-of true, in a sense that we will explain later in the chapter.

Moving from convexity and homogeneity of the profit function to convexity and homogeneity of the solution set, a few results can be harvested, even allowing for nonexistence of a solution. Keep in mind that, by definition, the empty set is trivially convex.

Proposition 9.4. *If Z is convex, then $Z^*(p)$ is convex for each p.*

Proof. Suppose z and z' are both in $Z^*(p)$. For all $\alpha \in [0,1]$, $\alpha z + (1-\alpha)z' \in Z$ because Z is convex, and $p \cdot (\alpha z + (1-\alpha)z') = \alpha p \cdot z + (1-\alpha)p \cdot z' = \alpha\pi(p) + (1-\alpha)\pi(p) = \pi(p)$; therefore $\alpha z + (1-\alpha)z' \in Z^*(p)$. ∎

In the spirit of earlier results on uniqueness of solutions, we'd like to give conditions under which $Z^*(p)$ is at most singleton. We say "at most" here because we aren't (yet) going to rule out that $Z^*(p)$ is empty. But if $Z^*(p)$ is nonempty, we'd like it to be singleton. Unhappily, the method we employed previously to get a unique solution result does not work here. That method invokes strict quasi-concavity of the objective function (typically, the utility function). But the objective function here is linear. What we need instead is an assumption that the feasible set Z is "strictly convex." This isn't a concept we've encountered; hence the scare quotes. But something like the following seems to capture what we might mean: If distinct z and z' are both in Z, points along the line segment that joins them are not on the boundary of Z but are instead interior to Z.

[4] Proposition A3.26 is about functions that are real valued, while π is allowed to take on the value $+\infty$. But if you go through its proof, you'll see that this presents no problems. Of course, π cannot have a subgradient at a price p where $\pi(p) = \infty$, as no affine function can take on the value ∞ at p.

In fact, we need something less than this to be true of Z, because we only need "interiority" in directions that increase profit.

Proposition 9.5. *Suppose Z has the property that, if z, z' are distinct elements of Z, then there exist an $\alpha \in (0,1)$ and a nonzero, nonnegative vector $\zeta \in R^k_+$ (depending on z, z', and α) such that $\zeta + \alpha z + (1-\alpha)z' \in Z$. Then for all strictly positive p, $Z^*(p)$ is either empty or singleton.*

Before giving the (pretty simple) proof, remarks about the property are worth making. We aren't looking at all convex combinations of z and z' because we only need one. And you should think of ζ as a small addition to the convex combination of z and z'; we will settle for any (small) nonnegative combination, because prices are strictly positive. Of course, this property is implied by the more restrictive assumption that, for all distinct z and z' in Z, every nontrivial convex combination of them (that is, $\alpha z + (1-\alpha)z'$ for $\alpha \in (0,1)$) is in the interior of Z.

Proof. Suppose z and z' are distinct elements of Z that, for some p, are both in $Z^*(p)$. Produce the ζ and α assumed to exist, and note that $p \cdot (\zeta + \alpha z + (1-\alpha)z') = p \cdot \zeta + \pi(p)$. Since ζ is nonnegative and nonzero and p is strictly positive, $p \cdot \zeta$ is strictly positive, and this immediately gives a contradiction. It is impossible for $Z^*(p)$ to contain two distinct production plans. ∎

Proposition 9.6. *For all p and $\alpha > 0$, $Z^*(p) = Z^*(\alpha p)$.*

In words, the set of solutions is homogeneous of degree 0 in p, as long as we don't go to the extreme of a price vector that is identically zero (that is, by taking $\alpha = 0$). I assume you don't need the details of a proof for this.

Existence of solutions, and a technical lemma

Proposition 9.7. *Suppose Z is closed and nonempty. For a given Z, a solution to the firm's profit-maximization problem exists for every strictly positive price vector p if and only if Z satisfies the recession-cone property (repeated here for convenience): If $\{z^n; n = 1, 2, \ldots\}$ is a sequence from Z such that $\|z^n\| \to \infty$, then every accumulation point of the set $\{z^n/\|z^n\|; n = 1, 2, \ldots\}$ lies in the negative orthant of R^k.*

Remark: It will become obvious in the course of the proof that if Z admits a solution to the profit-maximization problem for every strictly positive p, then Z has the recession-cone property, even if it is not closed. And if Z is empty, then clearly the profit-maximization problem never has a solution, so Z being nonempty is necessary for there to be solutions. The assumption that Z is closed is sufficient but not, strictly speaking, necessary for there to be solutions for all strictly positive p, since Z could fail to be closed in inessential places, places where the firm would never go to find a profit-maximizing production plan regardless of prices (such as, in the negative orthant, if $0 \in Z$).

Proof. First we show that the recession-cone property is sufficient: Fix a strictly positive price vector p. Take any $z^0 \in Z$ (Z is nonempty), and let $L = p \cdot z^0 - 1$.

Of course, L is then a lower bound on the feasible profit at the price vector p.

Take a sequence $\{z^n\}$ of production vectors in Z such that $p \cdot z^n$ approaches the value $\sup_{z \in Z} p \cdot z$. If this sequence lives inside a bounded set, or even if some subsequence of the sequence lies inside a bounded set, then an accumulation point (of the subsequence) can be extracted. This accumulation point will be in Z, because Z is closed, and (by continuity of $p \cdot z$ in z) it will be a solution to the firm's profit-maximization problem. The only case we must worry about, then, is if $\{z^n\}$ eventually leaves every bounded set, which implies that $\|z^n\| \to \infty$. Also, $p \cdot z^n > L$ for all sufficiently large n.

Let $\hat{z}^n = z^n/\|z^n\|$. (Do this for n large enough so that $z^n = 0$ no longer happens and so that $p \cdot z^n > L$.) The sequence $\{\hat{z}^n\}$ lives on the unit circle; hence it has accumulation points. Since $p \cdot z^n > L$, $p \cdot \hat{z}^n > L/\|z^n\|$. The limit in n of the right-hand side is zero, and hence, for any accumulation point, z^* of the sequence $\{\hat{z}^n\}$, $p \cdot z^* \geq 0$. But by the recession-cone property, any and all accumulation points z^* must lie in the negative orthant. Since p is strictly positive, $p \cdot z^* < 0$, a contradiction.

And to show that the recession-cone property is necessary: Suppose the recession-cone property fails. That is, for some sequence $\{z^n\}$ from Z, $\|z^n\| \to \infty$ and $z^n/\|z^n\| \to z^*$, which is not in the negative orthant. Let i be any component of z^* such that $z_i^* > 0$. Consider the price vector p^* that is 1 in all components but the ith, and has the value $(k+1)/z_i^*$ in the ith component. Since z^* lies on the unit circle, none of its components can have an absolute value greater than 1, so in $p^* \cdot z^*$, the contribution of the ith term in the inner product is at least $k+1$ (positive) and the contribution of all other terms can be no less than -1 (there are $k-1$ of these), so the inner product is at least 2. Moreover, by continuity of the inner product, there is some N sufficiently large so that for all $n \geq N$,

$$p^* \cdot \frac{z^n}{\|z^n\|} \geq 1.$$

Therefore, for all these n,

$$p^* \cdot z^n \geq \|z^n\|,$$

which goes to infinity, and the firm's profit-maximization problem has no solution at p^*. ∎

The proof of this proposition shows why the recession-cone property is just the thing for the result we want. If we can go arbitrarily far out (in norm) in a direction that is not in the negative orthant, we can find a strictly positive price vector that gives strictly positive profit in that direction, and going further and further in that direction (at those prices) will give unbounded profit. If there is a solution to the profit-maximization problem for every strictly positive price vector, the recession-cone property is necessary. On the other hand, while Z can be unbounded, if we know that there is some feasible profit level L, then we know that the solution to the profit-maximization problem at prices p must lie within $\{z \in Z : p \cdot z \geq L\} = Z \cap \{z \in R^k : p \cdot z \geq L\}$. The recession-cone property tells us, essentially, that for every strictly positive price vector p, this intersection of Z and a half-space is a bounded set. As long as Z is closed, it is moreover a compact set and, fixing the prices p, we can restrict our attention to a compact set when looking for a profit-maximizing production plan.

The following technical lemma extends the result announced at the end of the previous paragraph. Can you guess the purpose of this lemma?

Lemma 9.8. *Suppose Z is closed, nonempty, and has the recession-cone property. Then for any $z^0 \in Z$, the correspondence*

$$p \Rightarrow \{z \in Z : p \cdot z \geq p \cdot z^0\}$$

is locally bounded and upper semi-continuous.

Proof. Upper semi-continuity of the correspondence is easy: Suppose $\{(p^n, z^n)\}$ is a sequence of price–production plan pairs in the graph of the correspondence with limit (p, z). By assumption, p remains in the domain of the correspondence; we *assume* that p is strictly positive, and the key is to prove that z lies in the correspondence evaluated at p. Since Z is closed and z is the limit of points z^n in Z, z is certainly in Z. And since $p^n \cdot z^n \geq p^n \cdot z^0$ for each n and the dot product is jointly continuous, we know by continuity that $p \cdot z \geq p \cdot z^0$. That's it for upper semi-continuity.

Local boundedness is harder. If the correspondence is not locally bounded, then it fails at some strictly positive price vector p. At this price vector p, there is a sequence of prices $\{p^n\}$ with limit p and corresponding $\{z^n\}$ such that $z^n \in Z$ and $p^n \cdot z^n \geq p^n \cdot z^0$, and $\lim_n \|z^n\| = \infty$. Define $\hat{z}^n = z^n/\|z^n\|$. Each $\hat{z}^n$ lies in the unit circle, a compact set, so by looking along a subsequence if necessary, we can assume that the sequence $\{\hat{z}^n\}$ converges to some z^*. Since $p^n \cdot z^n \geq p^n \cdot z^0$ for each n, $p^n \cdot \hat{z}^n = p^n \cdot z^n/\|z^n\| \geq p^n \cdot z^0/\|z^n\|$. We know that the p^n converge to p, the $\hat{z}^n$ converge to z^*, and $z^0/\|z^n\|$ converges to 0, so we know that $p \cdot z^* \geq 0$. But p is strictly positive and z^* lies in the negative orthant by the recession-cone property, a contradiction. The correspondence is indeed locally bounded. ∎

Before we make (the obvious?) use of the lemma, one final remark on existence of solutions is in order. The recession-cone property is, essentially, just what is needed to ensure the existence of solutions to the firm's profit-maximization problems for all strictly positive p. But it isn't the most transparent property in the world, and you will find treatments of the theory of the firm that give more transparent properties on Z that are sufficient for solutions to exist. One that is particularly prevalent is the assumption that Z is, up to free disposal, generated by a compact set. To be precise, the property is that there is some compact set Z^0 such that $Z^0 \subseteq Z$ and, for every $z \in Z$, there is some z^0 in Z^0 (depending on z) such that $z^0 \geq z$. It is straightforward to see that, if such a Z^0 did exist, then all points $z \in Z$ and not in Z^0 are not candidates for solutions to the profit-maximization problem at any strictly positive price p, since any disparity between z and its z^0 is, at strictly positive prices, a recipe for lowering profit. Hence with such a Z^0, we can restrict attention in solving the profit-maximization problem to Z^0. And if Z^0 is compact, life becomes very easy.

Of course, this means that if such a Z^0 exists, then Z satisfies the recession-cone property. As a bit of drill, you might wish to prove that directly.

Berge's Theorem for the profit-maximization problem

Getting back to the lemma, it is the key step to proving the following:

Proposition 9.9 (Berge's Theorem for the profit-maximization problem). *If Z is closed, nonempty, and satisfies the recession-cone property, then the correspondence $p \Rightarrow Z^*(p)$ is nonempty valued, locally bounded, and upper semi-continuous, and the function $p \to \pi(p)$ is continuous (and real valued). For any (open) domain of prices over which $Z^*(p)$ is singleton valued, the function $p \to z^*(p)$ that is described by the correspondence is continuous.*

Proof. This is a straightforward application of Berge's Theorem, Proposition A4.7, and its Corollary A4.8. The parameter θ is the price vector, the variable is the production plan z. The objective function is $p \cdot z$, which is certainly jointly continuous. The A correspondence—the large feasible set—is the constant correspondence $A(p) \equiv Z$. Being constant, this is certainly lower semi-continuous. And the B correspondence—wherein all solutions are found—is constructed as follows: Letting z^0 be any fixed element of Z (here is where the nonemptiness of Z comes in), set $B(p) = \{z \in Z : p \cdot z \geq p \cdot z^0\}$. Of course, the maximum profit over all of Z is the same as the maximum over $B(p)$ for each p, and $B(p)$ contains $Z^*(p)$. And the lemma establishes that this correspondence is locally bounded (hence so is $Z^*(p)$) and upper semi-continuous. ∎

9.4. Afriat's Theorem for Firms

In the spirit of Afriat's Theorem (Chapter 4, remember?), suppose that you are given a finite amount of data alleged to be a firm's profit-maximizing production choices. Specifically, for a finite list of price vectors, $\{p^n; n = 1, \ldots, N\}$, it is alleged that z^n is "the" profit-maximizing choice of the firm at prices p^n, for $n = 1, \ldots, N$. We put *the* in scare quotes here because we don't preclude that there are other profit-maximizing choices the firm might have made at the prices p^n. The question is, Is there some production possibilities set Z that rationalizes these data; that is, such that each z^n is in Z, and $z^n \in \arg\max\{p^n \cdot z : z \in Z\}$ for each n? Compared to Afriat's Theorem, the answer is remarkably simple in this context.

Proposition 9.10. *Given a finite list of prices and production plans, $\{(p^n, z^n); n = 1, \ldots, N\}$ (where each $p^n \in R^k_{++}$ and $z^n \in R^k$), a set $Z \subseteq R^k$ exists such that*

$z^n \in \arg\max\{p^n \cdot z : z \in Z\}$ for each n if and only if

$$p^n \cdot z^n \geq p^n \cdot z^m \text{ for each } n, m = 1, \ldots, N. \tag{9.1}$$

Moreover, if (9.1) holds, the set Z works if and only if it satisfies

$$\{z^n; n = 1, \ldots, N\} \subseteq Z \subseteq \{z \in R^k : p^n \cdot z \leq p^n \cdot z^n, n = 1, \ldots, N\}. \tag{9.2}$$

To paraphrase: The necessary and sufficient condition is that, for each listed production plan z^m and each price vector p^n, the production plan z^n that is alleged to be profit maximizing at prices p^n must make at least as much profit at prices p^n as does z^m. And the last part of the proposition says: To work, a production-possibility set Z must contain *at least* all the listed production plans and cannot contain any production plan z that, at any of the prices p^n, makes a greater profit than does z^n.

If you think about it, this is obvious. First, (9.1) is necessary: For a Z to exist, it certainly has to contain (at least) all the z^n. And if at some price p^n, it is true that $p^n \cdot z^m > p^n \cdot z^n$ for some z^m, then z^n can hardly the be profit-maximizing choice out of Z, which must contain z^m, at the prices p^n.

As for sufficiency of (9.1), suppose it holds. Let $Z = \{z^n; n = 1, \ldots, N\}$. The condition says that, for each n, $p^n \cdot z^n \geq p^n \cdot z^m$ for all m; hence z^n is a profit-maximizing choice in this Z at the prices p^n. So this Z works.

Of course, no Z that works can be any smaller in the sense of set inclusion than the set $\{z^n; n = 1, \ldots, N\}$. And as long as the set Z contains nothing that gives greater profit at p^n than z^n, for each n, it will work. If it contains any plan z that, for some n, gives greater profit at p^n than does z^n, then this Z will not work. These two statements together give the right-hand set inclusion in (9.2). (If we had been formal and written *Proof* at the start of this argument, we would now conclude with an endproof mark.)

Recall that, in Afriat's Theorem for consumer choice, the continuity, nondecreasing, and convexity of preferences were all untestable: If any preferences rationalized a finite set of demand data, we would find continuous, strictly increasing, and convex preferences that did so. The corresponding properties in this context would be a Z that is closed, has free disposal, and is convex. We might also wish to insist that the Z produced has the recession-cone property.

Proposition 9.11. *Suppose a finite set of prices and production-plan data $\{(p^n, z^n); n = 1, \ldots, N\}$ satisfies (9.1) and so can be rationalized as the choice of a profit-maximizing firm in the sense of Proposition 9.10. Let*

$$\hat{Z} = \left\{ z \in R^k : z \leq \sum_{n=1}^{N} \alpha^n z^n, \alpha^n \geq 0, \sum_{n=1}^{N} \alpha^n = 1 \right\}.$$

(In words, $\hat{Z}$ is everything that lies (weakly) below points in the convex hull of the $\{z^n\}$.) Then $\hat{Z}$ works—the data are consistent with the firm having production possibility set $\hat{Z}$—and $\hat{Z}$ is closed, convex, and satisfies the free-disposal and the recession-cone properties. Moreover, $\hat{Z}$ is the smallest (by set inclusion) convex and free-disposal set that rationalizes the data.

Proof. To show that $\hat{Z}$ works, we need to show that, for each n, $p^n \cdot z^n \geq p^n \cdot z$ for all $z \in \hat{Z}$. But if $z \in \hat{Z}$, then $z \leq \sum_{m=1}^{N} \alpha^m z^m$ where the α^m are nonnegative and sum to 1. So, since p^n is strictly positive, $p^n \cdot z \leq p^n \cdot [\sum_m \alpha^m z^m] = \sum_m \alpha^m (p^n \cdot z^m) \leq \sum_m \alpha^m (p^n \cdot z^n)$ (because (9.1) holds) $= p^n \cdot z^n$. It is obvious that $\hat{Z}$ satisfies the free-disposal property. It is easy (and left to you) to show that $\hat{Z}$ is convex. To see that $\hat{Z}$ is closed, suppose that $\{z_\ell\}$ is a sequence from $\hat{Z}$ that converges to some z_∞; since each z_ℓ is from $\hat{Z}$, we have $z_\ell \leq \sum_m \alpha_\ell^m z^m$, where for each ℓ, the weights $\{\alpha_\ell^m; m = 1, \ldots, N\}$ are nonnegative and sum to 1. Therefore, all the weights lie in the unit interval, and by looking along a subsequence ℓ', we can assume that $\lim_{\ell' \to \infty} \alpha_{\ell'}^m$ exists for each m. Call this limit α_∞^m; then we know that these limits are all nonnegative and, by passing to the limit along the subsequence in the equation $\sum_m \alpha_\ell^m = 1$, sum to one. But then because $z_\ell \leq \sum_m \alpha_\ell^m z^m$, we can again look along this subsequence to conclude that $z_\infty \leq \sum_m \alpha_\infty^m z^m$, which means that $z_\infty \in \hat{Z}$.

To show that $\hat{Z}$ satisfies the recession-cone property: Let $\{z_\ell\}$ be a sequence from $\hat{Z}$ whose norms diverge to infinity and such that $z_\ell / \|z_\ell\|$ converges to some z'_∞ on the unit circle. Write $z_\ell \leq \sum_m \alpha_\ell^m z^m$, where the sum on the right-hand side is a convex combination of the z^m. Let me rewrite this as $z_\ell = \zeta_\ell + \sum_m \alpha_\ell^m z^m$, where $\zeta_\ell \leq 0$; then

$$\frac{z_\ell}{\|z_\ell\|} = \frac{\zeta_\ell}{\|z_\ell\|} + \frac{\sum_m \alpha_\ell^m z^m}{\|z_\ell\|}.$$

Now as ℓ goes to infinity, the term $\left[\sum_m \alpha_\ell^m z^m\right] / \|z_\ell\|$ must go to zero, because the norm of the numerator is bounded above by largest of the norms of the z^m (use the triangle inequality and the fact that the weights are all between zero and one for each ℓ), while the denominator goes to infinity. So

$$\lim_\ell \frac{z_\ell}{\|z_\ell\|} = \lim_\ell \frac{\zeta_\ell}{\|z_\ell\|},$$

and since the ζ_ℓ are all nonpositive, the latter limit must lie in the negative orthant.

Finally, suppose Z is a set that contains $\{z^m; m = 1, \ldots, N\}$ and is convex and has free disposal. Since Z is convex, it contains every convex combination of the z^m, and since it has the free-disposal property, it contains every z less than or equal to a convex combination of the z^m. Therefore, Z must contain $\hat{Z}$; $\hat{Z}$ is the smallest convex and free-disposal set that works. ∎

It is perhaps worth pointing out that the set on the right-hand side of (9.2), $\{z \in R^k : p^n \cdot z \leq p^n \cdot z^n \text{ for } n = 1, \ldots, N\}$ is closed, convex, and has the free-disposal property (recall that each p^n is strictly positive). But this set fails to satisfy the recession-cone property.

The own-price effect for profit-maximizing firms

You might also recall from Chapter 4 the discussion of the own-price effect for consumers, and the corresponding discussion of Giffen goods. For firms, once again, things are much simpler. We start with a lemma.

Lemma 9.12. *Suppose $z \in Z^*(p)$ and $z' \in Z^*(p')$. Then $(p - p') \cdot (z - z') \geq 0$.*

Proof. Since $z \in Z^*(p)$ and $z' \in Z^*(p')$, both z and z' are in Z. Therefore, $p \cdot z \geq p \cdot z'$ and $p' \cdot z' \geq p' \cdot z$. Therefore, $p \cdot z + p' \cdot z' \geq p \cdot z' + p' \cdot z$, or $p \cdot z - p \cdot z' - p' \cdot z + p' \cdot z' \geq 0$, which is $(p - p') \cdot (z - z') \geq 0$. ∎

Corollary 9.13. *Consider a profit-maximizing firm and its response to two price vectors, p and p', which differ only in the ith coordinate. That is, $p_j = p'_j$ for $j \neq i$. Suppose that $p_i > p'_i$. If z is a profit-maximizing choice by the firm at prices p, while z' is a profit-maximizing choice at p', then $z_i \geq z'_i$.*

Proof. From the lemma, $(p - p') \cdot (z - z') \geq 0$. By assumption, in $(p - p')$, the only nonzero component is the ith, which is strictly positive. Hence $z_i \geq z'_i$ is required if the dot product is to be nonnegative. ∎

A bit of interpretation is in order. Suppose first that good i is an output of the firm. The corollary then says that, as the price of output good i increases, the firm's profit-maximizing choice cannot be to decrease the amount of good i it produces. To say a word more about this, fixing all prices but the price of good i, let $Z_i(p_i)$ be the *set* of levels of output of good i consistent with profit maximization and a price p_i for good i. The correspondence $p_i \Rightarrow Z_i(p_i)$ is then the *supply "function"* of firm i, fixing all prices but the price of its output good i. I've put scare quotes around "function" because, of course, this is really a supply correspondence. What we've just seen is if $p_i > p'_i$, $z_i \in Z_i(p_i)$, and $z'_i \in Z_i(p'_i)$, then $z_i \geq z'_i$. Or, in words, *a profit-maximizing firm's supply "function" must be "upward sloping,"* where now we have two sets of scare quotes, the first because it is a correspondence, and and the second because we have no justification for using the term "slope" at this level of generality. (If we knew that it was a function—that each $Z_i(p_i)$ is singleton valued—would we know that the function described is continuous?)

On the other hand, suppose that good i is an input to the firm. Then the corollary says that, as the price if input i increases, the (profit-maximizing) firm will never increase the amount of this input that it uses. (Since inputs have negative signs, $z_i \geq z'_i$ for input i means that z_i is less negative than z'_i; it constitutes less of input i.)

9.5. From Profit Functions to Production-Possibility Sets

What we've done to this point in this chapter runs very much in parallel with results for the theory of the consumer in Chapters 3 and 4. In Chapter 3, we discuss the solution of the consumer's problem using calculus and the theory of constrained maximization, something we haven't done here (and will not do). But, except for that, we've replicated the results of Chapters 3 and 4.

Now we step off into territory we didn't cover in the theory of the consumer. (And, to foreshadow developments, this is territory we'll cover for the consumer in Chapters 10 and 11.) The plot line, overall, runs as follows. In the previous section, we investigated what one concludes from a finite set of data about the (alleged) activities of a profit-maximizing firm. Now we ask: Suppose you are handed what is alleged to be the full set of activities of a profit-maximizing firm. That is, we are told what the firm will choose to do not for a finite set of price vectors, but for every strictly positive price vector. Are these alleged profit-maximizing production plans really and truly the plans that would be selected by a firm with some production-possibility set Z?

The proof of Proposition 9.10 suggests a simple answer. We're being given, for each $p \in R^k_{++}$, an alleged profit-maximizing production plan $z^*(p)$. For a Z to exist that rationalizes this now infinite collection of data, we know that Z must be at least $\{z^*(p); p \in R^k_{++}\}$. That is, every production plan that, it is alleged, the firm chooses must be in any Z that rationalizes these choices. Adding more things to Z only makes it harder for these choices to be profit maximizing, so, as long as we aren't concerned with free disposal or convexity, why not stop with precisely this smallest possible set Z? Then we are fine, as long as

$$p \cdot z^*(p) \geq p \cdot z^*(p'), \text{ for all } p, p' \in R^k_{++}.$$

That's easy enough. However, it isn't quite useful, since those are a lot of conditions to check. We aim to find a condition that is easier to check in practice. And *that* is really where we are headed.

To get there, let me give an alternative formulation to the question. Suppose you are handed an alleged profit function π. That is, for each $p \in R^k_{++}$, you have a number $\pi(p)$ that is alleged to be the profit earned by a firm that is characterized by some unspecified Z. Is there some Z that generates this π and, if so, what can you say about it?

This sounds like a lot less data than are contained in a $z^*(p)$ function. And, in fact, the profit function cannot provide any *more* information than you have in a $z^*(p)$ function: If someone provides you with, for each $p \in R^k_{++}$, a production plan $z^*(p)$ that is meant to be the optimal production plan for some firm, you have also simultaneously been handed the profit function for this firm, since $\pi(p) = p \cdot z^*(p)$. So it can't be any easier to answer the question formulated this way, and it probably seems a lot harder.

Next, recognize that we know a number of *necessary conditions* for a candidate profit function π: π must be convex, continuous, and homogeneous of degree 1. Is it possible that these necessary conditions are also sufficient? Perhaps suprisingly, they are.

Proposition 9.14. *Suppose $\pi : R^k_{++} \to R$ is convex and homogeneous of degree 1.*[5] *Let*

$$Z^* = \{z \in R^k : p \cdot z \leq \pi(p) \text{ for all } p \in R^k_{++}\}.$$

Then Z^* is closed, convex, and has free disposal. And π is the profit function for a firm with production-possibility set Z^*; hence Z^* satisfies the recession-cone property.

Proof. Rewrite

$$Z^* = \bigcap_{p \in R^k_{++}} \{z \in R^k : p \cdot z \leq \pi(p)\}.$$

This is the intersection of half-spaces, each of which is closed and convex, so the intersection is closed and convex. To show that Z^* has free disposal, suppose that $z \in Z^*$ and $z' \leq z$. Since $z \in Z$, $p \cdot z \leq \pi(p)$ for each $p \in R^k_{++}$, and since $z' \leq z$ and each p is strictly positive, $p \cdot z' \leq p \cdot z \leq \pi(p)$ for each $p \in R^k_{++}$; therefore $z' \in Z^*$.

What is left? We need to show that, for each $p^* \in R^k_{++}$, there is some $z^* \in R^k$ such that $p^* \cdot z^* = \pi(p^*)$ and $p \cdot z^* \leq \pi(p)$ for all $p \in R^k_{++}$. This z^* will be a member of Z^*, and since $p^* \cdot z \leq \pi(p^*)$ for all $z \in Z^*$ by definition, it will be profit maximizing, producing profit $\pi(p^*)$, at p^*. If we do this, we have completed the proof. Please note: At this point, we don't even know that Z^* is nonempty. But we haven't used the convexity and homogeneity of π, yet. Now we do.

Since π is convex and each $p^* \in R^k_{++}$ is in the interior of the domain of π, there exists a subgradient of π at p^*. (See Appendix 3 and, in particular, section A3.6. The discussion there is about concave functions and supergradients, but all the results there work for convex functions and subgradients.) Since π is homogeneous of degree 1, its subgradients are linear functions (Proposition A3.26); that is, there exists some $z^* \in R^k$ such that $p^* \cdot z^* = \pi(p)$ and $p \cdot z^* \leq \pi(p)$ for all $p \in R^k_{++}$. That's what we needed to show.

The last conclusion follows from Proposition 9.7. ∎

Recall the second half of Proposition 9.3: For a given Z, p, and $z^* \in Z$, z^* is a subgradient of π at p if and only if $z^* \in Z^*(p)$. We said at the time that we would like to drop the condition that $z^* \in Z^*$ and conclude simply that $z^* \in Z^*(p)$ if and only if z^* is a subgradient of π at p. But, for general Z, we cannot do this, because the given Z may not be big enough. *Since z^* is a subgradient of π at p, adding it into Z^* won't affect π at all. But we don't know, a priori, that z^* is in the originally provided Z.* I have emphasized the previous two sentences, so don't rush past them too quickly. To reiterate: To say that z^* is a subgradient of π at p means

[5] I don't list continuity of π as one of its properties because, in the current context, it is redundant: since the domain of π is an open set, convexity of π implies continuity (Proposition A3.17g). But see two sections further on for more on this point.

that $p' \cdot z^* \leq \pi(p')$ for all p'. Hence, if z^* is not a member of Z already, adding it to Z does not increase the profit the firm can earn at any price p'. Being a subgradient at p also means that $p \cdot z^* = \pi(p)$; z^*, upon joining Z, will become a solution to the firm's profit-maximization problem at the price vector p. But it is possible (see Problem 9.1) that some subgradients of π at some prices p are not members of Z, initially. This raises the question that is the title of the next section.

9.6. How Many Production-Possibility Sets Give the Same Profit Function?

The answer to this question involves the *closure of the free-disposal convex hull* of a set Z.

Definition 9.15. *For any set $Z \subseteq R^k$, the **free-disposal convex hull** of Z, or* FDCH(Z), *is the set*

$$\Big\{ z \in R^k : z \leq \sum_n \alpha_n z^n \text{ for nonnegative scalars } \alpha_1, \ldots, \alpha_n \\ \text{such that } \sum_n \alpha_n = 1 \text{ and points } z^1, \ldots, z^n \text{ from } Z \Big\}.$$

*And the **closure of the free-disposal convex hull** of Z, or $\overline{\text{FDCH}}(Z)$, is the closure of* FDCH(Z).

In words, take Z, take its convex hull and then take everything that is in or below the convex hull, and you have FDCH(Z). Add in all the limit points of this set, and you have $\overline{\text{FDCH}}(Z)$. It is obvious, I hope, that if Z is convex, closed, and has free disposal, then $\overline{\text{FDCH}}(Z) = Z$.

With this concept in place, the answer to the title of this section is, almost,

Z and Z' give the same profit function if and only if $\overline{\text{FDCH}}(Z) = \overline{\text{FDCH}}(Z')$.

In one direction, this is exactly true.

Proposition 9.16. *If $\overline{\text{FDCH}}(Z) = \overline{\text{FDCH}}(Z')$, then Z and Z' have the same profit function.*

Remark. Before getting to the details of the proof, let me clarify the possibility of infinite-valued profit functions: In this section, they are allowed. That is, we will deal in this section with general production-possibility sets Z, with only one restriction: Z must be nonempty. Once we know that Z is nonempty, we know that its profit function π, defined for $p \in R^k_{++}$ as

$$\pi(p) = \sup\{p \cdot z : z \in Z\}$$

is never equal to $-\infty$. But unless we assume that Z is closed and has the recession-cone property, we cannot rule out the possibilities (a) that, for a particular p, the supremum is not attained by any $z \in Z$, even if $\pi(p) < \infty$, and (b) that, for a particular p, the supremum is $+\infty$, in which case the supremum is certainly not attained at any z. I don't wish to preclude either of these possibilities, and proofs of this proposition and Proposition 9.17 are valid, even if these possibilities are not precluded.

Compare with Proposition 9.14. The statement of that proposition begins with a function $\pi : R^k_{++} \to R$ that is convex and homogeneous of degree 1. *By assumption,* the range of π is the real line, not the extended real line (i.e., values of ∞ are ruled out by assumption), and so the Z^* that is produced (which we know is closed, convex, and has free disposal) must satisfy the recession-cone property. It is interesting to speculate on what would happen if we had a candidate profit function π that was allowed to take on values of ∞; of course, if we allow this, we'd better be clear what we mean by things like "convex" and "homogeneous of degree 1." We'll get back to this, although a bit informally, next section.

Proof. We prove this by showing that if π is the profit function generated by a set Z and $\hat{\pi}$ is the profit function generated by $\overline{\text{FDCH}}(Z)$, then $\pi \equiv \hat{\pi}$. This shows the result, since if this is true, and if π' is the profit function generated by some other Z' such that $\overline{\text{FDCH}}(Z) = \overline{\text{FDCH}}(Z')$, then $\pi' \equiv \hat{\pi} \equiv \pi$.

Since $Z \subseteq \overline{\text{FDCH}}(Z)$, it is clear that $\hat{\pi} \geq \pi$; maximizing over a larger set of production possibilities can only increase profits. So we are done if we show that $\hat{\pi}$ can never strictly exceed π.

Suppose by way of contradiction that it does. That is, for some strictly positive price p, $\hat{\pi}(p) > \pi(p)$. Then for some $\epsilon > 0$, we can find $z \in \overline{\text{FDCH}}(Z)$ such that $p \cdot z > \pi(p) + \epsilon$. By continuity of the dot product, we can find some $z' \in \text{FDCH}(Z)$ close enough to z so that $p \cdot z' > \pi(p) + \epsilon/2$. Since $z' \in \text{FDCH}(Z)$, there is some $z'' \in \text{CH}(Z)$ (the convex hull of Z) such that $z'' \geq z'$, which (since prices are strictly positive) implies that $p \cdot z'' \geq \pi(p) + \epsilon/2$. But z'' is a convex combination of elements of Z; write $z'' = \sum_{j=1}^n \alpha^j z^j$, where each $z^j \in Z$ and the scalars are nonnegative and sum to one. Since $p \cdot z'' = \sum_{j=1}^n \alpha^j (p \cdot z^j) \geq \pi(p) + \epsilon/2$, and since the α^j are nonnegative and sum to one, for some index j, $p \cdot z^j \geq \pi(p) + \epsilon/2$. Since this z^j is from Z, we have a contradiction. ∎

The converse is only almost true.

Proposition 9.17. *Suppose (nonempty) Z and Z' have different closed free-disposal convex hulls; that is, $\overline{\text{FDCH}}(Z) \neq \overline{\text{FDCH}}(Z')$. Then either (a) they generate different profit functions, or (b) they both generate profit functions that are identically $+\infty$.*

Proof. Z generates the same profit function as does $\overline{\text{FDCH}}(Z)$, and Z' generates the same profit function as does $\overline{\text{FDCH}}(Z')$, so we can rephrase this proposition as follows: If Z and Z' are closed, convex, and have free disposal, and if they are not identical, then either (a) they generate different profit functions or (b) they both generate the profit function that is identically $+\infty$. We'll prove the proposition stated this way.

So suppose Z and Z' are both closed, convex, have free disposal, and are different. Let π be the profit function for Z, and let π' be the profit function for Z'. If $\pi = \pi'$ and both are the constant function equal to $+\infty$, there is nothing to show, so suppose that one or the other of these functions is finite valued at some price.

Since Z and Z' are different, there are points in one that are not in the other. I need either

- a point $z^* \in Z \setminus Z'$ and a strictly positive price $\hat{p}$ such that $\pi'(\hat{p}) < \infty$, or
- a point $z^* \in Z' \setminus Z$ and a strictly positive price $\hat{p}$ such that $\pi(\hat{p}) < \infty$.

I claim that it must be possible to find z^* and $\hat{p}$ that satisfy one or the other (or both) of these joint conditions. Suppose $Z \subseteq Z'$. Then $\pi(p) \leq \pi'(p)$ for all strictly positive p. Of course, in this case, we can find a $z^* \in Z' \setminus Z$. And since either π or π' is finite valued for some price $\hat{p}$, π, being smaller, must be finite valued for some $\hat{p}$; that is, the second of the two bullet points holds. The case $Z' \subseteq Z$ is handled symmetrically, landing us in the condition of the first bullet point. And if neither Z nor Z' is a subset of the other, then there are points in either one not in the other one, and we pick the first or second bullet point depending on which of π or π' is not identically ∞.

So, it is without loss of generality to assume that z^* and $\hat{p}$ exist as in the first bullet point: z^* is in Z but not Z', and $\pi'(\hat{p}) < \infty$.

Since Z' is convex and z^* is not in Z', and since the set $\{z^*\}$ is compact, we can strictly separate z^* from Z'. That is, we can find a vector $q \in R^k$ and a scalar b such that $q \cdot z < b < q \cdot z^*$ for all $z \in Z'$. Since Z' has free disposal, q must be nonnegative: Suppose $q_i < 0$. Take any vector $z \in Z'$, and let d^N be the vector $(0, 0, \ldots, 0, -N, 0, \ldots, 0)$, where the $-N$ is in component i. Then $z + d^N \in Z'$ by free disposal, and $q \cdot (z + d^N) = q \cdot z - Nq_i$ which, as N goes to infinity, will certainly exceed any finite b.

Let $\delta = q \cdot z^* - b$. Let $\epsilon > 0$ be such that $|\epsilon\hat{p} \cdot z^*| < \delta/3$ and $\epsilon\pi'(\hat{p}) < \delta/3$, and then let $p^* = q + \epsilon\hat{p}$. Note that p^* is strictly positive. We have $p^* \cdot z^* = q \cdot z^* + \epsilon\hat{p} \cdot z^* > q \cdot z^* - |\epsilon\hat{p} \cdot z^*| > q \cdot z^* - \delta/3 = b + 2\delta/3$, while for all $z \in Z'$, $p^* \cdot z = q \cdot z + \epsilon\hat{p} \cdot z \leq q \cdot z + \epsilon\pi'(\hat{p}) \leq b + \delta/3$, and so

$$\pi(p^*) \geq p^* \cdot z^* > b + \frac{2\delta}{3} > b + \frac{\delta}{3} \geq \pi'(p^*).$$

Hence the two profit functions are different at p^*. ∎

This result gives us the following corollary, which may be obvious but is still worth stating explicitly.

Corollary 9.18. *Suppose that a production possibility set Z that is closed and convex and has free disposal generates a profit function $\pi : R^k_{++} \to R$. Then if*

$$Z^* := \{z \in R^k : p \cdot z \leq \pi(p) \text{ for all } p \in R^k_{++}\},$$

$Z^* = Z$. *Moreover,* $Z = Z^*$ *is closure of the free-disposal convex hull of all the subgradients of* π.

The proof is left for you to supply (it should be very quick and easy); it basically consists of juxtaposing results already provided.

Propositions 9.16 and 9.17 would be so much nicer if we could simply say that Z and Z' have the same profit function if and only if $\overline{\text{FDCH}}(Z) = \overline{\text{FDCH}}(Z')$. The caveat in Proposition 9.17 about them sharing the profit function $\pi(\cdot) \equiv \infty$, even when $\overline{\text{FDCH}}(Z) \neq \overline{\text{FDCH}}(Z')$, messes up an otherwise very pretty picture. It isn't a hugely offensive mess, but if you tracked the proofs closely, you may see a way around it.

We've defined the profit function π for strictly positive prices. Now enlarge its domain, to be all positive (that is, nonnegative) prices. Define for any set $Z \subseteq R^k$ the *extended*[6] *profit function* $\overline{\pi}_Z : R^k_+ \to R \cup \{\infty\}$ by

$$\overline{\pi}_Z(p) = \sup\{p \cdot z : z \in Z\}.$$

I'm subscripting $\overline{\pi}$ by the set Z that generates it as a notational convenience. As is true throughout this section, I allow $\overline{\pi}_Z$ to take on the value $+\infty$. (I assume throughout that Z is nonempty, so I don't need to worry about the value $-\infty$.)

Corollary 9.19. *For any* $Z, Z' \subseteq R^k$, $\overline{\text{FDCH}}(Z) = \overline{\text{FDCH}}(Z')$ *if and only if* $\overline{\pi}_Z \equiv \overline{\pi}_{Z'}$.

That is, allowing nonnegative (as opposed to only strictly positive) prices gets us the no-mess result. It is a bit of an abuse of language to call this a corollary, but it does follow fairly easily from the *proofs* of Propositions 9.16 and 9.17. If you aren't sure why, see Problem 9.7.

9.7. What Is Going On Here, Mathematically?

(You may skip this section if the mathematics is getting too thick for you, but if you want to understand what just happened, you should persevere.)

Except for the little bit of mess that is cleaned up by Corollary 9.18, Propositions 9.16 and 9.17 establish a one-to-one relationship between closed, convex, free-disposal production-possibility sets (or the equivalence classes of production-possibility sets that share the same $\overline{\text{FDCH}}$'s) and their profit functions. That there should be this one-to-one relationship may seem fuzzy to you, in which case consider the following.

Section 3 of Appendix 3 provides a fairly intuitive mathematical result, the Support-Function Theorem, which says that a closed and convex set $Z \subseteq R^k$ that is not all of R^k is the intersection of all the closed half-spaces that contain it. Once you have a good feel for separating-hyperplane theorems, it isn't hard to see why this should be: If $\hat{z}$ is any point not in Z, we can strictly separate $\hat{z}$ from Z with

[6] "Extended" here refers to the extended domain and not the extended-reals range.

a hyperplane, so $\hat{z}$ won't be in the intersection of all the closed half-spaces that contain Z. And, of course, Z is in that intersection.

But now write out in symbols "the intersection of all the closed half-spaces that contain Z": A half-space is a set of the form $\{z \in R^k : p \cdot z \leq \beta\}$ for some $p \in R^k$ and $\beta \in R$. Don't be confused here by the use of p; now we have no sign restrictions on the components of p. And the half-space $\{z \in R^k : p \cdot z \leq \beta\}$ contains Z if and only if $\sup\{p \cdot z : z \in Z\} \leq \beta$. So if we define $\tilde{\pi}_Z : R^k \to R \cup \{\infty\}$ by

$$\tilde{\pi}_Z(p) = \sup\{p \cdot z : z \in Z\}, \tag{9.3}$$

we know that Z is contained within the closed sub-space defined by p and β if and only if $\tilde{\pi}_Z(p) \leq \beta$, and the Support-Function Theorem says that

$$Z = \bigcap_{p \in R^k, \beta \geq \tilde{\pi}_Z(p)} \{z \in R^k : p \cdot z \leq \beta\}.$$

Moreover, in that big intersection, we can limit ourselves to one value of β for each value of p, namely $\beta = \tilde{\pi}_Z(p)$, since the half-space with any larger β is a strict superset of the half-space with this specific β. In other words, for this wonderful function $\tilde{\pi}_Z$, the Support-Function Theorem says that *For any closed and convex set* Z,

$$Z = \bigcap_{p \in R^k} \{z \in R^k : p \cdot z \leq \tilde{\pi}_Z(p)\} = \{z \in R^k : p \cdot z \leq \tilde{\pi}_Z(p) \textit{ for all } p \in R^k\}. \tag{9.4}$$

Therefore, *there is a one-to-one correspondence between each closed and convex set* Z *in* R^k *and its respective **support function*** $\tilde{\pi}_Z$, where the function $\tilde{\pi}_Z$ defined in (9.3) has been given its mathematical name, the support function.

This is nearly identical to what went on in the previous two sections, except that the *profit function* is defined only for strictly positive prices, and instead of getting a correspondence between closed and convex sets and their support functions, we (almost) got a correspondence between closed, convex, and free-disposal sets and their profit functions. But please note: A support function is defined precisely the way a profit function is defined, except for a larger domain (all $p \in R^k$ instead of strictly positive p), and recovering Z from its support function via (9.4) should look awfully familiar to you after reading earlier sections of this chapter.

But there are more parallels. You should have no problem proving the following result, if you understood the proofs of the previous two sections.

Proposition 9.20.

a. *Suppose* Z *and* Z' *are arbitrary sets in* R^k. *Then* $\tilde{\pi}_Z \equiv \tilde{\pi}_{Z'}$ *if and only if* $\overline{CH}(Z) = \overline{CH}(Z')$, *where* $\overline{CH}(Z)$ *is the closure of the convex hull of* Z.

b. Suppose Z is closed and convex. The support function of Z, $\tilde{\pi}_Z$, is finite valued for all $p \in R^k$ if and only if Z is compact. And, in this case, $\tilde{\pi}_Z$ is convex and homogeneous of degree 1.

c. Suppose $\tilde{\pi} : R^k \to R$ is convex and homogeneous of degree 1. Then it is the support function of the closed and convex set Z defined by (9.4), which is (of course) compact.

I leave the proof of this proposition for you (as Problem 9.9).

But now to dig still deeper, I assert that even if $\tilde{\pi}_Z$ is not finite valued for all p, it is still convex and homogenous of degree 1, if you define convexity and homogeneity appropriately (see Problem 9.10). Moreover, for any extended real-valued function $\tilde{\pi}$ on R^k that is convex and homogeneous of degree 1, the set $\{p \in R^k : \tilde{\pi}(p) < \infty\}$ is a convex cone. Call this convex cone $P^*_{\tilde{\pi}}$, and introduce another set,

$$Z^*_{\tilde{\pi}} = \{z \in R^k : p \cdot z \leq 0 \text{ for all } p \in P^*_{\tilde{\pi}}\}.$$

This set is also a convex cone; it is called the negative conjugate cone to $P^*_{\tilde{\pi}}$. Why look at these sets? Go back to the construction of Z from $\tilde{\pi}$ via (9.4), which is

$$Z = \{z \in R^k : p \cdot z \leq \tilde{\pi}(p) \text{ for all } p \in R^k\}.$$

If $p \notin P^*_{\tilde{\pi}}$, then $\tilde{\pi}(p) = \infty$, and $p \cdot z \leq \tilde{\pi}(p)$ for this p is no constraint at all on z. Hence we can rewrite our definition of Z as

$$Z = \{z \in R^k : p \cdot z \leq \tilde{\pi}(p) \text{ for all } p \in P^*_{\tilde{\pi}}\}.$$

Moreover, suppose $z^* \in Z^*_{\tilde{\pi}}$ and $z \in Z$. I assert that, automatically, $z + z^* \in Z$: For every $p \in P^*_{\tilde{\pi}}$, $p \cdot (z + z^*) = p \cdot z + p \cdot z^* \leq p \cdot z$, so if z satisfies the constraints, so does $z + z^*$. In words, the set Z explodes out in directions given by the cone $Z^*_{\tilde{\pi}}$.

Suppose, for instance, that $P^*_{\tilde{\pi}} = R^k_{++}$. That is, $\tilde{\pi}(p) = \infty$, or *is thought of as being equal to* ∞, for all vectors p that are not strictly positive. Then $Z^*_{\tilde{\pi}}$ is the negative orthant. That, pretty much, is the story for the profit function. We only look at strictly positive price vectors, so we generate no constraints on z for p outside of the strict positive orthant, and the sets Z we generate explode out in the direction of the negative orthant; in other words, we get free disposal.

Suppose then that we had a profit function π that had infinite value for some strictly positive prices. Its set of prices-for-which-π-is-finite is still a convex cone (as long as π is convex and homogeneous of degree 1), and when we go looking for the corresponding Z, we'll explode out in directions Z^* that are more than just the negative orthant; that is, we get free disposal plus.

There's a quite general theory lurking here, but I'm not going to develop it any further. To do justice to it would take an already long excursion away from the main lines of this chapter and make it very much too long. I hope this gives you either enough of a lead to do it on your own or enough of a taste for you to seek out the general theory. If you do seek out the general theory, look for conjugate convex functions and Fenchel duality.

9.8. Differentiability of the Profit Function

We know that if π is a profit function and $z \in Z^*(p)$ for some p, then z is a subgradient of π at this p. If π is differentiable at p, it has a unique subgradient, namely its derivative, and so $Z^*(p)$ must be the singleton set consisting of this derivative. This not-very-remarkable result will in fact prove to be quite useful (for instance, when we get to producer surplus in Chapter 12), and so has a name:

Corollary 9.21 (The Derivative Property, or Hotelling's Lemma). *Suppose the profit function π is continuously differentiable at price p^* and suppose that Z is closed.*[7] *Then $Z^*(p^*)$ is a singleton set consisting of the netput vector $z^*(p^*)$ whose ith component $z_i^*(p^*)$ is*

$$z_i^*(p^*) = \left.\frac{\partial \pi}{\partial p_i}\right|_{p^*}.$$

We can harvest one relatively quick and somewhat surprising corollary from this immediately. Suppose that, for whatever reason, we know that π is not only continuously differentiable, but twice continuously differentiable in some open region of prices. Hotelling's Lemma then implies that the optimal production plans of the firm, in that neighborhood of prices, can be written as a function $z^*(p)$. We already know that this function is continuous (How? Berge's Theorem), but now we know that it is continuously differentiable. And since the second partial derivatives of any twice-continuously differentiable function are symmetric, we know that

$$\frac{\partial^2 \pi}{\partial p_i \partial p_j} = \frac{\partial z_i^*}{\partial p_j} = \frac{\partial z_j^*}{\partial p_i}.$$

Think of i and j as two different inputs to the production process. This says that the rate at which the firm (optimally) changes its use of input i, as the price of input j changes, exactly equals the rate at which the firm changes its use of input j, as the price of input i changes. We're not just saying that the changes have the same sign. We're saying that the numerical rates of change are identical!

All very nice, but this is premised on smoothness of π. Is there any reason to believe that the profit function is differentiable, let alone twice continuously differentiable? Setting aside the harder question of two continuous derivatives momentarily, we see in the next proposition that the question about the first derivative of π has a simple answer.

---

[7] If Z is not closed, then $Z^*(p^*)$ could be empty.

Proposition 9.22. *The profit function π^* is differentiable at a price p^0 if and only if $Z^*(p^0)$ is singleton, in which case the gradient of π at p^0 is the single element of $Z^*(p^0)$.*

Proof. We already have one direction: If the profit function is differentiable at p^0, then $Z^*(p^0)$ is singleton, and the gradient of π is the single element of $Z^*(p^0)$. We need to show the converse. So suppose $Z^*(p^0)$ contains a single element, which we denote by z^0.

Suppose we have some sequence of price vectors $\{p^n\}$ with limit p^0. Write each p^n as $p^0 + \epsilon^n$. Let z^n be any element of $Z^*(p^n)$ (I assume there are solutions in at least an open neighborhood of p^0), and write $z^n = z^0 + \delta^n$. From Proposition 9.9 and the fact that $Z^*(p^0)$ is singleton, we know that $\{z^n\}$ has limit z^0 or, equivalently, $\{\delta^n\}$ approaches zero as n approaches ∞: Because $p \Rightarrow Z^*(p)$ is locally bounded, the sequence $\{z^n\}$ lives inside a bounded set. Hence every subsequence has a convergent sub-subsequence, and upper semi-continuity tells us that the limit of every convergent subsequence must be z^0. This implies that the limit of $\{z^n\}$ exists and is z^0.

To show differentiability at p^0 (and that the derivative is z^0), we must show that

$$\lim_{n\to\infty} \frac{\pi(p^n) - \pi(p^0) - (p^n - p^0)\cdot z^0}{\|p^n - p^0\|} = \lim_{n\to\infty} \frac{\pi(p^n) - p^0\cdot z^0 - \epsilon^n \cdot z^0}{\|\epsilon^n\|} = 0.$$

We have

$$\pi(p^n) = p^n \cdot z^n = (p^0 + \epsilon^n)\cdot(z^0 + \delta^n) = p^0\cdot z^0 + \epsilon^n\cdot z^0 + p^0\cdot\delta^n + \epsilon^n\cdot\delta^n;$$

substituting this into the numerator in the previous display, we must show that

$$\lim_{n\to\infty} \frac{p^0\cdot\delta^n + \epsilon^n\cdot\delta^n}{\|\epsilon^n\|} = 0. \tag{9.5}$$

To show this, we enlist two inequalities:

$$\pi(p^n) = (p^0 + \epsilon^n)\cdot(z^0 + \delta^n) \geq p^n\cdot z^0, \quad \text{or} \quad p^0\cdot\delta^n + \epsilon^n\cdot\delta^n \geq 0, \quad \text{and}$$

$$\pi(p^0) = p^0\cdot z^0 \geq p^0\cdot z^n = p^0\cdot(z^0 + \delta^n) \quad \text{or} \quad 0 \geq p^0\cdot\delta^n.$$

Putting these two together, we have

$$0 \geq p^0\cdot\delta^n \geq -\epsilon^n\cdot\delta^n. \tag{9.6}$$

So if we show that

$$\lim_{n\to\infty} \frac{\epsilon^n\cdot\delta^n}{\|\epsilon^n\|} = 0,$$

then we are done; the other term in (9.5) is clearly being driven to zero because of (9.6). And Berge's Theorem ensures that this last limit is true: Coordinate by coordinate, $\epsilon_i^n/\|\epsilon^n\|$ is bounded above by 1 by the triangle inequality, while δ_i^n goes to zero by Berge. ■

The profit function, then, is differentiable at p^0 if and only if $Z^*(p^0)$ is singleton. What does it take for this to be true? Referring back to Proposition 9.5, we need that Z is "strictly convex" in the sense of that proposition. (The scare quotes around *strictly convex* are certainly merited, since Z doesn't even have to be convex in areas where profit-maximizing production plans will not be found.) Conversely, if Z is not "strictly convex" in the sense of Proposition 9.5—if there are z and z' on the northeast boundary of Z, such that all convex combinations of z and z' are on the northeast boundary of Z—then prices can be found so that z and z' and all the convex combinations between them that are in Z are profit maximizing, and then we know that (at least) z and z' are in Z^* at those prices, and they and all their convex combinations will be subgradients of π at those prices. (Depending on Z, some of the convex combinations of z and z' will not be in Z^* at the prices in question. But all convex combinations will be subgradients of π at these prices. Be sure you understand this distinction.) Therefore, π will not be differentiable at those prices.

Suppose we know that π is differentiable on some open set of prices; hence Z^* is singleton for those prices, and we can write $z^*(p)$ for the *function* that gives the optimal netput vector as a function of prices. What (more) does it take to conclude that these optimal netput functions are differentiable? I will not give the answer here, prefering to reserve this discussion for Chapter 11, where we'll discuss the issue in the context of the theory of the consumer. But, anticipating what we'll say there, suppose one is able to describe the production technology in ways (typically, with production functions, which you may recall from intermediate microeconomics) that permit a solution of the firm's profit-maximization problem as a constrained maximization problem. Suppose there is enough convexity so that solutions to the first-order, complementary-slackness conditions are certain to be solutions of the profit-maximization problem. Then (with some technical conditions met) those first-order, complementary-slackness conditions implicitly define the optimal netput functions, and you can think of using the Implicit-Function Theorem to prove that the optimal netput functions are differentiable. However, where nonnegativity constraints (on the amount of an input being used, on the amount of a particular output being produced for sale) go from binding to no-binding, differentiability of the optimal netput functions will usually be lost. (And if you want to see what all this means, wait for the discussion in Chapter 11.)

Some practical criteria

So, to sum up, if someone hands you a function $\pi : R^k_{++} \to R$ and asserts that it is the profit function for a firm that has some Z and maximizes profits, you test whether π is indeed a profit function by asking: Is π homogeneous of degree 1?

Is π convex? If the answer is yes to both questions, then π is a profit function. (Remember, continuity of π is superfluous, since it follows from the convexity of π.) Moreover, you have a machine for resurrecting from π its Z or, rather, the closure of the free-disposal convex hull of the original Z. If π is differentiable (and Z is closed), $Z^*(p)$ will be singleton at each p, with the gradient of π at p being the optimal netput vector at p. More generally, subgradients of π at p are elements of $Z^*(p)$ or, rather, elements of $Z^*(p)$ *if* the original Z is convex, closed, and has free disposal.

And if someone hands you a vector-valued function $z^* : R^k_{++} \to R^k$ and asserts that it is the optimal netput function for a profit-maximizing firm, you construct the implicit profit function π by setting $\pi(p) = p \cdot z^*(p)$ for each p and proceed as above.

That summarizes the theory of the situation. But checking on convexity on first principles can be difficult. Happily, if you have sufficient differentiability, some simple criteria are available: If someone hands you a candidate profit function π that is twice-differentiable, you have to check that it is homogeneous of degree 1 and that the matrix of mixed second partials, whose ijth term is

$$\frac{\partial^2 \pi}{\partial p_i \partial p_j},$$

is positive semi-definite. While if someone hands you a candidate optimal netput (vector) function z^*, you must check that these functions are all homogeneous of degree 0 and that the *Jacobian* matrix whose ijth term is

$$\frac{\partial z_i}{\partial p_j}$$

is symmetric and positive semi-definite.

9.9. Cost Minimization and Input-Requirement Sets

This chapter has (so far) concerned the firm's profit-maximization problem. We specify the capabilities of the firm by a production-possibility set Z and then, given prices, find the optimal (profit-maximizing) levels of inputs and outputs simultaneously. A related treatment of the firm begins by assuming a clear distinction between the firm's inputs and outputs. Technological capabilities are given by so-called *input-requirement sets*, which tell us, for a given vector of outputs, what combinations of input are sufficient to obtain those outputs. And the problem studied is the firm's *cost-minimization problem*: For each vector of outputs and given prices for the inputs, what is the least-cost method for producing the specific output vector? One reason for studying this problem is that, while it may be hard to swallow the assumption that the firm is a price taker in its outputs, it is more reasonable to assume that its activities have no impact on the prices of its inputs.

In some ways, the firm's cost-minimization problem is simpler than its profit-maximization problem; for one thing, the required compactness assumptions arise very naturally (once strictly positive prices for inputs are fixed). In other ways, the story becomes more complex; in the firm's profit-maximization problem, prices are the only parameters and (so) the feasible set doesn't shift with changes in parameters; now prices of inputs and the level of outputs enter as parameters, and a shift in the level of outputs changes the feasible set over which the firm is optimizing. It turns out, moreover, that the cost-minimization problem shares a lot of mathematical structure with the consumer's expenditure-minimization problem (also known as the dual consumer's problem), the subject of next chapter. So in this section, we will give some results about the firm's cost-miminimization problem. But we won't be complete, and all the proofs are left as exercises for you. (Many of the proofs are provided in the *Guide*.) With regard to the incompleteness of results, you may want to take up the challenge of filling in the gaps. But if you do, it may be best to wait until you have finished Chapter 10.

Firms with fixed inputs and output, and input-requirement sets

Suppose for a firm (whose production-possibility set is denoted by $Z \subseteq R^k$), the k commodities are divided into inputs, outputs, and no-puts. Specifically, there are m possible outputs of the firm, and n inputs, with the first set disjoint from the second and with $n + m \leq k$. Assume for convenience that commodity labels are ordered so that the first m components of a netput vector z are the outputs of the firm, and the next n are inputs, and write $z = (y, -x, 0)$ for $z \in Z$, where $y \in R^m_+$ is an output vector and $x \in R^n_+$ is an input vector. The following assumptions are always made:

> *If* $z = (y, -x, w) \in Z$ *where* $y \in R^m$, $-x \in R^n$, *and* $w \in R^{k-m-n}$, *then* $x \geq 0$, $w \leq 0$, *and, if we write* y^+ *for the positive part of* y *(that is,* $y^+_i = \max\{y_i, 0\}$*), then* $(y^+, -x, 0) \in Z$.

The explanation is: The middle n coordinates are inputs for the firm, and they *must* be nonpositive in a netput vector z. The final $k - m - n$ coordinates are neither inputs nor outputs; to allow the firm to have free disposal, we allow it to dispose of some of these commodities (hence $w \leq 0$), but this disposal is inessential to the firm's actual production processes (hence we can replace w with 0 in these coordinates and still be feasible). And the first m coordinates are outputs: These are the only coordinates that can take on strictly positive values. Again to allow for free disposal in Z, we allow these coordinates to have negative values. But these are never net inputs to the firm's actual production process, and so if we replace any negative coordinate among these first m with zero, we remain feasible.

It goes almost without saying that, as long as prices are nonnegative and this assumption holds, the firm would never choose a production plan z in which one of the first m or the final $k - m - n$ coordinates are negative. So we can (and do) restrict our attention to that subset of Z where z has the form $(y, -x, 0)$, where y and x are both nonnegative. Let $\hat{Z}$ be the subset of the firm's Z of vectors of this form. Let Y denote the subset of R^m_+ such that $y \in Y$ if $(y, -x, 0) \in \hat{Z}$ for some

$x \in R^n_+$; that is, Y is the set of feasible output vectors for the firm. And, for each $y \in Y$, let $V(y) = \{x \in R^n_+ : (y, -x, 0) \in \hat{Z}\}$. *For a given output vector* y, *the set* $V(y)$ *is called the* ***input-requirement set*** *for* y.

Under the assumptions made, $\hat{Z}$ can be reconstructed from Y and, for each $y \in Y$, $V(y)$. (Alternatively, one can specify a $V(y)$ for all $y \in R^m_+$, where $V(y) = \emptyset$ if the firm is incapable of producing output vector y.) So instead of specifying the firm's production possibilities by Z (or $\hat{Z}$), one can begin with Y and the $V(y)$.

What properties of Y and the $V(y)$ correspond to the properties of Z given at the start of this chapter? Because the input-requirement sets tell us nothing about the structure of Z away from $\hat{Z}$, we will have to adapt some of the properties of Z to $\hat{Z}$. But with that caveat, we have the following result:

Proposition 9.23.

a. *Z has no free production if and only if $0 \notin V(y)$ for all y such that $y \geq 0$ and $y \neq 0$.*

b. *Z has the ability to shut down ($0 \in Z$) if and only if $0 \in Y$ and $0 \in V(0)$.*

c. *If Z has free disposal, then each $V(y)$ is* ***comprehensive upward****, meaning that if $x \in V(y)$ and $x' \geq x$, then $x' \in V(y)$. But the converse is not true. Instead, $\hat{Z}$ exhibits free disposal (if $(y, -x, 0) \in \hat{Z}$ and $0 \leq y' \leq y, x' \geq x$, then $(y', -x', 0) \in \hat{Z}$) if and only if $y \in Y$ and $0 \leq y' \leq y$ implies $y' \in Y$, each $V(y)$ is comprehensive upward, and the $V(y)$ sets nest in the sense that if $y, y' \in Y$ are such that $y \geq y'$, then $V(y) \subseteq V(y')$.*

d. *If Z is convex, then each $V(y)$ is convex. But each $V(y)$ can be convex and $\hat{Z}$ is not. Instead, $\hat{Z}$ is convex if and only if Y is convex and, for all $y, y' \in Y$, $x \in V(y)$, and $x' \in V(y')$, and for all $\alpha \in [0, 1]$, $\alpha x + (1 - \alpha)x' \in V(\alpha y + (1 - \alpha)y')$.*

e. *The correspondence $y \Rightarrow V(y)$ is upper semi-continuous if and only if $\hat{Z}$ is closed. As a corollary, if $\hat{Z}$ is closed, then each $V(y)$ is closed. But Y may not be closed, even if $\hat{Z}$ is closed.*

Proofs of parts of this proposition amount to little more than restating or rearranging definitions. But other parts have some substance, and examples that illustrate the negative statements are worth seeing. See Problem 9.11 and its solution in the *Student's Guide* for more on this.

The increasing/decreasing/constant returns to scale properties can be formulated in terms of input-requriement sets, but only in ways that, essentially, translate the old properties into the new context. So they are not interesting. The recession-cone property is also not of interest in this context, but for a very different reason: Once attention moves from Z to the V sets, maximizing overall profit gives way to minimizing cost and, as you will see momentarily, existence of a solution to the cost-minimization problem is never an issue if prices of inputs are strictly positive.

Cost minimization for a fixed level of output

Now we introduce prices for the inputs. Inputs are also called *factors of production*, and prices for them are often called *factor prices*. Regardless of the name, they are denoted by $r \in R^n_{++}$; note that we are looking only at strictly positive prices for the inputs.

Fixing some $y \in Y$ and prices r for the inputs, the firm's cost-minimization problem is to

$$\text{Minimize } r \cdot x, \quad \text{subject to } x \in V(y).$$

We can write $V^*(y, r)$ for the set of solutions to this problem and $\mathrm{C}(y, r)$ for $\inf\{r \cdot x : x \in V(y)\}$; C is called the *cost function*. Throughout this subsection, y will be fixed, and we'll abbreviate with $V^*(r)$ and $\mathrm{C}(r)$. Note that since $y \in Y$, $V(y)$ is nonempty, and hence $\mathrm{C}(r) < \infty$ for each r.

Proposition 9.24.

a. $\mathrm{C}(r) \geq 0$ *for all* $r \in R^n_{++}$.

b. If $V(y)$ *is closed, a solution to this problem exists for every* $r \in R^n_{++}$.

c. If $V(y)$ *is a convex set,* $V^*(r)$ *is convex for each* r.

d. The cost function $r \to \mathrm{C}(r)$ *is concave.*

e. The cost function C *is homogeneous of degree 1 in* r.

f. If $x \in V^*(r)$ *(for fixed* y*), then* x *is a supergradient of* C *at* r*. Conversely, if* $x \in V(y)$ *is a supergradient of* C *at* r*, then* $x \in V^*(r)$.

g. **(Berge's Theorem)** *For fixed* y*, if* $V(y)$ *is closed, then* $r \to \mathrm{C}(r)$ *is continuous and* $r \Rightarrow V^*(r)$ *is nonempty valued and upper semi-continuous.*

h. For $X \subseteq R^n_+$*, let* $\mathrm{CCH}(X) = \{x \in R^n_+ : x \geq \sum_{\ell=1}^L \alpha_\ell x^\ell$*, for nonnegative scalars* $\alpha_1, \ldots, \alpha_\ell$ *that sum to one, and* $x^1, \ldots, x^\ell \in X\}$*. And let* $\overline{\mathrm{CCH}}(X)$ *be the closure of* $\mathrm{CCH}(X)$*. Then the cost function associated with* X *—that is,* $\mathrm{C}(r) = \inf\{r \cdot x : x \in X\}$ *for* $r \in R^n_{++}$ *—is the same as the cost function associated with* $\overline{\mathrm{CCH}}(X)$*. Therefore, if* $\overline{\mathrm{CCH}}(X) = \overline{\mathrm{CCH}}(X')$*, then* X *and* X' *have the same cost function. Conversely, if* $\overline{\mathrm{CCH}}(X) \neq \overline{\mathrm{CCH}}(X')$*, then* X *and* X' *have different cost functions.*

i. Suppose that $\mathrm{C} : R^n_{++} \to R_+$ *is concave and homogeneous of degree 1. Define*

$$X = \{x \in R^k_+ : r \cdot x \geq \mathrm{C}(r) \text{ for all } r \in R^n_{++}\}.$$

Then X *is closed, convex, and comprehensive upwards, and for every* $r \in R^k_{++}$*,* $\mathrm{C}(r) = \min\{r \cdot x : x \in X\}$.

j. **(Hotelling's Lemma)** *The cost function* $\mathrm{C}(r)$ *is differentiable (in* r*) in an open neighborhood of* r^0 *if and only if the firm's cost-minimization problem has a unique solution for each* r *in that neighborhood, in which case the vector whose* i*th component is* $\partial \mathrm{C}/\partial r_i$ *—that is, the gradient of* C *—is the solution of the cost-minimization problem* *at each r. Moreover, if the solution is unique in an open neighborhood of r^0 and, writing $x^*(r)$ for the solution (in R^n_+) as a function of r, if this (vector-valued) function is continuously differentiable, then*

$$\frac{\partial x_i^*}{\partial r_j} = \frac{\partial x_j^*}{\partial r_i} \quad \text{for all } i, j = 1, \ldots, n.$$

That is, the rate of change in factor i per unit change in price of factor j exactly equals the rate of change in factor j per unit change in the price of factor i.

The proof of all parts of this proposition except part j is left as an exercise (Problem 9.12) for you; or see the solution to the problem in the *Guide*. Parts a through f are all fairly straightforward, but g, h, and i are good tests of whether you understood the details of the proofs in this chapter.

Note that, in parts h and i, the generic set X is a stand-in for an input-requirement set $V(y)$. Paraphrasing the two parts, the cost function can be used to recover $V(y)$ up to the closure of the comprehensive convex hull of $V(y)$. Two input-requirement sets with the same closures of their comprehensive convex hulls give the same cost function; if two input-requirement sets have different closures of their comprehensive convex hulls, they have different cost functions. And a candidate for a cost function (for a single output vector) is in fact a cost function for some input-requirement set, as long as it is nonnegative valued, concave, and homogeneous of degree 1.

Part j is easily proved if you understand the proof of Proposition 9.22, and so I omit it. The final pieces of part j have as premise that the solutions are differentiable in r; conditions that would guarantee this are developed in the context of consumer problems in Chapter 11. Otherwise, the symmetry of the partial derivatives derives from the fact that, under the conditions given,

$$\frac{\partial x_j^*}{\partial r_i} = \frac{\partial^2 C}{\partial r_i \partial r_j} = \frac{\partial x_i^*}{\partial r_j}.$$

Since C is concave in r, the matrix of these mixed second partials (assuming they exist) must be negative semi-definite.

The proposition does not provide the Afriat's Theorem analogue for input-requirement sets. That is relatively simple (for a single output level) and is left entirely to you.

Cost functions with varying output levels

Now we ask: What can be said about $C(y, r)$ as a function *jointly* of the target output vector y and input prices r?

If we are looking for properties such as convexity of C in y, it will take further assumptions on how the $V(y)$ knit together. Problem 9.14 asks you (in open-ended fashion) to see if you can find such conditions.

It is natural to suppose that the $V(y)$ nest. There are a variety of ways to formalize this, of varying strength. For instance:

- Say that the $V(y)$ satisfy *weak nesting* (or simply *nesting*) if $y \geq y'$ implies $V(y) \subseteq V(y')$. (In words, to produce less output, you can get by with just as much input.)
- And say that the $V(y)$ satisfy *strong nesting* if they satisfy weak nesting and, in addition, $y \geq y'$, $y \neq y'$, and $x \in V(y)$ imply that, for some $x' \leq x$, $x' \neq x$, we have $x' \in V(y')$. In words, to produce (somewhat) less output, you can get by with (somewhat) less input.

Proposition 9.25. *Suppose y and y', both in Y, satisfy $y \geq y'$, $y \neq y'$. If the input-requirement sets satisfy weak nesting, then $\mathrm{C}(y,r) \geq \mathrm{C}(y',r)$ for all r. And if the input-requirement sets are closed and satisfy strong nesting, then $\mathrm{C}(y,r) > \mathrm{C}(y',r)$.*

The proof of the first part is very easy: The infinimum taken over a smaller set (over $V(y)$) is necessarily as least as large as the infimum taken over a larger set ($V(y')$). The second part is nearly as easy: Fix some $r \in R^k_{++}$. If $V(y)$ is closed, let x be any element of $V^*(y,r)$. By assumption, there is some $x' \in V(y')$ that is $\leq x$ and $\neq x$, and at strictly positive prices, $\mathrm{C}(y',r) \leq r \cdot x' < r \cdot x = \mathrm{C}(y,r)$.

We'd like C to be continuous in y and r. The obvious vehicle for obtaining this is Berge's Theorem. But assuming that the $\hat{Z}$ corresponding to $V(y)$ is closed won't be sufficient: This only tells us that $y \rightrightarrows V(y)$ is upper semi-continuous; to apply Berge, we need that $y \rightrightarrows V(y)$ is lower semi-continuous (and that there is a locally bounded and upper semi-continuous sub-correspondence with all the requisite properties, but we're able to manufacture such a subcorrespondence in the proof, under the right conditions). This is not merely a lack of imagination on our part; we really need something more than that the corresponding $\hat{Z}$ is closed. To see why, consider the following simple example: $m = n = 1$, so there is one input good and one output. Suppose

$$V(y) = \begin{cases} [y, \infty), & \text{for } y \leq 1, \text{ and} \\ [y+1, \infty), & \text{for } y > 1. \end{cases}$$

(If the picture isn't immediately clear to you, graph the corresponding Z, assuming free disposal; a graph will be given in the *Guide*. The graph makes it clear that this $y \rightrightarrows V(y)$ is indeed upper semi-continuous.) Assuming the input good has price r, we get

$$\mathrm{C}(y,r) = \begin{cases} ry, & \text{for } y \leq 1, \text{ and} \\ r(y+1), & \text{for } r > 1. \end{cases}$$

This is, of course, discontinuous in y at $y = 1$. It is lower semi-continuous, and we can (in fact) settle for that (if we are not willing to assume more than $y \rightrightarrows V(y)$ is upper semi-continuous). Or we can assume that $y \Rightarrow V(y)$ is continuous, and get the desired continuity:

Proposition 9.26. *Suppose that the input-requirement sets (weakly) nest. Let Y^o denote $\{y \in Y$: There exists some $y' \in Y$ that is strictly greater than $y\}$. If $y \Rightarrow V(y)$ is upper semi-continuous, then $(y, r) \rightarrow \mathsf{C}(y, r)$ is lower semi-continuous on $Y^o \times R^n_{++}$. If $y \Rightarrow V(y)$ is continuous, then $(y, r) \rightarrow \mathsf{C}(y, r)$ is continuous and the correspondence $(y, r) \Rightarrow V^*(y, r)$ is upper semi-continuous on $Y^o \times R^n_{++}$.*

Restricting attention to Y^o is done for analytical convenience in the proof; other situations can be dealt with, but I've given the result in a form that permits a particular approach to the proof. (See Problem 9.23 and its solution in the *Student's Guide* for details.) I won't go any further with this development, except to leave you with two challenges, which are probably best pondered after you have consumed Chapter 10.

- If you assume that the $V(y)$ nest in the sense of Proposition 9.26, the lower semi-continuity of $y \Rightarrow V(y)$ is analogous to local insatiability. Recall what lower semi-continuity says: If $x \in V(y)$ and $\{y^n\}$ is a sequence with limit y, then we can produce a sequence $\{x^n\}$ with limit x, where $x^n \in V(y^n)$. In view of the nesting assumption, producing such a sequence is most difficult if the y^n approach y from above. The following property then is equivalent to lower semi-continuity (on Y^o, at least): If $x \in V(y)$, then in any neighborhood of x, however small, we can find an x' and a y' where $x' \in V(y')$ and y' is strictly larger (larger in every component) than y. How is this akin to local insatiability? Think of y as the utility level and x as the consumption bundle. The key here is that y' must be strictly larger than y; in the case of local insatiability, since there is only one dimension to utility, larger means strictly larger. Challenge number 1: Can you make everything just stated exact?
- Suppose a candidate cost function C with domain $R^m_+ \times R^n_{++}$ is nonnegative valued, concave and homogeneous of degree 1 in r, nondecreasing in y, and jointly continuous in (y, r). If, for each y, we define $V(y) := \{x \in R^n_+ : r \cdot x \geq \mathsf{C}(y, r)$ for all $r \in R^n_{++}\}$, then we know from Proposition 9.24i that each $V(y)$ is closed, convex, and comprehensive upwards and, for every $r \in R^k_{++}$, $\mathsf{C}(y, r) = \min\{r \cdot x : x \in V(y)\}$. It is relatively easy to show that these $V(y)$ sets nest. Challenge number 2: Is $y \Rightarrow V(y)$ a continuous correspondence?

9.10. Why Do We Care?

The bulk of this chapter has been about the connections between a firm's production technology, modeled by the production-possibility set Z, and its profit function π. Simplifying drastically, there is a one-to-one correspondence between production-possibility sets Z and profit functions π, where the many propositions we've developed make exact what is the real one-to-one correspondence.

Why do we care about this? The answer to this question takes us from the world of higher economic theory to more applied concerns, both theoretical and empirical. In terms of more applied theory, economists are often concerned with so-called comparative statics exercises; in the current context, this would mean asking and answering questions about how the maximizing decisions of a firm change as parameters of the firm's environment change. Knowing (directly) what is the class of optimal netput functions of the firm makes such results immediately available. And if we want to study data generated by a real firm, we may be lucky enough to be able to identify important aspects of the firm's technology and to obtain data that allow us to estimate that technology. But in many cases, the data available are economic and not technological in nature: We know that, facing one set of prices, the firm chose z; facing a second set of prices, it chose z', and so forth. The results that make up the bulk of this chapter tell us that economic data of these sorts identify (to some extent) the underlying technology of the firm, under the maintained hypothesis that the firm maximizes profit, taking prices as given. (Since for many firms the price of outputs is not given—that is, the firms have market power over their output prices—for many empirical purposes, the more useful version of this sort of thing is the theory of the cost function, in Section 9.9.) The next step, then, is to blend this theoretical development with empirical concerns, which often means identifying functional forms for the economic data we are likely to have—functional forms that permit estimation—and the corresponding technologies. Diewert (1974) and Fuss and McFadden (1978) are good places to begin your study of such matters.

Bibliographic Notes

The theory of the competitive, profit-maximizing firm is in some sense the poor relation of the theory of the utility-maximizing consumer in the literature of economics; not because it isn't important, but because it is, in comparison, relatively simple. Being simple, there isn't a lot to say, and what there is, is straightforward. (If this didn't seem straightforward to you, wait until you have finished Chapters 10 and 11!) But the theory is only the precursor to applications, and the chapter by Diewert and book by Fuss and McFadden just cited will begin to show how rich is the subject. These are also good, classic references to the theory developed here (in Fuss and McFadden, see Chapter 1), and both the article and the introduction to the book contain sketches of the history of thought on this topic.

Problems

■ 1. (a) On page 203, I suggest that you look at the example $k = 2$ and $Z = \{(-1,1), (-3,2), (0,0)\}$. What is π in this example? What is the connection between this example and the discussion there? What does the *sort of* in that discussion mean, precisely?

(b) Provide the (simple) proof of Corollary 9.18. How does this connect with part a of this problem?

■ *2. It is sometimes useful to know that $0 \in Z$; a firm has the ability to shut down. Suppose you are given the profit function π associated with some Z. To what extent does π alone tell you whether 0 is or is not a member of Z? (I am leaving this question somewhat open-ended; the challenge for you is to say as much as you can about whether $0 \in Z$, based on knowledge of π. To avoid complications, assume that π is real valued.)

■ 3. When we proved Berge's Theorem for the firm's profit-maximization problem, we assumed the recession-cone property, so that $\pi(p) < \infty$ for all $p \in R^k_{++}$. But suppose that π is infinite valued for some price vectors and finite for others. Suppose that, in such a case, we know that $\pi(p) < \infty$ for all p in an open neighborhood of some price p^0. Assume that Z is closed. Does Berge's Theorem work locally near p^0? Is $p \Rightarrow Z^*(p)$ upper semi-continuous, and is $p \to \pi(p)$ continuous, for all p in some (possibly smaller) open neighborhood of p^0?

■ *4. Suppose that a firm has a production-possibility set Z that is closed and nonempty and has the recession-cone property. Focus attention on good 1, by fixing strictly positive prices $p_2, p_3, \ldots, p_k$ for all the other goods, and let $Z_1^*(p_1)$ be the set of values of z_1 such that z_1 is part of a profit-maximizing production plan for the firm at prices $(p_1, p_2, \ldots, p_k)$; that is, $Z_1^*(p_1)$ is the projection along coordinate 1 of $Z^*(p_1, p_2, \ldots, p_k)$, or

$$Z_1^*(p_1) = \{z_1 \in R : \text{There exist } (z_2, \ldots, z_k) \in R^{k-1} \text{ such that } (z_1, z_2, \ldots, z_k) \in Z^*(p_1, \ldots, p_k)\}.$$

Suppose that, for some open interval of prices for good 1, say, $p_1 \in (\underline{p}_1, \overline{p}_1)$, we know that $Z_1^*(p_1)$ is a singleton set, say, $\{z_1(p_1)\}$. For p_1 in this interval, is $z_1(\cdot)$ a continuous function? (Hint: How is this connected to Corollary A4.8?)

■ 5. Production-possibility set Z is said to be *additive* if it has the property that if z and z' are both in Z, then so is $z + z'$. The idea is: If the firm can do z and can do z', then by setting up separate operations, it can do both z and z'.

(a) Show by example that additivity neither implies nor is implied by increasing returns to scale.

(b) Suppose Z is additive. What can you say about its profit function π?

■ 6. Proposition 9.10 concerns a finite set of price-and-production-plan data that is meant to come from a single Z. Suppose we imagine a firm whose production possibilities expand through time. Specifically, Z_t for $t = 1, 2, \ldots$ gives the production possibilities for this firm at time t, and with $Z_t \subseteq Z_{t+1}$ for all t. The data $(p_1, z_1), (p_2, z_2), \ldots, (p_T, z_T)$ are alleged to record the prices that face the firm and the production choice it made at times $t = 1, \ldots, T$, given this (expanding) production technology. Suppose we assume that the choice of the firm at time t maximizes the firm's profit at that time; that is, $z_t \in \arg\max\{p_t \cdot z : z \in Z_t\}$. (This is a very debatable assumption: Perhaps the firm's choice of production plan at time t affects the production possibilities it has at later times. Then its choice at time t should balance current profit against enhanced opportunities for profit in the future. But we do not take that possibility into account.) In the spirit of Proposition 9.10, give necessary and sufficient conditions for the data $(p_1, z_1), (p_2, z_2), \ldots, (p_T, z_T)$ to be consistent with this story, for some sets $Z_1, Z_2, \ldots, Z_T$.

■ *7. Concerning the messy caveat in Proposition 9.17 and Corollary 9.19, first show by example that the caveat is needed. That is, give two closed and convex free-disposal production possibility sets Z and Z' that both give $\pi \equiv \infty$ as their production function. Then provide a detailed and explicit proof of the corollary. (You are allowed to say stuff like "Now insert the text from xxxx to yyyy verbatim," assuming that what is in the text works in the context of the profit function defined for the extended domain.)

If you would like a further challenge (not answered in the *Student's Guide*: Suppose we had permitted nonnegative (instead of strictly positive) price vectors from the start in this chapter. What difficulties would this raise?

■ 8. Suppose we have two production-possibility sets Z and Z' (both in R^k for some k) and their corresponding profit functions π and π'. How are the following two relationships connected:

$$Z \subseteq Z' \quad \text{and} \quad \pi'(p) \geq \pi(p) \text{ for all } p \in R^k_{++}.$$

Does one of these imply the other? Are they equivalent? Do not just settle for answers to those two questions; you should develop as (economically) meaningful and general a proposition as you can about what it takes for one profit function to be everywhere at least as large as another in terms of the underlying production-possibility sets. (The term "develop" here means "state the result and give its proof," of course.)

■ *9. Prove Proposition 9.20.

■ 10. Recall (from the discussion just before Proposition 9.3) what it means for a function $f : R^k \to R \cup \{\infty\}$ to be convex and/or homogeneous of degree 1.

(a) Let Z be an arbitrary nonempty set in R^k, and let $\tilde{\pi}_Z : R^k \to R \cup \{\infty\}$ be defined by $\tilde{\pi}_Z(p) = \sup\{p \cdot z : z \in Z\}$. Show that $\tilde{\pi}_Z$ is convex and homogeneous of degree 1.

(b) Suppose that $f : R^k \to R \cup \{\infty\}$ is convex and homogeneous of degree 1. Show that the set $X^* = \{x \in R^k : f(x) < \infty\}$ is a convex cone.

(c) The next step in the development of this theory is to think about continuity properties of $\tilde{\pi}_Z$ as defined in part a. What can you say about this? It might be helpful to let $P_Z^* = \{p \in R^k : \tilde{\pi}_Z < \infty\}$ and consider separately the continuity of $\tilde{\pi}_Z$ on the interior of P_Z^*, on its boundary, and on the interior of its complement. (What if anything can you say about the value of $\tilde{\pi}_Z$ on the boundary of P_Z^*?) Before setting out to try to do this (it isn't easy), you might find it helpful to look at some examples. Begin with the following two: $Z = R_-^k$; $Z = \{(x_1, x_2) \in R^2 : x_1 \leq 0, x_2 \leq |x_1|^{1/2}\}$.

■ *11. Prove Proposition 9.23. and give examples that illustrate the negative statements in parts c, d, and e.

■ *12. Prove Proposition 9.24, omitting part j.

■ *13. Prove Proposition 9.26. For a hint on how to attack this (getting the locally bounded and upper semi-continuous sub-correspondence is a bit tricky), look ahead to the proof of Proposition 10.3 and, in particular, the paragraph at the end of the proof that begins "Now we resort to a trick."

■ 14. Consider the cost function C for a fixed r. Under what conditions is this a convex function of y?

■ 15. Suppose the firm has a single output good. The level of this output good will still be denoted by y, but now $y \in R_+$. A *production function* is a function $f : R_+^n \to R_+$ that gives, for a vector of inputs $x \in R_+^n$, the greatest amount of output that can be obtained from that vector of inputs. That is, if we start with a production-possibility set Z (where now the first component is the sole output good, and components 2 through $n+1$ give the vector of inputs), we define

$$f(x) = \sup\{y \in R_+ : (y, -x) \in Z\}.$$

Your assignment is to re-create the theory of the firm if the firm (a) has a single output and (b) has its technology specified by a production function f; begin with properties of f that correspond to the various properties of Z used in the chapter, and move on to either the firm's cost-minimization problem

$$\text{Minimize } r \cdot x, \quad \text{subject to } f(x) \geq y,$$

or the firm's full profit-maximization problem

$$\text{Maximize } qf(x) - r \cdot x, \quad \text{subject to } x \in R_+^n.$$

Warning: you may find it helpful to wait until you have finished Chapter 10.

Chapter Ten

The Expenditure-Minimization Problem

In this chapter, we return to the theory of consumer demand. Our ultimate objective is to get a theory as complete as the theory of the firm, with results similar to Propositions 9.14 through 9.19. Unhappily, the theory of the utility-maximizing consumer is more complex than the theory of the profit-maximizing firm, on two grounds:

1. The firm's profit-maximization problem has the price vector p as parameter. In the consumer's utility-maximization problem, prices enter parametrically, but so does the consumer's income y.
2. In the firm's profit-maximization problem, prices enter the objective function, but the feasible set never changes. In the consumer's utility-maximization problem, prices (and income) shift the feasible set.

Rather than take on both of these complications simultaneously, we take them one at a time: In this chapter, we examine a problem related to the consumer's utility-maximization problem, known as the *(consumer's) expenditure-minimization problem*, which has an extra parameter (beyond prices), but in which the feasible set does not shift with shifts in prices. Then in Chapter 11, we take on both complications at once, to finish off as best we can the theory of the consumer.

10.1. Defining the EMP

As in Chapters 3 and 4, we study a consumer whose preferences on R^k_+ are given by the utility function u, about which the following assumption is made.

Assumption 10.1. *Until otherwise indicated (near the end of the chapter), the utility function u is continuous and globally insatiable.*

We sometimes assume that u is quasi-concave and/or locally insatiable, but we will say so whenever either of those assumptions is made.

Recall the consumer's utility-maximization problem (abbreviated CP):

$$\text{Maximize } u(x), \text{ subject to } p \cdot x \leq y, x \geq 0,$$

for parameters $p \in R^k_{++}$, a strictly positive price vector, and $y \in R_+$, the nonnegative level of income. The *(consumer's) expenditure-minimization problem* (abbreviated

EMP) has as parameters the price vector $p \in R^k_{++}$ and a *level of utility* $v \in R$ and is to

$$\text{Minimize}\, p \cdot x, \text{ subject to } u(x) \geq v, x \geq 0.$$

That is, we are seeking the bundle x that gets the consumer the utility level v as cheaply as possible, given the prices p. (Since the utility function is u, and we will be working with values of the utility function, we use the letter v to denote values of utility; u will always be the utility *function*.) Pictures of the two problems are shown in Figure 10.1.

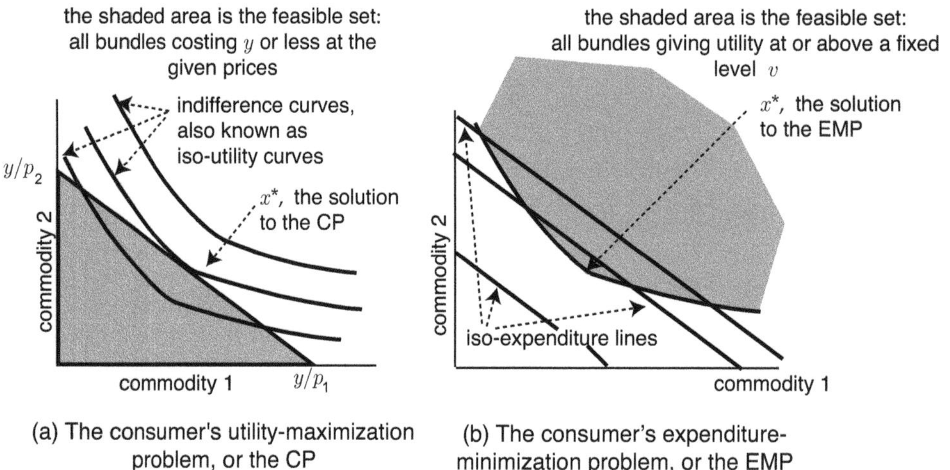

(a) The consumer's utility-maximization problem, or the CP

(b) The consumer's expenditure-minimization problem, or the EMP

Figure 10.1. The CP and the EMP in two pictures.

To tie back to the introduction, the target utility level v moves the feasible set, but not the objective function. Hence, the feasible set is not entirely free of all the parameters. But prices no longer impact the feasible set, which makes life a lot easier.

While the CP is a problem about which we could gather empirical evidence for a given consumer (at least, to the extent of asking hypothetical questions), the EMP as formulated is artificial. By this I mean, we can ask a consumer, "If you have so much income and face such-and-such prices, what will you buy?" And the answer that comes back is some bundle of goods. Both question and answer are concrete. Imagine, however, going to the consumer and asking, "Facing prices p, what bundle is the cheapest way for you to attain utility level, say, 36.5?" What, exactly, do we mean by utility level 36.5? Utility levels and the utility function u are artifices of our model of the consumer; they aren't anything tangible. Even so, the EMP has an important mathematical role to play.

We can render the EMP somewhat less artificial by reformulating it as, "For a given reference bundle x^0, what is the cheapest (at given prices p) bundle you could buy that would make you at least as well off as you would be if you had to consume x^0?"[1] Concerning this reformulation, see Problems 10.8 and 10.9.

10.2. Basic Analysis of the EMP

Before analyzing the EMP, consider the target utility level v.

- If $v \leq u(0)$, then the obvious solution to the EMP is $x = 0$, with a zero level of expenditure.
- Since we assume that u is globally insatiable, if we define $\bar{v} = \sup_{x \in R^k_+} u(x)$, then the problem is infeasible for $v \geq \bar{v}$. (No x can satisfy $u(x) \geq \bar{v}$, if u is globally insatiable.)

Therefore, whenever we talk about a target level of utility v for the EMP, we tacitly assume that $v \in [u(0), \bar{v})$, where $\bar{v} = \infty$ is of course possible.

Proposition 10.2. *Fix a consumer (characterized by her continuous and globally insatiable utility function u), prices $p \in R^k_{++}$, and a target utility level $v \in [u(0), \bar{v})$.*

a. *If x solves the EMP for this p and v, then x also solves the EMP for prices λp and utility level v, for $\lambda > 0$.*

b. *The EMP has a solution for this p and v.*

c. *If u represents convex preferences (if u is quasi-concave), the set of solutions of the EMP is a convex set. And if u represents strictly convex preferences, the EMP has a unique solution.*

d. *If x solves the EMP at p and v, then $u(x) = v$.*

The details of the proof are left for you (as Problem 10.1, solved in the *Student's Guide*), with a few hints:

1. Part b takes a bit of work, because the feasible set, $\{x \in R^k_+ : u(x) \geq v\}$, is not compact. But because $v \in [u(0), \bar{v})$ and because u is continuous, some $x^0 \in R^k_+$ satisfies $u(x^0) = v$ (why?). The set $\{x \in R^k_+ : u(x) \geq v \text{ and } p \cdot x \leq p \cdot x^0\}$ is compact (why?). And the set of solutions to the problem

$$\text{Minimize } p \cdot x, \text{ subject to } x \in R^k_+, u(x) \geq v, \quad p \cdot x \leq p \cdot x^0$$

   is the same as the set of solutions to the EMP (why?).

2. In part c, quasi-concavity of u is needed to show convexity of the feasible set. Also, the proof of uniqueness is *not* the standard proof, because $x \to p \cdot x$ is not a strictly quasi-concave function. You have to work at this one.

[1] In a similar manner, we could reformulate the CP as, "At given prices p, what is the best bundle you can purchase if your income is just sufficient to purchase the reference bundle x^0; that is, for $y = p \cdot x^0$?"

3. In contrast to the CP, where we need local insatiability of u to show that $p \cdot x = y$ at the solution, in the EMP we get $u(x) = v$ at solutions "for free." It isn't really for free, of course; continuity of u is required. But local insatiability is certainly not needed. This is because, in the EMP, the objective function $p \cdot x$ is "locally insatiable"; wherever you are, unless you are spending nothing, you can always spend a bit less locally. Please note, though, that continuity of u is needed in the argument; if you haven't used it in your proof, your proof doesn't work.

10.3. Hicksian Demand and the Expenditure Function

Recall that for the CP, we use $\mathbf{D}(p, y)$ to denote the solutions for given p and y, calling $\mathbf{D}(p, y)$ *Marshallian demand* at (p, y) and $(p, y) \Rightarrow \mathbf{D}(p, y)$ the *Marshallian demand correspondence.* We denote the value of the objective function at the solution by $\nu(p, y)$, calling ν the *indirect utility function.*

We use the following notation and names for the EMP:

- The set of solutions for given p and v is denoted $\mathbf{H}(p, v)$ and is called the *Hicksian demand* at (p, v). The correspondence $(p, v) \Rightarrow \mathbf{H}(p, v)$ is called the *Hicksian demand correspondence.*
- The value of the objective function at the solution is denoted by $e(p, v)$, and $(p, v) \to e(p, v)$ is called the *expenditure function.*

Next, we get the standard continuity results.

Proposition 10.3.

a. *For fixed $v \in [u(0), \bar{v})$, the function $p \to e(p, v)$ is continuous and the correspondence $p \Rightarrow \mathbf{H}(p, v)$ is nonempty valued, locally bounded, and upper semi-continuous.*

b. *If u satisfies local insatiability, the function $(p, v) \to e(p, v)$ is continuous and the correspondence $(p, v) \Rightarrow \mathbf{H}(p, v)$ is nonempty-valued, locally bounded, and upper semi-continuous.*

c. *If u is strictly quasi-concave, $\mathbf{H}(p, v)$ is singleton for each (p, v). Let $h(p, v)$ denote the single element of $\mathbf{H}(p, v)$ for each p and v; then the function $(p, v) \to h(p, v)$ is continuous.*

Proof. These "standard" continuity results are not so simple to obtain. Obviously, we want to apply Berge's Theorem, but the original constraint correspondence $(p, v) \Rightarrow \{x \in R_+^k : u(x) \geq v\}$ is not locally bounded. So we need to patch together some sort of fix.

Before tackling this issue, let's get the easy stuff out of the way. Part c claims uniqueness of the solution for each p and v, but that only repeats Proposition 10.2c. So this is a standard result about singleton-valued, upper semi-continuous, and locally bounded correspondences, once we know that $(p, v) \Rightarrow \mathbf{H}(p, v)$ is upper semi-continuous and locally bounded. Part b gives us this, if we know that u is locally insatiable. Fix arbitrary x. By global insatiability, $u(x') > u(x)$ for some x'. Because u is strictly quasi-concave, $u(\alpha x + (1 - \alpha)x') > u(x)$ for all $\alpha \in (0, 1)$.

But taking α arbitrarily close to 1 shows that u is locally insatiable at x. Since x is arbitrary, u is locally insatiable.

If v is fixed, the constraint set $\{x \in R^k_+ : u(x) \geq v\}$ is constant in the parameter p; hence it is lower semi-continuous. Since $v < \bar{v}$, there exists $\hat{x} \in R^k_+$ such that $u(\hat{x}) = \hat{v} > v$. Fix $\hat{x}$, and let $B(p) = \{x \in R^k_+ : u(x) \geq v, p \cdot x \leq p \cdot \hat{x}\}$. It is clear that $\mathbf{H}(p, v) \subseteq B(p)$ for all strictly positive p and that minimizing expenditure at prices p over $B(p)$ gives the same value as minimizing over the set of x such that $u(x) \geq v$. Upper semi-continuity and local boundedness of $p \Rightarrow B(p)$ is shown by the argument given back in the proof of Proposition 3.3. So Berge can be applied, giving part a.

Now for part b. To show that $(p, v) \Rightarrow \{x \in R^k_+ : u(x) \geq v\}$ is lower semi-continuous, reason as follows. The p argument plays no role here; so we don't carry it along in the notation. We need to show that, if $\{v^n\}$ is a sequence of utility targets with limit v and if x is such that $u(x) \geq v$, then there exist x^n such that $u(x^n) \geq v^n$ for each n and $\lim_n x^n = x$. The first step is to use local insatiability to produce, for $m = 1, 2, \ldots$, a point y^m such that $u(y^m) > u(x)$ and $\|y^m - x\| \leq 1/m$. Of course, this means that $\lim_m y^m = x$.

Now for each n, compare v^n with the set $\{u(y^1), u(y^2), \ldots, u(y^n)\}$. If v^n is strictly greater than all these values, set x^n to be any (arbitrary) point in R^k_+ such that $u(x^n) \geq v^n$. But if v^n is less than or equal to any of these n values, then let $x^n = y^m$ where m is the greatest index in the set $\{1, \ldots, n\}$ such that $v^n \leq u(y^m)$.

I assert that for any integer M, there is an N such that for all $n > N$, x^n will be chosen by this rule to be some y^m with $m > M$. We know that $u(y^{M+1}) > u(x) \geq v$, and we know that $v^n \to v$, so eventually (for all sufficiently large n), $v^n \leq u(y^{M+1})$. But then for $n \geq M + 1$ and large enough for this condition to hold, y^{M+1} is a candidate for assignment as x^n, and so if x^n is not assigned to be y^{M+1}, it must be because $x^n = y^m$ for some $m > M + 1$.

But this assertion finishes the proof of lower semi-continuity. The sequence $\{x^n\}$ that we've constructed has $u(x^n) \geq v^n$ for each n, and since x^n for large n is y^m for large m and the sequence $\{y^m\}$ converges to x, so does the sequence $\{x^n\}$.

Now we resort to a trick. We want to show upper semi-continuity and local boundedness of a correspondence and continuity of a function, jointly in p and v, for $v \in [u(0), \bar{v})$. These are local properties of the correspondence and the function in the sense that if we show that they hold for some open neighborhood of each (p, v), then they hold globally. So, as in the proof of part a, fix some $v^0 < \bar{v}$ and some $\hat{x}$ such that $v^0 < u(\hat{x}) = \hat{v} < \bar{v}$. For all $p \in R^k_{++}$ and $v' < \hat{v}$, define $B(p, v') = \{x \in R^k_+ : u(x) \geq v', p \cdot x \leq p \cdot \hat{x}\}$. Just as in part a, $\mathbf{H}(p, v') \subseteq B(p, v')$, and minimizing expenditure at prices p' over $B(p, v')$ gives the same infimum as minimizing over $\{x \in R^k_+ : u(x) \geq v'\}$ (as long as $v' < u(\hat{x})$, of course). And, again using the argument from the proof of Proposition 3.3, $(p, v') \Rightarrow B(p, v')$ is upper semi-continuous and locally bounded. So we conclude from Berge's Theorem that $(p, v) \Rightarrow \mathbf{H}(p, v)$ is upper semi-continuous and locally bounded, and $(p, v) \to e(p, v)$ is continuous, for $(p, v) \in R^k_{++} \times [u(0), \hat{v})$. But this domain contains an open neighborhood of (p, v^0) for any $p \in R^k_{++}$, and $v^0 \in [u(0), \bar{v})$ was arbitrary, proving part b. ■

10.4. Properties of the Expenditure Function

Now that we've gotten the basics and continuity properties out of the way, it is time to develop the theory of the EMP in a way that will give us some economic punch. This begins with a characterization of the expenditure function.

Proposition 10.4.

a. *The expenditure function is homogeneous (of degree 1) in p; that is, $e(\lambda p, v) = \lambda e(p, v)$ for $\lambda > 0$.*

b. *For all p, $e(p, v) = 0$ if $v = u(0)$ and $e(p, v) > 0$ if $v > u(0)$.*

c. *The expenditure function is strictly increasing in v and nondecreasing in p.*

d. *The expenditure function is concave in p.*

e. *The expenditure function $e(p, v)$ is unbounded above in v for each p.*

Proof. Part a follows from Proposition 10.2(a): If $x \in \mathbf{H}(p, v)$, then $x \in \mathbf{H}(\lambda p, v)$; hence if $e(p, v) = p \cdot x$, $e(\lambda p, v) = \lambda p \cdot x = \lambda e(p, v)$.

For part b, since $e(p, v) = p \cdot x$ for some $x \in R^k_+$, $e(p, v) \geq 0$ is obvious. If $v = u(0)$, $x = 0$ is a feasible way to achieve utility v, which gives the minimum possible expenditure, 0. If $v > u(0)$, then to achieve utility level v, we must choose a consumption bundle $x \neq 0$, and then $p \cdot x > 0$ for all strictly positive p. (Remember, the EMP always has a solution; for $v > u(0)$ and $p \in R^k_{++}$, there is some x^* that solves the EMP; hence $e(p, v) = p \cdot x^*$, and this is > 0.)

To prove part c, suppose $v' > v$. Pick $x \in \mathbf{H}(p, v')$, so that $e(p, v') = p \cdot x$. By part b and $v' > v \geq u(0)$, $e(p, v') > 0$. By continuity of u, we know that $u(\alpha x)$ approaches $u(x) \geq v'$ as α approaches 1; hence for some $\alpha^* < 1$, $v(\alpha^* x) \geq v$. But then $e(p, v) \leq p \cdot (\alpha^* x) = \alpha^* e(p, v') < e(p, v')$. Suppose $p' \geq p$. Pick $x \in \mathbf{H}(p', v)$, so that $e(p', v) = p' \cdot x$. Since x is feasible for the EMP at (p', v), it is feasible as well for (p, v); hence $e(p, v) \leq p \cdot x \leq p' \cdot x = e(p', v)$, where it is the last inequality that uses $p' \geq p$.

For part d, let x solve the EMP for $(ap + (1-a)p', v)$, so that $e(ap + (1-a)p', v) = (ap + (1-a)p') \cdot x$. Since $u(x) = v$, the bundle x is always a feasible way to achieve utility level v, although it may not be the cheapest way at prices other than $ap + (1-a)p'$. Accordingly,

$$e(p, v) \leq p \cdot x \quad \text{and} \quad e(p', v) \leq p' \cdot x.$$

Combining these two inequalities gives

$$\begin{aligned} ae(p, v) + (1-a)e(p', v) &\leq ap \cdot x + (1-a)p' \cdot x \\ &= (ap + (1-a)p') \cdot x = e(ap + (1-a)p', v). \end{aligned}$$

Finally, for part e, fix p and $K > 0$. Let x^0 maximize u on the set $\{x \in R^k_+ : p \cdot x \leq K\}$. Since preferences are globally insatiable, there is some $v < \bar{v}$ (that is, v is an attainable utility level) such that $u(x^0) < v$. It is immediate that $e(p, v) > K$ (since the best you can do spending K or less at prices p is x^0, which gives utility less than v. Since K is a free variable here, e must be unbounded in v for the fixed p. ∎

Two remarks about part d are worth making: First, once we know that e is concave in p, we know that it is continuous in p (since the domain of p is open). So the proof of part d constitutes an independent proof of the first part of Proposition 10.3a. Second, the proof of part d should remind you of how, in Chapter 9, we showed that the profit function in the firm's profit-maximization problem is convex. In fact, this is a proof that you should fully internalize; if shaken awake at 3:00 a.m. and asked to prove this, you should be able to do so.

Recall that after showing that the profit function was convex in p, we went on to show that any solution to the firm's profit-maximization problem was a subgradient of the profit function. You can guess, then, what comes next.

Proposition 10.5. *If $x \in \mathbf{H}(p^0, v)$, then x is a supergradient of e at (p^0, v) in p, which is to say that*

a. $p^0 \cdot x = e(p^0, v)$, and

b. $p \cdot x \geq e(p, v)$ for all p.

Hence, in particular, if e is differentiable in p at (p^0, v), the vector

$$\left(\frac{\partial e(p, u)}{\partial p_1}, \ldots, \frac{\partial e(p, u)}{\partial p_k} \right) \Bigg|_{(p^0, v)}$$

is the unique solution of the EMP at (p^0, v).

Proof. If $x \in \mathbf{H}(p^0, v)$, then part a follows immediately. And then, since we know that $u(x) = v$, we know that x is feasible for any prices p when the target utility is v, and part b follows immediately. The rest of the proposition is a simple consequence of what it means for a concave function to be differentiable at a point: Its gradient is its sole supergradient at the point. ∎

At least two partial converses could be stated for Proposition 10.5. One would be *If $x \in R^k_+$ is a supergradient of e in p at (p^0, v), then $x \in \mathbf{H}(p^0, v)$.* This is not true in general, because we have no way of knowing that $u(x) \geq v$. (Compare with the discussion beginning on the bottom of page 212 and with Problem 9.1, in the context of the theory of the firm. Can you construct a counterexample in this context along those lines?) But a second partial converse is true:

Proposition 10.6. *If the EMP at a given (p, v) has a unique solution x, then the expenditure function is differentiable in p at (p, v), and x is its gradient.*

The proof is very similar to the proof of Proposition 9.22, so I will not bother to give it in this context.

10.5. How Many Continuous Utility Functions Give the Same Expenditure Function?

We are now (almost) ready for a hoped-for, double-barreled climax to this chapter, namely answers to the following two questions:

1. *Given an expenditure function* e *generated from the utility function* u*, (how) can we recover* u*?*

2. *Given a function* e *that is purported to be an expenditure function, is it the expenditure function for some well-behaved utility function* u *(which we can then recover, once we have an answer to question 1)?*

This is similar to the recovery of the firm's production-possibility set Z from its profit function π, but with the added complication of the extra parameter v in the expenditure function. Of course, our experiences with this sort of thing in Chapter 9 warn us that we can't expect to recover *the* utility function u that generated e, since more than one utility function u will generate the same e. But we can hope to characterize all utility functions that generate the same expenditure function. We'll first tackle that.

The key geometric concept needed to answer the question that is the title of this section is the so-called *comprehensive convex hull* of a set. The setting is R^k, and we have the following definition.

Definition 10.7. *For any set* $X \subseteq R^k$*, the* ***comprehensive convex hull*** *of* X*, denoted* CCH(X) *is the smallest (by set inclusion) set* Y *that (a) contains* X*, (b) is convex, and (c) has the property that if* $x \in Y$ *and* $x' \geq x$*, then* $x' \in Y$*.*[2]

The *convex hull* part of this definition should be obvious from the general notion of a convex hull (see Appendix 3). The adjective *comprehensive* has to do with property c: If $x' \geq x$ and x is in this set, then x' is in the set.

It may not be obvious to you that a smallest set with these properties exists. But it isn't hard to show existence. Take the intersection of all sets that have these three properties. Since R^k itself contains X, is convex, and is comprehensive, we aren't taking the intersection over an empty collection of sets. If we take the intersection of an arbitrary collection of sets that all contain X, the intersection contains X. If all the sets in the collection are convex, the intersection is convex. And if all the sets are comprehensive in the sense the term is being used here, their intersection is comprehensive. So the intersection is in the collection of sets with these three properties. And, of course, it is automatically minimal in terms of set inclusion.

Thinking in terms of this intersection allows us to give a constructive definition of CCH(X):

---

[2] Cf. Proposition 9.24h; CCH(X) was used there, but was not set out in a formal definition.

Proposition 10.8 *For any set $X \subseteq R^k$, the* ***comprehensive convex hull*** *of X is the set of points*

$$\left\{x \in R^k : x \geq \sum_{n=1}^{N} \alpha_n x^n \text{ for a finite integer } N, \alpha_n \in [0,1], \sum_n \alpha_n = 1, x^n \in X\right\}.$$

Proof. Fix X, and call the set defined in the display Y. Y clearly contains X and is comprehensive. It is a bit harder (but not hard) to see that Y is convex (and I'm leaving that for you). So Y is one of the sets over which the intersection is taken when constructing CCH(X); CCH(X) $\subseteq Y$. But, at the same time, if Z is any convex and comprehensive set that contains X, then $Y \subseteq Z$; if $x \in Y$, then x is greater than or equal to a convex combination of points in X, and Z by definition contains all such points. Therefore, when we form CCH(X) by taking the intersection over all such Z, Y lies in that intersection, or $Y \subseteq$ CCH(X). Therefore, Y, the set in the display, *is* CCH(X). ∎

Please note: The characterization of CCH(X) just given can be rephrased as follows: CCH(X) = $\{x \in R^k : x \geq x' \text{ for some } x' \in \text{CH}(X)\}$, where CH($X$) is the convex hull of X.

The following general proposition will be needed.

Proposition 10.9. *If X is a closed subset of R^k_+, then* CCH(X) *is closed.*

There is more to this proposition than you may think at first. It isn't true that CCH(X) is necessary closed, if X is merely a closed subset of R^k (as opposed to R^k_+), and it isn't true that the convex hull of a general closed subset of R^k_+ is always closed. (Can you provide counterexamples?)

Proof. Fix X. Suppose $\{x^n\}$ is a sequence from CCH(X) with limit x. For each n, there are nonnegative weights α^{ni} that sum to 1 and bundles x^{ni} such that $x^{ni} \in X$, where $x^n \geq \sum_i \alpha^{ni} x^{ni}$. I haven't said how many i's there are for each n and, you might think, the number (call it K_n) might explode to infinity. But, in fact, Carathéodory's Theorem (Proposition A3.5) ensures that we can assume that, for each n, the index set of i is $\{1, 2, \ldots, k+1\}$.

Since each α^{ni} lies between 0 and 1, we can by looking along a subsequence of the n assume that, for each $i = 1, \ldots, k+1$, $\lim_n \alpha^{ni}$ exists. Call the limit α^i. For some of the i, α^i may be zero; for others, it is strictly positive; let I denote the subset of $\{1, \ldots, k+1\}$ such that $\alpha^i > 0$. Because $\sum_{i=1}^{k+1} \alpha^{ni} = 1$ for each n, the same is true in the limit, or $\sum_{i=1}^{k+1} \alpha^i = 1$. For $i \notin I$, $\alpha^i = 0$, so we know that $\sum_{i \in I} \alpha^i = 1$.

We know that $x^n \geq \sum_{i=1}^{k+1} \alpha^{ni} x^{ni}$. Since the α^{ni} are all nonnegative scalars, and the x^{ni} are all nonnegative vectors, if we drop some terms in the sum, we maintain the inequality. In particular, $x^n \geq \sum_{i \in I} \alpha^{ni} x^{ni}$. Now the x^n live inside a bounded set (they have limit x, so eventually they stay in neighborhoods of x, and there are only finitely many other terms to take into account). And the α^{ni} for $i \in I$ are all eventually strictly bounded away from zero (they have limits that are strictly positive). Therefore, the inequalities $x^n \geq \sum_{i \in I} \alpha^{ni} x^{ni}$ ensure the x^{ni} for $i \in I$ must, eventually, live inside a bounded set. So, by looking along a further subsequence, we can assume that, for each $i \in I$, $\lim_n x^{ni}$ exists; call the limit y^i. Since X is closed, $y^i \in X$. And, by taking limits on both sides of $x^n \geq \sum_{i \in I} \alpha^{ni} x^{ni}$, we get$x \geq \sum_{i \in I} \alpha^i y^i$. We already have established that $\sum_{i \in I} \alpha^i = 1$ and that $y^i \in X$ for each i, so this tells us that $x \in \text{CCH}(X)$. Therefore, CCH(X) is closed. ■

The next result links the concept of CCH sets with functions that are quasi-concave and nondecreasing.

Proposition 10.10. *A function $u : R_+^k \to R$ is quasi-concave and nondecreasing if and only if its upper-level sets are convex and comprehensive; that is, for all $v \in R$,*

$$\{x \in R_+^k : u(x) \geq v\} = \text{CCH}(\{x \in R_+^k : u(x) \geq v\}.$$

Proof. Suppose u is quasi-concave and nondecreasing. Then we know that the sets $\{x \in R_+^k : u(x) \geq v\}$ are convex and comprehensive. (For convexity of the sets, enlist Proposition A3.19. Showing that the sets are comprehensive is a matter of writing down a sequence of definitions.) Fix $v \in R$ and temporarily let $X = \{x \in R_+^k : u(x) \geq v\}$. Since CCH($X$) is the intersection of all convex and comprehensive sets that contain X, $X \subseteq \text{CCH}(X)$ and, on the other hand, since X is convex and comprehensive and contains X, it is among the sets in the intersection, so $\text{CCH}(X) \subseteq X$. Hence $X = \text{CCH}(X)$.

And suppose, for each v, the set $\{x \in R_+^k : u(x) \geq v\} = \text{CCH}(\{x \in R_+^k : u(x) \geq v\})$. Then this set is convex and comprehensive. But the convexity of such sets for all v implies that u is quasi-concave; again enlist Proposition A3.19. And if $x' \geq x$, then $x \in \{\hat{x} \in R_+^k : u(\hat{x}) \geq u(x)\}$; hence x' is also in that set (since the set is comprehensive), and so $u(x') \geq u(x)$. The function u is nondecreasing. ■

We come to the central result of this section.

Proposition 10.11. *Fix two* **continuous** *utility functions u and u'. Let e be the expenditure function defined from u, and e' be the expenditure function defined from u'. For $v \in R$, if*

$$\text{CCH}(\{x \in R_+^k : u(x) \geq v\}) = \text{CCH}(\{x \in R_+^k : u'(x) \geq v\}),$$

then $e(p, v) = e'(p, v)$ for all $p \in R_{++}^k$. Conversely, if u and u' are both continuous and, for some v,

$$\text{CCH}(\{x \in R_+^k : u(x) \geq v\}) \neq \text{CCH}(\{x \in R_+^k : u'(x) \geq v\}),$$

then for some $p \in R_{++}^k$, $e(p, v) \neq e'(p, v)$.

Before getting to the proof, two comments (one of which will give us a corollary) are in order:

- Note my emphasis on the utility functions being continuous. In view of Assumption 10.1, you may wonder why I even mention this; aren't all utility functions in this chapter assumed to be continuous? They are indeed, but if you go back to the proof of Proposition 10.10, you can see that the proposition is true even if u is not continuous. And the first half of Proposition 10.11—if the comprehensive convex hulls of the upper-level sets for a given v are the same, then the expenditure functions agree for that v—also doesn't need continuity of the utility functions. But the second half of Proposition 10.11 does need continuity, because it will be proven using the Strict-Separation Theorem (Proposition A3.11), for which we need the CCH sets to be closed.[3] However, I don't need to assume that the utility functions are globally insatiable for Proposition 10.10 or for *either* half of Proposition 10.11, which leads to the question, How much of our earlier results in this chapter needed the two parts of Assumption 10.1? Problem 10.3 asks you to go back and investigate this question.
- The proposition is stated one v at a time: The comprehensive convex hulls of the upper-level sets for a given v are the same if and only if the expenditure functions agree for that v. But this immediately implies a result for "all the v at once":

Corollary 10.12. *Fix two continuous utility functions u and u'. Let e be the expenditure function defined from u and e' be the expenditure function defined from u'. Then $e \equiv e'$ if and only if*

$$\text{CCH}(\{x \in R^k_+ : u(x) \geq v\}) = \text{CCH}(\{x \in R^k_+ : u'(x) \geq v\}) \quad \textit{for all } v \in R.$$

Proof of Proposition 10.11. Suppose first that, for some v,

$$\text{CCH}(\{x \in R^k_+ : u(x) \geq v\}) = \text{CCH}(\{x \in R^k_+ : u'(x) \geq v\}).$$

Fix any $p \in R^k_{++}$, and suppose that $e(p, v) < e'(p, v)$. Since $e(p, v)$ is the minimal expenditure needed to obtain utility level v at prices p under u, there is some x such that $u(x) \geq v$ and $p \cdot x < e'(p, v)$. Of course $x \in \text{CCH}(\{\hat{x} \in R^k_+ : u(\hat{x}) \geq v\})$ and, therefore, $x \in \text{CCH}(\{\hat{x} \in R^k_+ : u'(\hat{x}) \geq v\})$. This means that there exist nonnegative weights α^i summing to 1 and bundles x^i with $u'(x^i) \geq v$ such that $x \geq \sum_i \alpha^i x^i$. But then $p \cdot x \geq \sum_i \alpha^i (p \cdot x^i)$, and so $p \cdot x \geq p \cdot x^i$ for at least one i. And for that i, $u'(x^i) \geq v$. Hence $e'(p, v) \leq p \cdot x^i$, contradicting the assertion that $p \cdot x < e'(p, v)$.

As for the converse, note first that since u and u' are both continuous functions, both $\{x \in R^k_+ : u(x) \geq v\}$ and $\{x \in R^k_+ : u'(x) \geq v\}$ are closed. So by Proposition 10.9, both $\text{CCH}(\{x \in R^k_+ : u(x) \geq v\})$ and $\text{CCH}(\{x \in R^k_+ : u'(x) \geq v\}$ are closed.

---

[3] To foreshadow some later developments, what if u were only *upper semi*-continuous?

Now suppose that, for some v,

$$\mathrm{CCH}(\{x \in R^k_+ : u(x) \geq v\}) \neq \mathrm{CCH}(\{x \in R^k_+ : u'(x) \geq v\}).$$

Without loss of generality, suppose that $x^0 \in \mathrm{CCH}(\{x \in R^k_+ : u(x) \geq v\})$ but $\notin \mathrm{CCH}(\{x \in R^k_+ : u'(x) \geq v\})$. Temporarily denote $\mathrm{CCH}(\{x \in R^k_+ : u'(x) \geq v\})$ by X'. Since $x \in \mathrm{CCH}(\{x \in R^k_+ : u(x) \geq v\})$, we know that $x^0 \geq \sum_i \alpha^i x^i$ for nonnegative weights α^i that sum to 1 and vectors x^i such that $u(x^i) \geq v$. One of the x^i is not a member of X', since if they all were, so would be $\sum_i \alpha^i x^i$ (since X' is convex) and then so would be x^0 (since X' is comprehensive). So, without loss of generality, we can assume that the original x^0 is one of the x^i; specifically, it satisfies $u(x^0) \geq v$ but is not in the closed, comprehensive, and convex set X'.

Since X' is closed and convex, we can strictly separate x^0 from X'; that is, there exists a nonzero vector $q \in R^k$ such that $q \cdot x^0 < \inf\{q \cdot x : x \in X'\}$. Since X' is comprehensive upwards, the usual argument shows that q must be nonnegative. Now take any strictly positive vector, say $e = (1, 1, \ldots, 1) \in R^k$, and let $\epsilon > 0$ be small enough so that $(q + \epsilon e) \cdot x^0 = qx^0 + \epsilon e \cdot x^0 < \inf\{q \cdot x : x \in X'\}$. Let $p = q + \epsilon e$; clearly $p \in R^k_{++}$ and $p \cdot x^0 < \inf\{p \cdot x : x \in X'\}$ (since $p \cdot x \geq q \cdot x$ for all $x \in R^k_+$). But this means that the expenditure function for u, evaluated at p and v, or $e(p, v)$, is less than or equal to $p \cdot x^0$, since $x^0 \in \{x \in R^k_+ : u(x) \geq v\}$. And the expenditure function for u', evaluated at p and v, or $e'(p, v)$ is $\min\{p \cdot x : x \in X'\}$, by the first part of the proposition. Hence $e(p, v) < e'(p, v)$; u and u' have different expenditure functions. ■

We are almost ready for the two big questions posed at the start of this section. In particular, we know that if we are given an expenditure function e that is generated by some utility function u, we can't count on recovering the particular u from e: Other utility functions u' share e.

We do know, however, that if e was generated by a continuous, quasi-concave, and nondecreasing utility function u, then u is the *unique* continuous, quasi-concave, and nondecreasing utility function that generates e. We know this because, if u' is any *other* continuous, quasi-concave, and nondecreasing utility function, then u and u' must disagree at some x^0; that is, $u(x^0) \neq u'(x^0)$. Without loss of generality, suppose $u(x^0) > u'(x^0)$, and let $v = u(x^0)$. Then $x^0 \in \{x \in R^k_+ : u(x) \geq v\} = \mathrm{CCH}(\{x \in R^k_+ : u(x) \geq v\})$, while $x^0 \notin \{x \in R^k_+ : u'(x) \geq v\} = \mathrm{CCH}(\{x \in R^k_+ : u'(x) \geq v\})$, and hence by Corollary 10.12, they have different expenditure functions.

To make a neat package of these results, it would be nice to know that for *any* continuous utility function u, there exists some continuous, quasi-concave, and nondecreasing utility function $\hat{u}$ that gives the same expenditure function as does u. Then given an expenditure function e generated by some continuous utility function u, we can hope to be able to recover, if not u itself, the (necessarily unique) continuous, quasi-concave, and nondecreasing utility function $\hat{u}$ that shares u's expenditure function. (And, indeed, that hope will be realized next section.) So that is our final result for this section:

Proposition 10.13. *Suppose the utility function $u : R^k_+ \to R$ is continuous. Define utility function $\hat{u} : R^k_+ \to R$ from u by*

$$\hat{u}(x^0) := \sup \left\{ v \in R : x^0 \in \mathrm{CCH}(\{x \in R^k_+ : u(x) \geq v\}) \right\}. \tag{10.1}$$

The function $\hat{u}$ is continuous, quasi-concave, and nondecreasing, and for all $v \in R$,

$$\mathrm{CCH}(\{x \in R^k_+ : u(x) \geq v\}) = \{x \in R^k_+ : \hat{u}(x) \geq v\}. \tag{10.2}$$

Therefore, for the original u, $\hat{u}$ is the unique continuous, quasi-concave, and nondecreasing utility function that has the same expenditure function as u. Moreover, if u is locally insatiable, so is $\hat{u}$.

The definition in display (10.1) may make your head hurt, so let me recast it using the characterization of CCH sets developed in Proposition 10.8. The function $\hat{u}$ defined by (10.1) is equivalently

$$\hat{u}(x) := \sup\Big\{ v \in R : \text{ There exist a finite } N, x^i, \text{ and } \alpha^i, i = 1, \ldots, N, \text{ such that } \alpha^i \geq 0, \sum_i \alpha^i = 1, u(x^i) \geq v, \text{ and } x \geq \sum_i \alpha^i x^i \Big\}. \tag{10.1$'$}$$

Proof. As a first step, we will show that $\hat{u}$ is finite valued. Suppose instead that, for some x^0, $\hat{u}(x^0) = \infty$. That is, for each integer n, $x^0 \in \mathrm{CCH}(\{x \in R^k_+ : u(x) \geq n\})$. This would mean that, for each n, x^0 is greater than or equal to some convex combination of points, each of which has u value greater than n. By Carathéodory's Theorem, we can assume that the number of points in each of these convex combinations is no more than $k+1$. That is, $x^0 \geq \sum_{i=1}^{k+1} \alpha^{in} x^{in}$, where the α^{in} are nonnegative and sum to 1 and the x^{in} all satisfy $u(x^{in}) \geq n$. Looking along successive subsequences, we can without loss of generality assume that $\lim_{n\to\infty} \alpha^{in} = \alpha^i$ for each i. By the same argument used in the proof of Proposition 10.9, we know that not all of the $\alpha^i = 0$ and, in fact, $\sum_{i=1}^{k+1} \alpha^i = 1$. Let I be the subset of $\{1, \ldots, k+1\}$ such that $\alpha^i > 0$. The argument in the proof of Proposition 10.9 tells us that, since $x^0 \geq \sum_{i \in I} \alpha^{in} x^{in}$, each of the sequences $\{x^{in}; n = 1, \ldots\}$ for $i \in I$ lies within a compact set. So we can extract convergent subsequences. But letting i^0 be one index in I, if the limit along a subsequence of $\{x^{i^0 n}\}$ is some x^*, continuity of u and $u(x^{i^0 n}) \geq n$ present a contradiction.

Next we show that if $\hat{u}$ is defined from u by (10.1), then (10.2) holds. Fix some v, and suppose that $x^0 \in \mathrm{CCH}(\{x \in R^k_+ : u(x) \geq v\})$. When defining $\hat{u}(x^0)$ via (10.1), this implies that v is in the set over which the supremum is taken and, therefore, $\hat{u}(x^0) \geq v$. Therefore, for the fixed v, the set on the left-hand side of (10.2) is a subset of the set on the right-hand side.

Conversely, for fixed v, if x^0 is in the set on the right-hand side of (10.2), then $\hat{u}(x^0) \geq v$. Going back to (10.1), this means that for all $n = 1, 2, \ldots$, there is some

$v' > v - 1/n$ such that $x^0 \in \text{CCH}(\{x' \in R^k_+ : u(x') \geq v'\})$. That is, $x^0 \geq \sum_{i=1}^{k+1} \alpha^{in} x^{in}$ for the usual scalars $\alpha^{in}, i = 1, \ldots, k+1$ and for x^{in}, $i = 1, \ldots, k+1$ such that $u(x^{in}) \geq v - 1/n$. (We are using Carathéodory once again, of course.) Enlisting once again the argument in Proposition 10.9, we can assume that the α^{in} converge in n to α^i for $i = 1, \ldots, k+1$. Letting I be the index set of i such that $\alpha^i > 0$, we know that $\sum_{i \in I} \alpha^i = 1$ and that $x^0 \geq \sum_{i \in I} \alpha^{in} x^{in}$, which puts a uniform bound on the x^{in} for $i \in I$, so we can assume further that the x^{in} all converge in n to x^i. By continuity, $u(x^i) \geq v$ for $i \in I$, and $x^0 \geq \sum_{i \in I} \alpha^i x^i$, so $x^0 \in \text{CCH}(\{x \in R^k_+ : u(x) \geq v\})$. Therefore, x^0 is in the set on the left-hand side of (10.2), and the two sets are the same.

It is worth noting that, as a by-product of the argument just given, we've shown that the supremum in (10.1) is actually a maximum.

This means that the sets $\{x \in R^k_+ : \hat{u}(x) \geq v\}$ (for different v) are CCH sets and hence comprehensive and convex for each v, which implies that $\hat{u}$ is quasi-concave and nondecreasing (per Proposition 10.10).

To show that $\hat{u}$ is continuous, I'll show separately that it is upper and then lower semi-continuous. For upper semi-continuity, first note that the sets $\{x \in R^k_+ : u(x) \geq v\}$ are closed, since u is continuous. By Proposition 10.9, this implies that the sets $\text{CCH}(\{x \in R^k_+ : u(x) \geq v\}) = \{x \in R^k_+ : \hat{u}(x) \geq v\}$ are all closed. And one characterization of upper semi-continuity of a function is that its upper-level sets are closed. Since that result isn't given in Appendix 2, here it is: The definition of upper semi-continuity given in Appendix 2 is that, if $x^n \to x$, then $\limsup_n \hat{u}(x^n) \leq \hat{u}(x)$. Suppose to the contrary that, for some sequence $x^n \to x$, $\limsup_n \hat{u}(x^n) > \hat{u}(x)$. Then letting $v = \hat{u}(x)$, this would mean that for some $v' > v$ and for infinitely many n, $\hat{u}(x^n) \geq v'$, or (for those n), $x^n \in \{\hat{x} \in R^k_+ : \hat{u}(\hat{x}) \geq v'\}$. But looking along this subsequence, $x^n \to x$, and we know that $\{\hat{x} \in R^k_+ : \hat{u}(\hat{x}) \geq v'\}$ is a closed set, and hence $x \in \{\hat{x} \in R^k_+ : \hat{u}(\hat{x}) \geq v'\}$, a contradiction.

For lower semi-continuity, we need to show that if $x^n \to x$, $\liminf_n \hat{u}(x^n) \geq \hat{u}(x)$. Suppose by way of contradiction that, looking along a subsequence if necessary, we have a sequence $x^n \to x$ with $\lim_n \hat{u}(x^n)$ exists and is strictly less than $\hat{u}(x)$. Let $v = \hat{u}(x)$. We know that for some $i = 1, \ldots, N$, there are weights α^i and vectors x^i such that the weights are nonnegative and sum to 1, the x^i all satisfy $u(x^i) \geq v$, and $x \geq \sum_i \alpha^i x^i$. Consider, for $\beta < 1$, $\sum_i \alpha^i(\beta x^i)$. I assert that for all n sufficiently large, $x^n \geq \sum_i \alpha^i(\beta x^i)$. To see this, think about the inequality coordinate by coordinate. If $x_\ell = 0$, since $x_\ell \geq \sum_i \alpha^i x^i_\ell$ and since all the weights and coordinate values are nonnegative, we know that each x^i_ℓ must be 0, in which case x^n_ℓ (which is also nonnegative) is obviously $\geq$ the sum. And if $x_\ell > 0$ then $x_\ell \geq \sum_i \alpha^i x^i_\ell$ implies $x_\ell > \beta x_\ell \geq \sum_i \alpha^i(\beta x^i_\ell)$, and x^n_ℓ, having limit x_ℓ, will eventually be larger than $\beta x_\ell \geq \sum_i \alpha^i(\beta x^i_\ell)$.

Hence, for all sufficiently large n, it is true that $x^n \geq \sum_i \alpha^i(\beta x^i)$ (for fixed $\beta < 1$), and therefore $\hat{u}(x^n) \geq \min_i \{u(\beta x^i)\}$. But $u(x^i) \geq v$ for all i, and u is continuous, so $\lim_{\beta \to 1} \min_i \{u(\beta x^i)\} = \min_i \{u(x^i)\} \geq v$, a contradiction.

The "therefore" assertion following (10.2) follows from the argument given informally before the statement of Proposition 10.13.

Finally, suppose u is locally insatiable (as well as continuous). Fix x^0 and let $v^0 = \hat{u}(x^0)$. By (10.2), $x^0 \in \text{CCH}(\{x \in R^k_+ : u(x) \geq v^0\})$. Therefore, there exist, for $i = 1, \ldots, N$, weights α^i and vectors x^i such that $x^0 \geq \sum_i \alpha^i x^i$, the weights are nonnegative and sum to 1, and $u(x^i) \geq v^0$ for all i. Take any $\epsilon > 0$. By local insatiability of u, there exist $\check{x}^i$, each within ϵ/k of x^i, respectively, such that $u(\check{x}^i) > u(x^i) \geq v^0$. Letting $\check{v}$ be the smallest of the numbers $u(\check{x}^i)$, this implies that

$$\sum_i \alpha^i \check{x}^i \in \text{CCH}(\{x \in R^k_+ : u(x) \geq \check{v}\}),$$

or $\hat{u}(\sum_i \alpha^i \check{x}^i) \geq \check{v} > v^0$. And by the triangle inequality, since $x^0 \geq \sum_i \alpha^i x^i$ and each $\check{x}^i$ is within ϵ/k of x^i, there is some $\check{x}$ within ϵ of x^0 that is $\geq \sum_i \alpha^i \check{x}^i$; therefore $\hat{u}(\check{x}) \geq \check{v} > v^0$. This is local insatiability. ∎

10.6. Recovering Continuous Utility Functions from Expenditure Functions

The first of our two climax questions was *Given an expenditure function e derived from a utility function u, (how) can you recover u?* The previous section shows that we cannot recover u per se. However:

Proposition 10.14. *Suppose e is the expenditure function derived from a continuous utility function u. Let $\hat{u}$ be the expenditure-equivalent, continuous, quasi-concave, and nondecreasing utility function derived from u via the definition (10.1). Then for every $v \in R$,*

$$\{x \in R^k_+ : p \cdot x \geq e(p, v) \text{ for all } p \in R^k_{++}\} = \{x \in R^k_+ : \hat{u}(x) \geq v\}. \tag{10.3}$$

And if we define

$$\check{u}(x) := \max\{v \in R : p \cdot x \geq e(p, v) \text{ for all } p \in R^k_{++}\}, \tag{10.4}$$

then $\check{u}$ is identical to $\hat{u}$.

Comparisons with how we recovered a production-possibility set Z from the profit function are obvious, although this goes a step further, since there we recovered only a set; here we are recovering the upper-level sets defined from a function.

Proof. Fix u, $\hat{u}$, and e. Showing that the sets on the right-hand side of (10.3) are subsets of the sets on the left-hand side is trivial: Suppose x^0 is an element of $\{x \in R^k_+ : \hat{u}(x) \geq v\}$ for some v. Since e is the expenditure function for u, it is the expenditure function for $\hat{u}$, and so $p \cdot x^0 \geq e(p, v)$ for all $p \in R^k_{++}$; that is, x^0 is an element of the set on the left-hand side of (10.3) for the fixed v.

We show the reverse set inclusions by arguing the contrapositive: Suppose that for some fixed v, x^0 is not in the set on the right-hand side of (10.3); that is, $\hat{u}(x^0) < v$. Let $X = \{x \in R^k_+ : \hat{u}(x) \geq v\}$; the set X is closed, convex, and comprehensive. Being closed and convex, we can strictly separate it from x^0: There exists some nonzero $q \in R^k$ such that $q \cdot x^0 < \inf\{q \cdot x : x \in X\}$. Since the set X is comprehensive, the usual argument shows that $q \geq 0$. Therefore, we can find $\epsilon > 0$ sufficiently small (but still strictly positive) such that if $p = q + \epsilon(1, 1, \ldots, 1)$, then $p \cdot x^0 < \inf\{q \cdot x : x \in X\} \leq \inf\{p \cdot x : x \in X\}$. But p is strictly positive, and $\inf\{p \cdot x : x \in X\} = e(p, v)$, so this says that $p \cdot x^0 < e(p, v)$. Therefore, x^0 is not in the set on the left-hand side of (10.3).

Showing that if $\check{u}$ is defined by (10.4), then $\check{u}$ is $\hat{u}$, is now a matter of massaging definitions. Take any x^0. If $\hat{u}(x^0) = v^0$, then we know that $p \cdot x^0 \geq e(p, v^0)$ for all strictly positive p by (10.3). So v^0 is in the set over which the maximum is taken in (10.4), and $\check{u}(x^0) \geq v^0 = \hat{u}(x^0)$. Conversely, suppose that for some $v' > v^0$, $p \cdot x^0 \geq e(p, v')$ for all strictly positive p. Then applying (10.3) again tells us that x^0 is in the set of x such that $\hat{u}(x) \geq v'$. This isn't so, since v' was chosen to be greater than $v^0 = \hat{u}(x^0)$. Therefore, the largest possible v over which we are taking the maximum in (10.4) when defining $\check{u}(x^0)$ is $\hat{u}(x^0)$, and $\hat{u}(x^0) = \check{u}(x^0)$. Note, by the way, that this shows that, in (10.4), it is appropriate to write a maximum instead of a supremum. ■

10.7. Is an Alleged Expenditure Function Really an Expenditure Function?

The second of our two big questions is, *Given a function e that is alleged to be the expenditure function for some continuous (or possibly continuous and locally insatiable) utility function u, is it indeed?* Is there some continuous (and, perhaps, locally insatiable) utility function that generates e?

If the answer is yes, then we know that there is a continuous, (perhaps locally insatiable,) quasi-concave, and nondecreasing function u for which the answer is yes, namely the $\hat{u}$ that goes with u. And, in principle, we know how to find $\hat{u}$ if it exists: Employ equations (10.3) and (10.4), and check whether the $\hat{u} = \check{u}$ produced is continuous and, if desired, locally insatiable.

But running the "machine" defined by (10.3) and (10.4) for a specific e is certainly a nontrivial exercise. We'd like to know if there is a list of properties for e that guarantees, once we run this machine, we wind up with a nice utility function u.

We have accumulated a list of necessary conditions: First, e must have a domain of definition that is the cross product of R^k_{++} and a half-closed (on the bottom), half-open interval of real numbers. The bottom of this half-closed, half-open interval should be the value of $u(0)$ and, letting $\underline{v}$ denote this value, it should be true that $e(p, \underline{v}) = 0$ for all p. To avoid notational complications, we'll assume henceforth that $\underline{v} = 0$, which amounts to scaling the original utility function (if one exists) so that $u(0) = 0$.

Besides this, e should be concave and homogeneous of degree 1 in p. It should be nondecreasing in p, strictly increasing in v, and unbounded in v for each p.

And, if we want u to be locally insatiable, it should be jointly continuous in p and v.

Are these necessary conditions enough? If a candidate expenditure function has all these properties, is there a continuous and locally insatiable utility function that underlies it? The following proposition gives us considerable hope that the answer may be yes.

Proposition 10.15. *Suppose that $e : R^k_{++} \times [0, \bar{v}) \to [0, \infty)$ is continuous in all its arguments; concave, homogeneous of degree 1, and nondecreasing in p for each v; strictly increasing and unbounded in v for each p; and satisfies $e(p, 0) = 0$ for all p. Define, for each v in its domain,*

$$X_v := \{x \in R^k_+ : p \cdot x \geq e(p, v) \text{ for all } p \in R^k_{++}\}. \tag{10.5}$$

Then each X_v is closed, convex, and comprehensive. The X_v sets nest: if $v' < v$, then $X_v \subseteq X_{v'}$ and, moreover, $X_v \neq X_{v'}$. For every $x \in R^k_+$, there is some $v < \bar{v}$ such that $x \notin X_v$. And for every $p \in R^k_{++}$ and every v, there exists an $x(p, v) \in X_v$ such that $p \cdot x(p, v) = e(p, v)$ and (by definition) for every $x \in X_v$, $p \cdot x \geq e(p, v)$, so that the problem

$$\text{minimize } p \cdot x, \text{ over } x \in X_v$$

has a solution, and at that solution, $p \cdot x = e(p, v)$.

Proof. Parts of this are quite simple, while the rest is pretty straightforward, following what we did in Chapter 9.

To begin with the simple parts, rewrite definition (10.5) as

$$X_v = \bigcap_{p \in R^k_{++}} \{x \in R^k_+ : p \cdot x \geq e(p, v)\}. \tag{10.5$'$}$$

That's an intersection of half-spaces. Half-spaces are closed and convex, and (arbitrary) intersections of closed and convex sets are closed and convex. Since all the p are nonnegative (in fact, strictly positive), all the half-spaces are comprehensive, and (arbitrary) intersections of comprehensive sets are comprehensive. So each X_v is closed, convex, and comprehensive.

Since each $e(p, v)$ is strictly increasing in v, it is apparent that the X_v sets nest. (If $v > v'$, the half-spaces that are intersected to define X_v are all subsets of the half-spaces that are intersected to define $X_{v'}$.) Note: This only shows that if $v > v'$, then $X_v \subseteq X_{v'}$. We have "weak" nesting. The "moreover" part of the statement is proved later.

Take any $x^0 \in R^k_+$ and any $p^0 \in R^k_{++}$. Since $e(p^0, v)$ is unbounded in v (fixing p^0), there is some v such that $e(p^0, v) > p^0 \cdot x^0$, and so $x^0 \notin X_v$ for that v.

Fix v^0, and take any $p^0 \in R^k_{++}$. Since $e(p, v^0)$ is concave in p and p^0 is in the interior of the domain of e, a supergradient of $p \to e(p, v^0)$ at p^0 exists. Since e is homogeneous of degree 1 in p, we know (Proposition A3.26) that this supergradient is a linear function; that is, for some $x^0 \in R^k$, $p^0 \cdot x^0 = e(p^0, v^0)$ and $p \cdot x^0 \geq e(p, v^0)$ for all other $p \in R^k_{++}$.

Suppose x^0 had some coordinate value less than 0. Take p that is N in that coordinate value and 1 everywhere else; for N sufficiently large, $p \cdot x^0$ will be less than 0. But $e(p, v^0)$ is nonnegative (in fact, is strictly positive unless $v^0 = 0$), which would be a contradiction, so $x^0 \geq 0$. Setting $x(p^0, v^0) = x^0$ completes the proof of this part of the proposition.

Finally, we have the "moreover" left to prove. Fix v' and v with $v' < v$. Take any strictly positive price vector p. Then $e(p, v') < e(p, v)$. By the last paragraph, we know there is $x' \in X_{v'}$ such that $p \cdot x' = e(p, v')$. But this x' is then clearly not an element of X_v. ■

Definition (10.5) is, in essence, telling us how to find the no-worse-than-utility-level-v sets for the alleged utility function that (we hope) will generate e. It shows that these sets are closed, convex, and comprehensive. They nest, just like they should. Every bundle x is limited in how much utility it provides. And if we try to solve the expenditure-minimization problem with one of these no-worse-than-utility-level-v sets, it gives us back the alleged expenditure function $e(p, v)$. If there is any (quasi-concave and nondecreasing) utility function that gives us e, these would have to be the no-worse-than-utility-level-v sets for that utility function, because (as we already know) each expenditure function e uniquely defines these sets. In other words, if we go on from (10.5) and define

$$u(x) := \max\{v : x \in X_v\}, \tag{10.6}$$

assuming of course that the *max* is warranted, then either u is our utility function or there is no utility function that works.

So, to finish up and get an affirmative answer to our second big question (where the sufficient conditions are the conditions in Proposition 10.15), we only (!) need to show that the utility function u defined via (10.6) is continuous and locally insatiable. Unhappily, we can't take that last step.

To clear away some easy stuff, let's establish that we can use a maximum in (10.5) and harvest one piece of what we'd like to show.

Proposition 10.16. *Suppose e satisfies all the assumptions of Proposition 10.15 and so, in consequence, we define the sets X_v via (10.5). Then for each x^0, the set*

$$\{v \in R : x^0 \in X_v\}$$

contains its supremum, and it makes sense to write the max in (10.6). Moreover, the function u that is then defined in (10.6) is upper semi-continuous, quasi-concave, nondecreasing, and locally insatiable.

Proof. Fix x^0, and suppose that the supremum of the set $\{v \in R : x^0 \in X_v\}$ is v^0. This implies there is a sequence $\{v^n\}$ approaching v^0 from below such that, for each v^n, $p \cdot x^0 \geq e(p, v^n)$ for all $p \in R^k_{++}$. Continuity of e in the v argument assures us that $p \cdot x^0 \geq e(p, v^0)$ for all $p \in R^k_{++}$, and v^0 is indeed in the set over which the supremum is being taken.

That being so, for every v, for u defined via (10.6), $\{x \in R^k_+ : u(x) \geq v\} = X_v$. We have already shown that each X_v closed, convex, and comprehensive, so u is upper semi-continuous, quasi-concave, and nondecreasing.

And for local insatiability, I will show that, if $e = (1, 1, \ldots, 1) \in R^k_+$, then for any $x^0 \in R^k_+$, $u(x^0 + \delta e) > u(x^0)$ for all $\delta > 0$. Suppose this is not true; that is, we find x^0 and δ such that $u(x^0 + \delta e) = v^0 \leq u(x^0)$. Since u is nondecreasing, this implies that for every x such that $x^0 \leq x \leq x^0 + \delta e$, $u(x) = v^0$.

Let $Z = \cup_{v > v^0} X_v$. Of course, for any x such that $x \leq x^0 + \delta e$, $u(x) \leq v^0$, so $x \notin Z$. Therefore, we can put an open ball around x^0 that is disjoint from Z and, therefore, we can strictly separate x^0 from the closure of Z (which is convex, because Z is convex). That is, for some $p \in R^k$, $p \cdot x^0 < \inf_{x \in Z} p \cdot x$. Since Z is comprehensive upwards, $p \geq 0$, and by the usual argument, we can perturb p slightly so it is strictly positive, without affecting the strict separation from the closure of Z. Fix this p.

Per Proposition 10.15, for every v, if we minimize $p \cdot x$ over $x \in X_v$, the value of the solution is $e(p, v)$. So consider this problem for $v = v^0$ and for $v = v^0 + \epsilon$, $\epsilon > 0$. In the case $v = v^0$, the answer is no greater than $p \cdot x^0$, since $x^0 \in X_v$. In the case $v = v^0 + \epsilon$, the answer can be no smaller than the infimum over Z. But this then says that $\lim_{\epsilon \to 0} e(p, v^0 + \epsilon) =$ the infimum $> e(p, v^0)$, contradicting the assumed continuity of e. ∎

But for nice candidate expenditure functions, where "nice" means e *satisfies all the assumptions of Proposition 10.15*, the function u that is constructed by (10.5) and (10.6) will fail to be lower semi-continuous. Figure 10.2 (taken from Krishna and Sonnenschein 1990) indicates what can go wrong. The figure depicts the indifference curves of a utility function that is not continuous but that is strictly increasing and quasi-concave. The numbers on the indifference curves indicate the utility levels for the curves. The key point is $(x_0, 0)$. A number of indifference curves, all those with utility level between 2 and 4, meet at this point. (You can assign $(x_0, 0)$ any utility level you wish between 2 and 4.) All indifference curves approach the x-axis at slope approaching zero. To the left and right of the two extra heavy indifference curves (levels 2 and 4, respectively), the indifference curves are horizonal translates of the two (the level 4 curve to the right and the level 2 curve to the left); for utility levels between the levels of the two extra heavy curves, the transition is smooth.

Despite the fact that this utility function fails to be continuous at $(x_0, 0)$, we can still solve the expenditure-minimization problem using it, for every utility level and every strictly positive price p. The lack of continuity at $(x_0, 0)$ won't present a problem, because the indifference curves have slope 0 at that point; therefore, at any

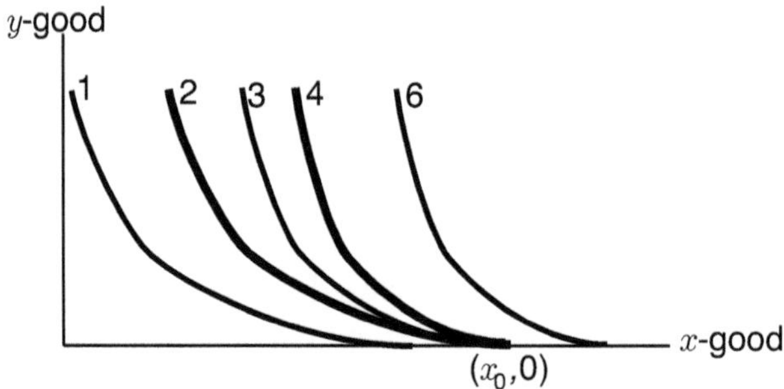

Fig. 10.2. Indifference curves for a counterexample. A utility function with the sort of indifference curves depicted will generate a continuous expenditure function, even though the utility function is not continuous. The key is that the indifference curves hit the x-axis with a slope of 0. The numbers by the indifference curves are the utility levels for each. The level of utility at the point $(x_0, 0)$ can be anything you choose between 2 and 4, but when the expenditure function is inverted using (10.5) and (10.6), $(x_0, 0)$ will be assigned the utility level 4.

strictly positive price, the solution will stay away. For this reason, the expenditure function $e(p, v)$ that is produced will be continuous in p and v. And if you use this expenditure function to reconstruct the utility function, you will get the function back, except that the process of reconstructing the utility function will give $(x_0, 0)$ the utility value 4 (which it will have to do, to keep the reconstructed utility function upper semi-continuous).

So what do we do with this unhappy state of affairs? The literature gives (at least) two answers.

We can give up on continuity. We've shown that a continuous expenditure function produces upper semi-continuous utility. If you want a theory in which everything fits together seamlessly, begin with upper semi-continuous utility, which would mean going back and redoing a lot of this chapter (and Chapter 3). In fact, you could go back even further, to Chapter 2: Debreu's Theorem is our excuse for assuming that the consumer's preferences have a continuous utility representation; this is ensured if her preferences are continuous. We can certainly talk about preferences that are upper semi-continuous—those would be preferences where the no-worse-than sets are all closed—and then the question is, If preferences are upper semi-continuous, do they necessarily have an upper semi-continuous utility representation?

If you do this—if you go back to reconstruct this entire theory assuming that u is (only) upper semi-continuous, some nice things will happen, but there will also be some snags. One nice thing will be that, in the CP, the existence of solutions is still guaranteed: If u is (only) upper semi-continuous, maximizing u over a compact set is guaranteed to have a solution. (We are *minimizing* in the EMP, but what is being minimized is the bilinear function $p \cdot x$, so that's not a problem. And we are minimizing over the set $\{x \in R_+^k : u(x) \geq v\}$; if u is upper semi-continuous, this set is closed.) However, go back to Proposition 10.2d, which says, if x solves the EMP at p and v, then $u(x) = v$. If u is only upper semi-continuous, that is no longer true. More significantly, expenditure functions will no longer be continuous in the v argument. They will be continuous in p, because concavity in p still holds (why is this enough?). But in v, we only get lower semi-continuity. In fact, this gives us a neat package: Upper semi-continuous utility functions are "dual" to expenditure functions that are lower semi-continuous in v.

You are asked to take the first step in a general development of this theory in Problem 10.4. But if you want to see the full-blown treatment, see Krishna and Sonnenschein (1990).

The second way to proceed is to find further conditions on (candidate) expenditure functions that are necessary and sufficient for continuous utility. Jackson (1986a) provides the missing link.

Proposition 10.17.[4] *Let $\mathcal{U}$ be the class of utility functions u on R^k_+ that are quasi-concave, continuous, nondecreasing, locally insatiable, and satisfy $u(0) = 0$ and $\sup_{x \in R^k_+} u(x) = \bar{v}$. Let $\mathcal{E}$ be the class of expenditure functions e with domain $R^k_{++} \times [0, \bar{v}) \to R_+$ that are continuous and unbounded above in v, nondecreasing in p and strictly increasing in v, concave and homogeneous of degree 1 in p, satisfy $e(p, v) = 0$ if and only if $v = 0$, and satisfy*

$$\begin{aligned} &\text{For every } x^0 \in R^k_+, \text{ for each } v \geq 0 \text{ and } \epsilon > 0 \text{ such that } p \cdot x^0 \\ &\quad \geq e(p, v + \epsilon) \text{ for all } p \in R^k_{++}, \text{ there exists } \delta, 0 < \delta < 1, \\ &\quad \text{such that } \delta p \cdot x^0 > e(p, v) \text{ for all } p \in R^k_{++}. \end{aligned} \tag{10.7}$$

Then every utility function $u \in \mathcal{U}$ generates a unique expenditure function $e \in \mathcal{E}$, and every expenditure function $e \in \mathcal{E}$ generates a unique utility function $u \in \mathcal{U}$, the latter by the construction described in this section.

Condition (10.7) is just what we need (obviously so, since it is necessary and sufficient). But it is hard to verify in practice: Jackson goes on to give a condition on e sufficient to guarantee (10.7), if e is differentiable in v.

Proof. In view of earlier results and, in particular, Proposition 10.16, we need to show (1) that if u is continuous (and all that other stuff), its expenditure function satisfies property (10.7), and (2), if e satisfies (10.7) (and all that other stuff), then its u (defined in (10.6)) is lower semi-continuous.

Taking these in order: Suppose u is continuous (and nondecreasing, quasi-concave, etc.); let e denote the corresponding expenditure function. Fix some x^0, v, and ϵ, such that $p \cdot x^0 \geq e(p, v + \epsilon)$ for all $p \in R^k_{++}$. Then from Proposition 10.14, $u(x^0) \geq v + \epsilon$. Therefore, there exists $\delta \in (0, 1)$ such that $u(\delta x^0) \geq v + \epsilon/2$. Therefore,

[4] If you consult Jackson (1986a), you'll see that I've changed the statement of his theorem somewhat. Some changes are cosmetic: He assumes $\bar{v} = \infty$. But where I say that u is nondecreasing and locally insatiable, he says that u is strictly increasing for strict increases in x (and continuous). On this point, see Problem 10.5. Note that Jackson's result also gives equivalent conditions on indirect utility functions; we'll discuss this in the next chapter.

for all $p \in R^k_{++}$, $\delta p \cdot x^0 = p \cdot (\delta x^0) \geq e(p, v + \epsilon/2) > e(p, v)$. That takes care of the first part.

For lower semi-continuity of a constructed u, fix a point x^0 and let $u(x^0) = v^0$. Let $\{x^n\}$ be a sequence of points with limit x^0. Since $u(x^0) = v^0$, for every $\epsilon > 0$, if we let $v = v^0 - 2\epsilon$, then $p \cdot x^0 \geq e(p, v + \epsilon) = e(p, v^0 - \epsilon)$ for all $p \in R^k_{++}$. So, by (10.7), there exists $0 < \delta < 1$ such that $\delta p \cdot x^0 > e(p, v)$ for all $p \in R^k_{++}$. Since $x^n \to x^0$ and all the components of all the x are nonnegative, we know that for sufficiently large N, $x^n \geq \delta x^0$ for all $n > N$. But then $p \cdot x^n \geq p \cdot (\delta x^0) = \delta p \cdot x^0 \geq e(p, v)$ for all p, and therefore, for all $n > N$, $u(x^n) \geq v = v^0 - 2\epsilon$. Since ϵ is arbitrary here, $\liminf_n u(x^n) \geq v^0 = u(x^0)$, which demonstrates lower semi-continuity. ∎

So what is the bottom line? If the criterion were mathematical elegance, my vote would be for the Krishna and Sonnenschein approach, which provides a nice duality between upper semi-continuous utility functions and lower semi-continuous expenditure functions. But continuity of preferences is pretty intuitive on economic grounds, or so it seems to me, so I vote for Jackson's necessary and sufficient condition. You are, of course, entitled to your own opinion on the matter.

10.8. Connecting the CP and the EMP

We are almost ready to get back to the consumer's problem and Marshallian demand, which will justify all the work we've done in this chapter. But there is one further bit of preparation to do: We have to connect the consumer's utility-maximization problem with the consumer's problem of minimizing expenditure.

Proposition 10.18. *Suppose the consumer has locally insatiable and continuous preferences. Then:*

for every $p \in R^k_{++}$ *and* $y \in R_+$, $\mathbf{H}(p, \nu(p, y)) = \mathbf{D}(p, y)$ *and* $e(p, \nu(p, y)) = y$*; and*

for every $p \in R^k_{++}$ *and* $v \in [u(0), \bar{v})$, $\mathbf{D}(p, e(p, v)) = \mathbf{H}(p, v)$, *and* $\nu(p, e(p, v)) = v$.

When rendered in symbols, this looks complex. But it couldn't be simpler. To paraphrase, solutions to the CP are the same as solutions to the corresponding version of the EMP.

If we were willing to substitute "proof by picture" for a real proof, the commentary surrounding the proof would go something like, The point where the indifference curve and the iso-expense line just touch in panel a of Figure 10.1 (the solution to the CP) is the same as the point where the iso-expense line and the indifference curve just touch in panel b of the same figure (the solution to the EMP). As for a real proof:

Proof. Fix p and y, and let x^* be any element of $\mathbf{D}(p, y)$, so that $u(x^*) = \nu(p, y)$ by definition. Let v^* be shorthand for $u(x^*) = \nu(p, y)$. Let h^* be any element of $\mathbf{H}(p, v^*)$, so that $e(p, v^*) = p \cdot h^*$:

1. Since $u(x^*) = v^*$, x^* is feasible for the EMP at (p, v^*). Since h^* is optimal for the EMP, this implies $y \geq p \cdot x^* \geq p \cdot h^*$. Therefore, h^* is feasible for the CP at (p, y). Since $u(h^*) = v^*$ by Proposition 10.2d, h^* is optimal for the CP. That is, $h^* \in \mathbf{D}(p, y)$.
2. By local insatiability, $h^* \in \mathbf{D}(p, y)$ implies that $p \cdot h^* = y \geq p \cdot x^*$. Since h^* is optimal for the EMP at (p, v^*) and x^* is feasible, this implies that x^* is optimal (as well) for the EMP. That is, $x^* \in \mathbf{H}(p, v^*)$.
3. By definition, $e(p, v^*) = p \cdot h^*$. The left-hand side is $e(p, \nu(p, y))$, while the right-hand side is y by steps 1 and 2. Therefore, $y = e(p, \nu(p, y))$.

Going the other way, fix p and $v \in [u(0), \bar{v})$. Let h^* be any element of $\mathbf{H}(p, v)$, so that $e(p, v) = p \cdot h^*$. Let y^* be shorthand for $e(p, v) = p \cdot h^*$, and let x^* be any element of $\mathbf{D}(p, y^*)$.

1. Since $p \cdot h^* = y^*$ by definition, h^* is feasible for the CP at (p, y^*). Since x^* is optimal for the CP, this implies that $u(x^*) \geq u(h^*) = v$ (the last by Proposition 10.2d). Therefore, x^* is feasible for the EMP at (p, v). Since $p \cdot x^* \leq y^* = p \cdot h^*$, this implies that x^* is optimal for the EMP. That is, $x^* \in \mathbf{H}(p, v)$.
2. By Proposition 10.2d, $u(x^*) = v$. By the definition of y^*, h^* is feasible for the CP at (p, y^*), and since $u(h^*) \geq v$ and x^* is optimal for the CP, h^* is also optimal for the CP. That is, $h^* \in \mathbf{D}(p, y^*)$.
3. Of course, $u(h^*) = v = u(x^*) = \nu(p, y^*) = \nu(p, e(p, v))$. ■

To build your understanding of this result and its proof, a useful exercise is to ask, What can be said (along these lines) if preferences are not locally insatiable? See Problem 10.6.

Bibliographic Notes

Diewert (1982) provides a survey of duality theory applied to the consumer's problem, including a history of the development of these ideas. I repeat references to Krishna and Sonnenschein (1990) and Jackson (1986a) for the "last word" on these results. Notwithstanding the dates of publication, my impression is that Krishna and Sonnenschein was written first, and Jackson (who did this work as part of his undergraduate senior thesis) wrote at least in part inspired by Krishna and Sonnenschein.

Problems

■ *10.1. Provide full details for the proof of Proposition 10.2.

■ 10.2. Give counterexamples to the following two false propositions. If X is a closed subset of R^k, then CCH(X) is closed. If X is a closed subset of R^k_+, then CH(X) is closed.

■ *10.3. In remarks following Proposition 10.11, I note that Assumption 10.1—that all utility functions are continuous and globally insatiable—is not needed for Proposition 10.10 or for the first half of 10.11. And in discussing the duality between utility functions and expenditure functions, I asserted (quoting Krishna and Sonnenschein 1990) that upper semi-continuous utility functions go with lower semi-continuous expenditure functions. Suppose that we restrict attention to utility functions $u : R^k_+ \to R$ for which $u(0) = 0$ and $\sup_{x \in R^k_+} u(x) = \infty$. (The first part of this involves an innocuous rescaling of utility, but the second part assumes that preferences are globally insatiable.) For such utility functions u, define $e : R^k_{++} \times R_+ \to R$ by

$$e(p, v) = \inf\{p \cdot x : x \in R^k_+ \text{ such that } u(x) \geq v\}.$$

Show that if $u : R^k_+ \to R$ is upper semi-continuous, then e is continuous in p and lower semi-continuous in (p, v).

■ 10.4. Continuing with the setup of Problem 10.3, what about the rest of the early propositions of this chapter, Propositions 10.2, 10.3, and 10.4? To what extent do the various pieces of those propositions require some form of continuity (full, upper semi-, or lower semi-) or local insatiability?

■ 10.5. In Jackson's statement of his basic result, which I've paraphrased in Proposition 10.17, his definition of the class of utility functions $\mathcal{U}$ does not include nondecreasing or local insatiability, but instead includes the condition that each $u \in \mathcal{U}$ is strictly increasing for strict increases in the argument (which he calls "increasing"). Prove that the difference is cosmetic; that is, if $u : R^k_+ \to R$ is continuous, then u is nondecreasing and locally insatiable if and only if u is strictly increasing for strict increases in its argument. (Hint: You may remember something like this, if you did the problems for Chapter 2.)

■ *10.6. Proposition 10.18 requires that the underlying utility function u is continuous and locally insatiable. What can be proven along these lines if you assume that u is not necessarily locally insatiable and is (only) upper semi-continuous? What if you assume u is continuous but not necessarily locally insatiable? What if u is locally insatiable but (only) upper semi-continuous?

■ 10.7. Fix a consumer with utility function u defined on R^k_+. Suppose we say that *good i is **normal** if for all prices $p \in R^k_{++}$ and income levels y and y' with $y > y' \geq 0$, if $x \in \mathbf{D}(p, y)$ and $x' \in \mathbf{D}(p, y')$, then $x_i \geq x'_i$.* Suppose we simultaneously say that *good i is **Hicks-normal** if for all prices p and utility levels v and v' with $v > v' \geq u(0)$, if $h \in \mathbf{H}(p, v)$ and $h' \in \mathbf{H}(p, v')$, then $h_i \geq h'_i$.* What can you say about the connections between normal goods and Hicks-normal goods? Under what conditions, if any, are the two concepts equivalent?

■ *10.8. In the text, I suggested that a more tangible version of the EMP would be the problem

$$\text{Minimize } p \cdot x, \text{ subject to } u(x) \geq u(x^0) \text{ and } x \geq 0,$$

where the parameters of this problem are strictly positive prices p and some reference consumption bundle $x^0 \in R^k_+$. Call this problem the MEMP(p, x^0), where the M abbreviates *modified.*

Similarly, for strictly positive prices p and a bundle $x^0 \in R^k_+$, consider the following modified consumer's problem:

$$\text{Maximize } u(x), \text{ subject to } p \cdot x \leq p \cdot x^0 \text{ and } x \geq 0.$$

In words, maximize the utility of consumption, subject to the constraint that the amount spent is no more than the cost of the bundle x^0. Call this problem the MCP(p, x^0).

Assume that the consumer's preferences are given by a continuous utility function u. If x^0 is a solution of the MEMP(p, x^0), is it (necessarily) also a solution of the MCP(p, x^0)? What about the converse? If one or both of these is false, can you give conditions under which the statement

$$x^0 \text{ solves the MEMP}(p, x^0) \text{ if and only if } x^0 \text{ solves the MCP}(p, x^0)$$

is true?

■ 10.9. Suppose we define $e : R^k_{++} \times R^k_+$ by

$$e(p, x^0) = \inf \{p \cdot x : u(x) \geq u(x^0)\}.$$

In the spirit of this chapter, develop a theory concerning this modified expenditure function. To keep matters relatively simple, assume that u is continuous, nondecreasing, quasi-concave, and locally insatiable.

Chapter Eleven

Classic Demand Theory

This chapter provides some return on the hard work of last chapter, describing how, in principle, one could start with consumer demand—that is, the solution to the CP for all prices and income levels—and recover the consumer's preferences. Along the way, we get several important results from the theory of consumer demand: Roy's Identity, the Slutsky Equation, and the Integrability Theorem (although the Integrability Theorem is given informally only). And we do for the indirect utility function the sorts of things we did for the expenditure function last chapter.

11.1. Roy's Identity and the Slutsky Equation

Assume that we have a consumer with strictly convex, continuous, and locally insatiable preferences. Continuity guarantees that the CP and the EMP have solutions for strictly positive prices, and strict convexity guarantees that those solutions are unique, so it makes sense to speak of the Marshallian and Hicksian demand functions, $(p, y) \to d(p, y)$ and $(p, v) \to h(p, v)$, respectively.

We know from last chapter that uniqueness of the solution implies that the expenditure function $e(p, v)$ is differentiable in p, holding v fixed, and that

$$\left.\frac{\partial e}{\partial p_i}\right|_{(p,v)} = h_i(p, v).$$

We *assume*, at least for the time being, that the indirect utility function $(p, y) \to \nu(p, y)$ is also differentiable (jointly in p and y), and that both the Marshallian and Hicksian demand functions are differentiable, Marshallian demand in both arguments and Hicksian demand in prices.

Consider the identity $\nu(p, e(p, v)) \equiv v$. That is, the indirect utility at prices p and the income level sufficient to get you utility level v at those prices is v. Differentiate this identity with respect to p_i:

$$\frac{\partial \nu}{\partial p_i} + \frac{\partial \nu}{\partial y}\frac{\partial e}{\partial p_i} = 0.$$

Replace $\partial e/\partial p_i$ with $h_i = d_i$ (for the corresponding arguments) and solve for d_i, to get

Roy's Identity: $$d_i(p, y) = -\left.\frac{\dfrac{\partial \nu}{\partial p_i}}{\dfrac{\partial \nu}{\partial y}}\right|_{(p,y)}.$$

Consider the identity $d_j(p, e(p, v)) \equiv h_j(p, v)$. Differentiate both sides with respect to p_i, to get

$$\frac{\partial d_j}{\partial p_i} + \frac{\partial d_j}{\partial y}\frac{\partial e}{\partial p_i} = \frac{\partial h_j}{\partial p_i}.$$

Replace $\partial e/\partial p_i$ with $h_i = d_i$, and you have

The Slutsky Equation: $$\left.\frac{\partial d_j}{\partial p_i}\right|_{(p,y)} = \left.\frac{\partial h_j}{\partial p_i}\right|_{(p,\nu(p,y))} - d_i \left.\frac{\partial d_j}{\partial y}\right|_{(p,y)}.$$

Intuition, step 1: Hicksian demand as compensated demand

Of course, we should at some point justify all the assumptions concerning differentiability that we just made. But first, let's look for the economic intuition behind Roy's Identity and the Slutsky Equation.

Intuitive explanations begin with the notion of *compensated demand*. Imagine a consumer who faces prices p with income y and selects the bundle x. If the price of some good, say good i, rises, we can think of two things having happened to the consumer.

1. The relative prices of the various commodities have changed. Relative to the price of all the other goods, good i is more expensive.
2. The consumer's *real income* has declined; that is, her y units of income are no longer sufficient to buy the bundle of goods she purchased before, as long as $x_i > 0$.

Suppose we want to isolate the effect of a shift in relative prices from the real-income effect, in terms of her utility and/or the amounts of the various goods that she consumes. A strategy for doing this is to *compensate* her for the increase in p_i, by increasing y so that her "real income" is what it was before. By how much should we increase y so that this is so? What does it mean to restore her to her old real income? Economists give two answers:

1. *Slutsky compensation* involves giving her enough income so that she can, if she wishes, buy back her old optimal bundle x. That is, if p'_i is the new price of good i, replace y with $y + (p'_i - p_i)x_i$. Another way to say the same thing is to define *Slutsky-compensated demand*, starting from the bundle x^0, as the demand function

$$s(p; x^0) := d(p, p \cdot x^0).$$

In words, Slutsky-compensated demand at the bundle x^0 and prices p is Marshallian demand at p and just enough income to buy x^0, or $p \cdot x^0$. Note that, at the new relative prices, the old optimal bundle, while affordable, may no longer be optimal. To the extent it is not, the consumer can increase her utility beyond what she had at the original prices and corresponding optimal bundle; in symbols, if $x^0 = d(p^0, y^0)$, then $u(s(p; x^0)) \geq \nu(p, y^0)$, and a strict inequality is a real possibility.

2. Since, in this sense, Slutsky compensation may *over*-compensate the consumer, economists also look at *Hicks compensation*, which involves giving the consumer just enough income so she can, if she optimizes, exactly maintain her utility level. In symbols, if the consumer, facing prices p^0 with income y^0 attains utility level $\nu(p^0, y^0)$, and if prices change to p, then Hicks compensation gives the consumer the income level y that enables her to remain at this utility level. This is $y = e(p, \nu(p^0, y^0))$, and the consumer's choice of bundle is $d(p, e(p, \nu(p^0, y^0))$ $= h(p, \nu(p^0, y^0))$. In other words, if we begin from p^0 and y^0, at which point the consumer achieves utility level $v^0 = \nu(p^0, y^0)$, *Hicks-compensated demand* is simply $h(p, v^0)$, or *Hicksian demand. Hicksian demand is a form of compensated demand.*

Figure 11.1 shows all this in a picture.

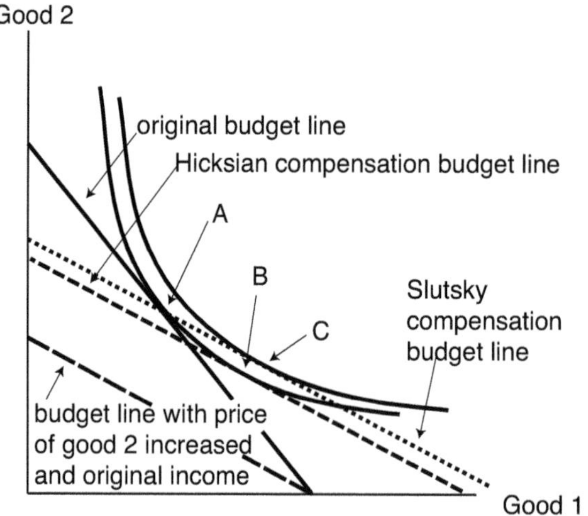

Figure 11.1. Hicks and Slutsky compensation. The consumer begins at the point marked A, with an optimal consumption bundle for given prices and income. This consumer's budget line is the solid line passing through A. Suppose the price of good 2 rises. The budget line pivots to become the line with long dashes. To compensate the consumer sufficiently to put her back on her original utility level—Hicks compensation—we have to push the new budget line up to the position of the line with medium dashes, and the consumer chooses the Hicksian demand point marked B. To compensate the consumer sufficiently to allow her to buy her original optimal bundle—Slutsky compensation—we have to push the budget line still further, to the line with the short dashes; the consumer then chooses the bundle marked C. Note that C is preferred to B and A, which are indifferent to one another.

The intuition for the Slutsky Equation and Roy's Identity

Now we can give the intuition for the Slutsky Equation. We are thinking of a consumer who chooses $x = d(p, y)$ at prices p and income y. The price of good i rises, changing relative prices and the consumer's real income. By how much does the consumer's consumption of good j change? First, the change in relative prices changes the consumer's demand for good j. Since Hicksian demand is compensated demand, it isolates this relative-price effect:

- The relative-price part of $\partial d_j/\partial p_i$ is $\partial h_j/\partial p_i$.

The real-income effect, on the other hand, depends on the rate at which a rise in the price of good i decreases the consumer's real income. If the consumer was consuming $d_i(p, y)$ units of good i, and if the price of good i increases by, say, a penny, then the consumer is $d_i(p, y)$ pennies poorer; to get back her old amount of good i, she needs to economize by $d_i(p, y)$ (in monetary units) somewhere else. Therefore,

- The real-income part of $\partial d_j/\partial p_i$ is $-d_i(p, y) \times \partial d_j/\partial y$.

The total rate of change in the consumption of good j per unit change in the price of good i is then the sum of these two pieces, which is precisely the Slutsky Equation.

Before turning to Roy's Identity, it may be worthwhile to think about the same thing in terms of Slutsky-compensated demand, or $s(p, x^0) = d(p, p \cdot x^0)$. Assuming that everything in sight is differentiable, the chain rule tells us that

$$\frac{\partial s_j}{\partial p_i} = \frac{\partial d_j}{\partial p_i} + x_i^0 \frac{\partial d_j}{\partial y}.$$

Rearrange terms, and you get the Slutsky Equation, except that $\partial h_j/\partial p_i$ is replaced by $\partial s_j/\partial p_i$, at least if Slutsky-compensated demand is based at the optimal consumption bundle at the prices and income at which you are taking these derivatives. Hence, these two partial derivatives are identical; Slutsky- and Hicks-compensated demand are "identical" for infinitesimal shifts in price.

As for Roy's Identity, the question is, What impact does an increase in the price of good i have on the *utility* the consumer obtains? Again think in terms of the change in p_i as affecting relative prices and the consumer's real income. If Hicks compensation and Hicksian demand capture the relative-price effect, then clearly the relative-price effect on utility is zero, by definition. But the dimunition of the consumer's real income has a first-order effect. If she had been consuming x_i units of good i and the price of good i goes up by a penny, her real income is reduced by x_i pennies. (Yes, you did just read this two paragraphs ago.) Hence

$$\frac{\partial \nu}{\partial p_i} = -x_i \frac{\partial \nu}{\partial y},$$

which is just Roy's Identity rearranged.

11.2. Differentiability of Indirect Utility

From Chapter 10, we know that the expenditure function is differentiable if the EMP has unique solutions (and vice versa). In this section, we prove that if the CP has unique solutions and if u is continuously differentiable and locally insatiable, then the indirect utility function is differentiable. Moreover, our proof will identify the derivatives, providing a proof of Roy's Identity under less restrictive assumptions.

Proposition 11.1 (Differentiability of the indirect utility function and its derivatives). *Suppose u is locally insatiable and continuously differentiable. If the CP has unique solutions in an open neighborhood of (p^0, y^0), $y^0 > 0$, then the indirect utility function ν is differentiable in (p, y) in that neighborhood. Writing x^0 for the solution to the CP at (p^0, y^0), the derivatives (at (p^0, y^0)) are*

$$\left.\frac{\partial \nu}{\partial p_i}\right|_{(p^0,y^0)} = -x_i^0 \frac{1}{p_j^0} \left.\frac{\partial u}{\partial x_j}\right|_{x^0},$$

*where j is **any** commodity index such that $x_j^0 > 0$, and*

$$\left.\frac{\partial \nu}{\partial y}\right|_{(p^0,y^0)} = \frac{1}{p_j^0} \left.\frac{\partial u}{\partial x_j}\right|_{x^0},$$

for the same j.

Corollary 11.2 (The value of the budget-constraint multiplier). *If u is locally insatiable and continuously differentiable, and if the CP has unique solutions in a neighborhood of some (p^0, y^0), then the Lagrange multiplier λ for the budget constraint in the first-order/complementary-slackness necessary conditions for the solution to the CP at (p^0, y^0) is*

$$\lambda = \left.\frac{\partial \nu}{\partial y}\right|_{(p^0,y^0)}.$$

Corollary 11.3 (Roy's Identity). *If u is locally insatiable and continuously differentiable, and if the CP has unique solutions in a neighborhood of some (p^0, y^0), then Roy's Identity holds:*

$$d_i(p^0, y^0) = -\left.\frac{\dfrac{\partial \nu}{\partial p_i}}{\dfrac{\partial \nu}{\partial y}}\right|_{(p^0,y^0)}.$$

Before proving the proposition, some comments are in order.

1. The assumption that u is continuously differentiable in this proposition was unnecessary in the proof of Proposition 10.6 (differentiability of the expenditure function). In Proposition 10.6, we were concerned with differentiability in p only; the shape of u matters because it determines the shape of the set $\{x : u(x) \geq v\}$ for each fixed v, but continuity of u is all that is needed. If we wanted to talk about differentiability of the expenditure function in v, however, we would need to assume more about u. (See Problem 11.2.)

2. As long as u is locally insatiable, we know (from Proposition 10.18) that the CP has a unique solution precisely where the EMP has a unique solution. Hence, differentiability of ν is essentially equivalent to differentiability of e. (I append *essentially* because we need continuous differentiability of u for one but not the other. But assuming differentiability of u is rarely a problem for economists. On the other hand, here we are showing differentiability of ν in p and y jointly; Proposition 10.6 shows differentiability of e in p only.)

3. In Roy's Identity, the possibility that the denominator (the partial derivative of indirect utility in income) equals 0 is real. But the proposition establishes that when this happens, the numerator is also zero, and in the sense that $0/0$ can be anything, Roy's Identity follows immediately from the proposition.

4. Corollary 11.2 is a simple consequence of the proposition, once we recall that for any good j that is consumed in strictly positive amount (at the optimal solution to the CP), the first-order condition is that $\partial u/\partial x_j = \lambda p_j$.

5. If we accept that the derivatives in the proposition exist, their values are relatively intuitive. Begin with $\partial\nu/\partial y$. This is the rate of increase in utility obtained per unit increase in the consumer's income. So the question is, if the consumer has \$1 more income, how should she spend it? Obviously (intuitively), this extra \$1 should be spent on goods that give the biggest bang for the buck. But we know that the goods consumed in positive amounts at x^0 have equal bangs for the buck, at least as great as the bangs for the buck of the other goods. So the answer is clear: The marginal \$1 can be spent any way the consumer chooses, *as long as it is spent on goods that are already consumed in positive amounts*. And if it is spent this way, ν will increase by approximately this bang for the buck; that is to say, $\partial\nu/\partial y = \mathrm{MU}_i(x^0)/p_i$ for any and every i such that $x_i^0 > 0$. (This argument should be vaguely familiar; it appears in Chapter 3.)

6. A similar argument works for $\partial\nu/\partial p_i$. If p_i rises by one unit, to stay budget feasible the consumer must cut back on her consumption. She obviously can't cut back on the consumption of goods whose current level is zero. And to a first-order approximation, it doesn't matter how she cuts back on the other goods, as long as she does so to stay budget feasible. When p_i increases by one unit, her old bundle costs x_i^0 more than she has, and she must economize by spending x_i^0 less on some package of goods. Therefore, a one-unit rise in p_i has the same marginal impact as an x_i^0-unit fall in income. This gives $\partial\nu/\partial p_i$.

7. As long as we are offering these intuitive explanations, we can offer one as well

for $\partial e/\partial p_i = h_i$. Suppose the price of good i increases by one (small) unit. If $h_i = 0$ at the original prices, no change is called for; the change in p_i has no impact on her expenditure. But if $h_i > 0$, perhaps she will wish to consume less of good i and more of other goods. Since the bangs for the buck of all other goods (at least, of those that are consumed in positive amounts) are all equal, the cost of replacing any lost utility will, to the first order, match the savings realized by consuming less of others. That is, to a first-order approximation, she might as well stay at the bundle optimal at the original prices. And then the impact of a one-unit increase in the price of p_i is to raise her expenditure by h_i.

8. The proposition does not cover the case of $y_0 = 0$, because in that case no commodity index j has $x_j^0 > 0$. See Problem 11.2.

The Proof of Proposition 11.1

Warning: This proof is a grind. It is *not* complex, but since it has many steps, it may seem so. Following all the details, I summarize its plotline, and you may do better to read that summary before launching into the details. (If anyone can suggest how to make it less of a grind, I would love to hear about it.)

Fix (p^0, y^0) in the open neighborhood in which the CP has unique solutions; let x^0 denote the solution to the CP there. Local insatiability implies $p^0 \cdot x^0 = y^0$, and hence, since $y^0 > 0$, that $x^0 \neq 0$. Pick any nonzero component of x^0; for expositional convenience we will assume it is the first; that is, $x_1^0 > 0$. To save on space later, let u' be the gradient function of u, and let u_i' be its ith coordinate; that is, $u_i'(x) = (\partial u/\partial x_i)|_x$. And let $b_1 = u_1'(x^0)/p_1$; b is a mnemonic for "bang for the buck." (If you've forgotten what this is, see page 61). Also, let $e^i \in R_+^k$ be the bundle of one unit of commodity i; that is, $e_j^i = 1$ if $i = j$ and $= 0$ otherwise.

Now suppose $\{(p^n, y^n)\}_{n=1,2,\ldots}$ is a sequence of price and income vectors that has limit (p^0, y^0). We need to show that

$$\lim_n \frac{\nu(p^n, y^n) - \nu(p^0, y^0) - \nu'(p^0, y^0) \cdot (p^n - p^0, y^n - y^0)}{\|(p^n - p^0, y^n - y^0)\|} = 0,$$

where $\nu'(p^0, y^0)$ is the gradient of ν, as given in the statement of the proposition.

Eventually this sequence lies within the open neighborhood of (p^0, y^0) in which solutions to the CP are unique; to simplify, we'll assume this is true for all n. (We only need to prove things about the tail of this sequence, so this assumption is innocuous.) Let x^n be the unique solution of the CP at (p^n, y^n).

The next step is, for each n, to adjust x^0 so that it just exhausts the budget y^n at prices p^n and to adjust each x^n so that it just exhausts the budget y^0 at prices p^0. These adjustments are done by varying the amounts of commodity 1 that are consumed; it is important here (to maintain feasibility) that $x_1^0 > 0$, that $x_1^n > 0$ for all sufficiently large n, and that the adjustments are small for large n. First, for each n, let

$$z^n := x^0 + \frac{y^n - p^n \cdot x^0}{p_1^n} e_1.$$

Note that $p^n \cdot z^n = p^n \cdot x^0 + y^n - p^n \cdot x^0 = y^n$. And let

$$\zeta^n := x^n + \frac{y^0 - p^0 \cdot x^n}{p_1^0} e_1.$$

Note that $p^0 \cdot \zeta^n = p^0 \cdot x^n + y^0 - p^0 \cdot x^n = y^0$. Therefore, as long as $\zeta^n \geq 0$, it is feasible at prices p^0 and income y^0, while if $z^n \geq 0$, then it is feasible at prices p^n and income y^n. And, therefore (assuming $z^n \geq 0$ and $\zeta^n \geq 0$),

$$\nu(p^0, y^0) = u(x^0) \geq u(\zeta^n) \quad \text{and} \quad \nu(p^n, y^n) = u(x^n) \geq u(z^n). \tag{11.1}$$

As a consequence of Proposition 3.3b (Berge's Theorem for the CP), $\lim_n x^n = x^0$. It is then obvious (since $\lim_n y^n = y^0$, $\lim_n p^n = p^0$, $p^n \cdot x^n = y^n$, and $p^0 \cdot x^0 = y^0$) that for n far enough out in the sequence, $z^n \geq 0$, $\zeta^n \geq 0$, and $\lim_n z^n = \lim_n \zeta^n = x^0$. As before, we will assume that $z^n \geq 0$ and $\zeta^n \geq 0$ for all n; this is still innocuous, and for the same reason.

Next we apply Taylor's Theorem, to evaluate $u(z^n)$, and $u(\zeta^n)$, the first in terms of its variation from $u(x^0)$ and the second in terms of its variation from $u(x^n)$. Rather than using Taylor's Theorem with a remainder term, we use the intermediate-value version of Taylor's Theorem, to get

$$u(z^n) = u(x^0) + u_1'(\hat{z}^n) \frac{y^n - p^n \cdot x^0}{p_1^n}, \quad \text{for some } \hat{z}^n = \beta^n x^0 + (1 - \beta^n) z^n, \beta^n \in [0, 1],$$

and

$$u(\zeta^n) = u(x^n) + u_1'(\hat{\zeta}^n) \frac{y^0 - p^0 \cdot x^n}{p_1^0}, \quad \text{for some } \hat{\zeta}^n = \gamma^n x^n + (1 - \gamma^n) \zeta^n, \gamma^n \in [0, 1].$$

Apply the two inequalities in (11.1) to the last two displays. From $u(x^0) \geq u(\zeta^n)$, we get

$$u(x^0) \geq u(x^n) + u_1'(\hat{\zeta}^n) \frac{y^0 - p^0 \cdot x^n}{p_1^0},$$

and from $u(x^n) \geq u(z^n)$, we get

$$u(x^n) \geq u(x^0) + u_1'(\hat{z}^n) \frac{y^n - p^n \cdot x^0}{p_1^n}.$$

These two inequalities can be rewritten as

$$-u_1'(\hat{\zeta}^n)\,\frac{y^0 - p^0 \cdot x^n}{p_1^0} \ge u(x^n) - u(x^0) \ge u_1'(\hat{z}^n)\,\frac{y^n - p^n \cdot x^0}{p_1^n}. \tag{11.2}$$

We want to show that

$$\lim_n \frac{\nu(p^n, y^n) - \nu(p^0, y^0) - \nu'(p^0, y^0) \cdot (p^n - p^0, y^n - y^0)}{\|(p^n - p^0, y^n - y^0)\|} = 0.$$

We know that $\nu(p^n, y^n) = u(x^n)$, and $\nu(p^0, y^0) = u(x^0)$. So we can rewrite the limit just displayed as

$$\lim_n \frac{u(x^n) - u(x^0) - \nu'(p^0, y^0) \cdot (p^n - p^0, y^n - y^0)}{\|(p^n - p^0, y^n - y^0)\|}.$$

The third term in the numerator, $-\nu'(p^0, y^0) \cdot (p^n - p^0, y^n - y^0)$, is

$$-\left[\sum_{i=1}^{k} (-x_i^0) b_1 (p_i^n - p_i^0) \;+\; b_1(y_n - y_0)\right] = -b_1\left[y_n - p^n \cdot x^0 \;- y^0 + p^0 \cdot x^0\right],$$

which is $-b_1(y^n - p^n \cdot x^0)$, where (recall) $b_1 = u_1'(x^0)/p_1$. So, rewriting our objective once again, we need to show that

$$\lim_n \frac{u(x^n) - u(x^0) - b_1(y^n - p^n \cdot x^0)}{\|(p^n - p^0, y^n - y^0)\|} = 0. \tag{11.3}$$

We do this using the two inequalities in (11.2).

From the right-hand side of (11.2), we know that the limit infimum in (11.3) is greater than or equal to

$$\liminf_n \frac{u_1'(\hat{z}^n)(y^n - p^n \cdot x^0)/p_1^n - b_1(y^n - p^n \cdot x^0)}{\|(p^n - p^0, y^n - y^0)\|}.$$

We can rewite this as

$$\liminf_n \left[\left(\frac{u_1'(\hat{z}^n)}{p_1^n} - b_1\right)\left(\frac{y^n - p^n \cdot x^0}{\|(p^n - p^0, y^n - y^0)\|}\right)\right].$$

Because $\hat{z}^n$ has limit x^0, p_1^n has limit p_1^0, and u is continuously differentiable, the first term inside the square brackets converges to zero. And the second term is bounded in n: Note that $y^n - p^n \cdot x^0 = (p^n - p^0, y^n - y^0) \cdot (-x^0, 1)$ (you do the algebra), so $|y^n - p^n \cdot x^0| \le \|(p^n - p^0, y^n - y^0)\| \|(-x^0, 1)\|$, so the second term is bounded by $\|(-x^0, 1)\|$. Therefore, the limit infimum of the sequence in (11.3) is greater than or equal to zero.

Now we'll show that the limit supremum is less than or equal to zero (which establishes that the limit is zero, finishing the proof). We use the other inequality from (11.2), to bound the limit supremum above by

$$\limsup_n \frac{-(u_1'(\hat{\zeta}^n)/p_1^0)(y^0 - p^0 \cdot x^n) - b_1(y^n - p^n \cdot x^0)}{\|(p^n - p^0, y^n - y^0)\|}.$$

Add and subtract $b_1(y^0 - p^0 \cdot x^n)$ to the numerator, to get

$$\limsup_n \frac{-(u_1'(\hat{\zeta}^n)/p_1^0)(y^0 - p^0 \cdot x^n) + b_1(y^0 - p^0 \cdot x^n) - b_1(y^0 - p^0 \cdot x^n) - b_1(y^n - p^n \cdot x^0)}{\|(p^n - p^0, y^n - y^0)\|}.$$

The limit supremum of a sum of two terms is less than or equal to the sum of the limit suprema of two summands, so look separately at

$$\limsup_n \frac{-(u_1'(\hat{\zeta}^n)/p_1^0)(y^0 - p^0 \cdot x^n) + b_1(y^0 - p^0 \cdot x^n)}{\|(p^n - p^0, y^n - y^0)\|} \qquad \text{and}$$

$$\limsup_n \frac{-b_1(y^0 - p^0 \cdot x^n) - b_1(y^n - p^n \cdot x^0)}{\|(p^n - p^0, y^n - y^0)\|}.$$

The numerator in the second of these two terms can be rewritten

$$\begin{aligned} -b_1(y^0 + y^n - p^0 \cdot x^n - p^n \cdot x^0) &= -b_1(p^0 \cdot x^0 + p^n \cdot x^n - p^0 \cdot x^n - p^n \cdot x^0) \\ &= -b_1(p^0 - p^n) \cdot (x^0 - x^n) \end{aligned}$$

and so the second of the two terms is

$$\limsup_n \; -b_1 \frac{(p^0 - p^n) \cdot (x^0 - x^n)}{\|(p^n - p^0, y^n - y^0)\|},$$

which is bounded above in absolute value by

$$\limsup_n \; -b_1 \frac{\|p^0 - p^n\|}{\|(p^n - p^0, y^n - y^0)\|} \|x^0 - x^n\|.$$

The first term ($-b_1$) is constant, the second term (the ratio of the norms) is bounded above by 1, and the third term vanishes as n goes to infinity. So this part of the limit sup is bounded above by 0.

This leaves us with

$$\limsup_n \frac{-(u_1'(\hat{\zeta}^n)/p_1^0)(y^0 - p^0 \cdot x^n) + b_1(y^0 - p^0 \cdot x^n)}{\|(p^n - p^0, y^n - y^0)\|}.$$

This can be rewritten

$$\limsup_n \left[\left(b_1 - \frac{u_1'(\hat{\zeta}^n)}{p_1^0} \right) \left(\frac{y^0 - p^0 \cdot x^n}{\|(p^n - p^0, y^n - y^0)\|} \right) \right].$$

The first term vanishes as n goes to infinity, since $\hat{\zeta}^n$ converges to x^0 and u is continuously differentiable. And the second term is bounded: rewrite the numerator as $(p^n - p^0, y^n - y^0) \cdot (x^n, -1)$ and bound the inner product by the product of the norms, noting that x^n is converging to x^0. ∎

Whew! That was indeed a grind but, if you look for the big picture of the proof and, in particular, compare with the proof of Proposition 9.22 (differentiability of the profit function), the basic idea of the proof is pretty simple. Recall how the proof of Proposition 9.22 went: We were looking at a sequence of prices p^n with limit p^0, and we pulled out the optimal production plan z^n for p^n and the optimal production plan z^0 for p^0. Then we looked at two inequalities:

$$p^n \cdot z^n \geq p^n \cdot z^0 \quad \text{and} \quad p^0 \cdot z^0 \geq p^0 \cdot z^n.$$

In words, at the price vector p^n, the production plan that maximizes profit at p^n is at least as profitable as the plan that is profit maxmizing at p^0, and vice versa. Those two inequalities, plus judicious use of Berge's Theorem (if solutions are unique, they define a continuous function), applied with brute force to the limit that defines the derivative of π, gave the result.

We are doing, pretty much, the same thing here. The key step is getting the corresponding two inequalities, which are the two inequalities in (11.2). Once we have those two inequalities, we apply them to the limit that defines the derivative of ν with sufficient brute force (a bit more than back in Chapter 9), and out comes the result. Two things make the proof harder: First, the objective function back in Chapter 9 is the bilinear form $p \cdot z$. So evaluating the differences $p^0 \cdot z^0 - p^0 \cdot z^n$ and $p^n \cdot z^n - p^n \cdot z^0$ is straightforward. In this case, we need to apply Taylor's Theorem to evaluate those differences in a way that is useful, which in turn is why we need the assumption that u is differentiable. And back in Chapter 9, the feasible set doesn't change as prices change. Here it does, and so when we compare x^0 with x^n in deriving the two inequalities, we first have to adjust x^0 to fit the problem (p^n, y^n) and we have to adjust x^n to fit the problem (p^0, x^0). Notice, though, that we do all our adjusting through adjustments in the consumption of good 1, under the hypothesis that, in x^0, $x_1^0 > 0$. That tells us (1) that when the adjustments are small, the adjusted values will still be nonnegative. And (2) we know from back in Chapter 3 that small adjustments in consumption levels to fit small changes in price or income are all equivalent (to the first order) as long as we change the levels of goods with the greatest bang for the buck, which are those goods that are consumed in strictly positive amounts. The proof takes a lot of steps and manipulation of symbols, but there is nothing especially deep in all those steps.

11.3. Duality of Utility and Indirect Utility

The climax of Chapter 10 is Proposition 10.17, showing a duality between expenditure functions that conform to a list of properties and the class of continuous, locally insatiable, nondecreasing, and quasi-concave utility functions. In this section, we match that result, for indirect utility functions.

Proposition 11.4. *Suppose that u is a continuous and locally insatiable utility function. Then ν, the indirect utility function generated from u, is continuous, strictly increasing in y, nonincreasing in p and strictly decreasing for strict increases in p if $y > 0$, homogeneous of degree 0 in (p, y), quasi-convex in (p, y), and satisfies $\nu(p, y) = u(0)$ if and only if $y = 0$. Moreover, $\lim_{y\to\infty} \nu(p, y) = \sup_{x\in R^k_+} u(x)$ for all $p \in R^k_{++}$.*

Proof. Proposition 3.3 established continuity and homogeneity of degree 0 in (p, y). To show that ν is strictly increasing in y, fix (p^0, y^0), and let x^0 be any solution of the CP at (p^0, y^0). Of course, $p^0 \cdot x^0 = y^0$. For any $y' > y^0$, local insatiability of u ensures that there exists x' (close to x^0) such that $u(x') > u(x^0)$ and $p^0 \cdot x' \leq y'$, and therefore $\nu(p^0, y') \geq u(x') > u(x^0) = \nu(p^0, y^0)$.

If $y = 0$, then it is obvious that $\nu(p, y) = u(0)$ for all p; the only bundle that is affordable is 0. And then, if $y > 0$, we know from the previous paragraph that $\nu(p, y) > \nu(p, 0) = u(0)$.

To show that ν is nonincreasing in p, fix (p^0, y^0) and let $p' \geq p^0$. Then $\{x \in R^k_+ : p' \cdot x \leq y^0\} \subseteq \{x \in R^k_+ : p^0 \cdot x \leq y^0\}$. But $\nu(p', y^0)$ is the maximum of $u(x)$ over the first of these sets, and $\nu(p^0, y^0)$ is the maximum over the second set. Maximizing over a larger set must produce a maximum at least as large: $\nu(p^0, y^0) \geq \nu(p', y^0)$.

Now suppose, in the notation of the last paragraph, that $y^0 > 0$ and p' is a strict increase over p^0. Let $\mathbf{D}(p^0, y^0)$ denote all the solutions of the CP at (p^0, y^0), and let x' be any solution of the CP at (p', y^0). Of course, because of local insatiability, $p^0 \cdot x = y^0$ for all $x \in \mathbf{D}(p^0, y^0)$, and $p' \cdot x' = y^0$. Since we know (now) that $\nu(p^0, y^0) > u(0)$, we know that every $x \in \mathbf{D}(p^0, y^0)$ is nonzero. This implies, since p' is a strict increase on p^0, that $p' \cdot x > p^0 \cdot x = y^0$ for every $x \in \mathbf{D}(p^0, y^0)$. Therefore, no $x \in \mathbf{D}(p^0, y^0)$ is feasible at (p', y^0), which implies that $x' \notin \mathbf{D}(p^0, y^0)$. But $p^0 \cdot x' \leq p' \cdot x' = y^0$, so x' is feasible at (p^0, y^0); since it is not a solution of the CP at (p^0, y^0) but is feasible, it must provide less utility than do members of $\mathbf{D}(p^0, y^0)$. That is, $\nu(p', y^0) = u(x') < \nu(p^0, y^0)$. (Can you construct a proof using the homogeneity properties of ν?)

Since ν is strictly increasing in y, $\lim_{y\to\infty} \nu(p, y)$ exists and is the same as $\sup_{y\in R_+} \nu(p, y)$. Since the CP has a solution for every set of parameter values, for any (p, y) there is some x such that $\nu(p, y) = u(x)$, and hence $\sup_{y\in R_+} \nu(p, y) \leq$

$\sup_{x\in R^k_+} u(x)$. To get the reverse inequality, suppose x^n is a sequence of bundles whose utilities approach $\sup_{x\in R^k_+} u(x)$ in n: For any price p, let $y^n = p\cdot x^n$, and we know that $\nu(p, y^n) \geq u(x^n)$ (since x^n is feasible); therefore $\sup_{y\in R_+} \nu(p, y) \geq u(x^n)$; taking n to infinity does it.

Finally, there is quasi-convexity: Fix (p, y), (p', y'), and $\alpha \in [0, 1]$, and let $(p'', y'') = \alpha(p, y) + (1 - \alpha)(p', y')$. Suppose x^* is a solution of the CP at (p'', y'').

I assert that x^* is either feasible for (p, y) or for (p', y'). Nonnegativity of x^* is not a problem, so the only way x^* could be infeasible for both (p, y) and (p', y') is if $p \cdot x^* > y$ and $p' \cdot x^* > y'$. But then $\alpha(p \cdot x^*) + (1 - \alpha)(p' \cdot x^*) > \alpha y + (1 - \alpha)y'$, which is $p'' \cdot x^* > y''$, contradicting the assumption that x^* is optimal, and hence feasible, at (p'', y'').

But if x^* is feasible for (p, y), then $u(x^*) \leq \nu(p, y) \leq v$. Similarly, if x^* is feasible for (p', y'), $u(x^*) \leq \nu(p', y') \leq v$. One of these must hold, so $u(x^*) = \nu(p'', y'') \leq \max\{\nu(p, y), \nu(p', y')\}$; hence ν is quasi-convex. ■

Recall that for a set $X \subseteq R^k_+$, CCH(X) is the comprehensive convex hull of X.

Proposition 11.5. *Suppose that u and u' are two continuous utility functions defined on R^k_+. Let ν denote the indirect utility function defined from u, and let ν' be the indirect utility function defined from u'. Then $\nu \equiv \nu'$ if and only if, for all $v \in R$, CCH($\{x \in R^k_+ : u(x) \geq v\}$) = CCH($\{x \in R^k_+ : u'(x) \geq v\}$.*

Corollary 11.6. *If ν is an indirect utility function derived from a continuous utility function, then it is the indirect utility function for a continuous, nondecreasing, and quasi-concave utility function, namely the function $\hat{u}$ derived from u via defining equation (10.1). And if ν is derived from a utility function that is moreover locally insatiable, then the corresponding $\hat{u}$ is also locally insatiable.*

Proof. Suppose that u and u' are continuous utility functions such that, for all v, CCH($\{x \in R^k_+ : u(x) \geq v\}$) = CCH($\{x \in R^k_+ : u'(x) \geq v\}$). Fix a price vector p and income level y, and let $\hat{x}$ be a solution to the CP for u at (p, y). Letting $v = u(\hat{x}) = \nu(p, y)$, it is obvious that $\hat{x} \in$ CCH($\{x \in R^k_+ : u(x) \geq v\}$) and, therefore, $\hat{x} \in$ CCH($\{x \in R^k_+ : u'(x) \geq v\}$). That is, $\hat{x} \geq \sum_i \alpha^i x^i$, for some vectors $x^1, \ldots, x^n$ such that $u'(x^i) \geq v$ for $i = 1, \ldots, n$ and nonnegative scalars $\alpha^1, \ldots, \alpha^n$ summing to one. I assert that $p \cdot x^i \leq y$ for at least one of the i's; were this not so, then $p \cdot \hat{x} \geq p \cdot \left(\sum_i \alpha^i x^i\right) = \sum_i \alpha^i (p \cdot x^i) > \sum_i \alpha^i y = y$, and $\hat{x}$ would not be feasible for (p, y), a contradiction. But for that x^i such that $p \cdot x^i \leq y$, x^i is feasible, so $\nu'(p, y) \geq u'(x^i) \geq v = \nu(p, y)$. By a symmetric argument, $\nu(p, y) \geq \nu'(p, y)$, so they are equal for all p and y.

Suppose, conversely, that u and u' are continous such that, for some v, CCH($\{x \in R^k_+ : u(x) \geq v\}$) $\neq$ CCH($\{x \in R^k_+ : u'(x) \geq v\}$. Without loss of generality, suppose x^0 is in CCH($\{x \in R^k_+ : u(x) \geq v\}$) but is not a member of CCH($\{x \in R^k_+ : u'(x) \geq v\}$). By the usual argument, we can strictly separate x^0 from the closed and convex set CCH($\{x \in R^k_+ : u'(x) \geq v\}$); that is, for some $q \in R^k$, $q \cdot x^0 < \inf\{q \cdot x : x \in$ CCH($\{x \in R^k_+ : u'(x) \geq v\}$)$\}$. Since CCH($\{x \in R^k_+ : u'(x) \geq v\}$) is comprehensive upwards, $q \geq 0$, and we can perturb q slightly so that it is strictly positive and still have the inequality. Let p be the strictly positive perturbation of q; that is, p is strictly positive and satisfies $p \cdot x^0 < \inf\{p \cdot x : x \in \text{CCH}(\{x \in R_+^k : u'(x) \geq v\})\}$. Now let $y = p \cdot x^0$. For the CP with parameters p and y, x^0 is feasible. Since $x^0 \in \text{CCH}(\{x \in R_+^k : u(x) \geq v\})$, by the argument from the previous paragraph we know that there is some x^i such that $u(x^i) \geq v$ and x^i is feasible at p and y. Therefore, $\nu(p, y) \geq u(x^i) \geq v$. On the other hand, for every x' such that $u'(x') \geq v$, we know $x' \in \text{CCH}(\{x \in R_+^k : u'(x) \geq v\})$ and, therefore, $p \cdot x' > y$, so x' is not feasible for (p, y). Therefore, $\nu'(p, y) < v$. The indirect utility functions are different.

The corollary is obvious given developments from last chapter. ■

The next step in the progression is to describe how to invert an indirect utility function, to recover "the" utility function that generated it. Based on the results just given and results from Chapter 10, we recover the original utility function *if* that function is nondecreasing and quasi-concave (and otherwise we recover "its" CCH-equivalent utility function).

Proposition 11.7. *Suppose that ν is an indirect utility function for a continuous, nondecreasing, and quasi-concave utility function u. Then, for all x,*

$$u(x) = \max\{v \in R : \nu(p, p \cdot x) \geq v \textit{ for all } p \in R_{++}^k\}. \tag{11.4}$$

Proof. Fix $x^0 \in R_+^k$. Since x^0 is feasible for the CP at the parameter values p and $y = p \cdot x^0$, $\nu(p, p \cdot x^0) \geq u(x^0)$ for all p. This implies that $v^0 = u(x^0)$ is among the values in the set on the right-hand side of (11.4). Therefore, the right-hand side of (11.4) is at least as large as $u(x^0)$.

Now take any $v' > u(x^0)$. We know that $x^0 \notin \{x \in R_+^k : u(x) \geq v'\}$ and that $\{x \in R_+^k : u(x) \geq v'\}$ is closed, convex, and comprehensive. Hence, by the usual argument, we can produce a strictly positive p^0 such that $p^0 \cdot x^0 < \inf\{p^0 \cdot x : u(x) \geq v'\}$. Therefore, if we look at the CP with the parameter values p^0 and $y = p^0 \cdot x^0$, we know that no x such that $u(x) \geq v'$ is feasible, and $\nu(p^0, p^0 \cdot x^0) < v'$. Since ν is defined as a supremum, we must be careful with this argument: The CP has a solution—denote it x^*—at $(p^0, p^0 \cdot x^0)$, and $\nu(p^0, p^0 \cdot x^0) = u(x^*)$. And, moreover, $x^* \notin \{x \in R_+^k : u(x) \geq v'\}$, since no point in $\{x \in R_+^k : u(x) \geq v'\}$ is feasible for the CP at $(p^0, p^0 \cdot x^0)$. Therefore $\nu(p^0, p^0 \cdot x^0) = u(x^*) < v'$.

This shows that for every $v' > u(x^0)$, $v' \notin \{v \in R : \nu(p, p \cdot x^0) \geq v$ for all $p \in R_{++}^k\}$, and therefore the "maximum" (which you should regard as a supremum until we prove that it is attained) on the right-hand side of (11.4) is no larger than $u(x^0)$.

And, since we showed in the first paragraph of the proof that $v^0 = u(x^0)$ is in the set on the right-hand side, we have established both the equality in (11.4) and that a maximum is appropriate. ■

The final question is: When is a candidate indirect utility function ν actually an indirect utility function? That is, when does a continuous (and, perhaps, locally insatiable) utility function exist, which generates the candidate function ν? For the sake of notational convenience, assume that $\nu(p,0) \equiv 0$ and $\lim_{y\to\infty} \nu(p,y) = \infty$ for all p; this amounts to assuming that, if there is a utility function that generated ν, it has $u(0) = 0$ and $\sup_{x\in R^k_+} u(x) = \infty$. Then:

Proposition 11.8. *Suppose that $\nu : R^k_{++} \times R_+ \to R_+$ is continuous, strictly increasing in its last argument, nonincreasing in its "p" argument and strictly decreasing for strict increases in the "p" argument when its last argument (the "y" argument) is strictly positive, quasi-convex, homogeneous of degree 0, satisfies $\nu(p,0) \equiv 0$, and $\lim_{y\to\infty} \nu(p,y) = \infty$ for all p. For $v^0 \in R_+$, define*

$$X_{v^0} := \{x \in R^k_+ : \nu(p, p\cdot x) \geq v^0 \text{ for all } p \in R^k_{++}\}. \tag{11.5}$$

Then X_{v^0} is closed, comprehensive, and convex. Also define, for $x \in R^k_+$,

$$u(x) = max\{v \in R : x \in X_v\}. \tag{11.6}$$

Then u is upper semi-continuous, quasi-concave, and nondecreasing. And if we define $\nu'(p,y) = max\{u(x) : x \in R^k_+, p\cdot x \leq y\}$, then $\nu' \equiv \nu$.

That is, we get everything *except* lower semi-continuity (hence, continuity) of the function u constructed from ν. (As part of the proof, we show that the two maxima embedded in the statement of the proposition are correct; that is, they are suprema that are attained.)

Proof. Rewrite the definition of X_{v^0} as $\bigcap_{p\in R^k_{++}} \{x \in R^k_+ : \nu(p, p\cdot x) \geq v^0\}$. Each set in the intersection is comprehensive upwards because ν is strictly increasing in its last argument, so the intersection is comprehensive upwards. Each set in the intersection is closed because ν is continuous, so the intersection is closed.

Each set in the intersection is convex: Fix p and take any pair of bundles x' and x'' such that both x' and x'' are in $\{x \in R^k_+ : \nu(p, p\cdot x) \geq v^0\}$. W.l.o.g., suppose that $p\cdot x' \geq p\cdot x''$. Then for any scalar $\alpha \in [0,1]$, $p\cdot(\alpha x' + (1-\alpha)x'') \geq p\cdot x''$, and since ν is strictly increasing in its last argument $\nu(p, p\cdot(\alpha x' + (1-\alpha)x'')) \geq \nu(p, p\cdot x'') \geq v^0$. Hence $\alpha x' + (1-\alpha)x'' \in \{x \in R^k_+ : \nu(p, p\cdot x) \geq v^0\}$.

And since each set in the intersection is convex, the intersection is convex. This, then, establishes that each X_{v^0} is closed, comprehensive, and convex.

Fix x^0. Since $\nu(p, p\cdot x^0)$ is finite valued for every p, it is obvious that $x^0 \notin X_v$ for some (finite and large) v. It is also clear from (11.5) that, if $x^0 \in X_v$, then $x^0 \in X_{v'}$ for all $v' \leq v$. Suppose $\{v^n\}$ is an increasing sequence of real numbers such that $x^0 \in X_{v^n}$ for each n; we know that the sequence is bounded above, so it has a limit, which we denote by v^0. Since $\nu(p, p\cdot x^0) \geq v^n$ for every p, of course $\nu(p, p\cdot x^0) \geq v^0$ for every p. But then $x^0 \in X_{v^0}$. This immediately implies that the *max* in (11.6) is appropriate. Moreover, $u(x) \geq v$ if and only if $x \in X_v$, so that the sets X_v are the upper-level sets of u. Since the X_v sets are closed, comprehensive, and convex, u is upper semi-continuous, nondecreasing, and quasi-concave.

Fix p^0 and y^0 and consider the problem of maximizing $u(x)$ subject to $p^0 \cdot x \leq y^0$. The set $\{x \in R^k_+ : p^0 \cdot x \leq y^0\}$ is compact, and upper semi-continuous functions attain their maxima on compact sets, so there is some $x^* \in R^k_+$ such that $p^0 \cdot x^* \leq y^0$ and $u(x^*) \geq u(x)$ for all other $x \in R^k_+$ that satisfy $p^0 \cdot x \leq y^0$. Let $v^* = u(x^*) = \nu'(p^0, y^0)$. We must show that $v^* = \nu(p^0, y^0)$.

Showing an inequality in one direction is easy: Since $x^* \in X_{v^*} = \{x \in R^k_+ : \nu(p, p \cdot x) \geq v^* \text{ for all } p \in R^k_{++}\}$, this is true in particular for p^0. That is, $\nu(p^0, p^0 \cdot x^*) \geq v^*$. Since $p^0 \cdot x^* \leq y^0$ and ν is strictly increasing in its second argument, $\nu(p^0, y^0) \geq v^*$.

To show that $\nu(p^0, y^0) \leq v^*$ takes a bit of an excursion. Recall that $y \to \nu(p, y)$ is strictly increasing and continuous (and the range is $[0, \infty)$), so for each $v \in [0, \infty)$ and p, there is a unique $y \in [0, \infty)$ such that $\nu(p, y) = v$. Denote this y by $e(p, v)$. The use of notation identical to that of the expenditure function is no coincidence—this is indeed the corresponding expenditure function—but we don't need to bother verifying this fact. Some facts about this function e are:

- For fixed p, it is the inverse function of $y \to \nu(p, y)$. Since $y \to \nu(p, y)$ is continuous and strictly increasing, so is $v \to e(p, v)$.
- The function is nonnegative valued: $e(p, v) \geq 0$ for all p and v. Moreover, $e(p, 0) = 0$ (since $\nu(p, 0) = 0$). And since $y \to \nu(p, y)$ increases to ∞, so does $v \to e(p, v)$.
- For fixed v, the function $p \to e(p, v)$ is homogeneous of degree 1: $e(\lambda p, v)$ must satisfy $\nu(\lambda p, e(\lambda p, v)) = v$. But since ν is homogenous of degree 0 in both arguments, and $\nu(p, e(p, v)) = v$, we know that $\nu(\lambda p, \lambda e(p, v)) = v$. Therefore, the unique value y that satisfies $\nu(\lambda p, y) = v$ is $e(\lambda p, v) = y = \lambda e(p, v)$.
- For fixed v, the function $p \to e(p, v)$ is concave: Fix v, and take any pair of price vectors p^1 and p^2 and scalar $\alpha \in [0, 1]$. Let $y^1 = e(p^1, v)$ and $y^2 = e(p^2, v)$, so that $\nu(p^1, y^1) = \nu(p^2, y^2) = v$. Because ν is quasi-convex, $\nu(\alpha p^1 + (1 - \alpha)p^2, \alpha y^1 + (1 - \alpha)y^2) \leq v$. Therefore, since ν is strictly increasing in its final argument, $e(\alpha p^1 + (1 - \alpha)p^2, v) \geq \alpha y^1 + (1 - \alpha)y^2$, which is concavity of e in p.
- We have the identities (for each p) $e(p, \nu(p, y)) = y$ and $\nu(p, e(p, v)) = v$.

Now go back to our fixed p^0 and y^0, and let $v^0 = \nu(p^0, y^0)$. Let x' be a supergradient of the concave and homogeneous-of-degree-1 function $p \to e(p, v^0)$ at $p = p^0$. That is,

$$p^0 \cdot x' = e(p^0, v^0) = y^0 \quad \text{and} \quad p \cdot x' \geq e(p, v^0) \text{ for all } p \in R^k_{++}.$$

(We are using the homogeneity-of-degree-1 property of e in p to conclude that the supergradient is linear, of course.) We know that x' is nonnegative: If x' had a negative component, we could find a strictly positive price p such that $p \cdot x' < 0$, contradicting the fact that $e(p, v^0) \geq 0$ for all p (and v^0).

The equation $p^0 \cdot x' = e(p^0, v^0) = y^0$ tells us that x' is feasible for the CP with parameters p^0 and y^0, and therefore $\nu'(p^0, y^0) \geq u(x')$. The inequality $p \cdot x' \geq e(p, v^0)$

tells us that for all p, $v^0 = \nu(p, e(p, v^0)) \le \nu(p, p \cdot x')$, which implies that $x' \in X_{v^0}$, or $u(x') \ge v^0 = \nu(p^0, y^0)$. Putting this together, $v^* = u(x^*) = \nu'(p^0, y^0) \ge u(x') \ge v^0 = \nu(p^0, y^0)$. This finishes the proof. ∎

Just as in Chapter 10, we nearly get everything we might want, but we can't show that, for a general candidate indirect utility function ν that is continuous, the u constructed via (11.5) and (11.6) is lower semi-continuous. The counterexample we described in Chapter 10 is a counterexample here as well and for the same reason: The point at which u fails to be lower semi-continuous is never a solution to either the CP or the EMP for strictly positive prices, so it doesn't cause the expenditure function or the indirect utility function to be discontinous.

And, just as in the case of Chapter 10, there are two ways to repair matters. You can give up on continuity of utility functions, settling for upper semi-continuity. This allows indirect utility functions to be upper semi-continous, just as (last chapter) it gave expenditure functions that can be lower semi-continuous in v. For the details of this approach, see Krishna and Sonnenschein (1990).

Or we can add a further regularity condition on our indirect utility functions:

Proposition 11.9. *Suppose ν is an indirect utility function generated by a utility function u that satisfies all the conditions of Proposition 11.4. Then ν satisfies*

$$\begin{aligned}&\text{For every } x^0 \in R^k_+, \text{ if } v \ge 0 \text{ and } \epsilon > 0 \text{ are such that } \nu(p, p \cdot x^0) \ge v + \epsilon \\ &\qquad \text{for all } p \in R^k_{++}, \text{ then for some } \delta \in (0,1), \nu(p, \delta p \cdot x^0) > v \text{ for all } p.\end{aligned} \tag{11.7}$$

Conversely, if ν is a candidate indirect utility function satisfying all the conditions of Proposition 11.8 and also Condition (11.7), then u defined from ν via (11.5) and (11.6) is continuous.

Condition (11.7) is due to Jackson (1986a). You should have no problem proving this proposition on your own, if you follow the model of the proof of Proposition 10.17; you are asked to do this in Problem 11.4. Please see Problem 11.5, as well.

11.4. Differentiability of Marshallian Demand

Conditions that guarantee differentiability of the two value functions (the indirect utility and expenditure functions) are relatively straightforward; uniqueness of the solution (essentially) yields differentiability of the value function. Moreover, differentiability of indirect utility is what we need for Roy's Identity. But to derive the Slutsky Equation, we need to know that the Marshallian and Hicksian demand functions are differentiable. We can provide conditions sufficient to guarantee this, but they are significantly less attractive. I cover the differentiability of Marshallian demand in this section, leaving Hicksian demand to you.

If we are to have any hope of showing that Marshallian demand is differentiable, it first must be a function, and a continuous function at that. Therefore, to begin this conversation, we must assume that the CP has a unique solution, at least in some open domain of parameter values. (Of course, continuity of the corresponding

Marshallian demand function follows from the application of Berge's Theorem.) So throughout this section, we maintain the assumption that the CP has a unique solution throughout some neighborhood of a specified point (p^0, y^0).

A motivating example

To motivate what comes next, consider the following simple example. Suppose that $k = 2$ and

$$u(x_1, x_2) = \ln(x_1 + 1) + \ln(x_2 + 10).$$

Because u is strictly concave, we know that the CP will have a unique solution for all p and y. Fix $p_1 = p_2 = 1$, and consider solutions to the CP as a function of y. If x_1 and x_2 are both strictly positive at the solution (for given y), the first-order conditions tell us that

$$\frac{1}{x_1 + 1} = \frac{1}{x_2 + 10}.$$

Clearly, this will be impossible unless $x_1 \geq 9$, which (in turn) requires $y \geq 9$. From this observation the solution is clear:

$$x_1((1,1), y) = \begin{cases} y, & \text{for } y \leq 9, \text{ and} \\ y/2 + 4.5, & \text{for } y \geq 9, \end{cases}$$

$$x_2((1,1), y) = \begin{cases} 0, & \text{for } y \leq 9, \text{ and} \\ y/2 - 4.5, & \text{for } y \geq 9. \end{cases}$$

Evidently, we do not get differentiability (in y, at least) for values where the set of binding nonnegativity constraints changes. If you fix $y = 9$ and $p_1 = 1$ (say), and then parametrically vary p_2, you will see that the same is true for differentiability in prices.

The utility function u in this example is continuously differentiable of all orders. It is bounded below and its derivatives are bounded on R^k_{++}. All in all, this is a very well-behaved utility function. Hence we conclude that looking for differentiability over changes in the set of nonzero consumption levels may be a problem.

The result for the CP

With this as prelude, we can state a positive result.

Proposition 11.10 (Differentiability of Marshallian demand). *Suppose that*

a. *u is locally insatiable and twice continuously differentiable;*

b. *the CP has a unique solution $d(p, y)$ for all (p, y) in an open neighborhood of some fixed (p^0, y^0); and* *c. in an open neighborhood of* (p^0, y^0), *the nonzero components of* $d(p, y)$ *do not change.*

Let n *be the number of nonzero components of* $d(p^0, y^0)$, *and let* $j_1, \ldots, j_n$ *be their indices. Use the notation*

$$u_i = \frac{\partial u}{\partial x_i} \quad \text{and} \quad u_{ij} = \frac{\partial^2 u}{\partial x_i \partial x_j}$$

and let $\mathcal{H}$ *be the* $(n+1) \times (n+1)$ *matrix*

$$\mathcal{H} = \begin{pmatrix} 0 & u_{j_1} & u_{j_2} & \cdots & u_{j_n} \\ u_{j_1} & u_{j_1 j_1} & u_{j_2 j_1} & \cdots & u_{j_n j_1} \\ u_{j_2} & u_{j_1 j_2} & u_{j_2 j_2} & \cdots & u_{j_n j_2} \\ \vdots & \vdots & \vdots & \ddots & \vdots \\ u_{j_n} & u_{j_1 j_n} & u_{j_2 j_n} & \cdots & u_{j_n j_n} \end{pmatrix}.$$

Suppose that

d. $\mathcal{H}$ *is nonsingular when evaluated at* $d(p^0, y^0)$.

Then $d(p, y)$ *is continuously differentiable over some open neighborhood of* (p^0, y^0).

The use of $\mathcal{H}$ in the statement of this result is slightly unfortunate, because it might be confused with the **H** in *Hicksian*. This $\mathcal{H}$ is for Hessian; more precisely, $\mathcal{H}$ is the *bordered Hessian* of the (twice-continuously differentiable) function u (restricted to the nonzero arguments that pertain around $d(p^0, y^0)$).[1]

Before launching into the proof, commentary on the four assumptions is in order.

- The assumption that u is twice continuously differentiable is, for most economists, fairly innocuous. It is also without any serious axiomatic basis.
- Uniqueness of the solution to the CP is far from innocuous, but we know that it follows if we assume that u is strictly quasi-concave. And there is no hope for this sort of result without this assumption (at least, for goods that are consumed; it is okay to have some goods that have no impact on utility and, therefore, are never consumed).
- The need for an assumption on nonchanging nonzero components of demand is shown by the simple example. We'll comment more on this assumption after the proof.
- Condition c in the proposition implies, of course, that $y^0 > 0$.
- Assumption d probably seems uninterpretable. Advanced books on this topic show that this assumption is "very likely" to hold at almost any point you pick,

[1] The *Hessian* matrix of u (restricted to its nonzero components) is not $\mathcal{H}$, but the $n \times n$ submatrix in the lower righthand part of $\mathcal{H}$. See Definition 11.11 next section. The adjective *bordered* refers to the first row and column of $\mathcal{H}$.

if u represents strictly convex preferences. But this doesn't change its inherent ugliness.

Proof. The proof uses the Implicit-Function Theorem; see Appendix 7.

Fix the point (p^0, y^0). Let x^0 denote $d(p^0, y^0)$ and let λ^0 be the Lagrange multiplier at the solution to the CP at (p^0, y^0).

As in the statement of the proposition, suppose that x^0 has n nonzero components. For typographical ease, renumber components so that these n are the first n components.

Recalling that $u_m = \lambda^0 p_m$ for $m = 1, \ldots, n$, nonsingularity of the matrix $\mathcal{H}$ implies that $\lambda^0 > 0$; otherwise the first row and the first column of $\mathcal{H}$ would both be identically zero.

Define the function

$$F(p, y, \lambda, x) = \begin{cases} p \cdot x - y \\ u_1(x) - \lambda p_1 \\ u_2(x) - \lambda p_2 \\ \vdots \\ u_n(x) - \lambda p_n \end{cases}.$$

The domain of definition of F is $R^n_{++} \times R_{++} \times R_{++} \times R^n_{++}$, and the range is R^{n+1}. By construction and the preceding paragraph, we know that $(p^0, y^0, \lambda^0, x^0)$ is in the domain of definition of F (if we restrict p^0 and x^0 to their first n components). By the first-order conditions, we know that

$$F(p^0, y^0, \lambda^0, x^0) = 0.$$

Now we apply the Implicit-Function Theorem to define implicitly functions $\hat{\lambda}(p, y)$ and $\hat{x}(p, y)$ that satisfy

$$F(p, y, \hat{\lambda}(p, y), \hat{x}(p, y)) = 0$$

in a neighborhood of $(p^0, y^0, \lambda^0, x^0)$. The Implicit-Function Theorem will apply if the $(n + 1) \times (n + 1)$ matrix of partial derivatives of F in the eliminated variables, evaluated at $(p^0, y^0, \lambda^0, x^0)$, is nonsingular. The derivative of F in λ is the vector

$$(0, -p_1, -p_2, \ldots, -p_n),$$

while the derivative of F in x_m is

$$(p_m, u_{1m}, u_{2m}, \ldots, u_{nm});$$

hence we are asking whether

$$\begin{pmatrix} 0 & -p_1 & -p_2 & \dots & -p_n \\ p_1 & u_{11} & u_{21} & \dots & u_{n1} \\ p_2 & u_{12} & u_{22} & \dots & u_{n2} \\ \vdots & \vdots & \vdots & \ddots & \vdots \\ p_n & u_{1n} & u_{2n} & \dots & u_{nn} \end{pmatrix}$$

is nonsingular. Nonsingularity of a matrix is unaffected by multiplying any row and/or any column by a nonzero scalar, so multiply the first row by $-\lambda$ and the first column by λ; from the first-order conditions, this gives us the matrix

$$\mathcal{H} = \begin{pmatrix} 0 & u_1 & u_2 & \dots & u_n \\ u_1 & u_{11} & u_{21} & \dots & u_{n1} \\ u_2 & u_{12} & u_{22} & \dots & u_{n2} \\ \vdots & \vdots & \vdots & \ddots & \vdots \\ u_n & u_{1n} & u_{2n} & \dots & u_{nn} \end{pmatrix},$$

evaluated at x^0. (To see that this is $\mathcal{H}$, recall that we renumbered our commodity indices.) But our final assumption is precisely that this matrix is nonsingular. That is, our final assumption was crafted so that at this step, we can invoke the Implicit-Function Theorem.

Therefore, we know that for an open neighborhood $\mathcal{N}_1$ of (p^0, y^0) and an open neighborhood $\mathcal{N}_2$ of (λ^0, x^0), there are unique solutions in $\mathcal{N}_2$ of the implicit equation

$$F(p, y, \hat{\lambda}(p, y), \hat{x}(p, y)) = 0,$$

and that the functions $\hat{\lambda}(p, y)$ and $\hat{x}(p, y)$ so created are continuously differentiable over $\mathcal{N}_1$. If necessary, shrink $\mathcal{N}_1$ so that for all $(p, y) \in \mathcal{N}_1$, $\hat{x}(p, y)$ has the same nonzero components as x^0.

The last step is to note that $\hat{x}(p, y)$ is Marshallian demand (and $\hat{\lambda}(p, y)$ gives the budget-constraint multiplier as a function of (p, y)): We know that $d(p, y)$ and $\lambda(p, y)$ (the true budget-constraint multiplier function) are continuous in (p, y) (the former by Proposition 3.3 and the latter by Proposition 11.1 and Corollary 11.2); hence for some open neighborhood $\mathcal{N}_1'$ of (p^0, y^0), they must lie within $\mathcal{N}_2$. The first-order conditions are necessary for solutions to the CP, and (since all this is in a region where the indices of commodities that are consumed in positive amounts are unchanging), the first-order conditions are just $F(p, y, \lambda(p, y), d(p, y)) = 0$. Since $\hat{\lambda}(p, y)$ and $\hat{x}(p, y)$ are the unique solutions of this equation within $\mathcal{N}_2$, it must be that $\hat{\lambda}(p, y) = \lambda(p, y)$ and $\hat{x}(p, y) = d(p, y)$, at least for $(p, y) \in \mathcal{N}_1 \cap \mathcal{N}_1'$. But then the continuous differentiability of $\hat{x}(p, y)$ tells us that $d(p, y)$ is continuously differentiable on $\mathcal{N}_1 \cap \mathcal{N}_1'$. ∎

How bad is it (from a practical standpoint) that we lose differentiability at points where nonnegativity constraints go inactive? A line of argument that says this isn't (practically) a terrible problem asserts that when we go to apply demand theory empirically, we will have to aggregate over goods to such an extent that expenditure on each aggregate commodity is strictly positive. That is, if we try to fit the consumption behavior of a consumer, we won't deal with her demand for bus service, air transport to New York, air transport to Los Angeles, and so on. Instead, we will create a composite commodity—transportation services—and try to fit her expenditure behavior at this aggregate level. The point is, while the individual consumer may spend (at some prices and income levels) zero on bus services, almost no one will spend nothing on transportation services. If we aggregate consumption commodities at a high enough level, the argument goes, we can safely assume that we will never see consumption on the boundary of R^k_+.

Differentiability of Hicksian demand

What about differentiability of Hicksian demand? Similar techniques work quite nicely. We assume that the EMP has a unique solution and that the binding constraints (the index set of the goods consumed in strictly positive amount) don't change over some neighborhood. We use the combined first-order, complementary-slackness conditions for the EMP to determine implicitly the Hicksian demand function, and then invoke the Implicit-Function Theorem. With this rather substantial hint, I leave the details to those of you fanatical enough to pursue it.

11.5. Integrability

The discussion two paragraphs ago, about applying demand theory empirically, probably struck you as coming out of left field. What is the relevance to this discussion of empirical applications of this theory? To answer this question, recall first why we are at all concerned with differentiability of the Marshallian demand function: We need it to derive the Slutsky Equation. (Given differentiability of Marshallian demand and Hicksian demand, our derivation of the Slutsky Equation is perfectly rigorous.) But why do we care about the Slutsky Equation?

- The Slutsky Equation, as we've already seen, gives us an intuitive decomposition of $\partial d/\partial p_i$ into relative-price and real-income pieces.
- As we shall see later in this section, economic notions of things like substitute and complementary goods are informed by the equation.
- The Slutsky Equation is central to the question of *integrability*.

And, to link two paragraphs ago to this section, the question of integrability has its roots in empirical applications of demand theory. In applied (econometric) work, it is often useful to have parametric functional specifications for a consumer's demand function. We can write down nice closed-form parametrizations for the utility function u, and then solve the CP to derive Marshallian demand. But for most analytically tractable specifications of u, the Marshallian demand function that results is a mess. It is often more convenient to specify a parametric form for Marshallian demand directly, being sure that this parametrization is analytically tractable. But then, to be sure that one's parametrization plays by the rules of microeconomic theory, one would want to know whether there is some (parameterized) utility function that gives the parametric family of Marshallian demand that is being used.

Integrability provides the answer. Given a specification of an alleged demand function—in the form of a function $\chi(p, y)$ (possibly with some free parameters to be estimated)—integrability gives sufficient conditions for $\chi(p, y)$ to be $d(p, y)$ for some well-behaved utility function u. To develop those conditions (and see to what extent they are necessary as well as sufficient), we begin with some definitions.

Definition 11.11.

a. *If $f : R^k \to R$ is twice continuously differentiable, the $k \times k$ matrix of its second partial derivatives—that is, the $k \times k$ matrix whose ijth element is $\partial^2 f / \partial z_i \, \partial z_j$—is called the* ***Hessian matrix*** *of f.*

b. *A $k \times k$ matrix M is* ***negative semi-definite*** *if $xMx \le 0$ for all $x \in R^k$.*

Mathematical facts: *Suppose f is a twice-continuously-differentiable function from (some open domain in) R^k to R.*

a. *The Hessian matrix of f is symmetric.*

b. *The function f is concave if and only if its Hessian matrix is negative semi-definite (evaluated at all points in the domain).*

I do not attempt to prove fact b, but you should note that fact a simply states that $\partial^2 f / \partial z_i \partial z_j = \partial^2 f / \partial z_j \partial z_i$.

Proposition 11.12. *Suppose, for a consumer with continuous and locally insatiable utility function u, e is the consumer's expenditure function and ν the indirect utility function. Suppose that for some open neighborhood of parameters, the solutions to the CP and the EMP are unique, and the corresponding Marshallian demand function d and Hicksian demand function h are both continuously differentiable. Then the $k \times k$ matrix whose ijth term is*

$$\frac{\partial d_j}{\partial p_i} + d_i \frac{\partial d_j}{\partial y} \tag{11.8}$$

is symmetric and negative semi-definite.

Proof. Since h is the gradient of e, and h is assumed to be continuously differentiable, e is twice continuously differentiable. We know that e is concave in prices, so its Hessian matrix must be symmetric and negative semi-definite. But as h gives the gradient of e, the ijth term in the Hessian matrix of e is just $\partial h_j / \partial p_i$, and the

Slutsky Equation tells us that this is identical to term in (11.8) ∎

Because of its importance to demand theory, the $k \times k$ matrix whose ijth element is given by (11.8) has a name: It is called the *Slutsky* Matrix.

Suppose someone hands you a differentiable function $\chi : R^k_{++} \times R_+ \to R^k_+$ and asserts that this function is Marshallian demand for some consumer with locally insatiable preferences. We now have a number of tests that this function must pass:

a. For each p and y, $p \cdot \chi(p, y)$ must equal y. Henceforth, we refer to this condition (that the consumer spends her entire income) as *Walras' Law.*

b. The function χ must be homogeneous of degree 0.

c. The Slutsky Matrix (with χ in place of d) must be symmetric and negative semi-definite.

The *Integrability Theorem* says that, with some technical conditions on the function χ, these conditions are sufficient as well. That is, if χ satisfies a, b, and c, and some technical conditions, it is the Marshallian demand function corresponding to a locally insatiable utility maximizer, whose preferences (moreover) are nondecreasing and convex.

I'm not going to try to prove this result, or even give an exact statement of it, because to do justice to it would require too much background on the theory of differential equations. Instead, I describe how integrability works, and then recommend further readings if you want to see the details.

Suppose $\chi(p, y)$ is indeed a Marshallian demand function. We know then that $u(\chi(p, y)) = \nu(p, y)$. Fix some price p^0 and income level y^0, and for all prices p, define

$$\mu(p;\, p^0, y^0) := e(p, \nu(p^0, y^0)).$$

In words, μ gives the amount of money needed at prices p to get the level of utility obtained at p^0 and y^0. This is called (by Hurwicz and Uzawa, in the classic paper on integrability) the *income compensation function.* Now fix p at, say, $\hat{p}$, and think of varying p^0 and y^0. In particular, define a function $\eta(p^0, y^0)$ by

$$\eta(p^0, y^0) := \mu(\hat{p}; p^0, y^0) = e(\hat{p}, \nu(p^0, y^0)).$$

Because e is strictly increasing in its second argument,

$$\eta(p^0, y^0) \geq \eta(p^1, y^1) \text{ if and only if } \nu(p^0, y^0) \geq \nu(p^1, y^1).$$

Hence if $x^0 = \chi(p^0, y^0)$ and $x^1 = \chi(p^1, y^1)$, we know that

$$u(x^0) = \nu(p^0, y^0) \geq \nu(p^1, y^1) = u(x^1) \text{ if and only if } \eta(p^0, y^0) \geq \eta(p^1, y^1).$$

In other words, if we define, for x in the range of χ,

$$U(x) := \eta(p, y), \quad \text{for } p, y \text{ such that } \chi(p, y) = x,$$

we know that U is a representation of the consumer's preferences (on the range of χ).

But how do we find $\eta(p, y)$? Go back to the equation $\mu(p; p^0, y^0) = e(p, \nu(p^0, y^0))$. Take the partial derivative of this in p_i:

$$\begin{aligned}\frac{\partial \mu(p; p^0, y^0)}{\partial p_i} &= \frac{\partial e(p, \nu(p^0, y^0))}{\partial p_i} = h_i(p, \nu(p^0, y^0)) \\ &= \chi_i(p, e(p^0, \nu(p^0, y^0))) = \chi_i(p, \mu(p; p^0, y^0)), \quad \text{for each } i.\end{aligned}$$

The first and last terms in this progression (for $i = 1, \ldots, k$ simultaneously) constitute a total differential equation for the function $\mu(\cdot; p^0, y^0)$, if you have the function χ. (Note that $\mu(p^0; p^0, y^0) = e(p^0, \nu(p^0, y^0)) = y^0$, which gives an initial condition for each p^0 and y^0.) Assuming you can solve (that is, integrate) this differential equation, you can construct the family of functions $\mu(\cdot; p^0, y^0)$. Invert these functions as above to construct η, and you have a utility function.

If this seems magical, think first about the differential equation

$$\frac{\partial \mu(p; p^0, y^0)}{\partial p_i} = \chi_i(p, \mu(p; p^0, y^0)).$$

The function μ tells you the amount of money needed to keep the consumer at the utility level $\nu(p^0, y^0)$, at prices p. The left-hand side of the differential equation asks: How much (more) money is needed, at the price vector p, if the price of good i increases by one unit? And the right-hand side says: It is the amount of money that is needed so that the consumer can continue to buy the bundle that she would buy at p, with enough money to get utility level $\nu(p^0, y^0)$. If she is buying none of good i, she needs no more money. If she is buying a positive amount of good i, then buying back her bundle is, to a first-order approximation, the optimal thing for her to do. This is just like the intuition we gave for the Slutsky Equation at the start of the chapter.

The other part of the argument is the realization that, if we fix the first argument in μ, it gives a utility function for the consumer. But that's not really magical either: If one bundle is chosen at p^0, y^0 and another at p^1, y^1, and if at prices $\hat{p}$ it takes more money to get the utility that the first bundle provides than to get the utility that the second bundle provides, then (of course) the first bundle has greater utility.

Of course, almost all of the heavy lifting remains to be done. Do the differential equations have a solution? Does the solution for different initial conditions behave nicely? Given the function η, does it really provide us with a utility function that gives back the demand functions χ? Assuming that we want utility functions that are locally insatiable and continuous, does the η that is constructed satisfy these conditions? And this only suggests how η can be defined for x in the range of χ. We want a (continuous and locally insatiable) utility function for all of R^k_+. How is η extended? If you are interested in details, I recommend both Border (2004) and Jackson (1986b).

11.6. Complements and Substitutes

The symmetry of the Slutsky Matrix bears some scrutiny. Putting this in terms of Hicksian demand, we know that

$$\frac{\partial h_i}{\partial p_j} = \frac{\partial h_j}{\partial p_i}.$$

So the income-compensated demand for good i is increasing in p_j if and only if the income-compensated demand for good j is increasing in p_i, and the magnitudes of the derivatives of each are identical.

The fact that the partial derivatives are identical and not just similarly signed is quite amazing. Why is it that whenever a \$0.01 rise in the price of good i means a fall in (compensated) demand for j of, say, 4.3 units, then a \$0.01 rise in the price of good j means a fall in (compensated) demand for i by approximately 4.3 units?[2] While I am unable to give a good intuitive explanation, at least the similar sign characteristic makes intuitive sense. If a rise in the price of good i causes demand for good j to rise, then in some sense j is substituting for i (the demand for which is reduced because of the rise in price). But then if j substitutes for i, i must substitute for j. And conversely, if i complements j, so a rise in the price of j lowers demand for i, the same effect must hold with i and j reversed.

Note that all this concerns Hicksian demand. For Marshallian demand, things are a bit more complex because there are income effects to worry about; we can't say that $\partial d_i/\partial p_j = \partial d_j/\partial p_i$, or even that they necessarily have the same sign.

In informal economics, the term *substitutes* is used to describe pairs of goods where an increase in the price of one good causes an increase in the demand of the second, and *complements* is used when an increase in the price of one good causes a decrease in the demand of the other. If we attempt to formalize this in terms of the signs of $\partial d_j/\partial p_i$, we run into the unhappy possibility that $\partial d_j/\partial p_i < 0$ and, at the same time, $\partial d_i/\partial p_j > 0$. The symmetry of the Hicksian demand derivatives precludes this unhappy possibility for Hicksian demand. So it has become common in more formal treatments of substitutes and complements to base the definition on the sign of $\partial h_j/\partial p_i = \partial h_i/\partial p_j$. But you should be careful when you encounter these terms in the literature, as different authors will use them somewhat differently.

---

[2] "Approximately" is inserted here because this is a discrete change in price. The derivatives are precisely equal.

11.7. Integrability and Revealed Preference

The question of integrability is, Does an alleged system of demand functions (for a single consumer), $\chi : R^k_{++} \times R_+ \to R^k_+$, arise from utility maximization for some (suitably regular) utility function? Up to some regularity conditions, the answer supplied by the Integrability Theorem is, Assuming differentiability, it does so if and only if χ is homogeneous of degree 0, satisfies Walras' Law ($p \cdot \chi(p, y) = y$), and has a symmetric and negative semi-definite Slutsky Matrix.

Back in Chapter 4, Afriat's Theorem addressed a seemingly similar question, Does a finite collection of demand data (from a single consumer), $\{(x^i, p^i, y^i); i = 1, \ldots, n\}$, where x^i is demand at p^i and y^i, arise from utility maximization according to a locally insatiable utility function? The answer given there was, It does if and only if there are no revealed preference cycles within the finite set of data, where at least one of the revealed preferences in the cycle is revealed strict preference.

To have a seamless theory, it would be nice to connect these two very different approaches to the same basic question. And in one direction, at least, the connection is very easy:

Corollary 11.13. *For an alleged system of demand functions $\chi : R^k_{++} \times R_+ \to R^k_+$ to be generated by a utility-maximizing consumer with locally insatiable, continuous utility, it is necessary that, for every finite collection of price-income pairs $\{(p^i, y^i); i = 1 \ldots, I\}$, the corresponding demands $\{\chi(p^i, y^i)\}$ together with those prices and income levels satisfy GARP.*

I label this a corollary, because it follows immediately from Afriat's Theorem and, for that matter, from the easy half of Afriat's Theorem.

But then one wonders: Suppose χ satisfies GARP for *every* finite collection of price-income pairs and the corresponding levels of demand. Is this sufficient to know that there is some underlying continuous and locally insatiable utility function that generates these demands? Please note: this is more of theoretical than practical interest, because checking that there are no violations of GARP for every finite collection of price-income pairs and the corresponding demands is utterly impractical. Compare this task with checking (presumably, algebraically) that χ is homogeneous of degree 0, satisfies Walras' Law, and has a negative semi-definite and symmetric Slutsky Matrix; the latter is something one could contemplate doing, given an algebraic specification of χ. But even if impractical, the question is of theoretical interest, since it unifies the two approaches.

Indeed, this is close to a fundamental—perhaps *the* fundamental—question in the historical development of the theory of the consumer. Why "close to"? GARP is based on the underlying maintained hypothesis that preferences must be locally insatiable. The historical developments referred to rely instead on an underlying maintained hypothesis that preferences give a unique solution to the CP for each p and y. Hence some constructions from Chapter 4 are modified:

> *If x is demanded at prices p with income y, say that x is* ***directly revealed as strictly preferred to*** *x', written $x \succ^d x'$, if $p \cdot x' \leq y$ and $x' \neq x$.*

The (alleged) demand function χ satisfies the ***Weak Axiom of Revealed Preference (WARP)*** *if $p \cdot \chi(p', y') \leq y$ and $\chi(p', y') \neq \chi(p, y)$ implies $p' \cdot \chi(p, y) > y'$.* (Restating this: if $p \cdot \chi(p', y') \leq y$, then $\chi(p', y')$ is affordable when prices are p and y. If, in addition $\chi(p, y) \neq \chi(p', y')$, then $\chi(p', y')$ is not chosen at p and y, and so must be strictly worse than $\chi(p, y)$ or, $\chi(p, y) \succ^d \chi(p', y')$, and so $\chi(p, y)$ must not be affordable at p' and y', or $p' \cdot \chi(p, y) > y'$. Or we can restate this as, if $\chi(p, y) \succ^d \chi(p', y')$, then it cannot be that $\chi(p', y') \succ^d \chi(p, y)$.)

The (alleged) demand function χ satisfies the ***Strong Axiom of Revealed Preference (SARP)*** *if for every finite collection of price-income pairs $\{(p^i, y^i); i = 1, \ldots, I\}$, such that $\chi(p^{i+1}, y^{i+1}) \succ^d \chi(p^i, y^i)$ for $i = 1, \ldots, I-1$, it is not true that $\chi(p^1, y^1) \succ^d \chi(p^I, y^I)$.* (Obviously, WARP is a special case of SARP.)

The questions to be answered are: How do WARP and SARP connect with the existence of a utility-maximizing consumer (with preferences that generate unique solutions to the CP)? How do they connection with the conditions in the Integrability Theorem?

At the risk (indeed, I fear, the certainty) of angering colleagues who are scandalized by its omission, I will not run these questions all the way down to definitive answers; the best results require some mathematical methods that outbid what I expect of readers of this book. But it is worthwhile to mention some of the easier bits of the theory:

- Walras' Law is not implied by SARP: Imagine strictly convex preferences with a global satiation point x^*; for any p and y such that $p \cdot x^* < y$, demand will be x^* and Walras' Law will fail. But if preferences are strictly convex, solutions to the CP are unique for all p and y, and (obviously) SARP holds. We can fix this by weakening the definition of $\succ^d$ to read: If x is demanded at p and y and *either* $p \cdot x' \leq y$ and $x' \neq x$ *or* $p \cdot x' < y$, then $x \succ^d x'$. Or we can simply add Walras' Law as a basic assumption about the demand function χ.

- If for some $\lambda > 0$, p, and y, we find that $\chi(p, y) \neq \chi(\lambda p, \lambda y)$—that is, if χ fails to be homogeneous of degree 0—then SARP is violated: Since $p \cdot \chi(p, y) \leq y$, $\lambda p \cdot \chi(p, y) \leq \lambda y$, so under the hypothesis that $\chi(p, y) \neq \chi(\lambda p, \lambda y)$, $\chi(\lambda p, \lambda y) \succ^d \chi(p, y)$. By a similar argument, $\chi(p, y) \succ^d \chi(\lambda p, \lambda y)$. This gives a $\succ^d$ cycle.

- If differentiable χ satisfies Walras' Law and is homogeneous of degree 0, then satisfaction of WARP implies that the Slutsky Matrix for x is negative semi-definite (at least, away from any boundaries). The argument, which I'll give a bit informally, has two steps. Throughout, we assume that χ satisfies Walras' Law, is homogeneous of degree 0 and differentiable, and satisfies WARP.

  First, fix any p and y, and let $x = \chi(p, y)$. Take any other price vector p', and let $y' = p' \cdot x$ and $x' = \chi(p'.y')$. Then

$$\begin{aligned}(p' - p) \cdot (x' - x) &= p \cdot x - p \cdot x' - p' \cdot x + p' \cdot x' \\ &= y - p \cdot x' - p' \cdot x + y' \\ &= y - p \cdot x' - p' \cdot x + p' \cdot x \\ &= y - p \cdot x' \leq 0,\end{aligned}$$

with a strict inequality at the end if $x \neq x'$. The first step is algebra, the second uses Walras' Law, the third uses the definition of y', and the final equality is just the cancellation of identical terms. As for $y \leq p \cdot x'$ with a strict inequality if $x \neq x'$, that is WARP: x' is demanded at p' and y' while x is affordable there (by construction), so $x' \succ^d x$. But then x', if it is not x, cannot be affordable at p and y.

Now again fix p and y, and let $x = \chi(p, y)$. Make a small change in prices, to $p' = p + dp$, and let $y' = p' \cdot x = (p + dp) \cdot x = y + dp \cdot x$. Let $x' = \chi(p + dp, y + dy)$. We know from the first step that $dp \cdot dx \leq 0$, where $dx = x' - x$. But, using Taylor's Theorem,

$$\begin{aligned}dx_j &= \sum_{i=1}^{k} \frac{\partial \chi_j}{\partial p_i} dp_i \ + \ \frac{\partial \chi_j}{\partial y} dy = \sum_{i=1}^{k} \frac{\partial \chi_j}{\partial p_i} dp_i \ + \ \frac{\partial \chi_j}{\partial y}(dp \cdot x) \\ &= \sum_{i=1}^{k} \left[\frac{\partial \chi_j}{\partial p_i} \ + \ \chi_i(p, y) \frac{\partial \chi_j}{\partial y} \right] dp_i.\end{aligned}$$

Hence $0 \geq dp \cdot dx = dp \cdot S \cdot dp$, where S is the Slutsky Matrix for χ. Since dp could have been taken in any direction, this shows that S is negative semi-definite.

That is the extent of the low-lying fruit on this topic. For the sake of completeness, let me give (but not prove) one result that connects SARP and the existence of a utility-maximizing consumer: *Suppose that every bundle $x \in R^k_+$ is demanded for some price-income pair; that is, $\{x \in R^k_+ : x = \chi(p, y)$ for some p and $y\} = R^k_+$. Suppose that χ satisfies Walras' Law and SARP. Then χ represents the utility-maximizing choices of a consumer, for some utility function.* This result is the corollary given by Richter (1966, p.641). For readers whose training in set theory is strong, I strongly recommend this article.

Bibliographic Notes

Roy's Identity is (first?) reported in Roy (1947). The earliest appearance of the Slutsky Equation that I have personally seen is in Samuelson's classic *Foundations of Economic Analysis* (1947); Samuelson in turn attributes this to Slutsky (1915).[3]

[3] If any reader can improve/correct this attempt at attribution, I'd be grateful.

As was the case last chapter, the material concerning the connections between utility functions and indirect utility functions comes from Krishna and Sonnenschein (1990) and Jackson (1986a).

The classic reference on integrability is Hurwicz and Uzawa (1971). I repeat my recommendations of Border (2004) and Jackson (1986b) for further discussion and detailed proofs.

I mentioned Richter (1966) as a good reference for chasing down revealed-preference approaches to the question *Is this alleged demand function really a demand function (does it arise from a utility-maximizing consumer)?*, as well as for related questions. The two classic references on the topic are Samuelson (1947) and Houthakker (1950).

Problems

■ *11.1. Suppose that $k = 3$ and $U(x_1, x_2, x_3) = \ln(x_1) + 3\ln(x_2) + \ln(x_3 + 10)$. Suppose that $p_1 = 1$, $p_2 = 2$, and $p_3 = 3$. At these prices, what is Marshallian demand as a function of y alone? What is the multiplier as a function of y? Verify mechanically Corollary 11.2 for these prices. (That is, compute ν, take its derivative in y, and compare with your earlier answer.)

■ 11.2. Proposition 11.1 (differentiability of the indirect utility function) leaves a few holes. Perhaps the most important is that we didn't give a result for differentiability of ν at (p^0, y^0) such that $y^0 = 0$. Please supply such a result (assume the CP has unique solutions in a relatively open neighborhood of (p^0, y^0), where $y^0 = 0$). Then, show by example that, if u is not differentiable, ν may not be differentiable in *either* p or y. (Hint: Work with $k = 1$.) Finally, we proved last chapter that the expenditure function is differentiable in p, for fixed v. Can you provide a result about differentiability in (p, v) jointly?

■ 11.3. Suppose that ν is continuously differentiable in p and y, and that $\partial\nu/\partial y > 0$ everywhere. (Assume that u is locally insatiable.) Prove directly that this implies that the expenditure function is continuously differentiable in p, using the Implicit-Function Theorem.

■ *11.4. Prove Proposition 11.9.

■ 11.5. You may think that Propositions 11.4 and 11.9 establish a one-to-one connection between a class of utility functions and a corresponding class of indirect utility functions, in the spirit of Proposition 10.17. But this is not true. I have omitted one or more important pieces of a full proof. (The propositions as stated are correct; I haven't lied to you. But the propositions miss one or more pieces of the puzzle. I did this intentionally so that, with this problem, I could force you to dig deeply into what the propositions say.) One thing that doesn't quite line up concerns the range of utility functions. But that is no more than a minor annoyance, easily repaired. Something else is missing. What is it? And can you fill in the missing piece of proof?

■ *11.6. Give and prove a result concerning differentiability of Hicksian demand. To do this, you must first explore the solution of the EMP using calculus, so there is a lot to do here.

■ 11.7. A particular consumer has Marshallian demand for two commodities given as follows

$$x_1(p_1, p_2, y) = \frac{y}{p_1 + 2p_2} \quad \text{and} \quad x_2(p_1, p_2, y) = \frac{2y}{p_1 + 2p_2}.$$

This is valid for all price and income levels that are strictly positive. This consumer assures me, by the way, that at prices (p_1, p_2) and income y, his Marshallian demand is strictly better for him than anything else he can afford.

Does this consumer conform to the model of the consumer we have created? That is, is there some set of preferences, given by a utility function, such that maximization of that utility subject to the budget constraint gives rise to this demand function?

If the answer to the first part of the question is yes, how much about the consumer's utility function and/or preferences can you tell me?

Chapter Twelve

Producer and Consumer Surplus

Most courses in microeconomics at some point engage in policy evaluation: What happens if the government taxes or subsidizes the sale of some good? What happens if a price ceiling or a price floor is established? What if imports into a particular domestic market are capped at some level?

The discussion of "what happens?" can begin and end with an analysis of changes in prices and quantities. But when it comes to evaluation, one typically seeks dollar-denominated measures of the impact such policies have on firms inside the industry and on consumers of the specific product. The concepts of *producer* and *consumer surplus* appear at this point; the former is advanced as a dollar-denominated measure of the impact the policy has on producers; the latter is asserted to be a dollar-denominated measure of its impact on consumers. These concepts are defined graphically, by pictures such as Figures 12.1a and b. In this chapter, we explore the foundations of these two concepts.

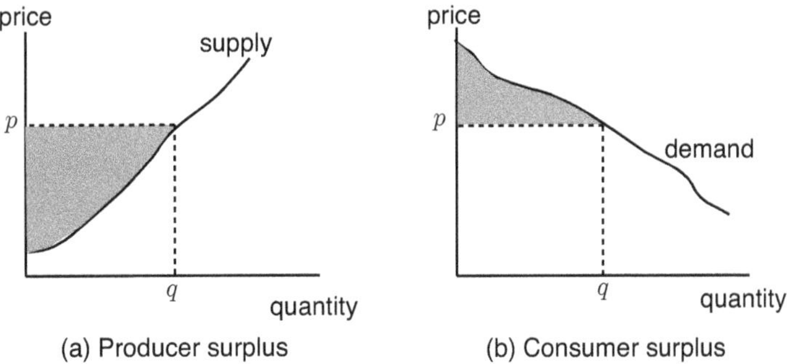

Figure 12.1. Producer and consumer surplus. Intermediate-level textbooks in microeconomics often have the pictures shown here, accompanied by text such as "The shaded region in panel a is producer surplus, a dollar-denominated measure of the value producers obtain from this market. The shaded region in panel b is consumer surplus, a dollar-denominated measure of the value obtained by consumers." The objective of this chapter is to make these notions as precise as we can.

12.1. Producer Surplus

Producer surplus has a relatively simple story, although one with a hidden trap. The story concerns the market for a particular good supplied by a number F of firms. We assume that the firms are all competitive, engaged in profit maximization in the sense and style of Chapter 9; Z^f will denote the production-possibility set of firm f. We let $p \in R^k_{++}$ be the vector of all prices, and we will suppose that coordinate indices have been chosen so that $i = 1$ is the index of the good that interests us.

Throughout this discussion, the following assumption is maintained.

Assumption 12.1. *For each firm f, Z^f is closed, nonempty, and satisfies the recession-cone property of Chapter 9.*

Upward-sloping supply

The first step is to construct a supply "curve" for this good. Fixing the prices of all other goods at $(\cdot, p_2, p_3, \ldots, p_k)$, we ask how much output will the firms in the industry produce as a function of the price p_1 of the one output good. Let $Z^{f*}(p_1)$ be the set of optimal netput vectors for firm f if the price of good 1 is p_1 and the price of all other goods is given by $(\cdot, p_2, p_3, \ldots, p_k)$. (I should indicate the dependence of $Z^{f*}(p_1)$ on those fixed other prices, but do not do so to keep the notation tidy. All prices except for p_1 are firmly fixed throughout the discussion of this section, unless and until I say otherwise.) And let Z^* denote the "full-industry optimal-netput set," or

$$Z^*(p_1) := \{z \in R^k : z = z^1 + \ldots + z^F, \text{ where } z^f \in Z^{f*}(p^1) \text{ for each } f = 1, \ldots, F\}.$$

The *individual-firm-f supply correspondence*, $p_1 \rightrightarrows Z_1^{f*}(p_1)$, is the projection along the first coordinate of Z^{f*} as p_1 varies—that is, $z_1 \in Z_1^{f*}(p_1)$ if there is some $z \in Z^{f*}(p_1)$ whose first coordinate is z_1—with the *industry-wide supply correspondence*, $p_1 \rightrightarrows Z_1^*(p_1)$ defined similarly.

In undergraduate-level textbooks on microeconomics, one finds supply functions, not supply correspondences. And the supply functions are always upward sloping. We'll keep the generality of correspondences: At some levels of p_1, individual firms (and hence the industry) may have several levels of output that are each part of (distinct) profit-maximizing netput vectors. But Corollary 9.13 ensures that supply, at both the individual-firm and the industry levels, is "upward sloping."

Proposition 12.2. *Suppose that $\hat{p}_1 > \check{p}_1$. If $\hat{z}_1^f \in Z_1^{f*}(\hat{p}_1)$ and $\check{z}_1^f \in Z_1^{f*}(\check{p}_1)$ for firm f, then $\hat{z}_1^f \geq \check{z}_1^f$. If $\hat{z}_1 \in Z_1^*(\hat{p}_1)$ and $\check{z}_1 \in Z_1^*(\check{p}_1)$, then $\hat{z}_1 \geq \check{z}_1$.*

Proof. The first part of this proposition simply restates Corollary 9.13: For a competitive, profit-maximizing firm, a rise in the price of good i with no change in any other price never leads to a "fall" in the level of good i. The scare quotes are there for the case where good i is an input: Then the corollary tells us that the profit-maxizing level of good i does not decrease, which is to say becomes no more negative, which is to say that the amount of the input used, measured as a positive quantity, does not *increase*. But in the current context, we're speaking of an output, and in that context the scare quotes are unnecessary: If the price of output good i rises, the level of output of good i (in any profit-maximizing plans for the two price vectors) does not fall.

The second part of the proposition follows very easily. Suppose $\hat{z}_1 \in Z_1^*(\hat{p}_1)$ and $\check{z}_1 \in Z_1^*(\check{p}_1)$. Then $\hat{z}_1 = \hat{z}_1^1 + \ldots + \hat{z}_1^F$, where each $\hat{z}_1^f \in Z_1^{f*}(\hat{p}_1)$, and $\check{z}_1 = \check{z}_1^1 + \ldots + \check{z}_1^F$, where each $\check{z}_1^f \in Z_1^{f*}(\check{p}_1)$. Then, because $\hat{z}_1^f \geq \check{z}_1^f$ for each f by the first part of the proposition (by Corollary 9.13), the same is true of the respective sums. ∎

It may be gilding the lily, but I want to reinforce the message of Proposition 12.2 with a picture. This picture shows what can (and cannot) happen in either $Z_1^{f*}(\cdot)$ or $Z_1^*(\cdot)$. Please recall that the variable p_1, the price of the good in question, is on the vertical axis, so you may want to tilt your head to the side as you look at this.

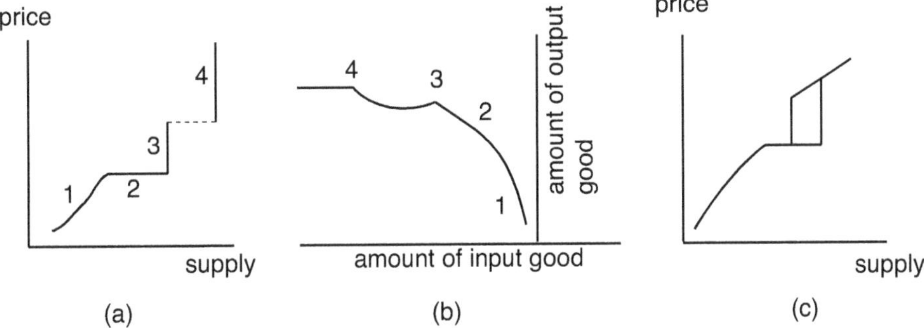

Figure 12.2. The geometry of supply. Panel a shows a supply correspondence and panel b the "northeast" frontier of the corresponding production-possibility set. Supply increases continuously if the frontier of Z is strictly concave, as in the regions marked by 1. Supply is is multivalued and "filled in" where the frontier of Z is flat; see the regions marked by 2. Where there are kinks in the frontier of Z, supply can be constant for a range of prices, and supply can by multivalued and discrete where the frontier "caves in"; points 3 and 4 mark kinks in the frontier of Z, while the region between them is a "cave in" or nonconvexity in Z. (For you to know that there is a kink at 3, you must convexify Z by drawing the line segment from 3 to 4 and see that the kink remains in the frontier of the convex hull.) Finally, panel c shows what cannot happen—there cannot be prices $\hat{p}_1 > \check{p}_1$ where the largest supply of output at $\check{p}_1$ exceeds the smallest supply of output at $\hat{p}_1$.

The legend of Figure 12.2 explains what is going on, but to reiterate: Panels a and b depict four possible shapes for a supply correspondence and the corresponding shapes of the underlying production-possibility set Z.[1] Where Z is strictly convex along its frontier, supply is singleton valued and rising; see the areas labeled 1 in the two panels. Where Z is flat, supply is multivalued and, moreover, all supply levels over an interval are in the supply correspondence; see the segments marked 2. Supply is constant over a range of prices where the set Z is kinked; see the point 3 on Z (in panel b) and the corresponding flat region 3 of supply in

[1] Panel a could be the supply correspondence of a single firm—that is, a Z_1^{f*}—and it could be the industry or aggregate supply correspondence, denoted Z_1^*. But once we introduce panel b and the production-possibility set Z, we seem to be speaking of a single firm. This isn't really so; for a given set of firms, we can speak of their aggregate production-possibility set. But we won't meet this concept until next chapter, when we discuss aggregation in more detail.

panel a. (Because the independent variable in panel a is price, "flat" means vertical. Also, the kink at point 3 in panel b is really only a kink in this sense if it remains a kink when we look at the convex hull of Z. In the figure, this happens.) Finally, the supply correspondence at the price for good 1 that spans the nonconvexity of Z between points 3 and 4 is multivalued, consisting of the two endpoints of the interval (only). In general, this happens whenever there are nonconvexities in the frontier of Z, even without the kinks.

We see, therefore, a fairly rich set of possibilities for supply correpondences. But what we can never see is the picture in panel c. The proposition tells us that while supply can be multivalued, the supply offered at two different prices $\hat{p}_1$ and $\check{p}_1$ can overlap at one level at most; if $\hat{p}_1 > \check{p}_1$, then the largest supply at $\check{p}_1$ can at most equal the smallest supply at $\hat{p}_1$; no other overlap is possible. And, moreover, if this happens, that common value is the *only* possible supply level at prices between $\check{p}_1$ and $\hat{p}_1$.

Supply and the profit function

Recall Proposition 9.22. The profit function π^f for firm f is differentiable at the price vector p^0 if and only if the firm's profit-maximization problem has a unique solution at p^0, in which case that unique solution is the gradient (derivative) of π^f. In this chapter, our concern is not with the full function π^f, because we are fixing all prices except for the price of the output good, indexed by $i = 1$. In this context, we have the following result:

Proposition 12.3. *Fix prices for all goods except the first at levels $p_2, p_3, \ldots, p_k$ and, for a given firm f, consider the function*

$$p_1 \rightarrow \pi^f(p_1, p_2, \ldots, p_k).$$

This function (of one variable) is differentiable at the price level p_1^0 if $Z_1^{f*}(p_1)$ is singleton at p_1^0, in which case the derivative is the unique $z_1 \in Z_1^{f*}(p_1^0)$.

We are only giving a one-directional implication (uniqueness of the output level of the firm implies differentiability in the price of the output) because, for our purposes, that is all we need. But if you want to be fastidious, you might want to answer the question, If π^f is differentiable in p_1 at the level p_1^0, does this imply that $Z_1^{f*}(p_1^0)$ is singleton? (Answer: Yes. So the task for the fastidious is to give the argument that shows this.)

Proof. The proof essentially mimics the proof provided for Proposition 9.22. Suppose $Z_1^{f*}(p_1^0)$ is singleton, with z_1 its single member. We must show that

$$\lim_{n \to \infty} \frac{\pi^f(p_1^n, p_2, \ldots, p_k) - \pi^f(p_1^0, p_2, \ldots, p_k) - (p_1^n - p_1^0)z_1}{|p_1^n - p_1^0|} = 0,$$

for every sequence of strictly positive prices for good 1, $\{p_1^n\}$, that has limit p_1^0 and such that $p_1^n \neq p_1^0$ for all n. We show this by the usual argument that, along every such sequence $\{p_1^n\}$, we have zero as a limit of the displayed fraction along some subsequence.

Fix a sequence $\{p_1^n\}$ (with $p_1^n \neq p_1^0$ for all n). Use p^n as shorthand for $(p_1^n, p_2, \ldots, p_k)$ (including for $n = 0$). Let z^n be any point selected out of $Z^{f*}(p^n)$. Since $\lim_{n\to\infty} p^n = p^0$ and the recession-cone property holds, we know that the z^n live in a compact set; looking along a subsequence, we can assume that $\lim_{n\to\infty} z^n$ exists and equals some z^0. Of course, by Berge's Theorem, $z^0 \in Z^{f*}(p^0)$, and so $z_1^0 = z_1$.

Because z^n is a profit maximizer for p^n and z^0 is a profit maximizer for p^0,

$$p^n \cdot z^n \geq p^n \cdot z^0 \quad \text{and} \quad p^0 \cdot z^0 \geq p^0 \cdot z^n.$$

Therefore,

$$p^n \cdot z^n - p^0 \cdot z^n \geq p^n \cdot z^n - p^0 \cdot z^0 = \pi^f(p^n) - \pi^f(p^0) \geq p^n \cdot z^0 - p^0 \cdot z^0.$$

But since all prices in each p^n are the same as the prices in p^0 except for the first, the first and last terms in this string of inequalities simplify, and we get

$$(p_1^n - p_1^0)z_1^n \geq \pi^f(p^n) - \pi^f(p^0) \geq (p_1^n - p_1^0)z_1^0.$$

Subtract $(p_1^n - p_1^0)z_1^0 = (p_1^n - p_1^0)z_1$ from each term and then divide by $|p_1^n - p_1^0|$ to get

$$\frac{(p_1^n - p_1^0)(z_1^n - z_1^0)}{|p_1^n - p_1^0|} \geq \frac{\pi^f(p^n) - \pi^f(p^0) - (p_1^n - p_1^0)z_1}{|p_1^n - p_1^0|} \geq 0.$$

The first term goes to zero as n goes to infinity, because $(p_1^n - p_1^0)/|p_1^n - p_1^0|$ is bounded by 1, while $\lim_n(z_1^n - z_1^0) = 0$ by construction. Therefore, the second term has limit zero as well. ∎

So, given the supply correspondence of a firm, what does its profit function (as a function of the output price alone, fixing all other prices) look like? The profit function is convex (we didn't need Proposition 12.3 to know that), and it is differentiable at any price where the supply correspondence of the firm is singleton. Since the supply correspondence is nondecreasing (in the strong sense of Proposition 12.2), the points of nondifferentiability of π^f are at most countable in number. (Wherever the supply correspondence is more than singleton, supply must span an interval of strictly positive length. The interiors of these intervals cannot overlap, and each contains a rational value. But there are only countably many rationals.) And except for those (at most) countable number of prices, the (single) level of supply at any price is the derivative of the profit function. The Fundamental Theorem of Calculus tells us the following:

Corollary 12.4. *Fix a firm f and prices for all goods except the first at levels $p_2, \ldots, p_k$. For any two prices for the first good, p_1' and p_1'',*

$$\pi^f(p_1', p_2, \ldots, p_k) - \pi^f(p_1'', p_2, \ldots, p_k) = \int_{p_1''}^{p_1'} z_1^{f*}(p_1)\, dp_1,$$

where $z_1^{f*}(p_1)$ is the supply of good 1 by firm f for prices p_1 such that the supply correspondence is singleton, and where it doesn't matter what you take for the integrand at prices where supply isn't singleton, because there are at most a countable number of those.

Because π can be nondifferentiable at countably many points (which could, in principle, be dense in any interval), this is not the plain-vanilla Fundamental Theorem of Calculus. But it is still true. The function π is convex; hence is it absolutely continuous. And absolutely continuous functions are the integrals of their (existing-almost-everywhere) derivatives. For details, see Royden (1968).[2]

Producer surplus

And except for some warnings to be supplied momentarily, that's all there is to producer surplus. Let me abuse notation and write $z_1^*(p_1)$ for the "industry supply function" of our good. The scare quotes around *industry supply function* are there because, at some prices, one or more firms might be willing to supply multiple quantities; at those prices, $z_1^*(p_1)$ is not well defined. But there are at most a countable number of such prices (finitely many firms, and a countable number of such prices for each firm), and I'll worry about them in a bit. *Producer surplus,* per most textbooks, is the *area "under" the industry supply curve,* where the scare quotes around *under* signify that economists typically graph supply with the independent variable price on the vertical axis, so *under* here really means, *to the left of.* The starting and ending points for this "area under the curve" also aren't so clear, but when it comes to application, economists are primarily concerned with changes in producer surplus. So let me give the following as a formal definition:

Definition 12.5. *Fixing all prices except for the price p_1 of some specific good, the supply "function" of which is given by $z_1^*(p_1)$, the* **change in producer surplus** *when the price of the good shifts from p_1^o to p_1^n is*

$$\int_{p_1^o}^{p_1^n} z_1^*(p_1) dp_1.$$

The superscripts n and o are mnemonics for *new* and *old*. Of course, in this integral, if price p_1^o exceeds that of p_1^n, you should understand this integral as being the negative of the integral with the upper limit being the higher price. What about

[2] I have the second edition of Royden, in which these results appear in Chapter 5, sections 4 and 5.

values of p_1 for which $z_1^*(p_1)$ is not well defined? Since there are at most a countable number of such values, they don't affect the integral. And we have:

Corollary 12.6. *The change in producer surplus is the sum of the changes in the profits of the firms that supply this good, resulting from the change in prices.*

Proof. Let $f = 1, \ldots, F$ ennumerate the firms that make up this industry, so that $z_1^*(p_1) = \sum_f z_1^{f*}(p_1)$, where $z_1^{f*}(p_1)$ is the unique supply by firm f at price p_1, for all points p_1 where Z_1^{f*} is singleton. (We don't worry about z_1^* at prices where one or more firms have nonsingleton Z_1^{f*}, as they don't affect the value of the integral.) Therefore, the change in producer surplus when price changes from p_1^o to p_1^n is

$$\int_{p_1^o}^{p_1^n} z_1^*(p_1)dp_1 = \int_{p_1^o}^{p_1^n} \left[\sum_{f=1}^{F} z_1^{f*}(p_1)\right] dp_1 = \sum_{f=1}^{F} \left[\int_{p_1^0}^{p_1^n} z_1^{f*}(p_1)\, dp_1\right],$$

and by Corollary 12.4, the terms being summed on the right-hand side are just the changes in the profits of the firms, firm by firm. ∎

Warning

The warning I've been threatening to give can now be given. In many applications of the concept of producer surplus, the "industry supply curve" is estimated empirically. You must be careful about this. Imagine an industry filled with small, price-taking firms. In particular, imagine that one of the inputs to the production process used by the firms in this industry is supplied by another industry, and the supply of that input is upward sloping. To be clear, no one firm in this industry buys enough of this input to affect its price materially, and so all firms in the industry have competitive conjectures about its price: They believe that they can buy as much as they want at whatever is the prevailing price, and they choose their production plans to be profit maximizing, based on that belief. But on an industry basis, this industry buys enough of this factor of production so that if the level of output in this industry changes, demand for the factor input will increase enough to drive up its price.

To compute the change in producer surplus, you are supposed to compute the area "under" the supply curve from the old to the new price of the output good. But in the situation I've described, there are two candidates for the industry supply curves. One, which might be called the empirical supply curve, takes into account the fact that, as the level of industry output rises, the price of the factor rises. The second, which can be called the notional supply curve, is just the sum of supplies by the individual firms, under the assumption that the price of this factor of production isn't going to change. It isn't hard to construct simple models of this situation where (as you might expect), the empirical supply curve responds less robustly to changes in the price of the output good than does the notional supply curve. They will certainly give different values for the change in producer surplus, as output prices change. If you go to the data, it is the empirical supply curve you will see. But in terms of the theory of producer surplus, if we are trying to measure the change in profits of firms in the industry as the result of changes in the price of the output good, it is the notional supply curve that gives the right answer. The key to producer surplus is Proposition 9.22 and its variants given here. This says "all other prices fixed." That's not what you get when you look at the empirical supply curve.

12.2. Consumer Surplus

While the story of producer surplus is nice, neat, and (relatively) simple, consumer surplus is trickier. In both cases, we are looking for a dollar-denominated measure of how firms supplying the good and consumers buying the good are affected by changes in the price of the good. For the profit-maximizing firms of this book, it is natural to measure this impact by the changes in their profit levels, which is what producer surplus does. But the welfare of consumers is measured in the first instance in utility. Unless there is a natural transformation from utility to dollars (which would happen, say, if utility were quasi-linear in money-left-over), it isn't clear how to proceed. That makes consumer surplus harder to pin down.

The compensating and equivalent variations

I will restrict attention in this discussion to the welfare impact on consumers of a change in the price they face for a given good, assuming they can (after the change in price) rearrange their consumption however they want, subject to their budget constraint, and assuming that the prices of all other goods stay the same. As with producer surplus, the good in question will be assumed to have index 1, its price will be denoted p_1, and the prices of all other goods will be fixed at $p_2, \ldots, p_k$. In parallel to Assumption 12.1, for the remainder of this section, I make the following assumption about all consumers.

Assumption 12.7. *Every consumer has continuous and locally insatiable utility.*

The question then is, What is the impact on a given consumer, whose income level is y, if the price of good 1 changes from p_1^o to p_1^n? In utility terms, we can talk about the consumer's levels of indirect utility $\nu(p_1^o, p_2, \ldots, p_k, y)$ and $\nu(p_1^n, p_2, \ldots, p_k, y)$. Let me denote the first utility level by v^o and the second by v^n. To measure the impact in dollars instead of utility, two measures of dollar compensation are employed.

Definition 12.8. *The* ***equivalent variation*** *is the amount of money* EV *that must be added to* y *so that the consumer is indifferent between having* y *at the new price* p_1^n *and* $y + \text{EV}$ *at the old price* p_1^o. *The* ***compensating variation*** *is the amount of money* CV *that must be subtracted from* y *so that the consumer is indifferent between having* y *at the old price* p_1^o *and* $y - \text{CV}$ *at the new price* p_1^n.[3]

[3] EV and CV are often defined more generally, for any pair of price vectors. But we will use them only for pairs of price vectors in which only one price changes.

Let me rephrase the definitions in terms of indirect utility. The equivalent variation EV is such that the consumer is equally well off with the new price and y, or with the old price and $y + \text{EV}$. In symbols,

$$\nu(p_1^n, p_2, \ldots, p_k, y) = \nu(p_1^o, p_2, \ldots, p_k, y + \text{EV}).$$

And the compensating variation CV is such that the consumer is equally well off with the new price and $y - \text{CV}$, or with y and the old price, which is

$$\nu(p_1^n, p_2, \ldots, p_k, y - \text{CV}) = \nu(p_1^o, p_2, \ldots, p_k, y).$$

The signs of CV and EV are designed to be positive when the change in price makes the consumer better off and negative when she is worse off. To see this, consider separately the cases $p_1^n > p_1^o$ and $p_1^n < p_1^o$.

- If $p_1^n < p_1^o$, then the consumer is presumably better off because the price of a consumption good has declined. (She is no worse off, certainly.) In this case, both the equivalent and compensating variations are positive: We know that $\nu(p_1^n, p_2, \ldots, p_k, y) \geq \nu(p_1^o, p_2, \ldots, p_k, y)$, so to increase the right-hand side up to the level of the left-hand side, we must *add* a positive amount to y on the right-hand side. And to get the left-hand side to decline to the level of the right-hand side, we must *subtract* a positive amount from y on the left-hand side. Going back to the definitions of EV and CV, this makes both positive (or, at least, nonnegative) numbers.
- On the other hand, if $p_1^n > p_1^o$, the change in prices makes the consumer somewhat worse off (or, at least, no better off). That is, $\nu(p_1^n, p_2, \ldots, p_k, y) \leq \nu(p_1^o, p_2, \ldots, p_k, y)$. To lower the right-hand side down to the level of the left-hand side, we must *add* a nonpositive amount to y on the right-hand side; to raise the left-hand side up to the level of the right-hand side, we must *subtract* a nonpositive amount from y on the left-hand side. That is, both variation measures are nonpositive.

In terms of our discussion of consumer surplus, the most useful equations that characterize the quantities EV and CV involve the expenditure function. I'll give these characterizations in the form of a proposition.

Proposition 12.9. *If v^o is the level of utility obtained by the consumer at the old prices, and v^n is the level of utility she obtains at the new prices, both with income y, then*

$$\text{EV} = e(p_1^o, p_2, \ldots, p_k, v^n) - e(p_1^n, p_2, \ldots, p_k, v^n), \quad \textit{and}$$
$$\text{CV} = e(p_1^o, p_2, \ldots, p_k, v^o) - e(p_1^n, p_2, \ldots, p_k, v^o).$$

Proof. To save space, I abbreviate $(p_1^o, p_2, \ldots, p^k)$ by p^o and $(p_1^n, p_2, \ldots, p_k)$ by p^n.
Then $e(p^n, v^n) = e(p^o, v^o) = y$, because v^n is the utility obtained at p^n with income y, and v^o is the utility obtained at p^o with that income. Furthermore,

$e(p^o, v^n)$ is the amount of income it takes to obtain v^n at the old prices. EV is defined to be the quantity such that, with income $y + \text{EV}$, the consumer can reach at the old prices the new level of utility, so

$$y + \text{EV} = e(p^o, v^n) \quad \text{or} \quad \text{EV} = e(p^o, v^n) - y = e(p^0, v^n) - e(p^n, v^n).$$

And $e(p^n, v^o)$ is the amount of money needed to attain utility v^o at the old prices, which is also $y - \text{CV}$, or

$$y - \text{CV} = e(p^n, v^o) \quad \text{or} \quad \text{CV} = y - e(p^n, v^0) = e(p^0, v^0) - e(p^n, v^0).$$

■

Hicksian demand, the expenditure function, EV, and CV

Having tied EV and CV to the expenditure function, the next step is to bring Hicksian demand into the mix. This step parallels Propositions 12.2 and 12.3 and Corollary 12.4; we collect the analogous results in a single proposition.

Proposition 12.10. *Fix all prices except for price of good 1 at levels $p_2, p_3, \ldots, p_k$, and, for a given consumer, fix a utility level v in the range of her utility function. Let $H_1(p_1)$ denote Hicksian demand for good 1 as a function of p_1, with p_2 through p_k and v fixed.*

a. *If $p_1' > p_1''$, $h_1' \in H_1(p_1')$, and $h_1'' \in H_1(p_1'')$, then $h_1' \leq h_1''$. In words, Hicksian demand for a good is "downward sloping" in its own price.*

b. *$H_1(p_1)$ is singleton for all but (at most) a countable number of prices p_1.*

c. *If $H_1(p_1^0)$ is a singleton set, then $p_1 \to e(p_1, p_2, \ldots, p_k, v)$ is differentiable in p_1 at p_1^0, and its derivative in p_1 is the single element h_1 of $H_1(p_1^0)$.*

d. *For two prices for good 1, p_1' and p_1'',*

$$e(p_1', p_2, \ldots, p_k, v) - e(p_1'', p_2, \ldots, p_k, v) = \int_{p_1''}^{p_1'} h_1(p_1)\, dp_1,$$

where $h_1(p_1)$ denotes the single element of $H_1(p_1)$ for all values p_1 at which $H_1(p_1)$ is singleton, and is defined arbitrarily (say, as some value in $H_1(p_1)$) at the countable number of prices where it is not singleton.

I will leave all parts of this for you to prove. You can virtually copy the arguments from Section 12.1. (For part a, there is no parallel result in Chapter 10 to Corollary 9.13, so you must prove it from first principles.)

Combining Propositions 12.9 and 12.10d gives us the following corollary.

Corollary 12.11. *Fix some consumer and a single good that the consumer demands. For convenience, label the good with index 1. Suppose that the consumer, at prices $p^o = (p_1^0, p_2, \ldots, p_k)$ and income y, has indirect utility $v^0 = \nu(p^0, y)$. Suppose that the price of good 1 changes to p_1^n, while the other prices all stay at their old levels; write $p^n =$*

$(p_1^n, p_2, \ldots, p_k)$, and let $v^n = \nu(p^n, y)$. Then if EV *is the equivalent variation for this change in prices (at the income level y), for this consumer, and* CV *is the compensating variation, we have*

$$\mathrm{EV} = \int_{p_1^n}^{p_1^o} h_1((p_1, p_2, \ldots, p_k), v^n)\, dp_1, \text{ and} \tag{12.1a}$$

$$\mathrm{CV} = \int_{p_1^n}^{p_1^o} h_1((p_1, p_2, \ldots, p_k), v^o)\, dp_1, \tag{12.1b}$$

where h_1 denotes Hicksian demand for good 1, which is single valued for all but (at most) a countable number of values of p_1.

Consumer surplus for one consumer, EV, and CV

This corollary is enticingly close to what we are after, if we agree that CV and EV are reasonable measures of the dollar-denominated change in the consumer's welfare, caused by the change in price of the good, and if, in constructing consumer surplus, we are allowed to use Hicksian demand functions rather than Marshallian demand functions.

Of course, since $h(\cdot, v^o)$ will, in general, be different from $h(\cdot, v^n)$, the corollary tells us something that you probably already realized: In general, the compensating and equivalent variations will be different. But if the change in the price of good 1 is small enough so that v^o and v^n are near to one another, and if (in consequence) $h(\cdot, v^o)$ and $h(\cdot, v^n)$ are close to one another (when evaluated at the same price arguments), then CV will be close to EV, and the consumer-surplus integral, evaluated using Hicksian demand instead of Marshallian demand, has a clear and pertinent interpretation.

And, to the extent that Marshallian demand for good 1, which I'll write in shorthand as $d_1(p_1)$, is approximately the same as Hicksian demand, then EV and CV are both approximately the same as the integral that conventionally defines "the change in consumer surplus" resulting from a change in the price of good 1.

The previous paragraph should set off a number of alarm bells:

- For one thing, Marshallian demand for good 1 is a function of the price of good 1, and also the prices of all other goods and income. So when I say that I write Marshallian demand for good 1 as $d_1(p_1)$, it is implicit (and now explicit) that I mean the function $p_1 \to d_1((p_1, p_2, \ldots, p_k), y)$, with those other arguments held fixed.

- And I (as yet) have no right to talk about a Marshallian demand *function*. Marshallian demand can be multivalued. Of course, the same is true of Hicksian demand. But what saves me in the case of Hicksian demand is that I know that if I vary p_1 over some interval p_1^o to p_1^n, where the other prices and the target utility level are fixed, Hicksian demand is multivalued at no more than a countable number of points. (If this statement confuses you, go back and reread the previous proposition.) I know this because the expenditure function is concave in price, and Hicksian demand provides supergradients of the expenditure function. No similar result holds for Marshallian demand. In fact, one can provide examples in which Marshallian demand for a good consists of an interval of values as the price of that good varies, for every price of the good in an interval of values. (See Problem 12.4.)

- This unhappy possibility (Marshallian demand is multivalued for every price between p_1^o and p_1^n, fixing all other prices and income) presents a formidable challenge for how we will formalize the conventional definition of *the change in consumer surplus* for this price change. The conventional definition involves the integral under (to the left of) the demand function for the good; what do we do when there is an interval of possible values to pick for the level of demand, for every price of the good?
- What does *Marshallian demand is approximately the same as Hicksian demand* mean? On the one hand, as long as the underlying preferences are locally insatiable (an assumption we maintain throughout), Proposition 10.18 seems to say that Marshallian demand is exactly the same as Hicksian demand. On the other hand, the arguments of Marshallian demand and Hicksian demand are different: Both are functions of the vector of prices, but Marshallian demand has income y as an argument, while Hicksian demand is a function of a target level of utility.

We can clear up at least the last of these possible confusions/complications: Supposing for the moment that Marshallian demand is a function, and writing it a bit less compactly as $d_1((p_1, p_2, \ldots, p_k), y)$, the conventional definition of the change in consumer surplus is

$$\int_{p_1^n}^{p_1^o} d_1((p_1, p_2, \ldots, p_k), y)\, dp_1. \tag{12.2}$$

Corollary 12.11 tells us that EV and CV are, respectively, similar integrals, but with respective integrands $h_1((p_1, p_2, \ldots, p_k), v^n)$ and $h_1((p_1, p_2, \ldots, p_k), v^0)$. Proposition 10.18 establishes that

$$d_1((p_1^n, p_2, \ldots, p_k), y) = h_1((p_1^n, p_2, \ldots, p_k), v^n),$$

but at arguments p_1 other than p_1^n, they aren't the same; instead what is true is that

$$d_1((p_1, p_2, \ldots, p_k), y) = h_1((p_1, p_2, \ldots, p_k), \nu((p_1, \ldots, p_n), y)),$$

so that when p_1 reaches the upper limit of the integral p_1^o, d_1 is the same as h_1 with target level of utility v^o. *In the integral that conventionally defines consumer surplus, (12.2), the integrand is the same as the integrand in (12.1a) (which gives* EV*) at the lower limit of the integral, but the integrands (presumably) move apart as we move toward the upper limit of the integral. And the integrands in (12.1b) (which gives* CV*) and (12.2) are* *the same at the upper limit of the integral, but are otherwise different.* The hope is that the divergence in integrands is not too large, so the integrals are approximately the same; indeed, to the extent that we don't have a particular reason to choose EV or CV as the appropriate measure of compensation, we'd like their integrands to be close together, so that if EV and CV are not the same, at least they are close to one another.

The obvious (and more difficult) thing to do at this point is to try to construct measures of how far apart the three integrands are from one another, based on underlying properties of the consumer's preferences. This line of attack is undertaken, for instance, in Willig (1976). We'll settle here for something much easier: Since we know that the integrand in (12.2) agrees with the integrand in (12.1a) on one endpoint of the integral and with the integrand in (12.1b) on the other end, we'll develop conditions under which, at all intermediate values, the integrand in (12.2) lies *between* the other two.

Before doing so, we must first confront the problem of multivalued Marshallian demand. In fact, confront is the wrong word; we simply assume the problem away:

Assumption 12.12. *For all values of prices, incomes, and target utility levels that are relevant (that appear in any of our integrals), Marshallian demand for good 1 (hence Hicksian demand for good 1) is single valued.*

An excuse for this assumption is that, in every application of consumer surplus of which I am aware, demand is single valued. Be that as it may, the assumption permits the next definition, which is key to the line of attack we will follow.

Let d_1 denote the (single-valued) Marshallian demand for good 1, and h_1 the corresponding Hicksian demand. Prices for all goods except good 1 are fixed throughout, so I suppress those arguments in d_1 and h_1. But I will want to vary the price of good 1, the consumer's income y, and the target utility level v, so I write things such as $d_1(p_1, y)$ and $h_1(p_1, v)$.

Definition 12.13. *For a region of prices, income levels, and utility levels: Good 1 is* ***normal*** *over the region if $d_1(p_1, y)$ is nondecreasing in y over that region, and it is* ***inferior*** *if $d_1(p_1, y)$ is nonincreasing in y (in both cases, for all values of p_1 in the region). Good 1 is* ***Hicks-normal*** *over the region if $h_1(p_1, v)$ is nondecreasing in v, and it is* ***Hicks-inferior*** *if $h_1(p_1, v)$ is nonincreasing in v (again, for all p_1).*

I am not being very precise with the qualifying phrase "over the region," but the idea is that, when we need these concepts, we won't need them to hold universally (for all prices, income levels, and utility levels), but only for prices, incomes, and utility levels in certain ranges. Indeed, the way this definition is rendered makes it impossible for a good to be inferior globally unless it is never consumed, since (obviously) $d_1(p_1, 0) = h_1(p_1, u(0)) = 0$.

Note that, according to this definition, if demand for a good is constant in y (or v), at least for some range of prices, income levels, and utility levels, then the good is said to be both normal and inferior (over those ranges). The more common expression in economese (the informal language of economists) is that demand for this good exhibits no income effects.

Lemma 12.14. *Good 1 is normal over a region of prices and incomes if and only if it is Hicks-normal over the corresponding region of prices and utility levels, and it is inferior if and only if it is Hicks-inferior.*

Proof.[4] Suppose $y > y'$. Fixing prices at p, let $v = \nu(p, y)$ and $v' = \nu(p, y')$. By local insatiability, $v > v'$. And then $d_1(p_1, y) \geq$ [resp., $\leq$] $d_1(p_1, y)$ if and only $h_1(p_1, v) \geq$ [resp., $\leq$] $h_1(p_1, v')$. So if good 1 is normal, it is Hicks-normal; and if it is inferior, it is Hicks-inferior. For the converse half, repeat the argument, noting that if $v > v'$ and we let $y = e(p, v)$ and $y' = e(p, v')$, then since e is strictly increasing in v, $y > y'$. ∎

Proposition 12.15. *Write ΔCS for the value of the integral defined in (12.2); that is, ΔCS is the change in consumer surplus, conventionally defined. Then if good 1 is (Hicks-) normal for prices of good 1 from p_1^o to p_1^n and target utility levels v^o to v^n,* EV $\geq \Delta$CS $\geq$ CV. *And if good 1 is (Hicks-) inferior over this range of prices and target utility levels, then* EV $\leq \Delta$CS $\leq$ CV.

Proof. The proof is almost obvious at this point (and can be rendered in a picture, Figure 12.3.) Suppose the good is normal and that $p_1^o > p_1^n$. This implies that $v^o \leq v^n$. Moreover, for every value of p_1 between p_1^o and p_1^n, the corresponding indirect utility at income level y satisfies $v^0 \leq \nu((p_1, p_2, \ldots, p_k), y) \leq v^n$. Therefore, since good 1 is normal,

$$h_1(p_1, v^n) \geq h_1(p_1, \nu((p_1, \ldots, p_k), y) = d_1(p_1, y) \geq h_1(p_1, v^0).$$

The integrand in (12.1a) is greater than or equal to the integrand in (12.2), which is greater than or equal to the integrand in (12.1b), and so the integrals inherit those inequalities.

On the other hand, if $p_1^o < p_1^n$ and good 1 is normal, these inequalities all flip, but also the integral's upper limit is less than its lower limit, which again reverses the sign, so the integrals keep this ordering. (Figure 12.3 is drawn to cover this case.) And the cases where the good is inferior reverse the inequalities. ∎

It is worth observing that, for normal goods, Marshallian demand is steeper (has a more negative slope) than Hicksian demand, assuming that these demand functions are all differentiable, so that we can speak of slope at all. But if we were willing to assume that the functions were differentiable, we'd get the picture of Figure 12.3 via the Slutsky equation, adapted to this context:

$$\frac{\partial x_1}{\partial p_1} = \frac{\partial h_1}{\partial p_1} - x_1 \frac{\partial x_1}{\partial y}.$$

[4] You were asked to prove this, more or less, in Problem 10.7.

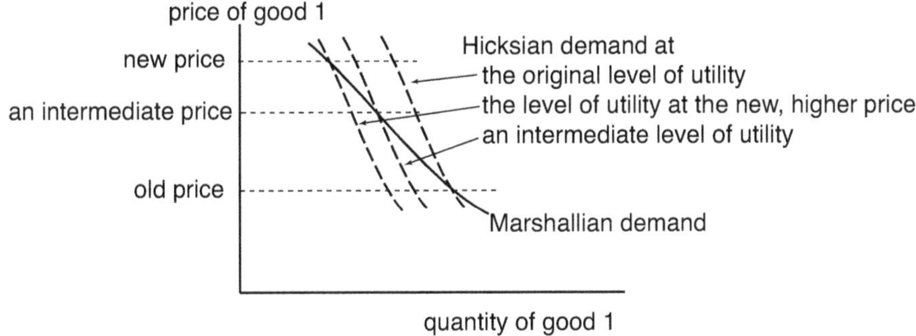

Figure 12.3. Consumer surplus and the equivalent and compensating variations. If the price of the good rises, the consumer's utility falls. For a normal good, this means the corresponding Hicksian demand functions, at the original price, at the new price, and at prices between the two, are arranged as shown. And so, in particular, Marshallian demand lies above new-utility Hicksian demand and below old-utility Hicksian demand. Hence the change in consumer surplus, the integral to the left of Marshallian demand, is greater (negative) than the intergral to the left of new-utility Hicksian demand, which is the change in expenditure at the new utility level, which is EV, and it is less negative than the integral to the left of old-utility Hicksian demand, which is the change of expenditure at the old utility level, which is CV.

We know that Hicksian demand is downward sloping, and if demand for the good is normal, the income effect term is a minus sign in front of a positive quantity, so the slope of Marshallian demand in own-price is even more negative than that of Hicksian demand.

The derivation we've supplied is more general than this Slutsky-equation-based argument, because we didn't make assumptions about the differentiability of our demand functions. I remind you, however, that we did need to assume that Marshallian demand (in the correspondence sense) is singleton valued (and, therefore, so is Hicksian demand). Can we do without this? We know that Hicksian demand is multivalued (for a given utility level) at no more than a countable number of prices, so the integrals that produce EV and CV are perfectly well defined, even if Hicksian demand is not singleton valued. You might hope for something like: *As long as a Marshallian demand function is selected from the Marshallian demand correspondence, however it is selected, the change in consumer surplus defined from the selected demand function lies between CV and EV.* To do this, though, we need to know that the selected demand function lies between the two Hicksian demand functions (for the old and new utility levels). And while the number of prices at which Hicksian demand can be multivalued for a given utility level is countable, the number of income levels for which it can be multivalued, fixing prices, can be a good deal larger. Depending on how you define a normal good (or an inferior good) for multivalued demand correpondences, results can be obtained. But those definitions become crucial. (And I leave you to it, if you are interested.)

Consumer surplus for multiple consumers

Our final task is to move from one consumer to an entire marketplace of consumers. But this is easy. Market demand is just the sum of demands coming from individual consumers. The change in consumer surplus is the integral "under" the market demand function, so if you interchange the summation and integration, you find that the change in aggregate (market) consumer surplus is just the sum of changes in individual-consumer consumer surplus. And each of those is a compromise between the two measures of appropriate dollar compensation, EV and CV, for the individual consumer.

Bibliographic Notes

The concept of consumer surplus is attributed in the literature to Dupuit (1844). Alfred Marshall developed and popularized (at least, among economists) the use of this concept; it use has been the subject of controversy ever since, with such luminaries as John Hicks promoting its use and Paul Samuelson decrying it. The strongest case for its use would seem to arise in situations where a tight (and small) bound can be put on the difference between the compensating and equivalent variations; see, for instance, Willig (1976) for such a bound. Producer surplus, being the change in profit, is relatively free of this sort of controversy.

But the general idea that one can sum in dollar-denominated terms the impact of a policy on individual firms and consumers and make on that basis social welfare judgments is controversial on a completely different plane and takes us back to Chapter 8 and the foundations of welfare economics and social choice. Arrow's (1963) chapter on the compensation principle is (once again) recommended.

Problems

■ *12.1. Proposition 12.3 says that if $Z_1^{f*}(p_1^0)$ is the singleton set $\{z_1^0\}$ (fixing all other prices), then π^f viewed as a function of p_1 is differentiable at p_1^0, and that derivative is z_1^0. Prove the converse: If π^f, viewed as a function of p_1, is differentiable in p_1 at p_1^0, then (a) $Z_1^{f*}(p_1^0)$ is singleton, and (b) the sole element of $Z_1^{f*}(p_1^0)$ is that derivative.

■ 12.2. Supply the details of the proof of Proposition 12.10.

■ 12.3. The developments of producer and consumer surplus in this chapter concerned supply coming from profit-maximizing firms and demand coming from utility-maximizing consumers. But in some cases, supply comes from consumers who sell out of their initial endowment of the good, and demand comes from firms that use the good as a factor input to their own production process. How do we interpret "producer surplus," when some or all of the supply comes from consumers (and when, in consequence, it would make more sense to speak of "seller surplus")? How about "buyer surplus," if purchasers of the good include both consumers and firms?

■ *12.4. Provide an example of a consumer with continuous and locally insatiable preferences where, fixing the prices of all goods but 1 and fixing income at some particular value, (Marshallian) demand is an interval of values for all prices in an interval of prices. (This is most easily done with an indifference curve diagram, with k [the number of commodities] = 2.)

■ 12.5. Make precise the following statement: *If there are no income effects in demand for the good over the relevant range of prices, etc., which is to say that Hicksian demand for the good is constant in the target level of utility, then the change in consumer surplus* = EV = CV.

Chapter Thirteen

Aggregating Firms and Consumers

With the exception of Chapter 8, concerning social choice, this book has so far been concerned with the choices of a single consumer or firm. In many places those choices have been in contexts where, presumably, other consumers and/or firms are around. Indeed, we've been particularly concerned with choices made in market settings in which other buyers and sellers, and even *many* other buyers and sellers, are found. But, with the exception of Chapter 8 and a bit last chapter, we haven't seriously considered the *interaction* of diverse consumers and firms.

That changes next chapter, when we take up issues of general equilibrium. In the models we will study, there will be (finite numbers of) consumers and firms, interacting through price-mediated markets. To prepare for this, in this chapter we address the question, What characterizes the (economic) aggregate behavior of collections of consumers and collections of firms? Answers to this question could be interesting on at least three grounds:

- It can be convenient to formulate specific stylized models at the aggregate-of-consumers and/or aggregate-of-firms level, rather than putting into the models hosts of consumers and firms. Readers with some exposure to so-called representative-agent (or -consumer, or -investor) models in the stochastic-general-equilibrium branches of macroeconomics and macro-finance will know about this; it is very convenient to suppose that equilibrium prices are determined by the first-order conditions of a single consumer's optimization, where that consumer (in equilibrium) must be consuming the social endowment.
- Part of our interest in results such as the Integrability Theorem has been rationalized on econometric grounds: To fit (say) a collection of demand data, it might be convenient to begin with a parametric set of demand functions, rather than with utility functions. But we then want to know that the demand functions we write down do, in fact, correspond to utility maximization according to some utility function. The Integrability Theorem provides the insurance sought: *If* the demand functions satisfy certain conditions, some utility function generates them.

  Those results concern demand by a single consumer. The rise of the internet and other electronic data-collecting devices increasingly provides the empirical economist with data on the behavior of single consumers, but still much of the data we see arrive in aggregate form. So on just the grounds that we had for wanting to know whether alleged Marshallian demand functions are legitimate, we want to know, When are alleged aggregate demand functions the aggregates of demand by a collection of legitimate (meaning, utility-maximizing) consumers? And, in the context of data on firm behavior, when are alleged aggregate netput functions the aggregates of netput decisions by profit-maximizing firms?

- Aggregation or, more precisely, *averaging*, can (asymptotically) produce desirable properties in aggregate supply and demand that may be unreasonable to assume for the supply and demand correspondences by single consumers and firms. If the production-possibility set Z of a firm is not convex, the firm's profit-maximizing netput correspondence can be nonconvex valued. If a consumer's preferences are not convex, her Marshallian demand correspondence can be nonconvex valued. As will be seen next chapter, such things are problematic in general equilibrium analysis or, put more positively, convexity in supply and demand is a useful assumption to make. Can aggregation "smooth over" this sort of difficulty? If so, how?

Please note, when thinking in terms of a single market, it is natural to think about the buying and selling sides separately, which means thinking about aggregate supply and aggregate demand. This is so even if some of the demand comes from firms purchasing inputs and / or if some of the supply comes from consumers selling from their endowment of goods. But the issues introduced in this chapter are, at least at the start, better thought of in terms of the aggregate behavior of (profit-maximizing) firms and the aggregate behavior of (utility-maximizing) consumers. Hence the terminology set forth in this chapter's title sets our agenda; we first aggregate the netput decisions of firms, then the demand and net demand decisions of consumers. And then we discuss the sense in which aggregation can "smooth out" the supply and demands of individual firms and consumers.

The Minkowski sum of a finite collection of sets

Thoughout this chapter, we have finite lists of nonempty subsets of R^k, such as $X_1, \ldots, X_n$, and we want to form the set that consists of all sums of selections from these sets, one element selected from each set. That is, we construct

$$\left\{x \in R^k : x = x_1 + \ldots + x_n \text{ for some selection } (x_1, \ldots, x_n) \in \prod_{i=1}^n X_i\right\}.$$

This "sum of the sets" is called the *Minkowski sum* of the sets X_1 through X_n; in what follows, when it is clear from the context that the X_i are sets, we will write $\sum_{i=1}^n X_i$ for this Minkowski sum. (When one or more of the sets in the list is empty, the standard convention is that the Minkowski sum of the list is similarly empty.)

13.1. Aggregating Firms

The firm half of the story is nearly trivial, as long as one assumption is met. The following proposition tells the whole story.

Proposition 13.1. *Suppose that, for $f = 1, \ldots, F$, firm f has nonempty production-possibility set $Z^f \subseteq R^k$. For $p \in R^k_{++}$, let $\pi^f(p)$ be the profit function of f evaluated at p and $Z^{f*}(p)$ be the profit-maximizing netput choices of firm f; that is,*

$$\pi^f(p) := \sup_{z \in Z^f} p \cdot z \quad \textit{and} \quad Z^{f*}(p) := \{z \in Z^f : p \cdot z = \pi^f(p)\}.$$

Define:

the aggregate production-possibility set $Z := \sum_{f=1}^F Z^f$;

for each $p \in R^k_{++}$, ***the aggregate profit function*** $\pi(p) := \sum_{f=1}^F \pi^f(p)$*; and*

for each $p \in R^k_{++}$, ***the aggregate optimal-netput set*** $Z^*(p) := \sum_{f=1}^F Z^{f*}(p)$.[1]

Then for each $p \in R^k_{++}$,

$$\pi(p) = \sup_{z \in Z} p \cdot z \quad \textit{and} \quad Z^*(p) = \{z \in Z : p \cdot z = \pi(p)\}.$$

Restating all this in words, we define: the *aggregate production-possibility set* is the Minkowski sum of the production-possibility sets of the individual firms; the *aggregate optimal-netput set* at the price vector p is the Minkowski sum of the optimal netput sets for the firms at that price vector; and the *aggregate profit function*, evaluated at p, is the sum of the profits of the individual firms at p. The proposition then says: The set of aggregate optimal netputs at the price vector p—the Minkowski sum of the optimal decisions firm by firm—is precisely the set of optimal netputs at p by a firm created by merging the production-possibility sets of the individual firms. And aggregate profit—the sum of the profits of the individual firms—is precisely the profit of this merged mega-firm. The firms in aggregate behave as if they were a single (price-taking) mega-firm.

Proof. Fix $p \in R^k_{++}$.

Since each Z^f is nonempty (by assumption), fix for each f some $\hat{z}^f \in Z^f$. Let $\hat{\pi}^f = p \cdot \hat{z}^f$. Clearly, $\pi^f(p) \geq \hat{\pi}^f > -\infty$, $\pi(p) = \sum_f \pi^f(p) > -\infty$ and, since $\hat{z} = \sum_f \hat{z}^f \in Z$, $\sup_{z \in Z} p \cdot z > -\infty$.

Suppose that $\sup_{z \in Z} p \cdot z$ is finite. Let $z_n \in Z$ be within $1/n$ of the supremum; that is, $p \cdot z_n + 1/n \geq p \cdot z$ for all $z \in Z$. Since $z_n \in Z$, there are $z_n^f \in Z^f$, $f = 1, \ldots, F$, such that $z_n = \sum_f z_n^f$. I assert that $p \cdot z_n^f + 1/n \geq p \cdot z$ for all $z \in Z^f$, for all f; suppose to the contrary that for some f', $p \cdot z_n^{f'} + 1/n < p \cdot z^{f'}$ for some $z^{f'} \in Z^{f'}$. Then $z = z^{f'} + \sum_{f \neq f'} z_n^f \in Z$, and $p \cdot z = p \cdot z^{f'} + \sum_{f \neq f'} p \cdot z_n^f > p \cdot z_n^{f'} + 1/n + \sum_{f \neq f'} p \cdot z_n^f = \sum_f p \cdot z_n^f + 1/n = p \cdot z_n + 1/n$, a contradiction. Therefore, $p \cdot z_n^f + 1/n \geq \pi^f(p)$ for all f, and hence $p \cdot z_n + F/n = \sum_f (p \cdot z_n^f + 1/n) \geq \sum_f \pi^f(p) = \pi(p)$. Hence, $\sup_{z \in Z} p \cdot z + F/n \geq \pi(p)$, and since n is arbitrary here, $\sup_{z \in Z} p \cdot z \geq \pi(p)$.

Of course, if $\sup_{z \in Z} p \cdot z = \infty$, then it is $\geq \pi(p)$.

---

[1] Hence, if one or more of the $Z^{f*}(p)$ is empty, $Z^*(p)$ is defined to be empty.

To get the reverse inequality, suppose that $\pi(p)$ is finite. (If it is infinite, we have the reverse inequality automatically.) Since we know that each $\pi^f(p)$ is $> -\infty$, $\pi(p) < \infty$ implies that each $\pi^f(p) < \infty$. For a given n, let z_n^f now be some element of Z^f that is $1/n$ within optimal; that is $p \cdot z_n^f + 1/n \geq p \cdot z$ for all $z \in Z^f$. Let $z_n = \sum_f z_n^f$, which is in Z. I assert that, for all $z \in Z$, $p \cdot z \leq p \cdot z_n + F/n$. To see this, suppose $z \in Z$ and write z as the sum of elements of the Z^f, one for each f, or $z = \sum_f z^f$. By assumption, $p \cdot z_n^f + 1/n \geq p \cdot z^f$ for each f, and summing on f gives the desired inequality.

Therefore, $p \cdot z_n + F/n \geq \sup_{z \in Z} p \cdot z$. But $p \cdot z_n^f \leq \pi^f(p)$ for each f, and $p \cdot z_n = \sum_f p \cdot z_n^f$, so $\pi(p) + F/n = \sum_f \pi^f(p) + F/n \geq p \cdot z_n + F/n \geq \sup_{z \in Z} p \cdot z$; let n go to infinity, and you have the desired (reverse) inequality. This implies that $\pi(p) = \sup_{z \in Z} p \cdot z$.

Suppose $z^* \in Z$ attains the supremum in $\sup_{z \in Z} p \cdot z$. Write z^* as the sum of elements, one from each Z^f, or $z^* = \sum_f z^{f*}$. Of course, $p \cdot z^{f*} \leq \pi^f(p)$, so $\sup_{z \in Z} p \cdot z = p \cdot z^* = \sum_f p \cdot z^{f*} \leq \sum_f \pi^f(p) = \pi(p)$, and since we know the first and last terms are equal, we must have equality everywhere. Moreover, we must have $p \cdot z^{f*} = \pi^f(p)$ for each f; if we had a strict inequality for any f, there is no way to make it up (to get the equality of the sum) for some other firm. Therefore, $z^{f*} \in Z^{f*}(p)$ for each p, which means that $z^* \in Z^*(p)$.

Conversely, suppose that $z^* \in Z^*(p)$, so that $z^* = \sum_f z^{f*}$ where each $z^{f*} \in Z^{f*}(p)$. Then $p \cdot z^{f*} = \pi_f(p)$ for each f, and therefore $p \cdot z^* = \sum_f p \cdot z^{f*} = \sum_f \pi^f(p) = \pi(p) = \sup_{z \in Z} p \cdot z$, where the last equality follows from what was shown previously. That is, $z^* \in Z^*(p)$ implies that z^* achieves the supremum. That gives us the full proposition.[2] ∎

That is a lot of proof for something that is (at worst) just the other side of obvious, but if you take it a step at a time, there is nothing hard happening.

And the result is worth the tedious hassle. We have simple necessary and sufficient conditions for an alleged profit function to be the profit function for some production-possibility set, given to us in Propositions 9.3 and 9.14: the function must be homogeneous of degree 1 and convex. Given a finite set of such functions, their sum is homogeneous of degree 1 and convex, so the aggregate profit function (obtained by summing individual profit functions) has all the properties of a single-firm profit function. In fact, we don't even need to know that the two necessary-and-sufficient conditions survive addition, since Proposition 13.1 tells us that the sum of the individual-firm profit functions is the profit function of a firm formed by summing the individual-firm production-possibility sets. And, moreover, the sum of their optimal-netput correspondences is the aggregate optimal-netput correspondence for this mega-firm. Aggregating the netput decisions of profit-maximizing firms gives us an aggregate that has precisely the properties we've derived for the individual firms.

---

[2] It is implicit here that there is no maximizer of $p \cdot z$ for $z \in Z$ if and only if one or more of the $Z^{f*}(p)$ is empty, so that $Z^*(p)$, which is defined as the Minkowski sum of the $Z^{f*}(p)$, is empty. But if you do not see how this is implied by what has been shown, you might prove this implicit "if and only if" directly.

Now recall the first sentence of this section: *The firm half of the story is nearly trivial, **as long as one assumption is met.*** Since we didn't add any assumptions, you may wonder what is that assumption. (We did assume that each firm in the collection of firms had a nonempty production-possibility set, but that's not it.) The implicit assumption is that *no firm, by its netput decision, affects the production possibilities of the other firms*. To use terminology that we'll develop more fully in Chapter 15, no firm generates an externality for any other firm.

Recall from last chapter the one caveat we inserted into the simple story of producer surplus: While every firm in an industry may be small enough so that it takes the prices it faces as given, when an entire industry shifts its production level, that may cause the price of some factor of production to change. Therefore, the "empirical" supply curve for an industry—what we see in the data—may not be the same as the sum of the individual-firm supply curves, which are based on the price-taking assumption. In a sense, that is a form of externality exerted by firms in the industry on each other—collectively, the firms change the prices of factor inputs that each faces. The caveat in this chapter is a bit different, because in the story here, we're talking about aggregating optimal netput choices as a function of the whole price vector. But it is still possible, not through prices but by other means, that one firm's production possibilities are influenced by the choices made by other firms. If, for instance, two of the firms are located along a river, and if both use the river water both as an input and as a means for disposing of unwanted by-products from their production, then the firm upstream, by disposing of its unwanted by-products, may make it impossible (or more costly) for the downstream firm to use river water in its production process. (This is a very standard example of a production externality.) The point is, Proposition 13.1 and the wonderful result it provides concerning the aggregation of firms' netput decisions and profit functions, implicitly rules all such things out.

13.2. Aggregating Consumers

When it comes to aggregating consumers, the story is much less nice. We begin with a commodity space R^k_+ and a list of consumers, indexed $h = 1, \ldots, H$.[3] Consumer h is characterized by preferences $\succeq^h$, defined on R^k_+, and a level of income y^h. We'll always assume that $\succeq^h$ is continuous, so it has a continuous representation u^h. We'll also always assume that $\succeq^h$ is locally insatiable.

For consumer h, we let $(p, y^h) \Rightarrow \mathbf{D}^h(p, y^h)$ denote the Marshallian demand correspondence, where the innovation in notation is the superscript h on $\mathbf{D}$. *Aggregate consumer demand* (at p and $(y^h)_{h=1,\ldots,H}$) is the Minkowski sum $\sum_h \mathbf{D}^h(p, y^h)$, and the ideal situation is for this sum to be $\mathbf{D}(p, y)$, which is Marshallian demand at prices p and aggregate consumer income or wealth $y = \sum_h y^h$, for some *representative consumer* with preferences or a utility function that somehow aggregates the preferences/utility functions of the H individual consumers.

[3] We continue the use of $h = 1, \ldots, H$ to enumerate consumers, or households, for the remainder of this volume. Compare with Chapter 8, where we used $h \in H$ instead.

Clearly, this is a lot to hope for. But there are very special cases in which, remarkably, it works.

Proposition 13.2 (Antonelli 1886). *Suppose that each consumer h has the same utility function u and, moreover, that utility function represents* **convex and homothetic preferences.**[4] *Let $\mathbf{D}(p, y)$ denote Marshallian demand according to this (one) utility function at p and y. Then for any income distribution $(y^h)_{h=1,\ldots,H}$ and price vector p,*

$$\sum_{h=1}^{H} \mathbf{D}(p, y^h) = \mathbf{D}\left(p, \sum_{h=1}^{H} y^h\right).$$

Note that, in the statement of the proposition, we can omit a superscript h on $\mathbf{D}$ because all the consumers, by assumption, have the same preferences.

Proof. If any $y^h = 0$, then $\mathbf{D}(p, y^h)$ must be $\{0\}$, and $\mathbf{D}(p, y^h)$ does not contribute to the sum of individual demands. For this reason, we can eliminate all h such that $y^h = 0$ from consideration (unless they all equal zero, in which case the result is trivial). Or, in other words, we can assume without loss of generality that $y^h > 0$ for each h. Let $y = \sum_h y^h$ and let $\alpha^h = y^h/y$. That is, α^h is h's share of the total income.

We now show that the left-hand side of the display is a subset of the right-hand side. Choose $d^h \in \mathbf{D}(p, y^h)$ for each h; we know that d^h is weakly preferred by h to any bundle x such that $p \cdot x \leq y^h$, so by homotheticity of preferences, d^h/α^h is weakly preferred to any bundle x/α^h where $p \cdot x \leq y^h$, which by a simple change of variables is any bundle x' such that $p \cdot x' \leq y^h/\alpha^h = y$. That is, for each h, $d^h/\alpha^h \in \mathbf{D}(p, y)$. This is true for each h, and so by convexity of preferences,

$$\sum_h \alpha^h \left(\frac{d^h}{\alpha^h}\right) = \sum_h d^h$$

is weakly preferred to any x such that $p \cdot x \leq y$, which is what we need to conclude that $\sum_h d^h \in \mathbf{D}(p, y)$.

Conversely, suppose $d \in \mathbf{D}(p, y)$. Then an easy argument, similar to the one in the previous paragraph, shows that $\alpha^h d \in \mathbf{D}(p, y^h)$ for each h. But then $\sum_h \alpha^h d = d$ is in the Minkowski sum $\sum_h \mathbf{D}(p, y^h)$. This gives set inclusion of the right-hand side in the left-hand side, and we're done. ∎

Identical homothetic (and convex) preferences is a special case, but it is not hard to see why such a special case is (nearly) required. (Concerning the convexity assumption, see Problem 13.1.) To keep the discussion simple, suppose we are looking at an open domain of prices and income levels over which (1) each consumer's demand is single valued and differentiable and satisfies Walras' Law

[4] If you need a refresher on homothetic preferences, see Definition 2.17 on page 44.

and (2) aggregate demand for each good is independent of how aggregate income is divided among the consumers, as long as the division keeps us in this region. Write $d^h(p, y^h)$ for the demand by consumer h at p and y^h. Since demand for each good i is independent of how we split the total income y over the consumers (at least, locally), then the change in demand for good i by consumer h if we increment her income by a small amount δ has to be just offset by the amount the demand for good i changes if we decrease the income of some other consumer h' by δ. (We do assume that there are at least two consumers.) Since we are assuming differentiability, Taylor's Theorem tells us that this means that

$$\left.\frac{\partial d_i^h}{\partial y}\right|_{(p,y^h)} = \left.\frac{\partial d_i^{h'}}{\partial y}\right|_{(p,y^{h'})},$$

at least inside the open set of prices and income levels for which aggregate demand is independent of the distribution of income. But if this is true when h has income y^h and h' has income $y^{h'}$, then it must also be true when we keep the income of h' at $y^{h'}$ but move h's income to some other level inside the region. That is, if y^h and $\hat{y}^h$ are two income levels for h inside this region, then the partial derivative of d_i^h in y at y^h must equal the partial derivative in y at $\hat{y}^h$ (for fixed p), since both must equal the right-hand side of the display above. But this means that, inside this region, demand for each good i by each consumer h must be affine in y, where the slope and intercept terms can depend on p. And the slope for h must also be the slope for every other h' (given p). That is, within this region,

$$\text{for each } h,\, d_i^h(p, y^h) \text{ must take the form } a_i^h(p) + b_i(p)y^h, \tag{13.1}$$

where (so that Walras' Law continues to hold) we need that $p \cdot b_i(p) = 1$. If this is to hold at all levels of p and y, then since $d_i^h(p, y^h)$ must approach zero as y^h approaches zero, we would need to have $a_i^h(p) = 0$, and while that isn't quite enough to know that preferences are homothetic, it is only because there could be regions in the consumption space that are never demanded, and hence for which preferences are not constrained by this aggregation property.

Suppose that, over some open set of prices and income levels smaller than all possible prices and income levels, each consumer's demand takes the form of (13.1), for some functions a_i^h and b_i. Obviously, aggregate demand is independent of the distribution of income, at least for prices and distributions of income within this region. Of course, this doesn't prove that aggregate demand is "as if" it came from a single utility-maximizing consumer; I won't attempt to prove that here. But it is easy to show (and you are asked to do so in Problem 13.2) that if each consumer's demand function satisfies the conditions of integrability and the demand functions take the form (13.1) over some open region, then aggregate demand satisfies the conditions of integrability over that region. Assuming that local satisfaction of the conditions of integrability is sufficient to be "as if" a single utility-maximizing consumer was behind the demand function for this region of prices and aggregate income (and this is the part we do not show), this tells us that (13.1) is both necessary and sufficient for aggregation of demand to work independently of the distribution of income, even locally.

And, as a local condition, (13.1) is less restrictive than identical homothetic preferences: For instance, suppose every consumer had preferences that are quasi-linear in, say, the kth good, that is, taking the form, $u^h(x) = v^h(x_1, \ldots, x_{k-1}) + x_k$ for some functions $v^h : R_+^{k-1} \to R$ that (to keep matters simple) are strictly concave. One can show (see Problem 3.9) that for prices p such that the relative prices p_i/p_j are all uniformly bounded, if each consumer has enough income, her demand for the first $k-1$ goods doesn't change in y^h (fixing p). That is, as long as the consumer has enough income, we have the displayed form, where $b_i(p) = 0$ for $i < k$ and $b_k(p) = 1/p_k$. So, locally, we have the required property.

Fixed shares of aggregate income

It is, clearly, a lot to ask that aggregate demand depends only on prices and aggregate income and not on how that income is divided among the consumers. So we might set our sights a bit lower. One way to do this is to specify that aggregate income is allocated to the consumers in fixed proportions. Specifically, we fix positive constants $\{\alpha^h\}_{h=1}^H$ that sum to one, and for aggregate demand, we look at

$$\mathbf{D}(p, y) = \sum_{h=1}^{H} \mathbf{D}^h(p, \alpha^h y).$$

Does this aggregate demand correspondence behave like the demand correspondence of a utility-maximizing consumer?

In general, the answer is no. Here is a simple example: Suppose that $H = k = 2$ (two consumers, and two goods). The income shares are $\alpha^1 = \alpha^2 = 0.5$. At the price vector $(1, 2)$ with total income 40 (so each consumer has 20), consumer 1 demands $(7, 6.5)$ and consumer 2 demands $(6, 7)$, making aggregate demand $(13, 13.5)$. At the price vector $(2, 1)$, also with total income 40, consumer 1 demands $(7, 6)$ and consumer 2 demands $(6.5, 7)$, making aggregate demand $(13.5, 13)$. Per Afriat's Theorem (Proposition 4.3), the data given here are consistent with both consumer 1 and 2 being utility maximizers. But aggregate demand is problematic: At the price vector $(1, 2)$, the bundle chosen is $(13, 13.5)$, which costs 40 (as it should, according to Walras' Law). But the bundle $(13.5, 13)$ costs only 39.5 at these prices. Apparently, if our supposed aggregate consumer is a utility maximizer with locally insatiable preferences, $(13, 13.5)$ is strictly better than $(13.5, 13)$. But, looking at the price vector $(2, 1)$, $(13, 13.5)$ costs 39.5 while the chosen bundle $(13.5, 13)$ costs 40. So we have a strict preference cycle (with a maintained hypothesis of local insatiability).

On the other hand, here is a positive result.[5]

[5] Shafer and Sonnenschein (1982) attribute this result to Eisenberg (1961) and the form in which it is given here to Chipman and Moore (1979).

Proposition 13.3 (Eisenberg; Chipman and Moore). *Suppose that each consumer has continuous and homothetic preferences $\succeq^h$, and that for each h there is some bundle x such that $x \succ^h 0$, while for all $x \in R^k_+$, $x \succeq^h 0$. Let u^h be a utility function that represents $\succeq^h$ and is homogeneous of degree 1 and continuous.*[6] *Fix weights $\{\alpha^h\}$ that are nonnegative and sum to one, and define a function $U : R^k_+ \to R$ by*

$$U(x) := \max \prod_{h=1}^{H} (u^h(x^h))^{\alpha^h}, \quad \text{subject to} \sum_h x^h \le x.$$

Then if, for a fixed price vector p, $d^h \in D^h(p, \alpha^h y)$, the aggregate demand $\sum_h d^h$ is among the Marshallian demands for a consumer with utility function U, facing prices p with income y.[7]

This shows that, if we fix income shares, we get aggregation of demand in all its glory (it is as if aggregate demand came from a single, utility-maximizing consumer, whose preferences turn out to be homothetic) if each consumer has homothetic preferences, although (because income shares have been fixed) they don't need to be identical homothetic preferences.

The proof of this proposition is not particularly difficult, but it is rather tedious. You are asked to provide it in Problem 13.4, which provides a step-by-step roadmap; the proof is given in the *Student's Guide*, if you want to see it worked through.

The consumer's problem with endowments rather than income

A different way to fix the distribution of income is to reformulate the problem in the manner of general equilibrium theory. We don't get to general equilibrium until next chapter but, anticipating a bit, suppose that consumer h's income derives entirely from the market value of an endowment $e^h \in R^k_+$ of goods with which she begins.[8] With endowment e^h and facing prices p, the consumer has $p \cdot e^h$ to spend on consumption, and she solves the problem

$$\text{Maximize } u^h(x), \text{ subject to } p \cdot x \le p \cdot e^h,\ x \in R^k_+.$$

(You may recall this variant on the consumer's problem from Problem 10.8 and then from Chapter 11, where it was connected to so-called Slutsky-compensated demand.) This problem will be abbreviated CP-E, for the *consumer's problem with*

---

6 See Proposition 2.19.

7 If $0 \succ^h x$ for some x, then in any homogeneous u^h we would have $u^h(x) < 0$, and U is not well defined. We can finesse this difficulty by restricting the x^h in the definition of U to be those that satisfy $u^h(x^h) \ge 0$, and in this sense the assumption that $x \succeq^h 0$ for all x is not needed. (Nonetheless, it seems innocuous, and I add it to simplify matters.) But we certainly need that $x \succ^h 0$ for some x, as if this is not true, then the definition of U, even if modified to avoid negative values of u^h, leads to U being the constant function 0.

8 Next chapter, she will also own shares in firms in the economy, and some of her income will derive from her share of the profits the firms make. But for current purposes, we'll keep it simple; in the language of next chapter, we're looking here at a *pure-trade* economy, rather than an economy *with production*.

endowments, rather than income. The CP-E is only a minor variation on the CP, and many of the results we obtained for the CP extend easily to the CP-E:

Proposition 13.4. *Consider the CP-E, where u^h is a continuous utility function on R^k_+, $p \in R^k_{++}$, and $e^h \in R^k_+$. Let $\mathbf{D}^h(p, e^h)$ denote the set of solutions to this problem, depending on the parameters p and e^h, and let $\nu^h(p, e^h)$ equal the value of the objective function (that is, $\nu^h(p, e^h)$ is the supremum of $u^h(x)$ for x within the constraint set).*

a. *A solution exists for each p and e^h; that is, $\mathbf{D}^h(p, e^h)$ is nonempty. Therefore, $\nu^h(p, e^h)$ is finite for every p and e^h.*

b. *If u^h is quasi-concave, $\mathbf{D}^h(p, e^h)$ is convex, and if u^h is strictly quasi-concave, $\mathbf{D}^h(p, e^h)$ is singleton.*

c. *The correspondence $(p, e^h) \Rightarrow \mathbf{D}^h(p, e^h)$ is upper semi-continuous and locally bounded, and the function $(p, e^h) \to \nu^h(p, e^h)$ is continuous.*

d. *$\mathbf{D}^h(\lambda p, e^h) = \mathbf{D}^h(p, e^h)$ and $\nu^h(\lambda p, e^h) = \nu^h(p, e^h)$ for all $\lambda > 0$.*

e. *If u is locally insatiable, then $p \cdot x = p \cdot e^h$ for all $x \in \mathbf{D}^h(p, e^h)$.*

Note that we're recycling the notation $\mathbf{D}$ for Marshallian demand (but now with endowment-driven wealth) and ν for indirect utility; I hope this isn't confusing. Some other fairly obvious immediate-corollaries-to or simple-extensions-of results could be given; for instance, ν is quasi-convex in p, nonincreasing in p, nondecreasing in e^h (and strictly increasing in e^h if u is locally insatiable), and so forth. But the results listed in Proposition 13.4 are what we'll need.

Individual and aggregate excess demand

Now we introduce a bit of terminology and a change of variables. The vector x in the CP-E is consumer h's final consumption bundle. We use the symbol ζ to mean $x - e^h$, calling ζ the consumer's *net trade* or *excess demand.* Excess demands can have positive and negative components; they are elements of R^k (not R^k_+), although as long as we insist on consumption bundles being nonnegative (and we will continue to insist on this), we know that excess demands for consumer h must satisfy the inequality $\zeta \geq -e^h$. When $\zeta_i > 0$, h consumes all of her endowment of good i *and ζ more in addition*; when $\zeta_i < 0$, she sells $-\zeta$ out of her endowment, retaining $e^h_i + \zeta_i$ to consume.

Definition 13.5.

a. *For a given consumer h (specified by her utility function u^h or preferences $\succeq^h$, define*

$$\mathcal{Z}^h(p, e^h) := \{\zeta \in R^k : \zeta + e^h \in \mathbf{D}^h(p, e^h)\},$$

calling $(p, e^h) \Rightarrow \mathcal{Z}^h(p, e^h)$ the ***excess-demand correspondence*** *of consumer h. If consumer h has strictly convex preferences, so that $\mathbf{D}^h(p, e^h)$ is singleton for all p and e^h, we let $\zeta^h(p, e^h)$ denote the single member of $\mathcal{Z}^h(p, e^h)$ and call $(p, e^h) \to \zeta^h(p, e^h)$ the* ***excess-demand function*** *for consumer h.*

b. For a finite collection of consumers $h = 1, \ldots, H$, each specified by her utility function or preferences, and for a fixed vector of endowments $(e^h)_{h=1,\ldots,H}$, define

$$\mathcal{Z}(p) := \sum_{h=1}^{H} \mathcal{Z}^h(p, e^h).$$

We call $p \Rightarrow \mathcal{Z}(p)$ the ***aggregate excess-demand correspondence*** *for this collection of consumers and their (fixed) endowments. When every consumer has strictly convex preferences, we define*

$$\zeta(p) := \sum_{h=1}^{H} \zeta^h(p, e^h),$$

calling $p \to \zeta(p)$ the ***aggregate excess-demand function*** *for this collection of consumers and endowments.*

Obviously, each individual excess-demand correspondence $(p, e^h) \Rightarrow \mathcal{Z}^h(p, e^h)$ inherits a bunch of properties from Proposition 13.4; I leave it to you (in Problem 13.5) to provide them and to prove the following:

Proposition 13.6. *Fix a collection of consumers indexed by $h = 1, \ldots, H$, specified by their preferences $\succeq^h$. Assume that these preferences are continuous and locally insatiable, represented by continuous utility functions u^h. And fix endowment vectors $e^h \in R^k_+$ for each consumer. Then the aggregate excess-demand correspondence $p \Rightarrow \mathcal{Z}(p)$ (for strictly positive p) is upper semi-continuous, locally bounded, homogeneous of degree 0 in the sense that $\mathcal{Z}(p) = \mathcal{Z}(\lambda p)$ for all $\lambda > 0$, and satisfies: If $\zeta \in \mathcal{Z}(p)$, then $p \cdot \zeta = 0$. Moreover, if each $\succeq^h$ is convex, then $\mathcal{Z}(p)$ is convex for every p.*

We return to general excess-demand correspondences next section. For the remainder of this section, we assume that each $\succeq^h$ is strictly convex, so we can speak of individual and aggregate excess-demand functions. We continue to fix each consumer's endowment and focus on the excess-demand functions $p \to \zeta^h(p)$, with dependence on e^h suppressed, and on the aggregate excess-demand function $p \to \zeta(p)$, with dependence on the vector of endowments $(e^h)_{h=1,\ldots,H}$ suppressed.

Corollary 13.7. *For a collection of consumers $h = 1, \ldots, H$ with fixed endowments $(e^h)_{h=1,\ldots,H}$ and strictly convex, continuous, and locally insatiable preferences $(\succeq^h)_{h=1,\ldots,H}$, the individual excess-demand functions $p \to \zeta^h(p)$ are each continuous in p, homogeneous of degree 0 in p, and satisfy* ***Walras' Law for individual excess demand:*** *$p \cdot \zeta^h(p) = 0$ for all p.*

Moreover the aggregate excess-demand function $p \to \zeta(p)$ is continuous, homogeneous of degree 0, and satisfies ***Walras' Law for aggregate excess demand:*** *$p \cdot \zeta(p) = 0$ for all p.*

This is a corollary to Proposition 13.6 for aggregate excess demand and to the unstated translation of Proposition 13.4 to individual excess-demand correspondences, once you recall that an upper semi-continuous correspondence that is singleton valued and locally bounded describes a continuous function.

The Sonnenschein-Mantel-Debreu Theorem

Individual excess-demand functions necessarily satisfy more than the three properties given in the first half of Corollary 13.7. For instance, the logic of revealed preference can be applied: We can never have (for some consumer h) two prices p and p' such that $p \cdot \zeta^h(p') < 0$ and $p' \cdot \zeta^h(p) < 0$. For if $p \cdot \zeta^h(p') < 0$, then $\zeta^h(p')$ is a net trade that is strictly affordable for h at prices p. Local insatiability implies that $e^h + \zeta^h(p) \succ^h e^h + \zeta^h(p')$. But the reverse inequality, $p' \cdot \zeta^h(p) < 0$, would symmetrically imply that $e^h + \zeta^h(p') \succ^h e^h + \zeta^h(p)$, and the two together are impossible.

If aggregate excess demand ζ could be rationalized as the individual excess-demand function for some utility-maximizing aggregate consumer, it would, likewise, need to obey this and other strictures of revealed preference. But aggregate excess demand is not so restricted, in general. The Sonnenschein-Mantel-Debreu Theorem says that, more or less, the only restrictions on an aggregate excess-demand function are those given by the second half of the corollary.

Proposition 13.8 (The Sonnenschein-Mantel-Debreu [S-M-D] Theorem). *If $\zeta : R^k_{++} \to R^k$ is continuous and homogeneous of degree 0 and satisfies Walras' Law, then for any $\epsilon > 0$ there exist k consumers with continuous, strictly convex, and nondecreasing preferences and endowments such that ζ is the aggregate excess-demand function for those k consumers, for all p such that $p_i/\|p\| \geq \epsilon$ for all i.*

The "more or less" in the sentence preceding the proposition is because the proposition only works for prices p that are strictly bounded away from the boundary (although ϵ can be chosen as small as you wish, as long as it is strictly positive). This version of the result is due to Debreu (1974). Sonnenschein (1973) provided the first result along these lines, but only for a set of aggregate excess-demand functions that is dense within the set of all continuous and homogeneous functions satisfying Walras' Law. Mantel (1974) then extended the result to any continuously differentiable excess-demand function, using $2k$ consumers; Debreu (1974) gave the result stated above, dropping Mantel's restriction to continuously differentiable functions and providing a proof with only k consumers needed.

A number of proofs of this result (some with added assumptions) have been given, but none of them are particularly simple, and I will not provide one here. (See Problem 13.6 for the relatively easy start of Debreu's proof.) Perhaps the most direct proof adds the assumption that ζ has uniformly bounded second-order partial derivatives on the domain of prices $\{p \in R^k_{++} : p_i \geq \epsilon$ for some $\epsilon > 0.\}$ Then it is possible to construct ζ as the aggregate demand of k consumers, each of whom has homothetic preferences. This version of the result is due to Mantel (1979); Shafer and Sonnenschein (1982) sketch a proof (which they attribute to Richter).

Bottom line: In this context of aggregate excess-demand functions, we (more or less) can do no better than continuity, homogeneity, and Walras' Law.

13.3. Convexification through Aggregation

A quick summary of this chapter so far: Aggregating the supply-and-demand decisions of firms is simple: Absent externalities, the aggregate decisions of a collection of competitive (price-taking) firms looks the same as the decisions of a single competitive mega-firm. But aggregating the (excess-) demand decisions of consumers is not so simple: Except under very restrictive assumptions, aggregate consumer behavior is not the same as the behavior of some utility-maximizing aggregate or representative consumer.

This neutral-to-bleak report card on aggregation is incomplete, however. Aggregation of supply and demand can sometimes have beneficial consequences, at least from the perspective of economic theory. In particular, aggregation can eliminate or, at least, reduce nonconvexities.

Results along these lines take two forms: limiting and "in the limit." This section provides you with details about one result of the first variety, and then informally discusses the second.[9]

Nonconvexities shrink: The Shapley-Folkman-Starr Theorem

Imagine an economy in which consumers have nonconvex preferences and/or firms have nonconvex production-possibility sets. Figure 13.1a shows indifference curves for preferences that are nonconvex; panel b shows a nonconvex production-possibility set. In either case, the demand correspondence (or excess-demand correspondence) of the consumer and the optimal netput correspondence of the firm will not be convex valued; for prices in a ratio of one to one in the figure, the consumer's demand correspondence (and excess-demand correspondence) and the firm's netput correspondence will consist of two points.[10] You will not learn why this is problematic until next chapter, but if you are willing to trust me on this for the time being, the theory to be developed next chapter "wants" aggregate supply and demand correspondences to be convex valued. So, when we get to next chapter, we'll be assuming that firms have convex production-possibility sets and consumers have convex preferences.

But now imagine that we have lots of consumers whose indifference curves look like Figure 13.1a and/or lots of firms whose production possibility sets look

---

[9] Aggregation can have other beneficial consequences besides convexification. For instance, under the right conditions, even if individual demand or excess demand is multivalued (that is, if $\mathcal{Z}^h(p)$ is not singleton for some p), aggregate (excess) demand, measured on a *per capita* basis for large numbers of consumers, can be nearly a function in the sense that the radius of the set of aggregate *per capita* (excess) demand at every price shrinks to zero. To show this, one must show that, for each consumer, the prices where $\mathcal{Z}^h(p)$ is not singleton are rare and then argue that, as the number of consumers grows, consumers will exhibit enough variation in their characteristics so that, at each price p, the number of consumers having nonsingleton (excess) demand at p will be small. I won't supply details about this strand of the literature.

[10] For the consumer, the level of income or endowment has to be "right" for this to happen.

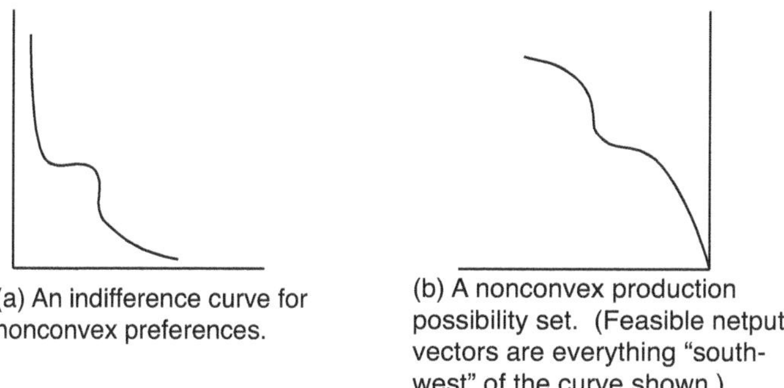

(a) An indifference curve for nonconvex preferences.

(b) A nonconvex production possibility set. (Feasible netput vectors are everything "south-west" of the curve shown.)

Figure 13.1. Nonconvexities in demand and netput. Panel a shows the indifference curve of a consumer with nonconvex preferences; panel b, a nonconvex production-possibility set of firm. At the right ratio of prices (for this figure, the ratio is one to one), the consumer's Marshallian demand will be nonconvex, as will the firm's optimal set of netput vectors.

like Figure 13.1b. To be very concrete, imagine we have 100 consumers with the indifference curve shown, so that, at the prices (1, 1) and the "right" level of income or endowment, the set of Marshallian demands for each consumer consists of two distinct points, $\{x_A, x_B\}$. At the problematic prices (1, 1) and the right income distribution, aggregate demand then has 101 points: $100x_A$, if all 100 consumers choose x_A; $99x_A + x_B$, if 99 choose x_A and one chooses x_B; $98x_A + 2x_B$; and so forth. Is this better? If we measure demand on a *per capita* basis, it may be, at least insofar as convexity is desirable. Because on a *per capita* basis, demand at these prices is $\{x_A, 0.99x_A + .01x_B, 0.98x_A + 0.02x_B, \ldots, 0.01x_A + 0.99x_B, x_B\}$. This isn't a convex set. But, at least intuitively, it is in the way of becoming closer to convex; the nonconvexity is being filled in.

Is this sort of "getting closer to convex on a *per capita* basis" useful? Since we won't know until next chapter why convexity is desirable, this is obviously a question we cannot address formally. But let me appeal to your intuition: The reason convexity is desirable, roughly, is that it is important to knowing that, at some set of prices, supply equals demand (or, as we'll phrase it next chapter, markets clear). Without convexity, you can't guarantee that this will happen. But "almost convexity on a *per capita* basis" ensures that, at some prices, supply nearly equals demand or markets nearly clear, both measured *per capita*. And, it can be argued, that's an economically desirable state of affairs.[11]

For now, I'll assume this intuition convinces you that "getting close to convex on a *per capita* basis" is desirable. But does aggregation give convexity-in-the-limit in general, or is it merely an artifact of the very special example two paragraphs ago? It is general, as long as (1) the number of items in the aggregate—that is, sets

[11] If you want to see the argument made more formally, finish Chapter 14 and then consult the seminal paper on this topic, Starr (1969).

in the Minkowski sum—(in the current context, sets of excess demands or netputs) goes to infinity, and (2) there is a uniform bound on how nonconvex is each of the sets. We begin the formal development with a definition.

Definition 13.9. *The **inner radius** of a subset X of R^k is the smallest scalar r such that every point x^* in the convex hull of X is a convex combination of points from X that are no more than r distant (in the usual Euclidean metric) from x^*.*

If X is bounded, its inner radius is necessarily finite. If X is convex, its inner radius is zero. In a sense, the inner radius of a set is a measure of how far from being convex is the set.

For any set $X \subseteq R^k$, write CH(X) for the convex hull of X.

Proposition 13.10 (Shapley-Folkman-Starr). *If $X_1, \ldots, X_n$ are all nonempty subsets of R^k, and if $X = \sum_{i=1}^n X_i$, then:*

a. $\mathrm{CH}(X) = \sum_{i=1}^n \mathrm{CH}(X_i)$.

b. Every point in CH(X) *can be written as $\sum_{i=1}^n x_i$ where $x_i \in \mathrm{CH}(X_i)$ (this is just restating part a, so far) and, moreover, no more than k of the x_i in the sum need to be taken from their respective* CH(X_i)*; at least $n - k$ can come from the original (nonconvex) X_i. (This is only meaningful if $n > k$, of course.)*

c. The inner radius of X is less than or equal to the sum of the k largest inner radii of the sets X_i.

The proof will be given shortly, but first I'll show how this can be employed.

Corollary 13.11. *Suppose $X_1, X_2, \ldots$ is a sequence of nonempty subsets of R^k for some k. For $n = 1, 2, \ldots$, let $S_n = \sum_{i=1}^n X_i$, the nth Minkowski partial sum, and let $Z_n = \{z \in R^k : z = (1/n)s \text{ for some } s \in S_n\}$. If the inner radii of the sets X_i are uniformly bounded by B, then the inner radius of S_n is bounded above by kB (a bound that is uniform in n), and the inner radius of Z_n is bounded above by kB/n.*

This is an obvious corollary to the proposition, once you recognize that if the inner radius of a set X is r, then the inner radius of $(1/n)X = \{z : z = (1/n)x, x \in X\}$ is r/n.

Apply this as follows: Suppose we have a collection of H consumers, participating in a pure-exchange economy with commodity space R^k, each of whom has (in the spirit of Proposition 13.6) fixed endowments e^h and a continuous and locally insatiable utility function that is not necessarily convex. Suppose there is a uniform upper bound on the consumers' endowments. Fix a strictly positive price vector p. The ratio of relative prices combined with the upper bound on endowments gives us an upper bound on how much of any good any consumer can afford: The bound on her endowment provides a bound on her wealth (if we normalize prices), and even if her endowment is entirely in the most expensive good, and she uses all of this endowment to buy the least expensive good, there is an upper bound on how much of that good she can purchase. Suppose B is that bound. Then B is also an upper bound, probably a very gross upper bound, on the inner radius of each $\mathcal{Z}^h(p)$.

Now consider $\mathcal{Z}(p) = \sum_h \mathcal{Z}^h(p)$. The proposition and corollary tell us that this set has inner radius of kB or less. And the inner radius of the set of *per capita* (aggregate) net trades is kB/H or less. As H goes to infinity, the sets of *per capita* net trades at the prices p are getting closer and closer to convex, at least in the sense that the inner radii of these sets approach zero.

Of course, this depends on the endowments being uniformly bounded; if, as we add more consumers, we add increasingly fantastically wealthy consumers (in the sense that one or more has a fantastically large endowment), problems can arise. And, to get a bound on the individual's net trade or demand, we need to bound the ratio of the highest priced good to the lowest.

Similar things can be done for per firm aggregate netputs, although the bound we are able to put on the inner radius of a single consumer's demand or excess demand, based on endowment size and relative prices, will be unavailable; one generally needs to assume a bound on the nonconvexities in an individual firm's production possibilities.

Proof of Proposition 13.10. First we prove part a. In one direction, it is easy: If $x \in \mathrm{CH}(\sum_i X_i)$, then $x = \sum_\ell \alpha^\ell x^\ell$ where the scalars α^ℓ are nonnegative and sum to 1, and each $x^\ell \in \sum_i X_i$ and so $x^\ell = \sum_i x_i^\ell$ where each $x_i^\ell \in X_i$. But then

$$x = \sum_\ell \alpha^\ell x^\ell = \sum_\ell \alpha^\ell \left[\sum_i x_i^\ell\right] = \sum_i \left[\sum_\ell \alpha^\ell x_i^\ell\right],$$

and each term $\sum_\ell \alpha^\ell x_i^\ell$ is clearly in its respective $\mathrm{CH}(X_i)$, so that the final term is an element of $\sum_i \mathrm{CH}(X_i)$. Hence $\mathrm{CH}(X) \subseteq \sum_i \mathrm{CH}(X_i)$.

The converse direction is a bit more difficult. We prove a more general result in linear algebra:

Suppose that

$$x = \sum_{i=1}^{n} \sum_{\ell=1}^{N_i} \alpha_i^\ell x_i^\ell,$$

where the scalars α_i^ℓ are all strictly positive and satisfy $\sum_{\ell=1}^{N_i} \alpha_i^\ell = \beta$ for some $\beta > 0$, for all i. Then we can write

$$x = \sum_{j=1}^{J} \gamma_j \left[\sum_{i=1}^{n} \hat{x}_i^j\right]$$

for some integer J, nonnegative scalars γ_j such that $\sum_j \gamma_j = \beta$, and vectors $\hat{x}_i^j$, where each of the $\hat{x}_i^j$ is an x_i^ℓ.

We need this result for the special case $\beta = 1$; for $\beta = 1$ then (assuming each $x_i^\ell \in X_i$) the first displayed double sum represents an arbitrary point in $\sum_i \text{CH}(X_i)$, while the second represents a point in $\text{CH}(\sum_i X_i)$. The proof for general β is by induction on the number of x_i^ℓ. Note that this number can never be smaller than n (since we require that at least one $\alpha_i^\ell > 0$ for each i) and in the case that $N_1 + \ldots + N_n = n$, then $N_i = 1$ for each i, and we have the desired form automatically.

Assume, then, that the result is true for all $N_1 + \ldots + N_n \leq M$, for $M \geq n$, and take a case in which $N_1 + \ldots + N_n = M + 1$. Some α_i^ℓ is smallest among all these scalars (if there is a tie for smallest, pick any one). Renumber if necessary so that this is true for $i = 1$ and $\ell = 1$. Write

$$x = \sum_{i=1}^{n} \sum_{\ell=1}^{N_i} \alpha_i^\ell x_i^\ell = \sum_{i=1}^{n} \alpha_1^1 x_i^1 + \sum_{i=2}^{n} (\alpha_i^1 - \alpha_1^1) x_i^1 + \sum_{i=1}^{n} \sum_{\ell=2}^{N_i} \alpha_i^\ell x_i^\ell.$$

The first summation of the three on the right-hand side is $\alpha_1^1(x_1^1 + \ldots + x_n^1)$, while the second and third summations are (no more than) M terms that satisfy the induction hypothesis, but with $\beta - \alpha_1^1$ instead of β. Applying the induction hypothesis to the second and third summations taken together says that they can be written in the form

$$x = \sum_{j=1}^{J} \gamma_j \left[\sum_{i=1}^{n} \hat{x}_i^j \right],$$

where $\sum_j \gamma_j = \beta - \alpha_1^1$; substituting this form for the second two summations completes the induction step, the proof of the general lemma, and hence the proof.

Part b is proved by a clever argument due to Zhou (1993), which employs another general result from linear algebra:

If $z = \sum_{j=1}^{n} \alpha_j z_j$ where z and the z_j all come from R^ℓ and the scalars α_j are all nonnegative, then z can be written in this form where no more than ℓ of the coefficients α_j are nonzero.

We essentially give the argument in the proof of Carathéodory's Theorem (Proposition A3.5) in Appendix 3, but to repeat it here: Suppose $z = \sum_{j=1}^{n} \alpha_j z_j$, where $n \geq \ell + 1$. Suppose we have expressed z in this manner with as few nonzero α_j's as possible, and suppose that number is $m \geq \ell + 1$. Renumber so that the nonzero α_j and corresponding x_j are listed as 1 through m. Since the vectors z_j for $j = 1, \ldots, m$ lie in R^ℓ and there are more than ℓ of them, they are linearly dependent, and we can write $0 = \sum_{j=1}^{m} \beta_j z_j$ for some coefficients β_j, not all zero. Moreover, it is without loss of generality to assume that at least one of the coefficients β_j is strictly positive; if they are all either 0 or less than zero, simply reverse their signs. Therefore, $z = \sum_{j=1}^{m} (\alpha_j - \gamma\beta_j) z_j$, and as we increase γ from zero, eventually one (or, simultaneously, more than one) of the coefficients $\alpha_j - \gamma\beta_j$ hits zero. Stopping with the smallest $\gamma > 0$ so that this is true (so that $\alpha_j - \gamma\beta_j \geq 0$ for all j and $= 0$ for one or more), we have reduced by one the number of nonzero coefficients needed, contradicting the supposed minimality of m.

Now suppose $x \in \mathrm{CH}(X)$ is written as $\sum_{i=1}^{n} x_i$ for $x_i \in \mathrm{CH}(X_i)$. Write each x_i as $\sum_{j=1}^{k+1} \beta_{ij} x_{ij}$ where each $x_{ij} \in X_i$ and the nonnegative β_{ij} satisfy $\sum_{j=1}^{k+1} \beta_{ij} = 1$. (This is all taking place in R^k, recall, and I've used Carathéodory's Theorem in expressing x_i as a convex combination of $k+1$ vectors from X_i.) Create the following vectors in R^{k+n}:

$$\begin{aligned} z &= (x, 1, 1, \ldots, 1), \\ z_{1j} &= (x_{1j}, 1, 0, \ldots, 0), \quad \text{for } j = 1, \ldots, k+1, \\ &\quad \cdots \\ z_{nj} &= (x_{nj}, 0, 0, \ldots, 1), \quad \text{for } j = 1, \ldots, k+1. \end{aligned}$$

We have

$$z = \sum_{i=1}^{n} \sum_{j=1}^{k+1} \beta_{ij} z_{ij}.$$

Apply the general result from linear algebra. We have written z as a nonnegative combination of the z_{ij} vectors, so we can assume that this can be done with no more than $k+n$ nonzero coefficients. That is, we can express

$$z = \sum_{i=1}^{n} \sum_{j=1}^{k+1} \gamma_{ij} z_{ij}$$

with no more than $k+n$ of the γ_{ij} being nonzero. To get equality in the last n coordinates (all those 1s and 0s), we must have $\sum_j \gamma_{ij} = 1$ for each i. For each i, this means at least one γ_{ij} must be nonzero. This leaves us with no more than k of the i's for which there can be two or more nonzero γ_{ij}, which proves part b.

Take any point $x \in \mathrm{CH}(X)$ and write it as $\sum_{i=1}^{n} x_i$ where $x_i \in \mathrm{CH}(X_i)$ for all i and $x_i \in X_i$ for all but (at most) k of the i's. Renumbering as necessary, we can assume that $x_i \in X_i$ for all $i > k$ (if $n \leq k$, there are no i for which this needs to be true), and so

$$x = \sum_{i=1}^{k} x_i + \sum_{i=k+1}^{n} x_i ,$$

where $x_i \in \mathrm{CH}(X_i)$ for $i \leq k$ and $x_i \in X_i$ for $i > k$. Let R_1 through R_n be the inner radii of X_1 through X_k, respectively. Then for each $i = 1, \ldots, k$, x_i can be written as a convex combination of points from X_i that are no more than R_i distant from x_i. (That's the definition of the inner radius.) That is,

$$x = \sum_{i=1}^{n} \sum_{\ell=1}^{N_i} \alpha_i^{\ell} x_i^{\ell} ,$$

where $\sum_\ell \alpha_i^\ell = 1$ for each i, the $\alpha_{i\ell}$ are all nonnegative, $x_i^\ell \in X_i$ for all i and ℓ, $N_i = 1$ (and $\alpha_i^1 = 1$ and $x_i^1 = x_i$) for $i > k$, and $\|x_i - x_i^\ell\| \leq R_i$ for $i \leq k$ and all ℓ. Now the argument we used for the second half of part a tells us that we can write x as

$$\sum_{j=1}^{J} \lambda_j \left[\sum_{i=1}^{n} \hat{x}_i^j \right],$$

where each $\hat{x}_i^j$ is one of the x_i^ℓ and the scalars γ_j are nonnegative and sum to one. Of course, for $i > k$, $\hat{x}_i^j = x_i$. So x is now a convex combination of the $\sum_{i=1}^n \hat{x}_i^j$. Once we uniformly bound the distance between $x = \sum_{i=1}^n x_i$ and $\sum_{i=1}^n \hat{x}_i^j$, we know that this upper bound is a bound on the inner radius of $\sum_i X_i$.

By the triangle inequality

$$\left\| \sum_i x_i - \sum_i \hat{x}_i^j \right\| \quad \leq \quad \sum_i \|x_i - \hat{x}_i^j\|.$$

And in the sum on the right-hand side, the ith summand is less or equal to R_i for $i = 1, \ldots, k$ and is 0 for $i > k$. This gives part c. ∎

Nonatomic spaces of agents and Aumann's Lemma

(This subsection will require the reader to have at least a nodding acquaintance with the mathematics of measure and integration. It is just a discussion, so a nodding acquaintance is all that is needed. But please skip it, if this isn't you.)

The Shapley-Folkman-Starr Theorem doesn't provide a lot of intuition as to why aggregation convexifies on a *per capita* basis, as the number of firms or consumers goes to infinity, so let me try to provide some. Imagine that you have an infinite sequence of sets $X_1, X_2, \ldots$ as in Corollary 13.11, and just as in the corollary, you are interested in the degree of nonconvexity of the *per capita* Minkowski partial sums, for n large relative to k. If there is a particular nonconvexity in some of the X_n sets, but this nonconvexity doesn't happen too often (think, only finitely often, although it can be more than this), then it will shrink away in the *per capita* sets as $n \to \infty$. And if it recurs frequently enough, then by judicious choosing on either side of the nonconvexity, you will (asymptotically) be able to get any convex combination you want. If you want, say, a 2/3, 1/3 combination, then 2/3 of the time you pick points on one side of the nonconvexity and 1/3 on the other. The point is, the very condition that says "this nonconvexity won't disappear of its own accord as n goes to infinity," namely that it reappears in a lot of the X_n, means that you will have lots of opportunities to balance your selection on one side or the other.

Obviously, this is very rough intuition, especially if the balancing act involves multiple dimensions and the nonconvexity is different for different consumers. But this idea points us in the direction of a very powerful variation on the aggregation-convexifies theory. I'll describe this in terms of consumers and their sets of net trades, but if you follow this description, it will be clear how it generalizes.

The price-taking assumption is based on the intuition that each consumer is small relative to the economy and has no impact on prices. Suppose that, rather than having a finite number of consumers, we imagine that there are uncountably many of them: For some measure space $(T, \mathcal{T})$, each $t \in T$ is a "type" of consumer, described by the type's preferences $\succeq^t$ and endowment e^t. The weight or proportion of consumers whose type t is drawn from some (measurable) subset $A \in \mathcal{T}$ is given by the measure $\mu(A)$,where μ is a (nonnegative) measure on the space $(T, \mathcal{T})$, such that $\mu(T) = 1$ (100% of the agents are of a type drawn from the set T).

For each type t, suppose that at some fixed price vector p (the commodity space will remain R^k for some finite k) the set of optimal net trades is given by $\mathcal{Z}(p;t)$. Assumptions are made so that the correspondence $t \Rightarrow \mathcal{Z}(p;t)$ is well behaved; think in terms of $\succeq^t$ being represented by a parameterized function $u(x;t)$ that is (say) jointly continuous in x and t, and $t \to e^t$ is continuous. (What would Berge's Theorem then tell you about $t \Rightarrow \mathcal{Z}(p;t)$ for some fixed p?)

What is *per capita* aggregate demand? With finitely many agents, it is the Minkowski sum, summing over agents (and, to make it *per capita,* divided by the number of agents); the corresponding concept to a sum is an integral, and so Aumann defines the integral over t of the sets $\mathcal{Z}(p;t)$ as:

> $\int_T \mathcal{Z}(p;t)\mu(dt)$ *is the set* $\{ \int_T \zeta(p;t)\mu(dt) : \zeta(p;t) \in \mathcal{Z}(p;t)$ *for each* t*, and* $t \to \zeta(p;t)$ *is well-enough behaved so the integral is well defined*$\}$.

If, for instance, we assume there is a uniform bound on the e^t, then there will be a uniform bound on elements of the set $\mathcal{Z}(p;t)$ (if prices p are strictly positive), so "well-enough behaved" can be taken to be "measurable." This so-called *Aumann integral* of the correspondence, the parallel concept to the Minkowski sum of a finite collection of sets, is the set of all integrals of measurable selections from the correspondence. The punch line to all this setup is

> *Suppose that* μ *is a nonatomic measure (that is, the weight or measure of every singleton set* $\{t\}$ *is 0). If* $t \Rightarrow \mathcal{Z}(p,t)$ *is "well-behaved,"*[12] *the set* $\int_T \mathcal{Z}(p;t)\mu(dt)$ *is convex, regardless of the convexity of the sets* $\mathcal{Z}(p;t)$.

Or, for nonatomic measures, meaning no single type t has positive weight *per capita,* aggregation convexifies. Not "convexifies in the limit" or "gets you closer and closer to convexity," but "convexifies, period."[13]

---

[12] A sufficient condition is that there is an integrable function $\underline{\zeta} : T \to R^k$ such that $\zeta \in \mathcal{Z}(p;t)$ implies that $\zeta \geq \underline{\zeta}(t)$.

[13] In this description, I've identified each $t \in T$ as a *type* of consumer, with the notion that there may be more than one consumer of type t. But by assuming that μ is nonatomic, I've assumed that the weight of type-t consumers is infinitesimal relative to the whole population. Note, in this regard, that in the definition of the Aumann integral, one $\zeta(p;t)$ is selected from $\mathcal{Z}(p;t)$ for each t; if there are multiple consumers of type t, they are all treated the same in the selection.

A different interpretation is that each $t \in T$ is an individual consumer, specified by her preferences and endowment. Then in the Aumann integral, we are allowing $\zeta(p;t)$ to be selected from $\mathcal{Z}(p;t)$ on a consumer-by-consumer basis (up to measurability constraints); we could allow distinct types to have positive weight, because we are allowing different copies of the same type to be treated differently in the Aumann integral. But in this interpretation, it probably makes most sense to assume each $t \in T$ has equal weight, which means something like: $T = [0,1]$ and μ is Lebesgue measure on T.

The intuition is, more or less, the intuition given earlier in the subsection: If μ is nonatomic, then we can chop up T into as many pieces of any size (measured by μ) needed to balance out individual nonconvexities that occur with positive μ-measure. (Nonconvexities that appear in $\mathcal{Z}(p;t)$ for a set of μ-measure 0 obviously are irrelevant to the integral.) Of course, this is just intuition: This result, sometimes called *Aumann's Lemma or Aumann's Theorem*, is a deep result in mathematics. But owing to it, and for other reasons, it provides the economic theorist who can handle the math a very felicitous environment for doing economic theory and, in particular, general equilibrium theory. The mathematics is at too high a level to be tackled in this book, but (especially after consuming the next two chapters), the reader who is prepared to handle this level of math should look in the literature for economies with a continuum of agents (that is, consumers and/or firms). The seminal references are provided below.

Bibliographic Notes

As stated at the start of the chapter, aggregation is very important on a number of grounds: in empirical studies, data are apt to come in aggregated form; it is often vastly simplifying to be able to assume that an economy consists of a representative consumer and/or a representative firm; and to the extent that aggregation helps justify assumptions like convexity or continuity, it justifies a lot of theory. For these reasons, there is a very substantial literature on the topic, and one that goes back a long way: The first aggregation result for consumers comes from Antonelli (1886). This chapter has only scratched the surface and, at that, the theoretical end of the surface.

For aggregation of consumers, I have relied very heavily on on Shafer and Sonnenschein (1982), who provide some historical notes. The three seminal papers for the S-M-D Theorem are Sonnenschein (1973), Mantel (1974), and Debreu (1974). It is probably worth noting that there are other senses in which one might talk about aggregation of consumers besides the adding up of their demands or market demands; see Mas-Colell, Whinston, and Green (1995, Section 4D).

What I call the Shapley-Folkman-Starr Theorem first appears in the economic literature in Starr (1969). Starr credits Shapley and Folkman as the originators of part b and a weaker version of part c; he himself provides the definition of inner radius and sharpens the original Shapley-Folkman Theorem to get part c.

The seminal papers on models with a continuum of agents are Aumann (1964, 1965, 1966).

Problems

■ *13.1. In the statement of Proposition 13.2, it is assumed that the preferences of the various consumers are identical, homothetic, and convex. What happens if we assume that they are (only) identical and homothetic?

■ 13.2. The chapter argues (informally) that if every consumer's demand d^h takes the form $d_i^h(p, y^h) = a_i^h(p) + b_i(p)y^h$ over some open region of prices and income levels, then over that region, aggregate demand is independent of the distribution of aggregate income and resembles the demand by a single consumer.

(a) One part of the informal argument is that, assuming each individual demand function satisfies the conditions of integrability, so does aggregate demand. Show that this is so.

(b) Suppose that each consumer's indirect utility function ν^h takes the form $\nu^h(p, y^h) = \alpha^h(p) + \beta(p)y^h$ over an open domain of prices and income levels. Making all the differentiability assumptions you care to, show that this implies that demand functions take the form indicated. (Use Roy's identity.) (This is called *Gorman form* indirect utility.)

■ 13.3. (This is purely a finger-exercise problem): Verify that the individual-consumer demand information given in the example on the bottom of page 313 is consistent with utility maximization by each consumer.

■ *13.4. Your task in this problem is to prove Proposition 13.3. If you follow the steps given here, it should not prove too hard.

(a) Consider the problem

$$\max \prod_{h=1}^{H} (\beta^h y^h)^{\alpha^h}, \quad \text{subject to } \sum_h y^h \leq y, y^h \geq 0,$$

where the scalars β^h are all strictly positive, the α^h are nonnegative and sum to one, and $y \geq 0$. (Warning: The superscript h's are all counters, so α^h means the hth α, not α raised to the power h. But the superscript α^h denotes raising the quantity inside the parentheses to the power of the hth α, α^h. Prove that the unique optimal solution is $y^h = \alpha^h y$.)

(b) Now fix a price vector p and consider the problem of consumer h, max $u^h(x)$ subject to $p \cdot x \leq 1$. Let the solution be $\hat{x}^h$, and let $u^h(\hat{x}^h) = \beta^h$. (If there are multiple solutions, choose any one.) Describe the solution to max $u^h(x)$ subject to $p \cdot x \leq y$ in terms of $\hat{x}^h$ and the value of the solution in terms of β^h.

(c) Let x^0 be the solution of max $U(x)$, subject to $p \cdot x \leq y$, and let $(\check{x}^h)_{h=1,\dots,H}$ be the solution of

$$\max \prod_h (u^h(x^h))^{\alpha^h}, \quad \text{subject to } \sum_h x^h \leq x^0.$$

Let $\check{y}^h = p \cdot \check{x}^h$. How does $U(x^0)$ compare with

$$\prod_h (u^i(\check{y}^h \hat{x}^h))^{\alpha^h} ? \tag{13.2}$$

(d) Let $\hat{x} = \sum_h \alpha^h y\hat{x}^h$. How does $U(x^0)$ compare with $U(\hat{x})$, and how does $U(\hat{x})$ compare with

$$\prod_h (u^i(\alpha^h y\hat{x}^h))^{\alpha^h} \text{ ?} \tag{13.3}$$

(e) Compare the two quantities (13.2) and (13.3) using part a, then finish the proof of the proposition.

■ *13.5. Write out a corollary to Proposition 13.4 that transforms each piece into a corresponding statement about consumer h's excess demand and excess-demand correspondence. Then prove Proposition 13.6.

■ 13.6. While we will not supply a full proof of the S-M-D Theorem, here is a piece of Debreu's (1974) proof: Let Q denote the set of all prices $p \in R^k_+$ such that $\|p\| = 1$, and for $\epsilon > 0$, let Q^ϵ be the set $\{q \in Q : q_i \geq \epsilon \text{ for all } i = 1, \ldots, k\}$. Suppose $\zeta : Q^\epsilon \to R^k$ is a continuous function that satisfies Walras' Law, or $p \cdot \zeta(p) = 0$ for all $p \in Q^\epsilon$. Since Q^ϵ is compact, we can produce continuous functions $\alpha : Q^\epsilon \to R_{++}$ such that $\zeta(p) + \alpha(p)p \geq 0$ for all $p \in Q^\epsilon$. Indeed, we can take α to be a constant function, as long as the constant $\alpha > \max\{-\zeta_i(p)/p_i : p \in Q^\epsilon, i = 1, \ldots, k\}$.

Debreu's proof involves finding k utility-maximizing agents whose excess demand functions ζ^h sum to ζ (on Q^ϵ). (We use homogeneity to extend to all price vectors p such that $p/\|p\| \in Q^\epsilon$.) So fix $\zeta(\cdot)$ and $\alpha(\cdot)$ as in the previous paragraph, and for $h = 1, \ldots, k$, define

$$\zeta^h(p) = (\zeta_h(p) + \alpha(p)p_h)(e^h - p_h p),$$

where $e^h = (0, 0, \ldots, 0, 1, 0, \ldots, 0)$, with the 1 in coordinate position h. (Remember, h here runs from 1 to k; there is one consumer for each of the k commodities. Indeed, if you examine $\zeta^h(p)$, you'll see that it is, by construction, a positive scalar [depending on p] times a vector that is positive in coordinate position h and negative in all other coordinate positions. So consumer h sells all commodities except for h out of her endowment, and purchases positive amounts of commodity h to consume in addition to her endowment.)

(a) Prove that $\sum_h \zeta^h(p) = \zeta(p)$ for all $p \in Q^\epsilon$.

(b) Prove that $p \cdot \zeta^h(p) = 0$ for $h = 1, \ldots, k$ and for all $p \in Q^\epsilon$.

(c) Prove that each $\zeta^h(p)$ satisfies the weak axiom of revealed preference: If $p' \cdot \zeta^h(p) \leq 0$, then $p \cdot \zeta^h(p') > 0$.

The "only" thing left to do is to prove that each ζ^h is the excess-demand function for some utility-maximizing consumer (specified by her preferences and endowment), for prices $p \in Q^\epsilon$. Of course, the scare quotes around the word *only* are sarcastic; this task is quite difficult. See Debreu (1974) or Geanakoplos (1984) for details.

■ *13.7. What is inner radius of the set $\{1, 2, 3, 4\}$ in R^1? What is the inner radius of the set $\{(z_1, z_2) : z_1, z_2 = 1, 2, 3, \text{or } 4\}$ in R^2?

Chapter Fourteen

General Equilibrium

In this chapter and the next two, we move with a vengeance beyond the behavior of a single consumer or a single firm, and beyond all the producers or consumers within the market for a single good, as we study the behavior of an entire economy, with multiple consumers and firms and with markets for all commodities simultaneously. But we stick to the assumption that consumers and firms are all price takers, basing their consumption and production decisions on the hypothesis that they can buy and sell as much as they would like at the going prices.

The topic is *general equilibrium*, and in many ways it is the climax of microeconomics, if you are willing to limit attention to price-taking actors who have access to common information, as we have done in this volume. Entire books have been written about the theory of general equilibrium, and we'll only cover the basics here. In particular, in this chapter we cover:

- the basic definitions of an economy and a Walrasian equilibrium;
- basic properties of a Walrasian equilibrium; and
- the existence and other mathematical properties of Walrasian equilibria.

Chapter 15 concerns the efficiency of Walrasian-equilibrium allocations. And in Chapter 16, we discuss how time and uncertainty can be accommodated within the framework of general equilibrium.

14.1. Definitions

The first set of definitions concerns the context of our analysis, an *economy*. The following pieces make up an economy:

- A finite integer k, the *number of commodities*. R^k is called the *commodity space*.
- A finite number F of *firms*. Firm f is characterized by a nonempty production-possibility set $Z^f \subseteq R^k$.
- A finite number H of *consumers*.[1] Consumer h is characterized by:
    - her *consumption space* X^h, which is a nonempty subset of R^k
    - her *utility function* $u^h : X^h \to R$ (We might specify instead the consumer's preference ordering $\succeq^h$, but since we momentarily assume that preferences

[1] H and h are mnemonics for *household*. We don't use I and i because we use i for the typical commodity index; that is, we write $i = 1, \ldots, k$, and so forth.

are continuous, starting with utility functions is without loss of generality. That said, I will feel free, when convenient, to write $x \succeq^h x'$ meaning $u^h(x) \geq u^h(x')$, and so forth.)

- her *(commodity) endowment*, $e^h \in X^h$
- her *shareholdings*, given by nonnegative numbers s^{fh} for $f = 1, \ldots, F$ and $h = 1, \ldots, H$, and such that $\sum_h s^{fh} = 1$ for each f

The symbol $\mathcal{E}$ is used to denote an economy.

In some cases, we will work with an economy without firms: consumers have endowments that they trade, but no transformation of commodities is possible. In such cases, we say that the economy is a *pure-exchange economy*.

Various assumptions about pieces of this definition will be made at various times in the chapter. But the following assumptions are *nearly always* made.

Assumption 14.1. *Each consumer's commodity space X^h is R^k_+. Each consumer's utility function u^h is continuous. Each firm's production-possibility set Z^f is nonempty and closed.*

To explain the "nearly" in "nearly always": Unless explicitly contravened, these assumptions hold throughout the chapter. When we get to questions of existence of equilibrium, we will (temporarily) assume that the consumption space X^h of consumer h is something smaller than R^k_+.

The second definition (this one set out formally) concerns the object we are studying, in the context of some economy $\mathcal{E}$.

Definition 14.2. *A* ***Walrasian equilibrium*** *for the economy $\mathcal{E}$ is a* ***price vector*** *$p \in R^k$, a* ***consumption allocation*** *$\{x^h; h = 1, \ldots, H\}$, and* ***production plans*** *$\{z^f; f = 1, \ldots, F\}$, such that*

a. For each consumer h, $x^h \in X^h$ and solves the problem

$$\text{maximize } u^h(x), \text{ subject to } x \in X^h \text{ and } p \cdot x \leq p \cdot e^h + \sum_f s^{fh} p \cdot z^f.$$

b. For each firm f, $z^f \in Z^f$ and solves the problem

$$\text{maximize } p \cdot z, \text{ subject to } z \in Z^f.$$

c. Markets clear: $\sum_h x^h \leq \sum_h e^h + \sum_f z^f$.

(For a pure-exchange economy, a Walrasian equilibrium is a price vector p and a consumption allocation such that requirement a holds, where the summation in the right-hand side of the budget constraint is omitted, and requirement c holds, where the final summation over firms is omitted.)

Several remarks about this definition are in order:

- Implicit in requirement a is the assumption that consumers are utility maximizers. In requirement a, and more specifically in the problem displayed there, which is the consumer's utility-maximization problem, the inequality $p \cdot x^h \leq p \cdot e^h + \sum_f s^{fh} p \cdot z^f$ is the consumer's *budget constraint*. For most of this book, budget constraints have taken the form $p \cdot x \leq y$, for some given income y. But in general equilibrium, the consumer's level of wealth or income is endogenized: The consumer comes endowed with a vector of commodities e^h; this endowment acquires value $p \cdot e^h$ depending on equilibrium prices. And the consumer obtains wealth from her shareholdings in the firms: At the equilibrium prices p, the firm chooses a production plan z^f (which is a netput vector just as in Chapter 9), so that $p \cdot z^f$ is the net profit of the firm. Consumer h owns an s^{fh} share in firm f, where shares in each firm are normalized to sum across consumers to one. Hence, consumer h receives her share $s^{fh} p \cdot z^f$ of firm f's profit. In total, then, the consumer's wealth or income is the value of her endowment, plus the sum, taken over all firms, of her share in the profits of the firms.

- Implicit in requirement b is the assumption that firms are profit maximizers.

- We have assumed in our definition of an economy that each consumer's endowment e^h lies in X^h, the consumer's consumption space. This is done, more or less, so we can be sure that the consumer's utility-maximization problem has a feasible solution; that is, there is some $x^h \in X^h$ that satisfies the budget constraint. But if that is why the assumption is made, it isn't (yet) enough: The consumer is assumed to get her share s^{fh} of the profit of firm f, and we have not yet made assumptions to guarantee that firms make nonnegative profit. If we assume $0 \in Z^f$ for each f—so that a profit-maximizing choice must give nonnegative profit—then we're okay on this score.

- The consumer's budget constraint says $\leq$, which means that the consumer can choose not to use all the purchasing power she receives from her endowment and shares in the firms' profits. And, in the market clearing condition c, we have an inequality $\leq$. Both of these inequalities are sometimes made equations, in other treatments of general equilibrium. The inequality in the budget constraint is not of much consequence as long as consumers are locally insatiable; if a consumer is locally insatiable, we know that she will spend her full budget. But if she could be locally satiated, we aren't forcing her to spend more than it takes to reach this point.

  The inequality (instead of an equality) in the market-clearing condition has greater economic interest. Imagine that one of the goods is a "bad," meaning that it lowers the utility of consumers. A concrete example might be some form of pollution. If a firm produces this bad commodity, and if we have an equality in requirement c, then we are forcing some consumer (in a Walrasian equilibrium) to consume this commodity. That, in itself, is not impossible to do: Note that we have not restricted prices to be nonnegative (let alone strictly positive), and if this bad commodity has a negative price, a consumer might be willing to "consume" it, as doing so loosens her budget constraint, giving her more resources to purchase good commodities.

But by having an inequality in c, we are allowing (as part of a Walrasian equilibrium) this bad commodity to go unconsumed after everything is said and done. In the case of noxious goods, then, the inequality in c may be inappropriate as a modeling assumption.

There is no bottom line to these considerations; no single way to model goods that are "bads" is unambiguously best. I will proceed with the definition of a Walrasian equilibrium given above; but if you consider applying this sort of model to a situation with goods that are bad, you should probably think carefully about this part of the definition.

- In requirements a and b, consumers and firms are price takers. They believe they can buy and/or sell any amount of any of the commodities at the going market price, without changing that price. The excuse for this assumption is the usual rationale: It is probably approximately true, if consumers and firms are both many and small. In any case, it is part of the story of general equilibrium.
- When, in previous chapters, we discussed the consumer's utility-maximization problem and the firm's profit-maximization problem, we made assumptions guaranteeing that solutions exist, at least for strictly positive prices. (Given that Z^f is closed and u^h is continuous, those assumptions guarantee that we can bound the set of feasible *and relevant* consumption bundles/production plans.) But it is part of the *definition* of a Walrasian equilibrium that prices are arranged so that consumers and firms can solve their respective problems. If, for instance, we specify an economy $\mathcal{E}$ in which a firm has a constant-returns-to-scale technology, then prices in any equilibrium must be such that the firm, at those prices, cannot make a positive profit.
- In some treatments, the definition includes the condition $p \neq 0$. We don't insist on this, but see Proposition 14.4 upcoming.

To economize on notation, the following conventions are adopted:

$\boldsymbol{X}$ denotes the space of consumption allocation vectors, or $\boldsymbol{X} = \prod_{h=1}^{H} X^h$, with typical element $\boldsymbol{x}$. For $\boldsymbol{x} \in \boldsymbol{X}$, write $\boldsymbol{x}^h$ for h's part of the allocation.

$\boldsymbol{Z}$ denotes the space of production plans for all the firms, or $\boldsymbol{Z} = \prod_{f=1}^{F} Z^f$, with typical element $\boldsymbol{z}$. For $\boldsymbol{z} \in \boldsymbol{Z}$, we write $\boldsymbol{z}^f$ for f's part of the overall production plan.

Therefore, a Walrasian equilibrium consists of a triple $(p, \boldsymbol{x}, \boldsymbol{z})$, where p gives the equilibrium prices, $\boldsymbol{x}$ is the consumption allocation, and $\boldsymbol{z}$ is the production plan.

In the next chapter, we will be in the business of comparing the consumption allocation portion of Walrasian equilibria with other consumption allocations that are feasible, using all the resources (endowments and firms' technologies) this economy has to offer. So the following definition is made:

Definition 14.3. *For a given economy $\mathcal{E}$, the* ***space of socially feasible consumption allocations****, denoted $\mathbf{X}^*$, is defined as*

$$\mathbf{X}^* := \left\{ \mathbf{x} \in \mathbf{X} : \sum_{h=1}^{H} x^h \leq \sum_{h=1}^{H} e^h + \sum_{f=1}^{F} z^f, \text{ for some } \mathbf{z} \in \mathbf{Z} \right\}.$$

Note that, in this definition, we allow for the disposal of goods; that is, the feasibility constraint is an inequality. This lines up with our use of an inequality in part c of the definition of a Walrasian equilibrium.

14.2. Basic Properties of Walrasian Equilibria

Proposition 14.4.

a. *If $(p, \mathbf{x}, \mathbf{z})$ is a Walrasian equilibrium for some economy, then so is $(\lambda p, \mathbf{x}, \mathbf{z})$ for all $\lambda > 0$.*

b. *If consumer h is locally insatiable, then in any Walrasian equilibrium $(p, \mathbf{x}, \mathbf{z})$, $p \cdot x^h = p \cdot e^h + \sum_f s^{fh} p \cdot z^f$. (In other words, locally insatiable consumers must satisfy Walras' Law.)*

c. *If any consumer is globally insatiable, then every Walrasian-equilibrium price vector p satisfies $p \neq 0$.*

d. *If any consumer has a nondecreasing and globally insatiable utility function, or if any firm has a free-disposal technology, then every Walrasian-equilibrium price vector p must satisfy $p \geq 0$.*

e. *If $(p, \mathbf{x}, \mathbf{z})$ is a Walrasian equilibrium for some economy in which every consumer is locally insatiable,*

$$p \cdot \left(\sum_h x^h \right) = p \cdot \left(\sum_h e^h \right) + p \cdot \left(\sum_f z^f \right).$$

(In words, the economy as a whole must satisfy Walras' Law.) And if, in addition, $p \geq 0$, then for each commodity i, $\sum_h x_i^h < \sum_h e_i^h + \sum_f z_i^f$ implies $p_i = 0$. (In words, for nonnegative prices and locally insatiable consumers, any good in excess supply must have a price of zero.)

Proof. Part a is entirely straightforward. Part b follows more or less immediately from Proposition 3.1d; that proposition is stated in the context of a consumer with a set amount of income y, but the logic is unchanged. The first half of part e results from summing up the equation in part b across all consumers and noting that shares in each firm sum to one. Given this, rewrite Walras' Law (for the whole economy) as $p \cdot \left(\sum_h x^h - \sum_h e^h - \sum_f z^f \right) = 0$. Each component of the term inside the parentheses must be nonpositive by the market-clearing condition. So if $p \geq 0$, for the dot product to be zero, each individual product in the dot product must be zero. This immediately implies the second half of e.

As for parts c and d: Suppose that p is part of an equilibrium and consumer h is globally insatiable. Were $p = 0$, the consumer would be unconstrained; she could afford any bundle and, therefore, her utility-maximization problem would have no solution. But in any Walrasian equilibrium, each consumer (and each firm) must have a finite solution to her (its) problem. So $p = 0$ is not possible, with one globally insatiable consumer.

Suppose p is part of a Walrasian equilibrium and $p_i < 0$. Suppose consumer h has nondecreasing and globally insatiable preferences. Let x^h denote h's equilibrium consumption. Then by global insatiability, we can find another bundle $\hat{x}^h$ that satisfies $u^h(\hat{x}^h) > u^h(x^h)$. If $p \cdot \hat{x}^h \leq p \cdot x^h$, then we have an immediate contradiction to the assertion that x^h solves consumer h's utility-maximization problem at prices p, so we can assume that $p \cdot \hat{x}^h - p \cdot x^h > 0$; define $M := p \cdot \hat{x}^h - p \cdot x^h$. Let b be the unit vector in the commodity-i direction; that is, $b = (0, \ldots, 0, 1, 0, \ldots, 0)$ where the 1 is at component position i. Then $\hat{x}^h + (M/|p_i|)b \geq \hat{x}^h$, and therefore $u^h(\hat{x}^h + (M/|p_i|)b) > u^h(x^h)$. But $p \cdot [\hat{x}^h + (M/|p_i|)b] = p \cdot \hat{x}^h + p_i(M/|p_i|) = p \cdot \hat{x}^h - M = p \cdot x^h$, contradicting the optimality of x^h at prices p. And suppose p is part of a Walrasian equilibrium, $p_i < 0$, and firm f has a free-disposal economy. Then whatever production plan, z^f, firm f is undertaking at the equilibrium, the plan $z^f - b$ is feasible for it (this alternative plan involves the firm doing what it would otherwise do, but buying and disposing of one more unit of commodity i), and this plan gives $-p_i$ more profit than does the plan z^f, contradicting the supposed optimality of plan z^f. ∎

Part d of the proposition gives conditions that ensure that the entire (equilibrium) price vector is nonnegative. But the proof makes clear that we can prove similar results one commodity at a time: *$p_i \geq 0$ in any Walrasian equilibrium if either (1) some consumer's utility function is nondecreasing in commodity i, and this consumer is globally insatiable, or (2) some firm can freely dispose of commodity i.*

In view of all the work we did earlier with strictly positive prices, we might want conditions that establish that equilibrium prices are strictly positive. An obvious result of this sort is the following:

Proposition 14.5 (Part 1). *Suppose that for some consumer h, u^h is strictly increasing in the consumption of commodity i. Then $p_i > 0$ in every Walrasian equilibrium.*

Proof. If (p, x, z) is alleged to be a Walrasian equilibrium with $p_i \leq 0$, then h can increase her consumption of good i without violating her budget constraint. So x^h cannot possibly be utility maximizing for h at the prices p, a contradiction. ∎

The assumption that u^h is strictly increasing in the consumption of commodity i doesn't apply to some commodities, of course. But the result of Proposition 14.5 can be "extended." Suppose, for instance, that we know commodity i has strictly positive market value (that is, $p_i > 0$ in any Walrasian equilibrium), and some firm

f, whatever else it is doing, can use a second commodity, j, as incremental input to produce a strictly positive incremental amount of i. Formally,

Proposition 14.5 (Part 2). *Suppose commodity i is ensured to have strictly positive price in every Walrasian equilibrium—because, for instance, it satisfies the conditions of part 1 of this proposition—and suppose for some commodity $j \neq i$, there is a firm f such that, if $z \in Z^f$, then there exists $\hat{z} \in Z^f$ such that $\hat{z}_i - z_i > 0$, $\hat{z}_j - z_j \leq 0$, and $\hat{z}_\ell = z_\ell$ for all ℓ other than i or j. Then $p_j > 0$ for every Walrasian-equilibrium price vector p.*

The proof is left for you as a simple exercise.

14.3. The Edgeworth Box

A number of insights into the nature of Walrasian equilibria can be gained by looking at caricature examples. Some caricatures are parametric examples. A selection is provided by Problems 14.2 through 14.5 at the end of this chapter; you should work through these.

The Edgeworth Box is a different sort of caricature. It depicts a simple yet still somewhat general case: pure exchange; two consumers; two goods. The generality (in terms of the ability to shape the two consumers' preferences, given by their indifference curves) allows for a fairly rich variety of phenomena. But with two consumers, two goods, and no firms, it allows for a visual representation of what is going on.

The two consumers, Alice and Bob, are abbreviated $h = A$ and B. Each has her ($h = A$) or his ($h = B$) endowment, $e^h \in R^2_+$. The *social endowment*, denoted by e, is the sum of the two endowments, or $e = e^A + e^B$.

Follow along in Figure 14.1.

The picture begins in panels a and b, with indifference curve diagrams depicting the preferences of, respectively, Alice and Bob. In Figure 14.1, and in most Edgeworth Boxes you will see, indifference curves are drawn to depict preferences that are strictly increasing and strictly convex. This isn't necessary, but it is common. Note in both panels the open circles representing the endowments of the two consumers, as well as the filled-in circle at the social endowment.

Then the box is constructed. Imagine rotating panel b by 180 degrees, giving you panel c. And then superimpose panel c on panel a, putting the origin of panel c on top of the social endowment of panel a, so that the social endowment of c lands on top of the origin of panel a. Panel d results. The "box" in the name Edgeworth Box is the box formed in panel d by the two sets of coordinate axes. Note that each point inside the box represents a way of dividing the social endowment between Alice and Bob, where everything not given to her is instead given to him.

Move on to Figure 14.2. I've depicted a more extreme version of panel d here, more extreme because the initial endowment point gives more of good 2 and less of good 1 to Alice, and the reverse for Bob.

In panel a (now Figure 14.2), the shaded region shows all the ways to divide the social endowment between Alice and Bob that leaves each at least as well off

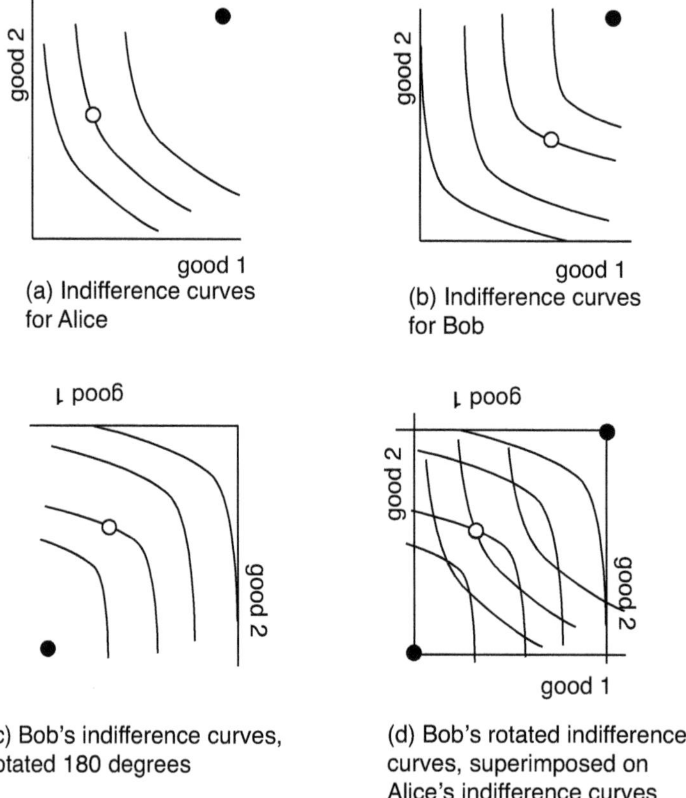

(a) Indifference curves for Alice

(b) Indifference curves for Bob

(c) Bob's indifference curves, rotated 180 degrees

(d) Bob's rotated indifference curves, superimposed on Alice's indifference curves

Figure 14.1. Constructing the Edgeworth Box. For two consumers, Alice and Bob, two goods, and pure exchange, begin with indifference curve diagrams for the two. Their endowment of the goods are marked on their indifference curve diagrams by the open circles, while the filled-in circle is the social endowment. This gives panel a for Alice and panel b for Bob. Then panel b is rotated 180 degrees (panel c) and superimposed on panel a, with the social endowment on one set of coordinate axes placed on top of the origin in the other set of axes. Panel d results. Note that, in panel d, each point inside the box formed by the two sets of axes represents a division of the social endowment between Alice and Bob in a way that wastes none of either good.

as they are at the initial endowment and that wastes none of either good. That is, these divisions are Pareto improvements on the initial endowment. Pareto-efficient divisions of the social endowment are divisions where any attempt to improve the utility of one party decreases the utility of the other; assuming indifference curves are smooth and preferences are quasi-concave, these would be points of tangency of two indifference curves, at least as long as the point is interior to the box. Panel b shows the full range of Pareto-efficient allocations as a heavy curve that runs from the origin in the southwest to the other origin in the northeast. The heavier portion of this consists of points that are Pareto efficient and that give each consumer as much utility as she or he gets at her or his initial endowment; in the next chapter we'll learn that these points are called *core* allocations. (I've drawn the picture

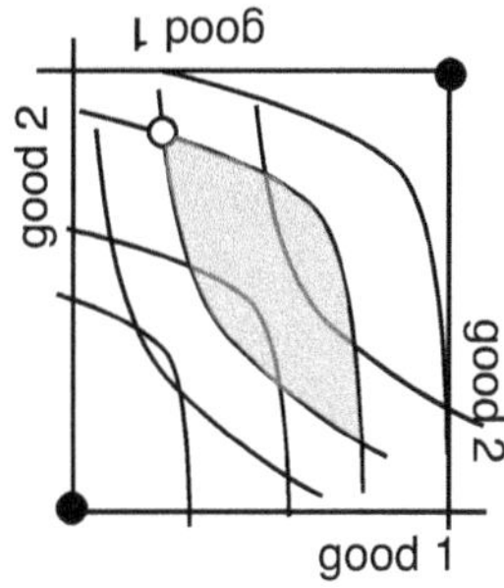

(a) Points that are Pareto improvements on the initial endowment

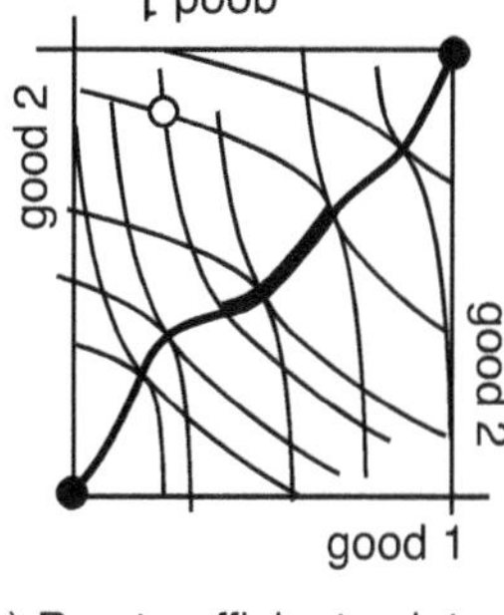

(b) Pareto-efficient points, and those that are better for both than the initial endowment

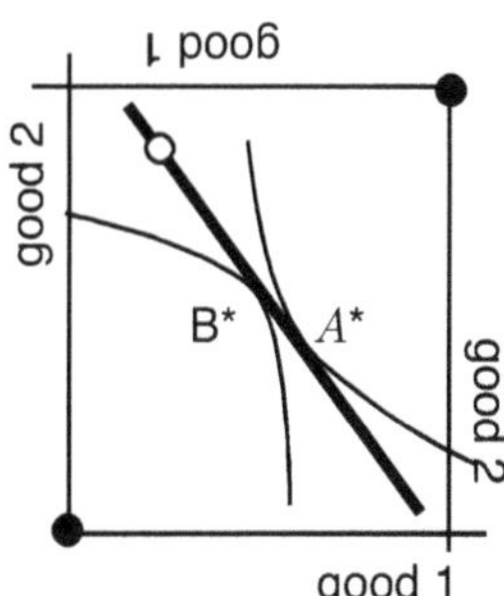

(c) At the relative prices given by the heavy line through the initial endowment, Alice demands the point labeled A^* and Bob the point labeled B^*. Too much good 1 is demanded. Markets don't clear; this is not an equilibrium.

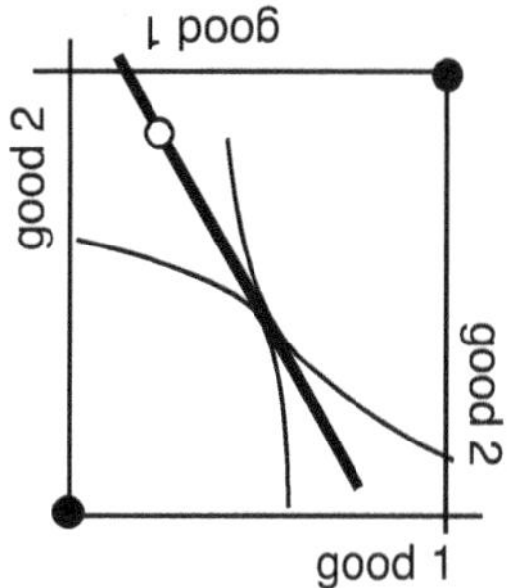

(d) At these relative prices, the demands by Alice and Bob, beginning from their endowments, are compatible with market clearing. This is a Walrasian equilibrium.

Figure 14.2. Efficiency and equilibrium in the Edgeworth Box

so that, except for the two "origins," the Pareto-efficient points lie inside the box. Depending on the slopes of the indifference curves, Pareto-efficient allocations could lie along the boundary of the box. See Problem 14.1.)

As for Walrasian equilibria: An equilibrium involves prices and price-driven choices by each consumer. For a two-good economy, relative prices are given by the slope of iso-cost lines, and the iso-cost line corresponding to a consumer's wealth is the iso-cost line through her initial endowment. A nice feature of an Edgeworth Box is that the same point represents (on their respective coordinate axes) the intial endowments of the two consumers, and a line through that common initial endowment point simultaneously depicts the iso-cost (equals initial wealth) line for both consumers. See, for instance, panel c, where the line drawn represents (approximately) a price ratio $p_1 : p_2 = 4 : 3$. The corresponding price-driven choice that Alice would make (marked with A^*) and the price-driven choice that Bob would make (marked B^*) are inconsistent with market clearing; demand for good 1 is higher than and demand for good 2 is less than the social endowment of these two goods. (Be sure you see this: Bob's demand for good 1 is measured as the horizontal distance from *his* origin, in the northeast corner, to the point B^*.) Panel d shows a Walrasian equilibrium: It is necessarily (!) a Pareto-efficient point (as you'll learn next chapter), where the line through the endowment point and this point has a slope that matches the slopes of the two indifference curves.

Before leaving the Edgeworth Box, let me be very clear on one point: The box allows you to depict divisions of the social allocation that do not waste any of the endowment. As long as one consumer or the other gets strictly higher utility from consumption of each good, the Pareto-efficient divisions will all have this no-waste property. But panel a of Figure 14.2 asserts that it shows divisions that are Pareto *improvements* on the initial endowment, and that, strictly speaking, isn't quite right. There can be Pareto improvements that waste some of either or both goods, as long as the waste isn't too high and the division of what is not wasted is pretty close to efficient.

14.4. Existence of Walrasian Equilibria

Does a given economy $\mathcal{E}$ possess a Walrasian equilibrium? Or, put somewhat differently, what assumptions about the economy $\mathcal{E}$ are sufficient to guarantee the existence of at least one Walrasian equilibrium? Answers to this question constitute a substantial literature; in his chapter on this topic in the *Handbook of Mathematical Economics* (1982), Debreu gives over 340 references. Although other methods for proving existence have been developed, the original methods employed fixed-point theorems.[2] Appendix 8 discusses fixed-point theorems; we will employ *Kakutani's Fixed-Point Theorem*, which I reproduce from the appendix here:

Proposition 14.6 (Kakutani's Fixed-point Theorem). *Suppose that X is a nonempty, compact, convex subset of R^n for some integer n. Suppose that $F : X \Rightarrow X$ is a correspondence from X to (subsets of) X that is upper semi-continuous, and convex and nonempty valued. Then for some $x \in X$, $x \in F(x)$.*

The idea, then, is to identify a set X and a correspondence ϕ from X to X for which fixed points ($x \in X$ such that $x \in \phi(x)$) are Walrasian equilibria; then make enough assumptions about the economy $\mathcal{E}$ so that a fixed-point theorem such as Kakutani's can be applied. This very general plan of attack admits a wide variety of specific approaches, beginning with identification of X; for instance, some approaches take for X the space of nonnegative, nonzero prices, normalized to sum to one (that is, $X = \{p \in R^k_+ : \sum_i p_i = 1\}$); this space is called *the unit simplex in* R^k, and is denoted by P. In other approaches, X is the space of relative weights put on consumers (that is, $X = \{(\alpha^h)^H_{h=1} \in R^H_+ : \sum_h \alpha^h = 1\}$), or the unit simplex in R^H, but with a

[2] The bibliographic notes at the end of the chapter give a cursory history, but for now it is worth observing that Arrow and Debreu (1954) and McKenzie (1954) are generally cited as the two papers that ignited this literature.

very different interpretation for the components of H. Some approaches take for X the product of these two spaces. Later in this section, the approach employed takes for X the product of P, the unit simplex of prices, and a compact set of excess demands (a compact subset of R^k).

A different dimension on which approaches to the question of existence vary concerns the starting point for the analysis. Very roughly, papers separate into two basic approaches. Some papers work directly with the consumers and firms that make up the economy. Others begin with an excess-demand correspondence or function. Of course, in the latter approach, consumers and, for economies with production, firms are at least implicitly present; assumptions are made about the excess-demand correspondence or function that are justified by appealing back to assumptions about the consumers and firms.

I will start with a result of the first type, working directly with consumers and firms, and following the approach of Arrow and Debreu (1954).[3] This presentation follows very closely some class notes of Vijay Krishna (2008). This approach starts with definitions and a result of independent interest.

Generalized games and their Nash equilibria

Definition 14.7. *An n-**player generalized game** $G = \{A_\ell, C_\ell, u_\ell\}_{\ell=1}^n$ for a finite integer n consists of, for each $\ell = 1, \ldots, n$,*

a. a set of strategies or actions A_ℓ,

b. a constraint correspondence $C_\ell : \prod_{m \neq \ell} A_m \rightrightarrows A_\ell$, and

c. a utility function $u_\ell : \prod_{\ell=1}^n A_\ell \to R$.

*A **Nash equilibrium** for this generalized game is a strategy profile $(a_\ell^*)_{\ell=1}^n \in \prod_{\ell=1}^n A_\ell$ such that, for each $\ell = 1, \ldots, n$,*

d. $a_\ell^* \in C_\ell\big((a_m^*)_{m \neq \ell}\big)$ and

e. a_ℓ^* maximizes $u_\ell\big(a_\ell, (a_m^*)_{m \neq \ell}\big)$ over $a_\ell \in C_\ell\big((a_m^*)_{m \neq \ell}\big)$.

Readers who know some (noncooperative) game theory will recognize that this is nearly the same as the definition of a *game in strategic form*, but with one complicating feature: In the usual definition of a strategic-form game, the set of strategies or actions available to a player is independent of the choices of other players. In this definition, the correspondence C_ℓ formalizes the notion that what is available to player ℓ can depend on the choices of the other players. Of course, this formulation, taken literally, presents significant problems of timing in the staging of the game: If the choices available to each player are constrained by the choices of all the other players, then how can choices be made? When are they made?

Consider in this regard the following simple example of a generalized game: There are two players; that is, $n = 2$. For $\ell = 1, 2$, $A_\ell = \{H, T\}$. $C_1(H) = \{H\}$,

[3] While the connection is a bit less direct, the results I give later, which begin with an excess-demand correspondence, are more in the spirit of the second seminal paper, McKenzie (1954).

$C_1(T) = \{T\}$, $C_2(H) = \{T\}$, and $C_2(T) = \{H\}$. (The assignment of utilities is irrelevant, as you will see momentarily.) The point of this example is probably obvious, but in case not: If 2 chooses H, then the only choice available to 1 is H. But if 1 chooses H, the only choice available to 2 is T, which makes T the only choice available to 1, which makes H the only choice available to 2. *No* strategy profile, or assignment of strategies/actions to the two players, satisfies the constraint that $a_\ell \in C_\ell(a_m)$ for $\ell, m = 1, 2$, $\ell \neq m$. There is no feasible way for the players to play this (generalized) game.

Our interest in this concept of a generalized game arises in the context of Walrasian equilibrium, and it is worth noting explicitly that this conundrum about how/when actions can be chosen if they are constrained by other actions taken simultaneously is inherent in the concept of a Walrasian equilibrium. Prices in an equilibrium presumably arise from the production and consumption choices of firms and consumers. But firms cannot make profit-maximizing choices without knowing the equilibrium prices, and consumers cannot make utility-maximizing choices without knowing their budget sets, which require equilibrium prices. Perhaps there is some mechanism that implements a Walrasian equilibrium, but the equilibrium concept itself is something of a reduced-form solution concept; it (perhaps) presumes the existence of some mechanism that gets the economy to an equilibrium, and being an equilibrium is a necessary condition for the outcome of this mechanism (again, perhaps), but the concept in no way tells us what is the mechanism, how it works, or whether in fact there is a mechanism.

Here, then, is the starting point for another branch of the literature of general equilibrium, a branch that we (in this volume, at least) ignore entirely: How is a general equilibrium to be implemented? We ignore this question not because it is uninteresting; it is vitally interesting if we are to take the concept seriously. But the tools needed to approach this question—at least the tools that are needed in modern approaches to this question—are tools from game theory, tools that are only developed in Volume 2.

Notwithstanding this hole, we can still theorize about generalized games. We will be using the notion of a strategy profile for all players except ℓ, or $(a_m)_{m \neq \ell}$ rather a lot; I'll henceforth denote this by $a_{\neg\ell}$.

Proposition 14.8. *Suppose that G is a generalized game for which*

a. *each A_ℓ is a nonempty, compact, convex subset of R^{k_ℓ} for some integer k_ℓ,*

b. *each C_ℓ is a continuous, nonempty-valued, and convex-valued correspondence, and*

c. *each u_ℓ is jointly continuous in the full vector of actions and quasi-concave in a_ℓ (for each fixed $a_{\neg\ell}$).*

Then G has a Nash equilibrium.

Remark. Since a Nash equilibrium strategy profile $a^* = (a_1^*, \ldots, a_n^*)$ must be feasible in the sense that each $a_\ell^* \in C_\ell(a_{\neg\ell}^*)$, the assumptions in the proposition (specifically, assumptions a and b) must imply that a feasible strategy profile exists. In other words, assumptions a and b rule out the sort of pathologies that the simple two-player example presents.

Proof. For each $\ell = 1, \ldots, n$, consider the parametric maximization problem

$$\text{Maximize } u_\ell(a_\ell; a_{\neg\ell}), \quad \text{subject to } a_\ell \in C_\ell(a_{\neg\ell}),$$

where the variable over which the maximum is being taken is a_ℓ, the strategies employed by others, or $a_{\neg\ell}$ (drawn from the full product set $\prod_{m \neq \ell} A_m$) is the parameter, and $u_\ell(a_\ell; a_{\neg\ell})$ means u_ℓ evaluated at the argument $(a_1, \ldots, a_n)$, with a_ℓ in the ℓth coordinate slot, and the other coordinates given by the "parameter" $a_{\neg\ell}$. Let $u_\ell^*(a_{\neg\ell})$ be the value of the maximized function (properly, the supremum, until we prove that the supremum is achieved), and let $A_\ell^*(a_{\neg\ell})$ be the set of maximizers. The assumptions made ensure that we can apply Berge's Theorem to this problem, concluding that $a_{\neg\ell} \rightarrow u_\ell^*(a_{\neg\ell})$ is a continuous function and $a_{\neg\ell} \Rightarrow A_\ell^*(a_{\neg\ell})$ is an upper semi-continuous correspondence. We moreover know that $A_\ell^*(a_{\neg\ell})$ is nonempty, and the quasi-concavity of u_ℓ in a_ℓ and convexity of $C_\ell(a_{\neg\ell})$ ensure that $A_\ell^*(a_{\neg\ell})$ is convex.

Piece together the various A_ℓ^* correspondences: Define

$$A^* : \prod_{\ell=1}^{n} A_\ell \Rightarrow \prod_{\ell=1}^{n} A_\ell,$$

as follows. At the argument $a = (a_1, \ldots, a_n)$, $(a'_1, \ldots, a'_n) \in A^*(a)$ if, for each ℓ, $a'_\ell \in A_\ell^*(a_{\neg\ell})$. I assert that this is an upper semi-continuous, nonempty-valued, and convex-valued correspondence. This takes some staring, but in the end is a fairly simple exercise in definitions, which I will leave to you as Problem 14.6.

And now we can invoke Kakutani's Fixed-Point Theorem. There exists some $a^* \in \prod_{\ell=1}^{n} A_\ell$ such that $a^* \in A^*(a^*)$, which means that each $a_\ell^* \in A_\ell^*(a_{\neg\ell}^*)$, which is precisely the definition of a Nash equilibrium. ∎

Existence of a Walrasian equilibrium for a very bounded economy

The next step in proving the existence of Walrasian equilibrium is to turn the problem of finding an equilibrium into a generalized game. To do this, and to apply Proposition 14.8, we need to satisfy the compactness assumptions of the proposition, which will mean some very strong boundedness assumptions imposed on the economy. In a final step (next subsection), we'll show how to relax these strong boundedness assumptions, requiring (only) weaker boundedness assumptions.

We work with an economy $\mathcal{E}$ in which there are H consumers and F firms, and we create a generalized game with $n = H + F + 1$ players. Each consumer is a player, choosing her consumption bundle x^h. Each firm is a player, choosing its production plan z^f. And the last player is a mythical auctioneer, who chooses prices p from the unit simplex P.

Of course, there is no problem with the set P being compact. But we are used to consumers who choose consumption bundles from R^k_+ and firms that choose production plans from sets Z^f that are (at least) unbounded below. That's where the very bounded assumptions come in: We will look at economies where consumer h selects a utility-maximizing consumption bundle from a compact set $X^h \subseteq R^k_+$, and where the production-possibility sets Z^f are compact. Otherwise, the assumptions made are reasonably standard:

Proposition 14.9. *Suppose the economy $\mathcal{E}$ satisfies the following conditions:*

a. For each consumer h, X^h is a compact and convex subset of R^k_+, e^h is interior to X^h, and $\succeq^h$ is continuous and convex.

b. For each firm f, Z^f is compact and convex and contains the origin.

Then $\mathcal{E}$ has a Walrasian equilibrium.

Proof. As already noted, we prove this by creating a generalized game, the Nash equilibria of which will be Walrasian equilibria.

The players in the game number $1 + H + F$:

- One player is a mythical auctioneer, who chooses a price p from the unit simplex P, unconstrained by the choices of the other players. (The auctioneer's utility function will be given momentarily.)
- Each consumer is a player, with full strategy set X^h, but with choices constrained by the choice of the auctioneer: If the auctioneer is choosing $p \in P$, then consumer h must choose x^h from the set $\{x \in X^h : p \cdot x \leq p \cdot e^h + \sum_f s^{fh}\pi^f(p)\}$, where π^f is the profit function of firm f, or $\pi^f(p) = \max\{p \cdot z^f : z^f \in Z^f\}$. The utility of consumer h is $u^h(x^h)$, where x^h is her choice of action.
- Each firm f is a player, with strategy set Z^f. Firm f's choice is unconstrained by the choices of the other players, and its utility depends on its own choice z^f and the choice of the auctioneer p, given by $p \cdot z^f$.
- The auctioneer's utility function, denoted by v, depends on all the choices by consumers, firms, and its own choice of price, and is given by $v(p, (x^h), (z^f)) = \sum_h p \cdot x^h - \sum_h p \cdot e^h - \sum_f p \cdot z^f$. That is, the auctioneer's objective is to choose p to maximize the value of the social net trade, given the choices by the consumers and the firms.

To apply Proposition 14.8, we must check that all (unconstrained) action sets are compact and convex subsets of some finite-dimensional Euclidean space, that the constraint correspondences are continuous and convex valued, and that each utility function is continuous in all the actions and quasi-concave in own action. That each (unconstrained) action set is a compact and convex subset of a finite-dimensional Euclidean space is by assumption. The constraint correspondences for the firms and the auctioneer are trivial (they give no constraints beyond choosing from Z^f or P), so they are clearly continuous and convex valued. As for the constraint correspondence of consumer h, budget sets are clearly convex. Continuity of each objective function in the full array of actions is quite clear, and quasi-concavity of each objective function in that player's own action is also easy: It is assumed for consumers; the objective functions of firms and the auctioneer are all linear in own actions.

What about continuity of the consumer's constraint correspondence? Results about the continuity of the budget set correspondence that we proved in earlier chapters are insufficient on two grounds: Each consumer's wealth is determined endogenously, and (more problematically) we allow individual prices (but not the full vector p) to be zero. So this takes some work: Fix consumer h, and temporarily, let $y^h(p) := p \cdot e^h + \sum_f s^{fh}\pi^f(p)$. That is, $y^h(p)$ is the budget constraint on consumer h in our generalized game; when the auctioneer chooses p from P, consumer h must choose an x^h such that $p \cdot x^h \leq y^h(p)$. Because $0 \in Z^f$ for all firms f (by assumption), $\pi^f(p) \geq 0$ for all p. Moreover, as a consequence of Berge's Theorem (and the assumed compactness of each Z^f), we know that $\pi^f(p)$ is continuous in p. Therefore, the function $y^h(p)$ is continuous in p and satisfies $y^h(p) \geq p \cdot e^h$ for all p.

Upper semi-continuity of the constraint-on-h correspondence is easy. Suppose $\{p_n\}$ is a sequence of prices from P approaching p, and x_n^h is feasible at p_n for each n and $\lim_n x_n^h = x^h$. Feasibility of x_n^h entails $x_n^h \in X^h$ for all n, so the compactness of X^h implies that $x^h \in X^h$. Feasibility also entails $p_n \cdot x_n^h \leq y^h(p_n)$ for all n; use continuity of the dot product on the left-hand side and of y^h on the right-hand side to conclude that $p \cdot x^h \leq y^h(p)$. That's upper semi-continuity.

Lower semi-continuity is harder and is where the assumption that e^h lies in the interior of X^h is employed. Because of this, we know there is some $\hat{x} \in X^h$ strictly less (less in all coordinates) than e^h; this implies that for some $\delta > 0$,

$$p \cdot \hat{x} + \delta \leq p \cdot e^h \leq y^h(p), \quad \text{or} \quad p \cdot \hat{x} \leq y^h(p) - \delta, \quad \text{for all } p \in P. \tag{14.1}$$

Now suppose that we are given an x that is budget feasible for h at some specific p^0; that is, $x \in X^h$ and $p^0 \cdot x \leq y^h(p^0)$. Suppose as well that we are given a sequence of prices $\{p^n\}$ with limit p^0. To show lower semi-continuity, we have to produce a sequence $\{x^n\}$ with limit x and where x^n is budget feasible at prices p^n. (We must do this for all n beyond some initial index, of course.) To do this, we look at convex combinations of x and $\hat{x}$. Since X^h is convex, all such convex combinations are in X^h. Fix (large) positive integer M. Since $y^h(p^0) - p^0 \cdot x \geq 0$ and $p^n \to p^0$, there exists N_M sufficiently large so that, for all $n > N_M$,

$$y^h(p^n) - p^n \cdot x \geq -\delta/M, \quad \text{or} \quad y^h(p^n) + \delta/M \geq p^n \cdot x. \tag{14.2}$$

Take the second inequality in display (14.1) for p^n (recall that it holds for all $p \in P$) and multiply by $1/(M+1)$, and combine it with the second inequality in (14.2) multiplied by $M/(M+1)$. We have that, for all $n \geq N_M$,

$$\left(\frac{1}{M+1}\right)p^n \cdot \hat{x} + \left(\frac{M}{M+1}\right)p^n \cdot x = p^n \cdot \left[\left(\frac{1}{M+1}\right)\hat{x} + \left(\frac{M}{M+1}\right)x\right] \leq$$

$$\left(\frac{1}{M+1}\right)(y^h(p^n) - \delta) + \left(\frac{M}{M+1}\right)\left(y^h(p^n) + \frac{\delta}{M}\right) = y^h(p^n).$$

Now choose $N_1, N_2, \ldots,$ so that $N_1 < N_2 < N_3 < \ldots$. And for each $n > N_1$, let M_n be the largest integer so that $n > N_{M_n}$ and

$$x^n = \frac{1}{M_n + 1}\hat{x} + \frac{M_n}{M_n + 1}x.$$

We know that $p^n \cdot x^n \leq y^h(p^n)$. And we know that $\lim_n M_n = \infty$; as soon as n exceeds N_M, M_n will exceed M. Hence $\lim x^n = x$, and we are done.

Therefore, we know that a Nash equilibrium to this generalized game exists, which I'll denote by $(p, (x^h), (z^f))$. The assertion, obviously, is that this Nash equilibrium is a Walrasian equilibrium of the original economy. The profit-maximization and utility-maximization conditions hold by design, once it is noted that a profit-maximizing choice by firm f means that $p \cdot z^f = \pi^f(p)$. But what about market clearing?

We know that each consumer satisfies her budget constraint, or

$$p \cdot x^h \leq p \cdot e^h + \sum_f s^{fh} p \cdot z^f.$$

Summing this inequality over all the h, reversing the order of summations in $\sum_h \sum_f$, and recalling that shares sum to 1, this gives

$$p \cdot \left(\sum_h x^h\right) \leq p \cdot \left(\sum_h e^h\right) + p \cdot \left(\sum_f z^f\right), \text{ or } p \cdot \left(\sum_h x^h - \sum_h e^h - \sum_f z^f\right) \leq 0.$$

That is, the auctioneer's optimized objective function is less or equal to zero at the Nash equilibrium. But suppose there was excess demand for some good; that is, for some $i = 1, \ldots, k$, $\sum_h x_i^h > \sum_h e_i^h + \sum_f z_i^f$. The auctioneer can pick the price vector p that is 1 in coordinate i and zero in all other coordinates to achieve a strictly positive value of her objective function. Since we know that, at its optimum, the auctioneer gets a nonpositive objective value, no good is in excess demand: Markets must clear. ∎

Existence for a somewhat bounded economy

The very strong bounds imposed on the pieces of economy $\mathcal{E}$ in Proposition 14.9 render it less than ideal. We can use the proposition as a step in proving a result that is a good deal less restrictive (although it does add one strengthened assumption on consumer preferences):

Proposition 14.10. *Suppose the economy $\mathcal{E}$ satisfies the following conditions:*

a. *For each consumer h, X^h is a convex subset of R^k_+, e^h is interior to X^h, and $\succeq^h$ is continuous and semi-strictly convex.*

b. *For each firm f, Z^f is convex and contains the origin.*

c. *There exists a large (scalar) β such that: If $(z^f)_{f=1}^F$ is a selection of production plans, where $z^f \in Z^f$ for each f, such that $\sum_h e^h + \sum_f z^f \geq 0$, then $\|z^f\| \leq \beta$ for all f.*

Then $\mathcal{E}$ has a Walrasian equilibrium.

Before giving the proof, some comments are in order.

- The definition of *semi-strictly convex preferences* was given back in Chapter 2, but has not been used since, so here it is again: Preferences are semi-strictly convex if they are convex and if, whenever $x \succ^h x'$, $ax + (1-a)x' \succ^h x'$ for all $a \in (0,1)$. As a special case, if preferences have a concave representation, they are semi-strictly convex.
- Condition c is the boundedness condition we impose. It says, more or less, that production technologies are not such that an unbounded amount of any good can be produced from the resources that can be provided by the economy. This does *not* mean that firms cannot have constant-returns-to-scale technologies. But if (say) firm f can produce unlimited amounts of an output good as long as it can get unlimited amounts of some input good, then it must not be possible for it to get unlimited amounts of that input good. This precludes, for instance, the production equivalent of a "perpetual motion machine," such as (for instance) where firm 1 can turn one unit good 1 into 1.1 units of good 2 on an unlimited scale, while firm 2 can turn one unit of good 2 into 1.1 units of good 1. It also precludes the knife-edge case where firm 1 can turn one unit of good 1 into one unit of good 2 (on any scale), while firm 2 can do the reverse.
- If $\mathcal{E}$ is a pure-exchange economy, then condition c holds automatically. So, as long as the conditions in a are acceptable, this gives a pretty general proof of existence for pure-exchange economies.

Proof. The idea of the proof is to use the bound in c to create an artificial economy $\hat{\mathcal{E}}$ from $\mathcal{E}$ that satisfies the conditions of Proposition 14.9, use 14.9 to extract a Walrasian equilibrium for $\hat{\mathcal{E}}$, and then prove that this is also an equilibrium for $\mathcal{E}$.

Let $\alpha = \|\sum_h e^h\|$, and let $\gamma = \alpha + F\beta + 1$. Repeated applications of the triangle inequality tell us that for any selection of production plans (z^f) such that $\sum_h e^h + \sum_f z^f \geq 0$, $\|\sum_h e^h + \sum_f z^f\| < \gamma$, and also $\|z^f\| \leq \beta < \gamma$ for each f.

Create $\hat{\mathcal{E}}$ from $\mathcal{E}$ as follows: For each consumer h, limit her consumption space $\hat{X}^h$ to be $\{x \in X^h : \|x\| \leq \gamma\}$. For each firm f, limit its production possibilities set $\hat{Z}^f$ to be $\{z \in Z^f : \|z\| \leq \gamma\}$. The preferences of the consumers and their endowments are unchanged. (It might be worth observing that the definition of γ ensures that each e^h is still in the interior of $\hat{X}^h$.)

Then $\hat{\mathcal{E}}$ satisfies the conditions of Proposition 14.9, and there exists a Walrasian equilibrium $(p, (x^h), (z^f))$ for $\hat{\mathcal{E}}$. I assert that $(p, (x^h), (z^f))$ is in fact a Walrasian equilibrium for the original economy $\mathcal{E}$:

- Market clearing (for the economy $\mathcal{E}$) of course holds, since it holds in $\hat{\mathcal{E}}$.
- Take any consumer h. Suppose that at prices p, with income given by $p \cdot e^h + \sum_f s^{fh} p \cdot z^f$, some affordable bundle $\hat{x} \in X^h$ is strictly better than x^h. Since X^h is convex and preferences $\succeq^h$ are semi-strictly convex, this implies that for all $a \in [0, 1)$, $ax^h + (1-a)\hat{x} \succ^h x^h$. Of course, all these convex combinations of x^h and $\hat{x}$ are affordable for h (at the equilibrium prices and her equilibrium wealth). But since each $x^{h'} \geq 0$ and $\sum_{h'} x^{h'} \leq \sum_{h'} e^{h'} + \sum_f z^f$, we know that $0 \leq x^h \leq \sum_{h'} e^{h'} + \sum_f z^f$; hence $\|x^h\| < \gamma$. Therefore, for some $a < 1$ (but, presumably, close to 1), $ax^h + (1-a)\hat{x} \in \hat{X}^h$, which would contradict the optimality for h of x^h among all budget-feasible bundles from $\hat{X}^h$. No such $\hat{x}$ can exist, and x^h is best for h from all budget-feasible bundles in her original (unconstrained) consumption space.
- Take any firm, say f. Suppose that, at prices p, there is some production plan $\hat{z}$ in f's unconstrained production-possibility set Z^f that gives higher profit than does z^f. Since Z^f is convex, all convex combinations $az^f + (1-a)\hat{z}$ are in Z^f, and (since profit is linear), all convex combinations for $a < 1$ must give greater profit than does z^f. But since $0 \leq \sum_h x^h \leq \sum_h e^h + \sum_f z^f$, we know that $\|z^f\| \leq \beta < \gamma$, which implies that for some $a < 1$ (but, perhaps, close to 1), $az^f + (1-a)\hat{z} \in \hat{Z}^f$, which would be a contradiction to z^f being profit maximizing (at prices p) in $\hat{Z}^f$. No such $\hat{z}$ can exist; z^f is profit maximizing at prices p in all of Z^f.

This means that $(p, (x^h), (z^f))$ is a Walrasian equilibrium for $\mathcal{E}$. ∎

Existence using aggregate excess demand

The alternative approach to beginning with consumers and firms is to work with an aggregate excess-demand correspondence $p \Rightarrow \mathcal{Z}(p)$ and seek a result along the lines, *If* $p \Rightarrow \mathcal{Z}(p)$ *satisfies ... [fill in some conditions], then there exists at least one* p *and* $\zeta \in \mathcal{Z}(p)$ *such that* $\zeta \leq 0$.

To be clear, this correspondence is meant to aggregate not only the excess demands of consumers in the economy, but also the netput decisions of individual firms. Specifically, if $Z^{f*}(p)$ represents the set of optimal (price-maximizing) netputs for firm f at prices p, and $\mathcal{Z}^h(p)$ is the set of optimal (utility-maximizing) excess demands by consumer h (for some given and fixed endowment vector e^h), and if we have finitely many firms and finitely many consumers, then

$$\mathcal{Z}(p) = \sum_h \mathcal{Z}^h(p) - \sum_f Z^{f*}(p),$$

where we are taking a Minkowski "sum" of the sets. The scare quotes around "sum" are there because the sign is reversed for netput vectors by firms; we want demands to be positive and supplies to be negative, which means positive signs on inputs and negative signs on outputs, the reverse of what we did in Chapter 9. In other words, $\zeta \in \mathcal{Z}(p)$ means that $\zeta = \sum_h x^h - \sum_h e^h - \sum_f z^f$ for a selection of x^h from the set of optimal demands for h and z^f from the set of optimal netputs for f, both at prices p.

This is only one possibility of the genesis of $\mathcal{Z}$. We might alternatively imagine a pure-trade economy with a continuum of consumers, and then (if you read the last parts of last chapter) $\mathcal{Z}(p)$ is the Aumann integral of the individual consumers' excess-demand sets at p. Or we might imagine that firms choose their netputs by some criterion other than maximizing profit. The point is, we *start* the formal developments with $p \Rightarrow \mathcal{Z}(p)$, making assumptions about this correspondence. For instance, it is typical to assume that

- $\mathcal{Z}(p)$ is homogeneous of degree 0 in p, or $\mathcal{Z}(p) = \mathcal{Z}(\lambda p)$ for $\lambda > 0$,
- $p \to \mathcal{Z}(p)$ is upper semi-continuous,
- *Walras' Law*: If $\zeta \in \mathcal{Z}(p)$, then $p \cdot \zeta = 0$, and
- Each $\mathcal{Z}(p)$ is a convex subset of R^k.[4]

The justification for these assumptions (and others that we will make) derives from those in-the-background consumers and firms. For instance, with finitely many consumers and firms, firms with closed and convex production-possibility sets that satisfy the recession-cone property, and consumers with convex, continuous, and locally insatiable preferences, you have all the results needed to justify these four assumptions for strictly positive prices. Or, alternatively, suppose that we have instead a pure-trade economy populated by consumers with continuous and locally insatiable but not necessarily convex preferences. And suppose we have a continuum of such consumers, the distribution of which is given by a non-atomic measure. Then (if you read through to the end of last chapter) you know that Aumann's Lemma guarantees the convexity of each $\mathcal{Z}(p)$, even if the various $\mathcal{Z}^h(p)$ are not necessarily convex.

Specific results add various boundedness assumptions to the list above (and, as we'll see, may relax Walras' Law), the justification for which also (sometimes implicitly) is played back to the in-the-background consumers and firms. And, very importantly, specific results differ concerning the assumed domain of $\mathcal{Z}$; for which prices are aggregate excess-demand sets well defined? If, for instance, one wants to have in the background firms with constant-returns-to-scale technologies, aggregate excess demand may be undefined for some prices; namely those for which the firms can make strictly positive, and hence infinite, profit. I won't try to chase those variations down here (the *Handbook* chapter by Debreu [1982] is a good starting point). Instead, I'll assume that $\mathcal{Z}(\cdot)$ is defined *at least* for all

[4] The literature does extend to analyses where the commodity space is infinite dimensional, but I won't tackle any of that here.

strictly positive prices p. (So, to the extent that I'm imagining firms making up a portion of aggregate excess-demand, their production-possibility sets *must* satisfy the recession-cone property.)

But there is still the question: Is $\mathcal{Z}$ defined only for strictly positive prices, or does it extend to all nonnegative prices? Even in a pure-exchange economy, excess demand for prices some of whose coordinate values are zero is problematic; if consumers' (or even one consumer's) preferences are never satiated in that good, they will demand infinite amounts of the good. If, however, we are willing to assume (in the background) that every consumer is eventually fully satiated in every good, and if firms cannot make use of (and so will not demand) infinite amounts of any input good, then it could be reasonable to suppose that $\mathcal{Z}$ is defined for all nonnegative p. However, in such cases, we lose some of the motivation for Walras' Law, which depends on local insatiability. The following result is classic:

Proposition 14.11 (The Debreu-Gale-Kuhn-Nikaido Lemma). *Let P be the unit simplex in R^k, that is $P = \{p \in R^k; p \geq 0, \sum_{i=1}^k p_i = 1\}$. Suppose that $\mathcal{Z}$ is a correspondence with domain P and range R^k (which is to say, $\mathcal{Z}(p) \subseteq R^k$ for each p). Suppose that $p \rightrightarrows \mathcal{Z}(p)$ is upper semi-continuous, nonempty valued, and convex valued, that $p \cdot \zeta \leq 0$ for all $\zeta \in \mathcal{Z}(p)$, and that there is a uniform bound on all the sets $\mathcal{Z}(p)$. Then there exists $p \in P$ and $\zeta \in \mathcal{Z}(p)$ such that $\zeta \leq 0$.*

Remarks. The obviously "difficult" additional assumption here is that the $\mathcal{Z}(p)$ are uniformly bounded. This would seemingly go best with assumptions about (eventual) global satiation in each good separately—that is, past a certain level, each consumer (or firm) has no use for more of each good. Since this could conceivably play havoc with Walras' Law, the lemma supposes only that $p \cdot \zeta \leq 0$ for $\zeta \in \mathcal{Z}(p)$, which (for those in-the-background actors) amounts to an assumption that consumers obey their budget constraints. Note that $\mathcal{Z}$ is defined in this proposition only for prices p in the unit simplex; hence no mention of homogeneity is needed.

One can imagine using this result as part of the proof of less restrictive results, where one bounds a given economy in something like the way we did earlier this section and then proves that the bound can be removed. Hence its name is the D-G-K-N *Lemma*. The multiple names attached to this result are not because the four did this collaboratively, but instead because they came up with proofs virtually contemporaneously and independently. In fact, the result as stated here is a simplified version of the full result, which concerns bounded $\mathcal{Z}$ whose domain is a closed and convex cone of prices.

The ingenious proof that follows is due to Debreu (1956).

Proof. Let B be a compact and convex subset of R^k such that $\mathcal{Z}(p) \subseteq B$ for all $p \in P$. The existence of B is guaranteed by the uniform boundedness assumption. Define a correspondence Φ on the domain $P \times B$ as follows:

$$\Phi(p, \zeta) = \{(p', \zeta') : \zeta' \in \mathcal{Z}(p),\ p \in P,\ p'_i > 0 \text{ only if } \zeta_i \geq \zeta_j \text{ for all } j = 1, \ldots, k\}.$$

The ζ' part of the definition is straightforward, but think for a minute what is going on with the p' part: At the argument (p, ζ), the price portion of vectors in $\Phi(p, \zeta)$ are prices that only put positive weight on the largest components of ζ. This should remind you of the auctioneer in the generalized game: Φ, like that auctioneer, is "picking" prices p' that maximize the market value of the vector that is playing the role of excess demand. (This proof strategy can be found in a lot of existence proofs.)

I assert that $\Phi(p, \zeta)$ is nonempty and convex and that $(p, \zeta) \Rightarrow \Phi(p, \zeta)$ is upper semi-continuous. Nonemptiness is obvious. For convexity, note that $\Phi(p, \zeta)$ is the product of two sets, $\{p' \in P : p'_i > 0 \text{ implies } \zeta_i \geq \zeta_j \text{ for all } j\}$ and $\mathcal{Z}(p)$. That $\mathcal{Z}(p)$ is convex is an assumption of the proposition; to show that the other set is convex, simply note that if p' and p'' are both in the set, then they only put positive weight on the largest components of ζ, and so (obviously) does any convex combination of them. And the product of two convex sets is obviously convex.

Now suppose that $(p^n, \zeta^n) \to (p^0, \zeta^0)$ and, for each n, we have a $(\hat{p}^n, \hat{\zeta}^n) \in \Phi(p^n, \zeta^n)$ where $(\hat{p}^n, \hat{\zeta}^n) \to (\hat{p}^0, \hat{\zeta}^0)$. Because of the upper semi-continuity of $\mathcal{Z}$, it is immediate that $\hat{\zeta}^0 \in \mathcal{Z}(p^0)$. And suppose that, for some i, $\hat{p}^0_i > 0$. Then for all large n, $\hat{p}^n_i > 0$; hence $\zeta^n_i \geq \zeta^n_j$ for all j, and hence $\zeta^0_i \geq \zeta^0_j$ for all j. Together these imply that $(\hat{p}^0, \hat{\zeta}^0) \in \Phi(p^0, \zeta^0)$, which is upper semi-continuity.

This means that Φ satisfies all the required conditions to apply Kakutani's Fixed-Point Theorem. (The domain $P \times B$ is clearly compact.) Therefore, there is some (p, ζ) such that $(p, \zeta) \in \Phi(p, \zeta)$. Of course, this means that $\zeta \in \mathcal{Z}(p)$, and also that $p_i > 0$ only if $\zeta_i \geq \zeta_j$ for all j. Were it the case that $\zeta_i > 0$ for some i, then p would only charge (be strictly positive for) js such that $\zeta_j > 0$, which would imply $p \cdot \zeta > 0$. This contradicts $p \cdot \zeta \leq 0$ for all $\zeta \in \mathcal{Z}(p)$, and so $\zeta \leq 0$, which is what we needed to show. ∎

The obvious weakness in this result is in the assumption that $\mathcal{Z}$ is defined (in an upper semi-continuous and uniformly bounded manner) out to the boundary of the price simplex. If we imagine that goods are always desirable, it is more likely that demand for a given good, and hence excess demand, grows without bound as the relative price of that good approaches zero (and assuming that the consumers' incomes are not simultaneously vanishing) and is undefined when the relative price of the good is zero. To accommodate this sort of situation, we have the following result.

Proposition 14.12.[5] *Let P^o be the open unit simplex in R^k; that is, $P^o = P \cap R^k_{++}$. Suppose $\mathcal{Z}$ is a correspondence from P^o to R^k that is nonempty and convex valued, upper semi-continuous, satisfies Walras' Law ($p \cdot \zeta = 0$ for all $\zeta \in \mathcal{Z}(p)$), is uniformly bounded below, and satisfies the following boundary condition: If $\{p^n\}$ is a sequence of strictly positive prices from P^o that approaches p^0 that is not strictly positive, and if $\zeta^n \in \mathcal{Z}(p^n)$ for each n, then $\lim_n \|\zeta^n\| = \infty$. Then there exists $p \in P^o$ such that $0 \in \mathcal{Z}(p)$.*

5 The form given here is attributed by Debreu (1982) to Hildenbrand (1974).

Remarks. As in Proposition 14.11, we are restricting attention to $\mathcal{Z}$ defined on prices normalized to lie in the unit simplex, so we don't need to mention homogeneity. The assumptions that $\mathcal{Z}(p)$ is nonempty and convex, that $p \Rightarrow \mathcal{Z}(p)$ is upper semi-continuous, and that Walras' Law holds, should all seem standard at this point.

The uniform lower bound is easiest to justify if we think of this excess-demand correspondence emerging from a pure-exchange economy; in that case, a lower bound on excess demand is provided by the sum of all the endowment vectors. With firms around, it is a little harder to justify; the sort of no-perpetual-motion-machines assumption we encountered in Proposition 14.10 is required.

The boundary condition deserves the most attention. Suppose that we have a sequence of prices $\{p^n\}$ from P^o converging to some $p^0 \notin P^o$. Of course, p^0 is nonnegative, and since the sum of its components is 1, there are j such that $p^0_j > 0$. If we imagine that at least some consumers have strictly positive endowments of such goods j, then those consumers will have income or wealth that, along the sequence, is strictly bounded away from zero. And then, the idea is, as the price of some good i goes to zero, these consumers will demand increasing, and unboundedly increasing, amounts of good i. Of course, this is just the underlying idea; to be turned into a result requires assumptions on the preferences of the consumers. But it is the sort of logic that makes the boundary assumption reasonable. It should be observed that in saying that $\|\zeta^n\| \to \infty$, it is only the components of ζ^n whose prices are going to zero that can diverge; Walras' Law implies that the excess demand for any good whose price is bounded away from zero must be bounded above (by a bound that depends on the consumer's overall endowment size and the amount by which the price of the good is bounded away from zero).

Finally, note that the conclusion is $0 \in \mathcal{Z}(p)$ for some p. Before we said that our general goal was to find a p and $\zeta \in \mathcal{Z}(p)$ such that $\zeta \leq 0$. But here the price p must be strictly positive, and if Walras' Law holds—if $p \cdot \zeta = 0$ for strictly positive p—then $\zeta \leq 0$ implies $\zeta = 0$.

Proof.[6] We mimic Debreu's proof of the D-G-K-N Lemma. To begin, let P^ϵ for $\epsilon > 0$ be the unit price simplex in R^k but with each price constrained to be at least ϵ; that is, $P^\epsilon = \{p \in P : p_i \geq \epsilon \text{ for all } i = 1, \ldots, k\}$. Let $B < 0$ be the uniform lower bound on each component of $\zeta \in \mathcal{Z}(p)$; I assert that each component of ζ for $\zeta \in \mathcal{Z}(p)$, $p \in P^\epsilon$, is bounded above by $B^\epsilon = -B/\epsilon$. This follows from Walras' Law: Suppose $\zeta \in \mathcal{Z}(p)$ for $p \in P^\epsilon$. We know that $p \cdot \zeta = 0$. The dot product is $\sum_i p_i \zeta_i$, which we can separate into

$$\sum_i p_i \max\{0, \zeta_i\} + \sum_i p_i \min\{0, \zeta_i\}.$$

[6] This proof was suggested to me by Phil Reny. Debreu's chapter in the *Handbook* provides a significantly more complicated proof, albeit for a more complex version of the result. This leads me to suspect that the proof I'm about to give has a problem; if so, I don't see it. And if it doesn't have a problem, it is so natural following Debreu's proof of the D-G-K-N Lemma that it probably has been given elsewhere; if someone has a reference, I'd be grateful to be told of it.

The entire sum must be zero, the second term is bounded below by B, and each $p_i \geq \epsilon$, so if $\zeta_i \geq 0$ it must be that $\zeta_i \leq -B/\epsilon$.

Next, for every $\epsilon > 0$ (and $\epsilon < 1/k$), construct a correspondence Φ^ϵ on the domain $P^\epsilon \times \{\zeta \in R^k : B \leq \zeta_i \leq B^\epsilon\}$ as follows: $(p', \zeta') \in \Phi^\epsilon(p, \zeta)$ if $\zeta' \in \mathcal{Z}(p)$, $p' \in P^\epsilon$, and $p'_i = \epsilon$ if, for some $j \neq i$, $\zeta_j > \zeta_i$. In other words, given a pair (p, ζ), $\Phi^\epsilon(p, \zeta)$ is the product of (1) the set of all prices in P^ϵ that put weight greater than ϵ only on the "largest" components of ζ and (2) the set $\mathcal{Z}(p)$. Note that since $p \in P^\epsilon$, every $\zeta' \in \mathcal{Z}(p)$ satisfies $B \leq \zeta'_i \leq B^\epsilon$, so $\Phi^\epsilon(p, \zeta)$ is a subset of the domain of the correspondence. The domain is clearly compact. By the arguments given in the proof of the D-G-K-N Lemma, $\Phi^\epsilon(p, \zeta)$ is convex and nonempty for every (p, ζ), and $(p, \zeta) \rightrightarrows \Phi^\epsilon(p, \zeta)$ is upper semi-continuous. Hence for every $\epsilon \in (0, 1/k)$, we can find at least one fixed point of the correspondence; select one such fixed point for each $\epsilon = 1/n$ $(n > k)$, calling the fixed point (p^n, ζ^n). Note well, this means that $\zeta^n \in \mathcal{Z}(p^n)$ and $p_i^n = 1/n$ if, for some $j \neq i$, $\zeta_j^n > \zeta_i^n$.

The sequence of prices $\{p^n\}$ lies in P, which is compact, so looking along a subsequence if necessary, we can assume that $\lim_n p^n$ exists and equals some p^0. I assert that p^0 must be in the interior of P. Suppose it is not: By the boundary condition, we know that $\lim_n \|\zeta^n\| = \infty$. Since the components of ζ^n are bounded below, this means that as $n \to \infty$, some components of ζ^n are growing (positively) without bound. Let $z^n = \max_{i=1,\ldots,k} \zeta_i^n$; of course, $\lim_n z^n = \infty$. Let $I^n = \{i : \zeta_i^n = z^n\}$; we know that $\sum_{i \in I^n} p_i^n \geq 1 - k/n$, since p_j^n must equal $1/n$ for $j \notin I^n$. But then $p^n \cdot \zeta^n \geq B + (1 - k/n) z_n$, which for large enough n will be strictly positive, contradicting Walras' Law.

Hence, p^0 is interior to P. Letting $r = \min_i p_i^0$, this implies that $p^n \in P^{r/2}$ for all sufficiently large n; hence there is a uniform upper bound on the ζ^n. Looking along a subsequence as necessary, we know that ζ^n converges to ζ^0, and by upper semi-continuity of $\mathcal{Z}$ on the interior of P, $\zeta^0 \in \mathcal{Z}(p^0)$. Moreover, the argument used in the proof of the D-G-K-N Lemma shows that all the coordinate values of ζ^0 must be the same, so by Walras' Law, they all must be 0. ■

To close this section, let me reiterate: There are many, many existence-of-Walrasian-equilibrium results in the literature. There are many that use variations on fixed-point arguments as here, but with different (and, usually, weaker) assumptions, and then there are other methodologies that have been employed. We've barely scratched the surface.

14.5. The Set of Equilibria for a Fixed Economy

Having proved (under conditions) that an economy has at least one Walrasian equilibrium, it is natural to wonder, How many? Economists brought up on the classic picture of supply equals demand (Figure 1.1) are fond of the definite character of the "answer"; there is one and only one price at which the rising (and continuous) supply curve hits the falling (and continuous) demand curve, and hence the theory makes a very definite prediction about the outcome. Moreover, in many cases one is able to engage in fruitful comparative statics exercises concerning the single equilibrium; as this parameter rises, equilibrium price rises (or falls). Obviously, such results are helped by uniqueness of the equilibrium.[7] Is the set of Walrasian equilibria for a given economy well behaved in this sense?

The literature provides three sorts of results. The first sort of result provides conditions under which there is, for the given economy, a unique Walrasian equilibrium. Following the analogy with Figure 1.1, the conditions are not hard to envision conceptually: We want conditions that guarantee that, as the relative price of any good rises, its excess demand falls. Formalizing this conceptual vision is not trivial, but it can certainly be done; see, for instance, Mas-Colell, Whinston, and Green (1995, Section 17F).

On the other hand, it is easy to give examples of economies that admit multiple equilibria. Consider, for instance, the following caricature exchange economy featuring two goods and two consumers, Alice and Bob. Alice and Bob have identical preferences, given by the utility function $u((x_1, x_2)) = \min\{x_1, x_2\}$. Alice is endowed with one unit of good 1 and none of good 2; Bob with one unit of good 2 and none of good 1. Then for any price vector $(p_1, p_2) \in P$ (that is, normalized so that $p_1+p_2 = 1$), Alice has initial wealth of p_1 and so will choose the bundle (p_1, p_1), while Bob has initial wealth p_2 and chooses (p_2, p_2). (If this isn't obvious to you, write down Alice's problem, noting that at her optimal bundle, $x_1 = x_2$. Or draw the Edgeworth Box representing this economy, which may be a good idea in any case. If p_1 or p_2 is zero, the choices indicated are not the only utility-maximizing choices for one of the two, but they are utility-maximizing choices.) Of course, these choices are market clearing; *every* price vector is a Walrasian-equilibrium price vector for this economy.

So what, if anything, can be said about the set of Walrasian equilibria? For one thing, the set of equilibria is (under mild conditions) closed. I will not state this as a formal proposition, but instead indicate two ways to interpret and prove the result. The first and easiest way is if we take as primitive an excess-demand function ζ (defined, say, on the unit simplex P of prices) that is continuous among its other properties. The set of equilibrium *prices* (in P) is then $\{p \in P : \zeta(p) \le 0\}$, which is certainly closed if ζ is continuous. Or suppose we use the sort of "full" formulation provided at the start of the chapter and in Definition 14.2. Suppose that, for a fixed economy $\mathcal{E}$, we have a sequence of Walrasian equilibria $\{(p_n, (x_n^h), (z_n^f)); n = 1, 2, \ldots\}$ (where the subscript n denotes the index of the sequence) that converges to a price, consumption allocation, and set of production plans $(p_0, (x_0^h), (z_0^f))$. As long as enough assumptions are made so that each consumer's Marshallian demand correspondence and each firm's optimal netput correspondences are upper semi-continuous, it is clear that the limiting $(p_0, (x_0^h), (z_0^f))$ will satisfy the conditions of being a Walrasian equilibrium.

But that's pretty much all one can say (beyond the results in Propositions 14.4 and 14.5). Mas-Colell (1977) proves the following remarkable result. As always (in

[7] This is not meant as a precise statement and, indeed, if one uses the methods of monotone comparative statics, it is not only imprecise, but somewhat incorrect.

this chapter) P denotes the unit simplex in R^k.

Proposition 14.13 (Mas-Colell's Theorem). *Let Q be any nonempty and closed subset of P that lies entirely within the interior of P. Then there exists a pure-exchange economy $\mathcal{E}$ (for k commodities), with consumers that have continuous, strictly convex, and monotone preferences, such that Q is the set of Walrasian-equilibrium prices for $\mathcal{E}$ (restricted to P).*

The remarkable thing is, the proposition says that this is true for *any* closed subset of P that stays away from the boundaries of P. If $k = 3$, then P is a triangle, and we can draw pictures. For instance, suppose we take for Q the set shown in Figure 14.3; that is, points that are "filled in" within the simplex. This is a closed set within the interior of P, so Mas-Colell's Theorem tells us that there exists an economy, meaning a collection of well-behaved consumers with endowments, for whom the Walrasian-equilibrium price vectors in P spell out the names of three fathers of modern general equilibrium theory.

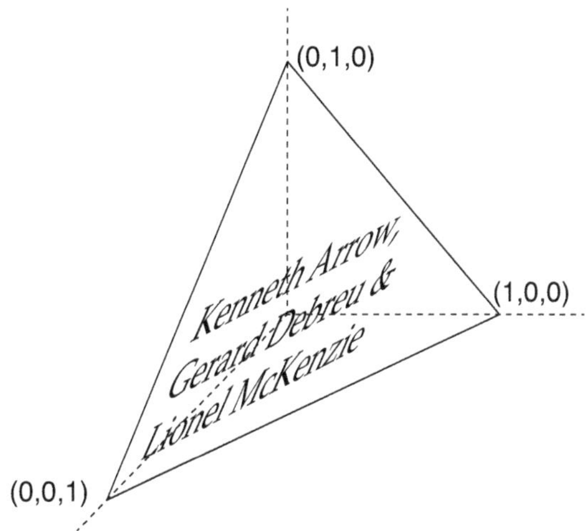

Figure 14.3. Equilibrium prices. Mas-Colell's Theorem (Proposition 14.13) tells us that we can find an exchange economy for which the set of Walrasian-equilibrium prices spell out the names of the three fathers of modern general equilibrium theory. The example is for $k = 3$, and we are looking (only) at the projection of equilibrium prices onto the unit simplex in R^3; that is, on price vectors p such that $\sum_{i=1}^{3} p_i = 1$.

This result is, in fact, an extension of the Sonnenschein-Mantel-Debreu Theorem from last chapter. The key is to find a continuous excess-demand function (on P) that satisfies $p \cdot \zeta(p) = 0$ for all p and whose zeros coincide with the set Q. In fact, this isn't quite enough; even using Debreu's version of the S-M-D Theorem, we have to worry about what happens near the boundary, where one price or another goes to zero. But Mas-Colell (1977) sharpens the S-M-D Theorem sufficiently to deal with this. (If you didn't fully appreciate the S-M-D Theorem before, perhaps this will convince you of its power.) See Problem 14.10 for the easier part of the proof of this result.

So, if we allow for any economy, very little can be said in the way of restrictions on the set of Walrasian-equilibrium prices. The third sort of result found in the literature then asks, What can be said about the set of Walrasian equilibria (and their prices) for "most" economies. Short of showing that there is a unique equilibrium, which takes fairly strong assumptions on the underlying economy, what one hopes (and strives) for is a result that "most" economies have a finite number of (necessarily isolated) equilibria. Using the methods of differential geometry and topology, such results are accessible; I will not pursue them here but strongly recommend the excellent introduction to this topic in Mas-Colell, Whinston, and Green (1995, Section 17D).

14.6. The Equilibrium Correspondence

An economy $\mathcal{E}$ will, in general, have a nonempty set of Walrasian equilibria. Suppose we think of economies being drawn from some topological space of economies; then we might be interested in the *Walrasian-equilibrium correspondence*, the correspondence from the space of economies to the space of prices $\times$ allocations $\times$ production plans that, for each economy, identifies the Walrasian equilibria of that economy.

To illustrate how this sort of thing might proceed and to give the simplest result available, fix a finite collection of consumers $h = 1, \ldots, H$, specified by their continuous and complete and transitive preferences $\succeq^h$ or, equivalently, their continuous utility functions u^h, with domain (consumption sets) $X^h = R^k_+$. And fix a finite collection of firms $f = 1, \ldots, F$, specified by their nonempty and closed production-possibility sets $Z^f \subseteq R^k$.[8] If you are wondering "What about consumer endowments?," this is what varies parametrically: For $e \in (R^k_+)^H$, economy $\mathcal{E}(e)$ is the economy made up of the fixed consumers and firms, where the vector of endowments for the consumers is given by e. For each economy, $\mathcal{E}(e)$, let $\mathbf{W}(\mathcal{E}(e))$ be the set of Walrasian equilibria for $\mathcal{E}(e)$, where each equilibrium is given by a price vector, consumption allocation, and array of production plans. We'd like to say that the correspondence $e \rightrightarrows \mathbf{W}(\mathcal{E}(e))$ is upper semi-continuous, but this isn't quite true. Instead, we have the following result.

Proposition 14.14. *For a sequence of endowment vectors $\{e_n\}$ with limit e, suppose that $(p_n, \mathbf{x}_n, \mathbf{z}_n) \in \mathbf{W}(\mathcal{E}(e^n))$ for each n. If $\lim_n(p_n, \mathbf{x}_n, \mathbf{z}_n) = (p, \mathbf{x}, \mathbf{z})$, and if $p \in R^k_{++}$, then $(p, \mathbf{x}, \mathbf{z}) \in \mathbf{W}(\mathcal{E}(e))$.*[9]

This is left to you to do as Problem 14.11.

Bibliographic Notes

Formulations of general equilibrium go back to (at least) the work of Walras. Questions of existence were "settled" by counting equations and unknowns and noting

[8] Recall that Assumption 14.1 holds throughout this chapter, so this adds no new assumptions.

[9] What if p is only nonnegative? See the discussion in the *Student's Guide*.

that they matched, after the redundant equations are removed; that is, unrigorously. The modern formulation and (rigorous) existence results date from the early 1950s. As noted already, the two pioneering papers devoted to existence are Arrow and Debreu (1954) and McKenzie (1954). There are many book-length treatments of the subject, which typically include material we will cover in the next two chapters: Debreu (1959) is truly classic, and I first learned the subject from Arrow and Hahn (1971), which, sadly, seems to be out of print. Among other things, Arrow and Hahn begin with a "Historical Introduction" chapter that sets the subject in its broad historical context. Scarf (1973) presents a computational approach, using methods of bilinear complementarity. I have skimped on mathematical considerations beyond existence, in part because it is pointless to try to compete with the wonderful exposition on the topic found in Mas-Colell, Whinston, and Green (1995); the discussion of Mas-Colell's Theorem here is lifted from Shafer and Sonnenschein (1982).

Problems

■ *14.1. (a) Draw an Edgeworth Box in which both consumers have strictly increasing and strictly convex preferences (strictly quasi-concave utility) and where the Pareto-efficient divisions of the social endowment lie entirely along the boundary of the box. Is it possible to have a case (with strictly increasing and strictly convex preferences) where the southeast corner of the box (all of good 1 is given to consumer 1, and all of good 2 is given to consumer 2) is Pareto efficient, but other Pareto-efficient points involve each consumer getting a strictly positive amount of both goods?

(b) Suppose we have a two-consumer, two-good, pure-exchange economy in which consumer 1 only wants to consume good 1 (and she wants as much of that as she can get), and consumer 2 only wants to consume good 2. Their initial endowments are identical: Each has 10 units of good 1 and 10 units of good 2. What does the Edgeworth Box for this pathological economy look like? Which allocations lie in the core, and what are the Walrasian equilibria?

■ *14.2. Consider the following two-person, two-commodity, pure-exchange economy. Consumer 1, Alice, has utility function $u^A(x_1, x_2) = 0.4\ln(x_1) + 0.6\ln(x_2)$. Consumer 2, Bob, has utility function $u^B(x_1, x_2) = 0.5\ln(x_1) + 0.5\ln(x_2)$. Alice's endowment is $(e_1^A, e_2^A) = (10, 10)$, while Bob's endowment is $(e_1^B, e_2^B) = (5, 10)$. What are the Walrasian equilibria of this economy?

■ *14.3. Consider the following economy: There are three goods, two consumers, and two firms. Good 3 is used as an input to the production process, and provides no utility of consumption. Firm 1, which is owned entirely by Alice, has a technology that allows good 3 to be made into good 1, according to the simple linear technology $x_1 \leq 3x_3$. That is, if firm 1 uses x_3 units of the input good, it can make up to $3x_3$ units of the first consumption good. Firm 2, owned entirely by Bob, uses the third good to make the second consumption good, and its technology is described by $x_2 \le 4x_3$. Each consumer initially owns 5 units of good 3; that is, $e^A = e^B = (0, 0, 5)$. Alice's utility function is $u^A(x_1, x_2, x_3) = 0.4\ln(x_1) + 0.6\ln(x_2)$, while Bob's utility function is $u^B(x_1, x_2, x_3) = 0.5\ln(x_1) + 0.5\ln(x_2)$.

What are the Walrasian equilibria of this economy? What would be the equilibria if the shareholdings were reversed?

■ 14.4. Redo Problem 14.3, where the only change is that, this time, $e^A = e^B = (5, 5, 5)$.

■ 14.5. Redo Problem 14.3, but where the technology of the first firm is described by $x_1 \le 3x_3^{1/3}$ and the technology of the second firm is described by $x_2 \le 2x_3^{1/2}$.

■ *14.6. In the proof of Proposition 14.8, I asserted (in the penultimate paragraph of the proof) that if we pasted together the various A_i^* correspondences to create A^*, then A^* is an upper semi-continuous, nonempty-valued, and convex-valued correspondence. Provide the details to support this assertion.

■ 14.7. In the proof of Proposition 14.9, the constraint on the actions of consumer h imposed by the actions of the other players (firms and the auctioneer) was set as follows: Consumer h is constrained to choose an x^h from X^h that satisfies the further constraint $p \cdot x^h \le p \cdot e^h + \sum_f s^{fh}\pi^f(p)$. Suppose we modified this, to say that consumer h must satisfy the further constraint $p \cdot x^h \le p \cdot e^h + \sum_f s^{fh} p \cdot z^f$, where z^f is the production plan chosen by firm f. If you try to redo the proof with this seemingly innocuous change, you will run into substantial difficulties. What are they?

■ *14.8. The proofs of Proposition 14.11 and 14.12 can be simplified or, at least, changed, if we assume that we begin with an excess-demand function instead of an excess-demand correspondence. In this problem, I point you in the direction of a different proof of Proposition 14.11 for excess-demand functions; Problem 14.9 will concern Proposition 14.12.

Suppose that $\zeta : P \to R^k$ is continuous and satisfies $p \cdot \zeta(p) \le 0$ for all p. For each $p \in P$ and $i = 1, \ldots, k$, let $\xi_i(p) := \max\{p_i, \zeta_i(p) + p_i\}$, and let

$$\phi(p) = \frac{\xi(p)}{\sum_{i=1}^k \xi_i(p)}.$$

Prove that ϕ is a continuous function that maps P into itself. Now apply Brouwer's Fixed-Point Theorem (see Appendix 8), and argue that if $\phi(p) = p$, then $\zeta(p) \le 0$.

■ *14.9. Let P^o be the interior of the unit simplex, and suppose we have an excess-demand function $\zeta : P^o \to R^k$ that is continuous, satisfies Walras' Law ($p \cdot \zeta(p) = 0$ for all $p \in P^o$), is bounded below, and satisfies the boundary condition: If $\{p^n\}$ is a sequence of prices drawn from P^o with limit p^0 that is not strictly positive, then $\lim_n \|\zeta(p^n)\| = \infty$.

Under these assumptions, construct a correspondence ϕ on the unit simplex of prices $P = \{p \in R_+^k : \sum_i p_i = 1\}$. For $p \in P^o$, let $\phi(p) = \{p' \in P : p'_i > 0$ only if $\zeta_i(p) \geq \zeta_j(p)$ for all $j = 1, \ldots, k\}$. And for $p \in P \setminus P^o$, let $\phi(p) = \{p' \in P : p'_i > 0$ only if $p_i = 0\}$. Think of this as follows: For p in the interior of P, $\phi(p)$ consists of all price vectors in P that assign positive prices to those goods that, according to $\zeta(p)$, are in greatest excess demand. And for p on the boundary of P, $\phi(p)$ assigns positive prices to those goods that "in theory" would be in infinite net demand, if we had defined ζ at the boundary. (The second of these characterizations is a bit inaccurate, but it is in the rough spirit of the second extra assumption.)

Show that ϕ is nonempty valued, convex valued, and upper semi-continuous. Then apply Kakutani and prove that any fixed point of ϕ must be interior and satisfy $\zeta(p) = 0$.

■ 14.10. One piece of the proof of Mas-Colell's Theorem (Proposition 14.13) is to generate, for a given closed set $Q \subseteq P$, which is entirely interior to P, an excess-demand function ζ that is continuous on the interior of P, that satisfies $p \cdot \zeta(p) = 0$, and that is zero (only) on the set Q. (Mas-Colell's extension of the S-M-D Theorem depends as well on this excess-demand function exploding in norm for any sequence of prices that approach the boundary of P, but don't worry about that.) Fixing the set Q, let $d(p, Q) = \min_{q \in Q} \|p - q\|$; because Q is closed, we know that the min here is appropriate and that $p \to d(p, Q)$ is a continuous function of p. Let $\hat{q}$ be any arbitrarily selected member of Q, and let

$$\zeta(p) = d(p, Q)\left(\frac{\hat{q}_1}{p_1} - 1, \ldots, \frac{\hat{q}_k}{p_k} - 1\right).$$

It should be clear that, away from the boundary of p, this function is continuous in p. Prove that it satisfies $p \cdot \zeta(p) = 0$ for all p ($\in$ the interior of P) and that it is zero at p if and only if $p \in Q$. (In the chapter, we said that an equilibrium was any p such that $\zeta(p) \leq 0$. Why don't we need to worry about the possibility of $\zeta(p) < 0$?)

■ *14.11. Prove Proposition 14.14.

Chapter Fifteen

General Equilibrium, Efficiency, and the Core

From the earliest days of academic economics (which is to say, from the time of Adam Smith), economists have written paeans of praise to competitive markets. "The *invisible hand* of prices coordinates the activities of myriad producers and consumers in an efficient manner, and moreover in a manner that, experience has taught us, centrally planned and administered economies cannot match." (Cue background music with choirs of angels.) Indeed, taken a step or two further, some versions of this hymn of praise to markets become hymns of praise to greed, self-interest, and the profit motive.

Behind the ideological bombast of these claims are serious models and analyses that mix ideas about the incentive to innovate and the aggregation of information by prices; models and analyses that, when done well, point out serious limitations to the simple claim that "markets are good." Incentives (to innovate or otherwise) and information aggregation are topics well beyond the framework of general equilibrium that was created last chapter, so this is not something that we can seriously tackle at this point. But within the context of general equilibrium, fundamental results provide a starting point for assertions that price equilibria are "good." This chapter develops some of those fundamental results.

In essence, this chapter presents four types of results:

- The *First Theorem of Welfare Economics* shows that, under seemingly very mild conditions, the allocation portion of a Walrasian equilibrium is Pareto efficient. Using the resources (endowments and production capacities) provided in an equilibrium, no consumer can be made strictly better off than she is in a Walrasian equilibrium without making some other consumer worse off.

- But, as we discussed in Chapter 8, to say that some mechanism (in this case, the price mechanism) produces Pareto-efficient outcomes falls short of a justification for the mechanism: It may produce a particular Pareto-efficient outcome that is, at the same time, vastly inequitable. The *Second Theorem of Welfare Economics* repairs this flaw in the following sense: Under somewhat more restrictive assumptions, and subject to a technical caveat, it proves that any (feasible) Pareto-efficient allocation is the allocation portion of a Walrasian equilibrium (sort of), if you are allowed to redistribute endowments and shareholdings first.

- Pareto efficiency is one criterion of goodness of a social outcome, but imagine a situation in which, relative to a given Walrasian-equilibrium outcome, another feasible outcome (a) is better for some subset of all the consumers in the economy and (b) can (somehow) be enforced by this subset. Of course, for (a) to hold for an equilibrium outcome, which must be Pareto efficient by the First Welfare Theorem, it must be that this alternative outcome makes someone outside the subset worse off. But if this subset has the power to enforce this outcome, isn't (a) still a valid objection to the goodness of the original Walrasian equilibrium? This idea, suitably formalized and generalized, leads to the game-theoretic notion of the *core*. And the third result of this chapter shows that the hypothesized situation cannot happen: Under mild conditions, every Walrasian equilibrium lies in the core of the economy, meaning no subset of consumers has the power to make its members better off than at the equilibrium outcome, although (of course) this result is predicated on a particular specification of the power possessed by each subset of consumers.

- And, very roughly, if a consumption allocation is in the core, then it is a Walrasian equilibrium. At least, this is true if there is "enough" competition in the economy. We formalize this result as a limiting result as the number of consumers increases, in the *Debreu-Scarf Theorem*; and then we discuss how it is obtained as an exact result for "large" economies (economies with a continuum of agents).

All these results depend on the assumptions that markets are competitive (consumers and firms take prices as given) and that there are no externalities. The chapter ends with a discussion of externalities and a variant on Walrasian equilibrium, Lindahl equilibrium, which in theory if not in practice "solves" the problem of externalities.

15.1. The First Theorem of Welfare Economics

We continue in this chapter to adhere to Assumption 14.1. For the sake of completeness, here it is again (renumbered):

Assumption 15.1. *Each consumer's commodity space X^h is R^k_+. Each consumer's utility function u^h is continuous. Each firm's production-possibility set Z^f is closed and nonempty.*

For an economy $\mathcal{E}$, recall from Definition 14.3 that $\boldsymbol{X}^*$ is the set of feasible allocations for the economy:

$$\boldsymbol{X}^* := \left\{ \boldsymbol{x} \in \boldsymbol{X} : \sum_{h=1}^{H} x^h \leq \sum_{h=1}^{H} e^h + \sum_{f=1}^{F} z^f, \text{ for some } \boldsymbol{z} \in \boldsymbol{Z} \right\},$$

where $\boldsymbol{X} = \prod_{h=1}^{H} X^h$ and $\boldsymbol{Z} = \prod_{f=1}^{F} Z^f$. Also define

$$X^* = \left\{ x \in R^k : x \leq \sum_h e^h + \sum_f z^f \text{ for some } \boldsymbol{z} \in \boldsymbol{Z} \right\}.$$

Or, in words, X^* consists of all bundles of goods that are less than or equal to bundles that the economy is capable of producing (including the initial endowments). Of course, if $\boldsymbol{x} \in \boldsymbol{X}^*$, then $\sum_h \boldsymbol{x}^h \in X^*$. But note carefully; $\boldsymbol{x} \in \boldsymbol{X}^*$ means that each $\boldsymbol{x}^h \in X^h$; that is, each $\boldsymbol{x}^h$ is nonnegative. In defining X^*, we allow "bundles" of goods with negative components. (See Problem 15.1 for more on this point.)

Proposition 15.2 (The First Theorem of Welfare Economics). *Suppose $(p, \boldsymbol{x}, \boldsymbol{z})$ is a Walrasian equilibrium for an economy with locally insatiable consumers, such that $p \geq 0$. Then $\boldsymbol{x}$ is Pareto efficient within $\boldsymbol{X}^*$.*

Proof. Let $(p, \boldsymbol{x}, \boldsymbol{z})$ be the Walrasian equilibrium in question, and let $Y := \sum_{h=1}^{H} p \cdot \boldsymbol{x}^h$. That is, Y is the value at the equilibrium prices of the summed-up equilibrium consumption bundles of the consumers in the economy.

The proof consists of showing that the hyperplane $\{x \in R^k : p \cdot x = Y\}$ separates (in a strict sense) bundles of goods that the economy is capable of producing from bundles of goods that can be distributed to the consumers in a fashion that is Pareto superior to $\boldsymbol{x}$.

We have, first of all, that

$$p \cdot x \leq Y \text{ for all } x \in X^*. \tag{15.1}$$

To see why this is true, note first that by local insatiability, each consumer spends all of her endowment, or $p \cdot \boldsymbol{x}^h = p \cdot e^h + \sum_f s^{fh} p \cdot \boldsymbol{z}^f$. Summing this over all h, we get $Y = \sum_h p \cdot \boldsymbol{x}^h = \sum_h p \cdot e^h + \sum_h \sum_f s^{fh} p \cdot \boldsymbol{z}^f = \sum_h p \cdot e^h + \sum_f p \cdot \boldsymbol{z}^f$, where the last equation follows from the fact that the sum of the shares in each firm totals 1. But for any $z^f \in Z^f$, $p \cdot \boldsymbol{z}^f \geq p \cdot z^f$, because $\boldsymbol{z}^f$ is profit maximizing at the prices p. Hence, for any $\hat{\boldsymbol{z}} \in \boldsymbol{Z}$,

$$Y = \sum_h p \cdot e^h + \sum_f p \cdot \boldsymbol{z}^f \geq \sum_h p \cdot e^h + \sum_f p \cdot \hat{\boldsymbol{z}}^f.$$

Now take $x \in X^*$; we have $x \leq \sum_h e^h + \sum_f \hat{\boldsymbol{z}}^f$ for some $\hat{\boldsymbol{z}} \in \boldsymbol{Z}$. Since prices p are assumed to be nonnegative, we can dot this inequality by the prices p and, combining with the previous display, we have

$$p \cdot x \leq \sum_h p \cdot e^h + \sum_f p \cdot \hat{\boldsymbol{z}}^f \leq Y,$$

which is (15.1).

Fixing $\boldsymbol{x}$, the equilibrium allocation, let

$$\boldsymbol{PS}(\boldsymbol{x}) = \{\hat{\boldsymbol{x}} \in R_+^{kH} : \hat{\boldsymbol{x}} \text{ is Pareto superior to } \boldsymbol{x}\};$$

here $\boldsymbol{PS}$ is an obvious mnenomic for "Pareto superior." And let

$$\mathcal{PS}(\boldsymbol{x}) = \left\{ x \in R_+^k : x = \sum_h \hat{\boldsymbol{x}}^h \text{ for some } \hat{\boldsymbol{x}} \in \boldsymbol{PS}(\boldsymbol{x}) \right\}.$$

Or, in words, $\mathcal{PS}(\boldsymbol{x})$ is the set of bundles of goods that can be parceled out to the consumers in a manner that is Pareto superior to $\boldsymbol{x}$. The point of these definitions is that

$$p \cdot x > Y \text{ for all } x \in \mathcal{PS}(\boldsymbol{x}). \tag{15.2}$$

This is a consequence of two consumer-by-consumer inequalities: For $\hat{x} \in R_+^k$,

$$\begin{aligned} &\text{If } \hat{x} \succeq^h \boldsymbol{x}^h, \text{ then } p \cdot \hat{x} \geq p \cdot \boldsymbol{x}^h, \text{ and} \\ &\text{if } \hat{x} \succ^h \boldsymbol{x}^h, \text{ then } p \cdot \hat{x} > p \cdot \boldsymbol{x}^h. \end{aligned}$$

For the second of these, suppose $\hat{x} \succ^h \boldsymbol{x}^h$. Since $\boldsymbol{x}^h$ is optimal for consumer h facing prices p, it must be that $\hat{x}$ is unaffordable for h at these prices. But since (we assume) consumers are locally insatiable, $\boldsymbol{x}^h$ must exhaust h's budget at prices p; hence $\hat{x}$ must cost strictly more than $\boldsymbol{x}^h$ at prices p. And for the first, even if $\hat{x} \sim^h \boldsymbol{x}^h$, if $p \cdot \hat{x} < p \cdot \boldsymbol{x}^h$, then local insatiability implies that h can purchase some bundle near to (but strictly better than) $\hat{x}$ for less than $p \cdot \boldsymbol{x}^h$, which would contradict the optimality for h of $\boldsymbol{x}^h$ at prices p.

But with these two consumer-by-consumer inequalities, we have (15.2): If $\hat{x} \in \mathcal{PS}(\boldsymbol{x})$, then $\hat{x} = \sum_h \hat{\boldsymbol{x}}^h$ for some $\hat{\boldsymbol{x}} \in \boldsymbol{PS}(\boldsymbol{x})$. For this $\hat{\boldsymbol{x}}$, $\hat{\boldsymbol{x}}^h \succeq^h \boldsymbol{x}^h$ for all h, and $\hat{\boldsymbol{x}}^h \succ^h \boldsymbol{x}^h$ for at least one h. Hence, by the two consumer-by-consumer inequalities,

$$\sum_h p \cdot \hat{\boldsymbol{x}}^h > \sum_h p \cdot \boldsymbol{x}^h.$$

Pulling the p outside the sum on the left-hand side gives $p \cdot \hat{x}$, while the right-hand side is Y.

And, with (15.1) and (15.2) in hand, we conclude that $\boldsymbol{x}$ must be Pareto efficient. For if it were not, there would be some feasible allocation $\hat{\boldsymbol{x}}$ that Pareto dominates it. To be feasible, the bundle of goods that allows the allocation $\hat{\boldsymbol{x}}$ must have value (under prices p) no greater than Y. But to be Pareto superior to $\boldsymbol{x}$, the same bundle must have value (again, under prices p) strictly exceeding Y. The two are incompatible. ∎

It is worth emphasizing that the assumptions in the First Theorem—equilibrium prices must be nonnegative and consumers must be locally insatiable—are pretty minimal. Minimal or not, you might wonder whether we need them. We used $p \geq 0$ in one place, where we said that if $x \in X^*$, the physical feasiblity of x, which is the inequality $x \leq \sum_h e^h + \sum_f \hat{z}^f$ for some array of production plans $\hat{z}$, can be turned into a value inequality. That is, we can "dot" both sides of the physical feasiblity inequality and get a value inequality running in the same direction. A negative price might reverse the inequality. But if we had from the start defined physical feasibility with an equality—if dumpsters are not freely available—then we wouldn't need to assume that $p \geq 0$ at this (or any other) step.

Local insatiability, on the other hand, is absolutely at the heart of the First Theorem. If consumers are not (all) locally insatiable, Walrasian-equilibrium allocations can be Pareto inefficient. Roughly put, a consumer who has a local bliss point (a point that, locally, maximizes her preferences) can, at an equilibrium, waste resources that other consumers would like to have but cannot afford. For more on this, see Problem 15.2.

15.2. The Second Theorem of Welfare Economics

The proof just given for the First Theorem of Welfare Economics is written in a way that emphasizes its internal logic: If $(p, \mathbf{x}, \mathbf{z})$ is a Walrasian equilibrium with $p \geq 0$ and with locally insatiable consumers, then the price vector p and scalar $Y = p \cdot \left(\sum_h x^h\right)$ form a hyperplane that separates technologically feasible bundles of goods from bundles that can be allocated to consumers in a manner that is Pareto superior to $\mathbf{x}$. Hence, what is feasible cannot be Pareto superior to $\mathbf{x}$.

This suggests a possible converse. Suppose $\mathbf{x}$ is a Pareto-efficient allocation within some economy. By definition, this says that the set of bundles that can be allocated in a manner Pareto superior to $\mathbf{x}$ are disjoint from the set of bundles that are feasible for this economy. Suppose we use the Separating-Hyperplane Theorem to find a price vector that separates these two sets; that is, that separates X^* from $\mathcal{PS}(\mathbf{x})$. Perhaps this separating price vector is, in some sense, a vector of equilibrium prices.

Roughly speaking, this is the line of argument in the Second Theorem of Welfare Economics. But there are two—shall we say?—snags in getting this to work. First—and not really a snag but instead a technical requirement—is that to employ the Separating-Hyperplane Theorem, we will need to know that the sets being separated are convex. We'll need assumptions on the firm's production-possibility sets Z^f to ensure that X^* is convex and on consumer preferences to ensure that $\mathcal{PS}(\mathbf{x})$ is convex. And—this time a real snag—in the First Theorem, we got semi-strict separation between the two sets; we had a $\leq$ inequality on one side and a $>$ inequality on the other. Unless we can call upon the Strict-Separation Theorem—and if you think about it, we cannot; $\mathcal{PS}(\mathbf{x})$ is not closed, and neither set is likely to be compact—we will get two weak inequalities. Because of this, the Second Theorem deals not with Walrasian equilibria but with something slightly weaker:

Definition 15.3. *A **Walrasian quasi-equilibrium** for an economy $\mathcal{E}$ is a triple $(p, \mathbf{x}, \mathbf{z})$ such that $p \neq 0$, where*

a. $\mathbf{z}^f$ maximizes $p \cdot z$ over $z \in Z^f$, for each f,

b. $p \cdot \mathbf{x}^h \leq p \cdot e^h + \sum_f s^{fh} p \cdot \mathbf{z}^f$,

c. *If* $x^h \in X^h$ *is such that* $x^h \succ^h \mathbf{x}^h$, *then* $p \cdot x^h \geq p \cdot e^h + \sum_f s^{fh} p \cdot \mathbf{z}^f$, *and*

d. $\sum_h \mathbf{x}^h \leq \sum_h e^h + \sum_f \mathbf{z}^f$.

Comparing this with the definition of a Walrasian equilibrium, the difference comes in the consumer-maximization part of the definition. In a Walrasian equilibrium, the consumer maximizes her utility at the allocation, given prices and her wealth, where it is implicit in the consumer-maximization part of the definition that the equilibrium allocation is budget feasible for each consumer. Here, budget feasibility is explicit (part b), but in place of optimality of the equilibrium allocation, we have the slightly weaker condition c. How much weaker?

Proposition 15.4. *If* $(p, \mathbf{x}, \mathbf{z})$ *is a Walrasian equilibrum for economy* $\mathcal{E}$, *then it is a Walrasian quasi-equilibrium. Conversely, if* $(p, \mathbf{x}, \mathbf{z})$ *is a Walrasian quasi-equilibrium for* $\mathcal{E}$ *and if* $p \cdot e^h + \sum_f s^{fh} p \cdot \mathbf{z}^f > 0$ *for consumer* h, *then for this consumer, if* $x^h \succ^h \mathbf{x}^h$, *then* $p \cdot x^h > p \cdot e^h + \sum_f s^{fh} p \cdot \mathbf{z}^f$. *Or, put the other way around, for this consumer* h, $\mathbf{x}^h$ *maximizes her preferences over her budget set. So if each consumer's net wealth at the prices* p *is strictly positive, the quasi-equilibrium is a Walrasian equilibrium.*

Proof. If $(p, \mathbf{x}, \mathbf{z})$ is a Walrasian equilibrium for $\mathcal{E}$, then parts a, b, and d of Definition 15.3 are immediate. And if $x^h \in X^h$ satisfies $x^h \succ^h \mathbf{x}^h$, then (so that $\mathbf{x}^h$ is optimal) it must be that x^h is not budget feasible, or $p \cdot x^h > p \cdot e^h + \sum_f s^{fh} p \cdot \mathbf{z}^f$. So part c of the definition holds with a strict inequality.

Conversely, suppose $(p, \mathbf{x}, \mathbf{z})$ is a Walrasian quasi-equilibrium for $\mathcal{E}$ and, for consumer h, $p \cdot e^h + \sum_f s^{fh} p \cdot \mathbf{z}^f > 0$. Suppose that $x \in R^k_+$ is such that $x \succ^h \mathbf{x}^h$ and $p \cdot x \leq p \cdot e^h + \sum_f s^{fh} p \cdot \mathbf{z}^f$. Part c of the definition then tells us that $p \cdot x = p \cdot e^h + \sum_f s^{fh} p \cdot \mathbf{z}^f > 0$. Since preferences are continuous, for some α strictly less than (but, presumably, close to) 1, $\alpha x \succ^h \mathbf{x}^h$, but $p \cdot (\alpha x) < p \cdot x$ (since $p \cdot x > 0) = p \cdot e^h + \sum_f s^{fh} p \cdot \mathbf{z}^f$, which contradicts part c of the definition. Hence if $p \cdot e^h + \sum_f s^{fh} p \cdot \mathbf{z}^f > 0$ and $x \succ^h \mathbf{x}^h$, it must be that $p \cdot x > p \cdot e^h + \sum_f s^{fh} p \cdot \mathbf{z}^f$.

Therefore, if $p \cdot e^h + \sum_f s^{fh} p \cdot \mathbf{z}^f > 0$ for all h, every consumer maximizes her preference over her budget set with the bundle $\mathbf{x}^h$. The physical-feasibility condition of a Walrasian equilibrium is precisely d in Definition 15.3, and the firm-profit-maximization condition is a, so this is indeed a Walrasian equilibrium. ∎

In other treatments of these ideas, you may find condition b of the definition of a quasi-equilibrium omitted. This omission has the following explanation.

Proposition 15.5. *Suppose all consumers are locally insatiable.*

a. *If condition c in the definition of a Walrasian quasi-equilibrium holds for any triple* $(p, \mathbf{x}, \mathbf{z})$, *then* $p \cdot \mathbf{x}^h \geq p \cdot e^h + \sum_f s^{fh} p \cdot \mathbf{z}^f$ *for each* h, *and (hence)* $\sum_h p \cdot \mathbf{x}^h \geq \sum_h p \cdot e^h + \sum_f p \cdot \mathbf{z}^f$.

b. *Conditions c and d in the definition of a Walrasian quasi-equilibrium imply condition b for any triple* $(p, \mathbf{x}, \mathbf{z})$ *such that* $p \geq 0$.

c. *If you replace the inequality in condition d in the definition of a Walrasian quasi-equilibrium with an equality, then condition c and the modified condition d imply condition b for any triple* $(p, \boldsymbol{x}, \boldsymbol{z})$, *regardless of the signs of components of* p.

Proof. (a) Suppose that for some triple $(p, \boldsymbol{x}, \boldsymbol{z})$, $p \cdot \boldsymbol{x}^h < p \cdot e^h + \sum_f s^{fh} p \cdot \boldsymbol{z}^f$. By local insatiability, there is some x^h near enough to $\boldsymbol{x}^h$ so that $p \cdot x^h < p \cdot e^h + \sum_f s^{fh} p \cdot \boldsymbol{z}^f$ and yet $x^h \succ^h \boldsymbol{x}^h$, which would be a contradiction to condition c of the definition. Hence condition c implies that $p \cdot \boldsymbol{x}^h \geq p \cdot e^h + \sum_f s^{fh} p \cdot \boldsymbol{z}^f$. Adding this up over all h gives $\sum_h p \cdot \boldsymbol{x}^h \geq \sum_h p \cdot e^h + \sum_f p \cdot \boldsymbol{z}^f$.

(b) If $p \geq 0$, then condition d of the definition implies that $\sum_h p \cdot \boldsymbol{x}^h \leq \sum_h p \cdot e^h + \sum_f p \cdot \boldsymbol{z}^f$. Therefore, enlisting part a of this proposition, conditions c and d together imply equality. But then we must have equality for each consumer individually; if some consumer spent more than her wealth, to get equality in the adding up, we would need some other consumer to spend less, which would contradict part a.

(c) If condition d is redefined to have equality rather than an inequality, then regardless of the sign of components of p, we have $\sum_h p \cdot \boldsymbol{x}^h = \sum_h p \cdot e^h + \sum_f p \cdot \boldsymbol{z}^f$. Now proceed as in the previous paragraph. ∎

Now for the main result of this section:

Proposition 15.6 (The Second Theorem of Welfare Economics). *Suppose that, for a given economy* $\mathcal{E}$, *each* Z^f *is convex, and each* $\succeq^h$ *is convex and locally insatiable. Suppose* $\boldsymbol{x} \in \boldsymbol{X}^*$ *is Pareto efficient within* $\boldsymbol{X}^*$. *Then there exists a way to reallocate endowments and shareholdings among consumers such that, for the economy with the reallocated endowments and shareholdings, there are production plans* $\boldsymbol{z}$ *and a nonzero price vector* p *such that* $(p, \boldsymbol{x}, \boldsymbol{z})$ *is a Walrasian quasi-equilibrium.*

Proof. Recall how this is meant to go. We want to use the Separating-Hyperplane Theorem to separate X^*, the set of all bundles of goods this economy can produce, from the set of all bundles of goods that can be allocated among the consumers in a fashion that is Pareto superior to $\boldsymbol{x}$. The assumption that each Z^f is convex is easily seen to be enough to ensure that X^* is a convex set, but to get convexity of the other set, it is convenient to work with the set of bundles that can be divided in a fashion that is *strictly* Pareto superior to $\boldsymbol{x}$. Formally, define

$$\boldsymbol{SPS}(\boldsymbol{x}) = \{\hat{\boldsymbol{x}} \in R_+^{kH} : \hat{\boldsymbol{x}}^h \succ^h \boldsymbol{x}^h \text{ for all } h\}, \text{ and}$$

$$\mathcal{SPS}(\boldsymbol{x}) = \left\{ x \in R_+^k : x = \sum_h \hat{\boldsymbol{x}}^h \text{ for some } \hat{\boldsymbol{x}} \in \boldsymbol{SPS}(\boldsymbol{x}) \right\}.$$

Since each $\succeq^h$ is convex, the set $\mathcal{SPS}(\boldsymbol{x})$ is convex: Let $\hat{x} = \sum_h \hat{\boldsymbol{x}}^h$ and $\check{x} = \sum_h \check{\boldsymbol{x}}^h$ be any two members of $\mathcal{SPS}(\boldsymbol{x})$, where $\hat{\boldsymbol{x}}$ and $\check{\boldsymbol{x}}$ are the corresponding two members of $\boldsymbol{SPS}(\boldsymbol{x})$. For any $\alpha \in [0,1]$, $\alpha\hat{\boldsymbol{x}}^h + (1-\alpha)\check{\boldsymbol{x}}^h \succ^h \boldsymbol{x}^h$ for each h, since, for each h, the convex combination is at least as good for h as whichever of $\hat{\boldsymbol{x}}^h$ and $\check{\boldsymbol{x}}^h$

is less good, and both $\hat{\boldsymbol{x}}^h$ and $\check{\boldsymbol{x}}^h$ are strictly better for h than $\boldsymbol{x}^h$. Therefore, $\alpha\hat{\boldsymbol{x}} + (1-\alpha)\check{\boldsymbol{x}} \in \boldsymbol{SPS}(\boldsymbol{x})$, so $\alpha\hat{x} + (1-\alpha)\check{x} = \sum_h(\alpha\hat{\boldsymbol{x}}^h + (1-\alpha)\check{\boldsymbol{x}}^h) \in \mathcal{SPS}(\boldsymbol{x})$. (Why is it more convenient to work with strict Pareto superiority? See Problem 15.3.)

Of course, because $\boldsymbol{x}$ is Pareto efficient, the (now convex) sets $\mathcal{SPS}(\boldsymbol{x})$ and X^* are disjoint. So there is a hyperplane that separates them: For some vector $p \neq 0$ and some scalar Y, $p \cdot x \leq Y$ for all $x \in X^*$ and $p \cdot x \geq Y$ for all $x \in \mathcal{SPS}(\boldsymbol{x})$.

By the usual argument (X^* is comprehensive below), $p \geq 0$.

Some pieces of notation will be handy. We are assuming that $\boldsymbol{x}$ is in $\boldsymbol{X}^*$, which means that $\sum_h \boldsymbol{x}^h \leq \sum_h e^h + \sum_f \boldsymbol{z}^f$ for some array of feasible production plans $\boldsymbol{z} \in \boldsymbol{Z}$. Let x^0 denote $\sum_h \boldsymbol{x}^h$. Also, because of local insatiability, for each household h we can find a sequence of consumption bundles $\{\hat{x}_n^h\}$ that approach $\boldsymbol{x}^h$ and such that (1) $\hat{x}_n^h \succ^h \boldsymbol{x}^h$ and (2) $|p \cdot (\hat{x}_n^h - \boldsymbol{x}^h)| \leq 1/n$.

I assert that $p \cdot x^0 = Y$; that is, x^0 lies along the hyperplane that separates X^* from $\mathcal{SPS}(\boldsymbol{x})$. Of course, since $\boldsymbol{x}$ is feasible, $x^0 \in X^*$, so $p \cdot x^0 \leq Y$. On the other hand, for any n, the allocation $(\hat{x}_n^1, \ldots, \hat{x}_n^H) \in \boldsymbol{SPS}(\boldsymbol{x})$; therefore $\sum_h \hat{x}_n^h \in \mathcal{SPS}(\boldsymbol{x})$, and so $p \cdot \left(\sum_h \hat{x}_n^h\right) \geq Y$. But, by the triangle inequality,

$$\left|p \cdot \left(\sum_h \hat{x}_n^h\right) - p \cdot x^0\right| \leq \sum_h |p \cdot (\hat{x}_n^h - \boldsymbol{x}^h)| \leq H/n.$$

Therefore, $p \cdot x^0 \geq Y - H/n$. Since n is arbitrary here, $p \cdot x^0 \geq Y$, which proves the assertion.

Since $x^0 \leq \sum_h e^h + \sum_f \boldsymbol{z}^f$ and $p \geq 0$, $Y = p \cdot x^0 \leq \sum_h p \cdot e^h + \sum_f p \cdot \boldsymbol{z}^f$. But, of course, $\sum_h e^h + \sum_f \boldsymbol{z}^f \in X^*$, so $p \cdot \left(\sum_h e^h + \sum_f \boldsymbol{z}^f\right) \leq Y$. We conclude that $\sum_h p \cdot \boldsymbol{x}^h = \sum_h p \cdot e^h + \sum_f p \cdot \boldsymbol{z}^f = Y$. Moreover, $p \cdot \boldsymbol{x}^h \geq 0$ for each h, so if we let $\beta^h = p \cdot \boldsymbol{x}^h / Y$, we have that $\beta^h \geq 0$ for each h and $\sum_h \beta^h = 1$. (If $Y = 0$, any assignment of weights (β^h) that sum to one will do.) Consider endowing consumer h with a β^h share of the social endowment and a β^h share of each firm, and at the prices p, consumer h's wealth will be precisely $\beta^h Y$, which is precisely $p \cdot \boldsymbol{x}^h$.

I assert, then, that with these alternative endowments and shareholdings, $(p, \boldsymbol{x}, \boldsymbol{z})$ is a Walrasian quasi-equilibrium. Parts b and d of the definition hold by construction; we only have to verify parts a (firms are maximizing their profits) and c (a bundle that is better than $\boldsymbol{x}^h$ for consumer h costs at least as much as $\boldsymbol{x}^h$).

For part a, pick any firm f' and any production plan $z' \in Z^{f'}$. Consider the array of production plans where firm f' produces z' and all other firms $f \neq f'$ produce $\boldsymbol{z}^f$. This production plan produces the bundle of goods $\sum_h e^h + \sum_{f \neq f'} \boldsymbol{z}^f + z' \in X^*$. Since this is an element of X^*, its value under p is less or equal to Y, or

$$\sum_h p \cdot e^h + \sum_{f \neq f'} p \cdot \boldsymbol{z}^f + p \cdot z' \leq Y = \sum_h p \cdot e^h + \sum_{f \neq f'} p \cdot \boldsymbol{z}^f + p \cdot \boldsymbol{z}^{f'}.$$

Cancel the identical terms on either side of the inequality and you get $p \cdot z' \leq p \cdot \boldsymbol{z}^{f'}$. Hence $\boldsymbol{z}^{f'}$ is indeed profit maximizing for firm f'. Since f' is arbitrary here, we have part a of the definition.

And for part c, choose any consumer h' and any consumption bundle x such that $x \succ^{h'} \boldsymbol{x}^{h'}$. For integer n, consider the consumption allocation that gives x to h' and $\hat{x}_n^h$ to consumer h, for $h \neq h'$. This consumption allocation is in ***SPS***($\boldsymbol{x}$), and so

$$p \cdot x + \sum_{h \neq h'} p \cdot \hat{x}_n^h \geq Y = p \cdot \boldsymbol{x}^{h'} + \sum_{h \neq h'} p \cdot \boldsymbol{x}^h.$$

Rearrange this as

$$p \cdot x \geq p \cdot \boldsymbol{x}^{h'} + \sum_{h \neq h'} (p \cdot \boldsymbol{x}^h - p \cdot \hat{x}_n^h) \geq p \cdot \boldsymbol{x}^{h'} - (H-1)/n,$$

where the last inequality uses the triangle inequality. The integer n here is arbitrary; hence $p \cdot x \geq p \cdot \boldsymbol{x}^{h'}$, which is part c of the definition. ■

It is easy to get lost in the details, but the argument is really quite straightforward. The convexity assumptions on the Z^f and the $\succeq^h$ ensure that the sets X^* and $\mathcal{SPS}(\boldsymbol{x})$ are convex. They are disjoint if $\boldsymbol{x}$ is Pareto efficient. So a hyperplane separates them. Since $\boldsymbol{x}$ is feasible, $\sum_h \boldsymbol{x}^h$ is in X^*, but local insatiability puts $\sum_h \boldsymbol{x}^h$ on the boundary between X^* and $\mathcal{SPS}(\boldsymbol{x})$, and hence within the hyperplane itself. And from there, it is more or less a matter of bookkeeping to (1) find a way to redistribute endowments and shareholdings so that each consumer h can just afford $\boldsymbol{x}^h$ at the prices p, (2) verify that firms are maximizing profits with the plan that makes $\boldsymbol{x}$ feasible, and (3) verify that any consumption bundle for any consumer that gives the consumer more utility than $\boldsymbol{x}^h$ must cost at least as much as $\boldsymbol{x}^h$.

To reiterate from before, we only get a quasi-equilibrium because, when we do the separating, the Separating-Hyperplane Theorem only provides a weak inequality. But perhaps this is just a lack of imagination; you may wonder whether there isn't some argument that shows we wind up with a full-blown Walrasian equilibrium. We know, in fact, that if $p \cdot \boldsymbol{x}^h > 0$ for every consumer, we do have a full-blown Walrasian equilibrium. But one can construct examples in which some consumers have zero-value bundles assigned to them at the only prices p that separate X^* from $\mathcal{SPS}(\boldsymbol{x})$ and in which we produce (only) Walrasian quasi-equilibria. See Problem 15.4 (and its solution in the *Guide*) for more on this point.

15.3. Walrasian Equilibria Are in the Core

The First Welfare Theorem can be strengthened for the case of a pure-exchange economy by showing that any Walrasian-equilibrium allocation is in the *core* of the economy.

The concept of the *core*, from cooperative game theory, is one answer to the following question: *Which outcomes cannot be* ***blocked*** *by any subset of the individuals* *involved?* Recall that the set of consumers is $\{1, \ldots, H\}$, which we henceforth denote by $\mathcal{H}$. A nonempty subset of $\mathcal{H}$, typically denoted by $\mathcal{J}$, is called a *coalition* of consumers. In general (that is to say, in general games in coalitional form), one specifies which outcomes each coalition $\mathcal{J}$ can guarantee for its members, and an outcome is said to be *blocked* if some coalition can guarantee for its members some alternative outcome that is at least as good for every member of the coalition and strictly better for some members. A key part of the formulation, then, specifies the power of each coalition; what outcomes can each coalition guarantee for its members? In the context of a pure-exchange equilibrium, the natural definition is, Each coalition $\mathcal{J}$ is able to distribute among its members the endowments of those members.[1] This leads to the following double-barreled definition.

Definition 15.7 *For a pure-exchange economy $\mathcal{E}$:*

a. *For each nonempty subset $\mathcal{J} \subseteq \mathcal{H} = \{1, \ldots, H\}$, define*

$$\mathbf{X}^{\mathcal{J}} := \left\{ (x^j)_{j \in \mathcal{J}} \in (R^k_+)^{\mathcal{J}} : \sum_{j \in \mathcal{J}} x^j \leq \sum_{j \in \mathcal{J}} e^j \right\}.$$

b. *A feasible allocation $\mathbf{x} \in \mathbf{X}^*$ is a* **core allocation** *for $\mathcal{E}$ if, for every nonempty subset $J \subseteq \{1, \ldots, H\}$ and for every $(\hat{x}^j)_{j \in J} \in \mathbf{X}^J$, if $\hat{x}^j \succeq^j \mathbf{x}^j$ for each $j \in J$, then $\mathbf{x}^j \sim^j \hat{x}^j$ for each $j \in J$.*

A couple of comments are in order about this definition. In the paragraph preceding the formal definition, I spoke in terms of a coalition blocking an allocation x; condition b states in contrapositive form the condition that x is unblocked by any coalition $\mathcal{J}$ and any allocation $x^{\mathcal{J}}$ that is feasible for $\mathcal{J}$. Also game theorists usually call $\mathcal{H}$ the *coalition of the whole*; note that $X^{\mathcal{H}}$ is just X^*, and property b, applied to the case of $\mathcal{H}$, says that x is Pareto efficient. Therefore, being in the core entails being Pareto efficient, and it (conceivably) is a stronger requirement. In fact, you can see from an Edgeworth Box that it is a stronger requirement: Specialized to that case (two-person, two-good, pure exchange), and in the case depicted in Figure 14.2b back on page 337, the Pareto-efficient points are all the points from the southwest corner to the northeast corner, along the heavily shaded line. To be in the core, an allocation (in this two-consumer case) must also provide each individual (viewed as her own coalition) with at least as much utility as she gets from her endowment; therefore the core consists of the segment of the Pareto-efficient set that is extra-heavily shaded.

Even though being in the core entails more than Pareto efficiency, being a Walrasian-equilibrium allocation is stronger still:

[1] Let me qualify this. This is the natural definition in a political economy in which each individual's rights to her endowment cannot be abrogated. The political power to confiscate the property of others—for instance, to tax based on (super) majority rule—changes this.

Proposition 15.8. *If (p, x) is a Walrasian equilibrium for a pure-exchange economy $\mathcal{E}$ in which all consumers are locally insatiable and $p \geq 0$, then x is a core allocation of $\mathcal{E}$.*

Proof. The proof of this proposition is quite similar to the proof of the First Theorem of Welfare Economics, so I'll (only) provide an outline of the steps, leaving it for you to fill in the details. Suppose (p, x) is a Walrasian equilibrium for the pure-exchange economy $\mathcal{E}$ in which all consumers are locally insatiable and with $p \geq 0$. Let $Y^{\mathcal{J}} = \sum_{j \in \mathcal{J}} p \cdot e^j$; that is, $Y^{\mathcal{J}}$ is the value of the endowment of coalition $\mathcal{J}$ at prices p. Show that if $(\hat{x}^j)_{j \in \mathcal{J}} \in (R^k_+)^{\mathcal{J}}$ is such that $\hat{x}^j \succeq^j x^j$ for all j and $\hat{x}^j \succ^j x^j$ for at least one $j \in \mathcal{J}$, then $p \cdot \left(\sum_{j \in \mathcal{J}} \hat{x}^j\right) > Y^{\mathcal{J}}$. And show that $p \cdot \left(\sum_{j \in \mathcal{J}} \hat{x}^j\right) \leq Y^{\mathcal{J}}$ for all $(\hat{x}^j)_{j \in \mathcal{J}} \in \mathbf{X}^{\mathcal{J}}$. Apply these two results to conclude that anything feasible for coalition $\mathcal{J}$ cannot be Pareto superior for the members of $\mathcal{J}$ to their allocation under x. ∎

Is the definition of the core that we've given here the "right" concept on economic grounds? The question is too vague to have a definitive answer. But among the many objections (not the best word to use in the current context) to the concept of the core as defined here, two that are often heard are:

- In the definition as given, a coalition "objects" to an allocation x if the coalition can divide its own endowment among its membership in a way that is Pareto superior for its members, meaning that everyone is at least as well off, and at least one member is strictly better off, than at x. For an objection to x to succeed, you might ask for a more solid inducement for those objecting: Define, instead, that a coalition can only successfully object to x if it can find a way to divide its own endowment among its members that makes every member *strictly* better off than at x. With locally insatiable consumers, there is less to this difference than you may think (what if, in the first definition, the one coalition member who is strictly better off has a strictly positive allocation under the objection?). But it is still a difference.
- The definition allows any objection to x to go unchallenged. Suppose instead, if $\mathcal{J}$ objects to x, then consumers from outside $\mathcal{J}$ are given the opportunity to register counterobjections. Without trying to be precise, you could imagine that a counterobjection takes the form of a coalition $\mathcal{J}'$ that includes some members of $\mathcal{J}$ and some consumers not from $\mathcal{J}$, that is sufficient to break coalition $\mathcal{J}$ in the sense that it induces some members of $\mathcal{J}$ to bolt from $\mathcal{J}$ and join $\mathcal{J}'$. We might look, with such a structure, for allocations x such that, to any objection to x, there is a counterobjection that defeats the objection. To be a valid objection, it must be that no counterobjection that defeats it can be raised.[2]

Whatever you think of these considerations, note that they both make it *harder* to object to a proposed allocation and, therefore, *enlarge* the set of allocations that survive valid objections. The core as we've defined it is "small," at least as far as

[2] If you want to chase down this idea of counterobjections to objections, look in the literature of cooperative game theory for the *bargaining set*.

these considerations are concerned. And Walrasian-equilibrium allocations are in this small core.

The core and Walrasian equilibria with production

Proposition 15.8, and our discussion so far in this section, concerns pure-exchange economies only. The reason is that it isn't clear a priori how to allocate productive possibilities to coalitions of consumers less than the entire population. The issue here is, What production resources does coalition $\mathcal{J}$ command, as it thinks of objections to some $x \in X^*$? What is $X^{\mathcal{J}}$? Here are some possibilities:

1. A coalition of consumers less than the coalition of the whole (that is, $\mathcal{J}$ a strict subset of $\mathcal{H}$) can only redistribute its own endowment. It cannot use the productive capabilities of the firms. In symbols,

$$\mathbf{X}^{\mathcal{J}} := \left\{ (x^j)_{j\in\mathcal{J}} \in (R^k_+)^{\mathcal{J}} : \sum_{j\in\mathcal{J}} x^j \leq \sum_{j\in\mathcal{J}} e^j \right\}.$$

2. At the other extreme, any coalition of consumers can employ the production technology of any firm, or

$$\mathbf{X}^{\mathcal{J}} := \left\{ (x^j)_{j\in\mathcal{J}} \in (R^k_+)^{\mathcal{J}} : \sum_{j\in\mathcal{J}} x^j \leq \sum_{j\in\mathcal{J}} e^j + \sum_{f=1}^{F} z^f \text{ for some } z \in Z \right\}.$$

3. A coalition of consumers is allowed to use the productive capacity of firm f (only) if 100% of the shares of firm f are held by consumers of the set $\mathcal{J}$:

$$\mathbf{X}^{\mathcal{J}} := \left\{ (x^j)_{j\in\mathcal{J}} \in (R^k_+)^{\mathcal{J}} : \sum_{j\in\mathcal{J}} x^j \leq \sum_{j\in\mathcal{J}} e^j + \sum_{f\in F^{\mathcal{J}}} z^f \text{ for some } z \in Z \right\},$$

   where $F^{\mathcal{J}}$ is defined (for now) as the set of firms f such that $\sum_{j\in\mathcal{J}} s^{fj} = 1$.

4. We allow any coalition of consumers to use the productive capacity of any firm in which the coalition's shareholdings total strictly more than 50%; the formal definition is the same as in possibility 3, except that $F^{\mathcal{J}}$ is the set of firms f such that $\sum_{j\in\mathcal{J}} s^{fj} > 0.5$.

5. We allow coalition $\mathcal{J}$ to use the productive capacity of a scaled copy of each firm, scaled by the coalition's shareholdings. Formally, we first define $s^{f\mathcal{J}} = \sum_{j\in\mathcal{J}} s^{fj}$ and then

$$\mathbf{X}^{\mathcal{J}} := \left\{ (x^j)_{j\in\mathcal{J}} \in (R^k_+)^{\mathcal{J}} : \sum_{j\in\mathcal{J}} x^j \leq \sum_{j\in J} e^j + \sum_{f=1}^{F} s^{f\mathcal{J}} z^f \text{ for some } z \in Z \right\}.$$

And there are other possibilities, besides.

It should be clear that giving more power to each coalition $\mathcal{J}$ makes it easier to raise an objection to an allocation x from $\mathbf{X}^*$, and so giving more power to each coalition $\mathcal{J}$ shrinks the core. Therefore, if we want to conclude that Walrasian-equilibrium allocations are in the core, we have the best shot with possibility 1 above, and the worst shot with possibility 2. (This assumes that the technologies of firms are useful. To avoid cases where coalitions would be happy to be able *not* to have to use firms, we assume that $0 \in Z^f$ for each firm.) In fact, here is what we get:

Proposition 15.9. *Suppose* $0 \in Z^f$ *for each* f. *A Walrasian-equilibrium allocation is in the core of the economy, where the core is defined relative to feasible sets* $\mathbf{X}^{\mathcal{J}}$ *for each coalition, if* $p \geq 0$, *each consumer is locally insatiable, and:*

a. each $\mathbf{X}^{\mathcal{J}}$ *is defined using rule 1, 3, or 5, or*

b. each $\mathbf{X}^{\mathcal{J}}$ *is defined using any of the rules above, as long as all firms have constant-returns-to-scale technologies.*

The idea of the proof in every case is to mimic the proof of Proposition 15.8. Define, for each $\mathcal{J}$, its equilibrium aggregate wealth using equilibrium prices as $Y^{\mathcal{J}}$, and then show that if $(\hat{x}^j)_{j \in \mathcal{J}}$ is in $\mathbf{X}^{\mathcal{J}}$ (in any of the cases), we have $p \cdot \left(\sum_{j \in \mathcal{J}} \hat{x}^j\right) \leq Y^{\mathcal{J}}$. The details are left to you as an exercise, but they can be found in the *Student's Guide* if you get stuck.

15.4. In a Large Enough Economy, Every Core Allocation Is a Walrasian-Equilibrum Allocation

The First Theorem of Welfare Economics says that every Walrasian-equilibrium allocation is efficient, and the Second Theorem says that every efficient allocation is (more or less) Walrasian. We now know that every Walrasian-equilibrium allocation is a core allocation, so how about a converse to this? Since being in the core implies efficiency, the Second Theorem is already one sort of converse, if we are allowed to redistribute endowments. But what about the converse *if we aren't allowed to redistribute endowments?* Is there any truth to *Every core allocation for a given economy is a Walrasian-equilibrium allocation for the original endowments*?

This isn't true in general, of course. We see this for two-person, two-good, pure-exchange economies, depicted in an Edgeworth Box. All efficient points that lie between the two indifference curves through the initial endowments are in the core; to be a Walrasian equilibrium, the line tangent to the two indifference curves through this point (which are tangent to one another, assuming smooth indifference curves and that we are interior to the box) must pass through the initial endowment point. This simply won't happen at every point in the core, in general.

At least since Edgeworth (1881), though, there has been the notion that, "in large economies," the only outcomes that can survive a robust negotiation process are competitive equilibrium allocations. The literature provides several formalizations of this remarkable idea. One approach involves economies where each consumer has infinitesimal impact on others because each consumer is, in fact, infinitesimal: Instead of having a finite set of consumers, the economy is composed of a continuum of consumers; in this case, every core allocation is indeed a Walrasian-equilibrium allocation. A second approach allows there to be a finite number of consumers, but *assumes* that no single consumer has any power in the sense that, if we remove from the economy a consumer and her endowment, everyone who remains can achieve just as much utility as with her present. And, in a third approach, one starts with a finite economy, where some core allocations may not be Walrasian-equilibrium allocations, but then the number of consumers is increased, with the hoped-for result being that, as the number of consumers rises, the core shrinks to the set of Walrasian-equilibrium allocations. The key to such results is to add consumers in the right way: Imagine, for instance, a three-good economy, where two of the consumers are endowed with and enjoy the consumption of the first two goods, and all other consumers are endowed with and enjoy only the third good. However many of those other (third type of) consumers you add, they will have no impact on the core as regards the first two. Roughly put, what is needed is to increase the number of consumers in the economy in a way so that every consumer becomes insignificant to every other consumer; no one depends on anyone else to any great degree, but can do nearly as well, if necessary, dealing with others.

This is a rich literature, and we'll provide only a taste here. Specifically, we'll provide the seminal result of the third type, the *Debreu-Scarf Theorem* and then discuss briefly how results of the first type are constructed.

The Debreu-Scarf Theorem involves the notion of a *replica* economy. Begin with a finite, pure-exchange economy $\mathcal{E}$. That is, we have a finite list of consumers $h = 1, \ldots, H$, each of whom has preferences given by a utility function u^h defined on R^k_+ (for some positive integer k) and an endowment e^h. Attach a superscript 1 to this economy, so it is relabeled $\mathcal{E}^1$ and called the *one-replica version of* $\mathcal{E}$. Then for any finite integer N, the N*-replica version* of $\mathcal{E}$, denote $\mathcal{E}^N$, is an economy with NH consumers, N of whom have preferences given by u^1 and endowment e^1, N more of whom are characterized by u^2 and e^2, and so forth: There are N-replicas of each of the H consumers in the original economy. Whereas we have enumerated consumers with the symbol h so far, in replica economies we use counters hn, meaning the nth consumer (out of N) of type h (out of H).

Allocations for $\mathcal{E}^N$ can, of course, give different copies of a specific type of consumer different consumption bundles; a general allocation for $\mathcal{E}^N$ is a point $(x^{hn})_{h=1,\ldots,H;n=1,\ldots,N} \in (R^k_+)^{HN}$ such that $\sum_{h,n} x^{hn} \leq N \sum_h e^h$. We are interested, however, in what are called *equal-treatment allocations*, which are just what the name implies: allocations in which $x^{hn} = x^{hn'}$ for all h, n, and n'. We continue to reserve the symbol $\boldsymbol{x}$ for an allocation for the base economy; that is, $\boldsymbol{x} \in (R^k_+)^H$. But we also talk about the equal-treatment allocation $\boldsymbol{x}$ for all replica economies $\mathcal{E}^N$, with the understanding that, in the N-replica economy $\mathcal{E}^N$, consumer hn gets $\boldsymbol{x}^h$ in the equal-treatment allocation $\boldsymbol{x}$.

We can justify restricting attention to equal-treatment allocations at the cost of assuming that each consumer has strictly convex preferences:

Proposition 15.10 *Suppose that all consumers have strictly convex preferences. Then any (general) allocation (x^{hn}) that is in the core of N-replica economy $\mathcal{E}^N$ (for any N) is an equal-treatment allocation. (Since we know that every Walrasian-equilibrium allocation is in the core of the economy, this implies as well that every Walrasian-equilibrium allocation is an equal-treatment allocation.)*

Proof. Suppose (x^{hn}) is a feasible allocation for the N-replica economy, which means that $\sum_{h,n} x^{hn} \leq N \sum_h e^h$. Form a coalition of consumers consisting of one representative of each type by the following rule: For type h, choose one of the replicas whose utility $u^h(x^{hn})$ is least among $\{u^h(x^{h1}), u^h(x^{h2}), \ldots, u^h(x^{hN})\}$. If all consumers of type h have the same utility under this allocation, choose any one; in general, if there is a tie for least utility (among replicas of this type), any one that has this least level of utility will do. Then consider the allocation for this coalition in which the representative of type h receives $(1/N)\sum_n x^{hn}$. That is, the representative of type h gets the average amount obtained by all replicas of this type under (x^{hn}). It is obvious that since the full allocation (x^{hn}) is feasible, this allocation is feasible for this coalition of representatives. Of course, since $\succeq^h$ is convex, this average allocation given to the representative of type h leaves her at least as well off as she was under (x^{hn}); remember that she was selected on the basis of having utility less than or equal to all other replicas of type h. And if the full allocation was not an equal-treatment allocation—that is, if for some h the x^{hn} are not all identical—then because $\succeq^h$ is strictly convex, this average allocation gives the representative of type h strictly greater utility than she had under (x^{hn}). That is to say, if the allocation (x^{hn}) is not an equal-treatment allocation, it is "blocked" by the coalition we've constructed and is not in the core, which is the contrapositive of the statement we set out to prove. ∎

With this as justification or otherwise, ask the question: *Is the (feasible) equal-treatment allocation $\boldsymbol{x}$ in the core of $\mathcal{E}^N$ for large N?* Two remarks begin to answer this question:

- Suppose $\boldsymbol{x}$, viewed as an equal-treatment allocation for $\mathcal{E}^N$, is *not* in the core of $\mathcal{E}^N$. This means that there must be a coalition of consumers in $\mathcal{E}^N$ that block $\boldsymbol{x}$. But every coalition in $\mathcal{E}^N$ is also a coalition in $\mathcal{E}^M$ for $M > N$, so this same coalition would block $\boldsymbol{x}$ from being in the core of $\mathcal{E}^M$. *If the equal-treatment allocation $\boldsymbol{x}$ is not in the core of $\mathcal{E}^N$ for some N, then it is not in the core of $\mathcal{E}^M$ for all $M > N$.*
- Suppose $\boldsymbol{x}$ is a Walrasian-equilibrium allocation for the base economy $\mathcal{E}$, with corresponding prices $p \geq 0$. Then $\boldsymbol{x}$, viewed as an equal-treatment allocation, is a Walrasian-equilibrium allocation for $\mathcal{E}^N$ for all N, supported by the price vector p. So if all consumers are locally insatiable, *Walrasian-equilibrium allocations $\boldsymbol{x}$ for the base economy (for nonnegative price vector p) are, when viewed as equal-treatment allocations, in the core of $\mathcal{E}^N$ for all N.*

To paraphrase, as long as we restrict attention to equal-treatment allocations for replica economies—and, if preferences are strictly convex, we are fully entitled to do so according to Proposition 15.10, as long as our interest is in core allocations—we know that the core shrinks (at least, cannot grow) as the number of replicas increases, but it never shrinks to be less than Walrasian-equilibrium allocations for the original economy (for locally insatiable consumers, and as long as the equilibirum prices are nonnegative). The following remarkable result completes this picture:

Proposition 15.11 (The Debreu-Scarf Theorem). *Suppose $\sum_h e^h$ is strictly positive and $\succeq^h$ is nondecreasing and strictly convex for each h. If $x \in (R^k_+)^H$, viewed as an equal-treatment allocation, is in the core of $\mathcal{E}^N$ for all N, then it is a Walrasian-equilibrium allocation for the base economy $\mathcal{E}$ (and, hence, for all $\mathcal{E}^N$), for some strictly positive price vector p.*

Before giving the details of the proof, a few remarks are in order. We've added assumptions that the social endowment is strictly positive and that preferences are nondecreasing and strictly convex. Note that the assumptions on preferences are enough to guarantee that preferences are strictly increasing (if you don't see this immediately, think about it some more); hence local insatiability and nonnegativity of equilibrium prices will not be a problem. Of course, strict convexity of preferences justifies looking at equal-treatment allocations, at least insofar as we are interested in core allocations. But these assumptions are (also) required for small steps in the proof; without them, and if we assumed local insatiability of preferences directly, we'd still get a result about Walrasian quasi-equilibria; we'll state this result at the end of the proof.

It is easy to get lost in the details of the proof, so let me give the main idea before giving details: We have a pure-exchange economy $\mathcal{E}$ and an allocation x, and we want to know: When is x a Walrasian-equilibrium allocation, relative to a given endowment vector (e^h)? Compare this with the question asked and answered in the Second Welfare Theorem: There we have an allocation x, and we want to know when this is a Walrasian-equilibrium allocation, but where we allow ourselves the freedom of redistributing the social endowment, so the answer is (more or less): It is, as long as we can pass a separating hyperplane between the set of all bundles that provide a Pareto improvement on x and the set of bundles the economy can realize.

In this case, we aren't given the freedom to redistribute the social endowment; endowments (e^h) are fixed, and we want to know if x is a Walrasian-equilibrium allocation relative to those endowments. In this regard, consider consumer h and the set

$$\mathcal{Z}^h(x^h, e^h) := \{\zeta \in R^k : \zeta + e^h \succ^h x^h, \zeta + e^h \geq 0\}. \tag{15.3}$$

Translating from symbols to words: this is the set of *net trades* that h can make, starting from her endowment e^h, that will leave her in a feasible consumption position (hence the restriction $\zeta + e^h \geq 0$) and that are better for her than $\boldsymbol{x}^h$.[3] *If* there are prices p that support $\boldsymbol{x}^h$ as a utility-maximizing choice for her, starting from e^h, then $p \cdot \zeta$ must be strictly positive for all ζ from this set; otherwise, she could afford something better than $\boldsymbol{x}^h$. So p needs to define a hyperplane that puts $\mathcal{Z}^h(\boldsymbol{x}^h, e^h)$ on its strictly positive side. (If we are content with $\boldsymbol{x}$ being the allocation portion of a Walrasian quasi-equilibrium, we need p to define a hyperplane that puts $\mathcal{Z}^h(\boldsymbol{x}^h, e^h)$ on its nonnegative side.)

But the same price vector p needs to work for all consumers h simultaneously. This means that $\cup_h \mathcal{Z}^h(\boldsymbol{x}^h, e^h)$ has to lie on the strictly positive (or, for quasi-equilibria, nonnegative) side of the hyperplane defined by p. And if that is true, the same must be true of the convex hull of this union. To set some notation, fixing the consumers, their preferences, and their endowments, let

$$\mathcal{Z}^*(\boldsymbol{x}, e) := \mathrm{CH}\Big(\bigcup_{h=1,\ldots,H} \mathcal{Z}^h(\boldsymbol{x}^h, e^h) \Big), \tag{15.4}$$

where the CH stands as always for "convex hull." Please note that if we assume that each consumer's preferences $\succeq^h$ are convex, we'll know that each set $\mathcal{Z}^h(\boldsymbol{x}^h, e^h)$ is convex. But we have no reason to suspect that the union of these sets is convex. So the taking of the convex hull of the union will be necessary. We will, of course, be finding p by applying the Separating-Hyperplane Theorem, so this becomes the key question in the proof:

What does it take, in terms of assumptions about the basic economy $\mathcal{E}$ and/or replicas $\mathcal{E}^N$, to ensure that $\mathcal{Z}^*(\boldsymbol{x}, e)$ can be put on the strictly positive (or nonnegative) side of a hyperplane through the origin?

Geometrically, the answer is easy. If $\mathcal{Z}^*(\boldsymbol{x}, e)$ can be put on the strictly positive (or, at least, nonnegative) side of a hyperplane defined by $p \cdot x = 0$, for nonnegative p, it is necessary that $\mathcal{Z}^*(\boldsymbol{x}, e)$ cannot have any intersection with the strict negative orthant in R^k. But this is sufficient as well: Suppose $\mathcal{Z}^*(\boldsymbol{x}, e)$ does not intersect the strict negative orthant. The set $\mathcal{Z}^*(\boldsymbol{x}, e)$ is convex, by construction. The strict negative orthant is convex. So the Separating-Hyperplane Theorem tells us immediately that there exists p such that $p \cdot \zeta \geq 0$ for all $\zeta \in \mathcal{Z}^*(\boldsymbol{x}, e)$ and $p \cdot \zeta \leq 0$ for all strictly negative ζ. The second half of this also implies that $p \geq 0$. We don't quite have everything we need (even for showing that p makes $\boldsymbol{x}$ a quasi-equilibrium allocation); we need to show that $p \cdot \boldsymbol{x}^h \leq p \cdot e^h$ for each h. But that will be a matter of fairly simple bookkeeping. (You'll see why momentarily.) Now, to move from quasi-equilibrium to full Walrasian equilibrium will take a bit more cleaning up, as will showing that the prices that support this equilibrium are strictly positive. But the heart of the argument is this application of the Separating-Hyperplane Theorem and the answer to the reformulated question:

[3] In Chapters 13 and 14, we used the term *excess demand* for vectors ζ, but in those cases, a price vector p was specified, so the word *demand* was appropriate. Here, no price p is present (yet), so *net trade* seems the more appropriate name.

What does it take, in terms of assumptions about the basic economy $\mathcal{E}$ and/or replicas $\mathcal{E}^N$, to ensure that $\mathcal{Z}^*(x, e)$ does not intersect the strict negative orthant in R^k?

The genius in the Debreu-Scarf Theorem is in recognizing the connection between the answer to this question and the cores of the replica economies. With that bit of initial intuition, here are the details of the proof.

Proof. Fix the economy $\mathcal{E}$ and an allocation $\boldsymbol{x}$, and define $\mathcal{Z}^h(\boldsymbol{x}^h, e^h)$ for each h and $\mathcal{Z}^*(\boldsymbol{x}, e)$ as in (15.3) and (15.4) above.

Suppose that $\mathcal{Z}^*(\boldsymbol{x}, e)$ is not disjoint from the strict negative orthant in R^k. That is, there exists some ζ, strictly less than zero, that is also a member of $\mathcal{Z}^*(\boldsymbol{x}, e)$. We know that $\zeta = \sum_h \alpha^h \zeta^h$ for $\zeta^h \in \mathcal{Z}^h(\boldsymbol{x}^h, e^h)$, where the coefficients α^h are all nonnegative and sum to 1. (We can select one ζ^h from $\mathcal{Z}^h(\boldsymbol{x}^h, e^h)$ for each h because we know that the $\mathcal{Z}^h(\boldsymbol{x}^h, e^h)$ are all convex sets, since preferences are all (strictly) convex. If we didn't know that preferences were convex, we might have to select more than one ζ^h for a given h, to make up an arbitrary point in the convex hull. Keep this variation in mind as you read through the proof.)

Because $\zeta = \sum_h \alpha^h \zeta^h$ is *strictly* negative, we can perturb the weights slightly to ensure that they are all nonnegative rational numbers, they still sum to one, and the convex combination is still strictly negative. Assuming this has already been done in the initial selection of weights (α^h), we can then let M be the least common multiple of the denominators of the α^h, so we know that

$$\zeta = \sum_h \frac{M^h}{M} \zeta^h$$

is strictly negative, for integers M^h whose sum is M. Look at the economy $\mathcal{E}^N$ for $N \geq M$ and a coalition consisting of M^1 copies of consumer 1, M^2 copies of consumer 2, and so forth. This coalition can generate net trades for its members of ζ^1 for all copies of consumer 1, and so forth; the fact that $\sum_h (M^h/M)\zeta^h \leq 0$ implies $\sum_h M^h \zeta^h \leq 0$, which means this is a feasible reallocation of the endowments of the members of this coalition. And this reallocation leaves all members of this coalition strictly better off than they are with their part of $\boldsymbol{x}$, so $\boldsymbol{x}$ is not in the core of $\mathcal{E}^N$ for all $N \geq M$. We know that the cores of $\mathcal{E}^N$ are ordered by set inclusion; that is, if $\boldsymbol{x}$, viewed as an equal-treatment allocation for $\mathcal{E}^N$, is not in the core of $\mathcal{E}^N$, then it is not in the core of $\mathcal{E}^M$ for all $M \geq N$. Hence this shows by contraposition that, if $\boldsymbol{x}$ (viewed as an equal-treatment allocation) is in the core of $\mathcal{E}^N$ for all N, then $\mathcal{Z}^*(\boldsymbol{x}, e)$ must be disjoint from the strict negative orthant in R^k.

(If you read the previous paragraph too quickly, you may miss the genius of Debreu-Scarf. It just happened, so please take the time necessary to savor its beauty.)

Both $\mathcal{Z}^*(\boldsymbol{x}, e)$ and the strict negative orthant are convex sets, so there is a hyperplane that separates them; i.e., a nonzero price vector $p \in R^k$ and a scalar β such that $p \cdot \zeta \geq \beta$ for all $\zeta \in \mathcal{Z}^*(\boldsymbol{x}, e)$ and $p \cdot \zeta \leq \beta$ for all strictly negative ζ. By the usual argument (since the strict negative orthant is on one side), $p \geq 0$. Moreover, it is clear that $\beta \geq 0$, since we can drive $p \cdot \zeta_n$ to 0 with a sequence $\{\zeta_n\}$ from the strict negative orthant that approaches the origin.

I claim that $p \cdot (x^h - e^h) \geq \beta$. To see this, recall that u^h is strictly increasing, and so if we take any nontrivial, nonnegative commodity bundle z, $u^h(x^h + \epsilon z) > u^h(x^h)$ for all $\epsilon > 0$. But then $x^h + \epsilon z - e^h \in \mathcal{Z}^h(x^h, e^h)$, and (therefore) $p \cdot (x^h + \epsilon z - e^h) = p \cdot (x^h - e^h) + \epsilon p \cdot z \geq \beta$. Pass to the limit as ϵ approaches zero from above, and $p \cdot (x^h - e^h) \geq \beta$ follows. (Suppose we didn't assume that each u^h was strictly increasing, but only locally insatiable. Could you still prove the assertion of this paragraph?)

I claim that $\beta = 0$, and $p \cdot (x^h - e^h) = 0$ for each h. Begin with the feasibility inequality,

$$\sum_{h=1}^{H} x^h \leq \sum_{h=1}^{H} e^h,$$

evaluate each side with the price vector p (which is nonnegative, and so doesn't change the inequality), collect terms to one side, and you get

$$\sum_{h=1}^{H} p \cdot (x^h - e^h) \leq 0.$$

But, term by term, the terms in the last summation must each be at least β, and $\beta \geq 0$. So β must be zero, and each term in the sum must be zero.

We are virtually done. The claim, clearly, is that the price vector p together with x forms a Walrasian equilibrium. We certainly know that it is a Walrasian *quasi*-equilibrium:

- The market clearing condition $\sum_h x^h \leq \sum_h e^h$ holds, because we *assumed* that x is a feasible allocation.
- The bundle allocated to consumer h (or the various copies of consumer type h) is affordable: We just showed that $p \cdot x^h = p \cdot e^h$.
- Any bundle $\hat{x}^h$ that is strictly preferred to x^h by type h costs $p \cdot e^h$ or more: If $\hat{x}^h$ is strictly preferred to x^h, then $\hat{x}^h - e^h$ is in $\mathcal{Z}^h(x^h, e^h)$, and so $p \cdot (\hat{x}^h - e^h) \geq \beta = 0$, which is $p \cdot \hat{x}^h \geq p \cdot e^h$.

The only pesky part is that we need to argue that we can drop the "quasi" portion of the last piece, which means that we need to show that if $\hat{x}^h$ is strictly preferred to x^h, then $p \cdot \hat{x}^h > p \cdot e^h$.

The first step is to show that p must be strictly positive. If $k = 1$, then this is obvious, as the Separating-Hyperplane Theorem produces a nontrivial (nonzero) hyperplane. So suppose $k > 1$, and imagine that $p_i = 0$ for some good i. Since p is nontrivial, there is some good j for which $p_j > 0$. Good j is in positive total supply (this is the one place we use that assumption), and preferences are strictly increasing, so in any Pareto-efficient allocation x (and x must be Pareto efficient, if it is in the core even of $\mathcal{E}^1$), some consumer type h is ending up with a strictly positive amount of j. Fix that person h, and look at $\boldsymbol{x}^h$. Add one unit of good i to $\boldsymbol{x}^h$; consumer h is strictly better off. So we can take away some small amount of good j (and this consumer has some j to be taken away, which is why we needed all that fluff, getting to this point), and the consumer still prefers the new bundle to $\boldsymbol{x}^h$. Call this new bundle $\check{x}^h$; $\check{x}^h - e^h$ is in $\mathcal{Z}^h(\boldsymbol{x}^h, e^h)$, so $p \cdot (\check{x}^h - e^h)$ must be greater than or equal to zero. But we know that $p \cdot (\boldsymbol{x}^h - e^h) = 0$, and the difference between $\check{x}^h$ and $\boldsymbol{x}^h$ is that $\check{x}^h$ has one more unit of a good whose price is zero, and a bit less of a good with a positive price, so $p \cdot (\check{x}^h - e^h) < p \cdot (x^h - e^h) = 0$, a contradiction. Price vector p must be strictly positive.

And now, suppose $\hat{x}^h$ is strictly preferred to $\boldsymbol{x}^h$. Preferences are strictly increasing, and $\boldsymbol{x}^h \in R^k_+$, so it is inevitable that $\hat{x}^h \neq 0$. Since prices p are strictly positive, $p \cdot \hat{x}^h > 0$. And now we are in business: By continuity of preferences, for α close to one, $\alpha\hat{x}^h$ is strictly preferred to $\boldsymbol{x}^h$; hence $\alpha\hat{x}^h - e^h$ is in $\mathcal{Z}^h(\boldsymbol{x}^h, e^h)$, and therefore $p \cdot \alpha\hat{x}^h \geq p \cdot e^h$. But since $p \cdot \hat{x}^h > 0$, $p \cdot \hat{x}^h > \alpha p \cdot \hat{x}^h = p \cdot \alpha\hat{x}^h \geq p \cdot e^h$. Our quasi-equilibrium is a full-fledged Walrasian equilibrium. ■

Consider the following variation on Debreu-Scarf:

Proposition 15.12. *Fix a finite pure-exchange economy $\mathcal{E}$, in which each consumer is locally insatiable. Suppose that a feasible allocation $\boldsymbol{x}$ for this economy, when interpreted as an equal-treatment allocation for replica economies built from $\mathcal{E}$, is in the core of $\mathcal{E}^N$ for all N. Then $\boldsymbol{x}$ is the allocation portion of a Walrasian quasi-equilibrium of $\mathcal{E}$, with nonnegative prices. And, letting p denote (nonnegative) prices that accomplish this, if $\boldsymbol{x}^h$ is strictly positive for consumer h, then $p \cdot \hat{x}^h > p \cdot e^h$ for every $\hat{x}^h$ that is strictly preferred by h to $\boldsymbol{x}^h$.*

We've removed from Debreu-Scarf the assumption that preferences are strictly convex; indeed, we don't even assume preferences are convex. We've removed the assumption that preferences are nondecreasing; assuming (only) local insatiability. And we have removed the assumption that the social endowment is strictly positive. Now we don't have as good an excuse as we had earlier for restricting attention to equal-treatment allocations in the replica economies; it becomes an integral part of the proposition that we look (only) at such allocations. And we can no longer assert that the supporting prices are strictly positive or that they give a full-fledged Walrasian equilibrium. But we get to nonnegative prices and a Walrasian quasi-equilibrium, and the same basic argument works. We use the proof only as far as the three bullet points back one page. And in two places we have to make some changes. I'd challenge you to find those two places, but since they are clearly marked, the challenge is somewhat less: Make sure you understand how to get past these two places without losing the basic flow of the proof.

An alternative, intuitive proof (with lots more assumptions)

Notwithstanding the mathematical beauty of the proof of the Debreu-Scarf Theorem, it doesn't convey to many people an immediate intuitive sense in which "large numbers of a given type" leads to the result. (It does do so if your intuition has internalized the idea that large numbers convexify, so the set of Pareto-improving net trades becomes convex. But it takes a very well developed intutition to regard this as intuitive.) So here is an alternative proof that requires more assumptions but does a better job in conveying the intuition.

The assumptions we add are that every consumer h has a differentiable utility function u^h, that x is strictly positive, and that the marginal utility for each consumer h of each good i is strictly positive at the allocation x^h. If x is not efficient, we know it is not in the core of even $\mathcal{E}^1$, so suppose x is Pareto efficient. Then our extra assumptions imply that the ratios of marginal utilities for all consumers are equal; writing MU_i^h for $(\partial u^h/\partial x_i)|_{x^h}$, MU_i^h/MU_j^h is the same for all h, for each i and j. Let $p_1 = 1$ and, for $i = 2, \ldots, k$, let $p_i = MU_i^h/MU_1^h$; that is, we are creating relative prices that match the ratios of marginal utilities. We know, of course, that if x is a Walrasian-equilibrium allocation for any prices, it must be for this set of (relative) prices p.

So check whether $p \cdot e^h \geq p \cdot x^h$ for all h. If it is, then with all the convexity assumptions we've made, we know that we have a Walrasian equilibrium. So suppose it is not. Suppose that, for some h, $p \cdot e^h < p \cdot x^h$. Relabel the consumers so that this h is $h = 1$; that is, we suppose that $p \cdot e^1 < p \cdot x^1$. Type 1 is getting more value than her endowment is worth; can't the others do without her and improve their own lot?

They certainly can do so, "on the margin." Suppose all the consumers except for type 1 tried to do without type 1. They could keep their allocations x^h $(h \neq 1)$, but they would have to absorb the net trade $x^1 - e^1$. Imagine that they had to absorb only a small piece of this: That is, imagine they consume $x^h + (x^1 - e^1)/M$ instead of x^h for large M. Taylor's Theorem tells us that the change in their utility, if M is large, is

$$\frac{1}{M}\sum_{i=1}^{k} MU_i^h(x_i^1 - e_i^1) + o\left(\frac{1}{M}\right),$$

but since $p \cdot (x^1 - e^1) > 0$ and $(MU_i^h)_{i=1,\ldots,k}$ is proportional to p, the summation is strictly positive. For M large enough, every consumer $h \neq 1$ is strictly better off with $x^h + (x^1 - e^1)/M$ than with x^h. Indeed, this is even true of consumers of type 1; for M big enough, they strictly prefer $x^1 + (x^1 - e^1)/M$ to x^1.

Here is where "big numbers" come in. Suppose M is large in the sense of the previous paragraph. For any replica economy $\mathcal{E}^N$, $N \geq (M+1)/H$, take the coalition of everyone but one copy of consumer 1. We give each consumer in this coalition what she had before (x^h for type h), plus her equal share of the net trade $x^1 - e^1$ that must be absorbed because we leave one type 1 out. This gives each consumer of type h the allocation $x^h + (x^1 - e^1)/(NH - 1)$, which (as long as $N \geq (M+1)/H$, so $NH - 1 \geq M$) is strictly preferred by this consumer to x^h. This coalition blocks x.

Therefore, if x is in the core of $\mathcal{E}^N$ for all N, it must be that $p \cdot x^h \leq p \cdot e^h$ for all h, which makes (p, x) a Walrasian equilibrium.

Continuum economies

At the start of the previous subsection, I mentioned that, to a well-developed intuition, the key idea is that large numbers convexify. If you have been reading and consuming in the past two chapters the remarks made about economies with a continuum of agents, Aumann integrals, and Aumann's Lemma, you can probably guess how those remarks extend. In fact, the first article by Aumann concerning these "large" economies, in which he defines Aumann integrals and provides his lemma, namely Aumann (1964), demonstrated an immediate equivalence between the core of such economies (pure-trade, with a nonatomic measure of consumers) and their Walrasian-equilibrium allocations. The proof that every Walrasian-equilibrium allocation is in the core is, except for mathematical details, just like the proof we gave (or, more accurately, outlined, based on the proof of the First Theorem); equilibrium prices will separate for each coalition $\mathcal{J}$ (now a measurable subset of the set $\mathcal{H}$ of all consumers[4]) Pareto-improving bundles from bundles less than or equal to the coalition's overall endowment. And to show that every core allocation is (quasi-)Walrasian, the argument is very close to the one presented here in the formal proof of the Debreu-Scarf Theorem. Suppose x is a core allocation (for the given endowment vectors given by e). For each consumer h, define $\mathcal{Z}^h(x^h, e^h)$, the set of net trades that when added to e^h improve on x^h for h. Being in the core means that for each coalition $\mathcal{J}$, no (measurable) selection $\zeta^h \in \mathcal{Z}^h(x^h, e^h)$ can be feasible for the coalition, or

$$\int_{\mathcal{J}} \zeta^h \mu(dh) \notin R^k_-, \quad \text{for all selections } \zeta^h.$$

(Here, μ is the nonatomic measure of the consumers.) Of course, this is just saying that the Aumann integral of the $\mathcal{Z}^h(x^h, e^h)$ has no intersection with the negative orthant. Add to each $\mathcal{Z}^h(x^h, e^h)$ the element 0 (the origin in R^k), where in the Aumann integral for coalition $\mathcal{J}$, you assign the selection 0 for $h \notin \mathcal{J}$, and the statement x is in the core becomes

$$\int_{\mathcal{H}} \mathcal{Z}^h(x^h, e^h)\mu(dh) \ \cap \ R^k_- = \emptyset,$$

where the integral is the Aumann integral for the $\mathcal{Z}^h(x^h, e^h)$ augmented with the origin. But Aumann's Lemma tells us that the integral is a convex set. We have everything needed to pass a separating hyperplane p between the negative orthant and the Aumann integral in the display, and then do the bookkeeping needed

[4] In earlier discussion, I suggested that $h \in \mathcal{H}$ was a type of consumer, and the nonatomic measure on $\mathcal{H}$ measured the relative proportions of sets of types. Here, it makes more sense to think of each h as a consumer, with the measure giving "number" of consumers in a given measurable subset of $\mathcal{H}$.

to finish off the proof. (And, of course, please note that convexity assumptions on individual preferences and any discussion of equal treatment are unnecessary; Aumann's Lemma about the convexifying power of aggregation is doing all the hard work.)

Of course, this is just the idea of the proof. There are details both technical/mathematical and economic to which we must attend. To see those details properly handled, you will have to consult one of the original papers on the subject or a more advanced book. But this discussion shows, I hope, the basic lines of this marvelous result.

15.5. Externalities and Lindahl Equilibrium

The First Theorem of Welfare Economics (and the core-compatibility of Walrasian-equilibrium allocations) is a remarkable result that has been used polemically, to argue that unfettered markets produce very good (efficient) economic outcomes. Usually these arguments are propaganda—very few modern economies are perfectly competitive, this ignores entirely questions of equity, and economic performance is driven as much by processes of growth and innovation as by static allocation; general equilibrium, even as interpreted to incorporate time and uncertainty as in next chapter, doesn't seriously address the forces of innovation. But read appropriately—as a catalog of what it takes to get efficiency out of market equilibrium—the First Theorem still has a lot to say.

In particular, an important assumption hidden away in the result is that there are no externalities in consumption or production. An externality is simply a case in which the economic activities of one party—a consumer or a firm—have a direct impact on the utilities or production-possibility sets of others, where by a direct impact I mean, not via the price mechanism. It is easiest to work with consumption externalities, so I will do so: Formally, the idea is that the utility of consumer h depends not only on what she herself consumes, x^h, but on the entire vector (x, z). It matters to her what her neighbors consume, what the firm down the street does, and so on. We can think of there being specific externalities—h is affected only by the consumption decisions of her next-door neighbors, for example—but the idea is always, u^h (or $\succeq^h$) turns on more than x^h.

When there are these consumption externalities, Walrasian-equilibrium allocations are not (necessarily) Pareto efficient. Problem 15.11 gives a simple illustration. But it might be helpful as well to indicate where the proof of the First Theorem breaks down.

Recall the proof. We take a Walrasian equilibrium (p, x, z) (with $p \geq 0$) and some $(\hat{x}, \hat{z})$ which is meant to be Pareto superior to it. If this alternative plan is feasible, it satisfies

$$\sum_h \hat{x}^h \leq \sum_h e^h + \sum_f \hat{z}^f,$$

and by dotting both sides of inequality with the nonnegative prices, we get

$$\sum_h p \cdot \hat{x}^h \leq \sum_h p \cdot e^h + \sum_f p \cdot \hat{z}^f \leq \sum_h p \cdot e^h + \sum_f p \cdot z^f,$$

where the second inequality follows because z is profit maximizing at p. So far, externalities (in consumption) don't affect the proof at all. (If there were externalities in production, which means that Z^f depends nontrivially on (x, z), the second inequality step would already pose a problem.)

But this alternative plan is supposed to be Pareto superior to the equilibrium plan. In the proof, we concluded from $\hat{x}^h \succeq^h x^h$ and local insatiability that $p \cdot \hat{x}^h \geq p \cdot e^h + \sum_f s^{fh} p \cdot z^f$ for each h, with strict inequality for some h (the h for which there is strict preference of the hat allocation). When there are externalities, this simply doesn't follow. To begin with, it doesn't make sense to write $\hat{x}^h \succeq^h x^h$; instead the appropriate thing is that $(\hat{x}, \hat{z}) \succeq^h (x, z)$, with strict preference for at least one h. And so it is even possible that $\hat{x}^h < x^h$ for some h—that is, the hat plan gives h strictly less direct consumption and so is surely affordable—but h prefers the hat plan because it calls for less consumption of some noxious good by a neighbor, or because it calls for less production, and hence less pollution by some neighboring plant. And so the proof dies.

An important view on why externalities cause inefficiencies, due to Ronald Coase (1960), is that the inefficiencies arise because of ill-defined property rights. If I am adversely affected by the pollution of a firm down the street from me, we should establish whether (1) I have the right to clean air, and the firm must pay me if it wants to pollute, or (2) the firm has the right to pollute, and I have to pay it if I want its pollution abated. The Coase Theorem says that if property rights of these sorts are established and consumers and firms bargain in good faith, then an efficient outcome will be reached.

At the level of general equilibrium, this idea is expressed in what is called a Lindahl equilibrium.[5] In a Lindahl equilibrium, transfers are made between every pair of agents for every activity undertaken by one that might have an external effect on the other. In our current setting of consumption externalities, we have

(1) prices $p \in R^k$ for the goods themselves;

(2) for every h and h', a set of transfer prices $r_{hh'} \in R^k$ that records transfers from h to h' made for the choice of x^h by h, and

(3) for every f and h, a set of transfer prices $q_{fh} \in R^k$ that records transfers from f to h made for f's choice of z^f.

The profit of firm f, given all these prices and given that the firm chooses production plan z^f, is $p \cdot z^f - \sum_h q_{fh} \cdot z^f$. Given prices and a production set Z^f, the firm is meant to choose z^f to maximize these transfer-included profits.

[5] Lindahl proposed this equilibrium before Coase (in 1919, although in the references I provide a citation to an English translation of his original article as Lindahl, 1958), so to some extent he anticipates Coase.

Consumers maximize the utility $u^h(x, z)$ that they accrue from the entire vector of economic activity (x, z), subject to the following budget constraint:

$$p \cdot x^h + \sum_{h' \neq h} r_{hh'} \cdot x^h \leq p \cdot e^h + \sum_f s^{fh} \left[p \cdot z^f - \sum_{h'} q_{fh'} \cdot z^f \right] + \sum_f q_{fh} \cdot z^f + \sum_{h' \neq h} r_{h'h} x^{h'}.$$

That is, consumer h pays for the goods she consumes, and she pays transfers to other consumers for her consumption choice. Her resources are the value of her endowment, her share of the profits of the firms, and the value of transfers she receives from firms and from other consumers for their production/consumption choices.

A Lindahl equilibrium is a vector (p, q, r, x, z) where: firm f, taking prices as given, maximizes its net-of-transfer profits at z^f; consumer h, taking prices as given, maximizes her preferences at (x, z), given the budget constraint above; and markets clear, in the usual fashion. N.B., every consumer chooses the full vector (x, z), and it is a condition of equilibrium that these choices all agree.

Proposition 15.13. *Even with externalities in consumption, if (p, q, r, x, z) is a Lindahl equilibrium with $p \geq 0$ and consumers are locally insatiable, then (x, z) is Pareto efficient among all plans that are feasible given the production technology and endowments.*

Proof. Suppose (x, z) is not Pareto efficient. Then there is some Pareto-superior plan, $(\hat{x}, \hat{z})$. Since $(\hat{x}, \hat{z}) \succeq^h (x, z)$ for all h, it must be (by the usual argument of local insatiability) that, at the prices (p, q, r), each h can only just afford $(\hat{x}, \hat{z})$, or

$$p \cdot \hat{x}^h + \sum_{h' \neq h} r_{hh'} \cdot \hat{x}^h \geq p \cdot e^h + \sum_f s^{fh} \left[p \cdot \hat{z}^f - \sum_{h'} q_{fh'} \cdot \hat{z}^f \right] + \sum_f q_{fi} \cdot \hat{z}^f + \sum_{h' \neq h} r_{h'h} \hat{x}^{h'}.$$

Moreover, for some consumer h (who strictly prefers the hat plan to the equilibrium plan), this inequality must be strict. Hence if we sum these inequalities over h, we get

$$\sum_h \left[p \cdot \hat{x}^h + \sum_{h' \neq h} r_{hh'} \cdot \hat{x}^h \right] >$$

$$\sum_h \left[p \cdot e^h + \sum_f s^{fh} \left[p \cdot \hat{z}^f - \sum_{h'} q_{fh'} \cdot \hat{z}^f \right] + \sum_f q_{fh} \cdot \hat{z}^f + \sum_{h' \neq h} r_{h'h} \hat{x}^{h'} \right].$$

The interconsumer transfers cancel, and the shareholdings sum to 1 for each firm, so this is

$$p \cdot \sum_h \hat{x}^h > p \cdot \sum_h e^h + \sum_f \left[p \cdot \hat{z}^f - \sum_{h'} q_{fh'} \cdot \hat{z}^f \right] + \sum_f \sum_h q_{fh} \cdot \hat{z}^f.$$

Cancelling the common firm-to-consumer transfers gives

$$p \cdot \sum_h \hat{\mathbf{x}}^h > p \cdot \sum_h e^h + \sum_f p \cdot \hat{\mathbf{z}}^f .$$

Since prices p are nonnegative, this contradicts physical feasibility of the hat plan. ▪

Bibliographic Notes

Many of the references relevant for this chapter were given last chapter or in the course of this chapter. If one wishes to go back to the early development of the idea that competitive equilibria are efficient, Smith (1776) and his paean to the invisible hand is generally accorded precedence; Edgeworth (1881) and Pareto (1909) are more modern but still classic references. (In particular, Edgeworth provides the informal argument that bargaining among many individuals leads to price equilibria.) Through the first half of the 20th century, proofs of the efficiency of competitive price equilibria depended on the idea that, in an equilibrium, ratios of marginal utilities would all be equalized; see, for instance, Samuelson (1947, Chapter 8). The first proofs and discussion in the modern style (the style given here) are found in Arrow (1951b) and Debreu (1951).

The Debreu-Scarf Theorem is found in Debreu and Scarf (1963). References for Lindahl equilibria are provided in the text.

Problems

▪ 15.1. In our development of the First and Second Theorems of Welfare Economics, we defined X^* to be all "bundles" in R^k that are less than or equal to bundles the economy is technologically capable of producing. This includes "bundles" with negative components, which may strain the sense of "technologically feasible," even with dumpsters freely available. (Can we write an IOU to a dumpster as in, "We owe you six tons of steel, which we don't currently have"?) Suppose instead we defined X^* as $\{x \in R^k_+ : x \leq \sum_h e^h + \sum_f z^f$, for some selection of production plans$\}$? How if at all would this affect developments in Sections 1 and 2 of this chapter?

▪ *15.2. Consider the following two-person, pure-exchange economy. The two consumers are Alice and Bob (A and B). Alice's endowment is $e^A = (2, 0)$ and her utility function is $u_A(x_1, x_2) = x_1^{1/2} + x_2^{1/2}$. Bob's endowment is $e^B = (1, 3)$ and his utility function is $u_B(x_1, x_2) = x_1^3 - 9x_1^2 + 15x_1 + x_2^3 - 9x_2^2 + 15x_2$.

(a) Prove that the prices $p = (1, 1)$ are Walrasian-equilibrium prices for this economy.

(b) Are the equilibrium allocations at these prices Pareto efficient? (They are not, so...)

(c) Why has the First Theorem of Welfare Economics failed?

■ 15.3. In the proof of the Second Theorem, we worked with the sets ***SPS***(x) and $\mathcal{SPS}(x)$ instead of ***PS***(x) and $\mathcal{PS}(x)$ because, we said, it was "more convenient" to do so. Explain.

■ *15.4. The Second Theorem of Welfare Economics produces a Walrasian quasi-equilibrium, and at the end of Section 15.2, we asserted that one can't do better: An economy $\mathcal{E}$ and a Pareto-efficient allocation $\boldsymbol{x}$ for that economy can be constructed such that $\boldsymbol{x}$ is *not* the allocation portion of a Walrasian equilibrium, no matter how you reallocate endowments and shareholdings. In fact, one can find an example with pure exchange, two commodities, and two consumers (that is, with an Edgeworth Box). Produce such an example. (A picture will do.)

■ *15.5. Provide the details for the proof of Proposition 15.8.

■ 15.6. In the context of a pure-exchange economy, we said that an allocation $\boldsymbol{x} \in \boldsymbol{X}^*$ was in the core of the economy if for every coalition J and every $(x^j)_{j\in J} \in \boldsymbol{X}^J$, if $x^j \succeq^j \boldsymbol{x}^j$ for all j, then $\boldsymbol{x}^j \sim^j x^j$ for all j. This is equivalent to the following two-part definition:

> The allocation $\boldsymbol{x} \in \boldsymbol{X}^*$ is *blocked* by coalition J if, for some $(x^j)_{j\in J} \in \boldsymbol{X}^J$, $x^j \succeq^j \boldsymbol{x}^j$ for all j and $x^j \succ^j \boldsymbol{x}^j$ for at least one $j \in J$.
>
> The allocation $\boldsymbol{x} \in \boldsymbol{X}^*$ is in the core of the economy if it is not blocked by any coalition.

We'd make it harder to block an allocation if we changed the first part of this two-part definition to read:

> The allocation $\boldsymbol{x} \in \boldsymbol{X}^*$ is *blocked* by coalition J if, for some $(x^j)_{j\in J} \in \boldsymbol{X}^J$, $x^j \succ^j \boldsymbol{x}^j$ for all $j \in J$.

In the text, I asserted that there is less to this distinction than may meet the eye, and I then mumbled something about "suppose the objection by a coalition involves giving the person strictly better off a strictly positive allocation." Clarify my mumblings.

■ *15.7. Prove Proposition 15.9.

■ 15.8. Proposition 15.10 shows that, in the N-replica economy $\mathcal{E}^N$, if all consumers have strictly convex preferences, then every core allocation is an equal-treatment allocation. Therefore, this proposition has as corollary that, in $\mathcal{E}^N$, every Walrasian-equilibrium allocation is an equal-treatment allocation. Give an alternative and direct proof of this corollary. (Your alternative and direct proof should not invoke the notion of a coalition. In fact, in showing that, if (x^{hn}) is a Walrasian-equilibrium allocation, then $x^{hn} = x^{hn'}$ for all n and n', you should not invoke the presence of any type other than type h. This alternative proof is simple: If it takes you more than three lines, you should think harder about it.)

■ 15.9. Prove that a strictly quasi-concave function $u : R^k_+ \to R$ that is also nondecreasing is strictly increasing.

■ 15.10. Give the details concerning the proof of Proposition 15.12.

■ *15.11. Suppose Alice and Bob live in a two-person, two-good exchange economy. Letting (x^A, x^B) be an allocation for the two of them, where $x^A = (x^A_1, x^A_2)$ and $x^B = (x^B_1, x^B_2)$, suppose that Alice has quite standard (for this volume) preferences given by $u^A((x^A_1, x^A_2)) = \ln(x^A_1 + 1) + \ln(x^A_2 + 1)$. Bob, on the other hand, enjoys Alice's consumption of the first good (but not the second): His utility function is $u^B((x^A_1, x^B_1, x^B_2)) = \ln(x^B_1 + 1) + \ln(x^B_2 + 1) + 0.5\ln(x^A_1 + 1)$. Alice's endowment is $e^A = (4, 0)$; Bob's endowment is $e^B = (0, 4)$.

(a) What is the set of Pareto-efficient allocations of the social endowment $(4, 4)$?

(b) A (standard) Walrasian equilibrium is a price vector p and an allocation x such that markets clear and each consumer maximizes her or his utility through her or his choice of own-consumption (Alice chooses x^A; Bob chooses x^B) subject to her or his budget constraint and *taking the choice of the other consumer as given*. What are the Walrasian equilibria of this economy? Are they (is it) Pareto efficient?

(c) What is the Lindahl equilibrium of this economy? (There is only one—just produce it.) Is it efficient? (Of course it is. That's what Proposition 15.13 tells you. In fact, you may want to use that fact to find the equilibrium prices.)

■ *15.12. What does the front-cover design depict?

Chapter Sixteen

General Equilibrium, Time, and Uncertainty

The basic model of general equilibrium posits k commodities and competitive markets in each of those commodities. The commodities can be physical goods, measured in some units, such as bushels of wheat or, being more exact, bushels of a particular variety of wheat. And they can be services; a haircut, say, or transportation by taxi to the airport. In the basic model, each commodity has a price, with all trading seemingly done in a single instant. And, if we are going to adhere to the notion that all trade takes place simultaneously, any and all production by firms is also instantaneous.

By interpreting the notion of a commodity more broadly, however, we can bring both time and uncertainty into the story. We can imagine markets taking place at different points of time and in different contingencies. We can imagine production that takes time and produces random amounts of output. We can incorporate into the basic story the notion of financial markets, in which various sorts of financial securities are bought, held for a while, and then sold by consumers. We can even envision shares in the various firms being among the items traded in those financial markets. In this chapter, we describe how these interpretations can be made—more accurately, how they *are* made in general equilibrium theory—and the very substantial problems that arise.

By page count, this is the longest chapter in this volume. The ideas aren't complex and the mathematics isn't difficult. But the number of variations is quite large. You may find it helpful to take this in pieces; the natural break points are probably between sections 2 and 3, and then between 4 and 5.

16.1. A Framework for Time and Uncertainty

Time in the models we explore is discrete and finite: There is a first date, denoted by $t = 0$, and then a finite and discrete sequence of future dates, denoted $t = 1, 2, \ldots, T$. (We use the terms "date t" and "time t" completely interchangeably.) The literature also contains models with infinite sequence of future dates—that is, with time measured by $t = 0, 1, \ldots$; models with a doubly infinite sequence of dates, or $t = \ldots, -1, 0, 1, 2, \ldots$; and models with time measured continuously, with either finite or infinite horizon(s). But these all raise complications that, on this first pass, we ignore.

As for uncertainty, we imagine a set Ω of states of nature, with typical state of nature given by ω. As back in Chapter 5, the list of states of nature is meant to be a complete list of mutually exclusive and exhaustive states, encoding all relevant uncertainty (at least, that resolves by the end of the economy). We will assume throughout that Ω is a finite set; extensions to infinite Ω, especially in the literature of finance, are common. (In just a few paragraphs, you'll see that if we allow Ω to be infinite or for there to be an infinite time horizon, we encounter infinite-dimensional commodity spaces. That is, in fact, good motivation for extending the methods and ideas of Chapters 14 and 15 to allow for infinite-dimensional commodity spaces. But we do not do so in this volume.)

Time and uncertainty intertwine when we answer the question, *What do agents in the economy we are constructing know about the state of nature ω at a particular date t?* "Agents" here refers both to consumers and to firms or, at least, to the managers of firms who decide on the production plans of each firm. Of course, it is entirely possible that different agents know different things at a given time, a possibility that dramatically affects the nature of a lot of economic activity. But this is another complication that, in this volume, we ignore. Instead, we make the following formulation assumption: *Every agent at every point in time has access to the same information about the state of nature ω as has any other agent at that time.*

And, having made that assumption, we model the (common) information with an *information partition* of Ω. The symbol $\mathcal{F}_t$ is used to denote a partition of Ω, a collection of subsets of Ω that have pairwise empty intersection and joint union that is all of Ω. Elements of $\mathcal{F}_t$—that is, subsets of Ω—are denoted by f_t and are called *time-t contingencies*. The interpretation is that, at date t, (all) agents know which time-t contingency $f_t \in \mathcal{F}_t$ contains the actual state of the world and no more. We assume throughout that

- no uncertainty has resolved by date 0, so that $\mathcal{F}_0 = \{\Omega\}$,
- all uncertainty resolves by date T, so that for each $\omega \in \Omega$, $\{\omega\} \in \mathcal{F}_T$, and
- agents' information refines from one date to the next, meaning that if $f_{t+1} \in \mathcal{F}_{t+1}$, then $f_{t+1} \subseteq f_t$ for some $f_t \in \mathcal{F}_t$. In this case, we call f_t the *immediate predecessor* of f_{t+1}, and f_{t+1} is one of f_t's *immediate successors*.

The first two assumptions are made for notational convenience: If they didn't hold, and given where we are going, we could reformulate things so that they do hold. (Since you don't yet know where we are going, you'll have to trust me on this.) The third assumption, however, has content, going with the notion that $\mathcal{F}_t$ tells us what uncertainty has resolved for the agents by time t. Uncertainty that has resolved by time t will surely have (also) resolved by time $t+1$. But insofar as $\mathcal{F}_t$ is interpreted as the information agents possess about the state of the world at time t, the third assumption incorporates the idea that once agents have some information about the state of nature, they retain it; they do not forget.

Once these assumptions are made, we can depict the framework of time and uncertainty with a tree structure, as in Figure 16.1. Each *node* or slice of a branch at a point in time represents a contingency at that time. The passage of time is marked by moving from left to right. The receipt of new information is depicted by branches splitting from one time to the next. See the figure and its legend for more on this.

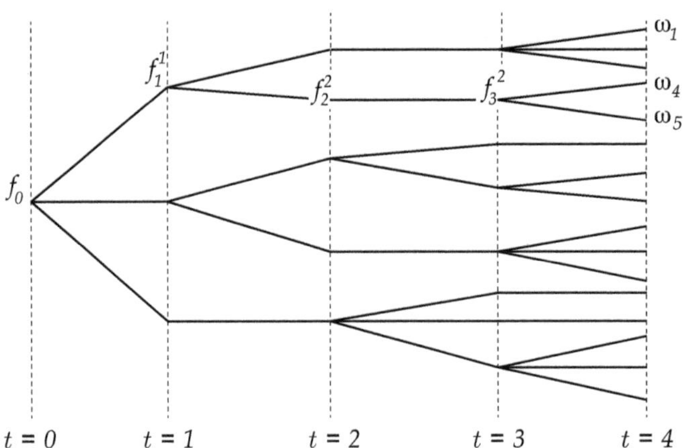

Figure 16.1. A time-uncertainty-information tree. This tree diagram provides a graphical representation for the type of time, uncertainty, and information structure used in this chapter. Time is discrete and finite, beginning with $t = 0$ and ending at some finite T; here $T = 4$. Time moves from left to right. States of nature $\omega \in \Omega$ are the tips of the tree, here 16 in number, with three of the states, ω_1, ω_4, and ω_5, marked. Information at a point in time, formally a cell f_t in a partition $\mathcal{F}_t$ of Ω, is depicted as a node in the tree. We always assume that there is no information received by time 0, or $f_0 = \Omega$, or (in the tree) a single root for the tree. In the diagram, at time 1, agents have learned that either $\omega \in \{\omega_1, \ldots, \omega_5\}$, which is marked as f_1^1, or $\omega \in \{\omega_6, \ldots, \omega_{11}\}$, or $\omega \in \{\omega_{12}, \ldots, \omega_{16}\}$. At date 2, there are five possible states of information or contingencies, including f_2^2 as marked; there are eight at date 3. Note that if the state of nature is ω_4, then agents learn that the state is one of ω_1 through ω_5 at date 1, they learn that is it either ω_4 or ω_5 at date 2, they learn nothing further at date 3, and then learn the truth (that the state is ω_4) at the final date, $t = 4$.

Note that, in this formal structure, a time-t contingency f_t is a subset of Ω. Therefore, f_t by itself does not (necessarily) distinguish its time. For instance, in Figure 16.1, $f_2^2 = \{\omega_4, \omega_5\} = f_3^2$. As a concession to less cluttered notation, we change things a bit and make the following convention: When we write f_t, it means the time-t contingency *marked with its date*. Think of f_t being the pair $(t, \{\cdot\})$, where the second component is the cell in the information partition $\mathcal{F}_t$. But, despite this, we write things like $\omega \in f_t$ or $f_t \subseteq f'_{t'}$; no confusion should result.

Having established this convention, we let $\mathcal{F} := \cup_{t=0}^{T} \mathcal{F}_t$; $\mathcal{F}$ is called the set of all *contingencies*. That is, a contingency is a time-and-information pair; in the tree diagram, it is any one of the nodes in the tree, including terminal nodes. The number of time-t contingencies will be denoted by N_t, with $N := N_0 + N_1 + \ldots + N_T$ denoting the total number of contingencies. Note that, in Figure 16.1, $N = 33$.

As already noted, each $f_t \in \mathcal{F}$ for $t > 0$ has a unique *immediate predecessor* in the tree, a time-$t-1$ contingency f_{t-1} that contains f_t. We write $\hat{f}_t$ for this immediate predecessor of f_t. The set of all predecessors of f_t (for $t > 0$) is denoted by $\mathbf{P}(f_t)$; this includes $\hat{f}_t$, as well as the immediate predecessor of $\hat{f}_t$, and so forth, stretching back to f_0. And we use $\mathbf{S}(f_t)$ to denote *all* the *successors* of f_t, for $t < T$.

16.2. General Equilibrium with Time and Uncertainty

With these pieces of framework in place, we can now repeat everything we did in Chapters 14 and 15, but with the notion that the commodity space is enlarged and enriched by time and uncertainty.

We suppose that there are k basic commodities, which means physical goods and services: think of "a bushel of wheat" or "a ride to the airport." Each of these commodities is now expanded into N different "contingency-labeled commodities": For each contingency f_t (for $t = 0, \ldots, T$), we have a commodity such as "a bushel of wheat in contingency f_t" or "a ride to airport in contingency f_t." We sometimes call this sort of thing a *contingency-stamped or -labeled commodity*.

Having commodities stamped by contingencies is clearly a godsend when it comes to more realistic models of production-possibility sets. If, say, we want to model a technology in which it takes two periods to achieve some production activity, we could require inputs be provided in date-t contingencies with output arriving at date $t+2$ in all successor contingencies. To model a production process in which the yield of usable output is random, we could have the output levels in date-$t+2$ contingencies vary. We can envision production plans by the firm in which they undertake production in some time-t contingencies but not in others. (And we can imagine consumers choosing to consume certain goods or services in some contingencies but not others.)

Of course, most tangible goods (not services) have a nontrivial shelf-life; wheat at date t can be stored and saved for, say, up to three periods. If the storing and saving is done by a firm, this means a more complex production-possibility set, with contingency-f_t wheat an input that leads to output contingency-f_{t+3} wheat, for all f_{t+3} that are successors of f_t, if we want to model the activity of storing for three periods. And we can easily take into account the cost of this storage activity, as a further required input to the production process, and/or spoilage, where, for instance, x units of input to the process gives only $(1-\alpha)x$ units of output, where α represents the spoilage rate. Accommodating storage by consumers is a bit trickier, but only a bit: essentially, you can provide for this with a clever definition of the utility of bundle of goods.

But, having contingency-stamped each commodity, we can then revert to the constructs and theorems of Chapters 14 and 15. The price vector p is now $k \times N$ dimensional, but a Walrasian equilibrium has the same structure, and all the theorems go through.

To be explicit, the idea in such a construction is that markets open once and once only, at (or just prior to) date 0, when consumers and firms essentially forward contract for all the activities they then will carry out as time passes and contingencies unfurl. If consumer h is endowed with 100 units of wheat in time-t contingency f_t, she can contract to supply this to the market in that contingency, receiving 100 times the price of f_t wheat, which she uses (say) to purchase 30 units of f_{t+2} corn, delivery of which occurs at time $t+2$, if the state of nature does indeed lie within f_{t+2}. In fact, she doesn't specifically exchange wheat for corn in this fashion; instead, she makes a full net trade, selling some goods and taking in profits from her shareholdings in firms, and using the wealth so generated to buy a consumption bundle that, through time and as uncertainty resolves, she consumes.

But all the *market* activity—all the buying and selling or, more accurately, the promises made to supply and taken to receive various goods and services at various times and in various contingencies—all this happens a priori. It's a very fanciful model of what really happens in the real world, but it is only a model, after all, and it greatly expands the scope of all the nice theory of Chapters 14 and 15.

Summing up, notation, and assumptions

This economy and its Walrasian equilibria set a benchmark for what follows, so let me sum up by making explicit a few things that have so far been implicit, creating some useful notation, and making some assumptions.

The setting has k *basic commodities* and a *time/uncertainty/information (t/u/i) structure* specified by the time index $t = 0, \ldots, T$, set of states of nature Ω, and information-partition structure $\{\mathcal{F}_t; t = 0, \ldots, T\}$. The t/u/i structure allows us to create sets of time-t contingencies for each t, the union of which is the set of all N contingencies. This then gives us the commodity space, where each basic commodity is copied N times, for a total of kN *contingency-stamped commodities*. Consumers and firms are introduced in the usual fashion, but now the consumption space of each consumer h is R_+^{kN}, endowments lie in this space, and preferences are defined over this space. For the firms, production-possibility sets Z^f are subsets of R^{kN}, in the usual fashion. The symbol $\mathcal{E}$ is used to denote such an economy.

We will use $x \in R_+^{kN}$ to denote consumption bundles and $z \in R^{kN}$ for production plans, appending the superscripts h and f, respectively, when we need to indicate the consumption bundle of consumer h and the production plan of firm f. (The use of f for firms and f_t for contingencies should not cause a problem.) For a consumption bundle x, the amount of basic good i in contingency f_t specified in x is denoted x_{if_t}; x_{f_t} denotes the vector in R_+^k whose ith component is x_{if_t}. The endowment of consumer h in an economy is denoted by e^h, with components $e^h_{if_t}$.

The *all-at-once market structure* for economy $\mathcal{E}$ consists of kN markets, all conducted at time $t = 0$ (or just prior), with one market in each of the kN contingency-stamped goods. Letting p be a price vector for these markets, with components denoted p_{if_t}, Walrasian equilibria for the all-at-once market structure are defined exactly as in Chapter 14; a Walrasian equilibrium consists of a price vector p, consumption plans $\boldsymbol{x}$ (with components $x^h_{if_t}$), and production plans $\boldsymbol{z}$.

We make the following assumptions about consumers:

Assumption 16.1. *Each consumer h has continuous, nondecreasing, and locally insatiable preferences. And, for each contingency f_t, some consumer is globally insatiable in the consumption of contingency-f_t commodity $i = 1$; that is, for each f_t there is some consumer h such that, for any $x \in R_+^{kN}$, there is an $x' \in R_+^{kN}$ such that x and x' are identical except on coordinate $1f_t$, and $u^h(x') > u^h(x)$. We hereafter refer to basic commodity 1 as **wheat**.*

Proposition 16.2. *In any Walrasian equilibrium, equilibrium prices are nonnegative, and the price of contingency-f_t wheat is strictly positive for all f_t. Moreover, every consumer satisfies her budget constraint with equality, and every Walrasian-equilibrium allocation is Pareto efficient.*

This follows from a combination of earlier results and, for the strict positivity of the prices of f_t wheat, an extension of an earlier argument. As something of a review, I'll leave it to you to supply all the details (in Problem 16.1a).

Bankruptcy and breach

In a Walrasian equilibrium (in general), it is implicit that all agents fulfill their obligations. If a consumer's equilibrium allocation calls for her to deliver some of her endowment of some good to the market, she does so. If a firm is supposed to provide the market with some quantity of output, it does so.

Back in Chapters 14 and 15, this sort of requirement didn't raise an eyebrow. If all economic activity takes place at once, we can envision simple enforcement mechanisms for this for consumers: Each consumer must deliver to the market any commodities that she is supplying, before she is allowed to take away commodities that she is (on net) demanding. For firms, it is a bit harder; it is bad enough that production is instantaneous, but how do we insist that firms deliver their outputs before they can take the inputs they need to produce those outputs?

What is a small worry concerning firms in Chapter 14 becomes a much bigger worry now. Consumer h contracts to deliver some amount of commodity i at date 3, in contingency f_3, and she uses this to purchase other goods and services at dates 0, 1, and 2. When date 3 rolls around, why doesn't she declare bankruptcy and renege on her promise? Why don't firms buy a lot of inputs early on and, in bad states of nature, renege on their promises to deliver output?

This sort of thing is ruled out in all the models of this chapter. The excuse for this modeling assumption goes back to our assumption of common information. In particular, everyone knows everything that everyone else knows. Once this assumption is made, it isn't that hard to follow it with the assumption that every agent in the economy evaluates every other agent's promises and plans, verifying that they can all be fulfilled. Then, some sort of legal mechanism is put in place to ensure fulfillment. Or, if we don't want to have every agent doing this, at least some entity checks on the *bona fides* of every agent's plans and, ex post, enforces all promises.

You hardly need me to tell you that bankruptcy and breach of promises, both oral and contractual (written), are real-life phenomena. But from the standpoint of economic theory, these are phenomena that mix differential information (different agents have access to different bits of information) and a lack of foresight for what the future may bring. They are important issues, but we don't have the tools to deal with them here, and so for the time being, we assume them out of existence.

16.3. Equilibria of Plans, Prices, and Price Expectations: I. Pure Exchange with Contingent Claims

The last section shows how to incorporate time and uncertainty into the basic model of general equilibrium, but at the cost of a market structure that is fairly unrealistic and, perhaps less obviously, with assumptions about individual behavior that begin to stretch credibility. (Are consumers really able to decide what foods they will want to eat many periods from now?) The plot for the rest of the chapter, more or less, is to try to bring the market institutions closer to reality, although, as you'll see, doing so stretches credibility on individual behavior even further.

Firms add significant complications to the stories we are about to tell, so for the next few sections, we suppress them. For now, we look only at pure-exchange economies.

Then, to make the market institutions more realistic, imagine that at each date t, and in each contingency f_t, markets will open (and clear) in each of the k basic commodities. Call these markets the *contingency-f_t spot markets*, and let prices in these markets be denoted by $r_{f_t} \in R^k_+$. (Hence, I've *assumed* that spot-market prices are nonnegative. But this restriction on the sign of spot-market prices is without substantial loss of generality given Assumption 16.1, or even a weakening of this assumption to be given later; see Problem 16.1b.) And, *in addition*, at time 0, in the sole time-0 contingency, f_0, additional markets are conducted in which consumers are able to transfer wealth among the various contingencies.

There are two ways to envision what is traded in these additional markets. The first, which goes with the name *contingent futures markets*, begins by fixing some tangible commodity that is certain to have a strictly positive price in every spot market.[1] The special role in Assumption 16.1 about commodity 1, wheat, was made for this purpose: At time 0, in addition to markets in the k spot commodities (f_0 wheat, f_0 corn, f_0 rides to the airport, etc.), we have $N-1$ *futures markets*, in which contracts to deliver f_t wheat (measured in the same units that are used in the f_t spot markets) are traded for immediate "cash." One such market exists for every contingency f_t except f_0. No one begins with an endowment of these contracts, and for every buyer, there must be a seller, so we allow consumers who trade in these contracts to take short positions, meaning that, at time 0, some consumers use their wealth to buy promised contracts in f_t wheat (for the various future contingencies) while others sell these contracts; they promise to deliver the wheat if and when f_t comes about, in return for which they get current cash with which to buy other things, which could be immediate (spot) consumption goods or futures contracts for wheat in other contingencies.

Think of a consumer with a large endowment of goods and services at date t for some t, or in some contingency f_t, but who is endowment-poor at some other date t' or contingency $f'_{t'}$. This consumer, knowing of her relative good fortune at t or f_t, anticipates that, should f_t come about, she can use her resources in that contingency to buy wheat and discharge obligations she makes at time 0. So she

[1] The second way to envision what is traded will be discussed near the end of this section.

sells futures contracts—if she is generally wealthy at date t, she might sell contracts in all the time-t contingencies; if she is wealthy in specific contingencies f_t, she might sell contracts in those contingencies only. And she uses the proceeds from this sale to purchase futures contracts for time-t' contingencies (all of them or some of them) in which she is endowment-poor.

Moreover, her purchases of wheat futures for, say, contingency $f'_{t'}$, aren't intended for consumption purposes, necessarily. Imagine that this consumer is completely neutral to the consumption of wheat; she has no desire to consume any of it. (This is consistent with nondecreasing preferences, as long as consuming wheat doesn't lower her utility.) But if she is endowment-poor in contingency $f'_{t'}$, she might buy $f'_{t'}$-wheat futures at time 0 with the intention, if $f'_{t'}$ happens, to take delivery of the wheat she bought and then sell it on the $f'_{t'}$ wheat spot market, using the proceeds from that sale to buy corn, or ice cream, or whatever it is that she wants to consume, in the then-functioning spot markets. Similarly, she need not be rich in endowed wheat in f_t to sell f_t-labeled wheat in the futures market: If, say, she is rich in f_t corn, she can sell f_t wheat futures and, should f_t eventuate, sell her f_t corn and buy f_t wheat in the spot market, with which she discharges her obligation to supply wheat.

Prices in these futures contracts are denoted by $q \in R_+^{N-1}$, where $q_{f_t} \in R_+$ is the price at date 0 for the promised delivery of a unit of wheat in contingency f_t. Note that I've assumed that these prices will all be nonnegative. In fact, given Assumption 16.1, they will be strictly positive in the sort of equilibrium about to be defined. (See Problem 16.1c.)

Definition 16.3. *An* ***equilibrium of plans, prices, and price expectations*** *(or* ***EPPPE****) for this (pure-exchange) economy is an array* $(r, q, \mathbf{x}, \mathbf{y})$ *consisting of:*

a. for each contingency f_t *(including* f_0*), a price vector* $r_{f_t} \in R_+^k$*, where* r_{f_t} *gives the (prospective) equilibrium prices for spot commodities in the* f_t *spot market;*

b. a price vector $q \in R_+^{N-1}$*, where* q_{f_t} *for each contingency* f_t *other than* f_0 *is the price (at time* 0*) of the contingency-*f_t *futures contract in wheat;*

c. for each consumer h*, a consumption plan* $\mathbf{x}^h \in R_+^{kN}$*, where* $\mathbf{x}^h_{if_t}$*, for* $i = 1, \ldots, k$ *and* f_t *a contingency, is the amount of contingency-*f_t *good* i *that* h *consumes in equilibrium; and*

d. for each consumer h*, a* ***contingent-futures-market position*** $\mathbf{y}^h \in R^{N-1}$*, where* $\mathbf{y}^h_{f_t}$ *(for each contingency* f_t *other than* f_0*) is the position taken in the contingent futures market for* f_t*-contingent wheat by* h*; if* $\mathbf{y}^h_{f_t} > 0$*, then* h *is a buyer of* f_t*-contingent wheat, while* $\mathbf{y}^h_{f_t} < 0$ *means that* h *is a seller of these contingent futures contracts.*

These must satisfy:

e. *Each consumer's plans* $\mathbf{x}^h$ *and* $\mathbf{y}^h$ *satisfy her contingency-by-contingency budget constraints, which are:*

$$r_{f_0} \cdot x^h_{f_0} + q \cdot y^h \le r_{f_0} \cdot e^h_{f_0}, \quad \text{and}$$
$$r_{f_t} \cdot x^h_{f_t} \le r_{f_t} \cdot e^h_{f_t} + r_{1f_t} y^h_{f_t}, \quad \text{for each } f_t \text{ other than } f_0, \tag{16.1}$$

where $e^h_{f_t} \in R^k_+$ *is* h*'s endowment of commodities in contingency* f_t.

f. *For each* h, $\mathbf{x}^h$ *maximizes* u^h *(*h*'s utility function), over all consumption plans* $x^h \in R^{kN}_+$ *for which there is a corresponding futures-market position* $y^h \in R^{N-1}$ *that, together with* x^h*, satisfy the budget constraints (16.1).*

g. *All markets clear:*

$$\sum_{h=1}^{H} \mathbf{x}^h_{f_t} \le \sum_{h=1}^{H} e^h_{f_t}, \quad \text{for each } f_t, \text{ and} \quad \sum_{h=1}^{H} y^h = 0. \tag{16.2}$$

One should be wary of definitions with seven clauses, but there is less to this definition (from a formal standpoint) than may at first seem. The idea is captured by the name of this creature, an *equilibrium of plans, prices, and price expectations.* Starting back at time $t = 0$, consumers in this economy think through everything that will happen and plan accordingly. In particular, they anticipate (accurately!) what will be the equilibrium prices in each contingency-f_t spot market. And they make their plans: They decide (optimally!) how to use the contingent futures contracts to move their wealth around, from one contingency to another, choosing at time 0 their immediate consumption as well as positions in futures contracts that will achieve this, while planning what they will buy and sell in the various contingent spot markets, based on their (accurate!) anticipation of future contingent spot prices.

Of course, consumer h faces budget constraints, one for each contingency f_t. For the initial contingency, her budget constraint is special, because that is when she takes positions in the futures markets; we get the budget constraint that is the first line of (16.1). On the "purchase" side are the cost of h's immediate consumption and the cost of her futures market position; recall that $y^h_{f_t} > 0$ when h is a buyer of contingency-f_t (future) wheat, so when $y^h_{f_t} > 0$, this is a drain on h's resources, while if $y^h_{f_t} < 0$, this loosens her time-0 budget constraint. On the "resource" side of this constraint is just the value of h's immediate endowment.

The second line of (16.1) gives h's budget constraint for all contingencies other than f_0. On the purchase or left-hand side is the cost of consumption; on the resource or right-hand side is the value of her endowment plus the value in that contingency of her position in the futures market. Again, if $y^h_{f_t} > 0$, then h is receiving wheat from the futures market, which increases her wealth. But if $y^h_{f_t} < 0$, she must make good on contracts she sold, which subtracts from her wealth.

And, what makes this an equilibrium, all of this fits together. Each consumer anticipates all future prices, each consumer maximizes her utility given those anticipations, and all markets clear. Note that we insist on equality in the time-0 futures markets; note also that, because of this, when we write out market clearing in the contingency-f_t-wheat spot market (part of the first inequality in (16.2)), we can ignore futures market positions, because they net out to zero.

Proposition 16.4. *(Recall Assumption 16.1, which remains in force.) Suppose (p, x) is a Walrasian equilibrium for the all-at-once market structure. Then (r, q, x, y) where*

$$r_{if_t} = p_{if_t}, \quad q_{f_t} = p_{1f_t}, \quad \textit{and} \quad y^h_{f_t} = p_{f_t} \cdot (x^h_{f_t} - e^h_{f_t})/p_{1f_t}$$

is an EPPPE for the economy with contingent futures markets. And if (r, q, x, y) is an EPPPE for the economy with contingent futures markets, then (p, x), where

$$p_{f_0} = r_{f_0} \quad \textit{and} \quad p_{if_t} = \left(\frac{q_{f_t}}{r_{1f_t}}\right) r_{if_t}, \textit{for } f_t \neq f_0,$$

is a Walrasian equilibrium for the all-at-once market structure.

A formal proof will be provided momentarily, but note what this is saying. We don't quite have a one-to-one correspondence between equilibria with one market structure and the other, because prices in the contingent spot markets can be arbitrarily scaled; that's why, in defining p from q and r, we must renormalize the spot-market prices. But in terms of what really matters, namely the consumers' consumption allocations, every equilibrium allocation for the all-at-once market structure is an equilibrium allocation for the contingent-futures-market market structure, and vice versa. Of course, this means that all the nice results of Chapters 14 and 15, concerning existence and, even more significantly, (Pareto) efficiency of Walrasian-equilibrium allocations, translate into the same results for this market structure. Moreover, note how we move from a Walrasian equilibrium to an EPPPE, in terms of the futures-market positions: We simply work out how much "cash" consumer h will need in the f_t-spot market and assign her the position that meets those needs.

At the same time, note the very heroic assumptions that are (implicitly) made about the powers of the consumers and, in particular, their predictive and strategic powers. They forecast with perfect accuracy what future spot prices will be and then they optimize their lifetime consumption plans given those forecasts (and current prices).

Proof. Now to prove the proposition. You are forewarned that this is a very tedious exercise; if you find yourself thinking, "It is amazing how things are working out," you are giving too much credit to what is going on. Once you understand how the two equilibria are related, this is all absolutely straightforward accounting (using Walras' Law as one of the available accounting identities).

Suppose that $(p, \boldsymbol{x})$ is a Walrasian equilibrium. Define r, q, and $\boldsymbol{y}$ as shown. To show that $(r, q, \boldsymbol{x}, \boldsymbol{y})$ is an EPPPE, we must verify that each consumer satisfies her budget constraints and is maximizing utility subject to those budget constraints, and that markets clear.

Concerning the budget constraints, since r is defined to be p, $\boldsymbol{y}$ can be rewritten as $\boldsymbol{y}^h_{f_t} = r_{f_t} \cdot (\boldsymbol{x}^h_{f_t} - e^h_{f_t})/r_{1f_t}$. Therefore, by definition, the second part of (16.1) holds with equality: $\boldsymbol{y}^h$ is defined to make this so. As for the first half, begin with the budget constraint in the Walrasian equilibrium, which holds with equality because all consumers are locally insatiable:

$$p \cdot \boldsymbol{x}^h = p \cdot e^h.$$

Break each sum into terms for contingency f_0 and for all others:

$$p_{f_0} \cdot \boldsymbol{x}^h_{f_0} + \sum_{f_t \neq f_0} p_{f_t} \cdot \boldsymbol{x}^h_{f_t} = p_{f_0} \cdot e^h_{f_0} + \sum_{f_t \neq f_0} p_{f_t} \cdot e^h_{f_t}.$$

Rearrange terms and substitute r for p (since they are identical), to get

$$r_{f_0} \cdot \boldsymbol{x}^h_{f_0} + \sum_{f_t \neq f_0} r_{f_t} \cdot (\boldsymbol{x}^h_{f_t} - e^h_{f_t}) = r_{f_0} \cdot e^h_{f_0}.$$

In the summation, multiply and divide each term by p_{1f_t}, and you get the top half of (16.1), with equality.

Next is to show that the consumer is maximizing. Let $\hat{x}$ be any consumption bundle for h that, together with a corresponding $\hat{y}$, satisfies the budget constraints (16.1) with $\hat{x}$ substituted for $\boldsymbol{x}^h$ and $\hat{y}$ for $\boldsymbol{y}^h$. Sum up over all f_t the budget constraints for $\hat{x}$ and $\hat{y}$, and you get

$$r_{f_0} \cdot \hat{x}_{f_0} + q \cdot \hat{y} + \sum_{f_t \neq f_0} r_{f_t} \cdot \hat{x}_{f_t} \leq r_{f_0} \cdot e^h_{f_0} + \sum_{f_t \neq f_0} (r_{f_t} \cdot e^h_{f_t} + r_{1f_t} \hat{y}_{f_t}).$$

Substitute p for r, while noting that $r_{1f_t} = p_{1f_t} = q_{f_t}$ and that $\sum_{f_t \neq f_0} q_{f_t} \hat{y}_{f_t}$ is just $q \cdot \hat{y}$, and you get

$$p_{f_0} \cdot \hat{x}_{f_0} + q \cdot \hat{y} + \sum_{f_t \neq f_0} p_{f_t} \cdot \hat{x}_{f_t} \leq p_{f_0} \cdot e^h_{f_0} + \sum_{f_t \neq f_0} p_{f_t} \cdot e^h_{f_t} + q \cdot \hat{y}.$$

Now cancel the common $q \cdot \hat{y}$, and recognize that the remaining terms amount to $p \cdot \hat{x}$ on the left-hand side and $p \cdot e^h$ on the right-hand side. Hence, $\hat{x}$ is a budget-feasible bundle for h in the economy with an all-at-once market structure and prices p. But since $\boldsymbol{x}^h$ is a Walrasian-equilibrium allocation at those prices, $u^h(\boldsymbol{x}^h) \geq u^h(\hat{x})$. That proves the maximization part of the definition of an EPPPE.

And to show that markets clear: The first half of (16.2) is the market-clearing condition for a Walrasian equilibrium (expressed a bit less succinctly than usual), so it holds immediately. And, we know that $p \geq 0$ and $\sum_h x^h \leq \sum_h e^h$, so clearly $p \cdot \sum_h (x^h - e^h) \leq 0$. Moreover, this dot product consists only of nonpositive terms. And, because consumers are all locally insatiable, each satisfies Walras' Law with equality in any equilibrium, so this dot product is zero, and hence each term in it is zero. That is, for each f_t,

$$p_{f_t} \cdot \sum_h \left(x^h_{f_t} - e^h_{f_t} \right) = 0.$$

We also know that $p_{1f_t} > 0$ for each f_t; hence for each f_t,

$$0 = \frac{1}{p_{1f_t}} p_{f_t} \cdot \sum_h \left(x^h_{f_t} - e^h_{f_t} \right) = \sum_h \frac{1}{p_{1f_t}} p_{f_t} \cdot (x^h_{f_t} - e^h_{f_t}) = \sum_h y^h_{f_t}.$$

That is market clearing in the futures market, and (r, q, x, y) is an EPPPE.

For the other half, suppose that (r, q, x, y) is an EPPPE. To show (p, x) is a Walrasian equilibrium (for p defined as indicated from r and q), we must show that each consumer is satisfying her (all-at-once) budget constraint, each is maximizing subject to that budget constraint, and that markets clear.

Market clearing is immediate from the first half of (16.2).

For the rest, I assert that, in any EPPPE, both q_{f_t} and r_{1f_t} must be be strictly positive. The distinguished consumer whose preferences are globally insatiable in f_t-contingent wheat provides this conclusion; you are asked to supply the argument in Problem 16.1c.

Now take the EPPPE budget constraint for consumer h, given by (16.1). For each f_t, multiply both sides of the inequalty by q_{f_t}/r_{1f_t} and then add all these constraints together to get

$$r_{f_0} \cdot x^h_{f_0} + q \cdot y^h + \sum_{f_t \neq f_0} \left(\frac{q_{f_t}}{r_{1f_t}} \right) r_{f_t} \cdot x^h_{f_t} \leq r_{f_0} \cdot e^h_{f_0} + \sum_{f_t \neq f_0} \left(\frac{q_{f_t}}{r_{1f_t}} \right) \left(r_{f_t} \cdot e^h_{f_t} + r_{1f_t} y^h_{f_t} \right).$$

Replace the (normalized) r's with p's, and cancel the common term $q \cdot y^h$, and you get $p \cdot x^h \leq p \cdot e^h$. So x^h is budget feasible for h at the prices p.

Finally, suppose that $\hat{x}$ is feasible for h at the prices p. Define $\hat{y} \in R^{N-1}$ by $\hat{y}_{f_t} = r_{f_t} \cdot (\hat{x}_{f_t} - e^h_{f_t})/r_{1f_t}$. I assert that the pair $(\hat{x}, \hat{y})$ satisfies (16.1), so that $\hat{x}$ is a feasible consumption bundle for h in the economy with futures markets and prices (r, q). Since x^h is an equilibrium bundle (in the EPPPE), once this is shown, we know that $u^h(x^h) \geq u^h(\hat{x})$, proving that x^h solves h's utility-maxmization problem in the all-markets-at-once economy, concluding the proof that (p, x) is a Walrasian equilibrium for that economy.

Note that $\hat{y}$ is defined so that for all f_t other than f_0, the second part of (16.1) holds with equality. We only need to verify the first part of (16.1). Since $\hat{x}$ is budget feasible in the all-markets-at-once economy at prices p, we know that $p \cdot \hat{x} \le p \cdot e^h$. Write this as

$$p_{f_0} \cdot \hat{x}_{f_0} + \sum_{f_t \neq f_0} p_{f_t} \cdot \hat{x}_{f_t} \le p_{f_0} \cdot e^h_{f_0} + \sum_{f_t \neq f_0} p_{f_t} \cdot e^h_{f_t}; \text{ hence}$$

$$p_{f_0} \cdot \hat{x}_{f_0} + \sum_{f_t \neq f_0} p_{f_t} \cdot (\hat{x}_{f_t} - e^h_{f_t}) \le p_{f_0} \cdot e^h_{f_0}.$$

In this inequality, replace each p with its definition in terms of q and r, and use the definition of $\hat{y}$, and you get

$$r_{f_0} \cdot \hat{x}_{f_0} + \sum_{f_t \neq f_0} \left(\frac{q_{f_t}}{r_{1 f_t}}\right) r_{f_t} \cdot (\hat{x}_{f_t} - e^h_{f_t}) = r_{f_0} \cdot \hat{x}_{f_0} + \sum_{f_t \neq f_0} q_{f_t} \hat{y}_{f_t}$$
$$= r_{f_0} \cdot \hat{x}_{f_0} + q \cdot \hat{y} \le r_{f_0} \cdot e^h_{f_0}.$$

That is the first half of (16.1), completing the proof. ■

Arrow-Debreu contingent claims

At the start of this section, I said that there were two ways to set up markets in which consumers can transfer wealth from one contingency to another. And, so far, I've only talked about one of those ways: So far, the extra markets at time 0 are contingent (commodity) futures markets, which pay off in units of a commodity (which we are calling wheat).

Imagine, instead, that we have at time 0, in addition to the time-0 spot markets in the k basic commodities, $N - 1$ *financial-claims markets*. One market exists for each f_t other than f_0, and if consumer h purchases (at time zero) y_{f_t} of these, then if and when contingency f_t (other than f_0) rolls around, her budget constraint is

$$r_{f_t} \cdot x_{f_t} \le r_{f_t} \cdot e^h_{f_t} + y_{f_t}.$$

Indeed, the same budget constraint applies if she sells some number of these claims; in that case, $y_{f_t} < 0$. In other words, one of these claims isn't a contingent claim to a unit of wheat or some tangible commodity; instead it is a claim to a unit of "money" or whatever is the numeraire (currency) in the f_t spot market.

This change in formulation doesn't make a serious economic difference to what emerges. In particular, we obtain the same sort of result as Proposition 16.4: The Walrasian-equilibrium allocations of the economy with the all-at-once market structure is the same as the EPPPE-equilibrium allocations of this market economy. Indeed, life is a little more convenient when it comes to writing stuff out with this second formulation, because you no longer need to worry about the market value in each contingency of "wheat" or whatever is playing the role of wheat. On the other hand, the scaling of prices does become an issue. In the formulation of the last subsection, prices in each contingent spot market can be rescaled independently, without affecting the price at time 0 of the f_t-contingent claim on wheat, because if you rescale all spot prices in contingency f_t, you rescale the spot price of wheat. The point is, a bushel of wheat in each contingency has some specific economic value (in equilibrium), and that is what q_{f_t} captures.

In this alternative framework, you can, say, double all the spot prices in contingency f_t. But when you do this, since the financial contingent claim for f_t pays off in units of account, you halve its value back at time $t = 0$. That is, it takes twice as many of these financial claims to transfer the same amount of real wealth into or out of contingency f_t. It isn't a big deal, if you are careful, but you do need to be careful.

With this alternative formulation, the commodity wheat no longer plays any special role, and so you might anticipate that we no longer need to assume the existence of a consumer whose preferences are globally insatiable in f_t wheat, for each f_t. We needed that to ensure that the spot price of wheat is strictly positive in all contingencies, so that the f_t-wheat futures contract would be a way to move resources between f_0 and f_t. *By definition,* a claim that pays in units of account will have positive value in any contingency. Or, rather, it will have a positive price (of one unit of account). However, if we no longer assume the existence of the wheat-loving consumer, we must make an assumption that ensures that units of account have real economic value in each contingency:

Assumption 16.1′. *Each consumer has continuous, nondecreasing, and locally insatiable preferences.* (This is just as before. What changes is:) *For each f_t, there is some consumer h who is* ***globally insatiable in f_t-contingent consumption****: For this consumer h, for any $x \in R_+^{kN}$, there exists $x' \in R_+^{kN}$ such that (1) x and x' are identical on any non-f_t component and (2) $u^h(x') > u^h(x)$.*

With this assumption in place of Assumption 16.1, Proposition 16.4, suitably modified, holds for contingent financial markets just as well as for contingent futures markets. (See Problem 16.2.)

You will often see the term *Arrow-Debreu contingent claims* used to decribe these financial securities. Arrow (1953) and Debreu (1959) both discuss the idea of contingency-stamping commodities in a general-equilibrium framework; Arrow (1953) goes on (in a two-period setting) to show that the combination of time-0 financial claims and subsequent contingent spot markets accomplishes the same thing. The term "equilibrium of plans, prices, and price expectations" is due to Radner (1968, 1972), although he deals as well with the more complex market structures we'll consider next section.

Economizing on markets, but not on calculations

Since the equilibrium outcomes (in terms of consumption allocations) are identical, why would we think that one or the other of the two market structures—contingent claims and spot markets versus all-markets-at-once— is better? Arrow (1953) suggests that the dynamic market structure, especially with financial claims, comes closer to what we see in the real world (and next section will bring us even closer to real-world institutions). And the dynamic market structure economizes on the number of markets that must be run:

In the all-at-once market structure, if there are N contingencies and k commodities, we need kN markets at time 0. In the dynamic economy, we need a spot market for each date, or $k(T+1)$, plus $N-1$ contingent-claims markets. Assuming T is a good deal smaller than N—and in Figure 16.1 (for example), $N = 33$ while $T = 4$—that is quite a savings. If, say, $k = 10$, then for the t/u/i structure of Figure 16.1, the all-at-once market structure involves 330 functioning markets (all functioning simultaneously), while in the sort of dynamic market structure studied in this section, we need 82. And, to the extent that markets need infrastructure, in the dynamic-market structure, we only have 42 markets to operate at time 0 and 10 at each subsequent date, rather than 330 markets all running simultaneously.

But while this market structure economizes on the number of markets required and, even more, on the number of markets that operate at any single time, it increases (if anything) the mental gymnastics required of consumers. In the all-at-once market structure, all the markets and hence all relevant prices are apparent to consumers at the one time the consumer makes her market decisions. With this market structure, once markets close, consumers can pretty much stop thinking; all that is required of them is to make good on promises to deliver and then consume. We have no serious story about how prices are set—recall the discussion of simultaneity back in Chapter 14, when we discussed generalized games—but it is intuitive that in any working mechanism, consumers learn about the terms of trade they face in, say, a date-3 contingency as they are asked to make trades for commodities stamped with that contingency.

In contrast, in the dynamic economy, consumers must work out for themselves what the terms of trade in every contingency are going to be. A consumer whose endowment in a date-3 contingency consists of a lot of corn and very little wheat will be vitally interested in the relative prices of these two commodities in that contingency. If, say, the price of corn will be low, this consumer may want to use her wealth from other contingencies to transfer wealth into this contingency. If the price of corn will be relatively high, perhaps (at time 0) she will want to sell futures or financial claims in this contingency, which her sizeable endowment in relatively high-price corn will allow her to cover. (It would help her, to some extent, if the futures markets dealt in contingent corn. But, if we have futures and not financial markets, those markets operate in wheat.) The amount of "figuring" she must do in the dynamic market economy is no less than in the all-at-once market structure and, since she is on her own in predicting what future prices will be, it seems intuitive that it is a good deal more. A story sometimes told about why price-mediated markets are good is that prices convey to each consumer in a low-dimensional way all relevant information about the preferences and endowments (and, in an economy with production, the production technologies) of other consumers. We have not formalized this story, but if you accept it, then note: In the dynamic economy, each consumer must contemplate the preferences and endowments of her peers, to assess accurately what equilibrium prices will emerge. Life is easier when the prices are posted.

Put it this way: Of course, these models are all idealizations. But the Pareto efficiency of the market outcome—the fruits of the First Theorem of Welfare Economics—is likely to be approximately correct only to the extent that our idealizations are approximately correct. The very rich market structure of the all-markets-at-once economy provides consumers with a lot of pertinent information for getting their own decisions right, and hence it increases our confidence in the approximate efficiency of the market outcome. The relatively sparse market structure of the dynamic economy can only cause our confidence in the efficiency of market outcomes to decrease.

Dynamic optimization?

And when we move to the dynamic market structure, we find the possibility of some curious dynamic optimizations.

Imagine that $k = 2$, with the two goods being corn and wheat. Imagine $T = 1$, and $\Omega = \{\omega_1, \omega_2\}$. This means we have three contingencies, and hence six contingency-stamped goods; I'll use $(c_0, w_0, c_{11}, w_{11}, c_{12}, w_{12})$ to denote a consumption bundle, where the first two components are time-0 consumption, the middle two are time-1, state-ω_1 consumption, and the final two are for time 1 and state ω_2. Now imagine a consumer whose utility function is

$$u(c_0, w_0, c_{11}, w_{11}, c_{12}, w_{12}) = (c_0 + 0.5c_{11} + 0.5c_{12})^{1/2} + w_0 + 0.5w_{11} + 0.5w_{12}.$$

Viewed as a utility function on the six-dimensional commodity space R^6_+, there is nothing particularly wrong or pathological about this function: It is strictly increasing, continuous, concave; all the things you'd want. So, in the all-markets-at-once economy, the optimizing behavior of this consumer raises no specific concerns.

But put this consumer into the dynamic economy and, in particular, consider her decision-making process in the $\{\omega_1\}$-spot market. She has a certain amount of resources, combining her endowment in that contingency with resources she has provided for herself by buying in the $\{\omega_1\}$-futures or -financial market at time 0 (or less any resources she must give up, to fulfill promises she made at time 0 by selling $\{\omega_1\}$ futures or financial claims). And she faces prices r_c for corn and r_w for wheat. So, she does the usual maximize-utility thing.

But it isn't quite so simple, because of the nature of her preferences. Phrasing this in terms of marginal utilities and bangs for the buck, her marginal utility of $\{\omega_1\}$-stamped wheat is a constant 0.5, so her bang for the buck in this commodity is 0.5 divided by the spot price in this contingency of wheat. But her marginal utility in $\{\omega_1\}$-stamped corn is $1/\big(4(c_0 + 0.5c_{11} + 0.5c_{12})^{1/2}\big)$, and her bang for the buck is this divided by the prevailing spot price in corn. The point is that, in contingency $\{\omega_1\}$, her marginal utility for corn is smaller the more corn she ate at time 0 *and the more corn she thinks she would have eaten, had the state of nature been* ω_2. The first part of this isn't too off-putting: If the time periods are close to each other, a big meal of corn at time 0 might put her off corn at time 1, at least to some extent. But the second part seems ... bizarre. She knows ω_2 isn't going to happen. She may have had plans to eat a huge amount of corn in contingency $\{\omega_2\}$ but, in contingency $\{\omega_1\}$, she knows that those plans are defunct. Yet her marginal utility for corn in contingency $\{\omega_1\}$, and hence her optimal allocation of her resources between wheat and corn, depends on that never-to-be-realized feast of corn. Taking this a step further, suppose state ω_2 represents a drought in corn-growing regions, so that corn endowments in that state are low, and spot prices for corn are correspondingly high. Suppose that, accordingly, her plans were to consume a *small* amount of corn consumption in contingency $\{\omega_2\}$. Then her demand for corn in the contingency-$\{\omega_1\}$ spot market is larger at every price, because of a drought that she knows will never take place and to make up for a small amount of corn she might have but now knows she will not consume. Hmmmm.

More than anything else, this is probably a good argument against this consumer's preferences. It seems intuitive that this sort of thing shouldn't happen. If, for instance, she was a subjective-expected-utility maximizer as in Chapter 5, this wouldn't happen. Indeed, justifications for axioms such as Savage's sure-thing principle come down, essentially, to an argument that this sort of thing is so bizarre that no consumer would behave in this fashion. So perhaps we should simply put this oddity down to "bad preferences" and not be concerned further.

But this does raise a point worth emphasizing. An EPPPE is an equilibrium of *prices*—in that it involves market clearing—and *price expectations*—in that consumers accurately anticipate future spot prices—and *plans*. And part of the *plans* piece of this is that agents formulate their plans in the standard fashion of dynamic choice in economic theory, as discussed in Chapter 7. For nearly all of this book, we've been concerned with static choice. But here we encounter dynamic choice, with a vengeance, and in an EPPPE, we are employing the standard paradigm that dynamic choice is no more than static choice of an optimal strategy, which is then carried out. To the extent that there is more to dynamic choice than this, we have another reason to be suspicious of this model.

16.4. EPPPE: II. Complex Financial Securities and Complete Markets

Building on the developments of the last section, we now consider economies with more complex securities. In this section, we continue to work with pure-exchange economies.

As before, we fix the list of basic commodities, indexed by $i = 1, \ldots, k$. And we fix a t/u/i structure, with time index $t = 0, \ldots, T$, state space Ω, and N contingencies, from f_0 to an $f_T = \{\omega\}$ for each $\omega \in \Omega$. Recall that $\mathcal{F}$ denotes the set of all N contingencies and that, for $f_t \in \mathcal{F}$, $t > 0$, $\hat{f}_t$ denotes the immediate predecessor of f_t. We also have a finite set of consumers, indexed by $h = 1, \ldots, H$, with utility functions u^h and endowments e^h.

In this setting, a *security* s is described by two things: a subset of contingencies $\mathcal{F}(s) \subseteq \mathcal{F}$ at which the security trades; and a dividend structure. For the balance of this section, we assume that, as at the end of last section, the securities are *financial*, meaning that dividends are paid in "units of account" or "numeraire."[2] As you will learn at the end of this section, this is problematic in some respects (more accurately, it leads to a massive amount of indeterminancy when it comes to prices), and we'll fix some of these problems next section. But it simplifies the account of results we can give, better for a first pass through the subject. Hence the dividend structure of security s is an element d_s of $R^{\mathcal{F}}$ (or, equivalently, R^N). We write $d_s(f_t)$ for the dividend paid in contingency f_t, and we make the following further assumptions:

Assumption 16.5. *The dividends paid by each security s are nonnegative, $d_s \in R^{\mathcal{F}}_+$. Securities are traded* **ex dividend***: Dividends paid in contingency f_t are paid to consumers who held the securities just prior to (any) contingency-f_t trading in the security. No security trades at date T. If $d_s(f_t) \neq 0$, then there is some contingency $f'_{t'}$ that precedes f_t at which s trades; or $f'_{t'} \in \mathcal{F}(s)$.*

The first part of this assumption isn't essential, but it does make later results easier to state. The bit about *ex dividend* has the following explanation: Suppose that in contingency f_t, which is a trading contingency for some security s, s pays a dividend of 4 units of numeraire. Suppose that consumer h enters contingency f_t holding 6 units of this security and, since this is a trading contingency for the security, sells 2 of her units, so she exits the period holding 4 units. Is her dividend payment 24, based on her initial holdings, or 16? We assume the former, which (more or less) is in accord with real-life practice.

But please note carefully: If our consumer h holds 6 units of a security, since securities are in zero net supply, there is some consumer h' out there with a strictly negative position in this security. And h' will have to come up with 4 units of numeraire for every unit of the security he is short (prior to contingency f_t trading), when and if contingency f_t comes around. The term "dividend" conventionally refers to a payout made by a firm to holders of its equity; short-sellers must make good on these dividends but, for the most part, payments go from the firm to agents who hold equity of the firm. In the model we are creating, there is some consumer short for every unit of the security that someone else is long, and all payments of "dividends" go from those who are short to those who are long. For this reason, "transfer" or "payout" might be a better term than "dividend." But "dividend" is conventionally used, and so we use it.

Also note why, with our *ex dividend* convention, it is pointless to have securities markets open at date T. Securities have value for two reasons: the buyer will receive a dividend at some future point; or she will be able to sell the security to some other buyer. At date T, there are no future opportunities to sell securities, and all dividends will have been paid, so all securities become worthless. And the

[2] This is a bit of an abuse of the adjective *financial*. It might be more accurate to call these *nominal* dividends and (so) nominal securities. But I'll continue to use *financial*.

ex dividend convention is the rationale for insisting that securities trade before they issue any (nonzero) dividends; if there have been no opportunities for trading in the security, no one holds any, and so there is no one to give or receive a dividend.

Some examples of securities are:

- An Arrow-Debreu contingent claim from last section is a security that, for some contingency f_t, $t > 0$, pays a dividend of 1 in contingency f_t, pays 0 in all other contingencies, and trades only in contingency f_0.
- A *simple time-t-to-time-t' debt*, for $0 \le t < t' \le T$, is a security that trades at all time-t contingencies—that is, $\mathcal{F}(s) = \mathcal{F}_t$—and pays nonzero dividend (only) at each $f_{t'} \in \mathcal{F}_{t'}$, when it pays one unit of numeraire. Or we could imagine that this asset is allowed to change hands—to be traded—at all contingencies f_τ, for $\tau = t, \ldots, t' - 1$. We can also imagine a debt asset for which trading initially opens at some specific $f_t \in \mathcal{F}_t$, and then trades at all dates prior to some t' in contingencies that are successors of the initial f_t.
- For each $f_t \neq f_0$, the *$\hat{f}_t$-to-f_t contingent claim* is a security for which trading takes place at the unique time $t - 1$ predecessor $\hat{f}_t$ of f_t—in symbols, $\mathcal{F}(s) = \{\hat{f}_t\}$—and that pays 1 unit of numeraire at f_t (and zero in all other contingencies).

Because we deal with financial securities in this section, Assumption 16.1′ rather than Assumption 16.1 is relevant. *For the balance of this section, Assumptions 16.1′ and 16.5 are maintained assumptions in all results.*

A full specification of a dynamic economy now consists of: a list of basic commodities; a t/u/i structure; consumers with preferences (utility functions) and endowments; a finite set S of securities; and a market structure consisting of whatever trade is permitted by the securities, plus spot markets in all basic commodities, in every contingency. Securities are in zero net supply, and in any contingency when security s is traded, any consumer can take a position (long or short) in that security; if the security has traded previously, she can *change* her position in the security.

Definition 16.6. *Fix a dynamic economy as described above. An equilibrium of plans, prices, and price expectations (EPPPE) for this dynamic economy is an array $(r, q, \mathbf{x}, \mathbf{y})$ consisting of:*

a. prices for each basic commodity in each contingency's spot market, given by r_{if_t}, as before;

b. prices for each security $s \in S$ in each contingency in which the security trades (or $f_t \in \mathcal{F}(s)$), given by q_{sf_t};

c. for each consumer h, a consumption plan $\mathbf{x}^h \in R_+^{kN}$; and

*d. for each consumer h, a **trading plan** for the securities, which is a vector $\mathbf{y}^h$ from $R^{\mathcal{F} \times S}$. Here, $\mathbf{y}^h(f_t, s)$ represents the number of units of security s held by h in contingency f_t, after trading takes place.*

These must satisfy the following:

e. *Each consumer's trading plan must respect the constraints on when securities can be traded:* $\boldsymbol{y}^h(f_0, s) \neq 0$ *only if* $f_0 \in \mathcal{F}(s)$*, and, for each* f_t *other than* f_0*,* $\boldsymbol{y}^h(f_t, s) \neq \boldsymbol{y}^h(\hat{f}_t, s)$ *only if* $f_t \in \mathcal{F}(s)$*.*

f. *Each consumer's trading plan and consumption allocation must together satisfy the consumer's budget constraints, one for each contingency. To write this as one inequality (without having to make a special case of* f_0*), we create an "immediate predecessor"* $\hat{f}_0$ *of* f_0*; every trading plan* y^h *for* h *satisfies* $y^h(\hat{f}_0, s) = 0$ *for all* s*, by convention. Then the budget constraints for* h*, which apply jointly to a consumption plan* x^h *and a trading plan* y^h*, are*

$$
\begin{aligned}
r_{f_t} \cdot x^h_{f_t} &+ \sum_{s \in \mathcal{S}} q_{sf_t}\left[y^h(f_t, s) - y^h(\hat{f}_t, s)\right] \\
&\leq r_{f_t} \cdot e^h_{f_t} + \sum_{s \in \mathcal{S}} y^h(\hat{f}_t, s) d_s(f_t), \text{ for each } f_t.
\end{aligned}
\tag{16.3}
$$

g. *Each consumer* h *maximizes her utility, subject to feasibility:* $x^h \in R^{kN}_+$ *is a feasible consumption bundle for* h *if there is some trading plan* y^h *that satisfies the constraints on when securities can be traded, as specified in e, such that* x^h *and* y^h *satisfy her contingency-by-contingency budget constraints (16.3).*

h. *Markets clear:*

$$
\sum_h \boldsymbol{x}^h_{f_t} \leq \sum_h e^h_{f_t} \quad \textit{and} \quad \sum_h \boldsymbol{y}^h(f_t, s) = 0 \quad \textit{for all } f_t \textit{ and } s.
$$

This definition is entirely straightforward, except perhaps for the budget constraints. In particular, q_{sf_t} appears on the left-hand side of the constraint for each f_t, but for security s, this price only exists for $f_t \in \mathcal{F}(s)$. The summation should read, "over s such that $f_t \in \mathcal{F}(s)$," but since q_{sf_t} is multiplied by a term that, per part e, must be zero if $f_t \notin \mathcal{F}(s)$, this bit of notational sloppiness can be excused.

And, then, the budget constraints are simply: In each contingency, the amount consumer h spends on consumption and (net) on securities cannot exceed the value of her endowment and any dividends she is receiving.

Arbitrage and the subspace of feasible wealth transfers

Because all dividends are financial, we can discuss and analyze the securities side of any consumer's activities without worrying about commodities, their prices, or the specific consumer's endowments:

Definition 16.7.

a. *The set of* ***feasible wealth transfers*** *for a given set of securities* $\mathcal{S}$ *and prices* q *for those securities is the set* $M(\mathcal{S}, q)$ *of* $\xi \in R^N$ *such that, for some legitimate trading plan* y *(that is, a trading plan that satisfies Definition 16.6e),*

$$
\xi(f_t) = \sum_{s \in \mathcal{S}} \left(q_{sf_t}\left[y(\hat{f}_t, s) - y(f_t, s)\right] + y(\hat{f}_t, s) d_s(f_t) \right).
$$

(Note that $0 \in M(\mathcal{S}, q)$ in all cases, since the trading plan $y \equiv 0$ is always available and legitimate.)

b. *If there exists some $\xi \geq 0$ and $\neq 0$ in $M(\mathcal{S}, q)$, we say that* ***the securities $\mathcal{S}$ and prices q admit an arbitrage opportunity.*** *If $M(\mathcal{S}, q) \cap R_+^N = \{0\}$, we say that $\mathcal{S}$* ***and q do not admit arbitrage.***

c. *If there is some full (pure-exchange) economy with securities $\mathcal{S}$ and with consumers (who satisfy Assumption 16.1′) such that, with a full set of spot markets open in each contingency, there is an EPPPE in which the equilibrium prices for the securities are given by q, we say that $\mathcal{S}$ and q are a* ***viable*** *model of the securities markets, while if there is no such economy, we say that $\mathcal{S}$ and q are* ***not viable.***

Proposition 16.8.

a. *$M(\mathcal{S}, q)$ is a linear subspace of R^N.*

b. *$\mathcal{S}$ and q are viable if and only if they do not admit arbitrage, which is true if and only if there exists $\pi \in R_{++}^N$ such that $\pi \cdot \xi = 0$ for all $\xi \in M(\mathcal{S}, q)$.*

c. *Suppose $\mathcal{S}$ and q are viable, and let $\Pi(\mathcal{S}, q)$ be the set $\{\pi \in R_{++}^N : \pi \cdot \xi = 0$ for all $\xi \in M(\mathcal{S}, q)\}$. Then $\Pi(\mathcal{S}, q)$ is a cone (less its vertex, the origin), whose dimension is N less the dimension of $M(\mathcal{S}, q)$. Moreover, $\xi \in M(\mathcal{S}, q)$ if and only if $\pi \cdot \xi = 0$ for all $\pi \in \Pi(\mathcal{S}, q)$.*

In particular, $M(\mathcal{S}, q)$ has dimension $N-1$ if and only if $\Pi(\mathcal{S}, q)$ is one-dimensional, in which case $\xi \in M(\mathcal{S}, q)$ if and only if $\pi \cdot \xi = 0$ for (any) $\pi \in \Pi(\mathcal{S}, q)$.

Proof. (a) Suppose that ξ and ξ' are elements of $M(\mathcal{S}, q)$, with ξ generated by the trading plan y and ξ' by y'. For any scalars α and β, $\alpha y + \beta y'$ is a legitimate trading plan, and it clearly generates $\alpha\xi + \beta\xi'$.

(b) Suppose that $\mathcal{S}$ and q admit an arbitrage opportunity. In particular, suppose that the trading plan y^0 generates $\xi^0 \in R_+^k$ which is nonzero. Then there is some contingency f_t such that $\xi^0(f_t) > 0$, while $\xi^0(f'_{t'}) \geq 0$ for all (other) $f'_{t'}$. Consider a consumer h who is globally insatiable in f_t-contingency consumption. (The existence of such a consumer is guaranteed by Assumption 16.1′.) Whatever consumption bundle $\boldsymbol{x}^h$ is consumed by h, and whatever trading plan $\boldsymbol{y}^h$ she is using, if she uses $\boldsymbol{y}^h + \alpha y^0$, she will be able to afford $\boldsymbol{x}^h$ and, in contingency f_t, have $\alpha\xi^0(f_t)$ left over, with which (for large enough α) she can improve on $\boldsymbol{x}^h$. So, $\mathcal{S}$ and q are incompatible with her having a utility-maximizing choice and hence are incompatible with being part of an EPPPE. If $\mathcal{S}$ and q admit an arbitrage opportunity, $\mathcal{S}$ and q are not viable. And, therefore, if $\mathcal{S}$ and q are viable, they cannot admit an arbitrage opportunity.

Now suppose that $\mathcal{S}$ and q do not admit an arbitrage opportunity. Let $\Delta = \{z \in R_+^N : \sum_{f_t} z_{f_t} = 1\}$.[3] That is, Δ is the unit simplex in R^N. Clearly, Δ is compact and convex. Since $M(\mathcal{S}, q)$ is a subspace, it is closed and convex. "No

[3] The N-element index set $\mathcal{F}$ is used here, since $M(\mathcal{S}, q) \subseteq R^N$ has $\mathcal{F}$ as its index set.

arbitrage" implies that $M(\mathcal{S},q) \cap \Delta = \emptyset$. Therefore, the Strict Separation Theorem can be applied: There is a nonzero $\pi \in R^N$ and a scalar β such that $\pi \cdot \xi < \beta$ for all $\xi \in M(\mathcal{S},q)$ and $\pi \cdot z > \beta$ for all $z \in \Delta$.

Since $M(\mathcal{S},q)$ is a subspace, it must be that $\pi \cdot \xi = 0$ for all $\xi \in M(\mathcal{S},q)$. For if $\pi \cdot \xi^0 \neq 0$ for some $\xi^0 \in M(\mathcal{S},q)$, then either $\alpha\xi^0$ or $-\alpha\xi^0$ for very large α, both of which are in $M(\mathcal{S},q)$, would violate $\pi \cdot \xi < \beta$ for all $\xi \in M(\mathcal{S},q)$. And, therefore, $\beta > 0$. Hence, π must be strictly positive: If $\pi_{f_t} \leq 0$ for some f_t, then π dotted into the unit vector in direction f_t (the vector of all zeros except for a 1 in coordinate position f_t) would be $\pi_{f_t} \leq 0 < \beta$, even though this unit vector is in Δ.

Now suppose that there is a strictly positive vector π such that $\pi \cdot \xi = 0$ for all $\xi \in M(\mathcal{S},q)$. Consider a one-agent, one-basic-commodity economy, where the single agent's preferences are given by $u(x) = \pi \cdot x$. (Since this is a one-basic-commodity economy, the consumption space R_+^{kN} is simply R_+^N.) Clearly, Assumption 16.1′ holds for this consumer. Suppose the consumer is endowed with one unit of the good in every contingency. I assert that if the agent chooses to consume her endowment and make no trades, we have an EPPPE for $(\mathcal{S},q)$, where the spot price in each contingency is 1: The only alternative to consuming her endowment that the agent can contemplate is to shift her consumption by a vector lying in $M(\mathcal{S},q)$. But since u is linear, the impact this will have on her utility is $\pi \cdot \xi$, where ξ is the shift, and this has zero impact. So she is maximizing her utility in this economy, with these prices, by sticking to her endowment. This is an EPPPE, and $\mathcal{S}$ and q are viable.

We've shown viability implies no arbitrage implies existence of π implies viability, finishing part b.

(c) Suppose both π and π' from R_{++}^N both satisfy $\pi \cdot m = 0$ and $\pi' \cdot m = 0$ for all $m \in M(\mathcal{S},q)$. Then for any strictly positive scalars α and α', it is evident that $(\alpha\pi + \alpha'\pi') \cdot m = 0$ for all $m \in M(\mathcal{S},q)$ and, of course, $\alpha m + \alpha' m'$ is strictly positive. So $\Pi(\mathcal{S},q)$ is a cone less its vertex.

The rest of part c is standard theory from linear algebra. Since $M(\mathcal{S},q)$ is a subspace in R^N, its orthogonal complement,

$$M(\mathcal{S},q)^{\perp} = \{\pi \in R^N : \pi \cdot \xi = 0 \text{ for all } \xi \in M(\mathcal{S},q)\},$$

is a subspace of R^N whose dimension is N less the dimension of $M(\mathcal{S},q)$. Moreover, $(M(\mathcal{S},q)^{\perp})^{\perp} = M(\mathcal{S},q)$, which means that $\xi \in M(\mathcal{S},q)$ if and only if $\pi \cdot \xi = 0$ for all $\pi \in M(\mathcal{S},q)^{\perp}$.

Note that $\Pi(\mathcal{S},q)$ is simply $M(\mathcal{S},q)^{\perp} \cap R_{++}^N$. Since $\mathcal{S}$ and q are viable, we know that $\Pi(\mathcal{S},q)$ is nonempty (by part b); fix some $\pi \in \Pi(\mathcal{S},q)$. If $M(\mathcal{S},q)$ has dimension $N-1$, then $M(\mathcal{S},q)^{\perp}$ and, therefore, $\Pi(\mathcal{S},q)$ are one dimensional. And if $M(\mathcal{S},q)$ has dimension less than $N-1$, then form a basis of $M(\mathcal{S},q)^{\perp}$ that starts with π; denote this basis by $\{\pi, \rho^1, \ldots, \rho^j\}$ (so that the dimension of $M(\mathcal{S},q)^{\perp}$ is $j+1$). For $i = 1, \ldots, j$, find scalar $\gamma^i \neq 0$ such that $\pi + \gamma^i\rho^i$ is strictly positive; since π is strictly positive, this can always be done by, if necessary, taking γ^i close to zero. But then $\{\pi, \pi + \gamma^1\rho^1, \ldots, \pi + \gamma^j\rho^j\}$ is a set of $j+1$ linearly independent vectors in $M(\mathcal{S},q)^{\perp}$. Since they are all strictly positive by construction, they all lie in $\Pi(\mathcal{S},q)$, which ensures the $\Pi(\mathcal{S},q)$ has the same dimension as $M(\mathcal{S},q)^{\perp}$.

In fact, being $j+1$ linearly independent vectors in $M(\mathcal{S},q)^{\perp}$, they form a basis for $M(\mathcal{S},q)^{\perp}$. This means that $\pi \cdot \xi = 0$ for all $\pi \in M(\mathcal{S},q)^{\perp}$ is equivalent to $\pi \cdot \xi = 0$ for all $\pi \in \Pi(\mathcal{S},q)$. But this, we know, is equivalent to $\xi \in M(\mathcal{S},q)$. ■

Complete-markets EPPPE

Proposition 16.9.

a. *Suppose $\mathcal{S}$ and q are viable, and $M(\mathcal{S},q)$ has dimension $N-1$. Choose π from $\Pi(\mathcal{S},q)$. If spot market prices are given by r, then consumer h, facing the prices q and r, can (affordably) attain the consumption bundle $x \in R^{kN}$ (in the dynamic economy) if and only if*

$$\sum_{f_t \in \mathcal{F}} \pi_{f_t} r_{f_t} \cdot (x_{f_t} - e^h_{f_t}) \le 0.$$

b. *Suppose $(r,q,\mathbf{x},\mathbf{y})$ is an EPPPE for a dynamic economy with (financial) securities $\mathcal{S}$. If $M(\mathcal{S},q)$ has dimension $N-1$, then $\mathbf{x}$ is the equilibrium allocation of a Walrasian equilibrium for the all-markets-at-once economy, where the Walrasian-equilibrium prices p are given by $p_{if_t} = \pi_{f_t} r_{if_t}$, for π chosen from $\Pi(\mathcal{S},q)$.*

Note that since $\Pi(\mathcal{S},q)$ is one-dimensional, the choice of π from $\Pi(\mathcal{S},q)$ amounts to nothing more than a strictly positive scaling of the prices in the Walrasian equilibrium. In view of part b, we say that an EPPPE $(r,q,\mathbf{x},\mathbf{y})$ where $M(\mathcal{S},q)$ has dimension $N-1$ is an EPPPE *with complete markets.*

Proof. (a) The constraint

$$\sum_{f_t \in \mathcal{F}} \pi_{f_t} r_{f_t} \cdot (x_{f_t} - e^h_{f_t}) \le 0$$

doesn't depend on how π is scaled, so it is without loss of generality to assume that π is the (unique) choice such that $\pi_{f_0} = 1$. Assume this is so.

Suppose x is a consumption bundle that satisfies the constraint. Let $\xi(f_t) = r_{f_t} \cdot (x_{f_t} - e^h_{f_t})$ for all f_t other than f_0, while for f_0, let $\xi(f_0) = \sum_{f_t \ne f_0} \pi_{f_t} r_{f_t} \cdot (e^h_{f_t} - x_{f_t})$. Since π_{f_0} is normalized to be 1, we have

$$\pi \cdot \xi = \sum_{f_t \ne f_0} \pi_{f_t} r_{f_t} \cdot (e^h_{f_t} - x_{f_t}) + \sum_{f_t \ne f_0} \pi_{f_t} r_{f_t} \cdot (x_{f_t} - e^h_{f_t}) = 0.$$

By the last part of Proposition 16.8c, we know that there is a trading plan that gives the wealth transfer vector ξ. And this plan immediately allows h to consume x and satisfy all her budget constraints: For $f_t \neq f_0$, $\xi(f_t)$ supplies exactly the financial resources she needs; for f_0, her net expenditure is

$$r_{f_0} \cdot (x_{f_0} - e^h_{f_0}) + \xi(f_0) = \sum_{f_t \in \mathcal{F}} \pi_{f_t} r_{f_t} \cdot (x_{f_t} - e^h_{f_t}) \leq 0.$$

Conversely, suppose she can afford x, which means that for some legitimate trading plan y,

$$r_{f_t} \cdot x_{f_t} \sum_{s \in \mathcal{S}} q_{sf_t} \left[y(f_t, s) - y(\hat{f}_t, s) \right] \leq r_{f_t} \cdot e^h_{f_t} + \sum_{s \in \mathcal{S}} y(\hat{f}_t, s) d_s(f_t), \text{ for each } f_t.$$

Multiply this inequality for f_t by π_{f_t}, and then rearrange terms and add the inequalities, to get

$$\sum_{f_t \in \mathcal{F}} \pi_{f_t} r_{f_t} \cdot (x_{f_t} - e^h_{f_t}) \leq \sum_{f_t \in \mathcal{F}} \pi_{f_t} \left[\sum_{s \in \mathcal{S}} q_{sf_t} \left[y(\hat{f}_t, s) - y(f_t, s) \right] + y(\hat{f}_t, s) d_s(f_t) \right].$$

But on the right-hand side we have $\pi \cdot \xi$ for the wealth-transfer vector created by the trading plan y, and so the right-hand side is 0.

(b) Market clearing in the Walrasian equilibrium (by $\boldsymbol{x}$) is immediately implied by market clearing in the EPPPE by $(\boldsymbol{x}, \boldsymbol{y})$; nothing more needs to be said about this. We must show that, for each h, $\boldsymbol{x}^h$ is affordable at the prices p in the all-markets-at-once economy and that it maximizes h's utility among those consumption bundles that are affordable.

We know that $\boldsymbol{x}^h$ is attainable by h in the dynamic economy in conjunction with trading plan $\boldsymbol{y}^h$. Of course, since $(r, q, \boldsymbol{x}, \boldsymbol{y})$ is an EPPPE, $\mathcal{S}$ and q are viable and so, by part a, $\boldsymbol{x}^h$ satisfies

$$\sum_{f_t} \pi_{f_t} r_{f_t} \cdot (\boldsymbol{x}^h_{f_t} - e^h_{f_t}) \leq 0.$$

But with prices p defined as in the statement of part b, this is nothing more than $p \cdot (\boldsymbol{x}^h - e^h) \leq 0$, the budget constraint in the all-markets-at-once economy. And if x is affordable by h in the all-markets-at-once economy, or $p \cdot (x - e^h) \leq 0$, then replacing each p_{if_t} with $\pi_{f_t} r_{if_t}$ and breaking the sum in the dot product into terms for each f_t, we see that x satisfies the inequality in part a and hence is affordably attainable by h in the dynamic economy at the prices r and q. But since $\boldsymbol{x}^h$ is optimal for h in the dynamic economy, this means that $u^h(\boldsymbol{x}^h) \geq u^h(x)$; this shows that $u^h(\boldsymbol{x}^h) \geq u^h(x)$ for all x that h can afford in the all-markets-at-once economy when prices are p, and $(p, \boldsymbol{x})$ is a Walrasian equilibrium for that economy.[4] ∎

[4] I reiterate an earlier admonition: If this seems like magic to you, think harder about it. It isn't magic. It's very simple bookkeeping.

What, in economic terms, does it mean that $M(\mathcal{S}, q)$ has dimension $N-1$? Why did we say (just after the statement of the proposition, before its proof) that this meant the equilibrium had *complete markets*? And what is the economic meaning of π?

The answers to these questions are (at least) implicit in the proof of Proposition 16.9a. But to be explicit: Consumers in dynamic economies with securities have two tasks when it comes to maximizing their utility, given prices. They must make trade-offs in each contingency concerning their spot-consumption of the k commodities. When we assume that a full array of k spot markets operates in each contingency, we are assuming they have all the market tools needed to accomplish this first task.

But, in addition, they would like to trade consumption in one contingency for consumption in others. They would like to move wealth from contingencies in which their endowments make them relatively rich, to contingencies in which they have low-market-value endowments. Securities are the means for effecting these trade-offs. And given a set of securities $\mathcal{S}$ and prices q, $M(\mathcal{S}, q)$ is the space of contingency-to-contingency wealth trade-offs they can make. The dimension of $M(\mathcal{S}, q)$ can't be N, because (for instance) the transfer that gives \$100 more wealth in every contingency—that is, $\xi = (100, 100, \ldots, 100)$, which is what we've called an arbitrage opportunity—is incompatible with equilibrium. But if the dimension of $M(\mathcal{S}, q)$ is $N-1$, and if $\mathcal{S}$ and q are viable, then the consumer has available a full set of possible trade-offs; if she is willing to give up enough wealth in one particular contingency, she can obtain any vector of transfers of wealth into all the others.[5] The vector π, the normal to $M(\mathcal{S}, q)$, is just the price vector for these trade-offs. And her budget constraint for transfers among contingencies is: She can achieve any $\xi \in R^N$, as long as $\pi \cdot \xi = 0$. If S and q are viable and $M(\mathcal{S}, q)$ has dimension $N-1$, then we know that she can move numeraire around from contingency to contingency as long as she meets that constraint; everything she can accomplish with a legitimate trading plan must satisfy that constraint (that is, if ξ is generated by a legitimate trading plan, then $\pi \cdot \xi = 0$), and everything that meets this budget constraint can be accomplished by a legitimate trading plan (that is, $\pi \cdot \xi = 0$ implies that ξ can be gotten by some trading plan). And, to gild this lily, if we know π, which gives contingency-versus-contingency trade-offs as measured in the numeraire, and we know the various spot-market prices r, we know the (implicit) trade-offs of one contingency-stamped commodity against another, given by the price vector $p = \pi r$ (or, more precisely, $p_{if_t} = \pi_{f_t} r_{if_t}$).

This implies, among other things, that if we find an EPPPE in which $M(\mathcal{S}, q)$ has dimension $N-1$, then the equilibrium consumption allocation is Pareto efficient. We therefore wish to know what it takes for $M(\mathcal{S}, q)$ to have dimension $N-1$. When is this guaranteed? When is it impossible? From the last section, we know one case where it is guaranteed: If we have a full set of financial contingent claims, it is certain (for any price vector q that, with these securities, is

[5] We need both parts of the premise; $M(\mathcal{S}, q)$ must have dimension $N-1$ *and* $\mathcal{S}$ and q must be viable. It is possible the $M(\mathcal{S}, q)$ has dimension $N-1$ *and* arbitrage opportunities exist. Can you see how?

viable) that $M(\mathcal{S},q)$ has dimension $N-1$. Moreover, we know that, in this case, *the set of consumption allocations in EPPPE for the dynamic economy is identical to the set of Walrasian-equilibrium consumption allocations for the all-markets-at-once economy.* This allows us, among other things, to extend our existence results for Walrasian equilibria to EPPPE, at least for a dynamic economy with this set of securities. Does this generalize?

To answer these questions, a couple of lemmas are needed, the first a tool for verifying that a set of securities $\mathcal{S}$ with prices q gives complete markets; the second a more general pair of results about viable prices for arbitrary sets of securities.

Lemma 16.10. *Suppose $\mathcal{S}$ and q are viable. For $M(\mathcal{S},q)$ to have dimension $N-1$, it is necessary and sufficient that a plan can be found that produces, for each f_t^0 other than f_0, the wealth transfer ξ given by*

$$\xi(f_t)=\begin{cases}\textit{some strictly negative amount}, & \textit{for } f_t=f_0,\\ 1, & \textit{for } f_t=f_t^0, \textit{ and}\\ 0, & \textit{for all } f_t \textit{ other than } f_0 \textit{ and } f_t^0.\end{cases}$$

Of course, the strictly negative amount is $-\pi_{f_t^0}/\pi_{f_0}$, for the π that is orthogonal to $M(\mathcal{S},q)$.

Proof. Suppose that $M(\mathcal{S},q)$ is viable and has dimension $N-1$. Choose π from Π. If "some strictly negative amount" in the display just above is $-\pi_{f_t^0}/\pi_{f_0}$, then it is immediate that $\pi\cdot\xi=0$, and the last part of Proposition 16.8 ensures that $\xi\in M(\mathcal{S},q)$. That is necessity.

For sufficiency, note that the set of ξ of the form shown, one for each f_t^0 such that $t>0$, is $N-1$ linearly independent vectors. Hence if each of these is in $M(\mathcal{S},q)$, $M(\mathcal{S},q)$ has dimension at least $N-1$. The proposition presumes that $\mathcal{S}$ and q are viable; hence $N-1$ is an upper bound on the dimension of $M(\mathcal{S},q)$, and so that is the dimension, and markets are complete. ∎

Recall that $\mathbf{S}(f_t)$ is the set of all successors of f_t, for $t<T$.

Lemma 16.11.

a. *If $\mathcal{S}$ and q are viable, then for any $s\in\mathcal{S}$ and any contingency f_τ^0 at which s trades, $q_{sf_\tau^0}>0$ if and only if there is at least one contingency $f_t\in\mathbf{S}(f_\tau^0)$ in which s pays a strictly positive dividend.*

   Indeed, if $\mathcal{S}$ and q are viable, then for all s and for all $f_\tau^0\in\mathcal{F}(s)$,

$$q_{sf_\tau^0}=\frac{1}{\pi_{f_\tau^0}}\sum_{f_t\in\mathbf{S}(f_\tau^0)}\pi_{f_t}d_s(f_t), \tag{16.4}$$

   for all $\pi\in\Pi(\mathcal{S},q)$.

b. *Fix a t/u/i structure, a set of securities $\mathcal{S}$, and $\pi \in R^N_{++}$. If, for each $s \in \mathcal{S}$ and $f^0_\tau \in \mathcal{F}(s)$, we* ***define*** *$q_{sf^0_\tau}$ by the formula (16.4), then $\mathcal{S}$ and q are viable and, moreover, $\pi \in \Pi(\mathcal{S}, q)$.*

I leave the proof of this lemma to you as Problem 16.5, with solution provided in the *Student's Guide.* Please see the directions provided in the problem statement.

Lemma 16.11 has an important paraphrase: *The equilibrium price of any security in any contingency is the "properly discounted" present value of the dividends it will pay in the future.* The proper discount is given by pricing vector π; part a then says that this statement is true in any viable price system and, moreover, for every $\pi \in \Pi(\mathcal{S}, q)$; part b says that if we use this formula for any strictly positive pricing vector π, the price process generated will, with $\mathcal{S}$, be a viable model of the securities market, with $\pi \in \Pi(\mathcal{S}, q)$ for the resulting q.

Now to generalize the results of the last section, concerning the full set of financial contingent claims. Recall how that went: We had one security s^{f_t} for each $f_t \in \mathcal{F}$, $t > 0$. The security s^{f_t} traded only in contingency f_0 (at time 0), and paid a dividend of 1 in contingency f_t (only). Label this set of securities $\mathcal{S}^{\text{FFCC}}$, where the superscripted FFCC is shorthand for *full (set of) financial contingent claims.* Immediately following the statement of Assumption 16.1′ (page 399), we asserted that the set of EPPPE consumption allocations for the dynamic economy with $\mathcal{S}^{\text{FFCC}}$ coincides with the set of Walrasian-equilbrium allocations for the all-markets-at-once economy. The formal statement of this specific result and its proof are provided in the *Student's Guide.* Alternatively, we can derive this as a corollary to the following more general proposition.

Proposition 16.12. *Suppose that, for a given t/u/i structure and set of (financial) securities $\mathcal{S}$, if $\mathcal{S}$ and q are viable, then $M(\mathcal{S}, q)$ has dimension $N-1$. Then the set of EPPPE consumption allocations for a dynamic economy with this set of securities coincides with the set of Walrasian-equilibrium allocations for the all-markets-at-once economy.*

Or, to paraphrase, if a set of securities is guaranteed (in any EPPPE) to give complete markets, then its equilibrium consumption allocations are precisely the Walrasian-equilibirum allocations.

Proof. Half of this is an immediate corollary to Proposition 16.9. Suppose that $(r, q, \boldsymbol{x}, \boldsymbol{y})$ is an EPPPE for this set of securities. Then S and q are, by definition, viable. Hence $M(\mathcal{S}, q)$ has dimension $N-1$. And, therefore, Proposition 16.9 tells us that $\boldsymbol{x}$ is a Walrasian-equilibrium allocation, for the prices $p = \pi r$.

Conversely, suppose $(p, \boldsymbol{x})$ is a Walrasian equilibrium for the all-markets-at-once economy. Let $\pi \in R^N$ be the vector $(1, 1, 1, \ldots, 1)$, and use equation (16.4) and this π to define securities prices q. Let $r_{if_t} = p_{if_t}$. I assert that, with an appropriate choice of $\boldsymbol{y}$ (to be given momentarily), $(r, q, \boldsymbol{x}, \boldsymbol{y})$ is an EPPPE for the dynamic economy. Note first that by Lemma 16.11, we know that $\mathcal{S}$ and q (defined in this fashion) are viable. By the premise of this proposition, this implies that $M(\mathcal{S}, q)$ has dimension $N-1$. By Proposition 16.9a, x is an affordably attainable consumption bundle for h in the dynamic economy if and only if $\sum_{f_t} \pi_{f_t} r_{f_t} \cdot (x_{f_t} - e^h_{f_t}) \leq 0$, but with π and r as defined, this is precisely the budget constraint $p \cdot (x - e^h) \leq 0$, the budget constraint in the all-markets-at-once economy with prices p. We know, therefore, that $\boldsymbol{x}^h$ is affordable and attainable by h in the dynamic economy, and it is as good (in terms of u^h) as any other affordable and attainable consumption bundle.

Market clearing in the real-commodities markets follows immediately from market-clearing in the Walrasian equilibrium. So all that needs to be done, to finish the proof, is to produce trading plans $\boldsymbol{y}^h$ for the consumers that (1) give each consumer her desired consumption bundle and (2) lead to market clearing in the securities markets.

For each consumer h, let $\xi^h(f_t) = r_{f_t} \cdot (\boldsymbol{x}^h_{f_t} - e^h_{f_t})$. That is, for each h, ξ^h is the wealth-transfer vector that h requires to consume $\boldsymbol{x}^h$. Because each consumer h is locally insatiable, we know that Walras' Law holds, or $p \cdot (\boldsymbol{x}^h - e^h) = 0$. But since $\pi = (1, 1, \ldots, 1)$ and $r_{f_t} = p_{f_t}$, we can rewrite Walras' Law for h as $0 = \sum_{f_t} r_{f_t} \cdot (\boldsymbol{x}^h_{f_t} - e^h_{f_t}) = \sum_{f_t} \xi^h(f_t) = \pi \cdot \xi^h$.

Choose a consumer h^0. For every other consumer $h \neq h^0$, since $\pi \cdot \xi^h = 0$, we know (Proposition 16.8c) a trading strategy $\boldsymbol{y}^h$ can be constructed that realizes ξ^h. Fix such a $\boldsymbol{y}^h$ for all $h \neq h^0$, and define $\boldsymbol{y}^{h^0} = -\sum_{h \neq h^0} \boldsymbol{y}^h$. Note that, with this definition, $\sum_h \boldsymbol{y}^h = 0$ by construction; we have market clearing in the asset markets. But does $\boldsymbol{y}^{h^0}$ provide h^0 with the ability to consume $\boldsymbol{x}^{h^0}$?

It does. Since h^0 is on the opposite side of the security-market trades of all other consumers, $\boldsymbol{y}^{h^0}$ generates the wealth-transfer vector $-\sum_{h \neq h^0} \xi^h$. So we must show that $\xi^{h^0} = -\sum_{h \neq h^0} \xi^h$, or $\sum_h \xi^h = 0$. This is $\sum_h r_{f_t} \cdot (\boldsymbol{x}^h_{f_t} - e^h_{f_t}) = 0$ for each f_t. Since Walrasian-equilibrium prices are nonnegative and all consumers are locally insatiable, we know (Proposition 14.4e) even more than this: For each i and f_t, $\sum_h r_{if_t} (\boldsymbol{x}^h_{if_t} - e^h_{if_t}) = \sum_h p_{if_t} (\boldsymbol{x}^h_{if_t} - e^h_{if_t}) = 0$. Summing over i for each f_t finishes the proof. ∎

As a corollary to this result, consider the set of securities $\mathcal{S}^{\text{FFCC}}$. Lemma 16.10 tells us almost instantly that, if q is any viable price system for $\mathcal{S}^{\text{FFCC}}$, then $M(\mathcal{S}^{\text{FFCC}}, q)$ has dimension $N - 1$. Proposition 16.12 then applies; the set of EPPPE consumption allocations for $\mathcal{S}^{\text{FFCC}}$ coincides with the set of Walrasian-equilibirum allocations for the corresponding all-markets-at-once economy. And there are other sets of securities, besides the set $\mathcal{S}^{\text{FFCC}}$ from last section, for which the space $M(\mathcal{S}, q)$ has dimension $N-1$ for any viable q and, hence, to which Proposition 16.12 applies. Here are two sets that work:

- Suppose $\mathcal{S}$ consists of as many securities as there are states of nature. The security corresponding to the state ω trades at every contingency f_t that contains ω except the time-T contingency $\{\omega\}$. The security corresponding to ω pays a dividend of 1 at time T, if ω is the state (that is, in the time-T contingency $\{\omega\}$), and nothing in all other contingencies. Call this set of securities $\mathcal{S}^{\text{SFCC}}$, where SFCC stands for *state-based financial contingent claims.*
- As in $\mathcal{S}^{\text{FFCC}}$, we suppose $\mathcal{S}$ consists of $N - 1$ securities, one for each f_t other

than f_0. And the security corresponding to f_t pays 1 in this contingency and 0 in all other contingencies. But, in this case, suppose that the security corresponding to f_t trades only in the contingency $\hat{f}_t$; that is, it trades only in the unique contingency that immediately precedes f_t. Call this set of securities $\mathcal{S}^{\text{RFCC}}$, where RFCC stand for *rolling financial contingent claims.*

I assert (and leave it to you to prove, in Problem 16.6), that for both these sets of securities, the special property required to apply Proposition 16.12 holds: For any viable prices q, they always give complete markets. And these are not the only possibilities: Problems 16.7, 16.8, and 16.10 are connected to this general idea.

Recall the discussion last section about how the creation of a full set of contingent claims reduced the number of markets required to achieve complete-markets equilibria, relative to the all-at-once market structure. It may be interesting to know how $\mathcal{S}^{\text{SFCC}}$ and $\mathcal{S}^{\text{RFCC}}$ do in this regard. Recall that we had two ways of measuring things: (1) How many markets must be opened at some time or other? (2) What is the maximum number of markets that must be open in any single contingency? And to these I add a third: (3) How many different securities are necessary? Table 16.1 answers these questions for the t/u/i structure of Figure 16.1, assuming $k = 10$. (Rules for how I computed these numbers are given in the legend of the table.) I hasten to reiterate: The dynamic market structures may economize on the number of markets needed and, especially, on the number of markets needed in any single contingency. But they impose severe demands on the ability of consumers to foresee the future.

As a bit of a converse to Proposition 16.12 and the three sets of securities $\mathcal{S}^{\text{FFCC}}$, $\mathcal{S}^{\text{SFCC}}$, and $\mathcal{S}^{\text{RFCC}}$, we can ask: Under what circumstances is it impossible for there to be complete markets? An answer to this question is given in contrapositive form.

Proposition 16.13. *For each f_t for $t < T$, let $\ell(f_t)$ be the number of f_t's immediate successors. That is, $\ell(f_t)$ is the number of f_{t+1} that have f_t as their immediate predecessor. Fix a set of securities $\mathcal{S}$ and their prices q, such that $\mathcal{S}$ and q are viable. Then a necessary condition for $M(\mathcal{S}, q)$ to have dimension $N - 1$ (and, therefore, for an economy with $\mathcal{S}$ to have a complete-market EPPPE) is that, for each f_t $(t < T)$, there are at least $\ell(f_t)$ securities that pay at least one strictly positive dividend in some contingency that follows f_t.*

Proof. Fix viable $\mathcal{S}$ and q. For any contingency f_t, call security s *defunct at* f_t if, in all contingencies that are successors of f_t, the security pays zero dividend. Note, this does not preclude s having just paid a strictly positive dividend in contingency f_t. Note also that once a security is defunct, is remains so. Using this terminology, we can paraphrase Lemma 16.11a as $q_{sf_t} > 0$ *if and only if s is not defunct in contingency f_t*. And this proposition can be paraphrased as, *For there to be the chance of complete markets in an EPPPE, for each f_t, there must be at least $\ell(f_t)$ non-defunct securities.*

Fix $\mathcal{S}$ and q where $M(\mathcal{S}, q)$ has dimension $N-1$. Let π denote the (essentially unique) element of $\Pi(\mathcal{S}, q)$.

	All-at-once market structure	Full financial contingent claims	State-based contingent claims	Rolling contingent claims
Number of spot markets	10	50	50	50
Maximum number of securities needed	320	32	16	10
Maximum number of financial markets needed	320	32	29	10
Maximum number of financial markets needed at any one time	320	32	16	3
Maximum number of markets open at any one time	330	42	26	13

Table 16.1. Comparisons of four ways to achieve complete markets. For the t/u/i structure of Figure 16.1 and assuming there are 10 basic commodities, this table gives some statistics on how many markets and securities are needed for each of four ways to get complete markets: all-markets-at-once, a full set of (financial) contingent claims at the outset, state-based contingent claims, and rolling contingent claims. In calculating these numbers, I used the following conventions: For the all-markets-at-once structure, the 10 f_0-commodity markets are counted as spot markets; the other 320 f_t-commodity markets are counted as securities markets. Any market in which no trading would take place is not counted as being opened. So, in terms of spot markets in any dynamic market structure, if there are T periods, I count this as $(T+1)k$ opened spot markets, with no more than k needing to be opened at any time. And, in terms of securities markets, I do not open a market in a security in any contingency in which it is known that the price of the security will be zero, because it is known that the security will not pay any further dividends. Nor do I consider a security having been created, if no market in it ever comes into existence. (This has bite, obviously, only for rolling contingent claims.) Note that for the state-contingent claims and rolling-contingent claims markets, some of the numbers are maxima; depending on the state, the number could be less.

The rules for trading the securities in $\mathcal{S}$ may not allow trading in some contingencies, but I assert that this can be relaxed without changing the space of available wealth-transfer vectors: Suppose that we look at $\mathcal{S}'$ and q' where (1) for each $s \in \mathcal{S}$, there is an $s' \in \mathcal{S}'$ with precisely the same dividend structure as has s, but s' trades at every date, and (2) the price $q'_{s'f_t}$ is given by (16.4) for the fixed π, for every contingency f_t, $t < T$. I assert that $q'_{s'f_t} = q_{sf_t}$ for s' and s corresponding securities and for $f_t \in \mathcal{F}(s)$; this is true because the formulas for both terms are given by (16.4). I assert that $M(\mathcal{S}, q) \subseteq M(\mathcal{S}', q')$, since every trading opportunity under $\mathcal{S}$ and q remains. But $\mathcal{S}'$ and q' are viable, by virtue of Lemma 16.11b; hence the dimension of $M(\mathcal{S}', q')$ cannot be larger than $N-1$. And, of course, it cannot be smaller, since $M(\mathcal{S}', q')$ contains $M(\mathcal{S}, q)$. But this implies immediately that $M(\mathcal{S}', q') = M(\mathcal{S}, q)$. (Or, you can reason as follows: By Lemma 16.11(b), we know that $\pi \in \Pi(\mathcal{S}', q')$. We know that $M(\mathcal{S}', q')$ has dimension $N-1$, so $\Pi(\mathcal{S}', q')$ consists (solely) of scale copies of π. Therefore, $\xi \in M(\mathcal{S}', q')$ if and only if $\pi \cdot \xi = 0$, which is precisely the criterion for $\xi \in M(\mathcal{S}, q)$.)

Finally, $s' \in \mathcal{S}'$ is defunct at f_t if and only if the corresponding $s \in \mathcal{S}$ is defunct at f_t. So we only need to show that, in $\mathcal{S}'$, for each f_t, there are at least $\ell(f_t)$ nondefunct securities.

Pick some f_t^0 for $t < T$. Let the $\ell(f_t^0)$ immediate successors of f_t^0 be denoted by f_{t+1}^j for $j = 1, \ldots, \ell(f_t)$. By Lemma 16.10, for markets to be complete, it must be possible to find $\ell(f_t)$ different trading strategies y^j for $j = 1, \ldots, \ell(f_t)$ that cost a positive amount of money in contingency f_0, generate 1 unit in contingency f_{t+1}^j, and generate 0 in all other contingencies.

Focus on trading plan y^j and, in particular, what holdings of securities it involves at contingency f_t^0 and then at each of the immediate successor contingencies to f_t^0. At contingency f_t^0, some of the securities may be defunct. Any nonzero amount of defunct-at-f_t securities held at f_t^0 in any of the y^j is irrelevant: These securities will never again pay a dividend and never again have a nonzero price, so they will have no further impact on the financial gains and/or losses from trading plan y^j.

Moreover, I assert that whatever y^j suggests doing at time $t+1$ and beyond, an equivalent outcome is generated if we suppose that y^j calls for complete liquidation of all securities at time $t+1$. (This is why we change from $\mathcal{S}$ and $\mathcal{S}'$; so that we know we can sell the securities in y^j at each immediate successor to f_t^0.) To see this, note that in contingency $f_{t+1}^{j'}$, the portfolio consisting of $y^j(f_{t+1}^{j'}, s')$ units of security s' must have a value at current (contingency-$f_{t+1}^{j'}$) prices of zero: If this portfolio has any other market value, then either buying or selling (depending on whether the value is negative or positive) and then following the prescriptions of y^j generates a positive amount of wealth in contingency $f_{t+1}^{j'}$ and 0 thereafter, which is an arbitrage opportunity. Hence, liquidation doesn't affect time $t+1$ wealth, either.

Hence, it is without loss of generality to assume that y^j calls for complete liquidation at time $t+1$. This means that

$$\sum_{s' \in \mathcal{S}'} y^j(f_t^0, s')\left(q'_{s' f_{t+1}^{j'}} + d_{s'}(f_{t+1}^{j'})\right) \quad = \quad 1 \text{ if } j = j' \text{ and } 0 \text{ otherwise.}$$

Ranging over the ℓ different j, this means that we have ℓ different linear combinations of the vectors $q'_{s' f_{t+1}^{j'}} + d_{s'}(f_{t+1}^{j'})$, giving ℓ linearly independent outcomes. There must, therefore, be at least ℓ of the vectors whose linear combinations are being formed. ∎

This proposition establishes a sense in which, if we want to economize on securities that are actively traded at any one time, we can't do any better than the security set $\mathcal{S}^{\text{RFCC}}$. At each point in time, in each contingency, this has precisely the minimum number of active securities needed to get complete markets, and this set is sure to give complete-markets equilibrium outcomes in the very strong sense of Proposition 16.12.

Where does the theory of complete-market EPPPE go from here? One important direction is to look beyond $\mathcal{S}^{\text{FFCC}}$, $\mathcal{S}^{\text{SFCC}}$, and $\mathcal{S}^{\text{RFCC}}$, for other sets of securities that guarantee complete markets. One version of this concerns derivative securities, or securities whose "dividends" depend on the prices and/or dividends of other securities.

A second direction specializes to the case where (1) securities trade in every contingency and (2) only pay dividends at time T. Prices q are given and the two questions to be answered are: Is the model (that is, the securities and prices for them) viable? Does it give complete markets? Assumptions (1) and (2) allow for fairly simple tests of this proposition.

You get to explore both these directions in the problems.

Security price indeterminacy

The analysis we've done on complete markets with financial securities has at least one unsavory aspect, which should be revealed. The starkest way to put this is the following:

> *Suppose that* $(r, q, \boldsymbol{x}, \boldsymbol{y})$ *is an EPPPE for some dynamic economy, where the set of securities* $\mathcal{S}$ *is* $\mathcal{S}^{\text{FFCC}}$. *Then* ***for any strictly positive*** $\hat{q} \in R^{N-1}$, *there is an EPPPE for this economy where the securities prices are given by* $\hat{q}$ *and the consumption allocation is* $\boldsymbol{x}$. *In other words, in this economy and for this equilibrium outcome, equilibrium security prices are completely indeterminate (except for being strictly positive).*

I'm not going to prove precisely this—you are asked to do it in Problem 16.12—but I will indicate why it is true. Go back for a moment to the proof of Proposition 16.12 and, in particular, the step where I said *Let* $\pi \in R^N$ *be the vector* $(1, 1, 1 \ldots, 1)$, after which this π was used to compute q via (16.4). This choice of π is, in some sense, natural; it says that consumers can transfer numeraire from one contingency to another on a one-to-one basis, which, of course, is automatically true in the all-markets-at-once economy. But this choice of π is both arbitrary and irrelevant to the proof. *The proof would work for any choice of strictly positive* π, as long as you are careful in moving between spot prices r and all-markets-at-once prices p. And the required care is established in part b of Proposition 16.9: $p_{if_t} = \pi_{f_t} r_{if_t}$. Of course, changing π will change the values of $\boldsymbol{y}$. The point is, though, that I could have chosen any π and proceeded along with the proof. And, to a large extent, the choice of π is what determines q. (Now you should have no problem tackling my italicized claim.)

Why does this happen? In all the economics of markets that we've seen in this volume, it is *relative prices* that matter. You can double all the prices, or halve them all, and nothing of economic import changes (as long as consumer wealth is similarly scaled, which it is in a general-equilibrium framework, where wealth comes from endowments). In these dynamic economies, the N spot markets establish relative prices for the k spot commodities in each of N contingencies. But if all that matters are relative prices, then we can double spot prices in one contingency and halve them in another. The securities markets are about moving wealth from one contingency to another, and when securities pay nominal or financial dividends, we gain a lot of degrees of freedom when it comes to equilibrium prices. If you want to pick the π vector first, you can always undo this (as far as the economics of the situation are concerned) by adjusting spot-price levels in the different contingencies.

If one *raison d'être* for economics is to say what determines equilibrium prices, this is not a pleasant place to end our analysis.

16.5. EPPPE: III. Complex Securities with Real Dividends and Complete Markets

One direction in which to go, at this point, is to try to explain connections between fiat money (numeraire) and real commodities. That is, we could launch ourselves into the theory of money. Rather than go in that direction, I want to make the point that the indeterminacy effectively goes away if we go back to where this chapter began, with securities that pay their dividends in real commodities.

In fact, this raises two possibilities. The first is to allow for securities that pay dividends in all manner of real commodities; one security is a wheat futures contract, another pays off in pork bellies, a third might issue a dividend that includes both wheat and iced broilers, and so forth. There is a literature on such things, but it is messy, and this chapter is already lengthy.

So I want to consider an economy in which all dividends are paid in one distinguished commodity. I'll assume this is commodity 1, wheat, and we go back to Assumption 16.1, so that we know that wheat must have a strictly positive price in every contingency. It is still true that $d_s \in R^{\mathcal{F}}$, but this now means that security s pays $d_s(f_t)$ units of wheat as dividend in contingency f_t. In fact, I'll assume that $d_s \in R^{\mathcal{F}}_+$; all wheat-dividends are nonnegative. And the rest of Assumption 16.5 is maintained.

And, I'll make one more ... not assumption, but normalization. *Assume that spot-market prices* r_{f_t} *are normalized so that the spot price of wheat is always 1, or* $r_{1f_t} = 1$, for all f_t. In words, we normalize prices in each contingency so that a unit of wheat becomes the numeraire.[6] This really pins down price levels; the indeterminacy

[6] This story would become almost realistic, at least in terms of economies a few centuries ago, if instead of wheat, commodity 1 was gold, and the units of gold were "gold coins." Then the spot price of, say, an orange in contingency f_t would be so many gold coins. We might even give gold coins a name, such as "doubloons." But this doesn't quite work in the framework of this chapter, because one doesn't consume gold; one might get utility from its use (as jewelry or in dental applications), but it isn't destroyed by the consumption of its services. This, of course, is one reason why gold became a medium of exchange. This takes us to the theory of money, which I want to avoid, so I'll stick with wheat.

that concerned us at the end of last section is completely gone. And, to nail things down (a nail being more than a pin), when we look at prices in all-markets-at-once economies, we'll assume that prices are normalized so that the price of wheat in contingency f_0 is 1.

This normalization has the wonderful effect, moreover, of making most of what happened last section continue to be true. The key is that the budget constraints in an EPPPE, which in the last section was (16.3), doesn't change in the least. We can still talk about $M(\mathcal{S}, q)$ and arbitrage and viability and $\Pi(\mathcal{S}, q)$; the propositions and lemmas survive virtually unchanged. What does change? Here's the very short list:

1. In the definition of an EPPPE, Definition 16.6, part a of the definition must specify that spot-market prices r_{f_t} should always be normalized so that $r_{1f_t} = 1$. (Without this, the budget constraints (16.3) are wrong.)

2. While for most uses, it doesn't really matter which $\pi \in \Pi(\mathcal{S}, q)$ is chosen (for instance, in Proposition 16.9a), the specific choice of π in which $\pi_{f_0} = 1$ has a lot of appeal. Then, at least when $M(\mathcal{S}, q)$ has dimension $N - 1$ (and $\mathcal{S}$ and q are viable), the interpretation of π_{f_t} is: This is how many units of wheat must be given up in contingency f_0 to get one unit of wheat in f_t. Relative to the all-markets-at-once equilibrium price vector $p \in R_+^{kN}$, normalized so that $p_{1f_0} = 1$, π_{f_t} is p_{1f_t}.

3. This particular normalization and choice of π becomes more transparent if you look at part b of Proposition 16.9 and the assertion that, if (r, q, x, y) is a complete-market EPPPE, (p, x) is an all-markets-at-once Walrasian equilibrium for p given by $p_{f_t} = \pi_{f_t} r_{f_t}$. If you don't normalize π so that $\pi_{f_0} = 1$, the statement is still true; Walrasian-equilibrium prices are not subject to any arbitrary normalization. But choosing $\pi_{f_0} = 1$ gives a corresponding p for which $p_{1f_0} = 1$.

4. While Proposition 16.12 remains true as stated, the proof needs some repair. This is where the arbitrary choice of $\pi = (1, 1, \ldots, 1)$ took place, but that choice is tied to the next line in the proof, *Let* $r_{if_t} = p_{if_t}$. We can't allow $r_{if_t} = p_{if_t}$, unless we give up on our fixed normalization of spot-market prices, which means changing the budget constraints (16.3). Instead, given a Walrasian equilibrium (p, x), we need to define π by $\pi_{f_t} = p_{1f_t}$, r by $r_{if_t} = p_{if_t}/p_{1f_t}$, and q by (16.4) applied to this specific choice of π. To be very pedantic about why these choices are necessary: Proposition 16.9a says that as long as a $\mathcal{S}$ and q are viable and $M(\mathcal{S}, q)$ has dimension $N - 1$, the consumer's choices are as if she faced a single budget constraint, where the "price" of commodity if_t is $\pi_{f_t} r_{if_t}$. We want this to be p_{if_t}, and so we require $p_{if_t} = \pi_{f_t} r_{if_t}$. We're okay with making p_{f_t} proportional to r_{f_t}, except for the forced normalization $r_{1f_t} = 1$, so we can take $r_{f_t} = p_{f_t}/p_{1f_t}$, which is $p_{1f_t} r_{f_t} = p_{f_t}$. That is, π_{f_t} must be p_{1f_t}. But if we use this choice of π and (16.4) to define q, Lemma 16.11b tells us that $\pi \in \Pi(\mathcal{S}, q)$, and everything fits together very nicely.

And, with this done, security prices have meaning. They are, of course, the *current value of future dividends*—that's what Lemma 16.11 tells us—but now the contingent discount factors for bringing a contingency-f_t dividend "back" to an earlier contingency $f'_{t'}$, which is always $\pi_{f_t}/\pi_{f'_{t'}}$, is the quite specific $p_{1f_t}/p_{1f'_{t'}}$, the relative value of f_t-labeled wheat to $f'_{t'}$-labeled wheat. Whatever determines those relative values in equilibrium is what drives (with complete markets) security prices.

16.6. Incomplete Markets

The story for complete markets is very nice. But if markets are incomplete, the possibilities are—well, *interesting* is a good and neutral adjective.

The literature on EPPPE with incomplete markets (and still without firms) is sizable, and I will not try to give anything like an organized tour. But to whet your appetite, I'll develop a simple example from a seminal paper on the topic, Hart (1975).

The dynamic economy in question has two consumers (Alice and Bob), two basic commodities ($i = 1, 2$), two dates ($t = 0, 1$), and two states of nature ($\Omega = \{\omega_1, \omega_2\}$). Therefore, there are three contingencies: f_0, the sole time-0 contingency; and two time-1 contingencies, $f_1^1 = \{\omega_1\}$ and $f_1^2 = \{\omega_2\}$. Both Bob and Alice have preferences that are additively separable across contingencies, both taking the form

$$u_0(x_{1f_0}, x_{2f_0}) + \gamma^h u^h(x_{1f_1^1}, x_{2f_1^1}) + (1 - \gamma^h) u^h(x_{1f_1^2}, x_{2f_1^2}),$$

for h = Alice or Bob, where $\gamma^{\text{Alice}} = 0.9$ and $\gamma^{\text{Bob}} = 0.1$. To explicate: Both Alice and Bob have the same preferences over consumption bundles in contingency f_0. Moreover, their endowments in this contingency are identical, say $e^h_{f_0} = (1, 1)$ for h = both Alice and Bob. In the two time-1 contingencies, each has the same preference as in the other contingency, although Alice's preferences and Bob's may differ. But Alice thinks that state ω_1 is very likely to happen, while Bob thinks ω_2 is very likely; they are both expected utility maximizers, where Alice assesses probability 0.9 for ω_1, while Bob assesses probability 0.1.

Their endowments in the two time-1 states are also identical across the states: Alice has the endowment (2,0) while Bob has (0,2). As for their preferences, I'll use an Edgeworth Box to depict those; if we look only at contingency f_1^1 (or, identically, at f_1^2), and *we do not allow any transfers of wealth between the different contingencies*, the situation is as depicted in Figure 16.2. There are two (and only two) Walrasian equilibia in the contingent spot market, the first where the relative prices are (1,2) and the second where they are (2,1). Note that Alice strictly prefers the second of these (because the higher-priced good is the one that she is endowed with), while Bob strictly prefers the first. Suppose in particular that

$$u^{\text{Alice}}(4/3, 4/3) = u^{\text{Bob}}(4/3, 4/3) = 2 \quad \text{and} \quad u^{\text{Alice}}(2/3, 2/3) = u^{\text{Bob}}(2/3, 2/3) = 1.$$

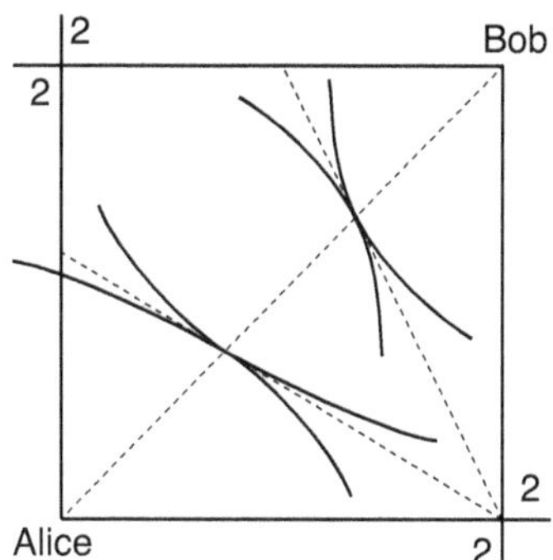

Figure 16.2. Alice and Bob in either time-1 contingency. If Alice and Bob cannot transfer wealth between contingencies, then in each time-1 contingency, they trade in their endowments in the spot markets. We depict the possibilities, including the two possible spot-market equilibria, with an Edgeworth Box.

And, now for the key to this example: Markets are supposed to be incomplete, meaning there are some transfers of wealth between contingencies that are not available to Alice and Bob. We will look at the extreme case where *there are no securities, so Alice and Bob can't make **any** transfers of wealth.*

This means that the possible EPPPE are arrays of spot-market equilibria; one for each contingency, based on the endowments in each contingency. The assumptions that Alice and Bob have the same f_0 endowment and the same preferences means (assuming convexity, which I do) that there is no trade in that contingency—they stick with their endowments (and prices are set to support that choice). Suppose that this gives each of them utility-in-the-contingency of 1.5 apiece. And in the two time-1 contingencies, we have a choice of two possible spot-market equilibria. So, althogether, this economy has four EPPPE.

Of course, Alice likes best of all the EPPPE in which the prices in the two time-1 spot markets are both (2,1), while Bob likes this least. Bob likes best of all the EPPPE in which the prices in the two time-1 spot markets are both (1,2), which is worst for Alice. But now compare their utilities in the two EPPPE that have different prices in the time-1 spot markets:

- In the EPPPE in which prices are (2,1) in contingency f_1^1 and (1,2) in f_1^2, Alice's overall utility is $1.5 + (0.9)(2) + (0.1)(1) = 3.4$, while Bob's is $1.5 + (0.1)(1) + (0.9)(2) = 3.4$.
- In the EPPPE in which prices are (1,2) in contingency f_1^1 and (2,1) in f_1^2, Alice's overall utility is $1.5 + (0.9)(1) + (0.1)(2) = 2.6$, while Bob's is $1.5 + (0.1)(2) + (0.9)(1) = 2.6$.

That is, this economy has four EPPPE, one of which is Pareto superior to a second!

You might think that this depends on the assumption that no trade is possible among contingencies. Or perhaps this is a knife-edge example, one that would disappear if we perturb the model slightly. But neither of these is true. At the cost of complicating the story, we can get the same phenomenon if we assume (1) that there is a single security, which allows wealth to be transfered between dates 0 and 1, but does not permit the transfer to distinguish between states (or that allows for transfer from 0 to 1 but only in a set proportion), (2) Alice and Bob have time-0 preferences where the marginal utilities of the goods near their endowments change very rapidly, so they will only want to shift a small amount of wealth, and (3) the Walrasian-equilibrium correspondence for each time-1 spot market is locally continuous in their endowments. And we'll get this phenomenon for all local perturbations of things like the consumers' endowments.

Incomplete markets, but all at once

Moreover, the phenomenon we're seeing here is very different from what we'd see in an incomplete-but-all-markets-at-once economy. To explain this cryptic remark:

Suppose we have k basic commodities and a t/u/i structure with N contingencies, so there are kN commodities. And we have H consumers, each with a utility function $u^h : R_+^{kN} \to R$ and an endowment $e^h \in R_+^{kN}$. It will be convenient in this discussion to shift attention from the final consumption bundles allocated to consumers to their net trades. So, for each h, let $\mathcal{X}^h := \{\zeta \in R^{kN} : e^h + \zeta \geq 0\}$, the set of feasible net trades for h, and define $v^h : \mathcal{X}^h \to R$ by $v^h(\zeta) := u^h(\zeta + e^h)$.

Imagine that markets are established for a nontrivial subspace of the goods. Let $\mathcal{M}$ be a subspace of R^{kN}; we imagine that consumers can buy and sell bundles from $\mathcal{M}$ and no others. You can think of some commodities not trading at all—if $m \in \mathcal{M}$, then $m_{if_t} = 0$ for some i and f_t—or that certain commodities only trade in preassigned bundles; for instance, if $m \in \mathcal{M}$, then $m_{if_t} = m_{if'_t}$ for all $f_t, f'_t \in \mathcal{F}_t$. The first case represents a situation in which there is no market in f_t-labeled commodity i; the second, a case in which the only market for commodity i to be consumed at date t involves the same amount of i in all time-t contingencies. Please note: in this second case, h may *consume* different amounts i in different time-t contingencies. But her *net trades* cannot vary; any differences across time-t contingencies result from differences in her initial endowment e^h.

The fact that $\mathcal{M}$ is a subspace is the start of a "competitive markets" story: If the consumer can buy m, she can sell m (assuming she has the resources in her endowment to do so and can afford these transactions; see below). If she can buy m, she can buy λm for any $\lambda > 0$, and if she can buy m and m', then she can buy $m + m'$ (both subject to budget constraints). Be careful about the word "buy" here, as m could mix some positive and some negative components.

The only restriction put on $\mathcal{M}$ (besides that it is a subspace) is that there is some $m \geq 0$, $m \neq 0$, such that $m \in \mathcal{M}$. That is, the opportunity to buy (really buy) some goods without having to sell others exists.

Definition 16.14.

a. *An* $\mathcal{M}$***-constrained Walrasian equilibrium*** *consists of a linear function* $\mathbf{p} : \mathcal{M} \to R$ *and, for each consumer* h*, a net trade* $\zeta^h \in \mathcal{M} \cap \mathcal{X}^h$*, such that:* $\mathbf{p}(\zeta^h) \leq 0$ *for* *each* h*; for each* h*, if* $\hat{\zeta}^h \in \mathcal{M} \cap \mathcal{X}^h$ *and* $p(\hat{\zeta}^h) \leq 0$*, then* $v^h(\zeta^h) \geq v^h(\hat{\zeta}^h)$*; and* $\sum_h \zeta^h \leq 0$.

b. *A linear functional* $p : \mathcal{M} \to R$ *is* ***nonnegative*** *if* $p(m) \geq 0$ *for all* $m \geq 0$.

c. *Consumer* h *is* ***locally insatiable constrained to*** $\mathcal{M}$ *if, for every* $\zeta \in \mathcal{M} \cap \mathcal{X}^h$ *and for every* $\epsilon > 0$*, there exists some* $\zeta' \in \mathcal{M} \cap \mathcal{X}^h$ *such that* $\|\zeta - \zeta'\| \leq \epsilon$ *and* $v^h(\zeta') > v^h(\zeta)$*. (Given our assumption that* $\mathcal{M}$ *contains some* $m \geq 0$*, the easiest way to guarantee this is to assume that each* u^h*, and hence* v^h*, is strictly increasing.)*

Proposition 16.15 (The First Theorem of Constrained Welfare Economics). *Suppose that* p *and* $(\zeta^h)_{h \in H}$ *constitute an* $\mathcal{M}$*-constrained Walrasian equilibrium, where* p *is nonnegative, and where each consumer is locally insatiable constrained to* $\mathcal{M}$*. If* $(\hat{\zeta}^h)_{h \in H}$ *is any other set of net trades for the consumers where each* $\hat{\zeta}^h \in \mathcal{M} \cap \mathcal{X}^h$ *and such that* $\sum_h \hat{\zeta}^h \leq 0$*, then* $(\hat{\zeta}^h)$ *does not Pareto dominate* (ζ^h).

Or, in other words, if consumers are constrained to net trades lying in some fixed $\mathcal{M}$, then $\mathcal{M}$-constrained-Walrasian-equilibrium net trades are (constrained) Pareto efficient. In particular, no economy with incomplete markets $\mathcal{M} \neq R^{kN}$ will admit two $\mathcal{M}$-constained-Walrasian-equilibrium allocations, one of which Pareto dominates the other.

The proof of Proposition 16.15 is left to you. If you remember the proof of the First Theorem of Welfare Economics, it should not be a challenge.

All-at-once versus dynamic market structures

With complete markets, EPPPE are more or less equivalent to the Walrasian equilibria of a corresponding all-markets-at-once economy. The cleanest statement of this is Proposition 16.12; if the set of securities $\mathcal{S}$ is such that any viable price system for $\mathcal{S}$ gives complete markets, then the set of Walrasian-equilibrium allocations is identical to the set of EPPPE consumption allocations.

Hart's example, compared to Proposition 16.15, shows that incomplete dynamic markets are different from incomplete all-at-once markets. Roughly speaking, when markets are complete, the many budget constraints of an EPPPE can be boiled together into a single budget constraint that works for all markets at once. But when markets are incomplete, the multiple budget constraints, one for each contingency, cannot generally be reduced to a single budget constraint with subspace restrictions on allowed net trades. In Hart's example, you can make trades in a subspace of R^{kN}, but you must satisfy three different budget constraints on those trades, which is mathematically a very different thing than satisfying a single budget constraint while choosing from a subspace.

And this is only the beginning of the ... interesting phenomena brought about by incomplete markets. In the incomplete-but-all-markets-at-once world, the existence results of Chapter 14 adapt very nicely. Obtaining existence results when markets are incomplete and dynamic is not at all easy and, in fact, very well behaved dynamic economies can fail to have any EPPPE (although such examples tend to be knife-edge cases). Hart (1975) provides an example of nonexistence.

Suppose we have a dynamic market economy and an EPPPE for it with incomplete markets. If we complete markets (say, by adding one of the $\mathcal{S}^{\mathrm{FFCC}}$ or $\mathcal{S}^{\mathrm{SFCC}}$ or $\mathcal{S}^{\mathrm{RFCC}}$), we know that any EPPPE for the market with augmented securities will not be Pareto dominated by the original EPPPE outcome. But Hart also provides an example where, starting with a set of securities $\mathcal{S}$ and an EPPPE, if securities are added to $\mathcal{S}$ that do not complete the markets, then the new economy can have an EPPPE whose outcome in terms of consumption is Pareto inferior to the original. Adding markets, if you don't add enough, can make everyone worse off.

If you want to study incomplete markets systematically, you should begin with Hart's paper; I'll supply further references in the bibliographic notes.

16.7. Firms

We come back, finally, to firms. What does it take to bring them back into the story? What problems arise?

In the basic general equilibrium model of Chapter 14, firms are formalized in three pieces: (1) Their ability to transform commodities is specified by a production-possibility set Z. (2) Their objective is to maximize their profits, taking prices as given. (3) Their connection with consumers is specified by exogenously given shareholdings. None of these need to change in the all-markets-at-once economy and, indeed and as we observed at the start of this chapter, by contingency-stamping commodities, our ability to model production more realistically (as taking time, as having uncertain outputs) is enormously enhanced.

When we move to markets with securities, however, a number of questions arise. These don't concern production possibilities for the firms; that part of the model of a firm continues to be enhanced. But:

- What is the profit of a firm, if there is no single market in which all transactions can be reckoned in a single numeraire?
- If a firm requires inputs for its chosen production plan early and only produces outputs late, how does it finance the purchase of those inputs?
- Securities that are tied to the fortunes of a firm are among the most important securities traded in the real world. So, presumably, in a model of a dynamic economy with securities and firms, we would want among the securities to be things like equity in the firm and debt issued by the firm. About these:

  In the real world, debt securities issued by firms—corporate bonds, commercial paper—carry the possibility of default, because limited-liability firms can and do go bankrupt. Bankruptcy is a not allowed in the models we have built so far; unless and until it is put into our models, there is no reason to distinguish one firm's "riskless" debt from another's, or from debt taken on by a consumer. However, there is no reason, if we allow firms to issue securities, to preclude a firm from issuing a security that, say, pays 1000 units of numeraire in some subset of the time-t contingencies, something less than 1000 units in other time-t contingencies, and 0 in still others. In other words, we can conceive of securities within the framework we've created that mimic risky debt.

As for equity, this is generally what determines ownership of a firm. If equity in a firm trades in securities markets, then ownership is not some exogenously given (and fixed) vector of shareholdings, but instead something that changes as securities are traded among consumers (and, perhaps, between consumers and firms, or among firms). Also, to this point, all securities have been in zero net supply. But equity in a firm is meant to total 100% of the firm. So equity as a security needs some new and special treatment. And, as we give it that treatment, who are the intial holders of the firm's equity?

In our models of securities so far, the set of securities is exogenously given, with the dividends issued by the security part of the exogenous specification of each security, along with a specification of when the security trades. The phrase "securities issued by a firm" immediately suggests something entirely more complex: The set of securities is endogenously determined by the actions of a single firm (with what as the objective function?). And even if we preclude this—we say that equity in every firm is traded and all other securities are exogneously specified—equity is a claim on the profit of the firm, which, admittedly, is a very vague concept, at this point. That being so, as the firm changes, or contemplates changing, its production plan, it will presumably be implicitly changing, or contemplating a change in, the dividends its equity pays. So even if the list of securities is fixed exogenously, it would seem that the dividends paid by at least some securities will have to be endogenously determined.

Back in Chapter 9, we never really rationalized profit maximization as an objective for the firm, but we did mention that many rationales that are offered begin with the contention that shareholders in a firm unanimously prefer profit maximization (and go on to offer reasons why managers of the firm act on behalf of its shareholders). How good is this rationale, when the shareholders in a firm may be a shifting lot of individuals?

These are all good questions. And they have tidy answers *if* markets are complete in a strong sense. The following meta-proposition applies:

Almost every reasonable way to answer questions about "what can/do firms do about securities" is fine, as long as (a) there are enough securities around so that markets are complete, (b) if firms' decisions affect the set of securities or the dividends paid by a security, these effects don't change the completeness of markets, and (c) firms, along with consumers, are price takers: The actions of firms don't change spot prices in any market, and they don't change the trade-offs in moving wealth from one contingency to another, which are given by the (essentially unique) vector $\pi \in \Pi(\mathcal{S}, q)$. Moreover, when markets are complete, there is no ambiguity as to what ***profit maximization*** *means for firms: Firms choose their production plans to maximize the* ***net present value*** *of all their activities, with the net present value defined as the value computed in contingency-f_0 prices, with cash flows in each f_t brought back to f_0 through the complete securities markets and their prices. This* *objective function is in the best interests of initial shareholders in the firm, and—subject to a reasonable assumption about the nature of production technologies*[7] *—remains in the continued best interest of subsequent shareholders, if trading in equity is allowed so that shareholdings change.*

This is a *meta-proposition*, which means that I'm not going to offer a proof. Before we can contemplate a proof, we have to specify answers to a lot of the questions asked; once that is done, then the proposition can be proved, and the proof runs along the lines of Proposition 16.12; if a, b, and c hold, then equilibrium outcomes will be the same as equilibrium outcomes in the all-markets-at-once economy. Just to give a for-instance, suppose we say

- In the model, F firms are given, each specified by a production-possibility set $Z^f \subseteq R^{kN}$ and an intial vector of shareholdings (σ^{hf}), where $\sigma^{hf} \geq 0$ for all h and f and $\sum_h \sigma^{hf} = 1$ for each f.[8] Assume that each Z^f is closed and contains 0.
- In the model, besides securities connected to firms, there is a set $\mathcal{S}$ of non-firm-related securities, rich enough so that for any viable prices q for $\mathcal{S}$, we know that markets will be complete. (So, for instance, $\mathcal{S}$ could be $\mathcal{S}^{\text{FFCC}}$ or $\mathcal{S}^{\text{SFCC}}$ or $\mathcal{S}^{\text{RFCC}}$.)
- Besides the securities in $\mathcal{S}$, the shares in the firms trade in securities markets that are open each contingency (prior to T). (Dividends are specified below.)
- Suppose firm f contemplates production plan $z \in Z^f$. It must simultaneously formulate a "financing and dividend payment plan," which involves it borrowing in the securities markets $\mathcal{S}$ in contingencies for which it needs cash to finance immediate operations and paying out dividends in contingencies where its operations (including discharging any debts it has contracted) leave it with a positive net cash flow. Dividends are paid, of course, to whoever are the shareholders of record as the particular contingency begins. (Or, if you prefer, you can have the firm finance operations where cash is needed by issuing debt. Or you can have it levy its shareholders.)
- In all this, each firm takes prices r and q as given, and it conducts its operations to maximize its profit, which is defined as

$$\sum_{f_t} \frac{1}{\pi_{f_t}} r_{f_t} \cdot z^f_{f_t},$$

[7] If you want an explanation of this mysterious caveat, see the solution to Problem 16.15 in the *Student's Guide*

[8] Since s is being used in this chapter for securities, σ is used for initial shareholdings. And for readers who might be interested in general equilibrium with entrepreneurs, nothing precludes the initial shareholdings in a firm f from being entirely concentrated in one consumer's hands (that is, $\sigma^{hf} = 1$ for some h), who is the *founder* or *entrepreneur* of f.

where π is selected from $\Pi(\mathcal{S}, q)$.[9]

With these assumptions in place, an EPPPE can be defined in fairly obvious fashion: The price portion consists of spot prices r for each contingency and securities prices q for the exogeously given $\mathcal{S}$, with the securities prices for equity in the firms (and, if allowed, other securities the firm might issue) determined by the formula analogous to (16.4). Consumers have consumption and trading plans, where they are allowed to trade in the securities in $\mathcal{S}$ and in other securities firms may issue; their budget constraints are much as before, except for contingency f_0, where you need to take into account their initial shareholdings in equity in the firms. Firms have production plans and "financing and dividend plans," which are required to clear the books in each contingency (the firm is left with neither a numeraire debt nor numeraire surplus in any contingency). Firms maximize profits as defined above, given r and q, and given the belief that their own securities will be priced by analogs to (16.4). Consumers maximize utility subject to budget constraints. And markets must clear; here you have to be careful about market clearing in the equity markets; the sum of shareholdings in each firm's equity must always total 1, instead of 0.

And, then, you prove that all equilibrium outcomes (in terms of consumption plans by consumers and production plans by the firms) for the all-markets-at-once economy are EPPPE outcomes for some trading plans, financing and dividend plans, and the corresponding spot and securities prices. And the EPPPE consumption and production plans are Walrasian-equilibrium plans in the all-markets-at-once economy. (Problem 16.15 asks you to continue along these lines.) For readers who know some financial market theory, you can also prove a general-equilibrium version of the famous Modigliani-Miller Theorem:[10] As long as the firm can finance its operations and clears its books in every contingency, the "financing and dividend" plan that it chooses is entirely irrelevant, fixing equilibrium prices.

Everything ties together, very nicely.

And if markets are not complete?

Which is not true at all, without the assumption that markets are complete irrespective of what firms do, and that their actions do not change prices. Then we aren't sure what profit is and, whatever we decide is the objective of the firm, it isn't clear that shareholders want the firm to maximize "it." An example that is even more of a caricature of reality than was Hart's example illustrates what can happen. Again there are two consumers, Alice and Bob, two states of nature, and two dates (hence, three contingencies), $t = 0, 1$. There is a single basic commodity ($k = 1$); I'll abbreviate contingency-stamped commodity bundles (elements of R^3) by (x_0, x_1^1, x_1^2) (in place of $(x_{f_0}, x_{f_1^1}, x_{f_1^2})$, which is more consistent with previous notation). Alice and Bob have identical utility functions, given by

$$u(x_0, x_1^1, x_1^2) = \ln(x_0 + 1) + 0.5\ln(x_1^1 + 1) + 0.5\ln(x_1^2 + 1).$$

[9] I apologize for the double use of f, for firms and contingencies. It won't happen again.

[10] Modigliani and Miller (1958).

Alice's endowment vector is $(10, 20, 0)$, while Bob's is $(10,0,20)$.

There is one firm, which is essentially useless: Its production possibility set is $Z = R^k_-$.

The key to the example is that only two securities are traded. The first is a "savings" security, which pays a dividend of 1 at time 1, in either contingency. The other is equity in the firm. The savings security is in zero net supply; there is 1 unit of the firm's equity. Bob and Alice each are initially endowed with half the firm's equity.

It may seem obvious that the firm should simply shut down, rather than engage in free disposal. Because both consumers have strictly increasing preferences, the one basic good will have strictly positive price in every contingency. In fact, we can immediately normalize the spot-market prices so that the price of the basic good in each contingency is 1. Therefore, any production will consist solely of destroying valuable goods.

So, going with the this obvious conclusion, if the firm contemplates the production plan $z = 0$, its shares are worthless, and Alice and Bob are left doing the best they can by trading in the savings security. They wish most of all to balance their endowments in the two time-1 contingencies; if markets were complete, they each would wind up with the consumption bundle $(10, 10, 10)$, which gives each one utility 4.79579055. But there is no way for them to do this. Depending on the price q of the savings security, they might want to transfer some of their contingency f_0 wealth into the two time-1 contingencies. But since they share this desire, there is no one to take the other side of the transaction. In an EPPPE, the price of the savings instrument must be set at the price q that makes this marginally undesirable, which is the solution to

$$\frac{q}{11} = \frac{0.5}{1} + \frac{0.5}{21} \quad \text{or} \quad q = 5.76190476, \text{ approximately.}$$

So, in equilibrium, $q = 5.76190476$, and Alice and Bob both consume their endowment, which gives each of them utility 3.92015649.

Suppose, however, that Alice and Bob convene a meeting of the shareholders of the firm and advance the proposition that the firm should throw away 0.01 in contingency f_1^1. To "clear its books," the firm will finance this with a levy of 0.01 units of the one good if the contingency is f_1^1, the levy being imposed on shareholders based on their shareholdings coming *into* this contingency.[11]

[11] Recall that we never have trading in securities at the final time T, which is 1. So there is no real distinction between shareholders coming into time 1 and those leaving time 1. But if you don't like the idea of a levy imposed on time-1 shareholders—or if you become unhappy with the fact that, in the example, the value of this firm's equity will be negative—the same point can be made in a more complicated model where the firm's equity has positive value: Suppose that the firm's technology allows it to input up to 1 unit of the good at time 0 and receive two times its input as output at time 1, regardless of the contingency. This output is paid as a dividend to the shareholders. This will make the firm profitable; the point will be that, ex ante shareholders would be better off if, in one of the two contingencies, the firm discarded a bit of its output. (This final conclusion will make sense in a paragraph or so.)

Suppose the firm fixes this production plan ("destruction plan" is more descriptive), in consequence of which the price of a full share of the firm at time 0 is some $q' < 0$. (The price is strictly negative because if Alice or Bob holds a share of the firm, they may have to fulfill the levy next period.) Alice must choose whether to demand any shares of the firm and, simultaneously, whether to use the savings instrument, whose price is q. If her trading plan is (α^A, β^A), where α^A is her position in the savings instrument and β^A, her position in shares of the firm, her consumption bundle will be

$$x^A(\alpha^A, \beta^A) = (10 - \alpha^A q - (\beta^A - 0.5)q', 20 + \alpha^A - .01\beta^A, 0 + \alpha^A).$$

(Note that in contingency f_1^2, holding position β^A in shares of the firm doesn't hurt her at all.) And, similarly, for Bob, we get

$$x^B(\alpha^B, \beta^B) = (10 - \alpha^B q - (\beta^B - 0.5)q', \alpha^B - .01\beta^B, 20 + \alpha^B).$$

We want to find prices q and q' so that when Alice maximizes her utility of $x^A(\alpha^A, \beta^A)$ and Bob his utility of $x^B(\alpha^B, \beta^B)$, we find that the optimizing choices satisfy $\alpha^A + \alpha^B = 0$ and $\beta^A + \beta^B = 1$. Doing this numerically, I obtained the approximate solution shown in Table 16.2.

Price of savings instrument	1.000227376
Price of equity of firm	-0.005002274

	Alice	Bob
Positions in savings instrument	10.00113688	-10.00113688
Positions in equity of firm	2000.500052	-1999.500052
Consumption time 0	10.00113688	9.998863121
Consumption time 1 state 1	9.99613636	9.99386364
Consumption time 1 state 2	10.00113688	9.998863121
Utility of outcome	4.79576992	4.7953565
Utility of "no trade"	3.92015649	3.92015649
Utility if markets complete without destroying any good	4.79579055	4.79579055

Table 16.2. Alice and Bob destroy to create. The values in this table are the (approximate) equilibrium values for the Alice-and-Bob example with firms and incomplete markets. To give them the ability to trade endowments across time-1 contingencies, they unanimously prefer that the sole firm, which can produce nothing, destroy a bit of commodity in one contingency. This provides trading opportunities that Alice and Bob otherwise wouldn't have and leaves both much better off than if the firm "maximizes profit" and nearly as well off as they would be with complete securities markets from the beginning. (The text gives more detail.)

The equilibrium price of the savings instrument is a bit more than 1, while the price of the equity in the firm is approximately -0.005. Alice buys 2000 shares in the firm (where each share represents 100% of the firm), to give her a net position of 2000.5; Bob sells his 0.5 share and shorts an additional 1999.5 shares. Since the price of the firm's equity is negative, Bob's short position is costly to him, and he generates the resources required to take this short position by shorting the savings instrument (in effect, borrowing). Alice's purchases of equity generate time-0 funds for her, and she buys the savings instrument (in effect, loans her resources to Bob). In contingency f_1^2, Bob has to pay back the loan from Alice, but he has endowment 20 with which to do this; Alice gets back her loan (via the dividends of the savings instrument)—in equilibrium, Alice winds up with a bit more than 10 units of consumption and Bob a bit less than 10. Both of their initial positions leave their time-0 endowments virtually untouched; Alice's time-0 consumption is a bit more than 10 and Bob's a bit less.

The key is what happens in contingency f_1^1. Bob owes Alice about 10 units of consumption and has no endowment. But because he is short around 2000 units of the equity of the firm, and the firm is about to destroy 0.01 units of the good, the firm levies its shareholders this amount. Alice, who is long 2000 units, has to pay the 0.01 levy to the firm, *and must pay Bob around 20 units, since his short position entitles him the minus the amount of levy.*[12] So, in equilibrium, Alice winds up with a bit more than half of what remains of the social endowment, after the 0.01 units are destroyed, and Bob winds up with a bit less than half. Note that their utilities are much greater than if the firm "maximizes profit" and chooses $z = 0$, and nearly as high as in the outcome that would result if markets were complete. So, compared to the firm "maximizing profit," both Alice and Bob like this a lot more.

Why does Alice come out ever so slightly ahead? The firm, by destroying commodity in the first state, increases the value of what remains in that state. And Alice is the person whose endowment is larger in the first state.

Note that, after time-0 trade is done, Alice owns 100% of the firm. In fact, she owns 200,000% of the firm, in a manner of speaking. Imagine she convenes another shareholders meeting. Bob no longer has a vote, and Alice, being long in the shares of the firm, prefers that the firm change its production plan and *not* destroy any good in contingency f_1^1. Of course, if she could get the firm to do this, and if contingency f_1^1 comes about, Bob has a problem: He owes Alice 10 or so units to pay off her loan, and he has no endowment for doing so. Be that as it may, you can see here that the preferences of shareholders can change in this sort of situation.

It should also be noted that trying to replace "profit maximization" (which, with incomplete markets, is anyway ambiguous) with "maximize the value of initial equity" won't work in this example. If the firm chooses $z = 0$, its equity is worthless. If it destroys the 0.01 unit in contingency f_1^1, its equity has negative value. And that's unanimously preferred, ex ante, by both Alice and Bob.

If you think about it, none of this is too surprising. The meme that shareholders

---

[12] I reiterate from last footnote; if you find aspects of this example hard to swallow, switch to the alternative formulation described there, and these oddities will disappear.

unanimously prefer profit maximization works for competitive firms and only for competitive firms. It works because the *only* impact a competitive firm has on its shareholders is to change the right-hand side of their budget constraint, and a firm, by maximizing its profit, makes that right-hand side (that is, shareholder wealth) as large as possible. The profits of other firms aren't affected (assuming no other externalities), and the prices faced by consumers on the left-hand side of their budget constraint are unchanged. To reduce this to its essence, two one-share shareholders in General Motors who *do not* want GM to maximize its profit are (1) someone who holds 10,000 shares of Ford Motor Company, if GM profit maximizing will reduce the profit of Ford, and (2) someone who buys a brand-new Cadillac every year; this individual would prefer that GM set the price of Cadillacs at $10 each, even if that reduces profit.

In dynamic economies, the backbone in the meta-theorem is that firms are competitive in every sense of the word: they don't affect prices, but more than that, they in no way affect the left-hand side(s) of consumer optimization problems. If by changing their production plans, they change the *space* of what consumers can buy, they affect that left-hand side profoundly, and the sort of weirdness seen in this second Alice-and-Bob example can ensue.

This does not mean that there isn't a literature on firms in incomplete markets. There is a large literature, which moreover is organized on the theme of "What should be the objectives of the firm?" (References will be supplied momentarily.) But the answers provided are bound to be strained; even without the complications of time and uncertainty, there is no solid answer to the question *What should be the objectives of the firm?* for firms that are not price takers or that can create new goods or take products "off the shelves." That's the issue here, although time and uncertainty may obscure this fact.

Moving beyond the microeconomics of this volume

And this begs the question, If markets are incomplete (before we start worrying about equity in firms), why is that? In our example, why don't Alice and Bob create the "missing" security (or otherwise contractually agree to mutually ensure one another)? The methods developed in this volume are not well suited to answer this question, or to deal with imperfectly competitive firms, or to deal with the realities of consumers and firms that have no hope of undertaking successfully the complex decision and assessment problems that they have been facing in this chapter. There is more that can be done with the models and methods we've explored, but it is probably more important to bring to the table models and methods better suited to some of the questions this chapter (as well as others) has raised. But that's material for another volume or two.

Bibliographic Notes

The idea of contingency-stamping commodities in general equilibrium models first appears in the literature in Arrow (1953) and Debreu (1959). Arrow (1953) pioneers the idea of using securities markets to transfer wealth among contingencies, with contingent spot markets then available to allocate wealth among commodities.

Arrow (1953) deals with a two-period model only. The basic structure of an EPPPE for more complex market structures is due to Radner (1968, 1972), and EPPPE are often called Radner equilibria, in consequence. Merton (1973) contemporaneously develops essentially the same concept (albeit in continuous time models). Guesnerie and Jaffray (1974) then redo Arrow's analysis for rolling sets of contingent claims and multiple time periods.

Assuming all securities are financial or that they pay dividends in a single commodity whose spot price is normalized to be 1 in all contingencies, the connections between no-arbitrage, viability, and the existence of strictly positive pricing vectors π can be attributed to several authors. I'm conflicted on this, being in the set of authors. But, with the caveat that I am conflicted, I list Ross (1978) and Harrison and Kreps (1979) as early general statements.

The analysis of the (in)efficiency of incomplete markets was spurred by Hart (1975). Problems with the objectives of firms in incomplete markets were analyzed around the same time; see in particular the symposium on the subject in the *Bell Journal of Economics and Management Science* (1974). A large literature on incomplete markets (with and without production) ensued; surveys of the literature at various points in time include Kreps (1979b), Marimon (1987), and Geanakoplos (1990).

Problems

■ 16.1. (a) Prove Proposition 16.2. You should mostly be citing previous results.

(b) In the definition of an EPPPE (for any dynamic economy with a full set of spot markets in each contingency), I assumed that spot-market prices were nonnegative. Suppose I hadn't restricted their sign. Prove: In any EPPPE for any dynamic economy (with a full set of spot markets in each contingency) in which Assumption 16.1′ is satisfied, all spot market prices must be nonnegative.

(c) Prove: In any EPPPE for any dynamic economy (with a full set of spot markets in each contingency) in which Assumption 16.1 is satisfied, the price of f_t-commodity 1 is strictly positive. Also prove: In the specific dynamic economy of Section 16.3 (with contingency futures markets), the price at time 0 of the futures will all be strictly positive.

■ *16.2. Concerning contingent financial versus contingent futures markets:

(a) What is the logical relationship between Assumptions 16.1 and 16.1′? (Does either imply the other?)

(b) Give a statement of Proposition 16.4, but for contingent financial markets instead of contingent futures markets.

(c) If we assume Assumption 16.1′ instead of 16.1 and work with contingent financial markets instead of contingent futures markets, where does the proof of Proposition 16.4 need amendment? Provide the needed amendments.

■ 16.3. Alice is a subjective expected-utility maximizer: For some nondecreasing function $U : R_+^{k(T+1)} \to R$ and probability distribution μ on Ω, if her consumption bundle through time is $(x_0(\omega), x_1(\omega), \ldots, x_T(\omega))$ in state ω, where each $x_t(\omega) \in R_+^k$, her overall utility is

$$\sum_{\omega \in \Omega} \mu(\omega) U(x_0(\omega), x_1(\omega), \ldots, x_T(\omega)).$$

Under what conditions is Alice globally insatiable in every contingency f_t?

■ 16.4. We know that, in an all-markets-at-once economy, if Assumption 16.1′ holds, every consumer will satisfy her budget constraint with equality in any Walrasian equilibrium. But what about in an EPPPE? If $(r, q, \boldsymbol{x}, \boldsymbol{y})$ is an EPPPE for some dynamic economy in which Assumption 16.1′ holds, is it true that the budget constraints (16.3) all hold with equality (for $\boldsymbol{x}^h$ and $\boldsymbol{y}^h$)? Show by example that the answer is no. Can you provide conditions under which the answer would be yes?

■ *16.5. Prove Lemma 16.11. Note that the second half of part a implies the first half, so you might content yourself with (only) proving the second half. But to understand the notion of an arbitrage opportunity, you might try to prove the first half directly, using arbitrage. For part b, you want to show that if ξ is a wealth-transfer vector generated from $\mathcal{S}$ given these prices, then $\pi \cdot \xi = 0$. (Why is this enough?) To do so takes some cleverness in changing the order of summations.

■ *16.6. Prove that $\mathcal{S}^{\text{SFCC}}$ and $\mathcal{S}^{\text{RFCC}}$ have the property that, with any viable price system, markets are complete. (Hint: Use Lemma 16.10.)

■ 16.7. Recall that for each f_t, $t < T$, we let $\ell(f_t)$ be the number of immediate successors of f_t. Suppose $\mathcal{S}$ consists of $\sum_{f_t, t<T} \ell(f_t)$ securities. Each one trades in only one contingency; precisely $\ell(f_t)$ trade in contingency f_t. Each security that trades in contingency f_t pays dividends (only) at time $t+1$ and only in contingencies that are immediate successors to f_t; the dividends paid are arbitrary except that the $\ell(f_t)$ patterns of dividends form a linearly independent set. (Hence, $\mathcal{S}^{\text{RFCC}}$ is a special case of this situation.) Prove that for such a set of securities $\mathcal{S}$, if $\mathcal{S}$ and q are viable, then the dimension of $M(\mathcal{S}, q)$ is $N-1$.

■ *16.8. This problem employs the following mathematical fact. (You can try to prove this, if you wish. It isn't hard if you know some linear algebra and multivariate calculus. But you can also just take the fact and use it.) Suppose $(x_{mn})_{m=1,\ldots,M,\ n=1,\ldots,N}$ is an $M \times N$ matrix in $R_+^{M \times N}$, where each component x_{mn} of the matrix is drawn randomly from a uniform distribution on $[0,1]$ (or any other probability distribution that is absolutely continuous with respect to Lebesgue measure on R_+). Moreover, these MN numbers are drawn independently. Suppose the set $\{1, \ldots, N\}$ is partitioned into K nonempty pieces, $\{1, \ldots, n_1\}$, $\{n_1+1, \ldots, n_2\}$, $\ldots$, $\{n_{K-1}+1, \ldots, n_K\}$ (where $n_K = N$), and we form the MK-dimensional matrix whose mkth element is $\sum_{n=n_{k-1}+1}^{n_k} x_{mn}$. Then with probability 1 (with respect to the original random draw of the components of the matrix (x_{mn})), every $J \times J$ square submatrix of this $M \times K$ matrix (where $J \leq \min\{M, K\}$) has full rank.[13]

Use this fact to prove: Suppose we have a dynamic economy with L financial securities, in which $L \geq \ell(f_t)$ for all f_t. Each of these securities trades at each contingency f_t for $t < T$, and each one pays a strictly positive dividend in each final contingency $\{\omega_T\}$. The dividends $d_s(\{\omega\})$ are all drawn at random, in independent and identically distributed fashion, according to a uniform distribution on $[0, 1]$ (or any probability distribution on R_+ that is absolutely continuous with respect to Lebesgue measure). Then for this economy, if (p, x) is a Walrasian equilibrium for the all-markets-at-once economy (with these consumers and commodity space), there is an EPPPE in which x is the consumption allocation portion with probability 1 (concerning the choice of dividends).

How does this result relate to Proposition 16.13? What would happen if the securities paid real dividends?

■ 16.9. Consider the following pure-trade economy. There are two consumers, Alice and Bob. There are three dates, $t = 0, 1, 2$. There are four states of nature, and the t /u/i structure is such that, at date 1, Alice and Bob know that the state is in either $\{\omega_1, \omega_2\} = f_1^1$ or $\{\omega_3, \omega_4\} = f_1^2$. This implies that there are seven contingencies, f_0 at time 0, f_1^1 and f_1^2 at time 1, and $\{\omega_i\}$ for $i = 1, 2, 3, 4$ at time 2. There is a single basic commodity, and hence, since there are seven contingencies, the consumption space is R^7. Both Alice and Bob are expected utility maximizers; both attach probability $1/4$ to each of the four states, and they share the same von Neumann–Morgenstern utility function (on consumption vectors (x_0, x_1, x_2) at the three dates) $U(x_0, x_1, x_2) = \ln(x_0) + \ln(x_1) + \ln(x_2)$. Both Alice and Bob have endowments of 1 unit of the good in contingency f_0 and 9 units of the good in each of the four time-2 contingencies. But their endowments are different in the two time-1 contingencies: Alice is endowed with 2 units of the good in f_1^1 and 6 units in f_1^2, while Bob is endowed with 6 units in f_1^1 and 2 units in f_1^2.

(a) There is a single Walrasian equilibrium of this economy, with an all-markets-at-once economy. Identify this equilibrium, and prove that it is the only one.

(b) This is not an all-markets-at-once economy but, instead, an economy with two *financial* securities and dynamic trading. Each security trades in each of the three before-time-2 contingencies. Each pays dividends in each of the four time-2 contingencies. The first pays the dividend 2 if the state of nature is ω_1, 7 if ω_2, 3 if ω_3, and 5 if ω_4. The second pays, in the same order, 12, 2, 4, and 4. Is there an EPPPE corresponding to $\pi = (1, 1, \ldots, 1)$? If so, what is it? (It is not necessary for you to produce the equilibrium trading plans of Alice and Bob; it is enough to identify r, q, and x.)

---

[13] Why? Because, roughly, linear dependence is a property that holds on lower dimensional subspaces of the space looked at, and the probabilities being considered put zero weight on lower dimensional subspaces.

(c) Suppose the securities paid their dividends in the consumption good, rather than in numeraire. Is the Walrasian-equilibrium allocation an EPPPE allocation?

(d) Go back to the case where the securities are financial. Is there an EPPPE corresponding to π given by

$$\pi_{f_t} = \begin{cases} 1/2, & \text{if } t = 2 \text{ and } f_t = \{\omega_1\}, \text{ and} \\ 1, & \text{for all other } t \text{ and } f_t? \end{cases}$$

If so, what is it? Warning: This is harder than part b.

■ 16.10. Suppose that $\mathcal{S}$ contains one *primary* security s^0, which trades at every contingency (before time T) and pays a dividend in every time-T contingency $\{\omega\}$ and that, moreover, pays a different dividend in each time-T contingency. Ennumerate Ω as $\{\omega_1, \omega_2, \ldots, \omega_J\}$, where J is the cardinality of Ω, and abbreviate $d_{s^0}(\{\omega_j\})$ as $d(j)$. Arrange the indices so that $d(J) > d(j)$ for all $j < J$. Suppose $\mathcal{S}$ also contains $J-1$ "European call options" on the primary security: For $j = 1, \ldots, J-1$, the jth of these, which is denoted s^j, trades at every contingency (before time T) and pays a dividend at time T given by

$$d_{s^j}(\{\omega_{j'}\}) = \max\{d(j') - d(j), 0\}.$$

(If you know about call options, s^j is, effectively, a European call option on the primary security with striking price $d(j)$ and exercise date T. If you don't know about call options, ignore what you just read.) Prove that for this set of J securities, one primary and $J-1$ derivative, if $\mathcal{S}$ and q are viable, then the dimension of $M(\mathcal{S}, q)$ is $N-1$. (The idea that markets are complete if there are one primitive security that distinguishes among states of nature and enough call options on that security is due to Ross, 1976.)

■ *16.11. Suppose the set of securities $\mathcal{S}$ has the following properties. All securities pay dividends only at time T. Security 1 pays \$1 in each and every terminal contingency $\{\omega\}$. Suppose prices q are advanced for these securities, and (through a choice of numeraire) the price of security 1 is 1 in each contingency prior to T.

I assert two propositions. First, $\mathcal{S}$ and q are viable if and only if probabilities can be assigned to the states of nature so that, at each time $t < T$ and for each security s, the price of s in contingency f_t is the conditional expected value (under those probabilities) of the price of security s at time $t+1$, conditional on the state of nature lying in f_t. For those who know some theory of stochastic processes, we can paraphrase this as: $\mathcal{S}$ and q are viable if and only if we can find a probability distribution that makes the stochastic process of the price of each security a *martingale* relative to the filtration of the $\mathcal{F}_t$, where for the case of $t = T-1$, q_{sf_t} will be the conditional expectation of the dividend to be paid.

And, second, markets are complete if there is a unique probability distribution that does this.

Prove these two statements.

(In the literature, you'll find this result in somewhat more complicated form, where the probability distribution is called an *equivalent martingale measure*. Things are more complicated because this is done with infinite state spaces; see Harrison and Kreps (1979) for the orignal paper on these things.)

■ 16.12. In the discussion of security price indeterminacy with financial securities (starting on page 417), I never justified the italicized claim. Please finish justifying this.

■ *16.13. Prove Proposition 16.15. If you would like more of challenge, state and prove a version of this proposition with firms included in the story.

■ 16.14. Hart's example (from the start of Section 16.6) involves two consumers, two commodities, two dates, and two states of nature. Replicate his phenomenon, but with only one state of nature.

■ *16.15. Suppose we wanted to state and prove a precise version of the meta-proposition that, if markets are complete without involving equity in firms as securities, and if firms are price takers, then the set of EPPPE consumption (and production) allocations is the same as the set of Walrasian-equilibrium allocations. To do this, you must give an exact specification of the general idea that a firm's plans will include both a production plan $z \in Z$ *and* a financial plan that enables the firm to carry out this production plan while meeting a contingency-by-contingency constraint that the firm always balances it books. The text gets you started on this, and this problem asks you to continue. Warning: The solution given in the *Guide* goes on for over five pages and, while it states propositions formally, it fails to do all the tedious work of a formal proof. If you tackle this problem and push all the way to the end, it will take considerable time and effort. Also, in the statement of the meta-proposition in the text, a mysterious caveat is inserted to the (meta-)result that subsequent shareholders will not try to convince the firm to change its production plans. The answer in the *Guide* explains (somewhat informally) what that is all about.

■ 16.16. With regard to the Alice-and-Bob example with a firm, provide a fully fleshed-out example along the lines outlined in footnote 12. That is, rewrite the text from the start of the subsection *And if markets are not complete?* until the end of the example, without unhappy phenomena such as negative prices for the equity of the firm and the firm imposing a levy on shareholders at date 1 in certain contingencies. You may find it helpful, in doing this, to change endowments a bit: Begin with Alice having endowment $(10.5, 18, 0)$, Bob having $(10.5, 0, 18)$, and both Alice and Bob beginning with a $1/2$ share of the firm.

Appendices

About the Appendices

Economic theory, and in particular the theory that makes up this volume, is mathematical in character. Formal definitions that make use of concepts from mathematics (sets, binary relations, functions) are followed by lemmas, propositions, and corollaries. Your ability to make it through this book depends crucially on your level of comfort with the various pieces of mathematics that are used and in particular with your level of comfort with theorem-proof exposition.

These appendices present two types of material. In some cases, they review mathematical concepts, tools, and results that I hope and expect you have learned elsewhere. I assume that most readers of this book are graduate students (or perhaps advanced undergraduates) in economics and related fields, who have a solid background in mathematics in general and in the specific types of mathematics (analysis, probability) that are employed in particular. If your background is both solid and recent, you will find yourself able to read through many of the appendices with little problem.

But in some cases, and this is particularly true of Appendix 4 (on the mathematics of correspondences) and Appendix 6 (on dynamic programming), it is likely that much of the material will be new to you.

In either case, these appendices are *not* substitutes for good courses on the subjects they cover. They do not, for the most part, provide problem sets for you to do, and what is true for economic theory is even more true for mathematics: You learn the subject not so much by reading about it as by doing it and, in particular, by doing the problem sets. (Where problems are provided, you should take advantage and do them, especially if the material is new to you.) If you find yourself struggling with the material in any appendix, or if the material is entirely new to you, I urge you to find and consume a good textbook that covers the material thoroughly. I asked colleagues and economics Ph.D. students at the Stanford Graduate School of Business for textbooks that they would recommend for such study, and I was surprised to find that books that I studied as a student (a long, long time ago) are still regarded as good sources: Rudin's *Principles of Mathematical Analysis* (3rd ed.), McGraw-Hill, 1976; Royden, *Real Analysis* (3rd ed.), Prentice-Hall, 1988; and Rockafellar, *Convex Analysis*, Princeton University Press, 1970. One more recent book that was strongly recommended by some students and that covers a wide variety of subjects is Ok, *Real Analysis with Economic Applications*, Princeton University Press, 2007. Concerning dynamic programming, Bertsekas, *Dynamic Programming and Optimal Control*, vols. 1 and 2 (3rd edition), Athena Scientific, 2005 and 2007, was recommended. I personally like Whittle, *Optimization Over Time: Dynamic Pro-*

gramming and Stochastic Control, vols. 1 and 2. But this is out of print, I fear. Perhaps copies can be found in your library.

I have not included in the appendices mathematics that is truly basic. In particular, basic (multivariate) calculus, linear algebra, set theory, and simple probability theory are for the most part omitted.

When writing the appendices, I struggled with the question, Which results should I prove and which should I simply state? For the most part, I omit proofs where the proof is straightforward, and I omit proofs where the proof is so difficult that giving the proof would derail the exposition. But I do give proofs, or sometimes sketches of proofs, whenever I think your comprehension of the result will benefit by going through the details.

Appendix One

Mathematical Induction

Mathematical induction (or just, induction) is a technique for proving that a given statement is true for any positive (or nonnegative) integer. For those readers who are unfamiliar with this very useful technique, or who need a quick refresher, I will illustrate with a very silly example: For my statement, I will use *Every nonnegative integer* n *is either even or odd, where* n *is even if* $n = 2m$ *for some integer* m*, and* n *is odd if* $n = 2m + 1$ *for some* m. (You probably think, and correctly, this is petty obvious. But did you ever think how such a thing is proved? Here is one way.)

Step 1: First, you prove the statement is true for $n = 0$ if you want to prove it is true for all nonnegative integers, or you prove it is true for $n = 1$, if you want to prove it is true for all strictly positive integers.

In this case, we'll begin with $n = 0$. Zero is even, since $0 = 2 \times 0$.

Step 2: The induction step. Second, you *assume* or *hypothesize* that the statement is true for all nonnegative/positive integers less than or equal to n, and, using this hypothesis, you prove the statement is true for $n + 1$. The assumption is called *the induction hypothesis,* and this step is called *the induction step.*

So assume inductively that every nonnegative integer n or less is either even or odd. Then, in particular, either $n = 2m$ (n is even) or $n = 2m + 1$ (n is odd). Consider $n+1$. If n is even, so $n = 2m$ for some m, then $n+1 = 2m+1$, hence $n+1$ is odd. If n is odd, so $n = 2m+1$ for some m, then $n+1 = 2m+1+1 = 2m+2 = 2(m+1)$, and $n + 1$ is even. Therefore, we have shown that $n + 1$ is either even or odd, completing the induction step.

Step 3: Write *end of proof*; you are done.

You should have a pretty good intuitive understanding of why this is a valid technique of logical proof. Basically, this is a "domino" technique. The positive integers are the dominos, and domino n is considered to be knocked over if the statement is true for integer n. In step 1 you prove that the first domino is knocked over. In step 2, you prove that if all the dominos up to n are knocked over, then so is $n + 1$. And then, because the integers are like an infinite sequence of dominos, this shows that the statement is true for every integer; every domino is knocked down.

Suppose I want to prove some statement is true for all the integers, positive and negative. I can use the technique of induction by, for example, showing that the statement is true for zero, and then showing that if it is true for all positive integers from 0 to $n > 0$, it is true for $n + 1$, while if it is true for all negative integers from 0 down to to $m < 0$, then it is true for $m - 1$.

Although it is probably overdoing things, let me close by noting that this involves in particular the idea that there is always a "next" integer. Statements about all the real numbers are not amenable to this technique. For example, suppose I wanted to prove that *All nonnegative real numbers are rational.* I could carry out, in each case, step 1: Zero is rational. But then the logic in step 2 is that I assume that the statement is true for all the numbers less than or equal to n and prove it is true for the "next" number. There is no next real number after 0, so the proof technique doesn't work.

Appendix Two

Some Simple Real Analysis

This appendix reviews basic concepts and results from real analysis that are used in the text. As mentioned in the overall introduction to the appendices, if you are able to read through this appendix at a healthy clip, with most of the material coming back to you from some previous course you took, you are ready to proceed to the text and most problems. If it is familiar, but only vaguely so, you may need to review seriously. And if your have never seen this material before, it may be dangerous to rely on this as your sole resource; study a good textbook on real analysis. The overall introduction to the appendices gives some recommendations.

A2.1. The Setting

The explicit setting is finite-dimensional Euclidean space, which is fancy math-talk for the space of k-dimensional vectors with real numbers for components, for some positive integer k. Most of what is discussed here extends to real vector spaces and even to various metric and topological spaces, but I do not comment further on those extensions. Euclidean space of dimension k is denoted by R^k, with $x = (x_1, \ldots, x_k)$ denoting a typical element of R^k. The positive orthant is denoted R^k_+; that is, $x \in R^k_+$ if $x \geq 0$. The strict positive orthant, vectors with all components strictly positive, is denoted R^k_{++}. The letters f, g, and h usually denote functions on subsets of R^k with range R^j, for some (possibly other) integer j. The function f is called *real valued* if its range is R (that is, R^1).

A2.2. Distance, Neighborhoods, and Open and Closed Sets

Definition A.2.1. *For two points x and y from R^k, the* **Euclidean distance** *between them is*

$$\|x - y\| = \sqrt{\sum_{i=1}^{k} (x_i - y_i)^2}.$$

(We always take the positive root.) This is the length of the line segment that joins these points, measured in the usual fashion. The notation $\|x - y\|$ implicitly recognizes that the distance between the vectors x and y is the same as the distance between the vector $x - y = (x_1 - y_1, \ldots, x_k - y_k)$ and $0 = (0, \ldots 0)$; distance is translation invariant.[1] Also, the double vertical lines in $\|\cdot\|$ may remind you of single vertical lines used to denote absolute value in R^1; in the case of $k = 1$, the Euclidean distance between numbers x and y is just the absolute value of their difference, or $|x - y|$. Euclidean distance has some standard properties:

1. $\|x - y\| \geq 0$, and $\|x - y\| = 0$ if and only if $x = y$.
2. $\|x - y\| = \|y - x\|$
3. For a scalar α, $\|\alpha x - \alpha y\| = |\alpha| \, \|x - y\|$.
4. *The triangle inequality:* For every x, y, and z, $\|x - y\| + \|y - z\| \geq \|x - z\|$, which is paraphrased: The shortest path between x and z is the straight line between them; going via a third point y will never shorten the distance.

Definition A2.2. *For every point $x \in R^k$ and for every $\epsilon > 0$, the ϵ-**open-neighborhood around** x is the set of points*

$$N_\epsilon(x) = \{y \in R^k \ : \ \|y - x\| < \epsilon\}.$$

Definition A2.3. *A set $X \subseteq R^k$ is **open** if for every $x \in X$, there exists some $\epsilon > 0$ such that $N_\epsilon(x) \subseteq X$. A set $X \subseteq R$ is **closed** if it is the complement of an open set. Per careful application of these definitions, both the empty set and the entire space R^k are open and, hence, both are closed.*

The picture is a simple one: A set is open if, around every point, you can draw some "ball" of postive radius that is completely contained within the original set.[2] The mental picture of a closed set will be developed momentarily. Many sets in R^k are neither open nor closed; for instance, in R^1, the set $(0, 1] = \{x \in R : 0 < x \leq 1\}$ is neither.

Proposition A2.4. *The union of any number of open sets is open. The intersection of a finite number of open sets is open. The union of a finite number of closed sets is closed, and the intersection of any number of closed sets is closed.*[3]

Relatively open and closed sets

In many contexts, we talk about functions defined not on all of R^k but instead on a *subset* of R^k or conduct analysis in such a subset. Perhaps most importantly, we often look at functions defined on the positive orthant of R^k. To deal with such

[1] A mathematician would say, R^k is a normed linear space, and the distance between x and y is the norm of their difference.

[2] Exercise: Show that for $\epsilon > 0$, $N_\epsilon(x)$ is an open set. Hint: Use the triangle inequality.

[3] If all this is brand new to you, you should go through the proof of these things. Proving the first should be easy, and the second only a bit harder. For the two statements about closed sets, you must learn De Morgan's laws: The complement of a union of sets is the intersection of their complements, the complement of an intersection of sets is the union of their complements. (You can even prove this, if you are feeling fanatical.) You should also develop or be shown the standard examples of a (non-finite) intersection of open sets that is not open.

cases, we say that a subset Y of a set X is *relatively open* in X if $Y = Z \cap X$ for some set Z that is open in all of R^k and Y is *relatively closed* if $Y = Z \cap X$ for some set Z that is closed in all of R^k. Note that if X is closed, then Y is relatively closed in X if and only if it is closed, and if X is open, then Y is relatively open in X if and only if it is open. When conducting analysis in some particular domain, authors will sometimes drop the modifier *relatively* and speak of open and closed sets, implicitly meaning relatively open and relatively closed.

Closure and interior

Definition A2.5. *For $X \subseteq R^k$, the **closure** of X is the smallest closed subset of R^k containing X, and the **interior** of X is the largest open subset of R^k contained within X.*

How do we know that for a given set X, there is a smallest closed set containing X and a largest open set contained in X? We use Proposition A2.4: To define the closure of X, note that R^k is closed and contains X. Now take the intersection of every closed set that contains X. Proposition A2.4 tells us that this is necessarily a closed set. Of course, X is entirely contained in this intersection (since X is in each set in the intersection). And this must be the smallest closed set containing X; anything smaller would have been in the intersection, and hence would have reduced the intersection to itself (at least). Similarly, the interior of X is the union of all open sets entirely contained within X. Note that the interior of X can be empty.

Please note as well that if x is in the interior of X, then there is some $\epsilon > 0$ such that $N_\epsilon(x) \subseteq X$. In words, there is a ball around x contained in X. Why? Because if x is in the interior of X, since the interior of X is open, there is an open ball around x in the interior of X, which (perforce) is entirely contained within X. Conversely, if for $x \in X$ we can find an $\epsilon > 0$ such that $N_\epsilon(x) \subseteq X$, we are certain that x is in the interior of X: The interior of X is the union of all open sets contained within X, and $N_\epsilon(x)$ is one such open set. Hence the interior of X is equivalently defined as the set of points in X such that we can put some open ball around x and stay entirely within X. (A corresponding equivalent definition of closure follows in a few pages.)

If you desire some finger exercises on this material, a good one at this point is to show that the closure of a set X is the complement of the interior of its complement, and vice versa.

Note that the relative interior of a set X, relative to another set Y, defined as the largest relatively open set (relative to Y) contained in X is not, in general, the relative interior of X intersected with Y; for instance, the relative interior of X relative to itself is itself. On the other hand, the relative closure of X, relative to Y, which is the smallest relatively closed set containing X, is the closure of X intersected with Y (prove this!).

Other measures of distance

The Euclidean distance between x and y, given above, can be mathematically cumbersome to work with. There are many other ways to measure distance in R^k, two of which can be more tractable in proofs. These two are based on the so-called *sup* or ℓ^∞ norm (read ℓ^∞ as "ell-infinity") and the *sum-of-absolute-values* or ℓ^1 (read "ell-one") norm. In the first, the distance between x and y is

$$\|x - y\|_\infty = \max\{|x_i - y_i| \ : \ i = 1, \ldots, k\};$$

in the second, the distance between x and y is

$$\|x - y\|_1 = \sum_{i=1}^{k} |x_i - y_i|.$$

(In this parlance, Euclidean distance is based on the ℓ^2 norm, and there is an ℓ^p norm for every p from 1 to ∞.) Thinking in terms of R^2, $\|x - y\|_1$ is the distance from x to y if you can only move north-south or east-west at a time; it counts the number of "city blocks" that must be walked to get from x to y, if the city is laid out like Manhattan; $\|x - y\|$ (without a subscript, meaning Euclidean distance) is the distance from x to y as the crow flies; and $\|x-y\|_\infty$ is the larger of the north-south or east-west distance between x and y.

Hence if $x = (1, 3)$ and $y = (5, 0)$, $\|x - y\|_1 = 4 + 3 = 7$, $\|x - y\| = \sqrt{4^2 + 3^2} = \sqrt{25} = 5$, and $\|x - y\|_\infty = \max\{4, 3\} = 4$. In fact, it is generally true that

$$\|x - y\|_1 \geq \|x - y\| \geq \|x - y\|_\infty$$

for all x and y. But it is also true that

$$\|x - y\|_\infty \geq \frac{1}{k}\|x - y\|_1,$$

where k is the dimension of the Euclidean space. For this reason, when it comes to defining open and closed sets, the three different ways of measuring distance are equivalent. If a set is open with respect to one way of measuring distance, it is open with respect to the other two. This last statement is not meant to be obvious, although it is not hard to prove. And this has the following consequence: Many of the concepts we are about to define—and in particular, continuity of functions and boundedness and compactness of sets—don't depend on which of these measures of distance are used. (In mathematical terms, continuity and compactness are *topological properties*, and since the different ways of measuring distance don't change which sets are open, they induce the same *topologies*.) Therefore, in the text, when I want to prove that some function is continuous or a some set is bounded or (after Appendix 4) some correspondence is locally bounded, I can and will use whichever of the three distance measures is most convenient mathematically. If you have never studied these ideas in detail before, when this happens I will be pulling the proverbial rabbit out of a hat; I hope this dicussion will at least indicate the nature of the rabbit and the hat, although to tranform the argument from magic to transparent logic, you must study the issue rather more deeply than is possible in this appendix.

A2.3. Sequences and Limits

A ***sequence*** in R^k is, formally, a function from the positive integers $\{1, 2, 3, \ldots\}$ to R^k. Being somewhat less formal, it is a countably infinite list of points $x^1, x^2, \ldots$ from R^k. The connection between the formal and informal definitions is that x^i is the value of the function at the argument i. We write $\{x^i\}_{i=1}^n$ as shorthand for a sequence, and $\{x^i\}$ as short shorthand.[4]

Note the use of superscripts here; we are reserving subscripts for components of the vector, so that (for example) x_j^i will mean the jth component of the ith vector in the sequence $\{x^i\}$. In math books, subscripts are most often used for sequence indices; indeed, in several places in the text we revert to this practice (announcing the fact when this happens).

Definition A2.6. *The sequence $\{x^i\}$ has **limit** x if for every $\epsilon > 0$ there is some integer I such that for all $i \geq I$, $\|x^i - x\| \leq \epsilon$. When this happens, we write $lim_{i \to \infty}\ x^i = x$, $lim\, x^i = x$, or $x^i \to x$.*

In words, the sequence has limit x if the points in the sequence get and stay arbitrarily close to x.

Proposition A2.7. *The set $X \subseteq R^k$ is open if and only if, for every point $x \in X$ and sequence $\{x^i\}$ with limit x, there is some large enough integer I such that $x^i \in X$ for all $i \geq I$.*

Proposition A2.8. *The set $X \subseteq R^k$ is closed if and only if, for every sequence $\{x^i\}$ with limit x, if $x^i \in X$ for all i, then $x \in X$.*

Proposition A2.8 gives the most useful mental picture of closedness of a set; X is closed means that whenever we take a sequence from X with a limit, that limit is also in X. In other words, X contains all its limit points.

The phrase "whenever we take a sequence from X with a limit..." implicitly makes the important point that some sequences do not have a limit. For example, in R^1, the sequence $\{x^i\}$ where $x^i = 10i$—the sequence $\{10, 20, 30, \ldots\}$—has no limit. A more intriguing example is the sequence $\{1.1, 2.1, 1.01, 2.01, 1.001, 2.001, \ldots\}$. This also has no limit. It might be said that both 1 and 2 are limits of this sequence, but that is not quite right, since the sequence gets arbitrarily close to both, arbitrarily late in the sequence, but does not *stay* arbitrarily close to either. The points 1 and 2 are not limits of this sequence; instead they are its accumulation points:

---

[4] This use of curly brackets to set off a sequence may cause confusion, since curly brackets are also used to delineate a set. Suppose, for instance, for a sequence $\{x^i\}$, we want to indicate the countable set of values taken on by the sequence. Following standard notational usage, this would be $\{x^i; i = 1, \ldots\}$. The first means an ordered sequence of points; the second an unordered countable set of points. As long as you are aware of the distinction, the context should indicate which is meant.

Definition A2.9. *For $\{x^i\}$ a sequence in R^k, the point $x \in R^k$ is an **accumulation point** of the sequence if for every $\epsilon > 0$ and for every positive integer I, there is some $i \geq I$ such that $\|x^i - x\| \leq \epsilon$.*

In words, the sequence has x as an accumulation point if arbitrarily late in the sequence, we get arbitrarily close to the point, even if we don't stay close forever after. That is, we return to every neighborhood of x over and over again, but we might leave that neighborhood repeatedly as well.

Definition A2.10. *For a sequence $\{x^i\}$, a **subsequence** of this sequence is a sequence $\{y^i\}$ where $y^i = x^{n_i}$ for some infinite increasing sequence of integers $\{n_1, n_2, \ldots\}$.*

If the definition confuses you, two simple examples should clarify matters: For a given sequence $\{x^i\}$, two subsequences are $\{x^2, x^4, x^6, \ldots\}$ and $\{x^1, x^{10}, x^{100}, x^{1000}, \ldots\}$. The point of this new terminology is to recast the definition of an accumulation point: x is an accumulation point of $\{x^i\}$ if and only if there is some subsequence $\{x^{n_i}\}$ of $\{x^i\}$ that has x as its limit. (For more finger exercises, prove that these two definitions are equivalent.)

Proposition A2.8 is generalized in two steps. First, x is an *accumulation point of the set $X \subseteq R^K$* if there is some sequence $\{x^i\}$, where $x^i \in X$ for all i, such that x is an accumulation point of $\{x^i\}$. (In view of the previous paragraph, this in turn is equivalent to requiring that x is the limit of $\{x^i\}$, for some (possibly different) sequence drawn from X.) And then: A set $X \subseteq R^k$ is closed if and only if it contains all its accumulation points.

In fact, if we take any set X—open, closed, or neither—and we add to X all of the accumulation points of X, we get the closure of the set X. (Another exercise: Definition A2.5 says that the closure of a set X is the smallest closed set containing X, the intersection of all closed sets containing X. Prove that an equivalent characterization of the closure of X is X and all its accumulation points.)

A2.4. Boundedness, (Completeness), and Compactness

Consider the sequences $\{10, 20, 30, \ldots\}$ and $\{1.1, 2.1, 1.01, 2.01, 1.001, 2.001, \ldots\}$. The second has accumulation points 1 and 2, while the first has no accumulation points at all. The first has no accumulation points, apparently, because the numbers "blow up." In fact, this is the only way a sequence from R^k could fail to have an accumulation point.

Definition A2.11. *A subset X of R^k is **bounded** if there exists some $M \geq 0$ such that $\|x\| \leq M$ for all $x \in X$. Equivalently, the set is bounded if there is some $M' \geq 0$ such that, for all $x = (x_1, \ldots, x_k) \in X$, $|x_i| \leq M'$.*

Proposition A2.12. *Every bounded sequence has at least one accumulation point.*

(A sequence is *bounded* if the set of its points is a bounded set; that is, if for some large-enough scalar M, $\|x^i\| \leq M$ for all i.) Proposition A2.12 depends on very basic and deep properties of the real numbers connected to their construction and, in particular, to the property of *completeness*, which is defined in two steps:

1. A sequence $\{x^n\}$ from R^k is called a *Cauchy sequence* if for every $\epsilon > 0$, there exists an N such that $\|x^n - x^m\| \leq \epsilon$ for all n and m, both $\geq N$.
2. The space R^k is complete, meaning that every Cauchy sequence $\{x^n\}$ from R^k has a limit in R^k.

If you are feeling very adventurous mathematically, prove Proposition A2.12 under the assumption that R^k is complete.

Definition A2.13. *A subset X of R^k is* ***compact*** *if it is closed and bounded.*

Corollary A2.14 to Propositions A2.8 and A2.12. *If $\{x^n\}$ is a sequence drawn from a compact set X, then $\{x^n\}$ has one or more accumulation points, all of which lie in X.*

I won't bother making it a formal proposition or corollary, but please note that every finite subset of R^k is compact. (If this is new to you, prove it.)

In most math books you encounter, A2.13 is not the definition of compactness. Instead, the definition runs: A set X is compact if it has the property that every open cover of X—a collection of open sets $\{Z_\gamma; \gamma \in \Gamma\}$ such that X lies within the union of the Z_γ—admits a finite subcover, or X is a subset of the union of finitely many of the Z_γ. The Heine-Borel Theorem shows that for Euclidean spaces (among others), this is equivalent to so-called sequential compactness, which is essentially the conclusion of the corollary, and then the definition given here (A2.13) is shown to be an equivalent definition to the more primitive definitions. But in terms of workaday economic theory, the characterization given in Definition A2.13 is most often used to verify that a set is compact, with the conclusion of the corollary the normal harvest, a harvest that is then turned into any number of other results. In this regard, it may be worth cross-referencing the answer to Problem 1.12 given in the *Student's Guide*, which uses the first and usually most primitive definition of compactness to show directly, without recourse to Debreu's Theorem, that for continuous preferences, $c_{\succeq}(A)$ is nonempty for nonempty and compact sets A.

A2.5. Continuous Functions

Definition A2.15. *For $X \subseteq R^k$ and a function $f : X \to R^j$, f is* ***continuous at the point*** *$x \in X$ if for every $\epsilon > 0$ there exists $\delta > 0$ such that $\|y - x\| \leq \delta$ for $y \in X$ implies $\|f(y) - f(x)\| \leq \epsilon$. The function is* ***continuous on*** *X if it is continuous for each $x \in X$.*

Whenever we say "the function f is continuous," we always mean, f is continuous on its entire domain of definition. The picture is just what you expect from calculus—if you change the argument of the function by a little bit, you change the value of the function by a little bit as well.[5]

[5] The "rate" at which changes in the argument translate into changes in value can be quite different from one point x to another. It is a bit more than we will need, but: a function is *uniformly continuous* when for every ϵ there is a single δ, independent of the base point x; f is *Lipschitz continuous* at x

Proposition A2.15.

a. *f is continuous at x if and only if, for every sequence $\{x^i\}$ from X such that $\lim x^i = x$, $\lim f(x^i) = f(x)$.*

b. *f is continuous if and only if, for every open subset O of R^j, the set $\{x \in X : f(x) \in O\}$ is relatively open in X, if and only if, for every closed subset C of R^j, the set $\{x \in X : f(x) \in C\}$ is relatively closed in X.*

Proposition A2.16.

a. *If f and g are continuous functions from X to R^j (for $X \subseteq R^k$), then $f + g$ is as well, where $f + g$ is shorthand for the function whose value at $x \in X$ is $f(x) + g(x)$.*

b. *If f and g are continuous functions from R^k to R, then fg is as well, where fg is shorthand for the function whose value at x is $f(x)g(x)$.*

c. *If f and g are continuous functions from X to R and $g(x_0) \neq 0$ for $x_0 \in X$, then f/g (shorthand for the function whose value at x is $f(x)/g(x)$) is continuous at x_0.*

d. *If f is a continuous function from $X \to R^j$, and if g is a continuous function from $R^j \to R^\ell$, then $g \circ f$ is a continuous function from X to R^ℓ, where $g \circ f$ is shorthand for the function whose value at $x \in X$ is $g(f(x))$.*

A2.6. Simply Connected Sets and the Intermediate-Value Theorem

Definition A2.17. *The set $X \subseteq R^k$ is* ***simply connected*** *if for every pair of points x and y from X, a continuous path from x to y lies entirely in X. More formally, X is simply connected if, for each x and y, there is a continuous function $\phi : [0,1] \to R^k$ such that $\phi(0) = x$, $\phi(1) = y$, and $\phi(t) \in X$ for all $t \in [0,1]$.*

Proposition A2.18 (The Intermediate-Value Theorem). *If f is a continuous function from X to R, for some simply connected $X \subseteq R^k$, then for all pairs x and y from X such that $f(x) \leq f(y)$ and real numbers r such that $f(x) \leq r \leq f(y)$, there is some $z \in X$ with $f(z) = r$.*

A2.7. Suprema and Infima; Maxes and Mins

Definition A2.19.

a. *A set $X \subseteq R^k$ is bounded above if there is some $\overline{x} \in R^k$ such that $\overline{x} \geq x$ for all $x \in X$. X is unbounded above if it is not bounded above. Similar terms and definitions are used for (un)bounded below.*

b. *For any set $X \subseteq R$ that is bounded above, the* ***supremum of*** *X, denoted $\sup X$, is the smallest $z \in R$ such that $z \geq x$ for every $x \in X$. If X is unbounded above, we write $\sup X = \infty$.*

---

if there exists some $K > 0$ such that for every $\epsilon > 0$, $\delta = K\epsilon$ "works"; and it is *uniformly Lipschitz continuous* on X if K can be picked independently of x.

c. *For any set $X \subseteq R$ that is bounded below, the* ***infimum of*** X*, denoted inf* X*, is the largest number $z \in R$ such that $z \le x$ for every $x \in X$. If the set X is unbounded below, we write inf $X = -\infty$.*

d. *For a set $X \subseteq R$, when sup $X \in X$, we write max X for this value, calling this* ***the maximum in*** *(or* ***of****)* X*. When sup$X \notin X$, we say that* ***the maximum in*** X ***does not exist****. Similarly, when inf $X \in X$, we write min X for this value, calling it* ***the minimum in*** *(or* ***of****)* X*.*

Part b of the definition implicitly assumes that any bounded-above set of real numbers has a finite supremum; part c makes a similar assumption about bounded-below sets and their infima. These things are true and are part of the deep structure of the real numbers, connected (as with Cauchy sequences) to the fact that the real numbers are complete. Although it will cause mathematicians to wince (because it is stating as a proposition something that is really an axiom of the real numbers), I state this result in the form of a proposition.

Proposition A2.20.

a. *If X is a nonempty subset of R, then inf$X \le$ sup$X$.*

b. *Every nonempty subset $X \subseteq R$ that is bounded above has a finite supremum and every subset $X \subseteq R$ that is bounded below has a finite infimum.*

c. *Every nonempty compact subset of R has a maximum and a minimum.*

Note in this proposition that X is assumed to be nonempty. We will encounter constructions in which the supremum and/or infimum of a set in R is taken, where the set (in some cases) is empty. It is conventional to regard the infimum of the empty set as ∞ and the supremum of the empty set as $-\infty$. In several propositions to follow, you'll find the formulation "for every nonempty and compact set X." In most cases that you find this formulation, the "nonempty" part is there to guard against suprema that are (1) $-\infty$ and (2) therefore, not in X.

A2.8. The Maximum of a Continuous Function on a Compact Set

Proposition A2.21. *Suppose $f : X \to R$ is continuous for some compact and nonempty $X \subseteq R^k$. Then sup$\{f(x) : x \in X\}$ is finite and, for some $x_0 \in X$, $f(x_0)$ equals this supremum. In short, max$_{x\in X} f(x)$ exists; said differently, every continuous function f achieves its maximum over any compact nonempty domain X.*[6]

This result is, in many ways, the climax of this appendix, and it is the reason we work so hard in Chapter 2 to ensure that preferences can be represented by a continuous utility function. Because it is the climax, I give two proofs, the second of which is very slick but requires a bit more mathematical sophistication.

[6] Since we have defined the maximum of a set, we ought to write the maximum of $f(x)$ as x ranges over X as $\max\{f(x) : x \in X\}$. The typographic construction $\max_{x\in X} f(x)$ is shorthand for this.

Proof 1. If $\{f(x) : x \in X\}$ is unbounded above, there exists $x^i \in X$ such that $f(x^i) > i$ for $i = 1, 2, \ldots$. Because X is compact, the sequence $\{x^i\}$ has an accumulation point $x^* \in X$; that is, along some subsequence $\{x^{i_n}\}$ of the sequence $\{x^i\}$, $\lim_n x^{i_n} = x^*$. By the continuity of f, $\lim f(x^{i_n}) = f(x^*)$; the right-hand side is finite while the left-hand side is infinity by construction, a contradiction. So $\{f(x) : x \in X\}$ is bounded above. Let $f^* = \sup_{x \in X} f(x)$. Since f^* is the smallest number greater than $f(x)$ for all $x \in X$, for each $i = 1, 2, \ldots$ there is some $x^i \in X$ with $f(x^i) + 1/i > f^*$. Use compactness again to show that, along some subsequence, $\lim_n x^{i_n} = x^*$, and thus $\lim_n f(x^{i_n}) = f(x^*) \leq f^*$. But if $f(x^*) < f^*$, we contradict $f(x^{i_n}) > f^* - 1/i_n$ for all n. Thus $f(x^*) = f^*$. ∎

Proof 2. For each x, define $W(x) = \{z \in X : f(z) < f(x)\}$. By continuity of f, each $W(x)$ is relatively open in X, and hence is the intersection of some open set $W'(x)$ and X. Now suppose that f does not attain its supremum on the set X, for some compact set X. This means that for each $x \in X$, $f(x) < f(y)$ for some other $y \in X$, and hence $x \in W'(y)$. This in turn implies that X is contained in the union of the $W'(y)$ as y ranges over all of X; that is, $\{W'(y) : y \in X\}$ is an open cover of X. Since X is compact, this open cover has a finite subcover: for some finite set $\{y_1, y_2, \ldots, y_n\}$, $X \subseteq \cup_{i=1}^n W'(y_n)$. The set of real numbers $\{f(y_1), \ldots, f(y_n)\}$ has a maximum; suppose it is $f(y_{i^*})$. Then $f(y_{i^*}) \geq f(y_i)$ for all the i; hence $y_{i^*} \notin W'(y_i)$ for any i, which contradicts the statement that the $\{W'(y_i)\}$ cover X. ∎

A2.9. Lims Sup and Inf

Definition A.22. *For a sequence $\{x^i\}$ from R, **lim sup**$_i\, x^i = \lim_{i\to\infty} \sup_{n\geq i}\{x^n\}$, and **lim inf**$_i\, x^i = \lim_{i\to\infty} \inf_{n\geq i}\{x^n\}$.*

To explain, given a sequence of numbers $\{x^i\}$, for each i you find the supremum of the set $\{x^i, x^{i+1}, x^{i+2}, \ldots\}$, and then take the limit of those suprema, to find the limit supremum (or lim sup) of the sequence. Note that $\sup\{x^i, x^{i+1}, x^{i+2}, \ldots\} \geq \sup\{x^{i+1}, x^{i+2}, x^{i+3}, \ldots\}$; that is, the sequence of suprema is a nonincreasing sequence of numbers. Therefore, the limit of these suprema exists (see the caveats immediately following); the lim sup and lim inf of any sequence are always well defined. There are two caveats for the lim sup and two for the lim inf: If $\{x^n\}$ is unbounded above, then each supremum is ∞, thus the lim sup of the sequence is ∞. And if the sequence has limit $-\infty$—if for each integer N, $x^i < -N$ for all $i > N'$, for some N'—then the lim sup is $-\infty$. Similar caveats hold for the lim inf.

An equivalent characterization of the lim sup of a sequence is, Given the sequence $\{x^n\}$, let $\text{Acc}\{x^n\}$ be the set of accumulation points of the sequence. Then lim sup x^n is the maximum of the set $\text{Acc}\{x^n\}$ (and lim inf x^n is the minimum of this set). Implicit in this statement is the assertion that $\text{Acc}\{x^n\}$ contains its supremum and infimum, but this can be proved. (It makes a nice exercise.)

Proposition A2.23. *For a given sequence of real numbers $\{x^i\}$, $\lim_i x^i$ exists if and only* *if lim* $\sup_i x^i = \liminf_i x^i$*, in which case* $\lim_i x^i = \limsup_i x^i = \liminf_i x^i$.

A2.10. Upper and Lower Semi-continuous Functions

Definition A2.24. *A function* $f : X \to R$*, where* $X \subseteq R^k$*, is* ***upper semi-continuous*** *at* $x \in X$ *if for every* $\epsilon > 0$ *there exists a* $\delta > 0$ *such that for all* $y \in X$ *with* $\|y - x\| < \delta$*,* $f(x) \geq f(y) - \epsilon$*. The function is* ***lower semi-continuous*** *at* $x \in X$ *if for every* $\epsilon > 0$ *there exists a* $\delta > 0$ *such that for all* $y \in X$ *with* $\|y - x\| < \delta$*,* $f(x) \leq f(y) + \epsilon$*. The function is upper semi-continuous on* X *if it upper semi-continuous at every* $x \in X$*, and similarly for lower semi-continuity.*

Proposition A2.25. *A function* $f : X \to R$ *(for* $X \subseteq R^k$ *for some* k*) is upper semi-continuous at* $x \in X$ *if and only if* $f(x) \geq \limsup_i f(x^i)$ *for every sequence* $\{x^i\}$ *drawn from* X *with limit* x*. It is lower semi-continuous at* x *if and only if* $f(x) \leq \liminf_i f(x^i)$ *for all such sequences.*

Proposition A2.26. *If* $f : X \to R$ *is upper semi-continuous and* X *is nonempty and compact, then* f *attains its maximum over* X*. That is,* $f(x^0) = \sup_{x \in X} f(x)$ *for some* $x^0 \in X$*.*

Therefore, as long as we produce an upper semi-continuous utility function, we know utility maximization leads to a choice on every (nonempty) compact set of alternatives.

In case you feel fairly comfortable reading all this and want to give yourself a final diagnostic, see if you can prove the following: Let $X_1, X_2, \ldots$ be a countable collection of closed subsets of R^k, and let $a_1, a_2, \ldots$ be a sequence of strictly positive numbers such that $\sum_n a_n < \infty$. For each $x \in X$, define

$$U(x) = \sum_{\{n=1,2,\ldots\,:\, x \in X_n\}} a_n.$$

Then U is an upper semi-continuous function. (What is the connection between this and Chapter 1?)

Appendix Three

Convexity

Notions of convexity—both convexity of sets and of functions—play an extraordinarily important role in microeconomic theory.

As in Appendix 2, the setting is finite-dimensional Euclidean space, R^k. All the functions we consider are from subsets (nearly always convex subsets) X of R^k to the real line R. A crucial notion, which does not rate a formal definition, is a *convex combination* of two points: If x and y are from R^k and a is a scalar (a real number) between 0 and 1, the point $ax + (1 - a)y$ is a convex combination of x and y. The set of all such points, fixing x and y and allowing a to vary from 0 to 1, is the set of convex combinations of x and y. Geometrically, this is the line segment that joins x and y. Strict convex combinations are points $ax + (1 - a)y$ for $a \in (0, 1)$, the open interval from 0 to 1, as long as $x \neq y$; geometrically this is the line segment less its endpoints.

A3.1. Convex Sets

Definition A3.1. *A set $X \subseteq R^k$ is* **convex** *if, for every pair of points x and y from X and $a \in [0, 1]$, $ax + (1 - a)y \in X$. In words, every convex combination of every pair of points from X is in X.*

This rules out sets with holes, sets with borders that "bend in," and sets that are composed of several unconnected pieces. In Figure A3.1a, I draw a typical convex set, while the sets in A3.1b, c, and d illustrate three ways convexity can fail.

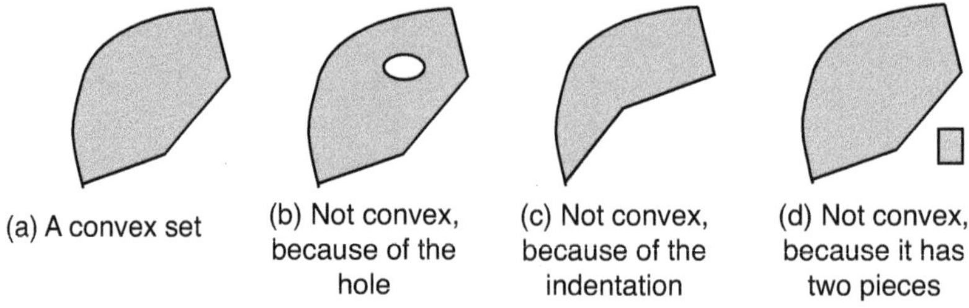

(a) A convex set
(b) Not convex, because of the hole
(c) Not convex, because of the indentation
(d) Not convex, because it has two pieces

Figure A3.1. Convex and nonconvex sets

By a strict reading of the definition (or, if you prefer, by convention), the empty set is a convex set.

It is perhaps overly pedantic, but let me state as a formal proposition the following:

Proposition A3.2. *If X is a convex set, $\{\alpha^\ell; \ell = 1, \ldots, n\}$ is a set of n nonnegative scalars such that $\sum_{\ell=1}^n \alpha^\ell = 1$, and $\{x^\ell; \ell = 1, \ldots, n\}$ are n points selected from X, then $\sum_{\ell=1}^n \alpha^\ell x^\ell$ is also an element of X.*

In words, convex combinations of finitely many elements from X are in X, if X is a convex set. This is proven by a standard induction argument from the definition of convexity (where $n = 2$), inducting on the number n. Another completely straightforward result is:

Proposition A3.3. *The intersection of any number of convex sets is convex.*

In Appendix 2, we discussed the notion of the closure of any set, the smallest closed set containing the original set. In similar fashion, we have:

Definition A3.4. *The* ***convex hull*** *of a set $X \subseteq R^k$, denoted CH(X) is the smallest convex set containing X. The* ***closed convex hull*** *of a set $X \subseteq R^k$, denoted $\overline{\text{CH}}(X)$ is the smallest closed-and-convex set containing X.*

Propositions A3.3 and A2.4 together guarantee the existence of CH(X) and $\overline{\text{CH}}(X)$ for any X: As in the definition of the closure, we simply take the intersection of all convex or closed-and-convex sets that contain X, noting that R^k is one such.

We have defined CH(X) as the smallest convex set containing X or, equivalently, as the intersection of all convex sets that contain X. But there is another way to characterize CH(X).

Proposition A3.4. *For any set X,*

$$\begin{aligned}\text{CH}(X) =\{y \in R^k : y = \sum_{\ell=1}^n \alpha^\ell x^\ell, \textit{where } x^\ell \in X \textit{ and}\\ \alpha^\ell \in [0,1], \ell = 1, \ldots, n, \textit{and } \alpha^1 + \ldots \alpha^n = 1\}.\end{aligned}$$

In words, the convex hull of X consists of all points that can be written as finite convex combinations of points in X.

Proof. As an instant corollary of Proposition A3.2, we know that for any convex set Y that contains X, every finite convex combination of elements contained in X is an element of Y. So the set on the right-hand side of the equation in the proposition is certainly in the intersection of all convex sets containing X; that is, it is a subset of CH(X). But it is easy to see that the set on the right-hand side is itself a convex set: The convex combination of any two (finite) convex combinations of members of X is itself a convex combination of members of X. Hence the set on the right-hand side of the equation is a convex set containing X, and as CH(X) is the intersection of all such sets, it contains CH(X). ∎

Carathéodory's Theorem

The following extension of Proposition A3.4 is quite useful.

Proposition A3.5 (Carathéodory's Theorem). *If $X \subseteq R^k$, any point in* CH(X) *can be written as a convex combination of* **no more than** $k+1$ *elements of* X.

A mental picture is easy to construct for $k = 2$. Take any number of points scattered in the plane. Their convex hull forms a convex polygon. Think of labeling the vertices (moving clockwise, say, around the polygon) as $v_0, v_1, \ldots, v_n$. Now picture the triangles formed by v_0, v_1, and v_2; by v_0, v_2, and v_3; by v_0, v_3, and v_4, and so forth. We take v_0 and each pair of (other) adjacent vertices. These triangles cover the polygon; each point in the polygon, being in one of the triangles, can be written as a convex combination of the vertices of "its" triangle. That, for $k = 2$, is the content of Carathéodory's Theorem.

Proof. Fix a set X and a point $y \in \text{CH}(X)$. By Proposition A3.4, we know that y can be written as a (finite) convex combination of points in X. It may take 100 points from X, or 1000, but some number n of points from X suffices. Therefore, there is some *least* number of points from X that suffices. That is, there is some n such that y can be written as a convex combination of n points from X but not as a convex combination of fewer than n.

Fix n and fix one of the convex-combination representations of y,

$$y = \sum_{i=1}^{n} \alpha^i x^i,$$

where the α^i are all strictly greater than zero (or else we could reduce n), less or equal to one, and sum to one, and the x^i are elements of X.

Suppose that $n > k+1$. The set of vectors $x^\ell - x^1$ for $\ell = 2, \ldots, n$ is a set of at least $k+1$ vectors in R^k, so it is a linearly dependent set; we can find scalars γ^ℓ, $\ell = 2, \ldots, n$, not all zero, such that

$$\sum_{\ell=2}^{n} \gamma^\ell (x^\ell - x^1) = 0.$$

Define $\gamma^1 = -\sum_{\ell=2}^{n} \gamma^\ell$ and this can be rewritten

$$\sum_{\ell=1}^{n} \gamma^\ell x^\ell = 0,$$

where $\sum_{\ell=1}^{n} \gamma^\ell = 0$. Since the γ^ℓ sum to zero and they are not all zero, at least one is strictly positive. But now

$$y = \sum_{\ell=1}^{n} \alpha^\ell x^\ell - \lambda \sum_{\ell=1}^{n} \gamma^\ell x^\ell,$$

for any $\lambda > 0$, because the second summation is zero. Rewrite this as

$$y = \sum_{\ell=1}^{n} (\alpha^\ell - \lambda\gamma^\ell)x^\ell.$$

And now, increase λ, starting from zero. At $\lambda = 0$, the coefficients are all strictly positive and sum to one, and as you increase λ, the coefficients still sum to one (since the γ^ℓ sum to zero). As λ increases, some of the coefficients increase (when $\gamma^\ell < 0$) and some decrease, but since at least one γ^ℓ is strictly positive, there is a minimum value of λ where some $\alpha^\ell - \lambda\gamma^\ell$ hits zero. For that value of λ, we have written y as a convex combination of $n-1$ of the x^ℓs (or fewer, if two or more $\alpha^\ell - \lambda\gamma^\ell$ hit zero simultaneously), contradicting the minimality of n.

Hence every $y \in \text{CH}(X)$ can be written as a convex combination of no more than $k+1$ of the members of X, which is the result sought. ∎

Convexity and closedness combined

We put Carathéodory's Theorem to work to prove the following result.

Proposition A3.6. *If $X \subseteq R^k$ is a compact set, then* CH(X) *is compact.*

Proof. The boundedness of CH(X) is easy: The characterization of CH(X) given in Proposition A3.4 shows that any bounding set for X effectively bounds CH(X). (You need to work out how a uniform bound on, say, the norm of elements of a set bounds the norm of convex combinations of elements of that set.) To show that CH(X) is closed, we use Carathéodory: Suppose $\{x^n\}$ is a sequence of points in CH(X) with limit x. Each x^n can be written as a convex combination of no more than $k+1$ elements out of X. Let me write this as

$$x^n = \alpha^{n,1}x^{n,1} + \ldots \alpha^{n,k+1}x^{n,k+1}.$$

Since X is compact (and so is the unit interval, from which all the scalars are drawn), we can extract a subsequence along which $\alpha^{n,\ell} \to \alpha^{*,\ell} \in [0,1]$ and $x^{n,\ell} \to x^{*,\ell} \in X$ for $\ell = 1, \ldots, k+1$, and then

$$x = \lim x^n = \alpha^{*,1}x^{*,\ell} + \ldots \alpha^{*,k+1}x^{*,k+1}.$$

Of course, as we pass to the limit, $\sum_{\ell=1}^{k+1} \alpha^{*,\ell} = 1$, so we conclude that x is indeed in CH(X). ∎

In this proof, the argument that the convex hull of a bounded set is bounded doesn't require that the set is closed. But the argument that the convex hull is closed relied on the compactness of the set X, to extract those convergent subsequences. It is *not* true, in general, that the convex hull of a closed (and unbounded) set is closed. For example, consider the set $\{x = (x_1, x_2) \in R^2 : x_1 \neq 0, x_2 \geq 1/|x_1|\}$. Draw the picture if you don't see this in your mind's eye; we have two hyperbolae, one in the positive orthant and the other in the quadrant where $x_1 < 0$ and $x_2 > 0$. This is indeed a closed set. But its convex hull is the set $\{x = (x_1, x_2) \in R^2 : x_2 > 0\}$, which is not closed.

This means that in constructing $\overline{\text{CH}}(X)$, it doesn't work (always) to take the convex hull of the closure of X. For X as in the example just given, $\overline{\text{CH}}(X)$ is the set of points where $x_2 \geq 0$, whereas the convex hull of the closure of X omits the x-axis. However:

Proposition A3.7. *The closure of a convex set X is convex. Hence, the closure of* CH(X) *is* $\overline{\text{CH}}(X)$.

Proof. Suppose X is convex. Suppose x and y are in the closure of X. That is, $x = \lim_n x^n$ and $y = \lim y^n$ for some sequences $\{x^n\}$ and $\{y^n\}$ from X. Take any $\alpha \in [0, 1]$: For each n, $z^n = \alpha x^n + (1 - \alpha)y^n \in X$, because X is convex and, passing to the limit, we see that $\lim z^n = \lim_n (\alpha x^n + (1 - \alpha)y^n) = \alpha x + (1 - \alpha)y$ is in the closure of X. The closure of X is indeed convex.

Since CH(X) is the intersection of all convex sets containing X, CH(X) is in any convex set that contains X; hence it is in the intersection of all closed and convex sets that contain X. That is, CH(X) $\subseteq \overline{\text{CH}}(X)$. Since $\overline{\text{CH}}(X)$ is a closed set, it is one of the sets whose intersection forms the closure of CH(x), and hence $\overline{\text{CH}}(X)$ contains the closure of CH(x). But the closure of CH(X) is closed (of course) and convex (by the first part of this proposition), so the closure of CH(X) is one of the sets over which an intersection is taken, to form $\overline{\text{CH}}(X)$. That is $\overline{\text{CH}}(x)$ is a subset of the closure of CH(X). The two halves of this paragraph together show that $\overline{\text{CH}}(X)$ is the closure of CH(X). ∎

If mixing together convex hulls and closures makes your head spin, just wait for Chapter 9, where another layer of complication is added.

Extreme points and the Krein-Milman Theorem

Definition A3.8. *For a set X, $x \in X$ is an* ***extreme point*** *of X if x cannot be written as the convex combination of some other points from X.*

Theorem A3.9 (The Krein-Milman Theorem). *A compact and convex set X is the convex hull of its extreme points.*

Krein-Milman holds, in fact, for well-behaved, infinite-dimensional spaces. Its proof requires the heavy machinery of the axiom of choice, so I won't give a proof. (See, for instance, Royden, *Real Analysis*, 1968)

While I will not give the proof, I do want to point out a corollary to the combination of Carathéodory and Krein-Milman. Suppose $X \subseteq R^k$ is compact. Then CH(X) is compact (Proposition A3.6) and convex, so every point can be written as a convex combination of its extreme points. But it is easy to see that no point in CH(X) that is not in X is an extreme point, so we can amend this to read: Every point in CH(X) can be written as a convex combination of the extreme points of X. That is, if X is compact, CH(X) is the convex hull of the extreme points of X. And then Carathéodory tells us: *If X is compact, every point in* CH(X) *can be written as a convex combination of no more than $k+1$* ***extreme*** *points in X.*

A3.2. The Separating- and Supporting-Hyperplane Theorems

The Separating- and Supporting-Hyperplane Theorems are some of the most important mathematical hammers in microeconomic theory. The term *hyperplane* may need a definition: We are working in R^k, and a hyperplane in R^k is, for $a \in R^k$, $a \neq 0$, and a scalar b, the set of points $\{x \in R^k : a \cdot x = b\}$. In words, it is almost a subspace of dimension $k-1$, where I say "almost" because it is translated away from the origin by the scalar term b.

Proposition A3.10 (The Separating-Hyperplane Theorem). *Suppose X and Y are two disjoint and nonempty*[1] *convex subsets of R^k; that is, $X \cap Y = \emptyset$. Then there exist a nonzero vector $a \in R^k$ and a scalar $b \in R$ such that*

$$a \cdot x \geq b \text{ for all } x \in X, \quad \text{and} \quad a \cdot y \leq b \text{ for all } y \in Y.$$

We could equivalently have written the consequent as *There exist a (nonzero) linear function $\phi : R^k \to R$ and a constant b such that $\phi(x) \geq b$ for all $x \in X$ and $\phi(y) \leq b$ for all $y \in Y$.* Or, also equivalently, *There exists a (nonzero) affine function $\phi : R^k \to R$ such that $\phi(x) \geq 0$ for all $x \in X$ and $\phi(y) \leq 0$ for all $y \in Y$.*[2] (We mention these alternatives, because sometimes you will see the Separating-Hyperplane Theorem written these ways.)[3]

I will not prove this result (or the two variations to follow). But I briefly discuss proofs after stating all three.

For $k = 2$, hyperplanes are straight lines, and then Figure A3.2 captures what is going on.

Proposition A3.10 is squishy on one point. The theorem only guarantees the weak inequalities $a \cdot x \geq b$ for $x \in X$ and $a \cdot y \leq b$ for $y \in Y$. The sets X and Y can both intersect the hyperplane. Indeed, in special cases both sets could lie entirely within the same "separating" hyperplane. We'd like to do better, sharpening the result so that $a \cdot x > b$ for all $x \in X$ and $a \cdot y < b$ for all $y \in Y$.

---

[1] As in Appendix 2, we have a qualifier about sets being nonempty. In this case, we are guarding against the possibility that $X = R^k$ and $Y = \emptyset$.

[2] A function $\phi : R^k \to R$ is *linear* if it satisfies $\phi(x+y) = \phi(x) + \phi(y)$. As you doubtless know from linear algebra, in R^k, every linear function has the form $\phi(x) = a \cdot x$ for some $a \in R^k$. A function is *affine* if it has the form $a \cdot x + b$, for $a \in R^k$ and $b \in R$.

[3] Indeed, if you ever see this generalized to infinite-dimensional spaces, the version that concerns *linear functions* is the most often observed form, and there will be some concern over whether the linear function in question can be assumed to be continuous. In this context, the Separating-Hyperplane Theorem is typically derived as a corollary to the Hahn-Banach Theorem.

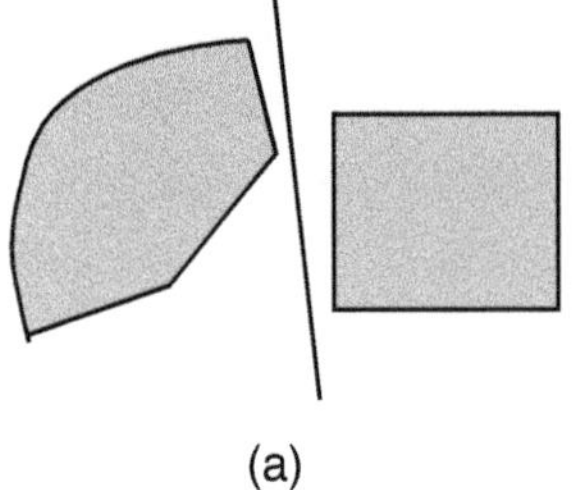

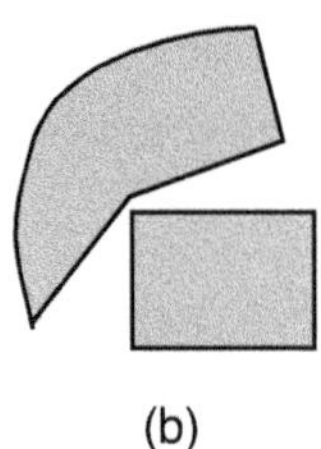

Figure A3.2. Separating hyperplanes. In panel a, the two disjoint convex sets are separated by a hyperplane. In panel b, the two sets are disjoint, but one is not convex, and there is no hyperplane that will separate them.

This may not be possible: For general convex disjoint sets X and Y, it may be necessary that both inequalities are allowed to be weak. Suppose, for example, that $k = 2$, $X = \{(x_1, x_2) : x_1 < 0 \text{ or } x_1 = 0 \text{ and } x_2 \geq 0\}$, and let Y be the complement of X. (Draw the picture, if this isn't clear to you.) And even if the sets are both closed, it may be necessary that at least one of the inequalities is weak. For instance, let $k = 2$, $X = \{(x_1, x_2) : x_1 \leq 0\}$, and $Y = \{(x_1, x_2) : x_2 \geq 1/x_1, x_1 > 0\}$.) However:

Proposition A3.11 (The Strict-Separation Theorem). *Suppose X and Y are closed, nonempty, and disjoint convex subsets of R^k. If either X or Y is compact, then we can find a nonzero vector $a \in R^k$ and a scalar b such that $a \cdot x > b$ for all $x \in X$ and $a \cdot y < b$ for all $y \in Y$.*

For a third variation, we need a definition.

Definition A3.12. *A point $x \in R^k$ is a* ***boundary point*** *of $X \subseteq R^k$ if x is in both the closure of X and the closure of the complement of X.*

Note that we do not require that x is an element of X. An alternative definition would be that x is a boundary point of X if we can find sequences $\{x^i\}$ and $\{y^i\}$, where $x^i \in X$ and $y^i \notin X$ for all i, such that both sequences have x as limit. Of course, the trivial sequence $x, x, \ldots$ serves as either the first or the second of these, depending on whether or not $x \in X$.

Proposition A3.13 (The Supporting-Hyperplane Theorem). *Suppose X is a convex subset of R^k and x^0 is a boundary point of X. Then there exist nonzero $a \in R^k$ and $b \in R$ such that $a \cdot x^0 = b$ and $a \cdot x \leq b$ for all $x \in X$.*

This is called the Supporting-Hyperplane Theorem because of pictures such as Figure A3.3: The hyperplane through x^0 "supports" (roughly, is tangent to) X at x^0.

We do not provide proofs of any of these results, but a few remarks about proofs may be helpful.

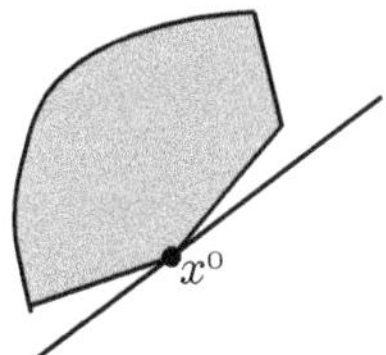

Figure A3.3. A supporting hyperplane. The point x^0, on the boundary of the convex set, is supported by the hyperplane shown.

1. Separating one convex set from another is really no harder than separating a convex set that doesn't contain the origin from the origin with a linear function; if X and Y are disjoint convex sets that we wish to separate, we can recast the problem as requiring the separation of 0 from the set $X - Y := \{z \in R^k : z = x - y, x \in X, y \in Y\}$. For if $a \in R^k$ is such that $a \cdot z \geq 0$ for all $z \in X - Y$, then $\inf_{x \in X} a \cdot x$ must be greater or equal to $\sup_{y \in Y} a \cdot y$.

2. Moreover, if X and Y are both closed, and one is compact, it is not hard to show that $X - Y$ is closed, so strict separation comes down to strict separation of the origin from a closed convex set Z that doesn't contain the origin. Put a ball of radius ϵ around the origin, where ϵ is chosen so that the ball doesn't intersect Z. Such balls are convex (why?), so apply the Separating-Hyperplane Theorem to the ball and Z.

3. And in the Supporting-Hyperplane Theorem, two cases need to be considered. If $x \notin X$, then this involves separating x from X; it is immediate from the Separating-Hyperplane Theorem. While if $x \in X$, we separate X from each in a sequence of points that approaches x from outside of X and pass to a limit along a subsequence.

A3.3. The Support-Function Theorem

A hyperplane $\{x \in R^k : a \cdot x = b\}$ defines two closed half-spaces, $\{x \in R^k : a \cdot x \geq b\}$ and $\{x \in R^k : a \cdot x \leq b\}$. The Strict-Separation Theorem then tells us the following.

Proposition A3.14. *Every closed and convex set X except for R^k itself consists of the intersection of all the closed half-spaces that contain it.*

Proof. Fix X. If $X \neq R^k$, some point y^0 lies in $R^k \setminus X$. The Strict-Separation Theorem tells us that there is some $a \in R^k$ and b such that $a \cdot x > b$ for all $x \in X$ and $a \cdot y^0 < b$. Therefore, at least one closed half-space contains X. Of course, the intersection of all closed half-spaces that contain X contains X. And if y is not in X, the Strict-Separation Theorem can be used once again to find a closed half-space that contains X but not y. So the intersection of all the closed half-spaces containing X contains no point not in X. (The proposition is true for the case of

$X = \emptyset$, but the proof just given doesn't quite work. Why not? And can you create a special argument for this special case?) ∎

Since the intersection of closed and convex sets is closed and convex, this provides us with another characterization of a closed and convex set (albeit not one that is useful): A set in R^k is closed and convex if and only if it is R^k itself or is the intersection of a collection of closed half-spaces. Also, this tells us that for any set X, $\overline{\text{CH}}(X)$ is either R^k or the intersection of all the closed half-spaces that contain X. (If it is not R^k, $\overline{\text{CH}}(X)$ is the intersection of all the closed half-spaces that contain $\overline{\text{CH}}(X)$, but each of these perforce also contains X. And no closed half-space that contains X omits any point from $\overline{\text{CH}}(X)$, since a closed half-space is closed and convex, and $\overline{\text{CH}}(X)$ is the intersection of all closed and convex sets containing X.)

One way to restate Proposition A3.14 begins with the following definition. For each closed and convex set X and for each $a \in R^k$, define

$$\phi_X(a) := \sup\{a \cdot x : x \in X\},$$

where we define $\phi_X(a) = \infty$ if $\sup_{x \in X} a \cdot x$ is infinite.[4] I claim that

$$\phi_X(a) = \inf\{b \in R : a \cdot x \leq b \text{ for all } x \in X\},$$

where the infimum equals ∞ if the set of such b's is empty. To show that these two are the same, first look at the case where the supremum is unbounded. This means that for every b, there is some $x \in X$ such that $a \cdot x > b$, and so the set over which the infimum is taken is empty. On the other hand, if the supremum is finite, then for any b that is greater than or equal to the supremum, $a \cdot x \leq b$ for all $x \in X$, and hence b makes it into the set over which we are taking the infimum, while if b is less than the supremum, then there is some $x \in X$ with $a \cdot x > b$, and b is not in the set of the infimum. Therefore, the infimum is precisely the supremum.

Proposition A3.15 (The Support-Function Theorem). *For the function ϕ defined as above for closed and convex sets X and $a \in R^k$,*

$$X = \bigcap_{a \in R^k} \{x \in R : a \cdot x \leq \phi_X(a)\},$$

where for given a, the set is interpreted as R^k when $\phi_X(a) = \infty$.

Proof. We know from Proposition A3.14 that X is either R^k or it is the intersection of all the closed half-spaces that contain it. If $X = R^k$, then it is easy to see that

[4] I have not been careful about the possibility that $X = \emptyset$, in which case $\phi_X(a) \equiv -\infty$. The fastidious reader may wish to go back to the start of this section and see whether it all works for the case where $X = \emptyset$ or if we need to qualify any of the results to rule out that case.

$\phi_X(a) = \infty$ for all $a \neq 0$, and so the intersection gives back R^k. (A special argument is needed for $a = 0$.)

Suppose $\{x : a \cdot x \leq b\}$ is a closed half-space containing X. That is, $a \cdot x \leq b$ for all $x \in X$. Then b is in the set over which the infinum is taken for a, and so $\phi_X(a) \leq b$. Therefore, the half-space $\{x : a \cdot x \leq \phi_X(a)\}$ is a subset of the half-space $\{x : a \cdot x \leq b\}$, and the intersection given in the proposition encompasses an intersection over $\{x : a \cdot x \leq b\}$. And if $\{x : a \cdot x \geq b\}$ is a closed half-space containing X, then (by a similar argument) the term in the intersection $\{x : -a \cdot x \leq \phi_X(-a)\}$ encompasses the intersection over $\{x : a \cdot x \geq b\}$.

Therefore, we know that the intersection in the proposition encompasses the intersection of all closed half-spaces containing X, which yields X, and this intersection can only be smaller than X. To finish, we must show that for $x \in X$, x is in the intersection in the proposition, which means we must show that $a \cdot x \leq \phi_X(a)$ for all $a \in R^k$. But using the original definition of $\phi_X(a)$, this is evident. ∎

The function $\phi_X(\cdot)$ is called the support function for the set X, and hence the name the Support-Function Theorem. You'll meet it (actually, variations on it) in Chapters 9 and 10, where (more or less) it will be called the profit function of a profit-maximizing firm and the expenditure function of a utility-maximizing consumer.

We haven't yet given the definition of a convex function—that is about to happen—and when we do, we won't define it for functions taking on the value ∞. But if you want a leg up on developments connected to the variations we'll see in the book, you can prove that *the support function as defined here is convex and homogeneous in* a, making due allowance for the possibility of infinite values of ϕ.

A3.4. Concave and Convex Functions

Definition A3.16. *Consider a function* $f : X \to R$ *for* X *a convex subset of* R^k.

a. The function f *is* ***concave*** *if for all* $x, y \in X$ *and* $a \in [0, 1]$, $f(ax + (1-a)y) \geq af(x) + (1-a)f(y)$. *The function is* ***strictly concave*** *if for all such* x *and* y, $x \neq y$, *and for all* $a \in (0, 1)$, $f(ax + (1-a)y) > af(x) + (1-a)f(y)$.

b. The function f *is* ***convex*** *if for all* $x, y \in X$ *and* $a \in [0, 1]$, $f(ax + (1-a)y) \leq af(x) + (1-a)f(y)$. *This function is* ***strictly convex*** *if for all such* x *and* y, $x \neq y$, *and for all* $a \in (0, 1)$, $f(ax + (1-a)y) < af(x) + (1-a)f(y)$.

In pictures, the functions in Figure A3.4 are, respectively, concave (panel a), strictly concave (panel b), and strictly convex (panel c). Note that the function in panel a fails to be strictly concave by virtue of the "linear" piece.

Some simple facts about convex and concave functions are recorded in the following proposition.

Proposition A3.17. *Assume throughout that the domains of functions in this proposition are convex.*

a. An affine function is both convex and concave.

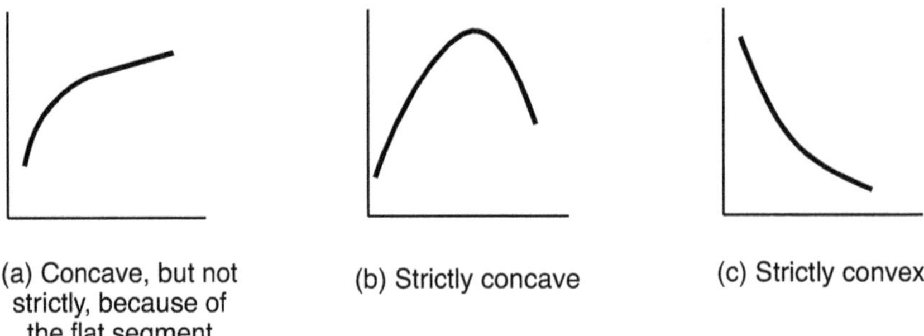

(a) Concave, but not strictly, because of the flat segment
(b) Strictly concave
(c) Strictly convex

Figure A3.4. Concave and convex functions

b. *If f_1 through f_n is a finite collection of concave functions, all with domain $X \subseteq R^k$, then the function $g = min\{f_1, \ldots, f_n\}$ defined by*

$$g(x) = min\{f_1(x), \ldots, f_n(x)\}, \quad \textit{for each } x \in X$$

is concave. For nonnegative scalars $a_1, a_2, \ldots, a_n$ and scalars k_1 through k_n and ℓ_1 through ℓ_n of any sign, the function $h : X \to R$ defined by

$$h(x) = \sum_{i=1}^{n} a_i f_i(k_i x + \ell_i), \quad \textit{for each } x \in X$$

is concave.

c. *If f_1 through f_n is a finite collection of convex functions, all with domain $X \subseteq R^k$, then the function $g = max\{f_1, \ldots, f_n\}$ (defined pointwise, like the min in part b) is convex. For nonnegative scalars a_1 through a_n and scalars k_1 through k_n of any sign, the function h defined by $h(x) = \sum_i a_i f_i(k_i x)$ is convex.*

d. *If f is concave, then for all $r \in R$, the set $\{x \in X : f(x) \geq r\}$ is a convex set.*

e. *If f is convex, then for all $r \in R$, the set $\{x \in X : f(x) \leq r\}$ is a convex set.*

f. *The function f is concave if and only if $-f$ is convex.*

g. *If f is concave (or convex), f is continuous on the interior of its domain X.*

Proof of part g. It isn't hard to prove parts a through f of this proposition; those are left to you. Part g, however, is less than trivial; here is a proof: First, without loss of generality, we can assume that 0 is in the interior of $X \subseteq R^k$ and it is at 0 that we wish to show continuity. Since 0 is in the interior of X, for some $\epsilon > 0$, all points $x = (x_1, \ldots, x_k)$ satisfying $|x_i| \leq \epsilon$ for all i are in X. By rescaling all the coordinates, we can (also without loss of generality) assume that $\epsilon = 1$. Let e^i be the vector whose ith coordinate is 1 and all the rest are zero.

We want to show that $\lim_n f(x^n) = f(0)$ for any sequence $\{x^n\}$ that approaches 0. Therefore, we will be looking at x^n that are close to zero; in particular, for any sequence approaching zero, consider x^n far enough out the sequence so that $|x_i^n| < 1/k$ for all i, where k is the dimension of the host space R^k. Write x^n as a convex combination of 0 and, for each i, either e^i or $-e^i$, depending on the sign of x_i^n; specifically, let $\text{sgn}(x_i^n) = +1$ if $x_i^n \geq 0$ and $= -1$ is $x_i^n < 0$ and then write

$$x^n = \sum_{i=1}^{k} |x_i^n| \, (\text{sgn}(x_i^n) \, e^i) + \left(1 - \sum_{i=1}^{k} |x_i^n|\right) 0.$$

As long as $|x_i^n| \leq 1/k$, this is a legitimate convex combination of points in X, so as f is concave, we have

$$f(x^n) \geq \sum_{i=1}^{k} |x_i^n| f(\text{sgn}(x_i^n) e^i) + \left(1 - \sum_{i=1}^{k} |x_i^n|\right) f(0).$$

Note that there are $2k$ possible values for the terms $f(\text{sgn}(x_i^n)e^i)$, so these terms are uniformly bounded. Therefore, as $x^n \to 0$, the right-hand side approaches $f(0)$, and f must be lower semi-continuous at 0.

And to show that f must be upper semi-continuous at zero, we write 0 as a convex combination of x^n and the e^i or $-e^i$ for all sufficiently large n. Specifically, we have

$$0 = \sum_{i=1}^{k} \frac{|x_i^n|}{M_n} (\text{sgn}(-x_i^n) \, e^i) + \frac{1}{M_n} x^n,$$

where M_n is the normalizing constant $1 + \sum_i |x_i^n|$. Concavity of f yields

$$f(0) \geq \sum_{i=1}^{k} \frac{|x_i^n|}{M_n} f(\text{sgn}(-x_i^n) \, e^i) + \frac{1}{M_n} f(x^n).$$

As $n \to \infty$, the coefficients on the terms in the sum converge to zero, so the sum converges to zero, while $M_n \to 1$. Therefore, $f(0) \geq \limsup_n f(x^n)$. Done. ■

A3.5. Quasi-concavity and Quasi-convexity

In microeconomic theory, the property of concavity given in Proposition A3.17(d), that sets $\{x \in X : f(x) \geq r\}$ are convex for $r \in R$, is very important. This property comes up in at least two places, as a property of consumer's preferences (leading to nicely behaved utility representations), and for its consequences in terms of constrained-maximization problems. To see the first, you should consult Chapter 2 in the text; the second is given (soon) in Proposition A3.21. But granting the significance of this property, it is natural to ask, Does this property *characterize* concave functions, or is there a broader class of functions with this property? The latter is true.

Definition A3.18. *Suppose $f : X \to R$ where X is a convex subset of R^k.*

a. *The function f is **quasi-concave** if $f(ax + (1 - a)y) \geq f(y)$ for all $x, y \in X$ such that $f(x) \geq f(y)$ and for all $a \in [0, 1]$.*

b. *The function f is **strictly quasi-concave** if $f(ax+(1-a)y) > f(y)$ for all $x, y \in X$, $x \neq y$, such that $f(x) \geq f(y)$ and for all $a \in (0, 1)$.*

c. *The function f is **semi-strictly quasi-concave** if it is quasi-concave and if $f(ax + (1 - a)y) > f(y)$, for all x and y with $f(x) > f(y)$ and for all $a \in (0, 1)$.*

d. *The function f is **quasi-convex** if $f(ax + (1 - a)y) \leq f(x)$ for all $x, y \in X$ such that $f(x) \geq f(y)$ and for all $a \in [0, 1]$.*

e. *The function f is **strictly quasi-convex** if $f(ax + (1 - a)y) < f(x)$ for x and y, $x \neq y$, such that $f(x) \geq f(y)$ and for all $a \in (0, 1)$.*[5]

In pictures, Figure 3.5a, shows a strictly quasi-concave function that is not concave, panel b shows a semi-strictly quasi-concave function that is not strictly quasi-concave, and panel c shows a quasi-concave function that is not semi-strictly quasi-concave. (See the caption for further remarks.)

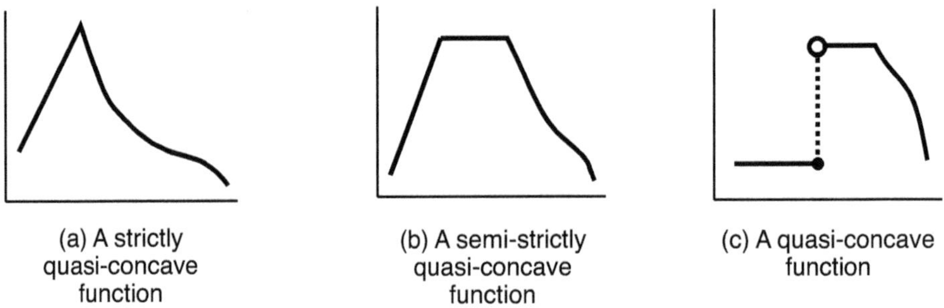

(a) A strictly quasi-concave function

(b) A semi-strictly quasi-concave function

(c) A quasi-concave function

Figure A3.5. Quasi-concavity. The function in panel a is strictly quasi-concave. Note that it is neither concave nor, where it is concave, is it strictly concave. The function in panel b is semi-strictly quasi-concave. Note the flat spot at the maximum. The function in panel c is quasi-concave; the dashed portion is not part of the function, and the open and closed circles indicate that the value of the function at its point of discontinuity is the "lower" value.

The reason for this definition is that quasi-concavity is equivalent to the property in Proposition A3.17d.

Proposition A3.19. *A function f with convex domain X and range R is quasi-concave if and only if the sets $\{x \in X : f(x) \geq r\}$ are convex for every $r \in R$.*[6]

[5] Semi-strictly quasi-convexity would be defined analogously to c, but it never comes up in the text, so we do not bother with it here.

[6] And the function f is quasi-convex if and only if $\{x \in R : f(x) \leq r\}$ is convex for every $r \in R$.

Proof. Suppose f is quasi-concave. Fix $r \in R$, and suppose x' and x'' are both elements of $\{x \in X : f(x) \geq r\}$. For all $a \in [0, 1]$, $f(ax' + (1-a)x'') \geq \min\{f(x'), f(x'')\} \geq r$, where the first of these inequalities uses the quasi-concavity of f. Thus $ax' + (1-a)x'' \in \{x \in X : f(x) \geq r\}$, and $\{x \in X : f(x) \geq r\}$ is necessarily convex. Conversely, suppose $\{x \in X : f(x) \geq r\}$ is a convex set for every $r \in R$. Choose any x' and x'', and suppose that $f(x') \geq f(x'')$. (If $f(x'') \geq f(x')$, the argument is symmetrical.) Then $x' \in \{x \in X : f(x) \geq f(x'')\}$ and $x'' \in \{x \in X : f(x) \geq f(x'')\}$. Convexity of the set $\{x \in X : f(x) \geq f(x'')\}$ implies that, for all $a \in [0, 1]$, $ax' + (1-a)x'' \in \{x \in X : f(x) \geq f(x'')\}$, and thus $f(ax' + (1-a)x'') \geq f(x'')$. ∎

Proposition A3.20. *If $f : X \to R$ is quasi-concave and $h : R \to R$ is a nondecreasing function, then $h \circ f$ (defined as, $h \circ f(x) = h(f(x))$) is quasi-concave. If f is strictly quasi-concave and h is strictly increasing, then $h \circ f$ is strictly quasi-concave.*

Note that this would not be true if we tried to replace quasi-concave with concave in this proposition. For more on this point, see Chapter 2.

The major reason for all the hoopla concerning quasi-concavity is the following proposition.

Proposition A3.21. *Suppose $f : X \to R$ is a quasi-concave function, for X a convex subset of R^k. The set of maximizers of f (over X) is a convex set. In symbols,*

$$\{x \in X : f(x) = \sup_{y \in X} f(y)\}$$

is convex (admitting the possibility that this set is empty, if f doesn't attain its supremum on X). And if f is strictly quasi-concave, the set of maximizers of f on X is either empty or consists of a single element.

Proof. The first part of this is virtually a corollary to Proposition A3.19. Let $r^* = \sup_{y \in X} f(y)$. Then we know that $\{x \in X : f(x) \geq r^*\}$ must be convex. By definition, there can be no $x \in X$ such that $f(x) > r^*$. Hence $\{x \in X : f(x) \geq r^*\}$ is $\{x \in X : f(x) = r^*\}$; that is, the set of maximizers of f on X (if there are any). For the second part, suppose x' and x'' are distinct elements of $\{x \in X : f(x) = r^*\}$. Then if f is strictly quasi-concave, we know that $f(0.5x + 0.5x'') > 0.5f(x') + 0.5f(x'') = 0.5r^* + 0.5r^* = r^*$, which contradicts the definition of r^* as the sup of $f(x)$ over X. ∎

The following results are easy to prove and left for you as exercises.

Proposition A3.22. *A concave function f is semi-strictly quasi-concave (hence quasi-concave). A strictly concave function f is strictly quasi-concave.*

3.6. Supergradients and Subgradients

While quasi-concavity (and quasi-convexity) of a function to be maximized (minimized) is the "right" property in terms of Proposition A3.21, concavity gives us one nice property that quasi-concavity lacks. This begins with a simple proposition.

Proposition A3.23. *For a convex domain X, the function $f : X \to R$ is concave if and only if the set $\{(x, r) \in X \times R : r \leq f(x)\}$ (which is called the **hypograph** of f) is convex.*

Proof. Suppose f is concave, and (x, r) and (x', r') are two points in the hypograph of f, so that $r \leq f(x)$ and $r' \leq f(x')$. For all $\alpha \in [0, 1]$, $\alpha r + (1 - \alpha)r' \leq \alpha f(x) + (1 - \alpha)f(x') \leq f(\alpha x + (1 - \alpha)x')$ and, therefore, $(\alpha x + (1 - \alpha)x', \alpha r + (1 - \alpha)r')$ is in the hypograph of f.

Conversely, suppose the hypograph of f is convex. Take any $x, x' \in X$ and $\alpha \in [0, 1]$. By definition $(x, f(x))$ and $(x', f(x'))$ are both in the hypograph of f and, therefore, so is $\alpha(x, f(x)) + (1 - \alpha)(x', f(x')) = (\alpha x + (1 - \alpha)x', \alpha f(x) + (1 - \alpha)f(x'))$, which means that $f(\alpha x + (1 - \alpha)x') \geq \alpha f(x) + (1 - \alpha)f(x')$; therefore f is concave. ∎

Why do we care about the convexity of the hypograph of f?

Definitions A3.24. *For a function $f : X \to R$, a **subgradient** of f at $y \in X$ is an affine function $\phi : X \to R$ such that $\phi(y) = f(y)$ and $\phi(x) \leq f(x)$ for all $x \in X$. A **supergradient** of f at $y \in X$ is an affine function $\phi : X \to R$ such that $\phi(y) = f(y)$ and $\phi(x) \geq f(x)$ for all $x \in X$.*

In Figure A3.6, you see a function $f : R \to R$ and a point y at which there are several supergradients; two are drawn in. The fact that f is kinked (not differentiable) at y should come as no surprise: If f is differentiable at y (for y in the interior of X), its derivative there gives the only possible candidate for a sub/supergradient. For an arbitrary function f and point $x \in X$, there may be neither a subgradient nor a supergradient; see the point y' and function f in Figure A3.6.

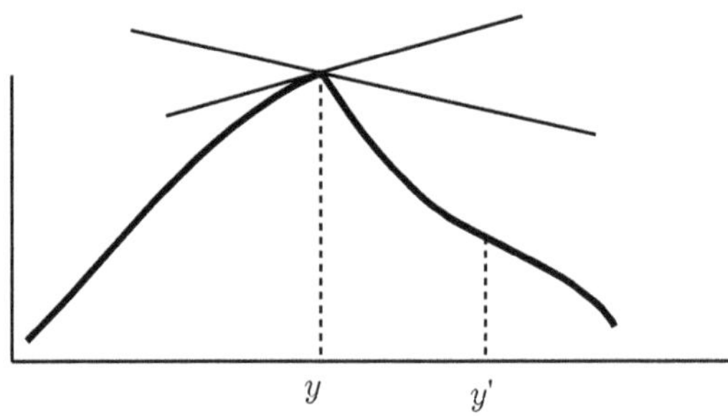

Figure A3.6. Supergradients. The function depicted has more than one supergradient at y and none at y'.

Proposition A3.25. *If $f : X \to R$ is concave (where X is a convex subset of R^k), then f has at least one supergradient at each point x in the interior of X. Therefore, f on the* *interior of X is the lower envelope of its supergradients. That is, if we let ∇_x denote the set of supergradients of f at the point x, then for each y in the interior of X,*

$$f(y) = \min\{\phi(y) : \phi \in \nabla_x,\ x \in X\}.$$

Proof. There is less to the second part of this proposition than you may think. Since every $f(y) \leq \phi_x(y)$ for all $y \in X$ and $\phi_x \in \nabla_x$ for any x, it is clear that $f(y) \leq \inf_{x \in X, \phi_x \in \nabla_x} \phi_x(y)$. That the infimum is attained (is a minimum) and equals $f(y)$ follows once we note that, for y in the interior of the domain of f, ∇_y is nonempty.

The real content of the proposition is the existence of a supergradient at each point y in the interior of the domain of f. Fix such a point y. Then I assert that the point $(y, f(y)) \in R^{k+1}$ is a boundary point of the hypograph of f. It is in the hypograph, of course, and it is approached from outside the hypograph by the sequence $(y, f(y) + 1/n)$. Because f is concave, its hypograph is convex, so there is a supporting hyperplane to the hypograph at $(y, f(y))$; that is, there exist $(a, b) \in R^k \times R$ and $c \in R$ such that

$$(a, b) \cdot (y, f(y)) = c \quad \text{and} \quad (a, b) \cdot (x, r) \geq c \text{ for all } (x, r) \text{ in the hypograph of } f.$$

Moreover, (a, b) is nonzero.

I assert that $b \leq 0$. Because if $b > 0$, then in the hypograph of f I can take r very, very large and negative, and $(a, b) \cdot (x, r)$ will get as small (large negative) as I want, violating the $\geq c$ condition. (The hypograph is all (x, r) such that $r \leq f(x)$, so there is no lower bound to r for any x.)

And I assert that $b \neq 0$. (Here is where y being interior comes in.) Suppose by way of contradiction that $b = 0$. Because y is interior, we can choose x in the domain of f to be y plus a small perturbation whose sign in the ith component is the reverse of the sign of a—for such an x, $(a, b) \cdot (x, f(x))$ would be strictly less than $(a, b) \cdot (y, f(y)) = c$; the contribution of $a \cdot x$ is strictly less than $a \cdot y$ by construction (if $b = 0$, a cannot be 0, and so in at least one component, we have a strictly negative contribution), and as $b = 0$, $bf(x) = bf(y) = 0$. But for such an x, $(x, f(x))$ is in the hypograph of f, contradicting the hypothesis that $(a, b) \cdot (x, r) \geq c$ for all (x, r) in the hypograph of f.

Therefore, $b < 0$. Normalize the supporting hyperplane so that $b = -1$, and $(a, b) \cdot (y, f(y)) = c$ becomes $a \cdot y - c = f(y)$, while the statement that $(a, b) \cdot (x, r) \geq c$ for all (x, r) in the hypograph of f, when specialized to $r = f(x)$, becomes $a \cdot x - c \geq f(x)$ for all x in the domain of f. The vector $a \in R^k$ and the scalar $-c \in R$ provide a supergradient to f at y. ∎

The obvious parallel result holds for a convex function f, the *epigraph* of f (the set $\{(x, r) \in X \times R : r \geq f(x)\}$), and subgradients of f.

Proposition A3.26. *Suppose $f : X \to R$ is homogeneous of degree 1, for a domain $X \subseteq R^k$ that is a cone (possibly lacking the vertex 0). If ϕ is a supergradient (or subgradient) of f at the point y, then ϕ is a linear function. That is, $\phi(x) = a \cdot x$ for some $a \in R^k$.*

Proof. We know that $\phi(x) = a \cdot x + b$ for $a \in R^k$ and $b \in R$; we need to show that $b = 0$. We know, of course, that $a \cdot y + b = f(y)$ and, since $2y \in X$, $a \cdot 2y + b \geq f(2y) = 2f(y) = 2(a \cdot y + b) = a \cdot 2y + 2b$. Hence $0 \geq b$. Repeat the argument with $0.5y$ in place of $2y$, and you get $.5b \geq 0$. This implies $b = 0$. The same argument works (with signs reversed) for subgradients. ∎

3.7. Concave and Convex Functions and Calculus

In Chapter 12, the following result will be needed:

Proposition A3.27. *Suppose f is a concave (respectively, convex) function of one real variable, with domain the open interval (a, b). Then f has a left- and right-hand derivative at every point $x \in (a, b)$. The left- and right-hand derivatives of f are both nonincreasing (resp., nondecreasing) functions, the left-hand derivative at x is greater or equal (resp., less or equal) to the right-hand derivative at x, and if $x > x'$, the right-hand derivative at x' is greater or equal (resp., less or equal) to the left-hand derivative at x. The left- and right-hand derivatives are equal to one another at all but (at most) a countable number of points in (a, b). And, over any closed subinterval of (a, b), $f(b) - f(a)$ is the integral of the "derivative" of f, where one can use for the integrand any value desired at the (at most) countable number of points at which the right- and left-hand derivatives do not agree.*

In other words, f has a derivative at all but a countable number of points, and the Fundamental Theorem of Calculus holds for f: It is the integral of its derivative. Most of this proposition is relatively straightforward to prove, if you know about the concept of absolute continuity and its connection to indefinite integration. See, for instance, Royden (1968).[7]

Finally, in several places in the book we use the following characterization of concavity (and convexity).

Proposition A3.28. *Suppose f is a twice-continuously differentiable function from a convex and open domain of R^k to R. Then f is concave if and only if the matrix of its mixed second partial derivatives (its Hessian matrix) is negative semi-definite, when evaluated at all points in domain of f. If its Hessian matrix is negative definite everywhere, it is strictly concave. For the case $k = 1$, this is: f is concave if and only if f'', its second derivative, is nonpositive, and if f'' is strictly negative, it is strictly concave.*[8] *(For convex functions, change negative to positive and nonpositive to nonegative.)*

---

[7] I am told that the third edition (and perhaps subsequent editions) of Royden doesn't give this result in its entirety. I'm relying on the second edition here.

[8] A strictly concave function can have a Hessian that is only negative semi-definite in some places; e.g., for the case $k = 1$, consider $f(x) = x^4$ at $x = 0$.

Appendix Four

Correspondences

In economics, problems frequently have more than one "answer" at a time. This "answer" can be the solution of a constrained optimization problem or the equilibrium of an economy, a market, or a game. Whatever it is, we need mathematical language for *sets* of answers / solutions / equilibria that change with changes in the parameters of the situation. The mathematical concept used in this case is a *correspondence*. This appendix introduces you to this concept and to important associated concepts, definitions, and results.

Marshallian demand

For purposes of illustration, we carry along two examples. The first comes from Chapter 3. A consumer's preferences are given by a continuous utility function $u : R^k_+ \to R$, and for strictly positive prices $p \in R^k_{++}$ and a nonnegative income level y, the consumer's problem is

$$\text{Maximize } u(x), \quad \text{subject to } p \cdot x \leq y, x \geq 0.$$

Per Proposition 3.1, continuity of u ensures that the problem has a solution (you are maximizing a continuous function over a compact set), the set of solutions is convex if u is quasi-concave, and the problem has a single solution if u is strictly quasi-concave. We do not generally assume strict quasi-concavity; hence there may be more than one solution. For given p and y, we write $\mathbf{D}(p, y)$ for the set of solutions of the problem, and we write $\nu(p, y)$ for the value of the optimal solution; that is, if $x \in \mathbf{D}(p, y)$, then $\nu(p, y) = u(x)$. As you learn in Chapter 3, $\mathbf{D}(p, y)$ is called *Marshallian demand* at the prices p and income level y, and $\nu(p, y)$ is called the *indirect utility* at that point.

Nash equilibria of a finite game

The second example comes from Volume 2, but it is simple and basic enough so that many readers will have seen it already. (If you've never seen anything like this, you may wish to skip this example.) Fix positive integers m and n, and imagine two $m \times n$ matrices of real numbers, A and B. Let e^m denote the m-dimensional vector all of whose components are 1, and let e^n be the n-dimensional vector of this sort. Let $S = \{s \in R^m : s \geq 0, s \cdot e^m = 1\}$, and let $T = \{t \in R^n : t \cdot e^n = 1\}$. That is, S is the space of probability distributions with m components or outcomes, and T is the space of probability distributions with n components or outcomes. We write sAt and sBt for the obvious scalar-vector-scalar products, thinking of t as a column vector for this purpose. Note that the dimensions are such that sAt and sBt are both scalars. Then for given A and B, we say that (s,t) is a *Nash equilibrium* for the bimatrix game (A,B) if $sAt = \sup\{s'At : s' \in S\}$ and $sBt = \sup\{sBt' : t' \in T\}$. For a given (A,B), there is no obvious reason to suppose that some pair (s,t) forms a Nash equilibrium for (A,B), but in fact a very nice application of fixed-point theory shows that this is so. For for any (A,B), let $\mathbf{E}(A,B)$ be the set of (s,t) that are Nash equilibria for (A,B).

A4.1. Functions and Correspondences

A *function* is a mathematical object that associates to every point in one set (the *domain* of the function) a single point in a second set (the *range*). The definition of a function specifies that each point in the domain is mapped into a single point in the range. (This is, two points in the domain may be mapped into the same point in the range; but a single point in the domain can't take on two different range values.)

A correspondence generalizes the idea of a function, allowing a point in the domain to be associated with more (or less) than one point in the range. Given sets X and Y, which are called the domain and range of the correspondence, a *correspondence* ϕ is a map that associates to every point $x \in X$ a *subset* $\phi(x)$ of Y.

In general, the domain X and range Y of a correspondence can be very general mathematical objects. In our work, however, X will always be a subset of R^n for some n, and Y will always be a *closed* subset of R^m, for some m. Accordingly, for all the applications we discuss, we can take limits of sequences of points in X or in Y, measure (Euclidean) distances between points in either set, and so on.

Note that a correspondence is nothing more than a fancy function, in the following sense. Let Y denote the set of all subsets of Y, then the correspondence ϕ is a function with domain X and range Y. But to emphasize that the targets are sets, the terminology *correspondence* is used. To write symbolically that ϕ is a correspondence from X to Y—that is, $\phi(x) \subseteq Y$ for each $x \in X$—we write $\phi : X \rightrightarrows Y$ and $x \rightrightarrows \phi(x)$, using a double arrow. (In comparison, $\phi : X \to Y$ is used to indicate that ϕ is a function from X to Y.)

In the example of Marshallian demand, two correspondences are worthy of attention. The more obvious, perhaps, is the correspondence that maps price–income pairs (p,y) into the consumer's Marshallian demand, or $\mathbf{D} : R^k_{++} \times R_+ \rightrightarrows R^k_+$. But there is also the *budget set* correspondence that defines, for each p and y, the consumer's feasible set: If $\mathbf{B}(p,y)$ denotes $\{x \in R^k_+ : p \cdot x \leq y\}$, then $\mathbf{B} : R^k_{++} \times R_+ \rightrightarrows R^k_+$ is a second correspondence.

In the example of equilibria of bimatrix games, $\mathbf{E} : R^{m\times n} \times R^{m\times n} \rightrightarrows R^m_+ \times R^n_+$ is the equilibrium correspondence; $\mathbf{E}(A,B)$ is the set of (s,t) that are Nash equilibria for (A,B). Note that (s,t) actually come from a smaller space than the range $R^m_+ \times R^n_+$ written here; they are probability distributions, whose components are both nonnegative (which is indicated) and sum to 1 (which is not).

Language commonly used concerning correspondences includes:

1. If the correspondence ϕ never maps a point in the domain into the empty set, we say that ϕ is *nonempty valued*. So, for example, because u is continuous and the budget sets are compact, **D** is nonempty valued; because of a fixed-point theorem, **E** is nonempty valued.

2. If $\phi(x)$ is convex for every $x \in X$, we say that ϕ is *convex valued*. So, if u is quasi-concave, **D** is convex valued. But (for those who know a smattering of game theory), because of games such as the Battle of the Sexes, **E** is most definitely *not* convex valued.

3. If the correspondence ϕ maps every point in the domain into a set containing a single element, we say that ϕ is *singleton valued*. Therefore, if u is strictly quasi-concave, the Marshallian demand correspondence is singleton valued.

4. If $\phi(x)$ is closed for every $x \in X$, we say that ϕ is *closed valued*. If $\phi(x)$ is compact for every $x \in X$, we say that ϕ is *compact valued*. As in: as part of the proof that **D** is nonempty valued, one must prove that **B** is a compact-valued correspondence. Or, since one can prove that the set of equilibria for any game is a closed set, and since equilibria (being pairs of probability distributions) are clearly bounded, **E** is compact valued.

5. The *graph* of the correspondence $\phi : X \rightrightarrows Y$ is the set of points $\{(x, y) \in X \times Y : y \in \phi(x)\}$.

A property of correspondences that we should spell out more formally is given in the following definition.

Definition A4.1. *The correspondence ϕ is* ***locally bounded*** *if for every $x \in X$, there exists an $\epsilon(x) > 0$ and a bounded set $Y(x) \subseteq Y$ such that $\phi(x') \subseteq Y(x)$ for all x' that are less than ϵ distant from x.*

To paraphrase, the range Y may be unbounded but, for every point x in the domain, we can simultaneously bound $\phi(x')$ for all x' in some (small) neighborhood of x.

Exercise 1. Construct a correspondence that is singleton-valued, and hence compact- and convex-valued, and whose graph is a closed set, but that is not locally bounded. (Hint: Consider the function $f(x) = 1/x$ around $x = 0$.)

A4.2. Continuity of Correspondences

In parallel with the idea of continuity of a function, correspondences have continuity properties. Specifically, three notions of continuity are important: upper semi-continuity, lower semi-continuity, and (full) continuity. Definitions vary from book to book, but for our purposes, the following will do.

Definition A4.2.

a. *The correspondence $\phi : X \rightrightarrows Y$ is* ***upper semi-continuous*** *if, whenever $\{x_n\}$ is a sequence in X with limit $x \in X$, and $\{y_n\}$ is a sequence in Y such that $y_n \in \phi(x_n)$ for all n and $\lim_n y_n$ exists, then this limit point is an element of $\phi(x)$.*

b. *The correspondence* $\phi : X \Rightarrow Y$ *is* ***lower semi-continuous*** *if for every* $x \in X$*, sequence* $\{x_n\}$ *from* X *with limit* x*, and* $y \in \phi(x)$*, we can find, for all* $n > N$ *for some sufficiently large* N*,* $y_n \in \phi(x_n)$ *such that* $\lim_n y_n = y$*.*

c. *The correspondence* $\phi : X \Rightarrow Y$ *is* ***continuous*** *if it is both upper and lower semi-continuous.*

The meaning of upper semi-continuity can be partially divined from the following alternative characterization.

Proposition A4.3. *The correspondence* $\phi : X \Rightarrow Y$ *is upper semi-continuous if and only if the graph of* ϕ *is (relatively) closed in* $X \times Y$*.*

Proof. This is less of a proposition than a remark, since it is just a matter of recalling the "sequential convergence" definition of a (relatively) closed set. ϕ is upper semi-continuous per Definition A4.2a, and $\{(x_n, y_n)\}$ is a sequence from the graph of ϕ with limit (x, y). Since $\{x_n\}$ has limit x, Definition A4.2a implies that $y \in \phi(x)$, holds. This is just another way of saying that (x, y) is in the graph of ϕ. Therefore, the graph of ϕ is a closed set. On the other hand, suppose the graph of ϕ is a closed set and that $\lim_n x_n = x$, $\lim_n y_n = y$, and $y_n \in \phi(x_n)$ for each n. Then $\{(x_n, y_n)\}$ is a sequence from the graph of ϕ with limit point (x, y), and since the graph of ϕ is closed, this means that (x, y) is in the graph, which is just to say that $y \in \phi(x)$.

The only part of this that requires more than a moment's thought concerns the parenthetical *relatively* in the statement of the proposition. Because X is not necessarily a closed set, when we say that the graph of ϕ is closed, we can't mean closed in the full Euclidean space that contains $X \times Y$, but instead we must mean that it is *relatively* closed within $X \times Y$. That characterization of a relatively closed set that we've used—that it contains all its limit points within the space—shows this. ∎

Here is another very simple result.

Proposition A4.4. *If a correspondence* ϕ *is upper semi-continuous, then* $\phi(x)$ *is closed for each* x*. Therefore, if a correspondence* ϕ *is upper semi-continuous and locally bounded, it is compact valued.*

Proof. If ϕ is upper semi-continuous, its graph is closed. Since the intersection of two closed sets is closed, and $\{x\} \times Y$ is a closed set, the intersection of the graph of ϕ and $\{x\} \times Y$, or $\{x\} \times \phi(x)$, is closed. Therefore, $\phi(x)$ is closed.[1] And if the correspondence is, in addition, locally bounded, then it is bounded at each x and, therefore, compact valued. ∎

Some examples with pictures may help you understand these definitions.

---

[1] Since Y is always a closed set, we don't need in this case to worry about relative closures.

1. Figure A4.1(a) shows the correspondence ϕ defined for $X = Y = R$ as follows:

$$\phi(x) = \begin{cases} \{4-x, 2-x\} & \text{for } x < 2, \\ [2-x, 4-x] & \text{for } 2 \leq x \leq 3, \text{ and} \\ \{x-3\} & \text{for } x > 3. \end{cases}$$

That is, $\phi(x)$ contains two points for $x < 2$, an entire interval of points for $2 \leq x \leq 3$, and a single point for $x > 3$.

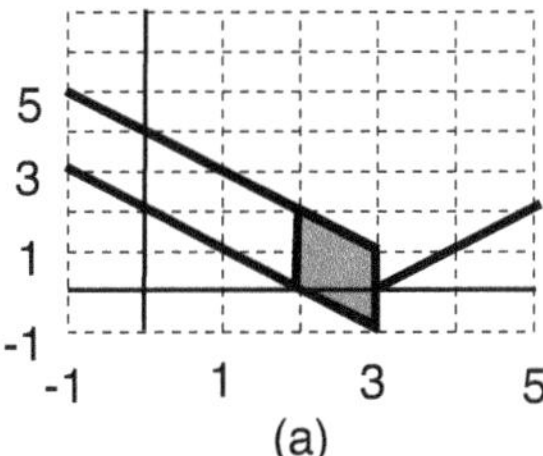

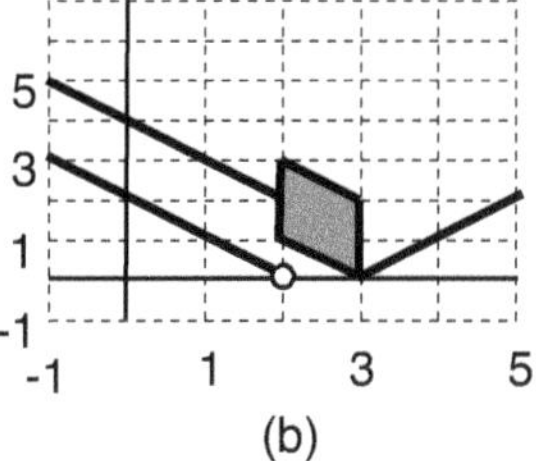

Figure A4.1. Two correspondences

This correspondence is upper semi-continuous. Perhaps the easiest way to see this is that its graph is a closed set. But it is not at all lower semi-continuous. It fails at $x = 2$ and at $x = 3$. For instance, $1 \in \phi(2)$. But as you approach $x = 1$ from below, say along the sequence in which $x_n = 2 - 1/n$, you can't get "close" to the value 1; you can find a sequence approaching the value $y = 2$ and another approaching $y = 0$, but $y = 1$ can't be approached.

2. Now consider the correspondence $\phi' : R \Rightarrow R$ defined by

$$\phi'(x) = \begin{cases} \{4-x, 2-x\} & \text{for } x < 2, \\ [3-x, 5-x] & \text{for } 2 \leq x \leq 3, \text{ and} \\ \{x-3\} & \text{for } x > 3. \end{cases}$$

This is graphed for you in Figure A4.1b; the open circle indicates a point that is not part of the correspondence. This is just like the previous example, except that for domain values $x \in [2,3]$, the correspondence has been "shifted up." This is not an upper semi-continuous correspondence: It should be clear to you that the graph is not closed; it lacks the accumulation point $(2, 0)$. (If it had that point, the graph would be closed and the correspondence would be upper semi-continuous.) It also fails to be lower semi-continuous, both at $x = 2$ and at $x = 3$. But imagine changing it at $x = 2$ and $x = 3$ as follows: Suppose the correspondence had $\phi(2) = \emptyset$ and $\phi(3) = \{0\}$. Then it would be lower semi-continuous. It is lower semi-continuous at $x = 2$ trivially; since $\phi(2) = \emptyset$, the definition has no bite there. And at $x = 3$, no matter how you approach x, there are values in the correspondence along the sequence that approach the one point, 0, in the correspondence at the limit.

Exercise 2. Are either the following correspondences upper semi-continuous? Why or why not? (You should begin by graphing them.)

$$\phi_1(x) = \begin{cases} \{4 - x, 2 - x\} & \text{for } x \le 2, \\ [2 - x, 4 - x] & \text{for } 2 < x \le 3, \text{ and} \\ \{x - 3\} & \text{for } x > 3. \end{cases}$$

$$\phi_2(x) = \begin{cases} \{4 - x, 2 - x\} & \text{for } x < 2, \\ [0, 6] & \text{for } x = 2, \\ [3 - x, 5 - x] & \text{for } 2 < x \le 3, \text{ and} \\ \{x - 3\} & \text{for } x > 3. \end{cases}$$

If either (or both) is not upper semi-continuous, what is the smallest change you can make to make it upper semi-continuous? And is either lower semi-continuous? If not, are there simple changes you can make at the values $x = 2$ and $x = 3$ to make them lower semi-continuous?

A4.3. Singleton-valued Correspondences and Continuity

For reasons that will become apparent next section, the case of singleton-valued correspondences is of special interest. Throughout this section, we deal with a function $f : X \to Y$ and a correspondence $\phi : X \rightrightarrows Y$ where $\phi(x) = \{f(x)\}$. We say that ϕ *describes* the function f, f is the function *associated with* the correspondence ϕ, and ϕ is the (singleton-valued) correspondence *associated with* the function f.

Proposition A4.5. *A singleton-valued correspondence ϕ is lower semi-continuous if and only if it describes a continuous function, in which case it is also upper semi-continuous.*

Proof. Suppose ϕ is lower semi-continuous. Take any $x \in X$ and sequence $\{x_n\}$ with limit x. Since $f(x) \in \phi(x)$, lower semi-continuity says that, for some sequences $\{y_n\}$ with $y_n \in \phi(x_n)$, $\lim_n y_n = f(x)$. But the only choice for y_n is $f(x_n)$. Therefore, f is continuous. Conversely, for $x \in X$ and $\{x_n\}$ with limit x, continuity of f ensures that $\lim_n f(x_n) = f(x)$. Therefore, for all $y \in \phi(x)$, and there is but one such y, namely $f(x)$, we can find $y_n \in \phi(x_n)$, namely $f(x_n)$, with limit $f(x)$. This is lower semi-continuity. And, in either case, for any $\{x_n\}$ with limit x, if $y_n \in \phi(x_n)$, then $y_n = f(x_n)$, and the (only) accumulation point of $y_n = \lim_n f(x_n) = f(x) \in \phi(x)$, which is upper semi-continuity. ∎

On the other hand, in this special case of singleton-valued correspondences, upper semi-continuity does not ensure continuity of the corresponding function. Consider $X = [0, \infty)$ and $f(x) = 1/x$ for $x > 0$ and $f(0) = 0$. This function is very discontinuous at $x = 0$, but the singleton-valued correspondence associated with this function is upper semi-continuous.

This example shows a sort of behavior we will want to avoid in applications, namely, where the function/correspondence "disappears" over the horizon as you get close to some value of x and then pops up at that x somewhere completely different. The definition we gave earlier of a locally bounded correspondence is just what is needed.

Proposition A4.6. *A singleton-valued correspondence ϕ that is locally bounded is upper semi-continuous if and only if it is lower semi-continuous if and only if the function it describes is continuous.*

Proof. Suppose ϕ is locally bounded and singleton valued. Let $f(x)$ denote the single element of $\phi(x)$, for each x. If f is continuous, then ϕ is clearly upper semi-continuous: If $x_n \to x$, $y_n \in \phi(x_n)$ for each n, and $y_n \to y$, then $y_n = f(x_n)$ and by continuity of f, $y = \lim_n y_n = \lim_n f(x_n) = f(x)$, so $y \in \phi(x) = \{f(x)\}$.

On the other hand, suppose ϕ is upper semi-continuous. Take any sequence $x_n \to x$. Since ϕ is locally bounded, there is a bounded set Y and an $\epsilon > 0$ such that $f(x') \in Y$ if $\|x' - x\| < \epsilon$. But $\|x_n - x\| < \epsilon$ for all by finitely many x_n (since $x_n \to x$), which implies that the set $\{f(x_n); n = 1, 2, \ldots\}$ is a bounded set. This implies that every subsequence of the sequence $\{f(x_n)\}$ has a further subsequence that converges to some y. But this y must be in $\phi(x)$ by the upper semi-continuity of ϕ. That is, $y = f(x)$. So, every subsequence of $\{f(x_n)\}$ has a further subsequence that converges to $f(x)$, which implies that the original sequence $\{f(x_n)\}$ converges to $f(x)$. This makes f continuous.

This shows that if ϕ is locally bounded and singleton valued, upper semi-continuity of ϕ is equivalent to continuity of the corresponding function f. Proposition A4.5 shows then that upper semi-continuity is equivalent to lower semi-continuity, since lower semi-continuity is equivalent to continuity of f. ∎

A4.4. Parametric Constrained Optimization Problems and Berge's Theorem

A constrained optimization problem takes the form

Maximize [or minimize] some objective function, subject to some constraints.

A parametric constrained optimization problem is a family of constrained optimization problems, where either the objective function or the constraint set (or both) varies parametrically. In what follows, we deal with maximization problems; everything we say works for minimization problems.[2]

We imagine that the parameter, denoted by θ, comes from a subset of R^n for some n, and the variables that are optimized, denoted by z, come from a subset of R^m for some m. The objective function is written $F(z, \theta)$, and for each θ, the set of feasible z values is denoted by $A(\theta)$. In notation, then, a parametric constrained maximization problem is written

[2] Mininimizing f is the same as maximizing $-f$, so this is almost immediate.

For each θ, maximize (in z) $F(z,\theta)$, subject to $z \in A(\theta)$.

For a parametric constrained maximization problem of this form, we let $Z(\theta)$ be the set of solutions of the problem for parameter value θ—that is, $Z(\cdot)$ is a correspondence with argument θ, giving (as values) sets of z—and we let $f(\theta) = \sup\{F(z,\theta); z \in A(\theta)\}$.[3]

An excellent example of a parametric constrained maximization problem is the consumer's problem (CP). The parameter θ is the vector of prices and income (p, Y), and the (vector) variable z is the consumption bundle x chosen by the consumer. The correspondence of solutions is the Marshallian demand correspondence, and the function f is the indirect utility function. Note that in this case, the objective function $u(x)$ is independent of the parameters (p, y), but the constraint set for x, $\mathbf{B}(p, y)$, does change with changes in (p, y).

Economic theory repeatedly uses the following proposition. The version given here is a bit "fancier" than is standard; see the comments following the statement of the corollary.

Proposition A4.7 (Berge's Theorem, also known as the Theorem of the Maximum). *Consider the parametric constrained-maximization problem*

$$\text{Maximize } F(z,\theta), \text{ subject to } z \in A(\theta).$$

Let $Z(\theta)$ be the set of solutions of this problem for the parameter θ, and let $f(\theta) = \sup\{F(z,\theta); z \in A(\theta)\}$. If

a. F is a continuous function in (z,θ),

b. $\theta \Rightarrow A(\theta)$ is lower semi-continuous and nonempty valued (that is, $A(\theta) \neq \emptyset$ for all θ), and

c. there exists for each θ a set $B(\theta) \subseteq A(\theta)$ such that $Z(\theta) \subseteq B(\theta)$, $\sup\{F(z,\theta) : z \in B(\theta)\} = \sup\{F(z,\theta) : z \in A(\theta)\}$, and $\theta \Rightarrow B(\theta)$ is an upper semi-continuous and locally bounded correspondence.

Then:

d. $Z(\theta)$ is nonempty for all θ, and $\theta \Rightarrow Z(\theta)$ is an upper semi-continuous and locally bounded correspondence; and

e. the function $\theta \to f(\theta)$ is continuous.

Identical conclusions hold if the optimization problem calls for minimizing F rather than maximizing F.

Before giving the proof of Berge's Theorem, we give a corollary that shows why we were interested last section in singleton-valued correspondences.

---

[3] We write *sup* instead of *max* in the definition of f to cover the case where there is no $x \in A(\theta)$ that is optimal.

Corollary A4.8. *In the situation of Proposition A4.7, if in addition you know that $Z(\theta)$ is a singleton set $\{z(\theta)\}$ for all θ in some (relatively) open set of parameter values, then $z(\theta)$ is a continuous function over that set of parameter values.*

Proof of the corollary. Berge's Theorem establishes that the solution correspondence Z is upper semi-continuous and locally bounded. Apply Proposition A4.6. ∎

In standard statements of this theorem, $B(\theta)$ doesn't appear; it is assumed that $A(\theta)$ is continuous. But the more general version of the result given here permits smoother application of the result in some cases encountered in the text.

Proof of Berge's Theorem. Since B is upper semi-continuous and locally bounded, it is compact valued. Since $A(\theta)$ is nonempty valued, $\sup\{F(z,\theta) : z \in A(\theta)\}$ is either finite or $+\infty$; since $\sup\{F(z,\theta) : z \in A(\theta)\} = \sup\{F(z,\theta) : z \in B(\theta)\}$ (condition c), we conclude that $B(\theta)$ is nonempty for each θ. Nonemptiness of $Z(\theta)$ for all θ then follows from Proposition A2.21, because F is continuous in z and $B(\theta)$ is nonempty and compact for each θ. This also implies that $f(\theta) < \infty$ for all θ.[4]

To establish continuity of f, suppose $\{\theta_n\}$ is a sequence of parameter values with limit θ. Let z be any solution to the problem at θ, so that $f(\theta) = F(z,\theta)$. Since A is lower semi-continuous, we can find $z_n \in A(\theta_n)$ for each n such that $\lim_n z_n = z$. But then, by continuity of F, $\lim_n F(z_n,\theta_n) = F(z,\theta) = f(\theta)$. And since $f(\theta_n) \geq F(z_n,\theta_n)$ for each n, $\liminf_n f(\theta_n) \geq f(\theta)$; f is lower semi-continuous at θ. Hence, continuity of f at θ can fail only if, for some sequence $\{\theta_n\}$ converging to θ and some $\epsilon > 0$, $f(\theta_n) > f(\theta) + \epsilon$ for all n. Suppose such a sequence exists; choose $z_n \in Z(\theta_n)$ (hence $f(\theta_n) = F(z_n,\theta_n)$) for each n. $Z(\theta_n) \subseteq B(\theta_n)$ implies $z_n \in B(\theta_n)$ for each n. Since B is locally bounded and $\theta_n \to \theta$, we can extract from the sequence $\{z_n\}$ a convergent subsequence $\{z_{n'}\}$, and since B is upper semi-continuous, the limit z of this convergent subsequence is in $B(\theta) \subseteq A(\theta)$. But then $f(\theta) \geq F(z,\theta) = \lim_n F(z_n,\theta_n)$ (by continuity of F) $= \lim_n f(\theta_n)$, contradicting the alleged hypothesis. The function f is continuous.

By assumption, B is locally bounded and $Z(\theta) \subseteq B(\theta)$, hence Z is locally bounded. Suppose $\{\theta_n\}$ and $\{z_n\}$ are sequences of parameters and variables such that: $\lim_n \theta_n = \theta$; $\lim_n z_n = z$; and $z_n \in Z(\theta_n)$, so that $f(\theta_n) = F(z_n,\theta_n)$, for each n. Continuity of F (assumed) and f (just proved) then tells us that $F(z,\theta) = \lim_n F(z_n,\theta_n) = \lim_n f(\theta_n) = f(\theta)$. Since $z_n \in Z(\theta_n) \subseteq B(\theta_n)$ and $\theta \Rightarrow B(\theta)$ is upper semi-continuous, $z \in B(\theta) \subseteq A(\theta)$, hence $z \in Z(\theta)$. We conclude that Z is upper semi-continuous and locally bounded. ∎

A4.5. Why This Terminology?

Why do we use the terminology upper and lower semi-continuity in Definition A4.2? What connects these definitions to how these terms are used for functions?

---

[4] Suppose $A(\theta) = \emptyset$ for some θ is permitted, with the convention that $\sup\{F(z,\theta) : z \in A(\theta)\} = -\infty$ when $A(\theta) = \emptyset$. In particular, suppose the domain of θ is R_+, $F(z,\theta) \equiv 0$, and $A(\theta) = \{1/\theta\}$ for all $\theta > 0$ and $= \emptyset$ for $\theta = 0$. For $A \equiv B$, do the rest of the conditions (besides assuming that A is nonempty valued) of Berge's Theorem hold? Does the conclusion hold?

When we discuss upper and lower semi-continuity of functions, two mathematical concepts are at work: we need a sense of convergence in the domain and the range, and we need a sense of order in the range. Order enters the story when we say stuff like, $\limsup f(x_n) \le f(x)$, for upper semi-continuity.

In this context, we know perfectly well what we mean by convergence in the domain space: The domain is a subset of Euclidean space. But the range space is a space of sets. What works for convergence there? And what works for order?

For order, the appropriate notion is pretty clear: One set is bigger than another if the first is a superset of the second. This is not a linear order, like $\ge$ or $\le$ for numbers. Instead, it is a partial order. But it is an order.

As for convergence among sets, *if* the sets are compact (in the subset of Euclidean space Y), then a well-known metric, the Hausdorff metric, can be used: The distance between two compact sets A and B is the smallest $\epsilon \ge 0$ such that, for every $a \in A$, there is some $b \in B$ no more than ϵ from a, and conversely. Putting these two ideas together, and assuming that all correspondences ϕ that we consider are compact valued, consider the following definitions:

Definition A4.9. *For any x and $\phi(x)$, and for any $\epsilon > 0$, let*

$$\phi_\epsilon(x) := \{y \in Y : y \text{ is within } \epsilon \text{ of some } y' \in \phi(x)\}.$$

That is, $\phi_\epsilon(x)$ is $\phi(x)$ "fattened" by ϵ. (It doesn't matter if you use a weak or a strict inequality in this fattening procedure.) Then

a. *The correspondence ϕ is* ***upper semi-continuous-alt*** *(for alternative) if for every $x \in X$ and $\epsilon > 0$ there exists $\delta > 0$ such that for all $x' \in X$ that are δ or closer to x, $\phi(x') \subseteq \phi_\epsilon(x)$.*

b. *The correspondence ϕ is* ***lower semi-continuous-alt*** *if for every $x \in X$ and $\epsilon > 0$, there exists $\delta > 0$ such that for all $x' \in X$ that are δ or closer to x, $\phi(x) \subseteq \phi_\epsilon(x')$.*

These are obvious parallels to upper and lower semi-continuity of functions.

But how do these two alternative definitions compare with the definitions we gave previously? The following is left for you to prove.

Proposition A4.10. *A compact-valued correspondence ϕ that is upper semi-continuous-alt is upper semi-continuous. A locally bounded, compact-valued correspondence that is upper semi-continuous is upper semi-continuous-alt. A compact-valued correspondence is lower semi-continuous-alt if and only if it is lower semi-continuous.*

(I have restricted attention to compact-valued correspondences so that the Hausdorff metric is both real valued and is a metric; i.e., if the distance between two sets is zero, then they are the same set. Notwithstanding this, portions of the proposition hold for more general correspondences.)

Appendix Five

Constrained Optimization

This appendix concerns the solution of constrained optimization problems using calculus. We will not strive for complete generality, but will (instead) give results in medium-level generality; enough for the applications of this book, but still special enough so that the proofs of the two basic propositions are fairly simple.

The problem is posed in R^k and involves an *objective function* $f : R^k \to R$, *constraint functions* $g_i : R^k \to R$ for $i = 1, \ldots, I$, and so-called *right-hand-side* values $y_i \in R$ for $i = 1, \ldots, I$. The problem is

$$\text{Maximize } f(x), \quad \text{subject to } g_i(x) \leq y_i, i = 1, \ldots, I.$$

It is assumed throughout that the functions f and all the g_i are continuously differentiable.

Note that this includes as a special case nonnegativity constraints, or constraints of the form $x_j \geq 0$. (The trick is to write the constraint as $-x_j \leq 0$.) But the case of nonnegativity constraints is so prevalent that they are covered in a separate section following.

Note also that this includes the case of equality constraints; constraints of the form $g_i(x) = y_i$. Equality constraints are (implicitly) included because we can write $g_i(x) = y_i$ as the intersection of two inequality constraints, $g_i(x) \leq y_i$ and $-g_i(x) \leq -y_i$. (But see the discussion under the heading *Equality constraints* following.)

To give the basic results about this problem, we need some notation: For any differentiable function $h : R^k \to R$, Dh is used to denote the *gradient* of h, the vector function D$h : R^k \to R^k$ given by

$$\mathrm{D}h = \left(\frac{\partial h}{\partial x_1}, \ldots, \frac{\partial h}{\partial x_k} \right),$$

and $\mathrm{D}(h)|_x$ and $\mathrm{D}(h)(x)$ are used interchangeably to denote the gradient evaluated at the point x; that is, $\mathrm{D}(h)|_x = \mathrm{D}(h)(x)$ is a point in R^k.

The constraint qualification

Definition A5.1.

a. *Fix a point x that satisfies all the constraints, or $g_i(x) \leq y_i$ for $i = 1, \ldots, I$. We say that constraint i **is binding** or **binds** at x if $g_i(x) = y_i$, and we write $I(x)$ for the index set of constraints that bind at x. (That is, $i \in I(x)$ if $g_i(x) = y_i$.) If constraint i is not binding at x, we say that it is **slack** at x.*

b. *Suppose x satisfies all the constraints. We say that the* **constraint qualification** *holds at x if the set of k-dimensional vectors $\{Dg_i(x) : i \in I(x)\}$ is a linearly independent set of vectors.*[1]

The optimality conditions

Definition A5.2. *Given our constrained maximization problem, we say that the* **optimality conditions hold at** x *if there exists a nonnegative I-dimensional vector $\lambda = (\lambda_1, \ldots, \lambda_I)$ such that*

a. $g_i(x) \leq y_i$ *for all* y,

b.
$$\frac{\partial f}{\partial x_j} = \sum_{i=1}^{I} \lambda_i \frac{\partial g_i}{\partial x_j},$$

for each $j = 1, \ldots, k$, *and*

c. $\lambda_i(y_i - g_i(x)) = 0$ *for* $i = 1, \ldots, I$.

Proposition A5.3 (Necessity of the optimality conditions). *Suppose the point x solves the constrained optimization problem, and the constraint qualification holds at x. Then the optimality conditions hold at x.*

Proposition A5.4 (Sufficiency of the optimality conditions). *Suppose f is concave and each g_i is quasi-convex. If the optimality conditions hold at x, x solves the constrained maximization problem.*

Proofs will be given after discussion.

Discussion

It is commonplace to refer to the variables λ_i as the *multipliers* on the constraints.

The optimality conditions have many names. They are often referred to as the Kuhn-Tucker conditions, after Harold Kuhn and Albert Tucker, mathematicians who were pioneers in this field. They are also referred to as *joint first-order, complementary-slackness conditions,* where (roughly) part b of the optimality conditions is the first-order conditions, and part c is complementary slackness.

One also often hears mention of Lagrangians and Langrange multipliers. Given the constrained maximization problem, some textbooks instruct you to construct the so-called *Lagrangian*

$$L(x, \lambda) = f(x) + \sum_{i=1}^{I} \lambda_i(y_i - g_i(x)),$$

and the first-order conditions (roughly) are that $\partial L/\partial x_j = 0$ for $j = 1, \ldots, k$. The language of Lagrangians fits better when all the constraints are equality constraints;

[1] The term "the constaint qualification" means different things in different references, so you should be careful if you see it in another book.

in which case the sign of the *multipliers* λ_i are not constrained, and complementary-slackness conditions do not intrude. Notwithstanding this, the language of Lagrangians gives an inkling as to why these optimality conditions "work": Maximizing f subject to the I constraints is akin to an unconstrained maximization of the Lagrangian, where a reward $\lambda_i(y_i - g_i(x))$ is given if the chosen x gives us a low value of $g_i(x)$. Complementary slackness (condition c) imposes the requirement that there is no reward if $g_i(x) < y_i$—you get no credit for making a slack constraint more slack (nor are you penalized for making it less slack), so a better way to say this is that one is *penalized* for violating the constraint. In essence, the propositions say that at a solution to the problem, the right "penalty weights" or multipliers can be found, so the constrained optimization problem becomes unconstrained optimization of the penalty-augmented Lagrangian.

How are these propositions used in practice? The common use runs as follows. You want to solve the constrained maximization problem, and you look for x (or, more properly, x and λ) that satisfy the optimality conditions. If you are very lucky, you'll have a nice problem with a concave objective and quasi-convex constraint functions, and you will know that any x (and λ) that satisfies the optimality conditions is a solution. Even if you aren't so lucky as that, if you can identify all x at which the optimality conditions hold, then you *almost* have the full set of candidates for the solution to the problem: x that do not satisfy the constraint qualification need not (according to Proposition A5.3) satisfy the optimality conditions. If you can show that every feasible x satisfies the constraint qualification, then the set of x at which the optimality conditions hold is a full set of candidate solutions to the problem.

Nonnegativity constraints on the variables

In economics the variables are often levels of consumption or levels of production or of activities, and it is natural to impose nonnegativity constraints. Hence it may be helpful to give the optimality conditions for this sort of problem directly.

The problem is

$$\text{Maximize } f(x), \quad \text{subject to } g_i(x) \le y_i, i = 1, \ldots, I, \quad \text{and } x \in R^k_+.$$

Definition A5.5. *The point $x \in R^k_+$* ***satisfies the optimality conditions*** *for this problem if there exist $\lambda \in R^I_+$ and $\mu \in R^k_+$ such that*

a. $g_i(x) \le y_i$ *for* $i = 1, \ldots, I$,

b.

$$\frac{\partial f}{\partial x_j} + \mu_j = \sum_{i=1}^{I} \lambda_i \frac{\partial g_i}{\partial x_j},$$

for each $j = 1, \ldots, k$,

c. $\mu_j x_j = 0$, *for each* $j = 1, \ldots, k$, *and*

d. $\lambda_i(y_i - g_i(x)) = 0$ *for* $i = 1, \ldots, I$.

With this as the revised definition of the optimality conditions, the two propositions hold *pari passu*, with one strong warning: In Proposition A5.3, the constraint qualification must hold for *all* the binding constraints, including any nonnegativity constraints that are binding.

Equality constraints

We observed earlier that equality constraints of the form $g_i(x) = y_i$ can be "handled" by writing them as two inequality constraints: $g_i(x) \leq y_i$ and $-g_i(x) \leq -y_i$. In terms of Proposition A5.4, things work fairly well if both g_i and $-g_i$ are quasi-convex—which happens, for example, if g_i is linear.[2] But Proposition A5.3 seems hopeless. If the constraints $g_i(x) \leq y_i$ and $-g_i(x) \leq -y_i$ must both hold, then (of course) they must both bind. And then the constraint qualification as we have defined it will not hold.

There are, happily, versions of Proposition A5.3 that work directly for equality constraints. Their proofs are more difficult than the proof of A5.3 that we are about to give, which is why we are content with the version given here. But most books on constrained optimization will give the more robust results.[3]

The multipliers as derivatives of the value function

Suppose we define a function $V : R^I \to R$ by

$$V(y) = \sup \left\{ f(x) : g_i(x) \leq y_i, i = 1, \ldots, I \right\}.$$

That is, we ask how the maximized value changes as a function of the vector y of right-hand-side variables. Results can be proved in the spirit of, *$V(y)$ is differentiable in y if and only if the problem for y has a unique solution, in which case $\partial V / \partial y_i = \lambda_i$, the multiplier for constraint i that goes with the solution for the right-hand side.* I won't try to give a precise statement of this result or prove it in any generality, but the result for the special case of the consumer's problem will be given and proved as demand theory unfolds.

Proof of Proposition A5.3

(The following simple proof was shown to me by Elchanan Ben Porath.) We will need the following result from linear algebra: If $\alpha^1, \ldots, \alpha^j$ are j linearly independent vectors from R^n, then for any $(b^1, \ldots, b^j) \in R^j$, there exists $x \in R^n$ such that

$$\alpha^i \cdot x = b^i, i = 1, \ldots, j.$$

[2] Linearity of g_i is not necessary. But cases of nonlinear g_i of more than one variable such that g_i and $-g_i$ are quasi-convex are not encountered very often in applications.

[3] And graduate students in economics can find statements of them in, for instance, Mas-Colell, Whinston, and Green (1995).

Now to prove the proposition. Suppose x solves the constrained optimization problem, and the constraint qualification holds there. First we will show that there exist λ_i that satisfy

$$\mathrm{D}f(x) = \sum_{i \in I(x)} \lambda_i \mathrm{D}g_i(x),$$

and then we will show that these λ_i are nonnegative.

Suppose, then, that no λ_i can be found that satisfy the displayed equation above. We know that the vectors $\{\mathrm{D}g_i(x) : i \in I(x)\}$ are linearly independent (this is the constraint qualification), and the nonexistence of such λ_i means that this set of vectors, augmented by $\mathrm{D}f(x)$, is also a linearly independent set. Thus we can find a vector $z \in R^k$ such that

$$\mathrm{D}f(x) \cdot z = 1, \quad \text{and} \quad \mathrm{D}g_i(x) \cdot z = -1, i \in I(x).$$

It follows nearly immediately by Taylor's Theorem that for $\epsilon > 0$ sufficiently small, $x + \epsilon z$ satisfies all the constraints (slack constraints at x are no problem, and for those that bind at x, the first-order impact of adding ϵz to x is to make them slack), and $f(x + \epsilon z) > f(x)$, contradicting the supposed optimality of x.

So λ_i can be produced such that

$$\mathrm{D}f(x) = \sum_{i \in I(x)} \lambda_i \mathrm{D}g_i(x).$$

Suppose that one or more of the λ_i is negative. In particular, suppose that $\lambda_{\hat{i}}$ is negative. Let $M < 0$ satisfy $M\lambda_{\hat{i}} > \sum_{i \in I(x), i \neq \hat{i}} \lambda_i$. Let $z \in R^k$ be a vector such that

$$\mathrm{D}g_{\hat{i}}(x) \cdot z = M \quad \text{and} \quad \mathrm{D}g_i \cdot z = -1 \text{ for } i \in I(x), i \neq \hat{i}$$

(the constraint qualification again). For small enough ϵ, Taylor's Theorem shows that $x + \epsilon z$ is feasible (same argument as before), and

$$f(x + \epsilon z) = f(x) + \epsilon \mathrm{D}f(x) \cdot z + o(\epsilon) = f(x) + \epsilon \sum_{i \in I(x)} \lambda_i \mathrm{D}g_i(x) \cdot z + o(\epsilon)$$

$$= f(x) + \epsilon \left[\lambda_{\hat{i}} M - \sum_{i \in I(x), i \neq \hat{i}} \lambda_i \right] + o(\epsilon).$$

The term of order ϵ is strictly positive by construction, and we again have a contradiction to the supposed optimality of x. ∎

Proof of Proposition A5.4

Suppose that x satisfies the optimality conditions, with multipliers λ. Let x' be any other feasible value; that is, $g_i(x') \leq y_i$ for all y.

I assert that for every constraint i that is binding at x, $\mathrm{D}g_i(x) \cdot (x' - x) \leq 0$. To see why, note that $g_i(x') \leq g_i(x) = y_i$ for i that binds at x. Since g_i is quasi-convex, this means that for all x'' on the line segment that joins x to x', $g_i(x'') \leq g_i(x)$. But by standard results in the calculus of several variables, $\mathrm{D}g_i(x) \cdot (x' - x)$ has the same sign as the directional derivative of g_i from x to x', which (immediately) is nonpositive.

Thus if x satisfies the optimality conditions, with multipliers λ,

$$\mathrm{D}f(x) \cdot (x' - x) = \sum_{i=1}^{I} \lambda_i \mathrm{D}g_i(x) \cdot (x' - x) \leq 0,$$

where the final inequality arises from the fact that λ_i is zero for constraints that don't bind at x, and it is nonnegative for those that do bind (so the previous paragraph applies).

But for any concave function f,

$$f(x') \leq f(x) + \mathrm{D}f(x) \cdot (x' - x),$$

and the previous paragraph ensures that $f(x') \leq f(x)$, since the rest of the right-hand side in the display is nonpositive. ■

Appendix Six

Dynamic Programming

This appendix concerns the solution of dynamic choice problems using the methods of dynamic programming. At nearly 50 pages, this the longest of all the appendices by far—it isn't longer than all the other appendices put together, but it comes close—and for a reason: I anticipate that, for many students of economics, this will be their first foray into this topic. (Unless macroeconomics changes direction, it is unlikely to be the last.) Even at this considerable length, this appendix does not provide a full treatment of the subject, and it is a good idea to supplement it with further study of a text devoted to the topic.[1] But since I anticipate that many students will not follow this up with further study, and most students will see the topic for the first time here, I will be much more pedantic than in other appendices.

Moreover, the treatment of the subject that I provide here is somewhat nonstandard. In every textbook treatment of which I know, and certainly in the vast majority of applications, the objective function takes an additive form: The decision maker chooses actions at a sequence of dates and, after each action, receives an immediate reward, where her overall objective is to maximize (or minimize) the expectation of the discounted sum of these rewards. This additive form obscures the basic mathematics of the key results of dynamic programming, and so I discuss the additive form as a special case, after developing the general theory. This approach, while clarifying the mathematics, adds length.

In the first section and, then, at the end, I provide a few specific problems that are solved using the techniques of this appendix. Some of these provide expository fodder for what comes later, but others are not solved here; you will improve your understanding of this material if you work through them. Solutions are provided in the *Student's Guide.*

A6.1. Several Examples

In economics, dynamic programming is applied to a wide variety of problems, some quite simple (at least, conceptually), and some with very complex and detailed formulations. We will build the tools of dynamic programming in sufficient generality to apply to complex formulations. But that means formulating and an-

[1] My recommendations are Bertsekas, *Dynamic Programming and Optimal Control,* Vols. 1 and 2 (3rd edition), Athena Scientific, 2005 and 2007, and Whittle, *Optimization Over Time: Dynamic Programming and Stochastic Control,* Vols. 1 and 2, John Wiley and Sons, 1982. Lucas and Stokey, *Recursive Methods in Economic Dynamics,* Harvard University Press, 1989, gives an account from which many economists have learned dynamic programming; their presentation varies considerably from mine, as readers familiar with their treatment will shortly learn.

alyzing the general problem in fairly abstract form, which may make it hard to digest. So here are several concrete problems to think about in conjunction with the general formulation.

1. A simple consumption-savings problem

Imagine a consumer with \$1000, to be used to finance consumption at four different times, $t = 0, 1, 2, 3$. At time $t = 0$, the consumer must decide how much to consume c_0, with the remainder $1000 - c_0$ being put into a savings account. At time 1, the savings account will be worth $1.05(1000 - c_0)$, and the individual must decide how much to consume c_1, with the remainder staying in the savings account, so that at time $t = 2$ the consumer will have resources $1.05(1.05(1000 - c_0) - c_1)$. And so on; money not spent for consumption is saved, with interest rate 5% per period.

The consumer seeks to maximize her utility of consumption, which is given by

$$u(c_0, c_1, c_2, c_3) = \sum_{t=0}^{3} (0.9)^t \ln(c_t).$$

(The variable c_t is the amount spent on a single consumption good, whose price is 1 at each date.)

2. A slightly harder consumption-savings problem

This is the same as problem 1, but instead of having four consumption dates, (a) the consumer must consume at dates $t = 0, 1, 2, \ldots$; (b) in each period t, any money that is saved either earns interest rate 5% or 12%, each with probability 1/2, with the rate of return on savings independent among periods; and the consumer seeks to maximize the expectation of

$$u(c_0, c_1, \ldots) = \sum_{t=0}^{\infty} (0.9)^t c_t^{1/2}.$$

3. A parking problem

You are trying to park in a long, linear parking lot. The parking spots in the lot are numbered $-100, -99, -98, \ldots, -2, -1, 0, 1, 2, 3, \ldots$, where spot 0 is right in front of the store you wish to enter, and spots whose number has higher absolute value are further away. You have a general desire to park as close to the front door as possible; more precisely, you wish to park in a way that minimizes the expectation of the absolute value of the spot in which you park.

As you proceed in the parking lot, you see whether each spot is occupied or not. You begin at spot -100: If it is occupied, you must continue to -99; if it is unoccupied, you can, if you wish, park there, or proceed to spot -98. You are quite near-sighted; you are only able to see the spot that you are currently approaching. So when you are deciding whether to park in spot n, if it is unoccupied, you are unable to perceive whether spots $n + 1, n + 2$, and so forth, are occupied or not.

You are not allowed to turn around—if you pass an unoccupied parking spot, you cannot go back to it.

Each spot is occupied with some probability $\rho < 1$, independent of the occupancy status of all other spots. So if, for instance, you are at spot -5 and it is unoccupied, the chance that spots -4 though 0 will all be occupied is ρ^5.

If you get to spot 0 and it is unoccupied, of course you should park. If you get to spot 0 and find it occupied, you must go on to spot 1; you park there if it is unoccupied, and you must go on to spot 2 if spot 1 is occupied, and so forth. That is, once you go past the front door of the store, you want to park at the first unoccupied spot you find. There are a (countably) infinite set of parking spots following 0, so if you get to spot 0, you will (eventually) find a parking spot with probability one.

Suppose $\rho = 0.9$, you are at parking spot -100, and it is unoccupied. What should be your strategy from here on? What if $\rho = 0.7$? And suppose you know that $\rho = 0.9$ or $= 0.7$ but you don't know which, and as you approach spot -100 (before you see its occupancy status), you assess probability 0.5 that $\rho = 0.9$.[2] What then?

4. A job-hunting problem

You are interviewing for a job at dates $t = 0, 1, 2, \ldots$ You may take the job offered at any date, but once you take a job, you must keep it forever. The job offered at date t pays a wage w_t for each following period. That is, if you take the job paying \$65 at date 5, you get \$65 at dates $5, 6, 7, \ldots$ Until you take a job, you get \$0. (Whatever payment you get at date t is called your *payoff* at that date.) You don't know the wage you will be offered at date t until date t. The sequence of wage offers $\{w_t\}$ forms an i.i.d. sequence, with each w_t uniformly distributed between \$0 and \$100. Once you pass on a job offer, you can't go back to it.

You discount payoffs at a rate δ per period. You want to maximize your expected total (discounted and summed) net present value of payoffs. What's the optimal strategy in terms of accepting a job offer to follow, as a function of δ? How, if at all, would your optimal strategy change, if you could go back to take up an offer made in a previous period?

5. Finding the best price (a variation on the previous problem)

You wish to buy a new flat-screen television (the model is fixed). Once you buy the television, you will receive a reward of \$3000 less the price you pay. You buy only once. There is an infinite sequence of stores from which you might purchase the television, indexed by $n = 0, 1, \ldots$. Store n charges the price p_n, and you can only learn p_n by going to store n.[3] From your perspective, $\{p_n\}$ is a sequence of independent and identically distributed random variables, each having a uniform

[2] In this case, my statement that the occupancy status of any parking spot is independent of the status of other spots isn't quite what I mean: The status of any spot is independent of others, conditional on the value of ρ. With uncertainty about ρ, the occupancy status of the various spots forms an *exchangeable* sequence, if you know that term from Bayesian statistics.

[3] The internet has made this classic *optimal search* problem somewhat anachronistic.

distribution on the interval [\$2000, \$3000]. You can visit as many stores as you wish, and there is no discounting, but each time you visit another store, you incur a cost of \$100. Once you leave a store (without buying), you cannot go back. You want to maximize the expected value of \$3000 less the price you pay and less the cost of all the visits to stores that you make; that is, if you visit stores $0, 1, 2, \ldots, n$ and then purchase at store n, your net reward is $\$3000 - p_n - 100(n+1)$; you seek to maximize the expected value of this quantity. (If you never purchase a television, your net reward is $-\infty$; you must keep visiting stores in succession until you buy.)

What is your optimal strategy for buying this television? What would be your optimal strategy if you could go back to a store you visited earlier, at no additional cost? What would be your optimal strategy if you could go back to a store you visited earlier, but at a cost of an additional \$100?

6. A button-pushing, letter-flashing machine problem

At dates $t = 0, 1, 2, \ldots$, a decision maker must push one of two buttons, the first marked X and the second, Y. Simultaneously, the machine flashes one of two signals, either A or B. (She doesn't get to see what the machine will flash before she chooses her button.) She is paid according to the button she pushes and the signal flashed by the machine: She gets \$10 if she pushes X and the machine flashes A, \$0 for X and B, \$15 for Y and A, and \$5 for Y and B.

If at date $t-1$ the decision maker pushes X *and* the machine flashes A, then the chance that the machine flashes A at date t is 0.75. While if at date $t-1$ either the decision maker pushes Y *or* the machine flashes B, then the chance that the machine flashes A at date t is 0.2. At date 0, the machine flashes A with probability 0.75 (that is, it behaves as if in the previous round X had been pushed and A flashed). (The machine's behavior at date t is otherwise conditionally independent of the past, conditional on what happened at date $t-1$.)

The decision maker wishes to maximize the expectation of the discounted sum of the payments she receives, discounted at a rate of 0.98 per period. What should she do?

7. The simplest multi-armed bandit problem

A decision maker must choose, at each date $t = 0, 1, \ldots$, whether or not to pull the arm of a very simple slot machine. It costs \$1 for each pull of the machine. If she puts in her \$1 and pulls the arm, she either wins back \$12 or she wins back \$0. (So her net, if she chooses to play the slot machine, is either \$11 or $\$-1$.)

There are two types of slot machines in the world. Type 1 pays back \$12 with probability $1/3$ and \$0 otherwise, with each round independent of all other rounds. Type 2 never pays back \$12—it just eats your \$1, each and every round. The decision maker doesn't know whether the slot machine in front of her is of type 1 or type 2, but at the outset, she assesses probability 0.8 that it is of type 1.

The decision maker wishes to maximize the expected value of the discounted sum of her net winnings, discounting at rate 0.9 per period. (That is, if she nets r_0

at date 0, r_1 at date 1, and so on, she evaluates her outcome as the sum

$$\sum_{t=0}^{\infty} (0.9)^t r_t,$$

and she wishes to play in a way that maximizes the expectation of this sum.)

What is the optimal strategy for this decision maker to follow?[4]

A6.2. A General Formulation

I reiterate that problems to which dynamic programming is applied range from the quite simple to the very complex. Giving an absolutely general formulation, which covers all the applications, is difficult if not impossible. And, if we tried to cover all the necessary technicalities for applications on the more complex end of the spectrum, we would quickly become bogged down in technical issues. I present a fairly general, but not completely general, formulation here, leaving a discussion of technical issues to the end of this section.

Decision dates or times. Dynamic programming concerns methods for solving optimization problems where, within the story of the problem, the decision maker chooses actions at a discrete series of dates. In some cases, the sequence of dates is finite, as in $t = 0, 1, \ldots, T$. In such cases, the problem is said to have a *finite horizon*. In other cases, the problem has a countably infinite sequence of dates, $t = 0, 1, \ldots,$ and is said to have an *infinite horizon*.

- The distinction between finite- and infinite-horizon problems is clearest if you contrast the four-period consumption-savings problem (finite horizon) with the infinite-horizon version of the problem.

- It is also clear that the two-button-machine problem and the simple multi-armed bandit problems have infinite horizons: The decision maker never stops having to decide which button to push or whether to pull the arm or not.

- In the take-a-job-offer problem (and the shopping-for-a-television problem), one assumes the individual will eventually accept an offer, after which no decisions remain. But the time of job acceptance can be delayed beyond any finite horizon, so this is an infinite-horizon problem: For a finite-horizon problem, there must be some finite and definite time T after which no decisions remain to be taken.

- The parking problem is perhaps the most subtle along this dimension. If and when parking spot 0 is reached, the best thing to do is to park at the first available unoccupied spot. Hence there are "real" decisions to make only (at most) at spots $-100, -99, -98, \ldots, -1$. (No decision needs to be made at an occupied spot, but there is some chance that a real decision is necessary at each of those

[4] Why is this called a multi-armed bandit problem, and why is it the "simplest" problem of that form? I'll explain that near the end of the appendix.

100 locales.) If a problem is such that, beyond some certain (finite and definite) time, the optimal strategy is obvious, then this is effectively a finite-horizon problem.

- The parking problem illustrates another bit of special formulation. In most formulations, the time index will begin with $t = 0$ as the first period, and we stick to that in the general formulation being built. But in some applications, and in particular in the parking problem, it is natural to index time differently; in the parking problem, if the first parking spot encountered is -100, it is convenient to index time by $t = -100, -99, \ldots$. For finite-horizon problems, having time count down to zero (instead of up to some T) is sometimes used.

Actions, information, histories. At date t, the decision maker chooses an action a_t. She does so based on information she possesses. Some of that information may have arrived just prior to making the decision. For instance, in the parking problem, whether the currently visited spot is occupied or not has just been learned; and in the job-acceptance problem, the wage currently on offer has just been learned. In other problems, information arrives during time period t but after the action is chosen. For instance, in the multi-armed bandit problem, if the decision in period t is to play the slot machine, whether it returns \$12 or \$0 this period is learned only after (and if) the arm is pulled. One could invent an abstract symbol i_t for the information received after the previous action was taken but before the current action, and you will find formulations in which pre-action and post-action information are encoded differently. In our general formulation, we eschew all symbols of this sort and instead encode, at each time t, everything the decision maker knows when she goes to make her time t decision: This is called the time t *(partial) history*, denoted by h_t, with H_t the set of all conceivable time t partial histories. So, for instance, in the multi-armed bandit problem, the results of the arm-pull at time t, if the arm is pulled at time t, is first encoded in h_{t+1}. Among the information contained within h_t is the sequence of actions taken previously, $(a_0, \ldots, a_{t-1})$.

In most applications of dynamic programming, and in the general formulation we use here, it is assumed that the decision maker never forgets anything she once knew. Therefore, the h_t "telescope"; h_t contains everything encoded in h_{t-1} and (perhaps) more besides.

We use h for a complete history of everything that happens over the course of the decision problem; H denotes the space of all conceivable complete histories.

In many applications, the actions available to the decision maker at time t depend on what has transpired so far. For instance, in the parking problem, whether the decision maker has the option to park in a particular spot depends on whether that spot is occupied. We write $A_t(h_t)$ for the set of actions available at time t, given the history up to this time, and let A_t be the union of $A_t(h_t)$ taken over all $h_t \in H_t$. We always assume that the decision maker is aware of the actions available to her.

Note that H_{t-1} is not a subset of H_t or of H, but rather can be thought of as a projected "subspace" of H_t and H. We sometimes use notation like $h_{t-1}(h_t)$, $h_t(h)$, and $a_t(h)$ to denote these projections. But, in many places, we also write

h_t alone when we mean the *date-t subhistory* of a particular full history h, when (I hope) this meaning is clear from the context.

Strategies. A strategy for the decision maker is a specification of which action she will take at every date, as a function of the history to that date. Formally, let Σ_t be the subset of $A_t^{H_t}$, such that, for $\sigma_t \in \Sigma_t$, $\sigma_t(h_t) \in A_t(h_t)$, and subject to any technical requirements (e.g., measurability) necessary. Therefore, Σ_t is the space of strategies for date-t action. And let Σ be the cross-product of the Σ_t for all decision dates; this is the space of full strategies for the decision problem.

For readers who know some game theory, the formulation just given does *not* permit a randomized choice of action. In most applications of dynamic programming, randomization is unnecessary. But where it is, you can formulate the strategy spaces to permit it, either using mixtures over Σ or using behaviorally mixed strategies, where each $\sigma_t(h_t)$ specifies a probability distribution over $A_t(h_t)$.

Laws of motion, probabilities, and expectations. Most problem formulations specify a *law of motion*, which says what will happen from the time-t action is taken until the next action must be taken; typically this is given by a transition probability distribution on H_{t+1}, conditional on h_t and the action taken a_t. We write $p_t(\cdot; h_t, a_t)$ for this transition probability (although we'll have little need for this bit of notation). From (a) the laws of motion or transition probabilities, (b) a starting point h_t for time t, and (c) a strategy σ, we build a conditional probability distribution $\mathbf{P}^\sigma[\cdot|h_t]$ on all of H: Starting at h_t, σ provides the action taken $\sigma_t(h_t)$, which gives the probability distribution on h_{t+1}, then σ provides the next action taken, and so forth. Note that σ may be inconsistent with h_t here; that is, h_t may record an action $a_{t-1} = a_{t-1}(h_t)$ for time $t-1$ and a time-$t-1$ history $h_{t-1} = h_{t-1}(h_t)$ where $a_{t-1} \neq \sigma_{t-1}(h_{t-1})$. That's okay; in constructing $\mathbf{P}^\sigma[\cdot|h_t]$, h_t specifies what happens up to time t, while σ is used to specify the action choice from time t on. We use $\mathbf{E}^\sigma[\cdot|h_t]$ to denote expectation taken with respect to $\mathbf{P}^\sigma[\cdot|h_t]$.

The objective function and optimality. The final piece of our general formulation concerns the objective function. Being very general, we imagine a utility function $u : H \to R$, such that the decision maker's objective is to maximize the expectation of u. For each strategy σ, we write

$$f_t^\sigma(h_t) := \mathbf{E}^\sigma[u(h)|h_t],$$

so that $f_t^\sigma(h_t)$ is the *expected (utility) value from using strategy σ, beginning at time t in the history h_t*.[5] By the law of iterated conditional expectations,

$$f_t^\sigma(h_t) = \mathbf{E}^\sigma[f_{t+1}^\sigma(h_{t+1})|h_t], \tag{A6.1}$$

[5] I debated whether to omit the subscript t in $f_t^\sigma(h_t)$, writing instead of $f^\sigma(h_t)$. Technically, the subscript is superfluous, as the argument of the function h_t implicitly identifies the time t. But at some crucial points in the exposition to follow, I think it helps clarify matters to have this subscript available, so I include it.

where in the h_{t+1}, what is random (perhaps) are those portions or components of h_{t+1} that are added to h_t between the time t and time $t+1$. One piece of new information is a_t, which is given by $\sigma_t(h_t)$, but other, random things may take place, driven by the law of motion that is part of the problem formulation.

(For finite-horizon problems, where decisions are taken at dates $t = 0, \ldots, T$, we define $h_{T+1} = h$ and $f^{\sigma}_{T+1}(h) = u(h)$, for all σ. Then (A6.1) is valid for all $t = 0, \ldots, T$.)

Dynamic programming is sometimes used in minimization problems; for instance, in the parking problem. But I work in this appendix with maximization problems. The *optimal value function* is defined at each h_t by

$$f^*_t(h_t) = \sup_{\sigma \in \Sigma} f^{\sigma}_t(h_t).$$

And *strategy σ is (everywhere) optimal* if

$$f^{\sigma}_t(h_t) = f^*_t(h_t), \quad \text{for all } t \text{ and } h_t.$$

We look for strategies that are *everywhere* optimal. (And, to be clear, we may not find an optimal strategy for some problems. But the optimal value function is defined as the supremum over all strategies, nonetheless.)

Please put a big star in the margin at this point. You might think it is enough to find a strategy that is optimal for some given initial history h_0. But the methods of dynamic programming depend crucially on the idea that we are searching for strategies that are optimal starting from every time t and in every starting point for time t, h_t. When you go to verify that a strategy is optimal, in the application of the methods of this appendix, you have to show it is optimal everywhere, in just this sense.

Technicalities

The formulation just given skirts some technical issues that must be addressed if we are going to be rigorous. But trying to address the technical issues in substantial generality (now and later, as we develop the theory) would add many more pages to an already too-long appendix and would probably obscure the basic ideas. So in this subsection I will signal the technical issues and offer some assumptions that make everything to follow legitimate, but that are limiting in terms of some applications you may meet.

The construction of the $\mathbf{P}^{\sigma}[\cdot|h_t]$

Most formulations of dynamic programming problems present the laws of motion in the form of transition probabilities: If the history to time t is this, and if the action selected is that, then here is the probability distribution over the new items that, together with the history and action selected, make up the next partial history. These transition probabilities are then employed to construct conditional probabilities $\mathbf{P}^{\sigma}[\cdot|h_t]$ on all of h. Moreover, this should be done so that laws of iterated conditional probabilities of the sort employed in writing (A6.1) hold. The chief mathematical hammer used here is an extension theorem (either Kolmogorov's or, a bit more generally, Tulcea's), which ensures that if consistent finite-dimensional probabilities are constructed, they can be extended to an appropriate (countably additive) probability on all of H. But a bit of care—and some measurability restrictions on the available strategies σ—are required.

Construction of strategies from other strategies
In later developments, we construct "contingent strategies" from other strategies; for instance, we might say, "Let $\hat{\sigma}$ follow the action choices mandated by σ up to time t; at time t with history h_t, let $\hat{\sigma}(h_t)$ prescribe an action that comes within ϵ of the optimal action in that history; and after time t, let $\hat{\sigma}$ be the same as σ'." If we are imposing measurability restrictions on strategies along the way, so that we can construct conditional probabilities as above, we must be sure that the contingent strategies we blithely define satisfy those restrictions. Often, this involves knowing whether and when certain *measurable selections* are feasible.

Integrating u
Finally, we defined $f_t^{\sigma}(h_t)$ as $\mathbf{E}^{\sigma}[u(h)|h_t]$. What guarantees do we have that this integral is well defined? For one (obvious) thing, the utility function u has to be measurable. But more than that, u has to be integrable with respect to $\mathbf{P}^{\sigma}[\cdot|h_t]$, for all σ and h_t.

I want to avoid discussions of measurability and worries about whether various contingent strategies can be constructed, and the easiest way to do so is to assume that H (and, therefore, each H_t) is countably infinite. Unhappily, taking this easy path excludes a lot of applications that arise in the economics literature. Of the seven examples with which we began, problems 1, 2, 4, and 5 would effectively be ruled out. But my desire to avoid discussions of measurability is strong, so I will engage in a bit of arm-waving: In the proofs and sketches of proofs to follow, I will eschew all discussion of measurability. If this worries you, what follows is rigorous for problems where H is countably infinite. In fact, the general results that follow can be extended to problems such as 1, 2, 4, and 5 (and I'll have no compunction about showing you solutions to those problems in what follows), but there are some issues that must be attended to, which I will not touch.

Regarding integrability of u, I can do a bit better: I will assume that either u is uniformly bounded above on H (where here I mean the set of histories that, per the problem formulation, might happen—formally, u is uniformly bounded above on a subset of H that has probability 1 under all $\mathbf{P}^{\sigma}[\cdot|h_t]$), or that u is uniformly bounded below on H. With either one of these two assumptions (and with unstipulated measurability assumptions on u), we are assured that u is always *quasi*-integrable; if u is uniformly bounded above, integrals of $-\infty$ are permitted, and if u is uniformly bounded below, integrals of ∞ are permitted, but in either case, they are well defined. (To be very precise, in cases where u is uniformly bounded above, I'm willing to have $u(h) = -\infty$ for particular histories h, and where u is uniformly bounded below, $u(h) = \infty$ is permitted.)

Note that one or the other of these conditions holds in all seven examples. I leave it to you to verify this; it is pretty simple except perhaps for Problem 1, but the fact that this problem has a finite horizon and wealth can grow no more than 5% per period gives a uniform upper bound. More generally, this assumption (that is, one of the two assumptions) holds in a wide variety of problems that arise in economics. Some exceptions are found in the literature: This is especially true in the context of consumption–investment budgeting problems in finance, where utility functions are unbounded on both sides, as are the supports of the distribution of per period returns. For such problems, you will need (if you are fastidious) to argue that the required integrals are well enough defined so that the theory to follow still holds. (Almost no one who writes in the literature is that fastidious.)

Because I am assuming only quasi-integrability, I am opening up the possibilities that one or more strategies have $f_t^\sigma(h_t) = \infty$ (when u is uniformly bounded below) or that all strategies have $f_t^\sigma(h_t) = -\infty$ (when u is uniformly bounded above). In the first case, any strategy that gives expected utility equal to ∞ is optimal; in the second case, all strategies are equally optimal. No distinction is made between the rate at which ∞ or $-\infty$ is reached. The broad theory of dynamic programming looks at finer optimal criteria for such cases (such as long-run average flow of utility or so-called overtaking optimality), but we will have nothing to say about them here.

A6.3. Bellman's Equation

Equation (A6.1) is "extended" to the optimal value function f_t^* in what is commonly called *Bellman's equation*.

Proposition A6.1.

$$f_t^*(h_t) = \sup_{\sigma \in \Sigma} \mathbf{E}^\sigma[f_{t+1}^*(h_{t+1})|h_t]. \tag{A6.2}$$

(For finite-horizon problems, because $f_{T+1}^\sigma \equiv u$ for all σ, f_{T+1}^*, which by definition is $\sup_\sigma f_{T+1}^\sigma$, is identically u. This implies that (A6.2) holds for all $t = 0, \ldots, T$.) Before discussing how one proves this remarkable equation, take careful note: The expectation is being taken over h_{t+1}. "Most" of h_{t+1} is set by the conditioning variable h_t. All that is not set is the immediate action taken, a_t, and any additional information that may be received before the next action must be taken at time $t+1$. And the law of motion of that additional information is determined by a_t and the history h_t. So in place of the $\sigma \in \Sigma$ in the supremum, we might just as well think of taking the supremum over $a_t \in A_t(h_t)$. That is all that matters.

Here is a sketch of the proof, for the case where f_t^* is finite valued: Fix h_t. Let $\hat{\sigma}$ be a strategy that is within ϵ of optimal at h_t, that is, such that $f_t^{\hat{\sigma}}(h_t) \geq f_t^*(h_t) - \epsilon$.

We know from (A6.1) that

$$f_t^{\hat\sigma}(h_t) = \mathbf{E}^{\hat\sigma}[f_{t+1}^{\hat\sigma}(h_{t+1})|h_t].$$

Since $f_{t+1}^{\hat\sigma}$ is everywhere less or equal to f_{t+1}^*, and since taking a supremum only increases the right-hand side, we know that

$$\begin{aligned} f_t^*(h_t) - \epsilon \le f_t^{\hat\sigma}(h_t) &= \mathbf{E}^{\hat\sigma}[f_{t+1}^{\hat\sigma}(h_{t+1})|h_t] \\ &\le \mathbf{E}^{\hat\sigma}[f_{t+1}^*(h_{t+1})|h_t] \le \sup_{\sigma\in\Sigma} \mathbf{E}^{\sigma}[f_{t+1}^*(h_{t+1})|h_t]. \end{aligned}$$

Since ϵ is arbitrary here, we have this inequality without the ϵ.

To go the other way, suppose $\hat\sigma$ comes within ϵ of the supremum on the right-hand side of (A6.2) for a particular t and h_t. That is,

$$\mathbf{E}^{\hat\sigma}[f_{t+1}^*(h_{t+1})|h_t] \ge \sup_{\sigma\in\Sigma} \mathbf{E}^{\sigma}[f_{t+1}^*(h_{t+1})|h_t] - \epsilon.$$

For each h_{t+1}, find some strategy $\sigma^{h_{t+1}}$ that is within ϵ of optimal starting at h_{t+1}, and we have

$$\mathbf{E}^{\hat\sigma}[f_{t+1}^{\sigma^{h_{t+1}}}(h_{t+1})|h_t] \ge \mathbf{E}^{\hat\sigma}[f_{t+1}^*(h_{t+1})|h_t] - \epsilon.$$

Now if we construct the strategy $\check\sigma$ that, at time t, employs $\hat\sigma$, and from time $t+1$ on employs $\sigma^{h_{t+1}}$ depending on h_{t+1}, then $(A6.1)$ can be rewritten

$$f_t^{\check\sigma}(h_t) = \mathbf{E}^{\check\sigma}[f_{t+1}^{\check\sigma}(h_{t+1})|h_t] \ge \mathbf{E}^{\hat\sigma}[f_{t+1}^*(h_{t+1})|h_t] - \epsilon.$$

Combine this inequality with the one two displays earlier, and we have

$$f_t^{\check\sigma}(h_t) \ge \sup_{\sigma\in\Sigma} \mathbf{E}^{\sigma}[f_{t+1}^*(h_{t+1})|h_t] - 2\epsilon.$$

This implies

$$f_t^*(h_t) \ge f_t^{\check\sigma}(h_t) \ge \sup_{\sigma\in\Sigma} \mathbf{E}^{\sigma}[f_{t+1}^*(h_{t+1})|h_t] - 2\epsilon,$$

and since ϵ is arbitrary here, we get what we need.

(If f^* is not finite, the argument needs some minor adjustments. Note that this is one of those places where we are constructing a strategy "contingently," out of pieces of other strategies, so this is a place where, if H is not countable, rigor demands that we worry about the measurability of the strategy we are constructing.)

A6.4. Conserving and Unimprovable Strategies

We come finally to the crux of the *theory* of dynamic programming. Begin by putting equations (*A*6.1) and (*A*6.2) side by side:

$$\text{For all } \sigma, f_t^\sigma(h_t) = \mathbf{E}^\sigma[f_{t+1}^\sigma(h_{t+1})|h_t] \quad \text{and} \quad f_t^*(h_t) = \sup_{\sigma\in\Sigma} \mathbf{E}^\sigma[f_{t+1}^*(h_{t+1})|h_t].$$

Suppose, on the one hand, that we could find some strategy $\hat{\sigma}$ that, for all t and h_t, attains the supremum in Bellman's equation. This calls for a definition:

Definition A6.2. *A strategy $\hat{\sigma}$ is* ***conserving*** *if it attains the supremum in Bellman's equation: For all t and h_t,*

$$f_t^*(h_t) = \mathbf{E}^{\hat{\sigma}}[f_{t+1}^*(h_{t+1})|h_t].$$

On the other hand, suppose we had a strategy whose value function satisfied Bellman's equation:

Definition A6.3. *A strategy $\hat{\sigma}$ is* ***unimprovable*** *if its value function satisfies Bellman's equation: For all t and h_t,*

$$f_t^{\hat{\sigma}}(h_t) = \sup_{\sigma\in\Sigma} \mathbf{E}^\sigma[f_{t+1}^{\hat{\sigma}}(h_{t+1})|h_t].$$

The terms *conserving* and *unimprovable* merit a moment's explanation. A strategy is *conserving* if using it conserves the optimal value, at least for a (finite) while. This isn't quite what the definition says; it says that using a conserving strategy for one round "conserves" the optimal value. But it is easy to show by induction and the law of iterated expectations that a conserving strategy conserves the optimal value for any finite number of rounds; that is, if $\hat{\sigma}$ is conserving, then for all t, $k > 0$, and h_t,

$$f_t^*(h_t) = \mathbf{E}^{\hat{\sigma}}[f_{t+k}^*(h_{t+k})|h_t]. \tag{A6.3}$$

In other words, if σ^* is an optimal strategy and $\hat{\sigma}$ is conserving, then an(other) optimal strategy is the composite strategy created by employing $\hat{\sigma}$ for k periods, where k is a finite integer, and then turning to σ^* for the rest of time.

On the other hand, to say that $\hat{\sigma}$ is unimprovable is to say that it cannot be improved upon in one step by any other strategy σ. If at any time t and history h_t, you know that you will revert to using $\hat{\sigma}$ next period, then you do as well as possible with $\hat{\sigma}$ this period. Because this is said a little differently from the definition, let me write it down: *Strategy $\hat{\sigma}$ is unimprovable if and only if, for every t, h_t, and alternative strategy σ,*

$$f_t^{\hat{\sigma}}(h_t) \geq \mathbf{E}^{\sigma}[f_{t+1}^{\hat{\sigma}}(h_t)|h_t].$$

And, by induction and the law of iterated conditional expectations, this easily extends to k periods: If $\hat{\sigma}$ is unimprovable, then for any other strategy σ, t, k, and h_t,

$$f_t^{\hat{\sigma}}(h_t) \geq \mathbf{E}^{\sigma}[f_{t+k}^{\hat{\sigma}}(h_{t+k})|h_t]. \quad (A6.4)$$

For later purposes, it is worth observing that if, for each t and h_t, the set of available actions $A_t(h_t)$ is finite, then the *supremum* in Bellman's equation is attained by some action for each h_t; that is, a conserving strategy exists.[6]

Bellman's equation, equation (A6.1), and the definition of an optimal strategy give the following immediate result:

Proposition A6.4. *If σ^* is optimal, then it is both conserving and unimprovable.*

For finite-horizon problems, the implications of Proposition A6.4 run both ways:

Proposition A6.5. *In any finite-horizon problem, every conserving strategy is optimal, and every unimprovable strategy is optimal.*

But in infinite-horizon problems, being either conserving or unimprovable is no guarantee of optimality of a strategy. Two examples illustrate how this can happen (and may help you understand the difference between a conserving and an unimprovable strategy).

The two examples share the following structure. There is no uncertainty. History to time t records (only) the sequence of actions taken up to that time, where to get things started we have a single time-0 history, $h_0 = (wait)$. There are three possibilities for h_t: it either looks like $(wait, wait, \ldots, wait)$—a total of $t+1$ *waits*—or $(wait, wait, \ldots, wait, take)$—a sequence of t *waits* and then *take*—or $(wait, wait, \ldots, wait, take, took, \ldots, took)$—a sequence of *waits*, then one *take*, then a sequence of *tooks*. As for actions available: If history is of the first type (all *waits*), then available actions are *take* or *wait* again. In any other history, the only available action is *took*. In essence, at the start of the problem, the decision maker has the opportunity to *take* a reward or *wait*. As long as she *waits*, she can *take* the reward

[6] Once again, where the partial history spaces are uncountably infinite, the legitimacy of this claim depends on a measurable selection argument. Readers with an interest in the deep mathematics of the subject may wish to consult the classic references on positive and negative dynamic programming, by Blackwell (1967) and Strauch (1966).

sometime in the future. But once she *takes* the reward, she is essentially done; she is offered no more choices.[7]

The examples differ in the specification of u. Suppose first that, if the decision maker *takes* in period t, her overall reward is $(t+1)/(t+2)$. If she never *takes*, her reward is zero. Obviously, the *never take* strategy gives 0. The function u is bounded above by 1, so $f_t^* \leq 1$. But if, at date t, the history is (*wait*, *wait*, ..., *wait*), then by continuing to wait and taking in the (relatively) distant future, you can get a value arbitrarily close to 1. Hence f_t^*(*wait*, *wait*, ..., *wait*) = 1. In this case, there is only one conserving strategy, which is *never take*. Note both why this is conserving and why it is the only conserving strategy. It is conserving because, if you *wait* (from a history of the form (*wait*, ...,*wait*), then you have conserved for the next round the optimal value of 1. If you *take*, you get something less than 1. Only *never take* is conserving, and it is very much sub-optimal.

Note that in this example, *never take* is certainly not unimprovable. To *take* at any time is a one-step improvement on what you get from the strategy *never take*. Also note that, in this example, there is no optimal strategy. This is clear on first principles—by delaying for a long time, you can get arbitrarily close to a reward of 1, but you can never get 1—or you can reason that it is true: We know (Proposition A6.4) that every optimal strategy must be conserving. But we also know that, in this example, the only conserving strategy is not optimal.

For the second example, the function u changes: For any history of the form (*wait*, *wait*, *wait*, ..., *wait*, *take*, *took*, *took*, ...), u has the value -1. And for the history of all *waits*, u has value 0. In other words, every strategy in which you *take* at some point nets -1, while *never take* nets 0. Clearly, the optimal strategy is *never take*. Of course (per Proposition A6.4), this strategy is both conserving and unimprovable. But there is another unimprovable strategy: the strategy that specifies *take* at every history of the form (*wait*, *wait*, ..., *wait*). This strategy nets -1 from such histories, of course. But it is unimprovable, since any one-step change (from *take* to *wait*) merely delays *taking* by one period, and delaying *take* by one period provides no improvement in the overall outcome. Needless to say, this other unimprovable strategy (and there are other unimprovable strategies, besides; can you see what they are?) is not optimal.

The two examples can be explained as follows: A conserving strategy, in essence, preserves for any finite length of time the possibility that complete gratification will be realized. As long as delayed gratification is, eventually, realized, to conserve the optimal value indefinitely means you will realize the optimal value. In the first example, this fails: Waiting conserves the optimal value indefinitely, but then it is never obtained. On the other hand, to employ an unimprovable strategy is, in essence, a bet that, if bad things are put off long enough, they will never arrive. In the second example, this fails: You can put off taking the -1 for any finite amount of time, but it is still there and still can (and, in the unimprovable but nonoptimal

[7] Such problems are often called *optimal-stopping* problems, although in most optimal-stopping problems, the reward if taken at time t depends on the position of a stochastic process that is being observed. In these two examples, the reward depends only on the time it is taken.

strategy, will) hurt you. These two intuitive explanations suggest the following definitions and results.

Definition A6.6. *For each history h in H and for each t, define*

$$\overline{u}_t(h) := \sup_{\{h' \in H: h_t(h') = h_t(h)\}} u(h') \quad and \quad \underline{u}_t(h) := \inf_{\{h' \in H: h_t(h') = h_t(h)\}} u(h').$$

*The utility function $u : H \to R$ is **upper convergent** if, for each h,*

$$\lim_{t \to \infty} \overline{u}_t(h) = u(h),$$

*and if there is a uniform upper bound on u. And u is **lower convergent** if, for each $h \in H$,*

$$\lim_{t \to \infty} \underline{u}_t(h) = u(h),$$

and if there is uniform lower bound on u.

Proposition A6.7. *In an infinite-horizon problem, if the utility function is upper convergent, then every conserving strategy is optimal. (Therefore, if the utility function is upper convergent and if, for each h_t, the set of actions available $A_t(h_t)$ is finite, an optimal strategy exists.) If the utility function is lower convergent, then every unimprovable strategy is optimal.*

Before proving the proposition, some discussion of the definitions may help. Anticipating somewhat developments in the next section, suppose that $u(h)$ takes the form $\sum_{t=0}^{\infty} r_t(h_t)$ for real-valued functions r_t. The idea is that the overall utility of a complete history is the sum of rewards received in each period, where the reward received at time t is a function of time-t history (at most). (Readers used to discounting the sequence of rewards should note that since the reward function has a time subscript, we can absorb any discounting into the functions r_t.) Then if each r_t takes on nonpositive values only, u is upper convergent, while if the r_t are nonnegative valued, u is lower convergent. (Why? Because in both cases, the infinite sum is bounded by and converges to the partial sums, although the limit may be $-\infty$ if the r_t are nonpositive and may be ∞ if the r_t are nonnegative.) Moreover, if the r_t have the form $\delta^t r(\cdot)$ for some $\delta < 1$ and bounded function r, then u is both upper and lower convergent. The theory was initially developed for additive u, so these three subcases are known in the classic literature of dynamic programming as negative, positive, and discounted dynamic programming.

And to relate the definition back to the intuition: If u is upper convergent, then the best that can happen in the far-off future is, asymptotically, what does happen. Hence conserving the optimal value for arbitrarily but finitely many stages, which is what a conserving strategy does, pays off with the optimal value. If you "stay in the game" (conserve the optimal value), eventually you win. If u is lower convergent, on the other hand, the worst that can happen in the far-off future is, asymptotically, no worse than what does happen. So if u is lower convergent and σ is unimprovable, no strategy σ' can beat σ in finitely many periods, and the worst that can happen after those periods, if you revert back to σ, is asymptotically of no consequence relative what you'd get if you finished the infinite horizon with σ'. Hence, an unimprovable strategy beats everything else, so it is optimal. The proofs of the proposition simply formalize these intuitive remarks:

Proof of Proposition A6.7. Suppose first that u is upper convergent and $\hat{\sigma}$ is conserving. Then for every t, h_t, and positive integer k, we have equation (A6.3), which I'll repeat here:

$$f_t^*(h_t) = \mathbf{E}^{\hat{\sigma}}[f_{t+k}^*(h_{t+k})|h_t]. \tag{A6.3}$$

Of course, $\overline{u}_{t+k}(h) \geq f_{t+k}^*(h_{t+k})$,[8] so (A6.3) implies

$$f_t^*(h_t) \leq \mathbf{E}^{\hat{\sigma}}[\overline{u}_{t+k}(h)|h_t].$$

But, for each h, $\{\overline{u}_{t+k}(h)\}$ is a nonincreasing sequence in k with limit $u(h)$ (since u is upper convergent), and so by monotone convergence,[9]

$$f_t^*(h_t) \leq \lim_{k\to\infty} \mathbf{E}^{\hat{\sigma}}[\overline{u}_{t+k}(h)|h_t] = \mathbf{E}^{\hat{\sigma}}\left[\lim_{k\to\infty} \overline{u}_{t+k}(h)\big|h_t\right] = \mathbf{E}^{\hat{\sigma}}[u(h)|h_t] = f_t^{\hat{\sigma}}(h_t).$$

Therefore, $\hat{\sigma}$ is optimal.

To prove that every unimprovable strategy is optimal if u is lower convergent, we employ equation (A6.4): If $\hat{\sigma}$ is unimprovable, then for every t, h_t, and alternative strategy σ,

$$f_t^{\hat{\sigma}}(h_t) \geq \mathbf{E}^{\sigma}[f_{t+k}^{\hat{\sigma}}(h_{t+k})|h_t]. \tag{A6.4}$$

Since $f_{t+k}^{\hat{\sigma}}(h_{t+k}) \geq \underline{u}_{t+k}(h)$, (A6.4) implies that

$$f_t^{\hat{\sigma}}(h_t) \geq \mathbf{E}^{\sigma}[\underline{u}_{t+k}(h)|h_t].$$

[8] It would be more precise to write $\mathbf{E}^{\hat{\sigma}}[f_{t+k}^*(h_{t+k}(h))|h_t]$ on the right-hand side of (A6.3), but here and in what follows, I'll use the more compact form shown.

[9] The usual statement of the Monotone Convergence Theorem states that, if f_n is a sequence of nonnegative functions converging pointwise and monotonically upwards to f, then $\lim_n \int f_n = \int f$. I'm adapting this result in the following ways: I'm integrating against a probability measure, the sequence of functions $\overline{u}_{t+k}$ converges monotonically downwards to u, everything is uniformly bounded above (instead of being nonnegative), and I don't preclude u having an expected value of $-\infty$, or even taking on the value $-\infty$ for some h. But this is all a legitimate extension of the usual Monotone Convergence Theorem.

But as k goes to infinity, $\underline{u}_{t+k}(h)$ converges monotonically (upwards) to $u(h)$ (since, by assumption, u is lower convergent), so an application of monotone convergence implies that

$$f_t^{\hat{\sigma}}(h_t) \geq \lim_{k\to\infty} \mathbf{E}^{\sigma}[\underline{u}_{t+k}(h)|h_t] = \mathbf{E}^{\sigma}[\lim_{k\to\infty} \underline{u}_{t+k}(h)|h_t] = \mathbf{E}^{\sigma}[u(h)|h_t] = f_t^{\sigma}(h_t).$$

Since σ is any other strategy, this shows that the unimprovable strategy $\hat{\sigma}$ is as good as any alternative; that is, $\hat{\sigma}$ is optimal. ∎

Propositions A6.5 and A6.7 provide the basic tools needed to solve many specific applications. But "many" is not "all"; these tools are inadequate for some specific applications (the problem of buying a flat-screen television, for instance), so we aren't done (yet) with high-level, general theory development. That said, I want to suspend working at this very high level of generality for a while, to show how to use the two propositions.

A6.5. Additive Rewards

Last section, we somewhat demystified the definitions of upper and lower convergent utility by citing the special case of additive rewards. This special case accounts for a huge percentage of the applications in the literature, including all the examples at the start of this appendix. In this section we formalize what we said last section and then gather further results for this special case.

We fix notation a bit differently than before. The idea is that, after the time that date-t decision is taken, but before the time that decision $t+1$ must be taken, an immediate reward is received. (When this reward is negative, language about costs that are incurred become more appropriate.) Overall utility is the discounted sum of these rewards (the discount factor is the difference), for a discount factor δ that is assumed to be nonnegative, but which could be 1 (or even > 1, although $0 < \delta \leq 1$ is almost always the case). We write $r_{t+1}(h_{t+1})$ for the reward received between times t and $t+1$, so that

$$u(h) = \sum_{t=0}^{\infty} \delta^t r_{t+1}(h_{t+1}).$$

(It would be more precise to write $r_{t+1}(h_{t+1}(h))$, to show the dependence of the time-$t+1$ partial history on h; cf. fn. 8.) Since the immediate reward function is subscripted by time, there is no need at this point to have the discount factor—it could be absorbed into the definition of the reward functions—but it helps later developments to carry this along from the start.

Now we can repeat formally what we said informally last section.

Proposition A6.8. *Suppose that* $u(h)$ *has an additive form as above. Then*

a. *If all rewards are* ≥ 0*, utility is lower convergent, and so every unimprovable strategy is optimal.*

b. *If all rewards are* ≤ 0*, utility is upper convergent, and so every conserving strategy is optimal.*

c. *If the functions* r_t *are uniformly bounded (both above and below) and* $\delta < 1$*, then utility is both upper and lower convergent, so every unimprovable strategy is optimal, and every conserving strategy is optimal.*

Your focus, for purposes of application, should mainly be on part c: Having a discount rate strictly less than one is very, very common in applications, and then part c says that as long as rewards in the various periods are uniformly bounded, you can verify that a strategy is optimal by verifying either that it is conserving or that it is unimprovable.[10] Proving that utility is both upper and lower convergent in this case is easy: Let K be the uniform bound on the absolute value of the functions r_t, and for any history h,

$$\overline{u}_t(h) - u(h) \leq 2K\delta^t/(1-\delta),$$

with the exact same bound on $u(h) - \underline{u}_t(h)$. Cases a and b require a bit of mathematical sophistication: In case a, for instance, which is known in the literature as *positive dynamic programming*, we allow $u(h) = \infty$ and, in the expectations, we only insist on quasi-integrability (since $u(h) \geq 0$, the "negative part" of any integral is certainly finite). Similar remarks apply to case b, known as *negative dynamic programming*.

Go back to the seven examples at the start of this appendix. The first and third problems have a finite horizon, so for them, both conserving and unimprovable strategies are automatically optimal. (Formally, they also have both upper and lower convergent utility.) The rest are infinite-horizon problems; of those, the fourth, sixth, and seventh have a discount factor less than one and rewards that are uniformly bounded. The second problem has a discount factor less than one, but the r_t functions are not bounded above; since they are nonnegative, we (at least) have lower convergent utility. And in the fifth problem, shopping for a big-screen television, u is upper convergent, although that takes an argument that we'll supply later, when we analyze that problem in full. (You can probably supply it on your own, now.)

A second use of an additive structure begins with a bit of bookkeeping. Fix

10 Take care here: While discounting with a discount rate strictly less than one is very common, the requirement that rewards are uniformly bounded can be problematic in some applications. In such cases, you can often find ways to extend c. For instance, if rewards in period t are bounded in absolute value by $K\beta^t$ for some fixed K and $\beta > 1$, and if $\delta\beta < 1$, then utility is both upper and lower convergent.

some σ, t, and h_t, and write

$$\begin{aligned} f_t^\sigma(h_t) = \mathbf{E}^\sigma[u(h)|h_t] &= \mathbf{E}^\sigma\left[\sum_{\tau=0}^{\infty}\delta^\tau r_{\tau+1}(h_{\tau+1})\,\middle|\,h_t\right] \\ &= \sum_{\tau=0}^{t-1}\delta^\tau r_{\tau+1}(h_{\tau+1}) \quad + \quad \delta^t\mathbf{E}^\sigma\left[\sum_{k=0}^{\infty}\delta^k\, r_{t+k+1}(h_{t+k+1})\,\middle|\,h_t\right] \\ &:= \sum_{\tau=0}^{t-1}\delta^\tau r_{\tau+1}(h_{\tau+1}) \quad + \quad \delta^t v_t^\sigma(h_t), \end{aligned}$$

where in the last line, we are defining a new function v_t^σ. What we've done is to separate, in f_t^σ, the *rewards received prior to time* t from the *(expected) discounted value of rewards received starting at time* t*, with history* h_t*, using strategy* σ. The latter is the function v_t^σ, with the proviso that we evaluate v_t^σ in "current-at-time-t" terms; that is, we also pull out the term δ^t that discounts after-date-t rewards from time-t units to time-0 units. Moreover, since $f_t^*(h_t) = \sup_\sigma f_t^\sigma(h_t)$ and, for each t and h_t the first set of terms is constant in σ, we can write

$$f_t^*(h_t) = \sum_{\tau=0}^{t-1}\delta^\tau r_{\tau+1}(h_{\tau+1}) \; + \; \delta^t v_t^*(h_t), \quad \text{where} \quad v_t^*(h_t) := \sup_\sigma v_t^\sigma(h_t).$$

We call $v_t^*(h_t)$ the *optimal (expected)* ***continuation*** *value function,* where the adjective *continuation* signals that it refers to the discounted sum of rewards received after time t. The terminology *continuation value function* is also used for the v_t^σ functions.

Having done this bookkeeping, we can use the functions v_t^σ and v_t^* to rewrite equations (A6.1) and (A6.2), as

$$v_t^\sigma(h_t) = \mathbf{E}^\sigma[r_{t+1}(h_{t+1}) + \delta v_{t+1}^\sigma(h_{t+1})\,|\,h_t], \text{ and} \tag{A6.1'}$$

$$v_t^*(h_t) = \sup_\sigma \mathbf{E}^\sigma[r_{t+1}(h_{t+1}) + \delta v_{t+1}^*(h_{t+1})\,|\,h_t]. \tag{A6.2'}$$

Readers who have studied dynamic programming from other texts will be familiar with these two equations (and may in fact be relieved to be seeing them); in particular, (A6.2′) is the common form of Bellman's equation. Of course, this common form depends on u having an additive structure.

And, as a final item for this section, we can (in this context of additive rewards) use this bookkeeping to recast what it means for a strategy σ to be optimal, conserving, and unimprovable:

- Strategy σ^* is optimal if $v_t^{\sigma^*}(h_t) = v_t^*(h_t)$ for all t and h_t,
- $\hat\sigma$ is conserving if $v_t^*(h_t) = \mathbf{E}^{\hat\sigma}[r_{t+1}(h_{t+1}) + \delta v_{t+1}^*(h_{t+1})\,|\,h_t]$ for all t and h_t, and
- $\hat\sigma$ is unimprovable if $v_t^{\hat\sigma}(h_t) = \sup_\sigma \mathbf{E}^\sigma[r_{t+1}(h_{t+1}) + \delta v_{t+1}^{\hat\sigma}(h_{t+1})\,|\,h_t]$ for all t and h_t.

Note carefully: We haven't changed the definitions, or any of our results. All we have done is to recast the old definitions, using the new from-time-t-on value and optimal (continuation) value functions. This is just bookkeeping.

A6.6. States of the System

Additive rewards "separate" the past from the future in terms of value functions. In many applications, the past and the future are also separated in terms of the laws of motion or evolution of the overall system, via *states of the system*.

Assume throughout that the utility function u has an additive structure, as in the previous section. (One can get by with less than this assumption, but the notation gets clumsy, and almost all applications are additive, so there is no point to it.)

Up to now, we have supposed that, at time t, when the partial history is h_t, the set of available actions A_t and the laws of motion that, depending perhaps on the action taken, determine (up to a probability distribution) h_{t+1}, are functions of the full history h_t.

But suppose that, for each date t, some *state of the system* s_t provides all the information needed to (a) tell you what actions are available, (b) given the action chosen a_t, what is the probability distribution of the next state, s_{t+1}, and (c) given the action chosen a_t and the next state s_{t+1}, what is the reward r_{t+1}. In view of (a), we would write $A_t(s_t)$. In view of (c), we would write $r_{t+1}(s_t, a_t, s_{t+1})$. And, if we were writing transition probabilities, in view of (b), we'd write the transition probability at time t as the probability distribution over s_{t+1}, given s_t and a_t.

The existence of such *states of the system* depends on the particular application. For example (drawing on our original examples):

- In the two consumption-savings problems, only the amount of wealth the individual has available at time t, to divide between immediate consumption and savings, is important going forward.
- In the parking problem, where the decision maker knows the value of ρ (the probability that any spot is occupied), you need to keep track of (a) whether you've already parked and (b) if not, whether the spot you currently face is occupied or not. (You also need to keep track of how far you are from the front door of the store or, in other words, what is the index of the spot you currently face, but the time parameter keeps a record of this for you.) But in the final variation described, where you begin uncertain whether ρ is 0.9 or 0.7, with a prior assessment of 0.5 that $\rho = 0.9$, you must keep track of the past insofar as it informs your current assessment about the value of ρ. That is, you might decide, at the outset, that you aren't going to park before spot -10, no matter what you learn. So for spots -100 to -11, you don't need to make any decision. But if, out of those 90 spots, 82 were occupied (suggesting that $\rho = 0.9$), your strategy (and, formally, the laws of motion concerning whether the next spot is occupied or not) will be quite different than if, of the first 90 spots, you find that

only 55 were occupied. A sufficient statistic, because it is sufficient to describe the laws of motion, is the Bayesian posterior on the value of ρ; this, together with the occupancy status of the current spot, becomes the state of the system

- In the job-hunting problem, you need to know whether you have already accepted a job or not and, if so, what was the wage. And if you haven't accepted a job, you need to know the wage you have just been offered.
- In the button-pushing, letter-flashing machine problem, your available actions never change, and your reward depends on what just happened; i.e., what button you pushed and what letter flashed. The button-letter combination from last time also tells you the odds for what the machine will flash this time. (From the perspective of the laws of motion, we could get by with only two states: Was last time XA or was it something else? But to know the reward, we need four states.)
- In the multi-armed bandit problem, you need to keep track of your posterior probability that the machine is of the first (versus the second) type.

Suppose we have this sort of *state of the system* for each time t. *If*, and it is a substantial *if*, we are looking at a strategy σ whose action choice at each time t depends on the past only through s_t, then what happens from time t on depends on the past only through s_t, and we can write $v_t^\sigma(s_t)$ in place of $v_t^\sigma(h_t)$. Of course, some strategies depend on more of history at date t than s_t; for such strategies, v_t^σ is not simply a function of s_t: To the extent that "historical facts" captured in h_t that go beyond s_t are material to the choice of actions, expected values can and, in general, will depend on those facts.

But notwithstanding the existence of strategies that depend at time t on more of h_t than s_t, the *optimal* continuation value functions v_t^* will depend on h_t *only* through s_t, so we can write $v_t^*(s_t)$. The reason is conceptually simple, but quite cumbersome to write out formally, so I'll explain conceptually why this is true. If it weren't true, there would be two histories h_t and h_t' that have the same state s_t but such that $v_t^*(h_t) \neq v_t^*(h_t')$. If these values are not equal, one must be larger: suppose $v_t^*(h_t) > v_t^*(h_t')$. Since $v_t^*(h_t)$ is the supremum over all strategies σ of continuing from time t in history h_t, there is some strategy $\hat{\sigma}$ such that $v_t^{\hat{\sigma}}(h_t) > v_t^*(h_t')$. But now, starting at time t with history h_t', imagine adopting the strategy "pretend that history up to time t was h_t instead of h_t' and proceed from there as prescribed by $\hat{\sigma}$." Since h_t and h_t' have the same state s_t, the same actions are available immediately, and as future states arise, the same actions (contingent on states) as well. Rewards, period by period, from this "pretend history was h_t" strategy are the same as if we had started with h_t, and the probabilistic laws of motion are the same. So the "pretend history was h_t" strategy, starting in h_t', generates the same probability distribution over rewards, current and future, as does $\hat{\sigma}$, starting in h_t, and so it provides the same expected (continuation) value. This contradicts the hypothesis that, starting in h_t and using $\hat{\sigma}$ gives you a better continuation value than the best you can do starting in h_t'.

This implies that, assuming an additive structure to u and this sort of state-of-the-system structure for the rest of the problem, we can rewrite Bellman's equation one more time:

$$\begin{aligned} v_t^*(s_t) &= \sup_{\sigma} \mathbf{E}^{\sigma}[r_{t+1}(s_t, \sigma_t(s_t), s_{t+1}) + \delta v_{t+1}^*(s_{t+1}) \mid s_t] \\ &= \sup_{a_t \in A_t(s_t)} \mathbf{E}^{(s_t,a_t)}[r_{t+1}(s_t, a_t, s_{t+1}) + \delta v_{t+1}^*(s_{t+1}) \mid s_t]. \end{aligned} \tag{A6.2''}$$

The second line recognizes that the choice of action at time t, together with the state s_t, determines the law of motion that gives the probability distribution over the next state s_{t+1}. Finally, a strategy will be conserving if, for every, t and s_t, the action it prescribes attains this supremum.

A6.7. Solving Finite-Horizon Problems

The purpose of this appendix is to teach you (or remind you) how to use dynamic programming to solve the sorts of problems given in the opening section. We finally have all the machinery in place to take on "half" of this: We can discuss the solution of finite-horizon problems.

In *theory*, the mechanics of solving a finite-horizon problem are straightforward. Let T be the horizon. Given each partial history h_T, find the optimal action to take in the final period T. This provides the function $f_T^*(h_T)$. Then move back to period $T-1$ and, for each h_{T-1}, find a strategy that is conserving at time $T-1$, starting from h_{T-1}. Do this for all h_{T-1}, and you have $f_{T-1}^*(h_{T-1})$. Now go back to time $T-2$, again find a conserving strategy, and so on. Since, in finite-horizon problems, conserving strategies are always optimal, this produces an optimal strategy.

In *practice*, if u has an additive structure and the problem otherwise has a nice *state of the system* structure, you use those to simplify: For each state of the system at time T, s_T, find the optimal (final) action to take, which gives you the value-of-continuation function $v_T^*(s_T)$. Use the form of Bellman's equation in (A6.2″) to find a strategy that is conserving for time $T-1$, and also $v_{T-1}^*(s_{T-1})$, for each s_{T-1}. And so forth.

The *in-practice* recommendation is, in effect, the same as the *in-theory* recommendation, but it is computationally a lot "cheaper." In typical problems, the dimension of the state-of-the-system space S_t for any t will be a lot less than the dimension of the space of all partial histories H_t and, indeed, in some problems there may only be a finite number of states. Simply put, you need to keep track of less stuff. But, effectively, you are doing what is called for *in theory*.

The sequence of iterated optimizations, first for the last period T, then for $T-1$, and so forth (which, in consequence, is sometimes referred to as *backward recursion* or *backward induction*), is sometimes done analytically and sometimes numerically. The finite-horizon consumption-savings problem illustrates an analytic approach:

Example. Finite horizon consumption-savings

Recall the problem: A consumer has \$1000, which must be used to finance consumption at four different times, $t = 0, 1, 2, 3$. At time $t = 0$, the consumer must decide how much to consume c_0, with the remainder $1000 - c_0$ being put into a savings account. At time 1, the savings account will be worth $1.05(1000 - c_0)$, and the individual must decide how much to consume c_1, with the remainder stating in the savings account, so that at time $t = 2$ the consumer will have resources $1.05(1.05(1000 - c_0) - c_1)$. And so on; money not spent for consumption is saved, with interest rate 5% per period. The consumer seeks to maximize her utility of consumption, given by

$$U(c_0, c_1, c_2, c_3) = \sum_{t=0}^{3} (0.9)^t \ln(c_t).$$

In fact, this problem doesn't really need dynamic programming: You can tackle it as a simple multivariate maximization problem, where the budget constraint on the four consumption variables c_0 through c_3 is

$$\sum_{t=0}^{3} \frac{c_t}{(1.05)^t} \leq 1000.$$

(It may not be apparent to you that this is the budget constraint, but a little bit of algebra should be enough to convince you.) Nonetheless, I will solve this problem using the methods of (finite-horizon) dynamic programming, to illustrate the technique.

Start from the "last" period, $t = 3$. Assume that consumer has w_3 in the bank. Since there is no period 4, it is clearly optimal for her to consume all of this, or $c_3 = w_3$, giving her a *optimal value*

$$v_3^*(w_3) = \ln(w_3).$$

Now go back to period $t = 2$, and suppose the consumer has w_2 in the bank. She can eat $c_2 \in [0, w_2]$ of this: If she does, she gets immediate reward $\ln(c_2)$, and next period she will have $w_3 = 1.05(w_2 - c_2)$ in the bank, which gives her the (still to be discounted) continuation value $\ln(1.05(w_2 - c_2))$. So her choice of action c_2 at time t_2 will be conserving (hence optimal) if it maximizes

$$\ln(c_2) + 0.9\ln(1.05(w_2 - c_2)) = \ln(c_2) + 0.9\ln(w_2 - c_2) + 0.9\ln(1.05).$$

The first-order condition for this maximization is

$$\frac{1}{c_2} = \frac{0.9}{w_2 - c_2},$$

which gives $c_2 = w_2/1.9$, and therefore

$$v_2^*(w_2) = \ln\left(\frac{w_2}{1.9}\right) + 0.9\ln\left(1.05\left(\frac{0.9w_2}{1.9}\right)\right) = 1.9\ln(w_2) + K,$$

where K is the constant $\ln(1/1.9) + 0.9\ln(0.945/1.9)$. And, continuing in like fashion, you can easily (if tediously) find the optimal consumption levels at dates $t = 1$ and then $t = 0$.

Example. The parking problem

The parking problem provides a good (if very simple) example of a finite-horizon problem that is solved numerically. The problem statement is too long to repeat here, so please go back and reread it before proceeding.

I will use the time index $t = -100, -99, \ldots, -1, 0, 1, 2, \ldots$, where time t refers to the index on the parking slot. In this problem, as long as you know the value of ρ, the state of the system is whether you've already parked and, if not, whether the spot you are at is occupied or not. There are no more decisions once you've parked, so I don't need to keep track of values in that state. So I'll use the following notation: v_t^* will be the expected cost of following the optimal strategy if you are at slot t and it is occupied, and w_t^* will be the expected cost of following the optimal strategy if you are at slot t and it is empty.

As already discussed, when (and if) you get to spot 0, it is obvious that the optimal thing to do is to park at the first open spot. Hence we know that $w_0^* = 0$—if slot 0 is empty, you park, and your cost is 0. As for v_0^*, there is probability $1 - \rho$ that the next spot ($t = 1$) is empty and you park there for a cost to you of 1; there is probability $\rho(1 - \rho)$ that spot 1 is occupied but 2 is empty, and the cost to you is 2; probability $\rho^2(1 - \rho)$ that spots 1 and 2 are occupied but 3 is empty, so the cost to you is 3; and so forth. This means that

$$v_0^* = \sum_{t=1}^{\infty}(1 - \rho)\rho^{t-1}t = \frac{1}{1 - \rho}.$$

(The evaluation of the infinite sum may not be obvious to you; if not, let $F(\rho) = 1 + \rho + \rho^2 + \ldots$, which you probably know how to evaluate, and take its derivative.)

Therefore, we have $v_0^* = 1/(1 - \rho)$ and $w_0^* = 0$. Now we can compute v_{-1}^* and w_{-1}^*. If spot -1 is reached and it is occupied, you must proceed to spot 0, for an expected cost

$$v_{-1}^* = \rho v_0^* + (1 - \rho)w_0^* = \frac{\rho}{1 - \rho}.$$

Taking this slowly: There are no decisions to make, so Bellman's equation has no optimization. You merely get the expected value of proceeding optimally starting in the next stage. (There is no immediate reward, and there is no discounting in this problem.) With probability ρ, the next spot is occupied, and the optimal continuation value is v_0^*. And with probability $1 - \rho$, it is empty, and you get optimal continuation value w_0^*.

As for w_{-1}^*, if you get to spot -1 and it is unoccupied, you may either park, with a total cost to you of 1, or you may drive on and take your chances with spot 0. Therefore,

$$w_{-1}^* = \min\left\{1,\ \rho v_0^* + (1 - \rho) w_0^*\right\}.$$

We take a minimum because we are minimizing in this problem (and this problem only, among all the problems in this appendix); the number 1 represents the immediate reward ("cost" would be a better term) if we park in spot -1 (and, having parked, we are done); the second term is the expected cost if we forego the opportunity to park in this spot and try our luck with spot 0, computed precisely as we computed v_{-1}^*, where we had no choice.

And, once we carry out these computations and have values for v_{-1}^* and w_{-1}^*, we can find v_{-2}^* and w_{-2}^*, and so forth. I leave to you the job of finishing this problem, but with the following substantial hint: In Table A6.1, I present the snapshot of an Excel spreadsheet, which gives the "results" of this sort of analysis for $t = -8$ through 0 and for $\rho = 0.9$, and which implicitly identifies the optimal strategy for $\rho = 0.9$ as..., well, you tell me. You should be able to replicate this spreadsheet, constructing it in a way that allows you to vary ρ. And there is still the final version of the problem, in which you have a Bayesian prior over the value of ρ—that's a lot harder to do, but if you can figure out how to do it, you understand finite-horizon dynamic programming.

	rho	0.9	
Slot number		v*	w*
0		10.000	0.000
-1		9.000	1.000
-2		8.200	2.000
-3		7.580	3.000
-4		7.122	4.000
-5		6.810	5.000
-6		6.629	6.000
-7		6.566	6.566
-8		6.566	6.566

Table A6.1. A spreadsheet for the parking problem

A6.8. Infinite-Horizon Problems and Stationarity

Solving infinite-horizon problems adds a significant complication: There is no "last period" from which you can begin. But they often add a final bit of structure with which you can overcome the complication: They present a stationary structure.

Assume that we have an infinite-horizon problem, that u has an additive form, and the problem otherwise presents a state-of-the-system structure, with s_t a typical state for time t. Now add to these assumptions one more: The states of the system, reward-payment functions, available actions, and laws of motion are all time homogeneous or time invariant or stationary. The adjectives *time homogeneous, time invariant,* and *stationary* are used more or less interchangeably in the literature, and in this context, they mean the same thing, namely:

- There is a single space S from which states of the system are drawn.
- Actions available at time t if the state is s, $A_t(s)$, are the same as actions available at time t' if at time t' the state of the system is s; we write $A(s)$, in consequence, dropping the subscript t.
- The reward $r_t(s_t, a_t, s_{t+1})$ is the same as the reward $r_{t'}(s_{t'}, a_{t'}, s_{t'+1})$ if $s_t = s_{t'}$, $a_t = a_{t'}$, and $s_{t+1} = s_{t'+1}$, so that we write $r(\cdot, \cdot, \cdot)$ for the time-invariant reward function.
- And the probabilistic law of motion that determines s_{t+1}, given s_t and a_t, is time invariant.

In such a context, consider a strategy σ in which the action chosen at time t depends only on the state s_t, and where by *depends only on* we mean: It doesn't depend on time, either. Such strategies are commonly called *stationary* (although calling them time homogeneous or time invariant would make equal sense). We write $\sigma(s)$ as the action prescription of stationary strategy σ when the current state of the system is s. For a stationary strategy σ,

- $v_t^\sigma(s_t) = v_{t'}^\sigma(s_{t'})$ if $s_t = s_{t'}$, in consequence of which we write v^σ for the (now time-invariant) value function,
- equation (A6.1′) can now be written

$$v^\sigma(s) = \mathbf{E}^\sigma[r(s, \sigma(s), s_{+1}) + \delta v^\sigma(s_{+1}) \mid s], \tag{A6.1''}$$

  (where the symbol s_{+1} will be explained momentarily, if it isn't obvious to you what this means),
- and, if rewards are bounded and $\delta < 1$, v^σ is the unique bounded solution of the functional equation (A6.1″).

Equation (A6.1″) can stand some interpretation: We are computing the expected value of rewards from time t on, discounted back to time t, if the stationary strategy σ is employed, and if the state of the system at time t is s. This is the expected value of the reward about to be received, plus the discounted value of using the strategy, beginning at the next state, where the random element over which expectation is being taken is the next state, denoted here by s_{+1}. Note that, in this expectation, all we need are the transition probabilities governing s_{+1}, starting from state s, if the action chosen is $\sigma(s)$. The significance of the last bullet point will become apparent next section.

The first two bullet points are straightforward to prove. As for the last, suppose $\hat{v}$ is another bounded solution to (A6.1″). We are assuming that $\hat{v}$ is not identical to v^σ, so for some state, they differ, and one is greater than the other (at that state). Suppose $\hat{v}(s) > v^\sigma(s)$ for some state(s). Let $M = \sup_s\{\hat{v}(s) - v^\sigma(s)\}$, and let s^* be any state such that $\hat{v}(s^*) - v^\sigma(s^*) > \delta M$. We have

$$\begin{aligned}\hat{v}(s^*)-&v^\sigma(s^*)\\ &= \mathbf{E}^\sigma[r(s^*, \sigma(s^*), s_{+1}) + \delta\hat{v}(s_{+1})|s^*] - \mathbf{E}^\sigma[r(s^*, \sigma(s^*), s_{+1}) + \delta v^\sigma(s_{+1})|s^*]\\ &= \mathbf{E}^\sigma[\delta\hat{v}(s_{+1}) - \delta v^\sigma(s_{+1})|s^*] = \delta\mathbf{E}^\sigma[\hat{v}(s_{+1}) - v^\sigma(s_{+1})|s^*].\end{aligned}$$

The integrand of the last term is everywhere less or equal to M, so the right-hand side is no larger than δM, a contradiction to how s^* was selected. (If $\hat{v} \le v^\sigma$, simply reverse the order, looking at the maximum value of $v^\sigma - \hat{v}$.)

Of course, these three bullet points don't work for strategies that are not stationary or, even worse, for strategies whose action choice at time t depends on more of h_t than the current state of the system. And the optimal value functions (both f_t^* and v_t^*) are defined as the supremum over all strategies, and not merely the stationary strategies. Even so, we have

- $v_t^*(s_t) = v_{t'}^*(s_{t'})$ if $s_t = s_{t'}$, in consequence of which we write v^* for the (now time-invariant) optimal continuation value function,
- Bellman's equation can now be written as

$$v^*(s) = \sup_{a\in A(s)} \mathbf{E}^{(s,a)}[r(s, a, s_{+1}) + \delta v^*(s_{+1}) \,|\, s], \qquad (A6.2''')$$

- and, if rewards are bounded and $\delta < 1$, then v^* is the unique bounded solution of the functional equation (A6.2‴).

Note that in the expectation, we superscript **E** with the state s and an action a (from $A(s)$), because they determine the probability distribution over s_{+1}, the next state of the system and the only stochastic element on the right-hand side of the equation. And the supremum is taken over all of $A(s)$.

The real punch in these three bullet points is in the first part; even though optimal value functions are defined over all manner of strategies, the optimal value function itself is "stationary." If you followed the argument for why v_t^* depends only on s_t when there is a state-of-the-system structure, back on page 505, you will probably see how to show this result. The second bullet point follows from the first, and the third involves an argument that is only a little more complex than the argument given for this third bullet point in the previous set. (Can you provide it?)

A6.9. Solving Infinite-Horizon (Stationary) Problems With Unimprovability

We solved finite-horizon problems by employing backwards induction, to find a conserving strategy. We can imagine using a similar technique for infinite-horizon problems or, at least, for an infinite-horizon problem for which conserving strategies are guaranteed to be optimal. But to do this, we need f^* or, for stationary problems, v^*, and it isn't a priori obvious how we find those. The last bullet point of the previous section suggests one possible technique, at least for stationary problems where $\delta < 1$ and r is a bounded function: v^* is characterized as the unique bounded solution to the functional equation (A6.2‴). Especially if the state space S is finite, finding the solution ought to be possible. We'll deal with this line of attack in Section A6.11.

But in this section, we take a different approach. In many cases, the most efficient way to find an optimal strategy, and in particular to prove that this strategy is optimal, is

Step 1. Use the structure of the problem and your intution to guess at the optimal strategy or, at least, at the form of the optimal strategy.

Step 2. Compute the "value of the strategy" function v^σ for your guess.

Step 3. Then show that your strategy is optimal by showing that it is unimprovable.

Of course, this only works if (a) you can guess at the form of the optimal strategy, (b) you can compute its value function, and (c) you know that you are dealing with a problem in which unimprovability implies optimality. I can't help you with (a), except to wish you and your intuition good luck. So, when I said that this is the "most efficient way to *find* an optimal strategy," I was being less than completely honest: *You* find the optimal strategy, or at least the form of the optimal strategy, based on your ability to see through the problem; this technique allows you to *verify* that your guess is correct.

As in the case of the finite-horizon problems, both analytic and numerical methods can be employed. I'll get you started with one example of each.

Example. The job search

Recall the problem: You are interviewing for a job at dates $t = 0, 1, 2, \ldots$ You may take the job offered at any date, but once you take a job, you must keep it forever. The job offered at date t pays a wage w_t for each following period. That is, if you take the job offered at date 5, and it pays \$65, you get \$65 at dates $5, 6, 7, \ldots$ Until you take a job, you get \$0. You don't know the wage you will be offered at date t until date t; the sequence of wage offers $\{w_t\}$ forms an i.i.d. sequence, with w_t uniformly distributed between \$0 and \$100. Once you pass on a job, you can't go back to it.

You discount payoffs at a rate $\delta \in [0, 1)$ per period. You want to maximize your expected total (discounted and summed) net present value of payoffs.

We said earlier that the "state" in this case is whether you've taken a job or not, what is the current offer if not, and what wage you are earning if you have already taken a job. I'll simplify this a bit by some clever bookkeeping: If you take a job in period t that pays a wage w_t, I'll credit you immediately with a reward $r_t = w_t/(1 - \delta)$, the net present value of all your future wages. (If you don't take a job, you get $r_t = 0$.) This way, I only need to keep track of (a) whether you've taken a job and (b) if not, what wage you are being offered. Also, once you take a job, there are no further decisions to take, so I only need to keep track of continuation values in states where you are still in the market for a job.

Step 1 says to guess at the optimal strategy or, at least, its form. My guess at this point is about the *form* of the optimal strategy, namely: For some w^* (which will depend on δ), take any job offer of w^* or more and turn down any offer less than w^*.

I don't know that the optimal strategy has this form—right now this is just a guess—but I do know how to compute the value of following this sort of strategy. I need to know $v^{w^*}(w)$, the continuation value of following this w^* strategy if I haven't taken an offer yet and w is the offer on the table. Clearly

$$v^{w^*}(w) = \frac{w}{1-\delta}, \quad \text{if } w \geq w^*,$$

because the strategy calls for me to accept the offer, giving me an immediate reward of $w/(1 - \delta)$ and (the way I'm doing things) a continuation value of 0, since I've accepted a job. On the other hand, if I turn down the job, which is if $w < w^*$, then I get another draw next time. My expected value (today, having just turned down the offer) doesn't depend on the offer (it has no influence on future offers), so let me denote this number by $\hat{v}$; I know that $\hat{v}$ solves the functional equation

$$\hat{v} = \delta\left[\int_0^{w^*} \hat{v}\,\frac{dw}{100} + \int_{w^*}^{100} \frac{w}{1-\delta}\,\frac{dw}{100}\right].$$

That's a lot to take in, so let me explain: Having rejected the job, I get no immediate reward, but I do get the discounted value of continuing with this strategy starting next time, which is what I'm computing: Next time, I'll get a fresh draw of a wage offer w. If it is between 0 and w^*, I'll turn it down again, and I'll get $\hat{v}$ for a continuation value. If it is between w^* and 100, I'll take it, receiving $w/(1 - \delta)$. I have to take the expectation over all possible values of w, which is uniformly distributed over the interval $[0, 100]$, which gives me the integrator (and density function) $dw/100$.

Of course, the first term inside the square brackets simplifies to $w^*\hat{v}/100$. And the second is $(100^2 - (w^*)^2)/(200(1 - \delta))$. So we have the equation

$$\hat{v} = \delta\left[\hat{v}\left(\frac{w^*}{100}\right) + \frac{100^2 - (w^*)^2}{200(1-\delta)}\right].$$

This gives

$$\hat{v} = \frac{\delta(100^2 - (w^*)^2)}{200(1-\delta)} \bigg/ \left(1 - \frac{\delta w^*}{100}\right) = \frac{\delta(100^2 - (w^*)^2)}{2(1-\delta)(100 - \delta w^*)}.$$

I've computed the v^{w^*} function, for any w^*. But, given δ, only one w^* will be best. Which is it? Our criterion for optimality is unimprovability, and checking unimprovability in this case is easy: For wage offers $w > w^*$, it has to be that $w/(1-\delta) \geq \hat{v}$; otherwise, turning down the offer is better than accepting. While for offers $w < w^*$, we need $\hat{v} \geq w/(1-\delta)$. So, apparently, we will require

$$\frac{w^*}{(1-\delta)} = \frac{\delta(100^2 - (w^*)^2)}{2(1-\delta)(100 - \delta w^*)}.$$

If you carry through all the algebra, you will find that this gives

$$w^*(\delta) = 100\left(\frac{1 - \sqrt{1-\delta^2}}{\delta}\right),$$

where I've now written the wage w^* that is optimal as a function of the discount rate δ. Note that if δ is close to 0, $w^*(\delta)$ is close to zero (use L'Hôpital's Rule); if you discount the future heavily, you accept virtually any wage offer. While as δ approaches 1, $w^*(\delta)$ approaches 100; you become very picky as you become very patient.

Is this truly the optimal strategy? If you think through what we've done, the way we learned the value of $w^*(\delta)$ was to verify the unimprovability of using it as the cutoff to determine whether to take a job offer or not. Rewards are bounded, and $\delta < 1$, so this strategy is optimal.

Example. The button-pushing, letter-flashing machine problem

Now for an example solved numerically. Recall the problem: At dates $t = 0, 1, 2, \ldots$, a decision maker must push one of two buttons, the first marked X and the second Y. Simultaneously, the machine flashes one of two signals, either A or B. (She doesn't get to see what the machine will flash before she chooses her button.) She is paid according to the button she pushes and the signal flashed by the machine: She gets \$10 if she pushes X and the machine flashes A, \$0 for X and B, \$15 for Y and A, and \$5 for Y and B.

If at date $t-1$ the decision maker pushed X *and* the machine flashed A, then the chance that the machine flashes A at date t is 0.75. While if at date $t-1$ either the decision maker pushed Y *or* the machine flashed B, then the chance that the machine flashes A at date t is 0.2. At date 0, the machine flashes A with probability 0.75 (that is, it behaves as if in the previous round X had been pushed and A flashed). (The machine's behavior at date t is otherwise conditionally independent of the past, conditional on what happened at date $t-1$.)

The decision maker wishes to maximize the expectation of the discounted sum of her rewards, discounted at a rate of 0.98 per period.

The problem has everything we want, namely additive rewards and a time-homogeneous state-of-the-system structure. So we go looking for a stationary optimal strategy. We know that one exists: Since the problem has a time-homogenous state-of-the-system structure, Bellman's equation (A6.2‴) has a time-homogeneous structure. There are finitely many actions available in each state, so the supremum in Bellman's equation is a max; that is, the supremum is achieved. This means that a stationary and conserving strategy exists, and every conserving strategy is optimal.

There are four states of the system, AX, AY, BX, and BY (recording what happened last time, which drives what will happen this time), and there are two possible actions in each state, so there are 16 possible stationary strategies. But it seems likely that whatever action is optimal in state AY, the same action will be optimal in states BX and BY, because the influence of the past on the future depends only on whether the state is AX or not. We keep track of all four states because we want the reward to be a function of the current and next state, as well as the action. But in terms of future values, only AX or not is of consequence.

So, having no particular feel for this problem, I'll take a random guess that *always push* X is optimal. Step 2 requires me to find the value function for following this strategy, and equation (A6.1") tells me that, if I use $v(\cdot)$ for the value function, I have

$$
\begin{aligned}
v(AX) &= 0.75(10 + 0.98 \cdot v(AX)) + 0.25(0 + 0.98 \cdot v(BX)) \\
v(BX) &= 0.2(10 + 0.98 \cdot v(AX)) + 0.8(0 + 0.98 \cdot v(BX)) \\
v(AY) &= 0.2(10 + 0.98 \cdot v(AX)) + 0.8(0 + 0.98 \cdot v(BX)), \text{and} \\
v(BY) &= 0.2(10 + 0.98 \cdot v(AX)) + 0.8(0 + 0.98 \cdot v(BX)).
\end{aligned}
$$

Taking this a step at a time, if last time we saw AX, there is 0.75 chance of A this time and 0.25 chance of B. We are pushing X, so we get 10 immediately and a discounted $v(AX)$ next time, with probability 0.75, and get 0 today and a discounted $v(BX)$ next time, with probability 0.25. Whereas if we saw BX, or AY, or BY last time, we get A this time with probability 0.2 and B with probability 0.8.

"Why," you may be asking, "do we need to compute $v(BY)$? If we are playing the strategy of always picking X, we'll never find ourselves in state BY." But, when we go to check unimprovability of this strategy, we have to ask what will happen if we deviate and play Y. And then we'll need to have a continuation value for state BY (as well as AY).

We have four linear equations in four unknowns to solve, although since it is evident now that $v(BX) = v(BY) = v(AY)$, it is really two equations in two unknowns. Working numerically, I get $v(AX) = 228.85$ and $v(BX) = v(BY) = v(AY) = 216.92$, to two decimal places. (It is worth pointing out that there is nothing special in this problem in this regard: In a stationary problem with a finite state space, solving for v^σ for any stationary strategy σ, involves as many unknowns as there are states—namely $v^\sigma(s)$ for each state s—and the same number of linear equations, given by (A6.1″). Uniqueness of the solution is guaranteed, essentially, if the discount factor δ is less than one.)

Is this strategy unimprovable? Suppose I'm in state AX. I'm meant to choose X, which will net for me $0.75(10 + 0.98 \cdot v(AX)) + 0.25(0 + 0.98 \cdot v(BX)) = 228.85$. Alternatively, I could push Y, which gives me an expected value of $0.75(15 + 0.98 \cdot v(AY)) + 0.25(5 + 0.98 \cdot v(BY)) = 225$ or so. That's good news. And if I'm in state AY (or BY, or BX), I'm meant to choose X, with a net of 216.92. The alternative is to choose Y, which will net $0.2(15 + 0.98 \cdot v(AY)) + 0.8(5 + 0.98 \cdot v(BY)) = 219.58$, or so. Too bad; this strategy is *not* unimprovable.

So what next? Back to the drawing board. Maybe the optimal strategy is to choose X in state AX and to choose Y in the other three states. Maybe it is to pick Y always. We must compute the value functions for whatever strategy we decide to test next, check if it passes the unimprovability test and, if not, move on to another strategy. Tedious, perhaps (although some clever work in Excel makes it less tedious), but you will get the answer if you persevere.

A6.10. Policy Iteration (and Transience)

In the discussion just concluded, we learned that the strategy *always choose* X is not optimal because it is not unimprovable: In states AY, BY, and BX, choosing Y gives a one-step improvement. So we concluded that the thing to do is to try a different strategy, and keep trying until we find one that is unimprovable.

This search must end successfully. Bellman's equation is time homogeneous, and the set of available actions is finite, so a stationary strategy that is also conserving (that attains the *sup* in Bellman's equation) must exist. And since, in this problem, the utility function is both upper and lower convergent, this conserving strategy will be optimal and, therefore, unimprovable.

But it would be nice if we didn't have to search randomly through all the stationary strategies to find one that is unimprovable. In this problem, there aren't so many strategies that this is a major issue. But if there were many more states or actions available, the effort involved in trying out strategy after strategy could be prohibitive.

Suppose though, that we try a strategy σ and find that σ' is a one-step improvement on σ. This might suggest that we try σ' next. The question is, If σ' is a one-step improvement on σ, in the sense that

$$f_t^\sigma(h_t) \leq \mathbf{E}^{\sigma'}[f^\sigma(h_{t+1})|h_t]$$

for all t and h_t, are we assured that $f_t^{\sigma'}(h_t) \geq f_t^\sigma(h_t)$? (I'm reverting back to notation appropriate for the most general formulations because the question is completely general, even if our motivation for it comes from the context of stationary problems with additive utility.) If the answer is yes, then we could begin our search with a strategy σ; if it is not unimprovable, find a one-step improvement on it, σ', and then if necessary move on to a one-step improvement on σ'; and so forth, knowing that until we find an unimprovable strategy, the value functions of the sequence of strategies are going uphill. This is known as *policy iteration* in the literature.

The first counterexample given Section A6.4 shows that the answer to this question may be no. In that example, a strategy of *always take* is improved upon for a single step by *always wait*: using *always wait* for one round and then *taking* is better than *taking* immediately, but using *always wait* forever is worse. At best, we can hope for conditions sufficient to guarantee that policy iteration will work.

I take the opportunity presented by this question to generalize the ideas behind upper and lower convergent utility. We start with two definitions.

Definition A6.9. *Strategy σ is **upper transient** if, for each t and h_t, there is a subset of histories H' such that $\mathbf{P}^{\sigma}[H'|h_t] = 1$, u is uniformly bounded above on H', and $\lim_{k\to\infty} \overline{u}_k(h) = u(h)$ on H'. Strategy σ is **lower transient** if, for each t and h_t, there is a subset of histories H' such that $\mathbf{P}^{\sigma}[H'|h_t] = 1$, u is uniformly bounded below on H', and $\lim_{k\to\infty} \underline{u}_k(h) = u(h)$ on H'.*[11]

If u is upper convergent, then every strategy is upper transient. If u is lower convergent, then every strategy is lower transient. But in some problems, u fails to be upper (or lower) convergent because of histories that have zero probability under certain strategies. In such cases, even though u is not universally "nice," nice things may still be true about strategies that avoid the "bad" histories.

Proposition A6.10.

a. *Suppose that σ' is everywhere a one-step improvement on σ in the sense that*

$$f_t^{\sigma}(h_t) \leq \mathbf{E}^{\sigma'}[f_{t+1}^{\sigma}(h_{t+1})|h_t] \quad \text{for all } t \text{ and } h_t.$$

If σ' is upper transient, then $f_t^{\sigma'}(h_t) \geq f_t^{\sigma}(h_t)$ for all t and h_t.

b. *Conversely, suppose that σ' is **nowhere** a one-step improvement on σ in the sense that*

$$f_t^{\sigma}(h_t) \geq \mathbf{E}^{\sigma'}[f_{t+1}^{\sigma}(h_{t+1})|h_t] \quad \text{for all } t \text{ and } h_t.$$

If σ' is lower transient, then $f_t^{\sigma'}(h_t) \leq f_t^{\sigma}(h_t)$ for all t and h_t.

c. *If $\hat{\sigma}$ is unimprovable, then $f_t^{\hat{\sigma}}(h_t) \geq f_t^{\sigma}(h_t)$ for every t, h_t, and every lower transient strategy σ.*

d. *If σ is conserving and upper transient, then σ is optimal.*

---

[11] To ensure that various integrals are well defined, from the outset I've assumed that u is either uniformly bounded above or uniformly bounded below. I am not backing off that assumption here. But, for example, in the buying-a-television problem, u is uniformly bounded above. I'll later want to show that some strategies in that problem are *lower* transient; so for those strategies, u must *also* be uniformly bounded below, at least on a set of histories that has probability one under those strategies.

Part c of this proposition is a direct corollary of part b. This generalizes the result that unimprovable strategies are optimal when utility is lower convergent, because when utility is lower convergent, every strategy is lower transient. Part d directly generalizes the result that conserving strategies are optimal when u is upper convergent by similar logic.

The proofs are extensions of the basic argument used in Proposition A6.7. Take part a: If σ' is a one-step improvement on σ in the sense given, then by induction and the law of iterated conditional expectations, we know that σ' is a k-step improvement on σ, in the sense that

$$f_t^\sigma(h_t) \leq \mathbf{E}^{\sigma'}[f_{t+k}^\sigma(h_{t+k})|h_t)] \quad \text{for all } t \text{ and } h_t.$$

Since $\overline{u}_{t+k}(h)$ is always an upper bound on $f_{t+k}^\sigma(h_{t+k})$ (where h_{t+k} is the $t+k$ partial history of h), this inequality tells us that

$$f_t^\sigma(h_t) \leq \mathbf{E}^{\sigma'}[\overline{u}_{t+k}(h)|h_t] \quad \text{for all } t \text{ and } h_t.$$

Fixing t and h_t, separate the integral on the right-hand side of the last inequality into the integral over the set H' that has $P^{\sigma'}[\cdot|h_t]$-probability 1 and on which u is "nice" (in the sense of the definition of upper transience) and over the complement of that set. The complement has zero measure and so is inconsequential to the integral, while on the set H', we can pass to the limit in k, using monotone convergence, to conclude that $f_t^\sigma(h_t) \leq \mathbf{E}^{\sigma'}[u(h)|h_t] = f_t^{\sigma'}(h_t)$. This is part a.

The arguments for parts b and d are similar and, as noted, part c is a direct corollary of part b.

A6.11. Value Iteration

As we noted at the start of Section A6.9, to solve a specific problem, we could search for a conserving strategy, as long as the problem is one in which conserving strategies are optimal, and as long as we have the ability to compute the optimal value functions f_t^* or, for stationary problems, v^*. Assume for now that the problem is indeed stationary; then if r is bounded and $\delta < 1$, we even have the means for producing v^*, namely as the unique bounded solution to (A6.2‴). This isn't quite as simple as finding v^σ for a given (stationary) strategy σ, in general. For instance, if S is finite, finding v^σ amounts to solving N linear equations in N unknowns, where N is the cardinality of S. To find v^* involves solving N equations in N unknowns, but because of the *sup* operators in (A6.2‴), these aren't linear equations.

Or we can try to find v^* by means of successive approximation. In the literature of dynamic programming, this is called *value iteration*.

Let $w_0^* \equiv 0$. Then, iteratively, define $w_n^* : S \to R$ by

$$w_n^*(s) := \sup_{a \in A(s)} \mathbf{E}^{(s,a)}[r(s,a,s_{+1}) + \delta w_{n-1}^*(s_{+1}) \,|\, s].$$

I'm using w here instead of v so that there is no confusion between w_n, the nth iteration in this attempt to compute v^* recursively, and v_t, a continuation-value function beginning at time t (which ought to have either a superscript σ or $*$).

The hope is that $\lim_{n\to\infty} w_n^*$ is v^*. Unhappily, this is not true, in general. A counterexample will be given momentarily, but both to get positive results of this sort and to understand better what value iteration means, it helps to give the w_n^* functions a concrete explanation:

Take a step back (in terms of assumptions) from the context of stationary problems, to problems with additive rewards only. Given any t, h_t, and $T \geq t$, we can imagine the *finite-horizon subproblem* where decisions are taken at dates $t, t+1, t+2, \ldots, T$, and rewards $r_{t+1}, \ldots, r_{T+1}$ are received. For each strategy σ and partial history h_t, define

$$v_{t,T}^{\sigma}(h_t) = \mathbf{E}^{\sigma}\left[\sum_{k=0}^{T-t} \delta^k r_{t+k+1}(h_{t+k+1}) \,\middle|\, h_t\right] \quad \text{and} \quad v_{t,T}^{*}(h_t) = \sup_{\sigma} v_{t,T}^{\sigma}(h_t).$$

These are finite-horizon value functions, which can be computed by backward induction. The connection to the w_n functions is that, in a stationary environment, where h_t is a history whose time-t state is s,

$$v_{t,T}^{*}(h_t) = w_{T-t+1}^{*}(s).$$

In words, the question of value iteration in a stationary environment—does $\lim_{n\to\infty} w_n^* = v^*$?—is subsumed by the broader question for problems with additive rewards: Do the value functions (both for a given strategy and the optimal value functions) for a finite-horizon subproblem of an infinite-horizon problem converge to the corresponding infinite-horizon value functions? That is, do

$$\lim_{T\to\infty} v_{t,T}^{\sigma}(h_t) = v_t^{\sigma}(h_t) \quad \text{and} \quad \lim_{T\to\infty} v_{t,T}^{*}(h_t) = v_t^{*}(h_t)?$$

In both cases (that is, both for the value of using a strategy and the optimal value functions), the answer is no, in general. For the value-of-using-a-strategy functions, counterexamples are extremely artificial, and conditions guaranteeing convergence are fairly weak. We have the following result:

Proposition A6.11. *For an infinite-horizon dynamic programming problem where U takes the additive form $U(h) = \sum_{t=0}^{\infty} \delta^t r_{t+1}(h_{t+1})$, let*

$$U^+(h) := \sum_{t=0}^{\infty} \delta^t \mathit{max}\{0, r_{t+1}(h_{t+1})\} \quad \mathit{and} \quad U^-(h) := \sum_{t=0}^{\infty} \delta^t \mathit{min}\{0, r_{t+1}(h_{t+1})\}.$$

If either $U^{+}(h)$ is uniformly bounded above (uniformly for all h) or $U^{-}(h)$ is uniformly bounded below, then for all t, h_t, and σ,

$$\lim_{T\to\infty} v^{\sigma}_{t,T}(h_t) = v^{\sigma}_t(h_t).$$

The proof of this is a mess of ϵ's and δ's, and I won't even give a sketch. You might want to try to prove the result for the following simpler cases: (a) the functions r_t are all nonnegative; (b) they are nonpositive; (c) the functions r_t are uniformly bounded and $\delta < 1$. These cases cover most applications you will encounter. However, for instance, the television-purchase example requires the more general statement given in the proposition.

But while the finite-horizon value functions for strategies converge to the infinite-horizon value functions fairly (but not completely) generally, it takes more to get convergence of the optimal value functions.

Consider the following example: Suppose that $\delta = 1$ and $S = \{00, 0, 1, 2, 3, \ldots\}$. The only state with any choice of action at all is state $s = 00$, where the available actions are $\{1, 2, \ldots\}$. Transitions are deterministic: From state $s = 00$, if the action taken is n, transition is to state n. From any other state n except for state 0, transition is to state $n-1$. From state 0, transition is back to state 0—state 0 is absorbing. As for rewards, $r \equiv 0$ with one exception: If you are in state 1 and make the (deterministic) transition to state 0, the "reward" is -1.

In this problem, $v^*(00) = -1$. No matter what action you choose in state 00, eventually the transition from 1 to 0 will happen and -1 is received. (There is no discounting, remember.) But for any finite n, $w^*_n(00) = v^*_{0,n}(00) = 0$, because with an n-stage horizon, by choosing (from state 00) an action $m > n+1$, you put off this -1 until after the problem "ends." The intuition here is simple: If you fix a strategy, then its value over a long-enough horizon converges to its value over the infinite horizon. But when it comes to optimal value functions, there can be strategies where this convergence happens arbitrarily far off in the future and, if you are in the sort of problem (with negative rewards) where this convergence is to be avoided, then in any finite-horizon subproblem, you may be able to do so.

This intuition suggests the following positive results for value iteration.

Proposition A6.12. *For an infinite-horizon dynamic programming problem where U takes additive form:*

a. *If the problem is such that $\lim_{T\to\infty} v^{\sigma}_{t,T}(h_t) = v^{\sigma}_t(h_t)$ for all strategies σ, dates t, and partial histories h_t (e.g., if the conditions of Proposition A6.11 hold), then for all t and h_t,*

$$\liminf_{T\to\infty} v^{*}_{t,T}(h_t) \geq v^{*}_t(h_t).$$

b. *If either the reward functions r_t are nonnegative, or the functions r_t are uniformly bounded and $\delta < 1$, then for all t and h_t,*

$$\lim_{T\to\infty} v^*_{t,T}(h_t) = v^*_t(h_t).$$

To prove part a, take any $\epsilon > 0$ and let σ be a strategy that is within ϵ of optimal starting at t and h_t. (If $v^*_t(h_t) = \infty$, a special argument needs to be constructed.) Take T' large enough so that for this σ and for all $T > T'$, $v^\sigma_{t,T}(h_t)$ is within ϵ of $v^\sigma_t(h_t)$. Then $v^\sigma_{t,T}(h_t)$ is within 2ϵ of $v^*_t(h_t)$ and, of course, $v^*_{t,T}(h_t) \geq v^\sigma_{t,T}(h_t)$.

For the first half of part b, note that if rewards are nonnegative, $v^*_t(h_t) \geq v^*_{t,T}(h_t)$, since the "added" rewards $r_{T+2}, r_{T+3}, \ldots$ can only increase the value of any strategy, and hence the optimal value. Apply part a. And for the second half of part b, note that, in this case, the difference between $v^\sigma_{t,T}$ and v^σ_t can be uniformly bounded by $\delta^T M/(1-\delta)$, where M is twice the uniform bound on the r_t functions; hence the same uniform bound applies to the difference between $v^*_{t,T}$ and v^*_t.

A6.12. Examples

We now have all the tools that we will develop in this appendix; what remains is to apply them to specific problems. Of the seven problems at the start of this appendix, we have already solved four; we will now analyze two of the remaining three. The purpose of this section is to show how these tools are used; even if you didn't follow all the proofs in earlier sections, you should make an effort to follow the logic of how the tools can be used in specific problems.

Infinite-horizon consumption and savings

The second problem given is an infinite-horizon consumption-savings problem, in which the decision maker seeks to maximize the expectation of the utility function

$$u(c_0, c_1, \ldots) = \sum_{t=0}^{\infty} (0.9)^t \, c_t^{1/2.}$$

The decision maker begins with \$1000 and, in each period, earns either 5% or 12% on any savings, each with probability 1/2, independent across periods. The problem doesn't say, but I assume that it is not possible for the decision maker to go into debt.

The problem has an additive and stationary structure, where the state variable at date t is the wealth held at the start of the period, which will be denoted y_t.

The "added-in" utility each period, $c_t^{1/2}$, is nonnegative, so this is immediately a problem with lower convergent utility. In fact, since the expected rate of return on wealth is less than the discount rate (and the per-period utility function is concave), you can prove that every strategy for this problem is upper transient. But I will proceed without that result, to show how you can work your way to the answer without it.

Because utility is lower convergent, any unimprovable strategy is optimal, and if we had a good guess as the form of the optimal strategy, we could proceed in the fashion of the job-search problem. In fact, since I know the answer, I have a good guess as to the form of the optimal strategy. But I'll pretend that I don't have such a good guess.

Instead, I'll employ value iteration. Because the "period-by-period rewards" are nonnegative, we know that by iterating Bellman's equation, we get (optimal, finite-horizon) value functions that converge to the infinite-horizon optimal value functions v^*. If there is only period 0, the optimal thing to do is to consume all wealth, so the iteration begins with $w_1^*(y_0) = y_0^{1/2}$. (This is the solution of the first iteration of Bellman's equation, beginning with $w_0^* \equiv 0$.) Dropping the subscript from the wealth term, we have the recursion

$$w_n^*(y) = \sup_c c^{1/2} + 0.9\big[0.5w_{n-1}^*(1.05(y-c)) + 0.5w_{n-1}^*((1.12(y-c)))\big].$$

To explain, the term over which we maximize is the utility of immediate consumption plus the discounted and expected continuation value: If we consume c out of y this period, next period's wealth is either $1.05(y-c)$ or $1.12(y-c)$, each with probability $1/2$.

If you use this general recursive equation with w_1^* in place of w_{n-1}^* to find w_2^*, you will learn that the optimal value of c (for a continuation value function $w_1^*(y) = y^{1/2}$) is $c = y/(1+k^2)$, where $k = 0.45(1.05^{1/2} + 1.12^{1/2})$, which is approximately 0.93734802. This then tells us that

$$w_2^*(y) = \left(\frac{y}{1+k^2}\right)^{1/2} + k\left(\frac{k^2 y}{1+k^2}\right)^{1/2} = ((1+k^2)y)^{1/2}.$$

If you stare at this for a moment, you see the pattern that emerges: By an inductive argument, if the value of continuation is $w_{n-1}^*(y) = k_{n-1}y^{1/2}$, then the recursion that determines w_n^* is

$$w_n^*(y) = \sup_c c^{1/2} + kk_{n-1}(y-c)^{1/2},$$

where k is the constant $0.45(1.05^{1/2} + 1.12^{1/2})$ and we begin with $k_0 = 0$ (or $k_1 = 1$). This produces an optimal $c = y/(1 + k^2k_{n-1}^2)$ and $w_n^*(y) = (1 + k^2k_{n-1}^2)^{1/2}y^{1/2}$, so that

$$k_n := (1 + k^2k_{n-1}^2)^{1/2}.$$

Letting $k_* = \lim_n k_n$, we know that $v^*(y)$ will equal $k_* y^{1/2}$. How do we know that this sequence of k_n must converge? Here's the argument:

- The recursion that determines w_n^* from w_{n-1}^* is increasing in the function w_{n-1}^*, meaning, put in a bigger value-of-continuation on the right-hand side, and a bigger value function must emerge on the left-hand side.
- Since $w_0^* \equiv 0$ and the immediate utility functions are all nonnegative, this means that $w_0^* \le w_1^* \le w_2^* \le \ldots$. Therefore, these value functions must "converge," albeit convergence to $+\infty$ is possible.
- In fact, since we know the form for each w_n^* is $k_n y^{1/2}$, this means that the scalars k_n are increasing in n.
- It is conceivable that k_n increases to $+\infty$, but since the expected return rate is less than the discount rate and the immediate-utility function is concave, this can't happen. (This last step is the only one that takes special pleading.)

Moreover, since any optimal strategy must be conserving (we know this, not the reverse!), the optimal strategy, if one exists, must be $c^*(y) = y/(1 + k^2 k_*^2)$. And now, to verify that this is indeed the optimal strategy, you can either prove that it generates the optimal value function or that it is unimprovable.

In case you do grind through the numbers, you should find that k_* is approximately 2.87030984 and the optimal strategy is to consume around 12.137869% of your wealth, each period.

(Had you been able to guess that the optimal strategy took the form of consuming a fixed fraction of wealth, you could have short-circuited much of this work by computing the value function associated with such a strategy and then found the fraction that made such a strategy unimprovable. But the analysis above shows how you can substitute a mixture of effort and value iteration for an inspired guess, if your powers of guessing are insufficient.)

Buying a flat-screen television

Recall the problem: You wish to buy a new flat-screen television. Once you buy the television, you will receive a reward of \$3000 less the price you pay. You only will buy once. There is an infinite sequence of stores from which you might purchase the television, indexed by $n = 0, 1, \ldots$. Store n charges the price p_n, and you can only learn p_n by going to store n: From your perspective, $\{p_n\}$ is a sequence of independent and identically distributed random variables, each having a uniform distribution on the interval $[\$2000, \$3000]$. You can visit as many stores as you wish, and there is no discounting, but each time you visit another store, you incur a cost of \$100. Once you leave a store (without buying), you cannot go back. You want to maximize the expected value of \$3000 less the price you pay and less the cost of all the visits to stores that you make; that is, if you visit stores $0, 1, 2, \ldots, n$ and then purchase at store n, your net reward is $\$3000 - p_n - 100(n+1)$; you seek to maximize the expected value of this quantity. (If you never purchase a television, your net reward is $-\infty$; you must keep visiting stores in succession until you buy.)

This seems very similar to the job-search problem, except that in the job-search problem, the forces pushing you to take a job are (a) that rewards are discounted, and (b) you get no wages until you take a job. In this problem, there is no discounting, but you have to keep paying \$100 per period until you purchase a television. The difference may seem small in terms of economics, but in terms of the difficulties faced in using the tools of dynamic programming, it is significant. In the job-search problem, rewards were all nonnegative (not to mention, discounted with a bound on per-period rewards), so the utility function is lower convergent, and (therefore) unimprovable strategies are optimal. In this case, the utility function is not lower convergent but upper convergent.[12] Since utility is not lower convergent, it seems at first blush that we cannot simply search for an unimprovable strategy and declare it optimal.

But it turns out that we can do this. The key is to enlist the result that says that an unimprovable strategy is as good as any lower-transient strategy. The lower-transient strategies, in this problem, are those that involve purchase before some fixed and definite time T. (Any strategy that has positive probability of delaying purchase beyond any horizon T is not lower transient, because there is no uniform lower bound on $u(h)$ for such strategies that holds with probability one under the strategy.) So, if we produce an unimprovable strategy $\hat{\sigma}$, it is at least as good as strategies that buy by some definite time. What about other strategies? Let σ be any strategy such that, for given t and h_t, $f_t^\sigma(h_t) = \mathbf{E}^\sigma[u(h)|h_t] > -\infty$. For each $T > t$, let σ^T denote the strategy: Beginning at t and history h_t, follow the prescriptions of σ until time T; but at time T, if a purchase has not yet been made, purchase no matter what price is quoted. Each σ^T is lower transient, and so for $\hat{\sigma}$ unimprovable, $f_t^{\hat{\sigma}}(h_t) \geq f_t^{\sigma^T}(h_t)$. And I assert that $\lim_{T\to\infty} f_t^{\sigma^T}(h_t) = f_t^\sigma(h_t)$, which then implies that $f_t^{\hat{\sigma}}(h_t) \geq f_t^\sigma(h_t)$. This in turn shows that $\hat{\sigma}$ is optimal, because it shows that $\hat{\sigma}$ is as good as any strategy that doesn't produce the disastrous outcome $-\infty$.

The key to the argument is to show that $\lim_T f_t^{\sigma^T}(h_t) = f_t^\sigma(h_t)$. This takes a bit of mathematical sophistication, and I'll just sketch the proof. Let H^T denote the subset of histories H on which (starting from h_t) a purchase is made by time T and G^T denote the complement of H^T. Then

$$f_t^{\sigma^T}(h_t) = \mathbf{E}^\sigma[u(h)1_{H_T}|h_t] + \mathbf{E}^\sigma[(3000 - p_T - 100T)1_{G^T}|h_t],$$

where 1_{H_T} indicates the standard indicator function. There is more going on here than you may first discern: I've substituted $\mathbf{E}^\sigma$ for $\mathbf{E}^{\sigma^T}$, but I can do that because using σ^T gives the same probability distribution of results as does σ, when σ calls for a purchase by time T (on the event H^T), and it calls for purchase at time T on the complementary event G^T. On the other hand,

$$f_t^\sigma(h_t) = \mathbf{E}^\sigma[u(h)1_{H_T}|h_t] + \mathbf{E}^\sigma[u(h)1_{G^T}|h_t].$$

So the difference between $f_t^{\sigma^T}(h_t)$ and $f_t^\sigma(h_t)$ is the difference between the two right-most terms. But since $f_t^\sigma(h_t) > -\infty$, the event on which no purchase is

[12] Why? Since you can only buy once, along every possible history, there is at most one positive entry. Along any history with that one positive entry, $\overline{u}_t(h)$ converges to $u(h)$ and, in fact, the convergence is exact at some finite time. And, along the history where you never buy, $\overline{u}_t(h)$ converges to $u(h) = -\infty$. Moreover, $u(h)$ is uniformly bounded above by 1000.

made has zero probability under $\mathbf{P}^\sigma[\cdot|h_t]$, and (by the continuity of probability) the probability of the events G^T goes to zero. More than that, because the integral $\mathbf{E}^\sigma[u(h)|h_t]$ has finite value, a standard argument (dominated convergence) shows that the contribution to the integral from integrating over the sets G^T goes to zero. From this argument, it is relatively easy to show as well that the second term that makes up $f_t^{\sigma^T}(h_t)$ also goes to zero, giving the desired convergence.

So, to conclude, we *can* hunt for an unimprovable strategy and, when we find one, we know it is optimal. Now that we know this is true, the methods used in the job-search problem work well: Hypothesize the form of the strategy—the obvious hypothesis is, take the first price below some critical price level $\hat{p}$—then find the value of using a cutoff price of $\hat{p}$, and finally find the value of $\hat{p}$ that makes this strategy unimprovable.

While this works, it takes substantial cleverness to see the argument that an unimprovable strategy is optimal. A more straightforward approach would be to recall that u is upper convergent in this problem, so we can find an optimal strategy by producing one that is conserving. The evident problem with this is that we don't know v^*. Moreover, it isn't evident that we can employ value iteration, since value iteration when rewards are undiscounted is only guaranteed to work (in Proposition A6.12) for problems with nonnegative rewards.

But we *can* use value iteration, because of part a of Proposition A6.12. Value iteration works for the v^σ functions, for all strategies σ, since there is a uniform upper bound (of 1000) on the sum of all positive rewards that can be received. Therefore, we know from Proposition A6.12 that the limit infimum of $v_{t,T}^*$ is at least as large as v_t^*. But, in addition (and for this specific problem!), we can show that $v_{t,T}^*$ is *nondecreasing* in T and that $v_t^* \geq v_{t,T}^*$ for all T. *Adding more periods to shop cannot decrease the optimal value!* A bit informally, the argument is: Take any strategy σ for the t to T horizon problem. In the last period, the sales price offered is necessarily less than the value 3000. So if σ doesn't prescribe accepting the last offer (if you get that far), σ is beaten (for the t-to-T-horizon problem) by the strategy that is: Do what σ prescribes, except make a purchase in the last period. Therefore, it is clear that $v_{t,T}^*$ is the supremum over all these purchase-at-date-T-if-you-haven't-already-done-so strategies. And those strategies are available for any longer-horizon problem and, in particular, for the infinite-horizon problem. So any longer-horizon problem, and the infinite-horizon problem, necessarily have optimal value functions that are no smaller than $v_{t,T}^*$.[13]

Therefore, we know that $\lim_{T\to\infty} v_{t,T}^*$ exists and equals v_t^*. Because (for this problem!) we can make a special argument about values only improving the longer is the horizon, we know that value iteration works. The job now is to compute v^* (where I use the stationarity of the problem to drop the subscript t).

To ease the computational burden, instead of computing the function v^*, I'm

---

[13] This argument depends on the fact that the price quoted in any store can be no greater than the value, 3000, of the television. What if the support of each p_t exceeds 3000? If you like mathematical challenges, see if you can adopt the simple argument I've given here to show that value interation does work, as long as the support of p_t is bounded below.

going to compute an "average" value of this function. Let me explain: When contemplating whether to purchase at the price quoted at the current store, which I'll call p, the decision maker reasons as follows: "If I purchase, my net from this point on is $3000 - p$. If I don't, I move on to the next store. I have to pay \$100 immediately and, in addition, I take my chances next time. Those chances aren't impacted by the current state of the system (which is the price p), since the next price I'll see (the next state) is independent of the current state. So, in essence, I'm comparing today between the value of buying today, $3000 - p$, and the expected value of where I'll be at the next store, which I'll denote ν^*, less the \$100 I have to pay to get there. That is, the number ν^* will be the average value of v^*, averaged over all the prices I may see next time, but not including the \$100 I have to pay to get to the next store."

In the recursion that determines ν^*, we start with $\nu_0 = 0$. (This corresponds to shopping with no more stores to visit.) Obviously, the optimal decision is to buy, since the price we're seeing today must be less than 3000. This means that $\nu_1 = 500$: The optimal value in the last period of shopping is $3000 - p$, where p is uniformly distributed between 2000 and 3000, and that averages to 500.

Suppose, then, that the decision maker is at the next-to-last store, seeing price p. Buying nets $3000 - p$, while going on to the next store nets an average value of $\nu_1 - 100 = 400$. So the best thing to do is to purchase if $p < 2600$ and go on to the final store if $p > 2600$. (If $p = 2600$, the decision maker can do either.) There is probability 0.6 that $p < 2600$, with an average value to the decision maker in this case of 700. And there is probability 0.4 that $p > 2600$, in which case the average value is 400. So $\nu_2 = (0.6)(700) + (0.4)(400) = 580$.

In general, suppose ν_{n-1} is the average value of shopping optimally, after paying the shopping fee of \$100, if this is store $n-1$ from the end. At store n from the end, facing price p, the choice is either (a) buy now, for value $3000 - p$, or (b) go to the next store, for value $\nu_{n-1} - 100$. It is better to buy now if $3000 - p > \nu_{n-1} - 100$ and to go on if not, which is when $3100 - \nu_{n-1} < p$. This then gives us the formula for ν_n (for $n \geq 2$):

$$\nu_n = \left(\frac{1100 - \nu_{n-1}}{1000}\right)\left(\frac{\nu_{n-1} + 900}{2}\right) + \left(\frac{\nu_{n-1} - 100}{1000}\right)(\nu_{n-1} - 100).$$

To explain, this is the probability of a price p less than $3100 - \nu_{n-1}$, times the average value accrued at prices between that price and the lowest price of 2000, plus the probability of a price above $3100 - \nu_{n-1}$, times the value of going on, which is ν_{n-1} less the 100 paid to continue shopping. Because we know that value iteration works, we know that these values will converge (upward) to ν^*, and, at the same time, the cutoff price $3100 - \nu_{n-1}$ that determines whether to buy today or keep shopping converges (downward) to the cutoff price that is conserving, and hence optimal, in the infinite-horizon problem. All that remains is to get out Excel and run the recursion; I did so and got $\nu^* = 652.7864$ (approximately, to four decimal points) and an optimal strategy of buying at the first price less (or equal to) \$2447.2136 (again, approximately) that is encountered.

What about the possibility of going back to an earlier price quote, either for free or at some cost? Even if this option were free, it is not worthwhile. It is better to pay \$100 and try a new store than to go back for any price greater than \$2447.2136, and if you had seen a price less than this in the past, you would have already bought. So, in the context of this problem (and, by a similar argument, in the context of the job-search problem), the option to go back, even for free, is worthless. It *could* be worth something if you didn't know the distribution of prices (or wage offers) and were learning about the distribution as you went along; then you might pass a price early on that, experience teaches you, was actually a good deal. But solving this sort of optimal search problem is a good deal harder when you are learning about the distribution of "offers" as you go. The parking problem where you don't know the probability ρ is a fairly simple finite-horizon problem of this sort, and the final example (number 7) from the start of the appendix gives you a fairly simple infinite-horizon example.

A6.13. Things Not Covered Here: Other Optimality Criteria; Continuous Time and Control Theory

This appendix has gone on more than long enough. The tools provided will be sufficient for many problems you encounter in the economics literature. But *many* is not *all*, and it may be helpful to point out (in this section and the next) two categories of problems the solution of which requires tools not covered here.

We've looked at optimality criteria that involve maximizing or minimizing the expected value of a function of the full history. More than that, the tools we've developed work when the utility function has the important property that the utility of an entire history is asymptotically "settled" by what happens in finite time, at least as an upper or a lower bound on the final outcome.

But imagine that rewards are received each period (that is, it looks like an additive structure), and those rewards are something like the per capita wealth of citizens alive in an economy in that period. (Take the perspective of a central planner who wishes to optimize institutional features of an economy that, in the model, lives for a countable infinity of generations of citizens.) Does it make sense to discount these values? Why should generations that come earlier be more important than those who come later? (These are not trivial questions. There is a large literature in economics on intergenerational equity.) If you don't discount per capita wealth and simply sum up the "rewards," you may well get $+\infty$ for a whole range of strategies. In this sort of setting, you may decide that it is sensible to evaluate institutional features of the economy in terms of which ones give the highest long-run average per capita wealth. That is, if W_t is the per capita wealth in period t, you want to maximize

$$\lim_{T\to\infty} \frac{W_0 + \ldots + W_T}{T}.$$

(If outcomes are uncertain, you might want to look at the expectation of this long-run average. If the long-run average doesn't exist, you might look at the limit infimum of the long-run average.) Or you might say that one set of institutional features is better than another if, eventually, the sum of per capita wealths of the first "overtakes" the second; that is, letting W_t be per capita wealth in the first set and W'_t in the second set, if there is T such that, for all $t > T$,

$$W_0 + \ldots + W_t \geq W'_0 + \ldots + W'_t.$$

(Of course, if one set of institutions "overtakes" the other in this sense, then it performs at least as well in terms of long-run averages.)

The point is: These are decision criteria in which what happens over any finite horizon is not only not dispositive, but even of no particular consequence. What matters is entirely what happens in the very long run. The tools developed here are pretty much useless for such criteria. So what does work? You'll need to consult a text on dynamic programming to get answers.

And, second, dynamic programming, at least as presented here, involves the selection of actions at a discrete (and possibly countably infinite) sequence of dates or times. In some economics problems, it is natural to have a formulation where actions are chosen continuously. The mathematical subject of control theory, in which the central result is the Pontryagin Maximum Principle, provides tools for solving these problems if there are no stochastic elements; the discipline of Stochastic Control Theory extends to problems with stochastic elements.

A6.14. Multi-armed Bandits and Complexity

Having slogged through an appendix of 50 pages, you are entitled to hope that you now have all the tools needed to solve all manner of complex dynamic choice problems where, at least, decisions are taken at a discrete sequence of dates, and the decision criteria conform to the restrictions we've imposed. But you should temper those hopes: Even with these stipulations, dynamic choice problems that arise in economics get very complex, very quickly.

A class of problems known as the *multi-armed bandit problems* illustrates the point. A multi-armed bandit problem is one in which, at each point in time $t = 0, 1, \ldots$, the decision maker has a number of different actions or policies she can try. But she can only try one in each period. At the outset, she isn't sure how efficacious the policies will be; she has a well-formed prior assessment about this, but as time passes, she will get better and better information about how different policies do. The feature that sends the complexity of this situation through the roof is, Suppose her decision which policy to try this period affects how much she learns about the efficacy of her options. At the extreme, imagine that the only way she can get information about the value of a given option is to try that particular option. If, say, she has a choice between A, B, and C, and if after some period of time, she decides that A looks better than B and C, she might abandon B and C altogether.

But if she does, she doesn't learn anything more about B and C and, in particular, she might miss out on the fact that C is actually better than A.

The name *multi-armed bandit* comes from a fanciful depiction of this problem. Imagine you sit in front of a slot machine. Each time t, you can put your coin (say, a silver dollar) into the machine and pull the arm. Most slot machines you will find in casinos have a single arm (hence the colloquialism *one-armed bandit*), but this slot machine has several arms. Different arms have different characteristics of payoff distributions: One arm might pay off small amounts frequently; a second might pay off rarely but in huge amounts, and a third (masquerading as the second) might eat your silver dollar each period and never pay back anything. The problem is, you don't know which arm is which or even what are the precise characteristics of each arm. You can "buy information" on an arm by putting up your silver dollar and pulling that arm. But the information costs you both a dollar and the time it takes to get the information; time you might spend more profitably by pulling a different arm.

Problem 7 from the first section is the simplest problem of this sort: It is really only a single-armed bandit, but (what makes it part of this category of models) you don't know a priori the characteristics of that arm, and while you can "buy" information, you do so only by playing that arm. If you ever stop playing, you learn nothing more; you might decide at some point that the arm looks bad (is the type that never pays you a reward), while in fact it is the sort that does pay a reward occasionally, and you've just had a run of bad luck with it.

While the depiction as a slot machine with multiple arms is fanciful, economic contexts for this category of problem abound. Think of a firm trying different production techniques (e.g., team-build versus assembly line), health authorities trying different treatment policies, or economic policymakers trying different forms of monetary policy. The decision maker isn't sure about the efficacy of any particular technique or policy and learns by trying. But the cost of trying a particular technique or policy to learn how well it functions includes not using another technique or policy that is known to work "adequately." Of course, in real-life applications, you may be able to analyze the impact of an untried policy through "what-if" analysis. But the law of unintended consequences often means that you learn best by implementing, and that comes at a cost.

Multi-armed bandit problems are hard dynamic programming problems. It took the community of dynamic programmers two decades or so to figure out how to solve these problems—look in the literature for the *Gittins Index*—and, at that, the methods developed only work if the arms are statistically independent (what you learn about one arm tells you nothing about any other arm). But in economic contexts, statistical independence is typically too strong an assumption: You may learn something about how well B would have done based on your experience with A, but not as much as you would have learned had you tried B. In this sort of situation, in general, the problem is just too hard to solve (at least, with a discounted sum of rewards criterion).

Why bother telling you all this (and discouraging you after reading through this appendix)? If you have already read Chapter 7 in the text itself, you know why. If not, please go and read that chapter now.

A6.15. Four More Problems You Can Solve

Of the seven examples given at the start of this appendix, you are left with some details to clean up in some of them, as well as two substantial tasks: In the parking problem, what happens if the decision maker is unsure whether $\rho = 0.7$ or 0.9? And all of the seventh example remains. And if you would like some more problems on which to try your hand, here are four.

■ 8. **Another two-button, flashing-light machine**

(a) A decision maker faces the following dynamic decision problem. At dates $t = 0, 1, 2, \ldots$, she must push one of two buttons, the first marked X and the second Y. Simultaneously, the machine flashes one of two signals, either A or B. (She doesn't get to see what the machine will flash before she chooses her button.) She is paid according to the button she pushes and the signal flashed by the machine: She gets \$10 is she pushes X and the machine flashes A, \$0 for X and B, \$15 for Y and A, and \$5 for Y and B.

Of course it matters to her what the machine flashes. If she pushed X at date $t-1$, then at date t the machine flashes A with probability 0.75 and B with probability 0.25. If she pushed Y at date $t-1$, the machine flashes B with probability 0.8 and A with probability 0.2. At date 0, the machine behaves as if she had pushed A at date -1; i.e., it will flash A with probability 0.75. (The machine's behavior at date t is otherwise conditionally independent of the past, conditional on what the decision maker did at date $t-1$.)

The decision maker wishes to maximize the expectation of the discounted sum of her payments, discounted at a rate δ per period. That is, if r_t is her reward at date t ($r_t = \$10, \$0, \$15$ or \$5), then she seeks to maximize the expectation of $\sum_{t=0}^{\infty} \delta^t r_t$.

As a function of δ, what is the optimal strategy for this decision maker?

(b) Redo this problem, but supposing that the machine behaves a bit differently. Specifically, if at date $t-1$ the decision maker pushed X *and* the machine flashed A, then the chance that the machine flashes A at date t is 0.75. While if at date $t-1$ either the decision maker pushed Y *or* the machine flashed B, then the chance that the machine flashes A at date t is 0.2. At date 0, the machine flashes A with probability 0.75. (The machine's behavior at date t is otherwise conditionally independent of the past, conditional on what happened at date $t-1$.)

■ 9. (This sort of problem arises in applications of game theory connected to the Folk Theorem with random observables.) A decision maker is controlling a random process that works as follows. At each date $t = 0, 1, \ldots$, the process is either in state X or state Y. If the process is in state Y, the decision maker has nothing to do; at the next date, the state will be Y again with probability 0.1 and it will be X with probability 0.9. Moreover, the decision maker receives \$0 on this date.

If, on the other hand, the process is in state X, the decision maker must choose one of two actions, either α or β. If the decision maker chooses α, she is paid \$1 and the state is X again next period with certainty. If she chooses β, she is paid \$2 and the state next period is Y with certainty.

The decision maker discounts her rewards at the rate 0.8 per period. That is, if she gets reward r_0 at date 0, r_1 at date 1, and so on, she evaluates her outcome as the sum $\sum_{t=0}^{\infty}(0.8)^t r_t$. If there is any uncertainty, she wishes to maximize the expectation of this discounted infinite sum.

What is the optimal strategy for this decision maker to follow?

■ 10. You are (eventually) going to manufacture a product for which you will be the monopoly producer. Demand for this product is given by the demand function $D(p) = 1000(10 - p)$ per period. Once you begin producing the product, you will set its price to maximize your per period profit, which will depend on your marginal cost of production c. (There are no fixed costs associated with production.) Specifically, given a value of c (less than 10), your optimal level of production per period is $500(10 - c)$, and your profit per period is $250(10 - c)^2$.

The marginal cost of manufacture c will be one of 7, or 4, or 1.

Which of these three will be your cost is partly determined by nature and partly by you. Specifically, there is a *theoretically best cost*, which is one of these three, and the chances of each value being the theoretically best cost is 1/3. (You know these probabilities; you do not (yet) know which is the true theoretical best cost and, as you will see, you may never learn which it is.)

At time $t = 0$, you know how to manufacture the good at a marginal cost of 7. But if you choose to, you can spend this period trying to get a better (lower) cost figure. If you choose to do this, and if the theoretical best cost figure is 7, you will make no progress. But if the theoretical best cost figure is either 4 or 1, there is a 1/2 probability that, in this period, you will learn how to manufacture the product at a cost of 4.

In general, in any period where you choose to do research to improve your costs of manufacture, you will either learn nothing or improve by one step, from 7 to 4 if you are currently at 7, and from 4 to 1 if you are currently at 4. *If* the true theoretical best cost is your current cost, then there is no chance you will better your cost. But if the true theoretical best cost is less than your current cost, there is probability 1/2 that you will improve your costs by one step. Moreover, this probability 1/2 is independent of anything that happened in prior periods and, if you are currently at a cost of 7, is the same whether the theoretical best cost is 4 or 1.

However, *if you choose to do research, to try to lower your costs, you cannot manufacture and sell this period.* There are no further costs to doing research, except for the profit you forego this period. But you must forego any profit this period. And *if you ever decide to stop research and manufacture, you can never go back to research. You are forever stuck with the cost at which you first decide to begin to manufacture and sell.*

You want to maximize the expected value of the discounted sum of profits you earn over an infinite horizon of time periods $t = 0, 1, 2, \ldots$, with a discount rate of $\delta = 0.9$. What is your optimal strategy? You must, of course, prove that the solution you propose is indeed optimal.

■ 11. Forest management

(This problem is very arduous. Proceed at your own risk!)

A firm manages a growing resource. (Think of a paper firm managing a forest.) In year t, the forest is of size x_t. The firm, seeing x_t, must decide whether to (i) *harvest the forest and replant* or (ii) *let the forest grow for another year*. If the firm harvests and replants in year t (after seeing x_t), it realizes a profit of $p_t(x_t - 1)$, where p_t is the price of wood in year t (which the firm also sees prior to its decision whether to harvest).

If the firm harvests in year t, the size of the forest in year $t+1$ is 1 and in year $t+2$ is 3. Thereafter, until harvested, the forest grows each year by either 4 units or 0 units.

When managing this forest, the firm wishes to maximize the net present value of its profits, discounted at a rate of 0.9 per year. Assume that in year 0, the forest is of size 1; i.e., it was just harvested and replanted in year -1.

(a) Suppose $p_t = 1$ in all periods. Moreover, the forest grows by 4 units in year 3 after harvest with certainty, and continues to grow by 4 units each year. What is the optimal (maximizing the net present value) harvesting strategy for the firm? (Prove that your allegedly optimal strategy is in fact optimal.)

(b) Suppose that the sequence $\{p_t\}$ is an sequence of independent and identically distributed random variables, where $p_t = 1$ with probability $1/2$ and $= 1.5$ with probability $1/2$. What is the optimal harvesting strategy for the firm? (Prove that your allegedly optimal strategy is in fact optimal.)

(c) Go back to the case where $p_t = 1$ in all periods. Suppose that, in year 3 after harvesting (i.e., in year $t = 2$ in the story above, and thereafter in the third year after any harvest decision), the forest grows by 4 units with probability 0.8 and by 0 units with probability 0.2. This continues until the forest is harvested according to the following law of motion: If the forest grew 4 units in the preceding period, it will grow 4 units in the current period with probability 0.8 and grow 0 units with probability 0.2; if it grew 0 units in the preceding period, it will grow 0 units in this period with probability 1. (In other words, once the forest stops growing, it never begins to grow again, until you harvest and replant.) What is the optimal harvesting strategy for the firm? (Prove that your allegedly optimal strategy is in fact optimal.)

(d) Complicate case c as follows. The forest, between each decision date, is either in *growth mode* or in *no-growth mode*. When it is in no-growth mode, its growth is 0, and it remains in no-growth mode. When it is in growth mode, its growth is either 4, with probability .9, or 0, with probability .1, and in the next period it is in growth mode with probabilty .8 and in no-growth mode with probability .2. The transition from growth to no-growth modes is conditionally independent of the size of the current growth, conditional on the previous mode. That is, if the forest is in growth mode between years t and $t+1$ and it grows 4 units over that period, its mode between years $t+1$ and $t+2$ is *growth* with probability .8, the same as if it had grown only 0 units between t and $t+1$. Assume that the forest is sure to grow 1 unit the first year after harvest and planting, 2 units the year following, and will be in growth mode the year following that. (Thereafter, the transition probabilities above kick in.) The firm cannot tell if the forest is in growth mode or not after the third year after harvest and planting; the only evidence is how much the forest grew.

What is the optimal harvesting strategy for the firm? (Prove that your allegedly optimal strategy is in fact optimal.)

Appendix Seven

The Implicit-Function Theorem

Suppose a continuously differentiable function $F : A \times B \rightarrow R^n$ is given, where A and B are open sets in the spaces R^m and R^n, respectively. A point $(a^0, b^0) \in A \times B$ is specified; let z^0 denote $F(a^0, b^0)$. We would like to find a function $\phi : A \rightarrow B$ with $\phi(a^0) = b^0$ and

$$F(a, \phi(a)) \equiv z^0. \qquad (A7.1)$$

In words, as we vary a, $\phi(a)$ finds a point in B that keeps the value of F fixed at z^0.

In general, a function ϕ that satisfies $(A6.1)$ cannot be found at all. Suppose, for instance, that F doesn't depend on b at all but varies nontrivially with a. To be able to find ϕ, F must be adequately "affected" by the b argument, where adequately means "enough so that we can undo the effects of varying a." Also, to find a function ϕ that works for every $a \in A$ is too much to hope for; the best we can do in general is to produce a function that works for a in a neighborhood of a^0. (In many applications, that is good enough.)

Proposition A7.1 (The Implicit-Function Theorem). *For the setting just described, write $b = (b_1, \ldots, b_n)$ and F_i for the ith component of the vector function F. Let M be the $n \times n$ matrix whose i, jth element is*

$$\frac{\partial F_i}{\partial b_j}, \quad i, j = 1, \ldots, n.$$

Then if M evaluated at the point (a^0, b^0) is nonsingular, there exist open sets $A' \subseteq A$ and $B' \subseteq B$ with $(a^0, b^0) \in A' \times B'$ and a continuously differentiable function $\phi : A' \rightarrow B'$ such that $(A7.1)$ holds for all $a \in A'$. Moreover, for each $a \in A'$, $\phi(a)$ is the unique $b \in B'$ such that $F(a, b) = z^0$.

For a proof, see Spivak (1965). If you have a good geometric intuition, you can probably intuit why nonsingularity of M means that F varies adequately in b, at least in a neighborhood around b^0: Whatever changes in the value of F are wrought by varying a (close to a^0), we can move in any direction we want by varying b.

Appendix Eight

Fixed-Point Theory

Proposition A8.1. *Suppose $f : [0,1] \to [0,1]$ is continuous. Then there exists a **fixed point** of f, meaning some point x^* such that $f(x^*) = x^*$.*

This is the simplest of all *fixed-point theorems*. Its proof is elementary to anyone who survived a course in calculus: Define the function $\phi : [0,1] \to R$ by $\phi(x) = f(x) - x$. This function ϕ is continuous, and $\phi(0) = f(0) - 0 = f(0) \geq 0$, while $\phi(1) = f(1) - 1 \leq 0$. The Intermediate-Value Theorem from calculus therefore tells us that there is some point $x^* \in [0,1]$ such that $\phi(x^*) = 0$, but this is $f(x^*) - x^* = 0$, or $f(x^*) = x^*$.

More generally, fixed-point theorems come in two basic forms, one for functions and one for correspondences:

If f is a function with domain X and range X, [and then conditions on X and f are given], there exists some $x^* \in X$ such that $f(x^*) = x^*$.

If F is a correspondence with domain X and range X (that is, $F(x) \subseteq X$ for all $x \in X$), [and then conditions on X and F are given], then there is exists some $x^* \in X$ such that $x^* \in F(x^*)$.

The fixed-point theorem will sometimes go on to say more, for instance, about the structure of the set of fixed points.

In economics fixed-point theorems and fixed-point theory are most often used to prove that an equilibrium to some system or other exists; for instance, in this volume, we use fixed-point theory to establish the existence of a Walrasian equilibrium for a general equilibrium economy. Economists use a variety of fixed-point theorems for these purposes. In Chapter 14 (the one place in this volume where fixed-point theory is employed), *Kakutani's Fixed-Point Theorem* is employed; in one of the problems, you are asked to use *Brouwer's Fixed-Point Theorem*. Here they are:

Proposition A8.2 (Brouwer's Fixed-Point Theorem). *If X is a nonempty, compact, and convex subset of R^k for some integer k, and $f : X \to X$ is continuous, then there exists a fixed point of f, meaning that for some $x^* \in X$, $f(x^*) = x^*$.*

Proposition A8.3 (Kakutani's Fixed-Point Theorem). *If X is a nonempty, compact, and convex subset of R^k for some integer k, and $F : X \rightrightarrows X$ is nonempty and convex valued and upper semi-continuous, then there exists a fixed point of F, meaning that for some $x^* \in X$, $x^* \in F(x^*)$.*

It is obvious (why?) that Bouwer's Fixed-Point Theorem is implied by Kakutani's; and Kakutani can be proved (not entirely trivially) if one assumes Brouwer. So, roughly speaking, the two are equivalent. But proofs of either are not trivial. Intuitive *demonstrations* can be provided. Perhaps the most typical is the following demonstration of Brouwer where X is a circle (interior and boundary) in R^2. Suppose $f : X \to X$ has no fixed point. For each point $x \in X$, find $f(x)$ and draw a ray from $f(x)$ through x; label the point on the boundary hit by this ray as $g(x)$. As long as $f(x) \neq x$, this is a well-defined process for defining $g(x)$, and it is intuitively clear that g is continuous. (If x moves a bit, then $f(x)$ moves only a bit; hence the ray moves only a bit and the intersection point moves only a bit.) Moreover, if x lies on the boundary of X, then clearly $g(x) = x$. But then g is a continuous map from X to its boundary that is the identity on the boundary. And (here's the intuitive part) it is intuitively clear that one can't do this. You must "tear" X somewhere to map the whole circle onto its boundary in a way that leaves the boundary fixed. Why does the existence of a fixed point rule this sort of thing out? If $f(x) = x$, then it isn't clear how to define $g(x)$. More to the point, perhaps, slight movements in x around such a fixed point can mean big movements in $g(x)$; the "proof" that g is continuous depends on some separation between x and $f(x)$.

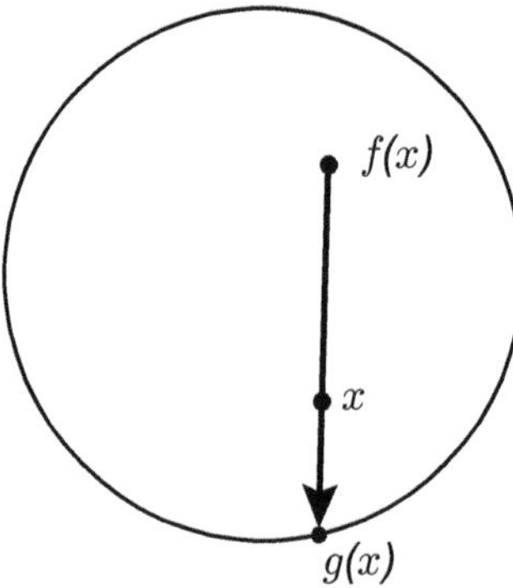

Figure A8.1. Demonstrating Brouwer's Fixed-Point Theorem on the circle in R^2. If continuous f has no fixed point, then let g map each x to the point on the boundary of X that is hit when you construct a ray from $f(x)$ through x. This g is continuous and seemingly maps the circle into its boundary in a way that keeps the boundary fixed. Intuitively, this does not seem possible, so every continuous f must have a fixed point.

But this is certainly no proof. It can be turned into one; a result in mathematics called Borsuk's Lemma shows that this sort of continuous map is impossible (in R^2 and in higher dimensions). And other, more direct proofs are possible. Perhaps the most accessible are "constructive" or computational: Using Sperner's Lemma, you can show how to find "approximate fixed points" to any degree of approximation desired, and then pass to a limit. For Brouwer proved in this fashion, see Border

(1990) or Scarf (1973). And if you know Green's Theorem from advanced calculus, it can be used as the basis of a proof.

While we use Kakutani in the text, other fixed-point theorems can be found in the literature. Some of these are in the same spirit as Kakutani and Brouwer. For example, in Brouwer, convexity per se of X is inessential. You should have no problem proving the following result:

Corollary A8.4. *If X is homeomorphic*[1] *to a convex and compact set $Y \subseteq R^k$, and if $f : X \to X$ is continuous, then there is some $x^* \in X$ such that $f(x^*) = x^*$.*

But other "extensions" of Brouwer and Kakutani are far less trivial; in the economics literature, you should watch in particular for the *Eilenberg-Montgomery Fixed-Point Theorem.*

Other fixed-point theorems found in the literature are distinctly different from Brouwer and Kakutani. Two of the most important are *Banach's Fixed-Point Theorem,* also known as *the Contraction-Mapping Theorem,* and *Tarksi's Fixed-Point Theorem.* Although we make no use of them in this volume, they are both relatively easy to prove, so I will give them here. Both concern fixed points of functions, but have relatively easy extensions to correspondences, which we also provide.

Banach's and Nadler's Fixed-Point Theorems

Because Banach's Theorem is sometimes used in contexts where the domain (and range) of the function are more complex than finite-dimensional Euclidean space, we will give it in greater generality.

The setting involves a function f defined from a complete metric space (X, d) to itself. To explain, a metric space is a nonempty set X for which the distance between any two points, x and x' from X, is given by $d(x, x')$. The distance function must satisfy (for all x, x', and x'' from X) $0 \leq d(x, x') < \infty$, $d(x, x') = 0$ if and only if $x = x'$, symmetry ($d(x, x') = d(x', x)$), and the triangle inequality: $d(x, x'') \leq d(x, x') + d(x', x'')$. The metric space is complete if every Cauchy sequence in it has a limit. For readers unfamiliar with this terminology, if X is a closed subset of R^k for some k, then X is a complete metric space if we measure distance by $d(x, x') = \|x - x'\|$. (And you can think in those terms for the rest of this subsection.)

Definition A8.5. *If, for some $\alpha < 1$, $f : X \to X$ satisfies $d(f(x), f(x')) \leq \alpha d(x, x')$ for all $x, x' \in X$, the function f is called a* ***contraction mapping.***

Proposition A8.6 (Banach's Fixed-Point Theorem, also known as the Contraction-Mapping Theorem). *If $f : X \to X$ is a contraction mapping defined on a complete metric space (X, d), then f has a unique fixed point x^*, a single point satisfying $f(x^*) = x^*$.*

---

[1] In general, sets X and Y are homeomorphic if there exists a function $\phi : X \to Y$ that is one-to-one and onto, and such that both ϕ and ϕ^{-1} are continuous. In the specific case of X compact, if $\phi : X \to Y$ is one-to-one, onto, and continuous, then ϕ^{-1} is automatically continuous. Given such a ϕ, to prove the corollary, let $g(y) = \phi(f(\phi^{-1}(y)))$.

Proof. Take any point from X and label it x^0. Let $x^1 = f(x^0)$ and, inductively, $x^{n+1} = f(x^n)$. Let $A = d(x^0, x^1)$, so that, inductively, $d(x^n, x^{n+1}) \leq \alpha^n A$. Applying the triangle inequality shows that $d(x^n, x^m) \leq A(\alpha^n + \ldots + \alpha^{m-1}) \leq \alpha^n A/(1-\alpha)$, (for $m > n$), and so $\{x^n\}$ is a Cauchy sequence. Since the space X is complete, this sequence has a limit x^*. That is $\lim_n d(x^n, x^*) = 0$. Since $d(f(x^n), f(x^*)) \leq \alpha d(x^n, x^*)$, this tells us that $\lim_n d(f(x^n), f(x^*)) = 0$, but this is $\lim_n d(x^{n+1}, f(x^*))$, so $\lim_n x^n = f(x^*)$. Using the triangle inequality, one shows that, in a metric space, a convergent sequence can have only one limit; hence $f(x^*) = x^*$, and x^* is a fixed point.

Now suppose $\hat{x}$ and $\check{x}$ are two fixed points of f. That is, $f(\hat{x}) = \hat{x}$ and $f(\check{x}) = \check{x}$. But then, because f is a contraction mapping,

$$d(\hat{x}, \check{x}) = d(f(\hat{x}), f(\check{x})) \leq \alpha d(\hat{x}, \check{x}),$$

for $\alpha < 1$, which implies $d(\hat{x}, \check{x}) = 0$, or $\hat{x} = \check{x}$; the fixed point is unique. ∎

Consider next the case of correspondences. For each $x \in X$, we have a set $F(x) \subseteq X$. We will assume that (X, d) is a metric space and that, for each $x \in X$, $F(x)$ is *compact*. Let Z be the space of all nonempty, compact subsets of X; a metric for Z, called the Hausdorff metric, is

$$d_H(z, z') = \max\{\max_{x \in z} \min_{x' \in z'} d(x, x'), \ \max_{x' \in z'} \min_{x \in z} d(x, x')\}.$$

It must be proved that d_H has all the properties required of a metric, but it does.

Definition A8.7. *If, for some $\alpha < 1$, $F : X \to Z$ satisfies $d_H(F(x), F(x') \leq \alpha d(x, x')$ for all $x, x' \in X$, the correspondence F is called* ***contractive****.*

Proposition A8.8 (Nadler's Fixed-Point Theorem). *If F is a contractive, nonempty-valued, and compact-valued correspondence defined on a complete metric space, then there is some $x^* \in X$ such that $x^* \in F(x^*)$.*

I'll leave the proof in your hands with the following (substantial) hint: Begin at any x^0 and let x^1 be a point in $F(x^0)$ that is closest to x^0. It is worth observing, perhaps, that uniqueness of the fixed-point is irrevocably lost: Suppose X is compact, and $F(x) = X$ for all x. This is a contractive mapping with a lot of fixed points.

Tarski's Fixed-Point Theorem

Tarski's Fixed-Point Theorem concerns functions on ordered sets. To set the stage, we need a slew of definitions.

Definition A8.9.

a. *A* ***partially ordered set****, or* ***poset****, consists of an abstract set X and a binary relation $\succeq$ on X that is reflexive ($x \succeq x$ for all x), transitive (you should know what that means), and anti-symmetric (if $x \succeq y$ and $y \succeq x$, then $x = y$).*

b. *If Y is a subset of X for some partially ordered set $(X, \succeq)$, an **upper bound** for Y is an element $x \in X$ such that $x \succeq y$ for all $y \in Y$. A **supremum** for Y is an upper bound x^* of Y that, moreover, satisfies $x \succeq x^*$ for all other upper bounds x of Y.*[2]

c. *A **join semi-lattice** is a partially ordered set $(X, \succeq)$ such that if x and x' are any two elements of X, then the set $\{x, x'\}$ has a supremum in X, which is denoted $x \vee x'$ and called the **join** of x and x'.*

Proposition A8.10 (Tarski's Fixed-Point Theorem). *Suppose $(X, \succeq)$ is a join semi-lattice with the following additional properties:*

- *The set X has a maximal and a minimal element: there exist $\overline{x} \in X$ and $\underline{x} \in X$ such that $\overline{x} \succeq x \succeq \underline{x}$ for all $x \in X$.*
- *Every nonempty subset Z of X has a supremum in X.*[3]

If $f : X \to X$ is a nondecreasing function, meaning $x \succeq x'$ implies $f(x) \succeq f(x')$, then the function f admits a fixed point: For some x^*, $f(x^*) = x^*$. Moreover, the supremum of the set of fixed points of f is itself a fixed point of f.

Proof. Given the function f, let $X' = \{x \in X : f(x) \succeq x\}$. Note that if $x \in X'$, then $f(x) \succeq x$ by the definition of X', which implies $f(f(x)) \succeq f(x)$, since f is an nondecreasing function, which implies $f(x) \in X'$.

Since $f(\underline{x}) \in X$ and $x' \succeq \underline{x}$ for all x', we know that $f(\underline{x}) \succeq \underline{x}$, and hence $\underline{x} \in X'$; X' is nonempty. Therefore, X' has a supremum x^*. I assert that $f(x^*) = x^*$; that is, x^* is a fixed point of the function: First, I assert that $f(x^*) \succeq x^*$. To see this, note that $x^* \succeq x'$ for all $x' \in X'$; hence $f(x^*) \succeq f(x')$ for all $x' \in X'$ (f is nondecreasing), and as $f(x') \succeq x'$ for all $x' \in X'$ by the definition of X', transitivity of $\succeq$ implies $f(x^*) \succeq x'$ for all $x' \in X'$. This means that $f(x^*)$ is an upper bound of X', and since x^* is its supremum, $f(x^*) \succeq x^*$.

But if $f(x^*) \succeq x^*$, then $x^* \in X'$ by definition, and so $f(x^*) \in X'$ (see the first paragraph). Since x^* is an upper bound of X', this implies $x^* \succeq f(x^*)$, which with the conclusion of the previous paragraph and anti-symmetry of $\succeq$ implies $x^* = f(x^*)$. This makes x^* a fixed point.

Since $\succeq$ is reflexive, for any fixed point $\hat{x}$, $f(\hat{x}) = \hat{x} \succeq \hat{x}$, and so $\hat{x} \in X'$. Therefore, x^*, being the supremum of X', is immediately also a supremum of the

[2] If a set Y has a supremum, that supremum is necessarily unique: If x^* is a supremum of Y, then x^* is an upper bound of Y, and so $x^* \succeq x^{**}$ for any other supremum x^{**} of Y. But if x^{**} is some other supremum of Y, then $x^{**} \succeq x^*$ by a symmetric argument, and anti-symmetry of $\succeq$ implies that $x^* = x^{**}$.

[3] This condition is sometimes phrased: Every nonempty set with an upper bound has a supremum. But the first bullet point ensures that every nonempty set has an upper bound. Readers with knowledge of lattice theory will recognize that if these two conditions hold, then X is a *lattice*; every pair of points has a *meet* as well as a join. Proof: If Z is a nonempty subset of X, the set B of its lower bounds is nonempty. Let b^* be the supremum of B. Since each $z \in Z$ is an upper bound of B and b^* is the supremum of B, we know that $z \succeq b^*$ for all $z \in Z$. That is, b^* is a lower bound of Z. Of course, since b^* is the supremum of B, $b^* \succeq b$ for all $b \in B$. But this implies that b^* is an *infimum* of Z. Applying this to two-element subsets of X gives us a meet for each pair out of X; moreover, every nonempty subset of X has an infimum as well as a supremum.

set of fixed points of f. ■

To see Tarski's Theorem at work (and where it fails to work), consider four examples: First, suppose X is the unit cube in R^k, or $X = [0,1]^k$, and $\succeq$ is the usual greater-than-or-equal-to relationship. Clearly, $(X, \geq)$ is a poset: $x \geq x$ for all x, $\geq$ is transitive, and if $x \geq y \geq x$, then $x = y$. X has maximal and minimal elements: The origin is minimal and the vector $(1, 1, \ldots, 1)$ is maximal. And suppose Z is any subset of $[0,1]^k$. Let x^* be defined as the component-wise supremum; that is, for $i = 1, \ldots, k$, $x_i^* = \sup\{z_i : z \in Z\}$. If x is any upper bound of Z, then $x_i \geq z_i$ for all $z \in Z$ and all i; hence $x_i \geq x_i^*$ and, therefore, $x \geq x^*$. And x^* is clearly an upper bound.

Now let f be any nondecreasing function from $[0,1]^k$ to $[0,1]^k$. Tarski's Theorem immediately implies that f has a fixed point.

Next, suppose $f : R_+^k \to R_+^k$ is nondecreasing. The simple case of $k = 1$ and $f(x) = x + 1$ shows that f need not have a fixed point. The problem, of course, is that R_+^k has no maximal element. (You could also say that there are subsets of R_+^k without suprema, but if we formulated the second bullet-point condition as *Every set with an upper bound has a supremum,* then the property holds; it is really the lack of a maximal element that is killing us.)

Or try $X = R_-^k$. The simple case of $k = 1$ and $f(x) = x - 1$ is an example with no fixed point. Note that in this case, X does have a maximal element and every nonempty subset does have a supremum. But we can never get the proof going, because we don't know that the set $X' = \{x \in X = R_-^k : f(x) \geq x\}$ is nonempty. (If we knew this set was nonempty for the f in question, we'd be in business.)

Finally, suppose X is the set of all rational numbers between 0 and 1, with the order $\geq$. We have a partially ordered set, and moreover the set has a minimal and a maximal element. But it is not *complete;* not every nonempty set has a supremum. Specifically, the set $\{q \in X : q \leq \pi/4\}$ (where π in this case is the standard irrational number 3.14159...) has no supremum in X. And we can produce nondecreasing f on this X with no fixed points. For instance, let $\{q_n\}$ be a sequence of rational numbers that are strictly increasing and approach $\pi/4$ from below, with $q_0 = 0$, and let $\{\hat{q}_n\}$ be any sequence of rational numbers that are strictly decreasing and approach $\pi/4$ from above, with $\hat{q}_0 = 1$. Then construct f as follows:

If q (a rational number) is less than $\pi/4$, then find q_n and q_{n+1} such that $q_n \leq q < q_{n+1}$, and let $f(q) = q_{n+1}$. And if q is greater than $\pi/4$, then find $\hat{q}_n$ and $\hat{q}_{n+1}$ such that $\hat{q}_n \geq q > \hat{q}_{n+1}$ and let $f(q) = \hat{q}_{n+1}$. I leave it to you to verify that f is nondecreasing, but has no fixed point (in X). (My f is not strictly increasing. Can you make a minor adjustment in my construction and provide an f that is strictly increasing on the rationals between 0 and 1 but still has no fixed point?)

Just as Kakutani's Fixed-Point Theorem provides a "correspondence version" of Brouwer, and Nadler provides a "correspondence version" of Banach, a "correspondence version" of Tarski's Fixed-Point Theorem has been given by Zhou (1994).

Proposition A8.11 (Zhou's Fixed-Point Theorem). *Suppose* $(X \succeq)$ *is a join semi-lattice with the two additional properties given in the statement of Proposition A8.10. Suppose that* $F : X \Rightarrow X$ *is a nonempty-valued correspondence on* X*, such that,*

- *for each* $x \in X$*,* $F(x)$ *contains its own supremum and,*
- *if* $x \succeq y$*,* $x' \in F(x)$*, and* $y' \in F(y)$*, then* $x' \vee y' \in F(x)$*.*

Then there is some $x^* \in X$ *such that* $x^* \in F(x^*)$*.*

Proof. For each x, let $f(x) = \sup(F(x))$. I assert that f is a nondecreasing function: If $x \succeq y$, since $f(x) \in F(x)$ and $f(y) \in F(y)$ by the first bullet point, we have $f(x) \vee f(y) \in F(x)$ by the second bullet point. Of course, $f(x) \vee f(y) \succeq f(x)$, but since $f(x) = \sup F(x)$ and $f(x) \vee f(y) \in F(x)$, it follows that $f(x) \succeq f(x) \vee f(y)$, and hence $f(x) \vee f(y) = f(x)$ by anti-symmetry. But then $f(x) = f(x) \vee f(y) \succeq f(y)$.

Now apply Tarski's Fixed-Point Theorem to f; there exists x^* such that $x^* = f(x^*)$. But $f(x^*) \in F(x^*)$ by the first bullet point, and so $x^* \in F(x^*)$. ∎

This is, in fact, a simplified version of Zhou's result: He provides conditions ensuring that the set of fixed points of an (appropriately conditioned) correspondence is a nonempty complete lattice.

References

Afriat, Sidney (1967). "The Construction of a Utility Function from Expenditure Data." *International Economic Review* **8**, 67–77.

Allais, Maurice (1953). "Le comportement de l'homme rationnel devant le risque, critique des postulates et axiomes de l'école américaine." *Econometrica* **21**, 503–46.

Anscombe, F., and R. Aumann (1963). "A Definition of Subjective Probability." *Annals of Mathematical Statistics* **34**, 199–205.

Antonelli, G. B. (1886). *Sulla Teoria Matemitica della Economia Politica.* Pisa: Nella Tipognafia del Folchetto. English translation published in J. S. Chipman, L. Hurwicz, M. K. Richter, and H. F. Sonnenschein (eds.), *Preferences, Utility, and Demand.* New York: Harcourt Brace Jovanovich, 333–60.

Arrow, Kenneth J. (1951a) (2nd edn. 1963). *Social Choice and Individual Values.* New York: J. Wiley and Sons.

Arrow, Kenneth J. (1951b). "An Extension of the Basic Theorems of Classical Welfare Economics." In J. Neyman (ed.), *Proceedings of the Second Berkeley Symposium on Mathematical Statistics and Probability.* Berkeley: University of California Press, 507–32.

Arrow, Kenneth J. (1953). "Le rôle des valeurs boursières pour la répartition la meilleure des risques." *Cahiers du Séminaire d'Econométrie.* English version published in 1964 as "The Role of Securities in the Optimal Allocation of Risk-Bearing," *Review of Economic Studies* **31** (2): 91–6.

Arrow, Kenneth J. (1959). "Rational Choice Functions and Orderings." *Economica* **26**, 121–7.

Arrow, Kenneth J. (1974). *Essays in the Theory of Risk Bearing.* Amsterdam: North-Holland.

Arrow, Kenneth J., and Gerard Debreu (1954). "Existence of an Equilibrium for a Competitive Economy." *Econometrica* **22**, 265–90.

Arrow, Kenneth J., and F. H. Hahn (1971). *General Competitive Analysis.* San Francisco: Holden-Day.

Aumann, Robert J. (1964). "Markets with a Continuum of Traders." *Econometrica* **32**, 39–50.

Aumann, Robert J. (1965). "Integrals of Set-Valued Functions." *Journal of Mathematical Analysis and Applications* **12**, 1–12.

Aumann, Robert J. (1966). "Existence of a Competitive Equilibrium in Markets with a Continuum of Traders." *Econometrica* **34**, 1–17.

Aumann, Robert J. (1987). "Correlated equilibrium as an expression of Bayesian rationality." *Econometrica* **55**, 1-18.

Bell Journal of Economics and Management Science, Vol. 5 (1974). "Symposium on the Objectives of the Firm When Markets are Incomplete." Includes articles by Ekern and Wilson, Leland, Merton and Subramanyam, and Radner.

Bersekes, Dimitri (2005, 2007). *Dynamic Programming and Optimal Control,* Vols. 1 and 2, 3rd edition. Belmont, MA: Athena Scientific.

Blackwell, David (1967). "Positive Dynamic Programming." In L. LeCam and J. Neyman (eds.), *Proceedings of the Fifth Berkeley Symposium on Mathematical Statistics and Probability,* **1**, 415–8.

Borch, Karl, (1968). *The Economics of Uncertainty.* Princeton, NJ: Princeton University Press.

Border, Kim (1990). *Fixed Point Theorems with Applications to Economics and Game Theory.* Cambridge: Cambridge University Press.

Border, Kim (2004). "The 'Integrability Problem.'" Notes posted at http://www.hss.caltech.edu/~kcb/Notes/Demand4-Integrability.pdf.

Caplin, Andrew, and Barry Nalebuff (1988). "On 64% Majority Rule." *Econometrica* **56**, 787–815.

Chipman, John S. (1974). "Homothetic Preferences and Aggregation." *Journal of Economic Theory* **8**, 26–38.

Chipman, John S., and J. Moore (1979). "On Social Welfare Functions and the Aggregation of Preferences." *Journal of Economic Theory* **21**, 111–39.

Chung, Kai Lai (1974). *A Course in Probability Theory,* 2nd edition. New York: Academic Press.

Coase, Ronald H. (1960). "The Problem of Social Cost." *Journal of Law and Economics* **3**, 1–44.

Debreu, Gerard (1951). "The Coefficient of Resource Utilization." *Econometrica* **19**, 273–92.

Debreu, Gerard (1954). "Representation of a Preference Ordering by a Numerical Function." In R. M. Thall, H. Coombs, and R. L. Davis (eds), *Decision Processes.* New York: John Wiley and Sons, 159–65.

Debreu, Gerard (1956). "Market Equilibrium." *Proceedings of the National Acaemy of Sciences of the United States* **42**, 876–8.

Debreu, Gerard (1959). *Theory of Value*. New Haven: Yale University Press.

Debreu, Gerard (1960). "Topological Methods in Cardinal Utility Theory." In Kenneth J. Arrow, Samuel Karlin, and Patrick Suppes (eds.), *Mathematical Methods in the Social Sciences*. Stanford, CA: Stanford University Press, 16–26.

Debreu, Gerard (1974). "Excess Demand Functions." *Journal of Mathematical Economics* **1**, 15–23.

Debreu, Gerard (1982). "Existence of Competitive Equilibrium." In Kenneth J. Arrow and Michael D. Intriligator (eds.), *Handbook of Mathematical Economics* **2**. Amsterdam: North-Holland, 697–743.

Debreu, Gerard, and Herbert Scarf (1963). "A Limit Theorem on the Core of an Economy." *International Economic Review* **4**, 235–46.

Diewert, Erwin (1974). "Applications of Duality Theory." In Michael D. Intriligator and David A. Kendrick (eds.), *Frontiers of Quantitative Economics* **2**. Amsterdam: North-Holland, 106–71.

Diewert, Erwin (1982), "Duality Approaches to Microeconomic Theory." In Kenneth J. Arrow and Michael D. Intriligator (eds.), *Handbook of Mathematical Economics* **2**. Amsterdam: North-Holland, 535–99.

Dupuit, A. J. E. J. (1844). "De la measure de l'utilité des travaux publics." *Annales des Ponts et Chaussées* **8**. Translated by R. H. Barback as "On the Measurement of the Utility of Public Works" and reprinted in Kenneth J. Arrow and Tibor Scitovsky (eds.), *Readings in Welfare Economics*. Homewood, IL: Richard D. Irwin, 1969, 255–83.

Edgeworth, Francis Ysidro (1881). *Mathematical Psychics: An Essay on the Application of Mathematics to the Moral Sciences*. London: C. Kegan Paul.

Eisenberg, B. (1961). "Aggregation of Utility Functions." *Management Science* **7**, 337–50.

Ellsberg, Daniel (1961). "Risk, Ambiguity, and the Savage Axioms." *Quarterly Journal of Economics* **75**, 643–69.

Fishburn, Peter (1970). *Utility Theory for Decision Making*. New York: John Wiley and Sons. Reprinted in 1979, Huntington, NY: R. E. Krieger Publishing.

Fudenberg, Drew, and David K. Levine (1998). *The Theory of Learning in Games*. Cambridge, MA: MIT Press.

Fuss, Melvyn, and Daniel L. McFadden (eds.) (1978). *Production Economics: A Dual Approach to Theory and Applications. Volume 1: The Theory of Production*. Amsterdam: North-Holland.

Geanakoplos, John (1984). "Utility Functions for Debreu's 'Excess Demands.'" *Journal of Mathematical Economics* **13**, 1–9.

Geanakoplos, John (1990). "An Introduction to General Equilibrium with Incomplete Asset Markets." *Journal of Mathematical Economics*, **19**, 1–38.

Guesnerie, Roger, and J.-Y. Jaffray (1974). "Optimality of Equilibrium of Plans, Prices, and Price Expectations." In J. Dreze (ed.), *Allocation under Uncertainty, Equilibrium, and Optimality*. London: Macmillan, 71–86.

Gul, Faruk, and Wolfgang Pesendorfer (2001). "Temptation and Self-Control." *Econometrica* **69**, 1403–35.

Gul, Faruk, and Wolfgang Pesendorfer (2005). "The Revealed Preference Theory of Changing Tastes." *Review of Economic Studies* **72**, 429–48.

Hadar, Josef, and William R. Russell (1969). "Rules for Ordering Uncertain Prospects." *American Economic Review* **59**, 25–34.

Harrison, J. M., and David M. Kreps (1979). "Martingales and Arbitrage in Multiperiod Securities Markets." *Journal of Economic Theory* **20**, 381–408.

Hart, Oliver (1975). "On the Optimality of Equilibrium When the Market Structure is Incomplete." *Journal of Economic Theory* **11**, 418–33.

Herstein, I. N., and J. Milnor (1953). "An Axiomatic Approach to Measurable Utility." *Econometrica* **21**, 291–7.

Hildenbrand, Werner (1974). *Core and Equilibrium of a Large Economy*. Princeton, NJ: Princeton University Press.

Houthakker, Hendrik S. (1950). "Revealed Preference and the Utility Function." *Economica* **NS 17**, 159–74.

Hurwicz, L., and H. Uzawa (1971). "On the Integrability of Demand Functions." In John S. Chipman, Leonid Hurwicz, Marcel Richter, and Hugo Sonnenschein (eds.), *Preferences, Utility, and Demand*. New York: Harcourt, Brace, and Jovanovich, 114–48.

Jackson, Matthew O. (1986a). "Continuous Utility Functions in Consumer Theory: A Set of Duality Theorems." *Journal of Mathematical Economics* **15**, 63–77

Jackson, Matthew O. (1986b). "Integration of Demand and Continuous Utility Functions." *Journal of Economic Theory* **38**, 298–312.

Kahnemann, D., and A. Tversky (1979). "Prospect Theory: An Analysis of Decision Under Risk." *Econommetrica* **47**, 263–71.

Kaneko, M., and K. Nakamura (1979). "The Nash Social Welfare Function." *Econometrica* **47**, 423–36.

Katzner, D. (1970). *Static Demand Theory.* New York: Macmillan.

Koszegi, B., and Matthew Rabin (2006). "A Model of Reference-Dependent Preferences." *Quarterly Journal of Economics* **121**, 1133–66.

Kreps, David M. (1979a). "A Representation Theorem for Preference for Flexibility." *Econometrica* **47**, 565–77.

Kreps, David M. (1979b). "Three Essays on Capital Markets." Institute for Mathematical Studies in the Social Sciences, Stanford University. Reprinted in *Revista Española de Economia* **4** (1), 1987, 111–46.

Kreps, David M. (1988). *Notes on the Theory of Choice.* Boulder, CO: Westview Press.

Kreps, David M. (1992). "Static Choice in the Presence of Unforeseen Contingencies." In Partha Dasgupta, Douglas Gale, Oliver Hart, and Eric Maskin, (eds.), *Economic Analysis of Markets and Games.* Cambridge, MA: MIT Press, 258–81.

Kreps, David M. (2004), *Microeconomics for Managers.* New York: W. W. Norton.

Kreps, David M., and Evan L. Porteus (1979). "Dynamic Choice Theory and Dynamic Programming." *Econometrica* , **47**, 91–100.

Krishna, Vijay (2008). "Notes on generalized games." Unpublished notes, PDF file, Pennylvania State University.

Krishna, Vijay, and Hugo Sonnenschein (1990). "Duality in Consumer Theory." In John S. Chipman, Daniel McFadden, and Marcel Richter (eds.), *Preferences, Uncertainty, and Optimality,* Boulder, CO: Westview Press, 44–55.

Lindahl, Erik (1958) [1919]. "Just Taxation—A Positive Solution." In R. A. Musgrave and A. T. Peacock (eds.), *Classics in the Theory of Public Finance.* London: Macmillan.

Lucas, Robert, and Nancy Stokey (1989). *Recursive Methods in Economic Dynamics.* Cambridge, MA: Harvard University Press.

Machina, Mark (1987). "Choice Under Uncertainty: Problems Solved and Unsolved." *Journal of Economic Perspectives* **1**, 121–54.

Machina, Mark, and John Pratt (1997). "Increasing Risk: Some Direct Constructions." *Journal of Risk and Uncertainty* **14**, 203–27.

Mantel, R. (1974). "On the Characterization of Aggregate Excess Demand." *Journal of Economic Theory* **7**, 348–53.

Mantel, R. (1979). "Homothetic Preferences and Community Excess Demand Functions." *Journal of Economic Theory* **12**, 197–301.

Marimon, Ramón (1987). "Kreps's Three Essays on Capital Markets almost Ten Years Later." *Revista Española de Economia* **4** (1), , 146–72.

Mas-Colell, Andreu (1977). "On the Equilibirium Price Set of an Exchange Economy." *Journal of Economic Theory*, **4**, 117–26.

Mas-Colell, Andreu, Michael D. Whinston, and Jerry R. Green (1995). *Microeconomic Theory*. New York: Oxford University Press.

McKenzie, Lionel W. (1954). "On Equilibrium in Graham's Model of World Trade and Other Competitive Systems." *Econometrica* **22**, 147–61.

Merton, Robert (1973). "An Intertermporal Capital Asset Pricing Model." *Econometrica* **41**, 867–87.

Modigliani, Franco, and Merton H. Miller (1958). "The Cost of Capital, Corporation Finance, and the Theory of Investment." *American Economic Review* **48**, 261–97.

Ok, Efe (2007). *Real Analysis with Economic Applications*. Princeton, NJ: Princeton University Press.

Pareto, Vilfredo (1909). *Manuel d'économie politique*. Paris: V. Giard et E. Brière.

Pratt, John (1964). "Risk Aversion in the Small and in the Large." *Econometrica* **32**, 122–36.

Radner, Roy (1968). "Competitive Equilibrium under Uncertainty." *Econometrica* **36** (1), 31–58.

Radner, Roy (1972). "Existence of Equilibrium of Plans, Prices, and Price Expectations in a Sequence of Markets." *Econometrica* **40**, 289–304.

Richter, Marcel K. (1966). "Revealed Preference Theory." *Econometrica* **34**, 635–45.

Robbins, Lionel (1998). *A History of Economic Thought*. Princeton, NJ: Princeton University Press.

Rockafellar, T. (1970). *Convex Analysis*. Princeton, NJ: Princeton University Press. Reprinted in paperback by Princeton University Press, 1997.

Ross, Stephen A. (1976). "Options and Efficiency." *Quarterly Journal of Economics* **90**, 75–89.

Ross, Stephen A. (1978). "A Simple Approach to the Valuation of Risky Streams." *Journal of Business* **51**, 453–75.

Ross, Stephen A. (1981). "Some Stronger Measures of Risk Aversion in the Small and the Large with Applications." *Econometrica* **49**, 621–38.

Rothschild, Michael, and Joseph Stiglitz (1970). "Increasing Risk. I: A Definition." *Journal of Economic Theory* **2**, 225–43.

Roy, R. (1947). "La distribution du revenu entre les divers biens." *Econometrica* **15**, 205–25.

Royden, H. L. (1968). *Real Analysis*, 2nd edition. London: Macmillan.

Rudin, Walter (1976). *Principles of Mathematical Analysis*, 3rd edition. New York: McGraw-Hill.

Rust, John (1987). "Optimal Replacement of GMC Bus Engines: An Empirical Model of Harold Zurcher." *Econometrica* **55**, 999–1033.

Samuelson, Paul A. (1947). *Foundations of Economic Analysis*. Cambridge, MA: Harvard University Press. Enlarged edition published 1983.

Sargent, Thomas J. (1999). *The Conquest of American Inflation*. Princeton, NJ: Princeton University Press.

Savage, L. J. (1954). *The Foundations of Statistics*. New York: John Wiley and Sons. Revised and enlarged edition published 1972, New York: Dover Publications.

Scarf, Herbert (1973). *The Computation of Economic Equilibria*. New Haven: Yale University Press.

Schelling, Thomas C. (2006). *Strategies of Commitment and Other Essays*. Cambridge, MA: Harvard University Press.

Sen, Amartya (1970). *Collective Choice and Social Welfare*, San Francisco: Holden-Day.

Shafer, Wayne, and Hugo Sonnenschein (1982). "Market Demand and Excess Demand Functions." In Kenneth J. Arrow and Michael D. Intriligator (eds.), *Handbook of Mathematical Economics* **2**, Amsterdam: North-Holland, 671–93.

Slutsky, E. E. (1915). "Sulla teoria del bilancio del consumatore." *Giornale degli Economisti* **51**, 1—26.

Smith, Adam (1776). *The Wealth of Nations*. Many modern printings of this book are available, for instance, by the Modern Library, New York: Random House.

Sonnenschein, Hugo (1973). "Do Walras' Identity and Continuity Characterize the Class of Community Excess Demand Functions?" *Journal of Economic Theory* **6**, 345–54.

Spivak, Michael (1965). *Calculus on Manifolds*. New York: W. A. Benjamin.

Starr, Ross (1969). "Quasi-Equilibria in Markets with Non-Convex Preferences." *Econometrica* **37**, 25–38.

Strauch, Ralph (1966). "Negative Dynamic Programming." *Annals of Mathematical Statistics* **37**, 871–90.

Strotz, R. (1955-56). "Myopia and Inconsistency in Dynamic Utility Maximization." *Review of Economic Studies* **23**, 165–80.

Varian, H. (1982). "The Nonparametric Approach to Demand Analysis." *Econometrica* **50**, 945–72.

Varian, H. (1992). *Microeconomic Analysis,* 3rd edition. New York: W. W. Norton.

von Neumann, John, and Oskar Morgenstern (1944). *Theory of Games and Economic Behavior*. Princeton, NJ: Princeton University Press.

Wakker, Peter (2008). "Uncertainty." In S. Durlauf and L. Blume (eds.), *The New Palgrave Dictionary of Economics,* 2nd edition. New York: Palgrave Macmillan.

Whittle, Peter (1983). *Optimization Over Time: Dynamic Programming and Stochastic Control,* Vols. 1 and 2. New York: John Wiley and Sons.

Willig, Robert D. (1976). "Consumer's Surplus Without Apology." *American Economic Review* **66**, 589–97.

Wilson, Robert (1968). "The Theory of Syndicates." *Econometrica* **36**, 119–32.

Zhou, Lin (1993). "A Simple Proof of the Shapley-Folkman Theorem." *Economic Theory* **3**, 371–2.

Zhou, Lin (1994). "The Set of Nash Equilibria of a Supermodular Game is a Complete Lattice." *Games and Economic Behavior* **7**, 295–300.

Index

www.ingramcontent.com/pod-product-compliance
Ingram Content Group UK Ltd.
Pitfield, Milton Keynes, MK11 3LW, UK
UKHW032327090225
454783UK00002B/2

9 780691 155838